THE CHRIST IN THE BIBLE COMMENTARY
Volume Four

THE
CHRIST IN THE BIBLE
COMMENTARY

Volume Four

Matthew

Mark

Luke

John

Acts

Dr. Albert B. Simpson

CHRISTIAN PUBLICATIONS
CAMP HILL, PENNSYLVANIA

Christian Publications
3825 Hartzdale Drive, Camp Hill, PA 17011

The mark of ✝ *vibrant faith*

ISBN: 0-87509-501-1
LOC Catalog Card Number: 92-70937
© 1993 by Christian Publications
All rights reserved
Printed in the United States of America

93 94 95 96 97 5 4 3 2 1

Cover Design: Step One Design

CONTENTS

Matthew

Mark

Acts

MATTHEW

CHAPTER 1

THE BIRTH OF THE KING

Where is the one who has been born king of the Jews? (Matthew 2:2)

Matthew is the Gospel of the Kingdom. The four gospels are not four different editions of the life of Christ, but four pictures of the Christ from different standpoints. Each presents a distinct aspect, and together they form the complete whole.

It is somewhat like attempting to obtain a photograph of Mount Blanc. They tell you in the valley that there is no single picture of the mountain, but they can give you a number of views from different standpoints, and then you can make your composite view of the mountain. So the four evangelists give us different views of the Lord Jesus, and out of the four comes the complete conception of His character and work.

SYMBOLS OF THE FOUR GOSPELS

In the ancient tabernacle and temple stood the figure of the cherubim. There were four faces: the first a lion, the second an ox, the third a man and the fourth an eagle. The lion represented Christ as our King; the ox, the toiling and suffering Christ; the man, the human Christ; and the eagle, His divine character. The ancient fathers justly applied these symbols to the four gospels. Matthew is the Gospel of the King, Mark, the Gospel of the Servant, Luke, the Gospel of the Son of Man, and John, the Gospel of the Son of God.

The very first picture in Matthew is the King of the Jews, and the last is the Supreme Lord, to whom all power is given both in heaven and in earth, sending forth His ambassadors to the nations and claiming their obedience and loyalty.

When we turn to Mark, we find a story of deeds, not words; a toiling Christ who has gone almost half through His ministry before the end of the first chapter.

In Luke we have the revelation of His human heart, and a series of most touching manifestations of His sympathy, tenderness and love. The first picture takes us to the cradle of the Babe, and the last gives us the walk to Emmaus, and the charming revelation of His human heart, unchanged even after the cross and resurrection.

When we turn to John, it is indeed the soaring eagle bearing us up to the sublime heights of His primeval deity and the mysteries of His oneness with the Father.

And yet none of these gospels attempts to give us a complete biography of Jesus Christ. Even the longest presents but a few fragments from the story of His life, the sketch of an occasional day or hour gleaned from much more that has been left unrecorded—so much indeed that the Apostle John could say that if all that He said and did were written, "even the whole world would not have room for the books that would be written" (John 21:25b).

It has been well said that the New Testament evangelists were not reporters but editors. They did not give a chronicle of complete facts so much as a selection of special incidents, clustered together for the purpose of illustrating certain points and principles which were more important than even the facts themselves.

THE GOSPEL OF THE KINGDOM

Returning to the gospel of Matthew, a brief analysis will show that it opens with the birth of the King, and after the briefest reference to His childhood, passes on to His forerunner and inauguration. Next comes the manifesto of the King, containing the laws and principles of the new kingdom which He was to set up. This is found in the Sermon on the Mount, as it is generally called, which is an unfolding of the righteousness of the kingdom which He came to establish, the reenacting of the Old Testament law with its larger liberty and deeper spirituality. Next come the credentials of the kingdom, the works of power in which His ministry began and by which it was approved of God to the faith of His followers. This in turn was followed by the rejection of the King and His preparation for the next stage of the kingdom after He has been condemned, crucified and called away from the earthly scene. This preparation consisted of the appointment of His apostles, the provision for the organization of His Church, the constitution and government of the new kingdom, the announcement of His second coming, and then the crown of thorns, the triumph over death, the revelation of the Prince of Life and the messages which He gave as the mediatorial King to those that were to represent Him during His absence and until He should come again. All this will come before us in due order. At present our subject calls us back to the first chapter, the royal birth of Israel's King.

SECTION I—*His Pedigree*

This, however, is preceded by the account of His pedigree. It was necessary that it should be demonstrated to Israel that He was her true King. The obvious design of this genealogical table is to show that Jesus was the actual and legal heir of David. Joseph, while not His actual father, was His legal father, and Jesus was the heir of Joseph. He was recognized by all the people as the son of Joseph, and entitled by every form of law and justice to inherit his rights and titles. If Joseph, therefore, was the lawful heir of David, Jesus must also be. This genealogical table was prepared with great accuracy, and establishes without question, the title of our Savior to sit on the throne of David. When He appears on earth again, no member of the Hebrew race will be able to lawfully dispute His title, that He is alive, and the only living heir to David's throne.

TWO GENEALOGIES

Many Bible students have been perplexed by the difference between the two genealogical tables given respectively by Matthew and Luke. Luke also gives us a long genealogy. The difference consists in this, that the genealogy of Luke is Mary's, not Joseph's. Luke has given us the human side of Christ; therefore it was natural that he should trace His mother's pedigree, and she also could trace back her lineage to David by an unbroken line through Nathan, the son of David, rather than through Solomon, from whose line the family of Joseph came; so that we have two lines of genealogy connecting Jesus with Israel's history and David's throne.

Matthew's genealogical table contains three groups of names, each group consisting of 14. The first consists of patriarchs from Abraham to David, the second of kings from David to the captivity, the third of persons of royal extraction, though not kings. Gradually the line descends until it reaches the carpenter's shop at Nazareth. These three groups form six series of seven each. Seven is the number of perfection, and six of imperfection. The six series that preceded Christ were all imperfect human links, the seventh is reached in Him, the perfect and golden link which makes the chain complete.

TYPES OF GRACE

Some names have been omitted among the kings, noticeably the wicked descendants of the house of Jezebel. The most remarkable feature, however, is the presence in this genealogy of four women, all of them women on whom rested a shadow of shame. The first was Tamar, of the family of Jacob, the story of whose dishonor is well known. The next was Rahab, the notorious woman of Jericho, who was saved by the spies because of her friendship. The third was Ruth, the daughter of Moab, herself a virtuous woman, but her race accursed. The fourth was Bathsheba, the mother of Solomon, but the partner of David's sin, when he stole her from her husband, Uriah. Why should these four dishonored women be named in the lineage of the Son of God and the Son of David? The reason is not far to seek. He came to be the Savior of sinners, and He was not ashamed to include even in His royal line the most lost and sinful of the race, and thus to set the pattern which the whole story of redemption has fulfilled that Christ "welcomes sinners" (Luke 15:2b).

SECTION II—*His Birth*

Having proved His pedigree and established His title, the evangelist next gives us the story of His royal birth. Seven witnesses stand forth to establish His lofty character and claims.

JOSEPH'S TESTIMONY

The first is Joseph, His reputed father. We are told that Joseph was a "righteous man," and when he found that Mary, his betrothed wife, was about to become a mother, with a rare blending of justice and gentleness, he had made up his mind to divorce her, but so privately that no disgrace would fall upon her (Matthew 1:19). Of course, he looked upon her as one of those unfortunates who appear all along the course of human history. The fact, however, that immediately after his determination we find him taking her to him as his wife and treating her with honor, affection and respect, is the strongest evidence that such a man must have had some convincing proof that she was innocent and virtuous. We are told what that proof was, namely, the vision of an angel from heaven bearing a divine message to Joseph, saying, "Do not be afraid to take Mary home as your wife, because what is conceived in her is from the Holy Spirit. She will give birth to a son, and you are to give him the name Jesus, because he will save his people from their sins" (1:20b–21).

Joseph, therefore, is the first witness to the spotless and supernatural incarnation of the Son of Man.

THE TESTIMONY OF THE ANGEL

The angel that appeared to Joseph is the second witness. His message has been already quoted, and so we have not only the testimony of Mary's husband, but of the supernatural messenger that brought his orders from the throne.

ISAIAH'S TESTIMONY

A third witness was the prophet Isaiah. For all this had been precisely in accordance with the announcement which for centuries had been waiting unfulfilled in the sacred Scriptures of the Jews. Recorded there in the seventh chapter of the book of Isaiah, in words which no Hebrew has ever dared to question to this day, is the strange announcement, "The virgin will be with child and will give birth to a son, and will call him Immanuel" (7:14b). Such a thought had never entered the human mind as a virgin bringing forth a son, but God had long ago announced it, and now it was at last fulfilled. How are we to explain this ancient prophecy and other repetitions of it in Micah and Jeremiah, if the miraculous conception of Christ is a delusion?

THE TESTIMONY OF THE STAR

The very heavens themselves were witnesses of the royal birth. A strange star appeared in the sky which brought from distant lands a company of the sages of other nations who knew, from their reading of astrology, that some distinguished ruler was being born in Palestine, and that they must come to visit the place of His birth and pay their worship at His feet. Astronomers tell us of remarkable combinations of the planets which certainly happened at that very time.

Just as the material universe shuddered over the cross of Calvary, so likewise it sent its signals to bear witness at His cradle, too.

THE MAGI

There was the witness of the world. The wise men that came from eastern lands represented the great heart of the world bearing witness to Jesus Christ. Humanity is crying out for God. In every age and every land there have been men whose attitude to the unseen world is well described by the apostle, who says, "God did this so that men would seek him and perhaps reach out for him and find him" (Acts 17:27). These sages had been watching the heavens for some light on the other world, and at last they felt the answer had come. Ancient legends love to represent three of these Magi as respectively a king, a priest and a prophet. The first represented the riches of the world, and brought his gold; the second represented his worship of the world, and brought his frankincense; and the third represented the sorrow of the world, and brought an offering of myrrh, the perfume with which they anointed the dead, and the old legend adds that in response to his touch, the infant Christ looked up and touched the worshiper's hand. It is perhaps a legend, but at least it suggests a truth, that the sweetest offering we can bring our King is the gift of our sorrow and our sin. These men were types of the myriads who all through the Christian age have pressed to the cross and found in the Incarnate One the answer to their sorrows and the remedy for their sins.

THE RULERS

The best of all the witnesses to the Holy Babe were the scribes and rulers of Jerusalem, the very men that afterwards condemned and crucified Him. When the wise men came to Jerusalem they inquired for the King that was born, and Herod called a council of the ecclesiastical rulers and asked them where the Christ should be born. They referred to the Hebrew Scriptures, and replied that it was Bethlehem, and quoted Micah's (5:2) prophecy locating the little village. The wise men followed and found the Holy Christ in the very place the prophecy had foretold. So the Scriptures of the Old Testament and the rulers of the Hebrew nation combine to identify Jesus, the Babe of Bethlehem, as the promised Messiah and Israel's King.

HEROD'S TESTIMONY

Herod himself, the false king of Israel, became unconsciously a witness to the true King by the jealous fear which the advent of the Babe of Bethlehem brought to his troubled mind, and the cruel, murderous hate with which he pursued Him and sought His very life. When Herod heard of His birth, we are told, "he was disturbed, and all Jerusalem with him" (Matthew 2:3). What a compliment to the lowly Babe in yonder manger that He should shake the very throne of the reigning monarch! The cruel tyrant never rested till he had butchered all the little boys of Bethlehem in the hope of exterminating his dreaded rival. But God had hidden His Son from his hate and wrath. Yet nonetheless does Herod's jealousy bear witness to the kingship of Jesus Christ.

SECTION III—*His Names*

This story presents to us a number of remarkable names and titles of Christ full of instructive meaning.

IMMANUEL

Immanuel (Matthew 1:23) means "God with us." It stands for the first great truth of redemption, namely, the *incarnation* of Jesus Christ, God in human form, God united to our nature and revealed in our flesh. This is the highest honor possible for humanity, to sit on yonder throne as the very form of deity.

JESUS

"You are to give him the name Jesus, because he will save his people from their sins" (1:21). This marks the second great truth in redemption, not only *incarnation*, but *atonement*. Not only has He visited us, but He has also redeemed us. It stands for the cross of Calvary, the blood of cleansing and the gospel of salvation. Have we accepted Him in this glorious name and has He indeed saved us, not only from the guilt, but the power of sin?

CHRIST

"Jesus, who is called Christ" (1:16). This marks a still higher spiritual meaning. Christ means "anointed" and it suggests the baptism of the Holy Spirit. Christ is the one that received the Holy Spirit and dispenses that precious gift to hungry and consecrated hearts. He is the One who not only saves, but sanctifies. Have we accepted Him as the Christ and have we received from Him that holy *chrism*, that sacred anointing which makes us Christians in the true sense, anointed ones, baptized and filled with the Holy Spirit?

THE KING

"Where is the one who has been born king of the Jews?" (2:2). What the world needs is a king. Human nature is made for obedience and subjection to a leader. Men want somebody to do their thinking for them, and that is the secret of the success of so many ambitious pretenders. We have our political bosses, and how subserviently they are followed; we have our industrial leaders, and how disgracefully they have abused their power; and we have our religious bosses, and with what blindness and fanaticism their disciples are following some of these impostors and false apostles. But none of them have ever done or ever will do anybody any good but themselves. The world is waiting for the true King, and Jesus is that King, the only One who will ever right our wrongs, and rule humanity with unselfish authority and righteousness.

THE HOLY CHILD

The Child, the Babe—this name also He bears. "They saw the child . . . and they bowed down and worshiped him" (2:11). Thank God our King has the spirit of a child. Jesus is crowned and enthroned tenderness, meekness, humility and self-sacrificing love. Although King of kings, and Lord of lords, He is as accessible, as simple, as lowly as a little child.

He comes to us in lowly disguise as the Babe of Bethlehem, the homeless wanderer, the Crucified of Calvary. But He is coming back in all His majesty and glory as the King of kings and Lord of lords, and only those who accept Him in His humiliation will be with Him in His kingdom. We must learn, like Joseph, to pass from the depths to the heights; we must go with Jesus from the manger to the throne.

It is said that one of the Russian emperors used to disguise himself and go out among his subjects at night as a poor tramp. One night, after having been turned from every door, at last he found refuge in a peasant's cottage, and lay all night upon a bed of straw, eating only of the crust the poor man shared with him. The next day he came back with his royal retinue round about him and called at that peasant's door. The poor man thought his doom had come, but it was to his amazement to have his sovereign take him by the hand, thank him for his kindness to him the night before and load him with rewards and honors.

Some day our King is coming back in majesty and glory, before which the sun and stars will cease to shine. Happy then for you if He who sits upon that throne shall meet your eye, shall stretch out His hand to welcome you, shall bid you rise, and seating you by His side, shall say, "Come, you who are blessed by my Father; take your inheritance, the kingdom prepared for you since the creation of the world. For . . . I was a stranger and you invited me in" (25:34–35).

CHAPTER 2

THE CHILDHOOD OF THE KING

"Thy holy child Jesus" (Acts 4:27, KJV)

"The child is the father of the man" is an adage which was as true of the childhood of Christ as it has often been of earth's distinguished men. In the story of Jesus recorded in Matthew 2, we see foreshadowed the larger story of His later life as unfolded in the Gospel of Matthew.

A careful study of this gospel will show that it may be divided into two sections, the first, up through the 10th chapter, setting forth the manifestation of Christ as Israel's King and the second recording the gradual and final rejection of the Messiah by His people, until at last it culminated in the betrayal, trial and crucifixion. All this we see in type in the story of His childhood, as given in the second chapter of Matthew.

SECTION I—*Visit of the Magi*

The revelation of the King is presented in the story of the visitation of the Magi to Jerusalem and Bethlehem. These men represented the wisdom and glory of the Gentile nations. It was true of the later history of Christianity that the Gentiles should be the first who recognized Him. These wise men stood for the merits of every tribe and tongue who have been flocking to His standard for 19 centuries, even as He said they would. "But I, when I am lifted up from the earth, will draw all men to myself" (John 12:32). When the times of the Gentiles are fulfilled, then Israel will seek and recognize her long rejected King.

These Magi brought the most distinguished recognition to the infant Messiah. They represented the priests and the prophets of the ancient world, and by their visit to Jerusalem and the answer given to them by the rulers of the Jewish nation identifying Bethlehem as the birthplace of the Messiah, they added to their testimony for Christ the testimony of the whole Jewish nation, too. The offerings they brought to Him were significant of the high character they ascribed to Him.

GOLD

They recognized Him as King and Lord by their offerings of gold. They counted Him the proprietor of all their wealth, and they brought to Him their gold in acknowledgment of this. This is what our gifts to God really signify. We do not give because He is poor, but because He is rich. The common idea of Christian giving is that the cause of Christ is in distress and we must help it out. This is an insult to God. He does not need our help. With sublime scorn of men's assumptions He says: "For every animal of the forest is mine,/ and the cattle on a thousand hills. . . . If I were hungry I would not tell you,/ for the world is mine, and all that is in it" (Psalm 50:10, 12). He accepts our gifts as a token of our allegiance and as a recognition of His sovereignty. He does not want them unless they mean this. The question for each of us is that which Christ put to the men that brought Him a coin of Caesar's: " 'Whose portrait is this? And whose inscription?' 'Caesar's,' they replied. Then he said to them, 'Give to Caesar what is Caesar's, and to God what is God's' " (Matthew 22:20–21). If God owns our gold, let us give it to Him in recognition of His claim; if we own it ourselves, and are our own proprietors, let us keep it and perish with it.

INCENSE (FRANKINCENSE)

They recognized Him as divine by the worship they paid and by the frankincense they offered Him. Frankincense was a precious perfume consecrated to religious worship. It was made by burning costly spices, and under the Jewish ceremonial it was protected by a prohibition so solemn that anyone who counterfeited it was guilty of sacrilege and sentenced to be cut off from among the people. In bringing this sacred offering to the Holy Babe, the Magi acknowledged Him as a divine being. This was what He always claimed to be, and this was one of the reasons why His enemies at last condemned Him to death, because He said that He was the Son of God. What He asks from us is worship. He does not want our service any more than our gold unless we first give Him ourselves. The homage He claims is the devotion of our hearts, and there is no finer figure of true worship than the burning frankincense—all the strength and sweetness of our being on fire with love to God and poured out as an offering of devotion. In the highest sense, every consecrated spirit is a sanctuary with its altar of incense and its Holy of Holies, where evermore ascends the breath of adoration, love and praise, and all our nature is ever voicing the divine doxology "For from him and through him and to him are all things./ To him be the glory forever! Amen" (Romans 11:36).

MYRRH

The last offering they brought Him was myrrh. This also had significance. It was for the anointing of the dead, and most distinctly it bore witness to His cross and precious blood. They recognized Him, not only as their King and Lord, but also as their Savior, whose life was to close with tragedy, and whose glory was to be humbled in the dust and buried in the tomb. The cross mark of Israel's Messiah was overlooked by them. There was so much of glory in the ancient picture of the Christ that they could not see the signs of suffering. We can see them clearly enough now that this is all past, but their eyes were blinded to the crown of thorns and the cross of Calvary. Alas there is a tendency today, in the liberal theology of our time, to pass by the cross once more, or at least, to explain it away in some lofty manner which will take out all its sacrificial significance. The latest theory is that the death of Christ was a sublime climax of heroism and self-sacrifice, intended to exalt human nature to such a height that it could claim acceptance with God, and also intended to inspire by the force of example our selfish lives to the nobility of self-sacrifice. This is not the cross in which Paul gloried, and of which the ransomed sing. Men are still ashamed of the myrrh.

One is reminded of the beautiful girl who had become ashamed of her mother's presence because that mother's face was scarred and her form disfigured in a most repulsive way. Patiently the mother suffered in silence until one day an old family friend took the daughter aside and asked her if she knew what caused that mother's disfigurement. And then she told the wondering and humbled girl how when she was a helpless babe, that mother snatched her from the flames, covered her with her own body, smothered the fire before it harmed her, but herself got the devouring blaze and was only saved from death with the marks of the fire upon her face and form for life. Do you suppose that daughter would have dared again to be ashamed of her mother's scars? Shame on the person that would blush because of our Savior's precious blood.

> Ashamed of Jesus, yes we may,
> When we've no guilt to wash away,
> No fears to hush, no good to crave,
> No tears to wipe, no soul to save.

SECTION II—*His Rejection*

Here also we have the foreshadowing of His future rejection in His public ministry.

BY HEROD

Instead of welcoming Him, we are told that Herod "was disturbed, and all Jerusalem with him" (Matthew 2:3). This represents the attitude of the political world to the Lord Jesus and His second coming. We read of it in the second Psalm: "The kings of the earth take their stand/ and the rulers gather together against the LORD/ and against his Anointed One" (2:2). Herod could only see in the birth of Christ a menace to his throne, and his natural resort was to violence and murder. In his cruel and relentless determination to put Jesus out of the way, he assassinated all the boys of Bethlehem under two years of age. Herod was of the race of Esau, and so he naturally represented the flesh in its enmity against the Lord; but he represented also the normal attitude of the world's political governments. We talk loudly of our Christian nations and our socialistic dreams, ideal communities and states that will be essentially theocratic. This will never be until Jesus Christ Himself shall come and establish His kingdom by divine authority and power. And when He comes He will find the world and its rulers not waiting to welcome and worship, but arrayed against Him in the last, dread battle of Armageddon.

BY THE RULERS

The ecclesiastical rulers, too, had the best of opportunities to examine His claims and accept His message. Their very Scripture pointed them to the place where He lay. But they, too, were disturbed as much as Herod. They made no effort to visit Him at Bethlehem, but treated Him with neglect and indifference, and afterwards rejected and crucified Him. And so the religious world, as well as the political, will be found arrayed against Christ when He comes again. There will be a little flock of true followers and friends, but the ecclesiastical rulers of Christendom are today not much in sympathy with the true spirit of Christ, and the Church is rapidly drifting toward the sad and solemn picture of the Laodicean Church, the last stage of nominal Christianity on earth, with Christ standing outside the door, and rejecting the lukewarm formalism which still wears His name, but which He is ready to spew out of His mouth (Revelation 3:14–16).

EXILE IN EGYPT

His flight into Egypt marked the next stage of His rejection. The Holy Babe and His mother, with Joseph, were forewarned of the threatened assassination, and immediately departed to the land which had always been associated with the sufferings of their people. Egypt was the land of exile and the house of bondage. It was necessary, therefore, that the Lord should pass through all that His people had suffered or should suffer. The journey was not made in royal state; no luxurious palace car conveyed this Leader and Master; no splendid hotel waited with open doors to entertain Him. Seated with His mother on a lowly ass, with Joseph leading it by the hand, along the rocky and desert road, with a leather bag of water and a few dates or figs and barley cakes, they traversed the long and desert way, and took refuge at last in some humble cabin in the land of their fathers' bondage. Still He is a King in exile. He does not sit on splendid thrones, or control the men and armies of the world, but like David in the cave of Adullam (1 Samuel 22:1–2), He has His humble followers gathered from the outcasts of the land. Christ is still an exiled King, and is despised and rejected of men. And if He were to appear once more, the majority of those who bear His name would probably be ashamed of Him.

THE NAZARENE

Nazareth was the last stage in the story of His rejection. The very root of the name Nazareth literally means a sprout or root out of a dry ground. It is quoted in Isaiah 11:1, "A shoot (sprout, KJV) will come up from the stump of Jesse," and in Isaiah 53:2, translated, "He grew up before him like a tender shoot,/ and like a root out of dry ground." It is the Hebrew word *nazar*. The town of Nazareth was worthy of its derogatory name. It held the lowest place, socially and morally in public estimation, and the question of Nathaniel was characteristic, "Nazareth! Can anything good come from there?" (John 1:46). It was enough to destroy a prophet's reputation to hail from the town of Nazareth, and the city of the Nazarenes was a term of reproach in apostolic times.

But the pressure of His life at Nazareth amounted to a good deal more than merely the reputation of the town. It was a life of poverty, toil and deep abasement. Read any literal description of the life of laboring people in Nazareth today and you will have a fair conception of the conditions of His childhood in the old, unchanging East. A carpenter's wages was an amount less than 25 cents a day. His home was a wretched hut cut out in the side of the hill, more like a cave than a dwelling, without windows or ventilation. The family huddled together, sleeping on rude pallets of straw and living on the crudest food. Their implements of toil were most antiquated and clumsy, and the hours of labor and the rates of pay were not regulated by labor unions, but were as long and hard as the light of day. There seems every reason to believe that Jesus, the eldest son of Mary's home, was early left with the care of His mother, for Joseph must have died at an early period in the life of the boy. Speaking of the family while He was still but a young man, His enemies said, "Isn't this Mary's son and the brother of James, Joseph, Judas and Simon? Aren't his sisters here with us?" (Mark 6:3), but they made no mention of His father as if alive. If this be so, the little lad

Jesus must have early taken upon Him the headship of the family at Nazareth and the burden of breadwinner for the rest.

HIS BOYHOOD

And so we can think of 20 years perhaps of His life, oppressed with the burden of care and toil, until He became familiar with every experience in our common lot of toil and sorrow. We read in olden legends of many a foolish romantic story connected with His childhood, but the gospel story gives no place for these idle, childish stories. It is a plain, unvarnished picture of a commonplace life, no relieving pictures except the light that shone from heaven in the secret chambers of His holy heart.

Such then is the picture of our Savior's childhood. Modern history tells us of the founder of the great Russian empire having spent his boyhood in the humblest toil and the most obscure disguise. So God was preparing His King for the grander destiny of the ages to come, and so God is preparing now the kings and princes that are to sit with Him on His throne and share His glory by and by.

LESSONS

What are some of the practical lessons of this New Testament picture?

1. It bids us recognize the Lordship of our King and bring Him the offerings of our wealth and sacrifice and acknowledge Him as our proprietor and Lord. He does not need our gold; but He will let us trust it to Him as a glorious investment, and some day He will make up to us the magnificent return that will fill our eternity with praise.

2. It bids us bring to Him our worship and offer up our hearts as the frankincense they brought to Bethlehem of old. He does not want our gold without our love.

3. It bids us recognize and love His precious cross. The best gifts we can bring Him are our sorrows and our sins. He is asking us for the myrrh as well as for the frankincense.

4. It reminds us that there is One that has gone through every stage of our earthly experience and is with us in loving sympathy in our life of toil and sorrow. The Christ of Nazareth is our Christ still, and we can take Him with us to the drudgery of the nursery, to the grime of the factory, to the whirl of the workshop, to the burning heat of the harvest field, to the petty cares and annoyances of our business and family life. He has been just where we are now. We can take Him with us into the commonplace life of every day. This is where most people fail, and this was where our Master spent the largest part of His own life. Let us not wait for the opportunity of doing some extraordinary thing, but let us do the ordinary things for Him in the spirit of His own lowly life at Nazareth of old. The story is told of an artist that

waited long to find a piece of sandalwood on which to carve the angel whose image had been painted on his brain. At last, finding no other material, he took a common piece of oak firewood and carved the image in the oak, and the work was so splendid that the image became a classic. And so many people are waiting for some great achievement. Let us take the materials of our everyday life, and God will help us to transform them into angels, too.

5. It teaches us that the true test of loyalty is humility. God's princes are recognized not by their uplifted heads and boasting claims, but by their ability to stoop. It is the kneeling soldier that is made by his sovereign a knighted noble, and the lower we stoop for Christ, the loftier the place He is preparing for us.

6. The picture of Christ's childhood has been stereotyped in the Acts of the Apostles and left with us forever as a lasting vision of God's Holy Son. Christ in one sense is a child forever. It is true that the child's face is typical of the highest beauty. How often some sweet old man becomes like a little child in the mellow beauty of glorified old age. Our Lord has Himself said, "Whoever welcomes one of these little children in my name welcomes me; and whoever welcomes me does not welcome me but the one who sent me" (Mark 9:37). Does He mean that when we see our Savior we shall see the face of a child, and that when we see our Father in heaven, it will be a blending of the simplicity, gentleness and the transcendent beauty of some lovely babe?

7. The Christ of Nazareth is a pattern for the children of today. Dear young friends, He is your Christ; He belongs to you. He knows the temptations, experiences and feelings of a boy. He was once your very age. Come to Him and test Him. Make Him your ideal; choose Him as your Master; and may He translate into your childhood the glory of the life at Nazareth of old.

Especially let parents remember that the Christ of Nazareth was the type for every other life. Too long we have had our children taught to look for their ideals in the proud successful leaders of human history, and to emulate the ambitions of an Alexander, a Napoleon, a Dewey. This is all wrong. The highest, truest pattern is not the splendor of earthly success, but the glory of self-denial, meekness and humility, self-restraint, and the moral heroism that can stoop to the humblest place and glorify the lowliest sphere. We hear of the strenuous life today, but there is a still higher and harder life—the life of meekness, the life of unselfish love. God give it to us and to our children!

CHAPTER 3

THE INAUGURATION OF THE KING

"This is my Son, whom I love; with him I am well pleased." (Matthew 3:17)

W hat a contrast the introduction of God's King presents to the splendid pageants with which earthly sovereigns ascend their thrones! The present chapter gives us the picture of Christ's inauguration.

SECTION I—*The Forerunner*

The prophet Malachi, 400 years before, had announced not only the coming of the Messiah, but also of His herald. He was to come as Elijah the prophet, and as God's messenger. In exact accordance with the prophecy and the Old Testament pattern, John the Baptist at length appeared, introduced by angelic messengers and supernatural signs, and proclaimed the advent of the greater Personage that was soon to follow.

ELIJAH

A good deal of confusion has arisen in the minds of superficial thinkers through the misleading theories of certain modern freaks, who are contending for the office of the prophet of Elijah and who very wrongly take it for granted that there is to be a third appearance of the ancient prophet. The Scripture gives no intimation of any such reincarnation of Elijah. In fact, they do not teach the doctrine of reincarnation at all. This is one of the wrong teachings of Eastern Buddhism. According to the Bible, John the Baptist was not an incarnation of Elijah, but a distinct individual, named John, who was to represent the same special prophetic ministry which Elijah fulfilled. This is expressed in the phrase, "He will go on before the Lord, in the spirit and power of Elijah" (Luke 1:17). But John was not Elijah; he was a distinct prophet, closing the Old Testament series of prophetic ministries, even as Elijah had opened it, and our Lord Himself explicitly declares that John fulfilled the prophecy of Malachi respecting the reappearance of Elijah. " 'But I tell you, Elijah has already come, and they did not recognize him, but have done to him everything they wished. . . .' Then the disciples understood that he was talking to them about John the Baptist" (Matthew 17:12a, 13).

FALSE PROPHETS

John was indeed a good deal more true to the ideal Old Testament idea of Elijah than his modern imitators. His personal appearance was rugged and his dress appropriate to a child of the wilderness. He lived in no sumptuous hotels, nor appeared in gorgeous ecclesiastical vestures; but his food was dried locusts and wild honey, and his gown a rough blanket of camel's hair, fastened with a belt of skin around his waist. His spirit and message, like Elijah's, represented the law rather than the gospel. He came to the Jewish people and was not a preacher of the gospel for the Gentiles.

His most distinguished mark was his humility. His one desire was to bear witness to the coming One and pass out of sight himself. Unlike modern imitators, he had no desire to occupy the center of the stage, but like the true Elijah on the Mount of Transfiguration, it was his business and his supreme delight to disappear and leave "no one except Jesus" (Matthew 17:8). He was the friend of the Bridegroom whose one occupation was to introduce the Bridegroom and then give place to Him. He was the morning star that shone to introduce the coming sunrise and then paled before the Lord of day. "He must become greater; I must become less" (John 3:30).

SECTION II—*The Preparation*

HIS MINISTRY OF MESSENGER

John's business was to prepare Israel for the presentation of their Messiah. The nation had backslidden until they practically lost their covenant rights as God's theocratic people. His ministry of repentance, and the sign of baptism that accompanied it, practically ignored all their ecclesiastical claims and rights and demanded of them that they should come back to God as proselytes from heathenism had to come.

The rite of baptism was not unknown among the Jews, but it was invariably associated with the receiving of proselytes or converts from the heathen. To require a Jew, therefore, to be baptized was an ignoring of his Jewish standing. It implied that he had forfeited his covenant rights and had to be born over again. It was indeed laying the axe to the root of the tree and hewing down all their pretensions and claims of birth and merit. That they should submit to this is the most profound proof of the marvelous power of the great revival introduced by John. Baptism in its own essential symbolism and significance is the figure of death and resurrection, and the baptism of the people of Israel was a death blow to all their religious pride and an acknowledgment of the need of an entirely new life before they could again stand on covenant ground.

An attempt has been made by some rigid dispensational teachers to show that John's ministry of repentance was intended only for Jews. They tell us that the gospel message to the Gentile is simply "Believe on the Lord Jesus Christ," and that repentance is involved but not expressed, that it belongs to the message of the law and not the gospel. These writers had better read again the statement of Paul (Acts 20:21), where he tells us that he "declared to both Jews and Greeks that they must turn to God in repentance and have faith in our Lord Jesus." We know the church at Ephesus largely consisted of Gentiles, and Paul's message to them had been the message of repentance as well as faith. Again, in Acts 26:20, the Apostle declares to Agrippa how his ministry and message began: "First to those in Damascus, then to those in Jerusalem and in all Judea, and to the Gentiles also, I preached that they should repent and turn to God and prove their repentance by their deeds." Paul had the same gospel for Jews and Gentiles, repentance toward God and faith toward the Lord Jesus Christ.

The message of repentance is always God's preparation for every advance moment. The hardened sinner has no use for God's message of grace until driven to self-despair by conviction of sin; then he is willing to listen to the gospel of the grace of God and believe on the Lord Jesus Christ.

John's message of repentance was not given merely to the coarse and criminal classes of his time, but to the learned Sadducees, the religious Pharisees and the cultured courtiers who thronged to hear him. It must have seemed very rude that he should class them all with publicans and sinners, but he did, and demanded of them a repentance so radical as to acknowledge that they needed a change as thorough as the publicans themselves.

It is said that John Wesley once preached one of his heart-searching sermons to a cultivated audience of fashionable people, and one of the ladies said at the close: "Why, Mr. Wesley, that sermon would just have suited the prisoners in Newgate jail." "Oh, no, madam," said the good evangelist, "if I had been preaching in Newgate jail, I would have preached: 'Behold the Lamb of God that taketh away the sin of the world.' The poor, self-convicted sinner could appreciate the gospel, but the proud, self-righteous moralist is not ready for it yet."

But John not merely demanded repentance, but restitution, righteousness, and a life bringing forth "fruit in keeping with repentance" (Matthew 3:8). The need of today in the Church of Christ is a revival of conscience and righteousness. This would impress an unbelieving world a good deal more than our learned answers to higher criticism. It is said that a farmer once called upon an infidel neighbor and told him that he had just been awakened to a sense of his sin, and wanted to restore to him four sheep that ought to be in his neighbor's pasture, with the offspring of these sheep for the past four years. The infidel was very much disturbed and said, "Go away; don't bother me about the sheep, you are welcome to keep them. If you go on this way much longer I will believe there is something after all in your religion. Keep the sheep and don't disturb my peace of mind." This is the gospel our conscienceless age needs, and this is the sort of repentance and practical righteousness that will make people want the fullness of Christ and lead the world to believe in Christ and His people.

SECTION III—*The Witness to Christ*

JOHN'S TESTIMONY

Notwithstanding his bold and faithful preaching of repentance, John knew that mere repentance would not permanently save them, and they must have a power supernatural and divine that would keep them from the sin that they had confessed and for a time put away. Therefore, he brought to them the promise of another and a greater Prophet, One who in His own personal character was so infinitely above him, that His very shoe strings he was unworthy to unloose, and One who was to bring a new power into our spiritual life as much greater than the mere power of repentance and reformation as fire is mightier than water. "He will baptize you with the Holy Spirit and with fire" (3:11c). Water is but external, fire is internal, penetrating and intrinsic in its cleansing power. This was what the prophet Ezekiel had announced centuries before as the radical need of fallen human nature, "I will put my Spirit in you and move you to follow my decrees and be careful to keep my laws" (36:27). This is the deeper Christian life which God is making so clear and so urgent in the life of His people today. This is Christ's baptism, not John's, and no converted soul is fully saved until it has passed on to this deeper life and received the Holy Spirit in His sanctifying and keeping fullness.

SECTION IV—*The Baptism of Christ*

Among the multitudes that came to John for baptism was one form so little different from the rest that speaking of Him later, John said, "I would not have known him, except that the one who sent me to baptize with water told me, 'The man on whom you see the Spirit come down and remain is he who will baptize with the Holy Spirit' " (John 1:33). John recognized the modest stranger as together they were going into the waters of the Jordan and at first refused to baptize Him: "I need to be baptized by you, and do you come to me?" (Matthew 3:14). But Christ insisted, explaining, "It is proper for us to do this to fulfill all righteousness" (3:15).

ITS MEANING

Christ had no sin of His own to bury, but He had the sin of the world. His baptism, therefore, was the assuming of the responsibility of human guilt and going down in a figure to death on account of it, and then coming forth in baptism again in a figure of the resurrection. As He did so, John expressed the deep significance of this sign on the following day, by pointing Him out and saying, "Look, the Lamb of God, who takes away the sin of the world!" (John 1:29). He had borne our sin into the waters of death figuratively, and, coming forth in resurrection, He had also figuratively borne it away. Then, a little later he was actually to go down into a real death on the cross, and come forth in a real resurrection. His baptism was the rehearsal in advance of the crucifixion and the resurrection. Therefore, it was followed by the Father's voice accepting Him, and declaring that He was well pleased, not only with Him for Himself, but henceforth and forevermore with all lost sinners who claimed Him as their Sacrifice and Righteousness.

THE HOLY SPIRIT

At the same time, there came to Jesus Christ another baptism, namely, the Holy Spirit, just as John declared that there would come this divine baptism to all who received Him. From this moment Jesus Christ stood in a new attitude to His work. Henceforth there was another Personality united with Him, in all His teachings, acts and sufferings. It was the third Person of the Deity, so that all Christ's public life was fulfilled in the power of the Spirit. While He was by His own divine right the Son of God, yet He deliberately suspended the exercise of His own divine rights, and took the position of a dependent man looking to God through the Holy Spirit to enable Him for all His ministry just as He enables us now.

Therefore, He delayed the commencement of His public ministry until after He had received the Holy Spirit. He did not attempt a single official act until He had been baptized with power from on high. What a lesson, what an example for us! His Spirit-baptism was intended to be the pattern of ours. This one feature marked the infinite difference between Christ's baptism and John's. John's was a baptism into death to the old life of sin; Christ's was a baptism into life and power, bringing to our aid something more than our own will power and our purpose to do better, and giving to us the divine cooperation of the Holy Spirit.

Not only so, it takes us into a new sonship. Even as He was recognized as the Son of God, united to Him by the Holy Spirit, we share His relation to the Father, and in infinite humility, and yet with infinite confidence we can hear the Father say, "accepted in the beloved" (Ephesians 1:6, KJV). "This is my Son, whom I love; with him I am well pleased" (Matthew 3:17).

LESSONS

In conclusion, what are some of the lessons of this story?

1. The first surely is repentance. If there is anything that is not right, we must put it right. God is not going to do for you what you can do. You can turn away from sin though you cannot keep away from it without His help; but the moment you make your new choice, He will give you His divine ability to keep it. "If you had responded to my rebuke,/ I would have poured out my heart to you/ and made my thoughts known to you" (Proverbs 1:23). It is ours to turn, it is His to meet us with His almighty grace and pour out His Spirit upon us without which all our doing is utterly vain.

2. Are you living under John's baptism or Christ's? The great majority of Christians today have gotten little farther than John's baptism, a conscientious turning to God with a desire and purpose to live a better life, but without any real touch of power from on high. No convert should be left in this place. The only guarantee of being kept is to go on to the baptism of the Holy Spirit.

3. Have you received the Holy Spirit since you believed (Acts 19:2)? That is the gift of Christ, that is the imperative need of every Christian. That is the special message of God to His people today, and the great work that He is doing preparatory to the coming of our Lord. Oh, listen to His appeal and "receive the Holy Spirit" (John 20:22).

4. Are you living under the opened heavens and in the fellowship and faith of God? That is what the baptism of the Spirit brings. The resurrection and ascension of Christ have opened heaven to the child of God, and it is our privilege to walk in the light of that upper world. We are dwelling in "heavenly realms in Christ Jesus" (Ephesians 2:6). We are the children of the day. Our feet may tread this earthly scene; but our hearts, our interests, our hopes, our lives are all invested yonder, and it is our privilege also to walk in the favor and love of God. "He hath made us accepted in the beloved" (1:6, KJV). We have no right to live like a prodigal in the kitchen or the swine house, but to take our place in our Father's love. Not for our righteousness are we accepted, not because of our unrighteousness are we excluded. But that day on Jordan's banks, one Man so pleased the Father, that forevermore He is pleased with every sinner that accepts Him and abides in Him, and He is willing to give us His grace, so that we may, moment by moment, "live a life worthy of the Lord and may please him in every way" (Colossians 1:10). Oh, let us walk with the heavens opened unto us and the Father ever whispering: "This is my Son, whom I love; with him I am well pleased" (Matthew 3:17).

CHAPTER 4

FIRST CONFLICT AND VICTORY OF THE KING

Then Jesus was led by the Spirit into the desert to be tempted by the devil. (Matthew 4:1)

Before David, the type of His greater Son, could be publicly called to the kingdom of Israel, he had to prove his prowess in single combat with the champion of the enemy, and his victory over Goliath vindicated his right to be recognized as the true leader of his people. In like manner the Lord Jesus Christ, immediately after the public inauguration of His ministry by the testimony of His Father, was called to meet the great enemy of God and overcome him in single combat and decisive victory.

MEANING OF THE TEMPTATION

The temptation in the wilderness had a threefold significance. First, it was intended to prove the divine character and the spotless righteousness of the Lord Himself.

In the next place, it was intended to defeat the devil from the very start and put him in the position henceforth of a conquered foe.

And in the third place, He fought the battle of the wilderness as the Captain of our salvation, and His conflict was the pattern and pledge of the conflict and victory through which all His followers should pass.

THE PLACE

The scene of the temptation was suggestive. The first chapter of human history began in a paradise, but it ended in a disaster. The first chapter of divine redemption began in a desert, but it shall end in a paradise restored. This contrast is typical of the old and new dispensations. The old dispensation gives promise of earthly blessing, the new dispensation starts in company with our Lord in poverty and humiliation and it leads up through great tribulation to the place where sorrow is unknown.

THE TIME

The time of our Lord's temptation was also full of significance. It came immediately after His baptism and the voice of the Father proclaiming from the open heavens: "This is my Son, whom I love; with him I am well pleased" (Matthew 3:17). Our severest temptations will come to us after our greatest blessings. The old line is full of meaning,

> If conqueror, of tomorrow's fight beware.

Indeed, it is only the soul that has met God and received the baptism of the Holy Spirit that really feels the full force of temptation. The man that is going along with the current of evil is insensible to its power. It is when he resists that he is conscious of the opposing force. It was when the Philistines heard that David had been made king that they came to "search for him" (2 Samuel 5:17). He was important enough now to be an object of their attack, and it is when we have yielded ourselves to God and committed ourselves to the purpose of full salvation that all powers of evil are combined to break us down and dishonor us with defeat and failure.

Then again the time of our Savior's temptation was significant in respect of His physical condition. He had just been fasting 40 days and nights, and it is added that after this "he was hungry" (Matthew 4:2). His body and mind were worn and exhausted with long fasting and privation in the wilderness and in this condition He was particularly susceptible to the assault of the enemy. Satan knows when we are weak and subject to his power, and he wisely chooses the time of attacking.

The story is told of a young student of blameless character who had struggled for years to win a valuable fellowship in the university that he might be able to support his widowed mother and continue his own studies. At length the crisis hour came on which all his future depended, and his friends were delighted when they learned at the close of a strenuous day that he had successfully passed the examinations and won his fellowship. Up to that time he had denied himself every needless indulgence and firmly resisted all temptation that might turn him aside from his high purpose. But it was the surprise and sorrow of one of his student companions on calling at his room that night to congratulate him, to find him lying on the floor in a condition of helpless drunkenness. The strain had been too great, the reaction had come, nature had given way, and the enemy had chosen that moment to wreck his life. And so we need to watch at all times, but especially to "stand your ground, and after you have done everything, to stand" (Ephesians 6:13).

THE ADVERSARY

The agent of the temptation is called the devil. This name is passing out of some of the modern theological dictionaries, but you will always find that with the passing out of the devil, there will also come the passing out of the blood, the cross, the Savior and even God Himself. The Bible recognizes a personal devil as definitely as a personal God. It is the very intensity of the light that flings on the street the shadow as you pass beneath the electric lamp. There is a real devil and a mighty army of demon spirits under his direction and control. It is probable that he himself, their mighty leader, only occasionally confronts any of God's servants. We may be very sure that he employs his time and his resources to the best advantage and wastes no needless ammunition on those that can be safely left to weaker hands.

There is no doubt that the story of the temptation describes a personal conflict between him and the Lord. At the same time, we do not need to believe that he was there in visible form, and that the instance described actually took place on a real mountain or the pinnacle of the very temple itself. We know that He was tempted as we are, and our temptations do not come to us in tangible manifestations of Satanic power. It is in our spirit that he meets us, with mental suggestions so vivid that they almost seem like voices, and yet, there is no visible presence. Had our Lord's temptation been a realistic incarnation and revelation of the devil, it would have been separated very far from the experience of His people. It is a question if Satan would be much of a temptation to us if he came in the traditional form, with cloven feet and dragon wings. The old Scotchman was not far from wrong when, after looking at a great painting of the temptation, with the devil in the background in the usual characters and colors, he said: "Yon deevil wouldna tempt me." He meant that he was too repulsive and terrifying to attract him very far in his direction. It is when he comes as an "angel of light" (2 Corinthians 11:14), with his insidious suggestions to the mind, that we have most reason to dread him. There is no difficulty in supposing that the mountain and the pinnacle of the temple were made real to Christ in vision, just as Ezekiel was present in the spirit in the temple at Jerusalem, although actually hundreds of miles away in Babylon.

THE CHEAP DEVIL

One of the strongest impressions which one receives in carefully reading this narrative is the utter poverty of the devil. He had nothing to offer Christ but stones. He couldn't even bring Him bread. True, he offered Him the kingdoms of the world and the glory of them, but these were all stolen goods, and the devil had no power to give title. Christ rejected his braggart bribe, and a little later was able to say Himself: "All authority in heaven and on earth has been given to me" (Matthew 28:18). The day is coming when the shout will be heard in earth and heaven: "The kingdom of the world has become the kingdom of our Lord and of his Christ" (Revelation 11:15b).

The devil is a liar and a fraud, and he will cheat you every time. Do not listen to his propositions. He is a promoter of worthless stocks; he will take your money and laugh at you after he has fooled you.

THE HOLY SPIRIT

There was another agent in this temptation, namely, the Holy Spirit. "Then Jesus was led by the Spirit into the desert to be tempted by the devil" (Matthew 4:1). Do not let us make our own temptations, but when God permits them, let us be very sure that He will go with us through them as He did with Jesus Christ. Then we shall have no need to fight in this battle. Hand over the devil along with all our other trials to His hands, then the battle will be the Lord's, and we shall learn to stand still and see Him conquer. "For the sinful nature desires what is contrary to the Spirit, and the Spirit what is contrary to the sinful nature" (Galatians 5:17). "When the enemy comes in like a flood,/ the Spirit of the LORD will put him to flight" (Isaiah 59:19b, margin).

AGAINST HIS FAITH

The form of the temptation is full of practical teaching and help. The first object of the enemy was to destroy His faith. This is always the primary object of the tempter. It is a trial of our faith. He came to Christ with an insinuating question, just as he came to our first parents in Eden. He did not dare to deny Jesus' divine Sonship, but he cunningly hinted at the obvious inconsistency of anybody in so deplorable a condition as He was, claiming to be the Son of God. It was as if he had said, "You, the Son of God, out here in this desolate wilderness, neglected by your Father, ready to perish with hunger? Surely it must be some wild delusion; and yet, if it be, why certainly you will have no difficulty in proving it by supplying yourself miraculously with all the bread you need?" And so he comes to us with some discouragement. He points to some mysterious trial or privation and he insinuates the subtle doubt of our Father's love, or of our own sonship; and we begin to wonder if, after all, we can be truly His children. Discouragement is back of many a life of sin and failure, and confidence in God is a "shield of faith, with which you can extinguish all the flaming arrows of the evil one" (Ephesians 6:16).

Then, when the adversary gets us discouraged, it is so easy for him to suggest to us some forbidden way of help—"make the stones bread," take some unauthorized way of deliverance, step out of the will of God, and accept the compromise of right or honor which the wicked one has always ready at our hand. But the Master would do no such thing. It was not so necessary for Him to have bread, as to do the will of God, and stand where His Father had placed Him in submission and obedience. And so He answered, "Man does not live on bread alone, but on every word that comes from the mouth of God" (Matthew 4:4).

A VICTORY OF RIGHTEOUSNESS

It has been finely said that the Lord Jesus did not defeat Satan by power, but by righteousness. It would have been very easy for Him, by a stroke of power, to have hurled the fiend into the abyss, but He did something better. He stood so panoplied by divine righteousness that the enemy could make no impression on the Son of God and was driven back helpless and defeated simply by the Master's breastplate of righteousness.

HIS HIGH NATURE

The next temptation appealed to His higher spiritual nature. It was a solicitation to His faith to go too far, venturing beyond the prescribed limits of God's own Word. "Throw yourself down" (4:6), he said, "and let God work a mighty miracle in your preservation, which will lead the people to acknowledge you in your divine character." When the enemy cannot tempt us through our lower nature, he will do so through our higher. He will use even our religious life and our very faith as the instrument of fanaticism, and push us to some rash, presumptuous extreme through which we shall take ourselves out of the hands of God, and really put ourselves in the hands of the enemy. Therefore, we see around us today, the numerous examples of well-meaning people that probably began with sincere faith and then allowed themselves to be controlled by the spirit of fanaticism until they have become the very instruments of the devil himself. Let us remember that even faith itself can go no farther than the Word of God. It must always be limited by "it is written" (4:4), and then "Everything is possible for him who believes" (Mark 9:23).

POWER

The next assault of Satan was aimed at the ambition of our Lord, and especially at what might be called a holy ambition. He showed Him all the kingdoms of the world, and the glory of them, and doubtless urged upon Him the good that He could do by accepting these seats of power and vast resources and using them to reclaim this earth from all its wrongs and grievances, and prove Himself the deliverer of humanity. But He asked this: that he be permitted to hold the helm, receive the homage and be the mastermind behind it all. " 'All this I will give you,' he said, 'if you will bow down and worship me' " (Matthew 4:9).

But he overreached himself. "Worship the Lord your God, and serve him only" (4:10b) was the answering blow with which his blasphemous demand was met, and he himself was driven, defeated, from the field. So still he comes with the alluring vision of power and ambition, pleading, no doubt, as of old, some beautiful motive, some dream of worldwide influence, some scheme of social reform or political utopia. The one fatal condition in it all is, "if you will bow down and worship me." His touch, his control, his partnership is enough. There can be no compromise with evil. Even the best things that he can give would be defiled by his fatal touch, and the true Christian will always remember that the only safe course is to have no fellowship with the unfruitful works of darkness and no partnership with evil in any form.

THE WORD OF GOD

The weapon which the Master used in this great conflict was the Word of God. "It is written" was His constant answer to the devil's approaches. It is very remarkable that the book of the Bible, from which Christ quoted all His answers to Satan, was that book which the higher criticism of today has rejected, the book of Deuteronomy. With divine foresight, the Lord chose this very portion of the Scriptures for His endorsement, and defeated Satan by the weapon which he himself pronounced the weakest in all the armory of truth. Satan seems to have been so much impressed with Christ's effective use of the Bible that he himself tried it once and began quoting Scripture, too, but he left out seven words in the quotation from the 91st Psalm. Those seven are the most vital of all, "to keep thee in all thy ways" (91:11b, KJV). All that Satan was thinking of was the physical keeping; but the clause he left out promised something besides this, namely, the keeping of the trusting soul in all his ways, so that it would be kept morally and spiritually as well as physically, and it was because of this very promise that Christ was kept from falling into his snare. You may always distinguish between the right and wrong use of Scripture by this test. The devil uses the Bible, too, but he uses it dishonestly to establish some special theory and without regard to the other Scriptures which appear upon the same point. We must remember always, not only that "it is written" (Matthew 4:4), but that "it is also written" (4:5).

THE RESULTS

Finally, let us note the results of this conflict. "Jesus returned to Galilee in the power of the Spirit" (Luke 4:14a). The Spirit led Him in and the Spirit led Him out with mightier power than He had entered in. The conflict of the wilderness left Him stronger than at the beginning. He was not only conqueror, but He was "more than conqueror" (Romans 8:37). So the Lord would have us gain spiritual power through the conflict. Let us not be content with merely escaping the devil's snare. Let us use the conflict for his defeat and dishonor and for the spoils of victory that will leave us richer and our adversary weaker than when the battle began.

"Blessed is the man who perseveres under trial, because when he has stood the test, he will receive the crown of life that God has promised to those who love him" (James 1:12). Not only is there the discipline of trial here and the strength it brings, but by and by there is a reward for the man that conquers.

There are four crowns promised to the victors. The first is the martyr's crown: "Be faithful, even to the point of death, and I will give you the crown of life" (Revelation 2:10). The second is the minister's crown: "And when the Chief Shepherd appears, you will receive the crown of glory that will never fade away" (1 Peter 5:4). The third is promised "to all who have longed for his appearing" (2 Timothy 4:8). But there is a fourth crown for the faithful soul that has battled with some hereditary temper, some long-established habit of evil, some trying surroundings and conditions in life, and perhaps feels that little service has been accomplished for God, and that it will be much to be saved at all "as one escaping through the flames" (1 Corinthians 3:15b). But some day, God will bring forth the crown of life for such tempted ones, and amid the acclamations of the skies, will place it upon your head, tried and struggling child of God, while the heavens shall ring with the echo of the promise, "Blessed is the man who perseveres under trial" (James 1:12).

CHAPTER 5

THE RIGHTEOUSNESS OF THE KINGDOM

Now when he saw the crowds, he went up on a mountainside and sat down. His disciples came to him, and he began to teach them . . . (Matthew 5:1–2)

After Moses had led the people across the Red Sea and they began their national history, he went up into a mountain and there promulgated God's great law from Sinai. In like manner, Jesus Christ, the Prophet greater than Moses, when He had been formally inaugurated and announced as the Messiah, also went up into a mountain and gave forth the great law of the New Testament.

ITS PLACE AND TIME

This is popularly known as the Sermon on the Mount. It is not introduced in the Gospel of Matthew in its chronological place, but was really delivered at a later period than the things recorded in the immediate context. This is in accordance with a principle already explained, that the writers of the Gospels were not mere reporters or historical chroniclers, but spiritual teachers, marshalling their facts, not in historical order, but rather in their logical relation to the central idea of their gospel.

It was the true order, that, having introduced the King and witnessed to His character and divine commission, He should now give to us a public declaration of the great principles of His kingdom and its relation to the teachings of the past and the plan of the future.

SCOPE OF THE DISCOURSE

This great discourse, which covers the next three chapters of Matthew (5–7), is an unfolding of the righteousness of the kingdom in contrast, first, with the teachings of Moses and the Old Testament; second, with the practice and conduct of the Scribes and Pharisees, the religious professors and teachers of the day; and thirdly, with the ungodly world who are traveling the broad road which leads to destruction.

It is necessary at the outset to clearly fix in our minds the purpose of this great discourse.

First, it is a summary of the law, presenting in concise form the essence of the teachings of Moses purged from the errors and corruptions which had grown around them through Jewish traditions.

Secondly, it is a summary of the ethical teaching of the New Testament, and therein marks a great advance upon the moral teaching of the Old Testament. It is a sort of frontispiece in the opening of the volume of Christ's life and teaching, like the first Psalm in the book of Psalms, which is a portrait of the godly man and primarily of the Lord Jesus Himself, the supreme type of all godliness and goodness. The Sermon on the Mount finds its only perfect realization in Christ Himself and so it stands like a portrait at the opening page of the Gospels.

NOT THE GOSPEL

But, in the third place, it must not be forgotten that even this sublime discourse falls short of the full spiritual teaching of the New Testament. It is not, therefore, in an unqualified sense, the law of Christ, and it is not correct to say, "If I regulate my life according to the Sermon on the Mount, I shall have reached the highest standard of character." We must bear in mind not only its advance on the teaching of the Old Testament, but its defects and shortcomings as compared with the deeper and higher teaching of the later portions of the New Testament. For example, we find nothing in this sermon about the name of Jesus and His mediation with the Father as our Intercessor and Great High Priest. The Lord's Prayer is offered to the Father direct without any reference to the Son. It is true that the "Our Father" of the first petition may be held, in the light of what Christ afterwards taught, to include the Intercessor along with us when we pray, but this certainly could not be obvious to an immediate listener to whom the great truth of Christ's Priesthood had not yet been explained. A good deal later, the Lord Himself refers to this and supplies the lack. "Until now you have not asked for anything in my name. Ask and you will receive, and your joy will be complete" (John 16:24).

Further, there is nothing here about the great work of the Holy Spirit, the next great revelation of the New Testament. This was to come later, and it would have been premature to introduce this teaching here before they were prepared to receive it. Later the Lord Himself made it preeminent in His parting messages, and the apostles of the New Testament re-echo the message on every page.

It is scarcely necessary to add that the Sermon on the Mount says nothing of the atonement, the crucifixion of the natural man, the resurrection life into which we enter through fellowship with Christ, and the indwelling of Christ Himself in the heart as the great Pattern of godliness and the only secret by which we can really live the Sermon on the Mount. It is a cold yet faultless vision of righteousness, revealing, like a mirror, our unrighteousness, but as helpless as that mirror would be to wash away impurities which it had exposed upon your face. While we give this glorious message its high preeminence, let us not put it in a false place, and let us not forget the Master's own later explanation, "I have much more to say to you, more than you can now bear. But when he, the Spirit of truth, comes, he will guide you into all truth" (16:12–13a). It is no reflection upon the honor of Christ to say these things, or frankly acknowledge the things that are lacking in His great law from the Mount. It was the message of the King and the Son of David, and it marked a transition between the Old and the New Testament dispensations, being the law of the kingdom rather than the law of the gospel. We find 10 great points in these New Testament laws.

CHARACTER

1. The Master does not speak of what we do, but of what we are, and the personal character which He here describes is strikingly different from the Old Testament ideal. The eight beatitudes mark the gradation of religious character by four steps downward and four steps upward. True spiritual character does not begin with self-effort, but self-renunciation. "Blessed are the poor in spirit" (Matthew 5:3a) is the first step; the people that are dissatisfied with themselves and have a deep and overwhelming sense of their failure and helplessness. The next step is also down, "Blessed are those who mourn" (5:4a). These are the people that not only realize their nothingness, but are deeply moved about it, and are tender and susceptible to the touch of God's Spirit. "Blessed are the meek" (5:5a) marks the next descending step; the people that are yielded, broken and so far from self-will that God can mold them to His will. Finally, the fourth step is a deep spiritual hunger, a longing for righteousness, a desire so earnest that all else is gladly sacrificed for the higher blessing sought. "Blessed are those who hunger and thirst for righteousness,/ for they will be filled" (5:6).

Now begins the spiritual ascent. The first step is love to others, that tender charity born of our own poverty of spirit and our own deep sense of nothingness and failure. "Blessed are the merciful" (5:7a). From love to man it is but a step to love to God, and so the next step is: "Blessed are the pure in heart" (5:8a). This is literally, the single in heart, the people that have but one aim, to please and glorify God. The third step in this advancing scale brings us to positive and practical service for Christ and others, "Blessed are the peacemakers" (5:9a). This does not mean the mere settling of personal grievances between people, but the sacred ministry of making peace between man and God, the reconciling of the world to Him, the seeking and saving of the lost. The last stage in spiritual life is suffering for Christ's sake. "Blessed are those who are persecuted because of righteousness. . . . Blessed are you when people insult you, persecute you and falsely say all kinds of evil against you because of me" (5:10–11). Christianity has its coronation in victorious suffering and patient submission to the will of God.

INFLUENCE

2. Character is not a cold and ethical quality; but it has a beneficent influence. Two fine figures are here employed to express it, the salt and the light. The salt is the figure of our silent influence, that which does not express itself in action, but spreads as a sweetening and conserving influence through human society. A very large part of our influence is unconscious and intangible, forces that are held in solution and yet that hold together the family, the Church and the whole social economy. True godliness is such salt, and for the sake of the saints of God, the world is saved from utter destruction.

There is also a positive influence in Christian character; it is like the light, diffused, far reaching, beneficent. It is not enough to have an absence of negative qualities. But rather, "let your light shine before men, that they may see your good deeds and praise your Father in heaven" (5:16). They must see our good works, but they must glorify not us, but our Father.

Salt and light! What beautiful figures of the influence of holy character. God help us to be as wholesome as the salt, and as bright, as pure, as far reaching in our influence for God and our usefulness to men as the beautiful light.

RIGHTEOUSNESS

3. From the 17th to the 37th verse, the Lord dwells upon the righteousness of the kingdom, showing, first, that it must not aim at a lower standard than the law, because instead of abrogating that law He has come to fulfill it. In the next place, it must surpass the righteousness of the Scribes and Pharisees, and we know that their righteousness was most scrupulous and elaborate. Above everything else, the righteousness of the kingdom must spring from the heart and control the secret motives of the soul. The hatred of a brother is recognized as murder, the spirit of evil desire as a real transgression of the seventh commandment, and the very thoughts of the heart as constituting moral acts and qualities. Under the heart-searching light of the holy law, human nature stands convicted and condemned, and "all our righteous acts are like filthy rags" (Isaiah 64:6).

LOVE

4. The last 10 verses of the fifth chapter of Matthew reach a height which

the Old Testament had not dreamed of. It teaches a love that not only sought to bless its neighbor but its enemy, and to be like the kind and beneficent heavenly Father, who "causes his sun to rise on the evil and the good, and sends rain on the righteous and the unrighteous" (Matthew 5:45). The law of Moses had nothing to correspond with the sublime ethics of the 44th verse: "Love your enemies and pray for those who persecute you." This is the high plane of the fifth beatitude, "Blessed are the merciful,/ for they will be shown mercy" (5:7). It is more than righteousness; it is divine love.

SINCERITY

5. Sincerity is the issue in chapter 6:1–18. Their good deeds, their alms, their prayers, their fasting, must all be in the sight of God and not in the sight of man. Ostentation and love of human praise must be denied, and our most sacred ministries inspired by two supreme motives: the glory of God and the approval of our Father in heaven. Human praise, if sought as a reward, will destroy all claim to higher recompense. The things we do to be seen of men may bring us their approval, but their value terminates there. "I tell you the truth, they have received their reward in full" (6:5c).

It is said a good man was once asked by a heavenly messenger what boon he would specially crave, and he asked that henceforth he might be made a blessing to everybody he came in contact with, but in such a way that his own shadow would never fall upon anyone else, and only God would recognize the service. The seraphim veil not only their faces, but their feet with their wings, and the highest ministry is that which is so lost in the thought of the Master that it forgets even its own footprints.

A SINGLE AIM

6. Singleness of heart is touched on in chapter 6:19–24. There must only be one Master. We cannot serve God and money. There must only be one goal, the home above. All our treasures must be there. The eye must be single to God alone, or the whole body shall be full of darkness. This is the meaning of the sixth beatitude. "Blessed are the pure in heart" (5:8a), literally this means, "the single in heart," people that have but one object and aim, to bless and glorify God, whether men praise or blame.

TRUST

7. Next, trust is present in chapter 6:25–34. The spirit of the Old Testament is work; the spirit of the New Testament is trust. Anxious care is forbidden and counted for sin. After the solemn words, "You cannot serve both God and Money" (6:24), the conjunction is introduced, "therefore." "Therefore I tell you, do not worry about your life" (6:25), and the inference is very plain that the taking of thought and the harboring of anxious care is a

form of serving money. Worldliness consists not merely in the love of the world, but quite as much in the fear of the world. True faith trusts the heavenly Father for the present life as well as for the life to come, and if we are not trusting Him now for the things that are present and real, what evidence have we that we are really trusting Him for the things that are unseen and about which we may only be deceiving ourselves? God gives us the tests and trials of the present life in order to prove that He is indeed real to us, and that our faith does take Him for help in time of need. Righteousness is not merely doing our duty to our fellow men, or even having an eye single to the will of God. The very root and principle of it is a confidence so simple and complete that like the sparrows of the field, we can leave all our interests in His hand and trust Him for the life that now is, as well as for that which is to come.

CHARITY

8. The spirit of consideration for others, especially in our judgments concerning our fellow men, is next enforced (chapter 7:1–16). The same principle by which we judge our brothers is to be applied to us by the Supreme Judge in the last day. With burning irony, the Master exposes the hollowness and insincerity of pretending to take a little speck of sawdust out of our brother's eye when there is something in our eyes as much greater than our brother's fault as a great piece of timber is greater than a little speck of sawdust floating in the sunbeam. The word "plank" here literally means "a rafter," a heavy piece of timber, and the keen logic of the comparison needs no emphasizing. We are not forbidden to judge of the moral quality of the actions of people; it is their motives that we are not to judge. Actual evil is obvious, and it is not wrong to call it by its right name. But this is a very different thing from sitting in judgment upon the motives and character of others. This is the prerogative of the divine Lawgiver, and He will not allow us to invade it.

At the same time there is a fine sentence added in the sixth verse. "Do not give dogs what is sacred; do not throw your pearls to pigs. If you do, they may trample them under their feet, and then turn and tear you to pieces." The spirit of charity does not require us to be weak and easily imposed upon. We should be so discriminating that we will not allow people to abuse our trustfulness. We should not commit ourselves to those that would take advantage of our frankness and rend us. We are to be "as shrewd as snakes and as innocent as doves" (10:16).

PRAYER

9. Two paragraphs are devoted to the subject of prayer in this discourse. The first is chapter 6:9–13, where the Lord's Prayer is given as the great model of prayer. This subject is resumed in chapter 7:7–11, "Ask and it will

be given to you; seek and you will find; knock and the door will be opened to you. For everyone who asks receives; he who seeks finds; and to him who knocks, the door will be opened" (7:7–8). The efficacy of prayer is most emphatically announced. Further, the various degrees and forms of prayer are finely expressed by the three words, "ask, seek and knock." Prayer is not only a matter of petition, but it is also a matter of patient and persevering search, and it is also a force that breaks down the barriers which interpose, and cooperates with God in bringing its own answer. Very beautifully does He tell us of the faithfulness of the great Hearer of prayer. He will not deceive us or put us off with a counterfeit blessing. From our own love to our offspring, He rises to the sublime argument, "If you, then, though you are evil, know how to give good gifts to your children, how much more will your Father in heaven give good gifts to those who ask him" (7:11).

THE FINAL TEST OF CHARACTER

10. Having finished the chief points of His discourse, He finally concludes by telling of the solemn test which is to come to every life and character.

He gives us a simple test to apply to our own actions. This is the Golden Rule (7:12), which shines like a star of light over all the teachings of human philosophy and morals: "So in everything, do to others what you would have them do to you, for this sums up the Law and the Prophets." This is the law of life by which we can determine for ourselves the right or the wrong of any action about which we may be in doubt. Is it according to the law of love? Will it bring happiness and blessing to my brother? Would I want him to do it to me? This will clear away every mist and enable us to act with a good conscience and a full assurance of pleasing God.

Next He gives us the test of the fruit men bear. "By their fruit you will recognize them" (7:16). The false prophet may come in sheep's clothing, but if we search him, we shall find him out by the influence of his life and the fruit of his teaching and practice. Is it humility, holiness, glory to God and lasting good to men? Or is it self-aggrandizement, self-glory and gain?

He gives us the test of obedience. This is to be the test of the judgment. "Not everyone who says to me, 'Lord, Lord,' will enter the kingdom of heaven, but only he who does the will of my Father who is in heaven. Many will say to me on that day, 'Lord, Lord, did we not prophesy in your name, and in your name drive out demons and perform many miracles?' Then I will tell them plainly, 'I never knew you. Away from me, you evildoers!' " (7:21–23).

God tests us now. The rain and the storm described in the closing paragraphs of this great Sermon on the Mount are not all to be revealed amid the tests of the Judgment Day. Many of these tests mercifully come to us now. God anticipates the day of judgment and gives to us the opportunity of finding out now whether we are prepared to stand the tests of the final day. Some day we shall thank Him for the trials and temptations that brought us to see whether we were wrong and saved us before the final crisis from the doom of the self-deceived.

The figure of the rock refers undoubtedly to the great Rock of Ages, Jesus Christ Himself. He alone is the foundation of holy character and final acceptance. It is not enough to know these lofty teachings or even to approve them. There is no power in poor human nature to fulfill them. The law of Christ, like the law of Moses, is but a mirror to reveal us to ourselves, not a fountain to cleanse us. For this we must go to Christ Himself.

The teaching of the Sermon on the Mount is not final but preparatory. It leads us up to Christ, but we must follow until we get there; and then from His indwelling light and His enabling Spirit, get the power to make this picture a living reality in our own experience. The great Teacher did not stop with the Sermon on the Mount. He has led us all the way to Calvary and Pentecost, and now, resting upon His finished work and His indwelling life and power, we can sing in a sense which the saints of the Old Testament could never know:

> On Christ, the solid Rock, I stand,
> All other ground is sinking sand.

CHAPTER 6

THE MIRACLES OF THE KINGDOM

"He has done everything well," they said. "He even makes the deaf hear and the mute speak." (Mark 7:37)

After the giving of the law by Moses, Israel's lawgiver, comes the record of the mighty works of Joshua, their great captain of faith and victory. And so, after the Sermon on the Mount, and the new law of righteousness proclaimed by the Lord Jesus, we are introduced to the victorious work of the Captain of our salvation.

The two chapters which follow the Sermon on the Mount, Matthew 8 and 9, contain a striking group of the miracles of our Lord, specially clustered together so as to set forth His mighty power in the most emphatic and convincing manner. They are not presented in their strict chronological order, but rather with special reference rather to their bearing upon His revelation as the Messiah and King. They are worthy of careful study in connection both with the kingdom and the King.

SECTION I—*The Kingdom*

Thoughtful students and teachers of dispensational truth see in these successive miracles a striking foreshadowing of the kingdom in its future developments. While we have no authority to say that the narrative was intended to set forth these future facts, yet there is nothing to forbid such an interpretation so long as it does not exclude the literal and immediate application of the truth to the present, or gospel, age.

One of the dangers of dispensational teaching is that it is apt to pigeonhole important portions of the Scriptures and limit them to the future when they are needed for the spiritual comfort of God's children in the present.

39

THE LEPER

In this view of their dispensational applications, the healing of the leper in the eighth chapter of Matthew is applied to Israel. The Lord was in the house when the leper came to Him, and so Israel in her sinfulness and helplessness, of which leprosy was the special Levitical type, is represented as coming to her King for healing.

CENTURION'S SERVANT

The next miracle, the healing of the centurion's servant, was quite different. Christ was absent from his house, and His healing virtue was transmitted through the intervening spaces to this Gentile believer, whom the Lord commended for a faith such as He had not found even in Israel. This represents Christ's healing and sanctifying power among the Gentiles through the Christian age, not through His visible and manifested presence, but through His Word, which is emphasized especially in this miracle.

PETER'S MOTHER-IN-LAW

The healing of Peter's mother-in-law, which follows, brings the Lord again into the house, and once more He is dealing with Israel, who is represented by the sick one here, whom He raises up to minister unto Him. This stands for the restoration of Israel at the coming of the Lord and the glorious ministry to which she shall be called during the Millennial age.

THE MULTITUDE

Then follows the healing of the people in Matthew 8:16, and the casting out of demon power without limitation. This, we are told by our dispensational friends, foreshadows the universal extension of the healing power of Christ after His second coming, when it shall be without limitation or restriction. Now some are healed, but then the promise will be fulfilled, "No one living in Zion will say, 'I am ill' " (Isaiah 33:24).

THE TEMPEST STILLED

The story of the stilling of the tempest in the eighth chapter of Matthew represents, according to this view, the trials and troubles of God's people during the present time, which are to be brought to an end at the appearing of the Lord, when He will rebuke the angry waves of this troubled world, and there shall be "a great calm" (Matthew 8:26, KJV).

This will be followed by the destruction of Satan's power in the Millennial earth, represented by the miracle of the healing of the Gadarene demoniacs, whom the Savior met on the other side of the lake after the stilling of the tempest.

THE PARALYTIC

Then follows the healing of the paralytic at Capernaum, accompanied especially by the statement, "the Son of Man has authority on earth to forgive sins" (9:6a). Our friends represent this as the appearing of Christ on earth and His restoring of His people Israel, raising them up from their paralysis of ages, and sending them forth to walk and work for Him.

OTHER MIRACLES

After this comes the resurrection of the daughter of Jairus, standing for the future resurrection.

And finally, the two miracles of the healing of the blind and the dumb complete the group, and tell of the time when the veil of blindness shall be taken away from Israel, and the promise shall be fulfilled, "then will . . . the mute tongue shout for joy" (Isaiah 35:6).

SECTION II—*The King*

But whatever may be the dispensational meaning of these miracles, there is no doubt about their present meaning. They present an impressive exhibition of the power of Christ over sickness, Satan, nature, death and sin.

POWER OVER DISEASE

This is illustrated in a series of striking cases of healing.

The Will of Christ Respecting the Healing of Disease, as Revealed in the Healing of the Leper

This poor sufferer came to Him representing a suffering world. His appeal expresses the attitude in which most people stand toward the Lord. They do not doubt His power, but will He? "Lord, if you are willing, you can make me clean" (Matthew 8:2b). The answer of Christ was prompt and unequivocal and leaves no doubt upon the mind of any candid sufferer about His attitude toward disease: "I am willing . . . be clean" (8:3b)! "Not only am I willing, but I am positively wanting to heal and help all who come within reach of My touch. But there must be a corresponding will on your part." Therefore, He adds, "be clean." You must bring a sanctified will, which is the true seat of faith, and meet His will, and when your will cooperates with His, then will come the manifestation of the healing power.

The Word of Christ for Healing

"Just say the word," said the centurion, "and my servant will be healed" (8:8b). This miracle is especially valuable for our dispensation. This represents the power of an absent Christ, through His Word, to reach our need. We do not need to

> Climb the heavenly steeps
> To bring the Lord Christ down.

His Word still holds in solution all His ancient power. Like that living seed they took from the mummy's hands, which had been lying there for 3,000 years, but which contained in its bosom a vital germ, so that the moment it touched the soil it germinated into life, and today our land is filled with Egyptian wheat. So the Word of Christ comes down to us across 2,000 years with unextinguished vitality in its every sentence, and if we will claim the promise, if we will plant our seed in the soil of a trusting heart, if we will commit ourselves to the promise and put our weight upon it, we shall find that it is as real as in the days of Galilee, and God's words will become living deeds in our life.

The Work of God

The next healing, Simon Peter's wife's mother, represents the purpose of divine healing. It is not for your selfish gratification or gain, but, like her, you must rise and minister to Him, and give back to God in loving service, the blessing that He has vouchsafed to you.

The Atoning Blood

The next reference connects our healing with the cross. The reason that He healed was because it was incumbent upon Him as the Messiah to fulfill the picture given by Isaiah the prophet, "He took up our infirmities/ and carried our sorrows" (53:4). This He did when He hung on the cross and bore in His own body all the physical liabilities of our bodies, making it true that "by his wounds you have been healed" (1 Peter 2:24b). It is the deep foundation of divine healing, the solid rock of Christ's atonement.

Sin and Sickness

The next example in the first part of the ninth chapter shows the connection between sickness and sin. They had brought this man to Christ with much faith on their part. But the Lord did not heal him at once. He saw a deeper need and at once He touched the real root of the trouble: "Take heart, son; your sins are forgiven" (Matthew 9:2b). Back of his sickness was the deep source of sin, and not until he was pardoned and prepared to take his place as an accepted child of God, was the Master ready to pass on to the healing. It is not true, therefore, that the Lord healed this man because of the faith of the four men that led him. Through their faith, the Lord took the case in hand and saved him first; and then, after he was saved, he had faith enough to take the Lord for healing and for anything, himself. It was through his own faith that he rose up and took his bed and walked. After we meet the Lord in salvation, it is easy to trust Him for everything besides.

The Touch of Faith

This is beautifully exemplified in Matthew 9:20–21, in the woman who pressed through the jostling crowd, and, with something in her own heart that had been awakened to apprehend God and feel its way to the living Christ, reached Him, and drew from Him the very dynamite of His power (the word "power" in Mark 5:30 literally is dynamite). The spiritual life has a set of senses corresponding to the outward senses of touch, taste, smell, sight and hearing. Just as the root of a tender grapevine feels after the hidden spring until it finds it, and then drinks from it its fertilizing nourishment, so there is something in a hungry heart that feels after God until it finds Him. And when it finds Him, it recognizes His reality just as sensibly as we know the light we see, the water we taste, the fragrance we breathe, the hand we touch.

We cannot take the Lord's healing till we have this sense of spiritual touch. God will give it to us. The beginning of it is the sense of need; and as we press this up to God and follow hard after Him, we shall surely find Him and a new life and revelation will come to our inmost being.

The Touch of Christ

"He touched their eyes" (Matthew 9:29). There are two touches. There is the touch of our trusting hand; there is the mighty touch of His healing hand. Both are necessary, but His will follow ours in every case. He did not touch them until they had answered his challenge to believe, and when He touched them, His message was: "According to your faith will it be done to you" (9:29).

Such is the picture of the power of Christ to heal. That power is still unchanged. "Jesus Christ is the same yesterday and today and forever" (Hebrews 13:8).

POWER OVER SATAN

Along with the healing of disease mentioned in Matthew 8:16, was also the casting out of evil spirits with His word. Indeed, in the healing of Simon's mother-in-law, there is a suggestion of demon power behind the disease. He "rebuked the fever," as Luke expresses it (4:39), and this implies that there was some evil power behind the fever with moral responsibility. In the same way, He rebuked the "winds and the waves" (Matthew 8:26), implying that they were controlled by the power of Satan.

The severest conflict, however, with the demon powers of the pit is recorded in 8:28–34. This occurred in the country of the Gadarenes, immediately after the stilling of the tempest and the crossing of the sea of Galilee. Immediately on landing, there met Him two demon-possessed men, so violent that no man might pass that way. They were possessed by a legion of evil spirits. There seemed to be a double personality in them. One power excited them to dread and try to escape Him and the other drew them to Him for mercy and help. This was usually the case with such victims. At times the human personality prevailed and cried out for deliverance; at other times it was the voice of the demon that controlled. In this case, a strange request was permitted and granted by the Lord, that they should not be driven from the country and forced back into the dark abyss, but allowed to enter into the herd of swine. This the Lord permitted. The result was the immediate destruction of the animals, who, frenzied with terror, fled headlong into the sea and perished. What a fearful exhibition not only of the violence and power of Satan, but also the power of the human soul in that it could endure the presence of a demon host sufficient to drive to madness 3,000 swine.

The effect of this miracle to the citizens of this country was a terrible dread that the presence of the Lord would be fatal to their forbidden trade in these unclean animals. The Lord granted their request, too, and departed out of their coasts.

The last case of the casting out of demons was the mute man (9:32–33), whose infirmity was evidently caused by the evil spirit, for when the demon was cast out, "the man who had been mute spoke. The crowd was amazed and said, 'Nothing like this has ever been seen in Israel' " (9:33).

POWER OVER NATURE

The story of the stilling of the tempest tells a larger story of Christ's providential control over all the forces of nature and all the events of time. He who stilled the waves of Galilee sits supreme above all the surges of human history, and is able to calm the storm and quiet the troubled heart. The ship in which He sails is always safe; and, although He may seem to be asleep in the hinder part, and we may not always be conscious of His presence, yet He is ever there, and in the hour of need will manifest Himself in power and deliverance.

POWER OVER DEATH

The raising of the daughter of Jairus from the dead tells of One who is the Conqueror of death. His own resurrection has confirmed His title as the Prince of Life. But the time of resurrection is not yet. "But each in his own turn: Christ, the firstfruits; then, when he comes, those who belong to him" (1 Corinthians 15:23). Soon the sad days that intervene will have passed away, and the glad morning of the resurrection will have come. This is the blessed hope that takes the sting from death and robs the grave of its victory (15:55–57).

POWER OVER SIN

This was His mightiest victory. He tells them, in connection with the healing of the paralytic, that it is easier to say to the sick and the paralytic, "get up and walk" than it is to say, "your sins are forgiven" (Matthew 9:5). But "the Son of Man has authority on earth to forgive sins" (9:6), and He has power in heaven, too. This is the age-long victory of His love. And this will be the everlasting song of heaven. "To him who loves us and has freed us from our sins by his blood" (Revelation 1:5b).

Matthew the Publican

The chapters we have just been following give several fine illustrations of His power over sin. We have one in the calling of Matthew, the publican. Here was a man that was engaged in the most degrading and disreputable occupation. He was a collector of taxes for the Roman government, and this was something which every loyal Jew recognized as a badge of shame and a sign, usually, of the lowest moral tendencies. The men engaged in this nefarious business were themselves largely the beneficiaries, and all that is now understood by the word graft was familiar to them. They demanded extortionate and oppressive taxes from the people in the name of a cruel government, and they reimbursed themselves abundantly for the trouble and humiliation. Matthew was doubtless like the rest of the tax gatherers, of whom Zacchaeus is held forth as a fair sample. The Lord Jesus met Matthew one day and uttered to him one single command—"Follow me" (Matthew 9:9). There is something sublime in the promptness with which the call was obeyed. Instantly he left his desk, his receipts and all his ambitious prospects and simply, wholly followed Christ. This is the power that still can turn us from the world and lead us to follow Jesus.

A little later we find the Master sitting down with publicans and sinners at the house of Matthew and giving His excuse for it: "I have not come to call the righteous, but sinners" (9:13b). That is still the supreme business of His life.

Shall we, as we read the story, repeat it yet once more in our own lives, or trust Him to repeat it in the lives of those we love? The same Christ is still "able to save completely those who come to God through him, because he always lives to intercede for them" (Hebrews 7:25).

CHAPTER 7

THE REJECTION OF THE KING

He was despised and rejected by men,
* a man of sorrows, and familiar with suffering.*
Like one from whom men hide their faces
* he was despised, and we esteemed him not. (Isaiah 53:3)*

He came to that which was his own, but his own did not receive
him. (John 1:11)

Then Jesus began to denounce the cities in which most of his miracles
had been performed, because they did not repent. (Matthew 11:20)

We have seen in the course of the last chapter the revelation of Jesus Christ as the Son of David and the King of Israel, in His power over sickness, Satan, nature, death and sin. The time had now come when His people must either accept Him or reject Him. The Light was so ample and the credentials were so divine and convincing, that evasion was impossible, and the issue faced them inexorably and immediately. Would they receive Him or reject Him? The answer is given by our text, "He came to that which was his own, but his own did not receive him" (John 1:11), and the old vision of Isaiah was fulfilled, "He was despised and rejected by men,/ a man of sorrows, and familiar with suffering./ Like one from whom men hide their faces/ he was despised, and we esteemed him not" (Isaiah 53:3).

Already in the previous chapters we have had no doubtful intimation of this result. In connection with the remarkable faith of the Centurion in the eighth chapter, He had said:

> I tell you the truth, I have not found anyone in Israel with such great faith. I say to you that many will come from the east and the west, and will take their places at the feast with Abraham,

Isaac and Jacob in the kingdom of heaven. But the subjects of the kingdom will be thrown outside, into the darkness, where there will be weeping and gnashing of teeth. (Matthew 8:10–12)

Again in the ninth chapter of Matthew we have already seen the spirit of hostility and opposition manifested when He undertook to forgive the sins of the paralytic, and they said in indignation, "This fellow is blaspheming" (9:3). But in the next three chapters (10–12) their opposition reaches its climax, and finally terminates in open blasphemy and murderous conspiracy, so that the Lord Jesus is obliged to change entirely His methods from this time. Instead of teaching openly, we find Him using the veil of parables, and commencing in the 13th chapter that extraordinary series of the parables of the kingdom in which He unveils the future development of His kingdom in a form fitted to hide the truth from those that were disposed to abuse it, and at the same time to reveal it to the earnest and sincere inquirer. Let us trace this story of rejection in those chapters.

THE APOSTLES SENT OUT

1. The first intimation of it is in connection with the sending out of the 12 apostles (10:1–42). They were to be His witnesses to Israel, and the terms of their commission are most explicit. "These twelve Jesus sent out with the following instructions: 'Do not go among the Gentiles or enter any town of the Samaritans. Go rather to the lost sheep of Israel' " (10:5–6).

The very fact of His appointing them indicates His realization of the fact that He Himself would soon be taken from the world, and therefore He appoints these representatives to carry on His kingdom after He shall have gone. Their message is to be rejected as well as His. "I am sending you out like sheep among wolves. . . . On my account you will be brought before governors and kings. . . . All men will hate you because of me. . . . A student is not above his teacher, nor a servant above his master. . . . If the head of the house has been called Beelzebub, how much more the members of his household" (10:16, 18, 22, 24, 25).

The principles of Christianity are not to bring about a state of universal peace, but "to turn a man against his father,/ a daughter against her mother,/ a daughter-in-law against her mother-in-law—/ a man's enemies will be the members of his own household" (10:35–36). "I did not come to bring peace, but a sword" (10:34). The radical teachings of the gospel arouse as much antagonism as love. On the other hand He tells them that those that received them will be recognized as receiving Him and the slightest ministry done to the disciple and the servant shall be acknowledged and rewarded by the Lord (10:40–42).

How different the prospect thus held out to them from the ideal which they had formed. How strange and sorrowful the ministry to which they went forth. But how necessary it is for us to understand the true spirit of the New Testament and realize today that the spirit of the age is as utterly opposed to Christ and true Christianity as it was in Galilee and Judea when these words were first uttered. We are not going forth to be received with open arms by our generation and to see a golden millennium arise around us during the present order of things, but rather as a "little flock" (Luke 12:32) of humble and separated men and women following still "outside the camp" (Hebrews 13:13) the lowly Nazarene, while the spirit of the age pursues its earthly aims and is satisfied with its own resources, hopes and destinies.

JOHN'S MESSAGE OF DOUBT

2. The next incident was the sending of two disciples from John the Baptist with a message of inquiry: "Are you the one who was to come, or should we expect someone else?" (Matthew 11:3). The Baptist was now a prisoner at the mercy of Herod, who was soon to behead him, and in the loneliness of his dungeon, the breaking down probably of his health, and the confused reports that doubtless came to him about Jesus Christ, he seems to have begun to doubt whether He was the true Messiah after all, and he sent two of his disciples to inquire.

It must have been discouraging to the Master to find that even John was beginning to doubt, but He sent back the self-evident answer, "Go back and report to John what you hear and see: The blind receive sight, the lame walk, those who have leprosy are cured, the deaf hear, the dead are raised, and the good news is preached to the poor," with the addition of a little hint to John himself not to lose faith: "Blessed is the man who does not fall away on account of me" (11:4–6). He then takes the opportunity of bearing high testimony to John as the greatest prophet of the old dispensation, but adds, as showing how much greater the gospel age is than the Old Testament: "yet he who is least in the kingdom of heaven is greater than he" (11:11b). The humblest disciple of Jesus raised through Him to the family of heaven as a son of God is greater than the highest of the Old Testament prophets. How lofty the dignity to which Jesus has brought us!

The Lord next proceeds to tell His disciples how the Jewish nation has rejected both John's ministry and His. "To what can I compare this generation? They are like children sitting in the marketplaces and calling out to others: 'We played the flute for you,/ and you did not dance;/ we sang a dirge,/ and you did not mourn' " (11:16–17). He means that the ministry of John with its solemn message of repentance has not really brought them to repentance, and that His ministry, so different, with its words of joy and hope, has likewise failed to evoke any real response from the heart of the nation. Israel refused the message of her God, and rejected John and Jesus, too.

THE CITIES OF GALILEE

3. Next follows His open upbraiding of the cities of Galilee, wherein most of His mighty works were done, because they had received His messages and the manifestations of His love and power in vain. Less terrible, He tells them, shall be the fate of Tyre and Sidon and even Sodom in the day of judgment than theirs. In proportion to their opportunity and privilege has been their indifference and unbelief. Today the ruins of Korazin, Bethsaida and Capernaum attest the awful fulfillment of these tremendous warnings.

Let not the modern hearer of the gospel forget that the privileges and opportunities which we are enjoying in this enlightened age will bring upon us also an equal or a greater guilt and doom if we receive the grace of God in vain.

HIS GRACIOUS WORDS

4. His mercy was in contrast with their unbelief. Over against the dark picture of their rejection stands the light of His love. It was in the very hour when His lips had uttered the dread woe against the cities of Galilee, that His tender and loving heart burst forth with the most touching and beautiful of all His messages of love,

> Come to me, all you who are weary and burdened, and I will give you rest. Take my yoke upon you and learn from me, for I am gentle and humble in heart, and you will find rest for your souls. For my yoke is easy and my burden is light. (11:28–30)

Perhaps in the crowd that surrounded Him, He saw the agonized face of some poor sinner; and from the hard unbelief of the self-righteous Pharisee, He turned to the earnest hearts even in that crowd that were longing for His mercy. It is a beautiful coincidence brought out by a careful study of the gospel harmony, that the story recorded in the seventh chapter of Luke of the sinful woman, who came and washed His feet with her tears and wiped them with the hairs of her head in the house of Simon, followed this incident in Matthew. How delightful to think that that appeal recorded in Matthew 11:28 had gone to her heart and led her to follow Him to the house of Simon and there to let Him know how His words of mercy had comforted and saved her. Yes, as the lone rose of the Alps grows amid the glaciers, so the fruits and flowers of grace are found even in the most forbidding soil and the most unlikely surroundings. Oh, that some heart that reads these lines might also come and repeat the story of her blessing.

NEW CONTROVERSIES

5. The next step of their opposition and rejection was a bitter theological fight with Him over their traditions concerning Sabbath observance. As He walked with His disciples through the grainfields they were hungry and without supplies, and they took the grain and rubbed it in their hands and satisfied their hunger in this crude way. The very poverty suggested by the act might well have touched the hearts of His cruel foes. It was indeed a sign of His rejection by a selfish world, and showed how true it was, as He said elsewhere, "The Son of Man has no place to lay his head" (8:20). But all they could see in it was a slight to their rigid traditions about working on the Sabbath. In their eyes it was a greater sin to rub out some grain than to let a man die of starvation.

The same spirit appears in the incident that follows in the 12th chapter of Matthew in connection with the healing of the man with the withered hand. They recognized His healing power by their question, "Is it lawful to heal on the Sabbath?" (12:10). It never seems to have occurred to them that if He had power to heal He must be greater than the Sabbath or the law. But all they could see was their theological bigotry. The Lord answered them by an appeal to common sense and humanity. He asked them what they would do if one of their sheep had fallen into a pit on the Sabbath. Would they help it out, or let it die there? The question needed no answer for every one of them knew that his self-interest quite as much as his humanity would lead him to save the sheep, Sabbath or no Sabbath. The Lord swiftly turns the argument on them by answering, "How much more valuable is a man than a sheep! Therefore it is lawful to do good on the Sabbath" (12:12), and immediately heals the man with the withered hand. These ancient theologians were types of a good many later followers, men who would fight to the death for a quibble or a doctrine, but who had no compunction about torturing to death an innocent martyr under the Spanish Inquisition, or treating a poor Hottentot as if he were a brute.

In passing, it is not out of place to refer to the question of the Sabbath. Our Lord undoubtedly recognized the Sabbath by His own distinct acknowledgment, "for the Son of Man is Lord of the Sabbath" (12:8). He distinctly revised it when He incorporated it into the New Testament and He established not only a new significance to it as His day, and the day that we hold in remembrance of His resurrection, but He also instituted as the essential principle of its observance the great law of liberty and love that runs through all the teachings of the gospel. The essential principle of Sabbath observance is love. It is not so much what you do not do, as what you do. It is to be spent in works of mercy and charity and therefore is to be kept in the spirit of holy liberty and loving service for God and man. Do not let us go back with the Seventh Day Adventists to the law of Moses. The gospel has set us free, but the liberty on which its freedom rests is "do not use your freedom to indulge the sinful nature; rather, serve one another in love" (Galatians 5:13).

PLOTTING TO KILL HIM

6. The outcome of this controversy is a bitter, malignant hatred that at length fully determines upon His destruction and at once begins to conspire for His death. They seem to have met at this time in a special conference and arranged the plot for His immediate arrest and destruction.

They seem never to have realized how futile all their plans and plots were against One that had the power of life and death in His hands, and that He could not die until His hour had come. But God let their malignity reach its full fruition and show itself in all its blackness and crime.

WITHDRAWS

7. We now read that when He knew of their conspiracy, He withdrew Himself from them and kept in retirement for a while (Matthew 12:15–16). This was but a type of His final withdrawal from Israel altogether. He was beginning to leave the nation to its fate, and, therefore, the evangelist quotes from Isaiah the prophecy concerning Him.

> Here is my servant whom I have chosen,
>   the one I love, in whom I delight;
> I will put my Spirit on him,
>   and he will proclaim justice to the nations.
> He will not quarrel or cry out;
>   no one will hear his voice in the streets.
> A bruised reed he will not break,
>   and a smoldering wick he will not snuff out,
> till he leads justice to victory.
>   In his name the nations will put their hope. (12:18–21)

The emphatic feature of this quotation is its reference to the Gentiles. Christ was now withdrawing from Israel and preparing for His ministry to the uncovenanted nations who have reaped the advantage of Israel's blindness and rejection. How solemn for us the thought that there comes a time in the individual's life when the Lord also withdraws Himself from the soul that has long rejected His grace.

> There is a time, we know not when,
> A point, we know not where,

That marks the destiny of men,
For glory or despair.

THEIR BLASPHEMY

8. This final climax of their long course of unbelief and opposition finally came through an outburst of popular enthusiasm on the part of the people after one of His miracles. Having healed the blind and the mute man, possessed of an evil spirit, so that the man both spoke and saw, the people were amazed and said, "Could this be the Son of David?" (12:23). The Pharisees could not stand this testimony and they broke out into wild and angry vituperation and immediately accused Him of being in league with Satan and casting out demons by Beelzebub, prince of the devils. Once before they had hinted at this, and the Lord had passed it over. But now He takes up their charge and answers it: first, with the most inexorable logic, showing them the absurdity of supposing that Satan would try to cast out himself, when this would be the surest way of breaking down his kingdom; and then, having exposed them to the ridicule of the people, He turns upon them with awful severity and pronounces upon them the fearful sentence of eternal judgment because they had committed the unpardonable sin of blaspheming the Holy Spirit by attributing the works of God to an evil spirit. Their sin had reached its culmination and at last their doom was sealed.

It is indeed a fearful picture and the question may well be asked, is it possible for us to commit their sin today? Certainly it is not possible in precisely the same way to commit it without our going to the extent of impious infidelity. But it may be possible for any sinful man to go to the terrible limit which they did in this essential principle, that is, in the face of light with full conviction and certainty that Jesus Christ is the Son of God, to reject Him deliberately and finally. This would indeed be an unpardonable sin. Let no one, however, be distressed and driven to despair by the enemy through this passage, if you still find that you really desire and are willing to accept the Lord Jesus as a Savior. For in this very passage He tells us that "every sin and blasphemy will be forgiven men" (12:31), the assumption of course is that they will accept forgiveness through Jesus Christ. It is the rejection of Christ that constitutes the fatal sin. For such there is no forgiveness, for there is no other Savior but He.

THE SIGN OF JONAH

9. They asked Him for a sign and He now gave them the sign of the prophet Jonah (12:38–42). It is somewhat sardonic that the Lord Jesus should choose as His witness the very man that the higher critics are trying to get rid of. Jesus at least had no doubt about the historical reality of Jonah

and the great fish, and we can safely stay in such good company, notwithstanding even the higher critics.

The two peculiarities of Jonah's significance as the type of Christ were, first, his death and resurrection. By referring to this the Lord Jesus clearly indicates now what He had incidentally hinted at before, that He is to be finally rejected and crucified. The next significant point, however, in Jonah's resemblance to Christ, was that after his resurrection Jonah was sent to the Gentiles and not to Israel. There is no mistaking the meaning of this in Christ's use of the figure. He is clearly intimating that through His death and resurrection He is to become the Savior not of the Jew only, but of the Gentile and the heathen.

In connection with the story of Jonah, the Lord adds a solemn warning to the men of that generation by telling them that their sin was greater than that of Nineveh, which repented at the preaching of Jonah, while "one greater than Jonah" (12:41) was appealing to them in vain.

PARABLE OF THE UNCLEAN SPIRIT

10. The parable of the unclean spirit follows (12:43–45). He applies it directly to Israel. They had been previously cleansed through John the Baptist, but they had failed to go on as John had bidden them, and receive Jesus Christ. And the result would be that their hearts, left "unoccupied, swept clean and put in order" (12:44b), would again be possessed by "seven other spirits more wicked than itself" and "the final condition . . . is worse than the first" (12:45).

How real, alas, all this has become to Israel, and it will become more sadly true in the judgments still awaiting them. It is also true of the individual soul. A temporary reformation, which is not followed by the filling of the heart with Christ and the Holy Spirit, will not suffice, but will surely be followed by a worse relapse. The only sure salvation is a full salvation. It is not enough to cast out Satan—you must receive the Holy Spirit and be filled with the fullness of the indwelling Christ.

HIS MOTHER AND BROTHERS

11. The last incident in the chapter is very pathetic. As we read it in the light of the other Gospels, we learn that His mother and His brothers were seeking for Him, not out of idle curiosity or family affection, but because they believed He was insane. "They said, 'He is out of his mind' " (Mark 3:21), and probably they wished to put Him under restraint. Yes, even His dearest ones at last had failed Him, and He takes advantage of the occasion to proclaim the law of the new relationship which He has established in the family circle of heaven.

"Who is my mother, and who are my brothers?" Pointing to his disciples, he said, "Here are my mother and my brothers. For whoever does the will of my Father in heaven is my brother and sister and mother." (Matthew 12:48–50)

And so to us, as we follow the Master, may come the keenest of all trials, the misunderstanding that separates from us our dearest friends and makes us as strangers and aliens to all human love. If it comes, let us go with Him all the way, but let us not be embittered against our friends. Let us love them still with His love and let us cease to need their love; loving with the love that seeks their good rather than ours, and God may be pleased at last to lead them even unto Him. But let us pass on in spirit to the heavenly family circle and the new circle of those whom He calls "brother and sister and mother" (12:50).

In conclusion, surely the one lesson that stands out above all other lessons is that the sin of sins is the rejection of Jesus Christ. Our eternal destiny hangs, not on our obedience or disobedience to any or all of the commandments, but our attitude toward Jesus Christ. As someone has said, "It is not the *sin* question, but the *Son* question."

How do you stand toward that question? "Whoever believes in him is not condemned, but whoever does not believe stands condemned already because he has not believed in the name of God's one and only Son" (John 3:18).

CHAPTER 8

THE PARABLES OF THE KINGDOM

The disciples came to him and asked, "Why do you speak to the people in parables?"

He replied, "The knowledge of the secrets of the kingdom of heaven has been given to you, but not to them. Whoever has will be given more, and he will have an abundance. Whoever does not have, even what he has will be taken from him. This is why I speak to them in parables:

"Though seeing, they do not see;
though hearing, they do not hear or understand."
(Matthew 13:10–13)

"I always did like the likes of Jesus" was the simple testimony of a child to the parables of Christ. He is the matchless Teacher and Illustrator. In this chapter we have the beginning of His wonderful parables and the group in the 13th chapter of Matthew is known as the parables of the kingdom. The formula with which each begins is "The kingdom of heaven is like . . ."

The purpose of Christ's parables was to present spiritual and moral truths under the veil of some incident, not in itself historically true, and yet not contrary to truth. His matchless stories were really works of imagination, but in beautiful harmony with truth, and setting forth the deepest and loftiest moral and spiritual teaching.

WHY IN PARABLES?

His reason for teaching them in parables is given by Himself as connected with their rejection of His previous messages. As we have already seen, all His words and works had been met by them with increasing hostility and malignant misrepresentation. They listened to Him only that they might in some way entangle Him in His talk. And so now He finally withdrew from the multitudes and began to teach His disciples in the veiled form of the parable in order, as He states Himself in this chapter, that the truth might be revealed to the diligent and earnest students and concealed from the indifferent and the prejudiced.

The present series of parables, as might be expected from the symbolic number seven, contains a complete unfolding of the future plan of His kingdom during the entire age up to His second coming. His own nation had now rejected the gospel of the kingdom and it was to be taken from them for a time and given to the Gentiles. In these parables He gives us the panorama of the age throughout the Christian dispensation.

KINGDOM OF HEAVEN

The phrase, "The kingdom of heaven," or "The kingdom of the heavens," really contains the keynote of the series. It does not mean the kingdom in relation to Israel, nor does it mean the history of the Church, but rather the progress of Christianity up to the coming of the Lord. It describes a mingled condition of good and evil, growing externally and marked by extraordinary prosperity and apparent success and yet full of corruption as well as righteousness, concealing the leaven as well as the treasure and the pearl, and only to be finally separated at the end of the age and the coming of the Lord.

This series of parables describes, first, the planting of the truth and then the sowing of the evil. This double work of good and evil is brought out in the first two parables. Then in the third parable of the mustard seed we see the rapid growth of this mingled system of good and evil until it fills the earth. But in the following parable of the oven, we get the inside view of this mingled system and we see that it is full of corruption. The next two parables, however, the treasure and the pearl, turn our attention to the brighter side of the picture, the hidden elements of good even in the heart of this mass of mingled elements. Finally, the parable of the draw net reveals the separation of the two elements in the day of judgment and at the end of the age.

THE SEVEN CHURCHES

These seven parables bear a strong resemblance to the seven letters of the risen and ascended Lord to the churches of Asia in the opening chapters of the book of Revelation (2:1–3:22). The first epistle to the church in Ephesus reminds us of the parable of the sower in Matthew 13; and the second, the dark picture of Smyrna and the power of evil recalls the parable of the enemy and the sowing of the weeds. The church in Pergamum is very much like the mustard tree. It is the picture of the outward prosperity and worldly power. The fourth church in Revelation, Thyatira, is the very counterpart of the leaven. "That woman Jezebel" (2:20) immediately recalls the woman that put the leaven in the three measures of meal. Both present to us a picture of inward corruption and impurity. The church in Sardis, which has "a few people . . . who have not soiled their clothes" (3:4), corresponds to the treasure hid in a field, and the glorious church of Philadelphia in Revelation is the very counterpart of the pearl in Matthew. Both describe the true and hidden followers of Christ in the midst of the present evil age. Finally, the church in Laodicea stands for the separation of the two classes when the Lord will spit out of His mouth the "lukewarm" and unfaithful and take the overcomers to sit with Him upon His throne (3:16, 21).

Both of these series present the plan of the age, substantially, and it does not take us long to see how utterly it is opposed to the popular theological ideas which underlie nearly all the current expositions of the gospel and the teaching of the great mass of the ministries of the Church today. At the risk of seeming to oppose so great a mass of prevalent teaching and belief, let us endeavor fairly and honestly to grasp the thought of the Master in this first unfolding of the mysteries of the kingdom.

THE SOWER

1. The Planting of the Kingdom (Matthew 13:3–8)

The parable of the sower represents the preaching of the gospel and its normal effects. The first thing that strikes us is that in three cases out of four it seems to fail. This is not from any defect in the seed, but because of conditions in the soil. In the first three cases there are hindrances either to the reception or the growth and fruition of the seed.

In the first case, the soil is hard and the devil is waiting to steal away the seed through the fowls of the air, who are always on hand before it really lodges in the soil. In the second case, the soil itself is shallow and although there is a sudden and apparent result, it soon passes away. The seed springs up for an hour, but withers on the rocky field and all the farmer's work is in vain. In the third case, there is a good beginning made, but later "thorns . . . grew up and choked the plants" (13:7), "the worries of this life and the deceitfulness of wealth" (13:22) and other things tear down the better purposes that had been formed in the heart and the harvest is brought to naught.

These three clauses represent the devil, the flesh and the world, that old trinity that has ever been arrayed against the kingdom of God. The devil steals the seed in the first case, the flesh fails in the second, and the world finishes the process in the third. In only one case does the seed germinate and mature, falling into good soil and honest hearts—souls that are sincere, consciences that are awakened, hearts that are hungering for God, wills that decide and settle their great resolves. The seed springs up and grows and "produces a crop, yelding a hundred, sixty or thirty times what was sown" (13:23b).

This has ever been the story of the progress of the gospel. It was the apostolic story; "Some were convinced by what he said, but others would not believe" (Acts 28:24), and it will be true to the end. This is no optimistic dream of the world rushing to embrace Christianity, but rather a somber picture of a small minority of the human race responding to the call of heaven and believing and obeying the gospel of Christ. It has ever been the case and it will be to the end.

THE WEEDS

2. The Sowing of the Weeds (Matthew 13:24–30)

"But while everyone was sleeping, his enemy came and sowed weeds among the wheat" (13:25). It is not hard to identify this enemy. A more difficult question is, "Where did he sow the weeds?" Does this parable teach that the Church is to be continually exposed to heresy, fanaticism and the unrestricted power of evil men and that we are to let this continue and make no effort to separate the evil from the good in the Church of God? No, not at all. It is not the Church that is here the field. "The field is the world" (13:38). This is the Master's own standard in interpreting these parables. It is right for us, as far as wise and watchful discipline can accomplish it, to purge out and keep out both error and wickedness from the Church of Christ. That is our business, but, as the apostle puts it so well, "God will judge those outside" (1 Corinthians 5:13a). It is in the world that the enemy sows his weeds—in immediate contact with the people of God and the Church of Christ. And these things surround us in our family, social, civil and business life, inexorably and incessantly. And the teaching of the parable is that this mingled condition will exist till the end of the age.

We are not going to see any of our modern crusaders clean out these evils—the saloons, the social evil or the political grafters. They will continue till the end. Our business is to plant and cultivate the good seed and let the good overcome the evil. But the separation God alone can make, and He will not make it until the end of the age. Our dreams of ideal social, ecclesiastical and political utopias are all in the air and will end like dissolving rainbows. Our hope is farther on—Christ and His blessed coming.

THE MUSTARD TREE

3. The Rapid and the Universal Growth of the Mingled System of Good and Evil (Matthew 13:31–32)

This appears in the mustard tree which suddenly shoots up its branches and spreads abroad its boughs and covers the earth with its shade until "the birds of the air come and perch in its branches" (13:32b). It has been customary to describe this as the encouraging symbol of the rapid growth of Christianity, and we have been deluged with figures of the millions that today comprise the Christian population of the globe. It is true that Christianity nominally controls the most powerful nations and holds under its influence the great proportion even of the non-Christian nations, but to call this the true kingdom of Jesus Christ would be a sad caricature. This great mass of several hundred millions of nominal Christians includes Roman Catholics, Greeks, Oriental Christians and vast numbers of Protestants, who are Christian only in name and who are worshiping mammon (Matthew 6:24, KJV) and following the spirit of the world quite as much as their less civilized fellowmen.

It is just what the parable was meant to express—a great mass of mingled good and evil, called Christendom. It is quite enough to condemn it that it is the harboring place of those "birds of the air" which in the first parable "ate" the good seed (13:4). It has room not only for God, but for every other god; not only Christ, but for all the "isms" that outnumber today the deities of the ancient Pantheism. It is the church of Laodicea: "You say, 'I am rich; I have acquired wealth and do not need a thing' " (Revelation 3:17), but so swollen with pride and self-complacency that it has no room for Christ, and He is only separating the few true hearts from the mass until He shall spit it out of His mouth.

THE YEAST

4. The Hidden Corruption of Nominal Christianity (Matthew 13:33)

The parable of the yeast now follows in true logical order and gives us the vision of the inward character of the great mass of nominal Christianity. This too has been perverted in most of our modern religious teaching. The yeast, according to these religious optimists, is the spreading of the gospel, permeating and pervading gradually the whole mass of humanity till the whole shall be leavened and the world shall awake some fine morning to find itself at last right side up and all the ills of all the ages ended in the poet's dream:

When the war drum throbs no longer and the battle flag is furled,
In the Parliament of man and federation of the world.

Unfortunately the analogy of the Scriptures is all against this, quite as much as the facts of human history. Flour, in the Old Testament, is always a type of the good and not of the bad. The grain offering was one of the five great offerings of Moses (Leviticus 2:1–16). It is the good seed we have already seen in the parable, ground into a form fitted for wholesome food. Yeast, on the other hand, is always the symbol of evil. It stands for fermentation, corruption, sin. It was forbidden in the ancient Jewish Passover, and it is forbidden in the New Testament epistles. We are not only to "get rid of the old yeast," but we are to be "without yeast" (1 Corinthians 5:7). Yeast, therefore, represents in the parable the influence of evil and its silent, pervading and far-reaching power. It is the secret working of the same enemy who sowed the weeds. It represents the unbelief, the worldliness, the selfishness, the license which today are slowly wearing down the barriers of faith, conscience and separation even in the Church itself, and reducing society to one broad level of liberalism, humanitarianism and easy-going selfishness. The process is so apparent that in order to understand the parable, we need only to look round us and see the conditions of the Christian church today.

THE TREASURE

5. The Hidden Elements of Good (Matthew 13:44–46)

But is this all, we naturally ask? Is there no brighter vision? Is there no other element? Is it all corruption? We turn to the next two parables and we behold a cheering contrast in the parable of the Treasure and the Pearl (13:44–46). These represent the good side of the inner life of Christendom. The first of these two parables, the Treasure hid in the field, appears to stand for Israel during the present age; the second, the Pearl, for the Church of Jesus Christ, containing only His holy and hidden ones. Israel was to disappear from the foreground because of her rejection of the Lord, but Israel was to have a remnant which would continue through the Christian age to represent God's chosen people and to claim at last their ancient covenant when Christ shall come again, and Israel shall come forth from the obscurity and suffering of all these sad ages to be the queen of nations on the Millennial earth. Israel is always God's earthly people, the Church, His heavenly people. Therefore, this treasure is "hidden in a field" (13:44), which means this world. Israel during the present age is hidden and in retirement from the stage of the prophecy, but it is for Israel's sake that God is preserving this old earth and is by and by to restore it and make it new.

Therefore we read that for the sake of that treasure, the Lord sold all that He had and bought the field in which the treasure was hidden. This is not said about the pearl. The pearl was taken out of the field, but the treasure remained in it. Israel is to remain on earth and at the Lord's return is to have the dominion of the earth. This is finely brought out in the symbolism of the parable, and as we thus understand it, a beautiful light is shed upon both the parable and the prophecies of Scripture concerning Israel.

The use of the word "treasure" is peculiarly appropriate to Israel. It is constantly employed in the Old Testament concerning God's chosen people. "For the LORD has chosen Jacob to be his own,/ Israel to be his treasured possession" (Psalm 135:4). "For the LORD'S portion is his people,/ Jacob his allotted inheritance" (Deuteronomy 32:9). These are but some of the numerous references to Israel as the Lord's treasure.

THE PEARL

6. The Place of the Church in the Plan of the Ages (Matthew 13:45–46)

This is finely set forth in the parable of the Pearl of Great Price. Unfortunately, this has been so often applied to Christ by inconsiderate teachers and expounders of the Scriptures that it is difficult to accustom Bible students to look at its true meaning. It does not describe Christ at all in this parable, for He is the One that found the pearl and gave all that He had to purchase it. Rather, it represents His people whom He describes as His jewels. More strictly speaking, it stands for the Bride of the Lamb, not Christians individually, but the whole body of His chosen ones as they shall at last be gathered and glorified at His coming, and as John describes them in the Apocalypse, in that vision of glory where the Lamb's wife is presented in the sublime imagery of all the combined jewels known to man. The description of the sacrifice by which the Lord obtained this pearl is applicable only to Him. How truly He "sold everything he had" (13:46) that He might buy His people! How true it is that He has bought them and redeemed them from sin, Satan, death and hell to be a peculiar people unto Himself, and how beautiful the figure of the Pearl under which they are represented as united and glorified to adorn His crown in the New Jerusalem!

It will be noticed that just before giving these two parables, the Lord Jesus withdrew from the multitude and "went into the house" (13:36), vividly signifying by His act that these parables that He was about to speak had a more personal and intimate relation to His own disciples, while the others related rather to the world and the multitude. His significant action should also be noted in the very beginning of this series of parables, when we are told that He went out of the house and sat down by the seaside (13:1). His going out of the house was significant of His leaving Israel and turning to the Gentiles. They had now rejected His overtures of grace and He went forth from them to the world, always represented in the Bible by the sea and its troubled waters. His first act, therefore, was to retire from Israel and give utterance to the parables that related to the Gentile world and the Christian age. His next symbolic act was to withdraw from the multitude and come into the house, again symbolizing His messages to His hidden ones in the parable of the Treasure and the Pearl.

THE NET

7. The Final Separation (13:47–50)

The parable of the Net is the picture of the separation that is to come at last when the Lord Himself shall appear. He and His angelic ministers alone can make this separation. Man has tried long and vainly to eliminate the evil from the world. Wiser and stronger hands are needed for the task and those hands are soon to undertake it.

Meanwhile the net is drawing "all kinds" (13:47) from the great sea of human life, and slowly the cords are being drawn to the eternal shore, where at last the hands of mighty angels "will come and separate the wicked from the righteous and throw them into the fiery furnace, where there will be weeping and gnashing of teeth" (13:49b–50), and "the righteous will shine like the sun in the kingdom of their Father" (13:43).

How very solemn is the picture of this mysterious net. How it suggests to us the silent and inevitable progress of time as the age is insensibly and yet inexorably rolling on to this awful crisis. What a touching spectacle those countless fishes, as they suddenly find themselves within the barriers of the enclosing net and vainly struggle to escape its meshes and get out into the freedom of the sea. Closer and closer draw those barriers as they dash from side to side and vainly struggle to escape. For a little they may think that they are free as they pass from one side to the other of prison; but lo, they strike again upon the farther side and are hurled back into the writhing mass in the center, until the cords are tightened and with a sudden jerk the whole mass is hurled upon the strand, struggling, writhing, gasping for breath, and finding themselves helpless and hopeless in a new element in which they have never lived before.

Such is the picture of human life as the age rolls on. For a time men think that they are free as they follow their own will in the great unconfined ocean of human life. But every little while there is something to remind them that God's great net of providence and destiny is thrown around them and that a force unseen is steadily drawing them to the eternal strand. Every little while, something reminds them that they are being drawn to that eternal shore. Sometimes, it is the death of a friend, sometimes it is the solemn voice of reason and conscience reminding them that they are born to die. Then they strike out again and claim their liberty and refuse to listen to their fears. Closer and closer the lines are drawing, and some day they shall find themselves swept into that strange eternal world which will be as foreign to them as the ocean strand to the helpless fishes of the sea. Then mighty hands will make the final separation. Our struggles, our pleas will be in vain and each of us will find himself and herself taking the place for evermore for which we have been preparing here.

Well might the Master ask His little class of wondering disciples, after they had listened to these strange, deep teachings, "Have you understood all these things?" (13:51a). God help us to understand them and live under "the powers of the coming age" (Hebrews 6:5).

CHAPTER 9

CHRIST'S FAREWELL TO GALILEE

When Jesus had finished these parables, he moved on from there.
(Matthew 13:53)

As we have already seen, the parables of the kingdom marked a stage in the rejection of the Lord Jesus and His withdrawal from the people that had refused these parables; we are now told that He departed from their midst.

Not all at once did He leave Galilee and the scenes of the past three years of His active ministry; but this was the beginning of the end. Gradually He commenced to withdraw. His back was turned on the scenes of His former labors, and after a few lingering visits and last messages, at length He took His final farewell and spent the last six months of His life in Judea and the regions about, returning no more to Capernaum, Bethsaida, Korazin and the cities where most of His mighty works had been done.

NAZARETH

1. His Last Visit to Nazareth

The first step in His retirement was one more visit to Nazareth, the city where He had been brought up (Matthew 13:54).

We may remember how, on a former occasion, He had been rejected here, and they had even sought His life and carried Him to the brow of the precipice on which the city was built, to hurl Him to death. We have also seen how even His mother and His brothers had concluded that He was insane, and had sought to restrain Him. Once more He visits these old scenes of His childhood, but His message is not received; His personality is altogether too familiar for these proud Jews; they know too much about Him to accept Him as a Rabbi, much less as a Prophet sent from God. They said, " 'Isn't this the carpenter's son? Isn't his mother's name Mary, and aren't his brothers James, Joseph, Simon and Judas? Aren't all his sisters with us?

Where then did this man get all these things?' And they took offense at him" (13:55–57).

This was the spirit of pure prejudice. What difference does it make about a man's family connections if he has a message from God and is himself a true man? It was the old spirit of prejudice that has so often kept people back from their best blessings. The effect of it was to send the Lord away and prevent Him from doing many mighty works because of their unbelief, and, as He left, He repeated the old proverb which has so often been true. "Only in his hometown and in his own house is a prophet without honor" (13:57b).

DEATH OF JOHN

2. The Death of John the Baptist, His Forerunner

A little while before this, John, languishing in prison because of his fearless courage in denouncing the sin of Herod and his paramour, had become discouraged and sent a message to Christ, pathetically asking whether He was indeed the Messiah that was to come, or whether they were to look for another. Now, at length, the tragedy reaches its climax (14:1–12).

That wicked woman had long been waiting for her opportunity to wreak her final vengeance on the brave man that had dared to challenge her crimes. At length the opportunity arrives. Seated in his banquet hall among his lords, and already half drunk with wine, Herod suddenly becomes infatuated with the bold and beautiful dancing of Salome, the fair daughter of his unlawful wife, and, in a fit of rashness, promises her with an oath to give her anything that she chooses to ask. Instructed by her cunning mother, who has been waiting for this hour, she immediately asks for the head of John the Baptist. The king was shocked and distressed, for he really was attached to John, but a false pride about the keeping of his oath left him no escape. So the executioner was dispatched, and in a few minutes the ghastly, bloody trophy was borne by those fair hands on a charger to her horrid mother, and the work of the great prophet was done. John's disciples, as soon as they heard of it, buried the body, and then "went and told Jesus" (14:12b). The effect of it upon Christ was very distressing. He loved John and grieved for his sad fate, but He also saw in it the certain harbinger of His own approaching death, and so He immediately retired for a little season that He might rest and also comfort the sorrowing disciples.

The story of John's murder has many fine lessons in which our present space will not permit us to dwell at length, but we cannot refrain from noticing the length to which human unbelief and sin will dare to go. The vile woman and weak man had refused the message of God through John, convicting them of their sin, and perhaps they never thought that they would go farther. But now we find their rejection of God's word leading them on to malignant hate and bloody crime. So sin pursues its terrible progression in every age, and, when we disobey God, we never know where the last step of our downward course is to land us. And what a lesson this is on worldliness. Mr. Spurgeon might well say that whenever he saw a dance he felt a little nervous about the throat, and remembered that the first Baptist preacher lost his head on account of one. Our business is not to start crusades against the ballroom, but rather to get men right with God; but when they are right with God they will not want these things. What a lesson also of the folly of recklessness. Herod's hasty words caused him the violation of his conscience, the murder of his friend, and the eternal ruin of his soul. If we have sinned by speaking rashly, let us not add to our sin by completing the rash act as well as the reckless word. Far better break the foolish vow than keep it, if it is wrong.

FEEDING OF THE FIVE THOUSAND

3. The Crisis and Climax of Christ's Galilean Ministry

In the next section of the Gospel of Matthew, chapter 14:14–21, our Lord's ministry in Galilee reached its crisis and its climax, the highest point of His love and power and the deepest depth of human unbelief and rejection.

After the death of John the Baptist, He retired for a time to the solitude of the eastern shore of the Sea of Galilee for the quiet that both He and His disciples needed. But the multitude would allow Him no rest. They thronged upon Him, and waited all day long in eager attention to His words of grace and His works of healing, love and power. At length, as the evening drew on, the Master felt the deepest compassion for the multitude, and He turned to His disciples and asked them about providing food for the people. But their little faith utterly broke down before such a prospect. Their limited means were only sufficient to purchase a mere morsel for such a crowd, and they had as yet no conception of the great miracle which He was waiting to perform. One among them, Andrew, in some degree was equal to the occasion and brought forward the little lad with his barley loaves and fishes as the only apparent solution of the difficulty, but even he gave up with the despairing cry, "how far will they go among so many?" (John 6:9b). Then the Master summoned the disciples to the great miracle which he had been planning all the time. Making the multitude sit down upon the grass, He distributed the loaves and fishes to the disciples, and they to the multitude, until all did eat and were filled, and they found remaining at the close 12 baskets full of the fragments of the fishes. This tremendous miracle demonstrated His power over nature as nothing else had done before. Little wonder that the crowd was filled with admiration and astonishment, and, as John tells us, they insisted at once upon taking Him by force and making

Him a King (6:14–15). This was what Matthew meant when he spoke of the Lord sending the multitudes away, while He at the same time sent His disciples across the sea in their little ship. Probably He knew that they would be just as likely as the crowd to join in the clamor that He should take upon Him the honors the multitude were thrusting upon Him. A nobler kingdom was coming to Him in a little while through His Father's gift and His own glorious victory over sin and Satan and the grave.

Therefore, He refused to accept the crown from the foolish and impulsive mob which was ready to worship Him today and crucify Him tomorrow. Refusing their proffered honors, He dismissed them to their homes and then withdrew to the solitude of the mountain to communion with His Father in prayer, while His little band of disciples were struggling with the waves and winds on their voyage to the other side. All this was strongly typical of the history of the age which was soon to follow.

That miracle of the feeding of the five thousand was a striking type of the gospel dispensation and the feeding of the world's famine with the bread of life through the faith of Christ's disciples. His ascension of the mountain was a type of His ascension to the Father's right hand, where today He is praying for the little flock as they battle with the winds and waves on the sea of life. His coming to them in the early morning watch is yet to be more closely fulfilled in His second advent; and, as of old, the moment He entered the ship they found themselves at the land whither they went, so again His coming is to bring all our ships ashore, to remedy all our wrongs, and to accomplish all the purposes that hitherto failed.

John's Account

The Gospel of John should be read in connection with the Gospel of Matthew in its picture of this series of incidents. Matthew tells us of the scribes and Pharisees that came up from Jerusalem at this time and got into another argument with the Lord about questions of ceremony and tradition (Matthew 15:1–9). But John tells us of a still more important conversation that occurred in the synagogue at Capernaum the Sabbath after the feeding of the five thousand. We find the account of it remarkably discussed in the sixth chapter of the Gospel of John (6:25–59ff). It is there in the Master's discourse on the living Bread that He reaches the loftiest height of spiritual teaching that His discussions had attempted heretofore. There He unfolds to them, with the deepest spirituality, the great mystery of our spiritual life and our personal union with Him as our living Head. The effect of these teachings was to perplex and alienate almost all His remaining followers in Galilee. They could not understand such deep spiritual teachings. They perfectly comprehended the supply of earthly bread, but how He could be their living Bread and supply the very life of their souls was mysticism to them, and they turned away, saying, "This is a hard teaching. Who can accept it?" (6:60). And John adds that from that day many of His disciples left Him and walked no more with Him, so that even to His own disciples He turned with deep pathos and asked, "You do not want to leave too, do you?" (6:67). Peter answered for them, "Lord, to whom shall we go? You have the words of eternal life" (6:68).

Turning Away of His Followers

Therefore, this whole incident marked the crisis, as we have already said, of His ministry in Galilee. He had reached its highest point, and from this time the multitude forsook Him as did the malignant leaders of the ecclesiastical party. They looked upon Him as a strained fanatic, impracticable and even unwilling to accept the earthly honors and powers they were willing to confer upon Him, that they might share with Him the temporal benefit which was the only advantage which they really understood or cared for. For deeper spiritual things they had no taste.

Alas, they were typical of multitudes today in the Church of Jesus Christ! The crisis which happened in Galilee will happen yet again in the story of the ages. Even in the Church today we are bound to find traces of a turning away from deeper spiritual teaching on the part of the followers of Christ. They are willing to accept the temporal advantages of Christianity and its universal moral and social benefits. They are willing to believe in it as a remedy for the future and a means of escaping future punishment for sin; but as marking a life of deliverance from the power of sin and communion and fellowship with God, they do not understand it; they do not desire it. All this is but mysticism and impractical dreaming, and the picture of the seven churches of Asia in the book of Revelation tells us that a time is coming when the great masses of Christendom will reject a deeply spiritual Christianity and turn away from the Lord, even as His Galilean followers.

From this time, the Lord's work in Galilee was practically closed. True, He lingered for a while on its borders, going and coming for a few weeks longer on His various detours, but He had practically withdrawn from the western shore of the Sea of Galilee. When we do see Him again among the Galileans it is in the country of Decapolis, on the farther shore, either among the Gentiles, or at their borders.

TYRE AND SIDON

4. His Journey to the Region of Tyre and Sidon

Mark tells us that He went away with the view of getting quiet, and had first stopped for privacy in a house, but he adds, "yet he could not keep his presence secret" (Mark 7:24). Immediately a woman of the country, a Gentile and a heathen, appealed first to His disciples and then to Him for help for her afflicted daughter, who was possessed with an evil spirit (Matthew 15:21–28). The disciples appealed to the Master in vain to grant her request or stop her clamor by sending her away. She turned from them and renewed her pleading with the Master Himself, but His first answer seemed to shut the door in her very face, by telling her that the limitations of His commission as a Son of David and the Messiah of Israel forbade His extending His ministry to those who, like her, were outside the pale of Israel. He was perfectly truthful in this, and His answer was in strict accord with the Gospel of Matthew and the picture of the King which it presents. But she must have seen something in His glance that gave her hope and assurance, for she still pressed her suit, and, when argument failed, she clung to His feet with impassioned entreaty and cried, "Lord, help me!" (15:25).

Then came the severest repulse of all, adding, it almost seemed, insult to injury, as He shut her out with harsh reproof, and answered, "It is not right to take the children's bread and toss it to their dogs" (15:26). It was then that her desperation inspired the highest faith of which we have any record in the New Testament. Without a word of self-defense, she took the place to which He had assigned her, as not only a Gentile dog, but as something far worse, for which that word always stood in the Old Testament—one of the degraded ones who had sinned even against nature itself. "I am a dog." she acknowledged. "I deserve all you say. I have no excuse, but I plead my very misery as my plea. I take the sinner's place, and I simply claim the sinner's portion. The very dogs eat of the crumbs that fall from the Master's table, and a crumb is all I ask." It was then that the Lord revealed the deep, intense love that had been waiting all through this trial of her faith to give it its great reward. "Woman, you have great faith! Your request is granted" (15:28).

Thus, the Master, rejected by His own people, had turned to the Gentiles and had been met by a faith which had not hitherto been found even in Israel. A type it was of the coming days, when the gospel should be given to the Gentiles of every tribe and tongue and should bring forth such fruits of faith as she had given the first example of. But, the very glory of this victory of human faith and divine power only deepened the more the dark shadow of Israel's unbelief. The Lord had now turned away from His own people and was beginning to find the door of faith closed to them and opening to the Gentile world.

FEEDING OF THE FOUR THOUSAND

5. His Last Visit to the Sea of Galilee

Returning from this Gentile region (15:29–16:12), the Lord made one more visit to the Galilean shores, remaining chiefly still on the eastern side, among the cities of Decapolis. Here a great multitude soon gathered around Him, and a second time He performed the miracle of multiplying the bread, feeding on this occasion 4,000, as a little before He had fed the 5,000.

CHAPTER 10

THE GLORY OF THE KING

After six days Jesus took with him Peter, James and John the brother of James, and led them up a high mountain by themselves. There he was transfigured before them. His face shone like the sun, and his clothes became as white as the light. Just then there appeared before them Moses and Elijah, talking with Jesus. (Matthew 17:1–3)

The transfiguration of Christ marked a turning point in His life and ministry. Up to that moment His path had ascended in successive revelations of His grace and glory until at last in that manifestation of His glory and majesty on Hermon's height, the veil of His humiliation for a moment was wholly cast aside and His disciples beheld Him in His primeval glory and in the glory of His second coming by-and-by.

But from this moment the pathway descended down through the lonely valley of humiliation, suffering and rejection until at last it led to the agony and mystery of the garden, the cross and the grave.

PURPOSE OF THE TRANSFIGURATION

The transfiguration also marked the close of His Galilean ministry. We have already seen that He was preparing for some time previously to leave the scenes of His three-year ministry. He had gone up to the heathen region of Tyre and Sidon, and on His return he had still lingered on the eastern shore of the Sea of Galilee in the country of Decapolis, which was semi-heathen. But soon after the transfiguration He withdrew altogether from the northern region, where most of His mighty works had been done, and, for the next six months, we find Him in Judea, Perea and the country round about Jerusalem.

The purpose of His transfiguration was perhaps, primarily, for His own encouragement and comfort, in view of the trying conditions through which He was passing and was soon to pass. His ministry of love and His miracles of power had been met by unbelief and bitter rejection, and before Him there loomed the darker shadows of His seeming failure and His cruel death.

Looking down the immediate pathway, the heavy shadows of that awful tragedy that ended at last on Calvary opened before Him, and the hour was one which needed, as never before, the encouragement of that heavenly vision which came to Him on the Mount of Transfiguration. Henceforth, He looked not at the valley of the shadow of death just before Him, but at the sunlit heights immediately beyond, and "for the joy set before him endured the cross, scorning its shame" (Hebrews 12:2).

But the second object of the transfiguration was for the comfort and encouragement of His disciples. They had just begun to understand from His own announcements that their fond dream of an earthly kingdom through the Messiah was to be rudely dispelled; and that, instead of honor, power and earthly prosperity, they were to go forth to share His shame and cross and to seek their kingdom not in this world but on the other side of the grave. It was therefore necessary that they, too, should have a vivid conception of the divine character of the Master they were following at such tremendous cost and the reward that they were expecting at the end of all their trials and sufferings. All this was assured them in that midnight vision on the Mount when they beheld, first, His glory, and, secondly, their own, as it was set forth in the appearance of Moses and Elijah, who "appeared in glorious splendor" (Luke 9:31) as patterns and types of the glory which awaits every believer who follows Christ to the end.

AN OBJECT LESSON

There was a further purpose in the heavenly vision, and perhaps the most important of all, namely: an object lesson of certain truths which the Lord had been proclaiming to His disciples during the past few weeks, and which were set forth in a most striking manner in the vision of the transfiguration. He had taken them up on this northern journey, through the beautiful regions of Caesarea Philippi, as a sort of summer school, for the purpose of talking to them calmly and fully of the great truths of the kingdom which it was necessary that they should fully understand. After He had fully explained these truths to them in word, He took them up on the Mount that night and gave them a vivid illustration of them in the glorious scenes of the transfiguration.

His Messiahship

The first of these truths was His own divinity and messiahship. "Who do people say the Son of Man is?" (Matthew 16:13), was the question with which the discussion had begun. After they had told Him the various opinions of the people, He asked them more directly, "But what about you?

... Who do you say I am?" (16:15). It was then that Peter uttered the great confession, "You are the Christ, the Son of the living God," which Jesus told him had been revealed to Him, not by flesh and blood, but by His Father in heaven (16:16–17).

Now, the transfiguration was a special and emphatic confirmation of this. First, the voice of God Himself from the overshadowing cloud: "This is my Son, whom I love; with him I am well pleased. Listen to him!" (17:5b). This was a distinct acknowledgment of the deity of Christ, accompanied with the manifestation of the glory of God in the illuminated cloud which was the unmistakable pledge of the divine Presence. The special command, "Listen to him," was a distinct acknowledgment of His superior claims to both Moses and Elijah. Hitherto, they had been hearing the voice of the Lawgiver and the voice of the Prophets, but now they were to hear Him as God's last and supreme Messenger to man. "In the past God spoke to our forefathers through the prophets at many times and in various ways, but in these last days he has spoken to us by his Son" (Hebrews 1:1–2a).

Further, the appearance of Moses and Elijah in a place of subordination to Him and as messengers and ministers who simply waited upon His superior Majesty was a still further confirmation to the disciples that He was indeed the Messiah whom Moses and the prophets had foretold, and that their authority ended with His coming, even as the stars pale at the rising of the sun. To make the dramatic scene more effective, they, after they had waited upon Him in the vision, vanished away as a token that their ministry and their messages had given place to His, and the disciples "when they looked up . . . saw no one except Jesus" (Matthew 17:8). Thus, the whole scene was a most striking and impressive confirmation of Peter's testimony and His own claim that He was indeed "the Christ, the Son of the living God" (16:16).

His Death

The next truth which He had unfolded to the disciples on their journey northward was quite different from this.

> From that time on Jesus began to explain to his disciples that he must go to Jerusalem and suffer many things at the hands of the elders, chief priests and teachers of the law, and that he must be killed and on the third day be raised to life.
> Peter took him aside and began to rebuke him. "Never, Lord!" he said. "This shall never happen to you!"
> Jesus turned and said to Peter, "Get behind me, Satan! You are a stumbling block to me; you do not have in mind the things of God, but the things of men." (16:21–23)

This was his first explicit announcement of His crucifixion. It came as a shock to the disciples, and Peter, their impetuous spokesman, had no hesitation in expressing their utter dissent and protest against any such doctrine. He did not want a crucified Savior. He wanted a glorious and popular Messiah, subduing all earthly as well as spiritual enemies and providing a kingdom in the present as well as in the future for His faithful followers. This doctrine of the cross was repugnant to all Peter's pride and ambition, and still more so to his love for his Master. But Peter only represented the natural thought of the human heart. Man does not want a crucified Savior. The doctrine of the cross too deeply recognizes the fact of human sin and the need of blood and sacrifice to wash it away. And further, it implies the painful and humbling truth that, for the disciple as well as the Master, there must also be a cross. If our Lord is crucified, we must also deny ourselves and take up our cross and follow Him. If the world rejects Him, it will also reject us; if He must die for our sins, we must die to our sins. Men do not like this at all, and, therefore, the cross has always been and always will be unpopular with the world.

Little wonder today that it is being questioned and even rejected by the worldly Church. But all such ideas are more repugnant to our Lord than His cross was to His disciples. "You are a stumbling block to me" (16:23), He says to His favorite disciple the moment he begins to question the precious doctrine of His death. What must He think of those in His very Church who today are heaping dishonor upon the doctrine of the blood and trying to find a way to heaven aside from the blood-stained pathway of Calvary's cross?

The transfiguration was a fine object lesson of the estimation in which the heavenly beings hold the cross of Christ. This scene was a sort of drama in which the disciples were spectators and stood gazing upon a stage on which great truths were being set forth in dramatic action. They stood listening to the strange conversation of the glorious beings that had come forth from the upper world to their Master. These two that appeared that night on Hermon's height were the most illustrious men that had ever lived. One of them was the great lawgiver himself, reverenced by every Hebrew next to Jehovah Himself, Moses, the founder of their Jewish theocracy and the giver of their venerated law. The other was the great Elijah, the mighty prophet who had come in the darkest hour of the nation's sin, and, after performing miracles unprecedented even among the mightiest of the prophets, including the raising of men from the dead, had at last himself been swept to heaven in a chariot of fire without the intervention of death.

There could be no doubt to any Hebrew mind about the authority and importance of such witnesses as these. But now, these two illustrious men appeared in a posture of inferiority to the Lord Jesus, their glorious Master, uniting in the Father's testimony to His majesty, and, still more, bearing witness to His sufferings and death by speaking of that event as the one sole theme of their conversation. Looking at this wonderful spectacle, it must have seemed to the wondering disciples that the chief theme in the heavenly world was the death of the Lord Jesus Christ. "They spoke about his departure, which he was about to bring to fulfillment at Jerusalem" (Luke 9:31). And it is still true that if we could pierce the heavens and listen for a moment to the songs and conferences of the heavenly beings above, we would find them engaged in the same great theme. In the book of Revelation the Apostle John has lifted the curtain upon that world, and the one song they sing and the one theme they celebrate is thus expressed: "Worthy is the Lamb, who was slain,/ to receive power and wealth and wisdom and strength/ and honor and glory and praise!" (Revelation 5:12b).

Dear friends, let us cherish and honor the cross of Jesus Christ, the badge of His shame before the world that rejected Him, but the glorious theme which ransomed saints and holy angels ever celebrate above.

His Coming

Once more, the transfiguration bore testimony to the Master's word concerning His second coming. This also had been one of the themes of conversation in their journey northward. The Lord had just reminded them of the utter worthlessness of every earthly thing compared with the value of the never-dying soul and then had added, "For the Son of Man is going to come in his Father's glory with his angels, and then he will reward each person according to what he has done" (Matthew 16:27).

The Lord had then added the very significant announcement, "I tell you the truth, some who are standing here will not taste death before they see the Son of Man coming in his kingdom" (16:28). At first sight, this almost looks like an announcement that some of the disciples should never die, but live on to the actual coming of the Lord Jesus. This, however, is not necessary. The words are sufficiently fulfilled if we understand them to mean that the transfiguration which followed shortly after was an actual exhibition and illustration of the words "coming in his kingdom," and that in seeing it they practically saw His kingdom come. This is more impressive when we note the next verse in the opening of the 17th chapter, which seems to follow as a direct explanation of this announcement: "After six days Jesus took with him Peter, James and John the brother of James, and led them up a high mountain by themselves. There he was transfigured before them" (17:1–2). This, then, was what He meant when He said that they should see Him coming into His kingdom. The transfiguration was a revelation of His coming, and the more we look at it the more will we be struck with its complete foreshadowing of the second advent.

In the first place, the Father was there standing behind the scene and manifesting to the world the glory of Jesus Christ as His Son. This is to be fulfilled when Christ shall come again. He will come in the glory of His Father; He will occupy the center of the stage, and He will be the Judge and the King, and all the splendors of that hour shall cluster around His person and His throne.

Next, the presence of Moses on the Mount represented the resurrection of the dead at Christ's second coming. Moses had died at Mount Nebo, and God had evidently raised him from the dead and brought him back to take part in the scenes of the transfiguration. He stands, therefore, for that glorious multitude who sleep in Jesus, whom the Lord will bring with Him at His return.

Then Elijah stands for another class, the living saints of God who shall be on earth at the time of Christ's coming and who shall suddenly be changed and caught up to meet Him in the air. Elijah did not die, but was translated to Heaven in a chariot of fire, and so we are taught that when our Lord returns "we who are still alive and are left will be caught up together with them in the clouds to meet the Lord in the air" (1 Thessalonians 4:17). And again we read, "We will not all sleep, but we will all be changed—in a flash, in the twinkling of an eye, at the last trumpet" (1 Corinthians 15:51b–52a).

The Apostle Peter was one of the three disciples who saw this glorious event on the Mount. He refers to it in his second epistle, and he speaks of it as specially designed to set forth "the power and coming of our Lord Jesus Christ" (2 Peter 1:16), and, as we take in all the circumstances of that glorious scene, there is nothing that more sublimely or accurately sets forth the chief events connected with the blessed hope of our Master's coming.

LESSONS

Let us gather up some practical conclusions from this sublime story.

1. It tells us of the closer fellowship into which the Lord Jesus brings some of His disciples. There were only three of the 12 who saw this vision. The other nine remained below and passed through that night, as we read a little later, in a troubled and fruitless conflict with the adversary; but the three were taken apart and caught up to meet the Lord on the mountain top and behold His glory. We find the same three disciples taken into His intimate fellowship on two other occasions, once at the raising of the daughter of Jairus from the dead (Mark 5:37), and again as the companions of His agony in the Garden of Gethsemane (Matthew 26:37). They represented that closer fellowship into which the Lord Jesus takes those who are willing to follow Him all the way. All that this means now and is to mean by and by would be difficult to express, but surely it means enough to make us covet that wondrous promise and let nothing rob us of its blessing. "To him who

overcomes, I will give . . . a white stone with a new name written on it, known only to him who receives it" (Revelation 2:17). There is a difference now, and oh, there will be a difference then, between those that have followed Him fully and those that have hesitated to go with Him all the way.

2. It tells us of the hours of elevation and revelation which come to us amid the trials and pressures of the present. That transfiguration then was given to comfort both them and Him at a real crisis in their lives and His, and so the Lord Jesus still gives His people hours of vision and revelation when they are elevated above the clouds and shadows of the present and permitted to come into closer touch with eternal things. Not always should we look for these celestial uplifts; it would not be wholesome. Two or three times in his life, the Apostle Paul had such special visitations from his Master, and then the ordinary current of his life and work was commonplace and without special revelation. Just as the mariner takes his observations when the stars shine out and the clouds flee away and sails by this light for many a stormy day, so God gives to us these uplifts and hours of elevation as we need them.

Let us thank Him for them and say with the Psalmist, "I will remember you/ from the land of the Jordan,/ the heights of Hermon" (Psalm 42:6)—that is, the heights of Hermon, where David also had his transfiguration hours.

3. It tells us that our loved ones who have left us are living, happy and glorified, and that they are coming back again some day to meet us. In the resurrection glory of Moses and Elijah, there shines a great light that drives away the darkness of the grave and wipes away the tears of the mourner. They are living beyond, they are not dead; they are active, intelligent, busy and happy, and we shall be with them in a little while and cease to sigh

> For the touch of the vanished hand
> And the sound of a voice that is still.

4. It tells us of the blessed hope of the Lord's coming as the pole star of our lives and the inspiration of our labors and sufferings. Let us never forget it, but be ever looking "forward to the day of God and speed its coming" (2 Peter 3:12a).

5. It tells us of something higher even than the transfiguration. The scene that followed the vision on the Mount is even finer than the vision itself. It is the victory of Jesus Christ at the foot of the Mount on the following morning over the power of Satan. When they came down, they found a terrible scene—an agonized father with a lunatic boy torn by demon possession and the little company of the disciples vainly trying to cast out the evil spirit while the people were looking on with mingled sympathy for the father and

scorn for the baffled disciples. There seems to have been something unusual even in the Lord's appearance, for Mark tells that as the people looked at Him, "they were overwhelmed with wonder and ran to greet him" (9:15). There must have been something in His face and bearing that bore the traces of the glory of the night before. Certainly there was a power that had not yet appeared, for in a moment the whole scene of defeat and despair was changed to victory, the demon cast out of the living child, and the father and multitude filled with wonder at the mighty power of God.

Need we pause to make the application—how it tells of the purpose of our transfiguration, to prepare us for the conflicts and the ministries that await us in this sad world below? We go not up to the Mount of Transfiguration to "put up three shelters" (Matthew 17:4), that we may stay forever there, but rather to get a touch of heaven to bring down to the dark, sad world in the valley below. Oh, that we might come forth clothed with the power which they beheld in Him, to live transfigured lives among our fellow man and to share with them the glory which we have caught upon the Mount of Vision. Surely, this is something higher than nursing our sanctification, seeking our blessing and being satisfied with our visions.

There was deep significance in the old legend of the two men that entered the celestial portals. The first was white-robed and stainless, and, when asked by the warder whence he had come and how his garments were so clean, he told how he had just passed a poor struggling traveler on the earth below whose cart had become entangled in a great swamp and how he had begged him to help him to extricate it, and with what difficulty and pain he had escaped the urgent call and kept his garments spotless to meet his Lord.

The second pilgrim followed, and his robes were soiled with mire and grime. Flushing crimson with shame, he explained that he had tried his best to keep his garments clean, but that, just as he reached the portals, he found a struggling wayfarer vainly trying to get his cart out of a quagmire, and that he could not refuse to put his shoulder to the wheel and help him out of his trouble, "and so," he added, "the marks are still on my once spotless robes."

But the angel smiled and said, "My brother, those stains will not hinder your welcome here, for, lo! while we speak, you will find that they are transformed into jewels of glory, and they are shining upon your garments as the badges and recompense of that love which is the highest glory of our sanctity and the brightest jewel in our crown."

Dear friends, shall we not only claim the Mount of Transfiguration with the Master, but oh, shall we learn to come down from the mountain to live the transfigured life of love below?

CHAPTER 11

THE KINGDOM AND THE HOME

He called a little child and had him stand among them. (Matthew 18:2)

The home is one of the few relics left us of the old Eden life before the Fall. Like some precious jewel shining out of its rocky bed in the midst of great rent fragments of dissolved mountains, so the family remains as a memento of the world's bright morning and a pledge of the eternal home in which the tragedy of sin and the drama of redemption are at last to end. No wonder that Christ recognized, both by His teaching and example, the sacredness of the home. The first half of both the 18th and 19th chapters of Matthew is devoted to His teaching concerning the family—the first section, with a verse or two in the second relating to children, the second section to the Christian law of marriage.

SECTION I—*Christ and the Children*

No more beautiful teaching was ever given than the Lord Jesus gave His disciples, and, through them, to the future Christian Church in these verses.

INFLUENCE OF A CHILD

1. "He called a little child and had him stand among them" (18:2). This is a typical picture. When the patriarchal age was at its crisis, it was the birth of a little child, Isaac, the seed of promise, that formed the central picture of God's dealings with Abraham and Israel, and through that little child came all the future history of the chosen people (Genesis 21). When Egypt's bondage had reached its height and deliverance was about to break upon their dark night, again it was a little child in that ark of bulrushes in the Nile that became the central figure of the world's history and the leader, lawgiver and founder of the theocracy of Israel (Exodus 2). When, centuries later, a still more bitter bondage had held the nation enslaved to the Canaanites,

again it was a little child who became the instrument of God's deliverance, and around Samuel's cradle clustered all the revelations of God and the hopes of Israel, and he became the great reformer and deliverer of his people and the real founder of the kingdom of David and Solomon (1 Samuel 1–2). And once again, when the world was waiting for its Redeemer, it was a little child that came to Bethlehem's manger as the incarnate Son of God and the Savior of mankind (Luke 2).

Enter the homes of any civilized, or almost any uncivilized land, and the strongest force still found on earth is the influence of a little child. What will that mother not do or dare for her babe? To her, notwithstanding all her toil and care, that child is the loveliest character on earth, and the true motive of every sacrifice and labor. The breadwinner, as he toils from day to day, finds his labor alleviated as he sits down at night in his humble home and dandles upon his knee the little child who is the motive and recompense of his toil. And, when that little one lies fever-stricken, sinking into the arms of death, what would not those parents give for that precious life, and what would they take in exchange for one little child. And when the tender lamb, as often happens, is removed to the upper fold, perhaps there is no power so strong to draw the hearts of men and women from earth to heaven. The Scotch fishermen, after toiling all day long under murky skies and amid stormy waves in their fishing craft, steer for home by the beacon lights held by their little children on the shore. When the mists are too dense to see the lights, they can hear the songs of the little ones as they call their fathers homeward.

So many a heart has heard the voices that are calling to the better land and has turned away from earth and sin to live for God and heaven for the blessed hope of meeting once more some little child. Yes, and could we enter within those curtains that hide the heavenly world, we would behold an innumerable company of happy spirits beyond, but more than 50 to one would be little children. If it be true that Christ has redeemed the little ones who die before the age of responsibility, and if it be also true that more than half the human family have died thus early, and if it be a fact, that out of the 60 generations that have passed since Christ ascended to heaven, it would be a large estimate to say that 10 millions of each generation has consisted of saved adults. It is an easy sum in arithmetic to compare these 600 millions with the 30 billions of little children that have died during the same period, so that in heaven as well as on earth it is still true that He has set the little children in the midst. Sometime we shall thank Him that He has taken our loved ones home in infancy, that we may have the beauty and gladness of childhood with us even there.

A TYPE OF TRUE CONVERSION

2. "Unless you change and become like little children, you will never

enter the kingdom of heaven" (Matthew 18:3). The spirit of a child is the true picture of a newborn soul, for childhood tells of birth, and salvation begins with a new birth. Childhood comes forth naked and empty-handed; so the newborn soul begins at nothing. Childhood has an infinite capacity for trusting and receiving; so conversion begins with believing in the Lord Jesus Christ and taking as a free gift His grace. Childhood is a state of utter dependence. A little child has to lean upon a strong arm, and the true child of God must learn to lean upon Christ and draw all his strength from Him as completely as the babe lives upon its mother's life and leans upon its mother's arm.

THE TYPE OF THE HIGHEST CHRISTIAN LIFE

3. "Whoever humbles himself like this child is the greatest in the kingdom of heaven" (18:4). While childhood represents the beginning of Christian life, it also represents its highest attainments. Especially is this noticeable in the one feature of humility. Older people often try to be humble, but the little child is humble without trying. It is that true humility which does not consist in demeaning ourselves, as some people seem to think, but of not thinking of ourselves at all. A little child may be placed in the most conspicuous place, or it may be crawling upon the carpet: it is alike unconscious of itself, and, the moment it becomes self-conscious, it loses the charm of childhood altogether. The greatest service you can render to your little ones is to keep them simple and free from self-consciousness and self-importance. This is the highest charm of Christian character, and it is uniform fruit and evidence of spiritual maturity and deep communion with the Master.

Again, the child teaches us much about unworldliness. It is as well pleased with the tinsel ornaments as the jeweled crown; it knows not and cares not for the difference. Its mother's smile is more to it than all the applause of shouting multitudes, and so it speaks to us of deadness to the world in that supreme sense which comes from devotedness to God and a heart absorbed and satisfied in Him.

Another thing about childhood is its instinctive life. It does not reason things out, but it senses them. It is largely a life of intuition. And the deepest spiritual life is not a life of great knowledge and human wisdom, as much as intense fellowship with the mind of the Master, and a perfect intuition of His very thought and will. It is Christ so living, thinking and working in us to will and do of His good pleasure, that we just think God's thoughts after God, and are in constant touch with the mind and heart of Christ. Great simplicity, therefore, characterizes the advanced saint, and his life becomes more and more leaning upon the Lord and walking in constant heart touch with Christ, like the beloved disciple on the Master's bosom. It is a sort of glorified childhood. And when we speak of the two qualities of faith and love that constitute the very heart of Christianity and the highest crown of sainthood, where shall we learn them, as from the little child, unless it be from Him who was not ashamed to compare Himself with the spirit of a child.

THE REPRESENTATIVE OF JESUS CHRIST

4. This is what He meant when He said, "And whoever welcomes a little child like this in my name welcomes me" (18:5). He has placed that babe in our midst as His own little ambassador to speak for Him, to remind us of Him, and to receive our ministries for Him. He Himself was once as young, as feeble, as helpless as that babe that lies upon your breast, and even in heaven He is still called "thy holy child, Jesus" (Acts 4:30, KJV). Perhaps, above all else, the little child is accessible. It is not hard to get acquainted with a child; it is not difficult to approach a little child. And oh, how easy it is to go to Jesus, and how simple His welcome, how prompt His forgiveness, acceptance and grace. You can find your Savior as easily as you can reach the heart of a little child.

And, busy mother, worrying perhaps about what you consider higher duties, and envying your happy sister, who has leisure to attend religious meetings and work for public charities and Christian objects, while you are busy all day long with the nursery and household, and sometimes grow impatient of the little hands that hold so tightly to your apron strings—if you would remember that your services to them are accepted by the Master as ministries to Him! They represent Him, and, in loving and caring for them, you are loving and caring for their Lord and yours. How beautifully this has been reflected in the old legend of St. Christopher, the knight that had long sought for the Master, whom he had chosen to serve, and at last one night he went to sleep in a little cabin on the banks of a stormy river. Late in the night, above the howling tempest, he heard the wail of a suffering child. He flew to its rescue and saved it from drowning in the winter torrent. As he brought it to the shore and placed it on the solid ground, himself chilled and almost exhausted with the struggle, lo, the child was suddenly transfigured, and the Savior stood before him instead of that rescued babe, His face all shining with light and His voice rewarding the services of the saint, and saying: "Inasmuch as you did it unto one of the least of these, you did it unto Me! Henceforth your name shall be Christ bearer (Christopher)—one that bears the burdens of the Christ." Beloved, let us be more willing to be Christ bearers, and we will never be heard saying again, "My work is only to look after children!"

CAPACITY FOR FAITH

5. By "these little ones who believe in me" (Matthew 18:6) He means that

the little children can trust Him. They are not too young to know their Savior. Earlier than you dream, their hearts can pray, believe, love and touch that spiritual realm that is reached not by strong reasoning, but with childish instinct.

Some of the most eminent servants of Christ became His happy followers as early as the age of three, four and five years. Dr. Isaac Watts was writing hymns at the age of five years. Some of us have parted with our little ones much younger on the brink of the dark river, and they have told us with shining faces and child faith that they knew they were going home to be with Jesus. Let us not chill them by our distrust. Let us not despise those little ones or think ignobly of them. They are very near to the Father, they are very dear to the Master, and they are not hard to bring to His blessed feet.

A STUMBLING BLOCK

6. The word "offend" (18:6, KJV) literally means to cause to stumble. It is not easy to offend a little child, for it has too much sense to take offense; but it means to cause them to stumble, to do them spiritual harm, and the Lord Jesus tells us that "it would be better for him to have a large millstone hung around his neck and to be drowned in the depths of the sea" (18:6), than that we should cause one of His little ones to stumble. Oh, how many are guilty of this! Sometimes it is through false teaching, and the adversary is wise in teaching the pagan mother, the Roman Catholic sister and the promoters of false religions, to do their best work with the children, for they know a prejudice learned in infancy is never forgotten. Perhaps the most serious way in which we cause the little ones to stumble is by our wicked example. Oh, the fearful influences in which many an innocent child is brought up—a drunken father, a passionate mother, family brawls alternating with family revels, cursing, Sabbath breaking, immorality and a school of vice and crime, which cannot possibly fail to leave its transcript upon the plastic and receptive mind of even the purest child. Fathers and mothers, if any motive stronger than another could appeal to you to become Christians yourself, surely it would be this—to save your children from the curse that sin has brought to you. Oh, how shall God ever forgive you, and how shall you forgive yourselves if you lead astray those little souls that have put their trusting hands in yours and said, "I go with mother; I will do what father does"!

Sometimes, again, even without these aggravated conditions, there are nominally Christian homes where the upbringing of childhood is sadly marred by lack of gentleness, tenderness and wisdom, the harsh word, the impatient rebuke, the quick and irritating blow, and then, perhaps, the foolish indulgence that tries to atone for it. The weakness of many a mother and father has crushed the sweetness out of childhood all too soon, and the bud that might have blossomed into a fair flower, has been crushed and changed into a thorn. That was what the apostle was thinking of when he wrote the touching verse, "Fathers, do not exasperate your children; instead, bring them up in the training and instruction of the Lord" (Ephesians 6:4). That literally means, bring them up as God brings you up. Remember, every time you treat them harshly: "How would I like my Father to treat me thus?" "Am I in the place of God?" (Genesis 50:19) was the beautiful language of Joseph to his brothers. Oh, that we might be to them instead of God!

But, above all other crimes against the little ones, is the crime of neglecting their souls' salvation, and letting them go astray, when it is so easy to bring them to the Savior. God save us from the blood of "the innocents," and the crime of causing the little ones to stumble.

THEIR HEAVENLY GUARDIANSHIP

7. An extremely beautiful truth is suggested in the 10th verse: "For I tell you that their angels in heaven always see the face of my Father in heaven" (Matthew 18:10). He means that the little ones have each a guardian angel, and that that angel has always access to the Father in heaven. Like that beautiful queen mother who always left word when called away by court ceremonies, "Remember that I am always at leisure for a call from the nursery," so the Father in heaven, amid all the care of countless worlds, is never too busy to listen to the report of the heavenly guardians who watch His little children. They may go to Him at any moment, and call upon Him for any need.

THEIR SHEPHERD AND THEIR SAVIOR

8. But they have a higher friend than even the angels. For He says, "The Son of Man came to save what was lost" (18:11, margin), and then He gives a special edition of the parable of the Good Shepherd, meant exclusively for the little children. There is another edition of the parable in Luke 15. That one is meant for adults, but this one belongs entirely to the little ones. He tells how the shepherd goes to seek his lost one and how he brings it home, and then He expounds the parable in one brief sentence: "In the same way your Father in heaven is not willing that any of these little ones should be lost" (Matthew 18:14). There is a very beautiful omission in the 11th verse. The same message occurs in Luke, when He was referring to the salvation of Zacchaeus, the publican. The Lord there adds one word to the phrase, "For the Son of Man came to *seek* and to save what was lost" (Luke 19:10). Zacchaeus, like us older sinners, needed to be sought as well as saved, but the little children come without effort, and He only needed to save them. Beautiful indeed was the comment of a little girl who was looking at a picture of the mothers of Jerusalem pushing their little children forward to the

Savior to receive His blessing, and as she watched the figures she turned to her mamma and said: "I don't like that; I'd go without pushing." This was the thought of Christ in this simple phrase.

The spirit of the disciples on this occasion was very offensive to Him. They had little sympathy with the crowd of mothers and children that were jostling the Savior, and they tried their best to keep them back, but the Savior was much displeased. These conservative disciples represent too many in the church today with whom our Lord is quite as much displeased. We have good cause to thank God for the greatly improved methods of Sunday School and Christian youth work, but none of these things can be substitutes for our individual love, sacrifice and service.

The act of the Lord Jesus in receiving these little children and publicly blessing them seems to suggest and authorize the beautiful custom in many churches of holding special dedicatory services for the little ones and offering them to God for His blessing. This was done in the case of our Lord Himself when a little child, and He seems to have repeated a similar service on this occasion in His earthly ministry. We cannot err in following His beautiful twofold example.

SECTION II—*The Christian Law of Marriage*

The first part of the 19th chapter of Matthew is devoted to the discussion of the relation of marriage to the kingdom.

THE LAW OF CREATION

1. He tells us in the fourth verse that the primeval law of marriage was the creation of one man for one woman and one woman for one man. The true reading here is, "He made them a male and a female." The law of creation made no provision for the vice of polygamy, but created an equal number of both sexes, and such has substantially been the case among all nations. Still further He goes on to tell us of the provision in nature itself and its instincts for the marriage relation and how it is the divine order that "a man will leave his father and mother and be united to his wife, and the two will become one flesh," and, "So they are no longer two, but one. Therefore what God has joined together, let man not separate" (Matthew 19:5–6). The element of personal affection and mutual attraction is clearly involved here. Marriage is not a conventional arrangement of convenience, but a cleavage of hearts so strong that it supersedes the previous attachment of father and mother to the extent at least of allowing a still closer union, the union which makes them truly one. Surely, it is needless to say that marriage without such unity and love is not a sacrament, but a sacrilege.

DIVORCE UNDER THE OLD TESTAMENT

2. He then takes up the Mosaic provision for divorce, and He admits that Moses did make liberal provision for divorce, but "it was not this way from the beginning" (19:8b). Moses, He tells them, did this "because your hearts were hard" (19:8a), that is to say, the age was not then prepared for the higher law of Christian marriage and God winked at certain provisions for a time, but His original conception of marriage and His ultimate law of marriage is the entering of one man and one woman in a heart fellowship of true affection as long as life itself.

DIVORCE UNDER THE NEW TESTAMENT

3. He then proceeds to lay down the Christian law concerning divorce. This is much more fully explained later by the Holy Spirit in the writings of the apostles, especially by Paul, in the seventh chapter of First Corinthians. There the great apostle tells us that Christian marriage must involve not only natural affection, but spiritual oneness. The child of God must not marry the unconverted, "but he must belong to the Lord" (1 Corinthians 7:39). Without such unity, marriage is indeed a rash venture and a sure disaster. As Dr. Arnot has well expressed it, it is like two ships joined together about 20 feet apart and sailing on a long ocean voyage. If they are really so close as to be one, they could breast the billows together and safely outride the storm, or if they were a hundred miles apart they would be safe, but so close they rasp and tear each other's side in every dash of the waves until at last they crush each other to destruction and go down together. Such is the picture of many an ill-mated marriage. The Lord Jesus does not take up this phase of it here, but He dwells on the side of divorce in the same terms as the apostle does in the chapter already referred to in Corinthians. There is provision for divorce under the law of Christ, but it is only on one condition, a breach of the marriage vows by literal unfaithfulness and immorality.

Then the innocent party has the right to divorce the guilty, and that carries with it the right of the innocent to remarry; but the divorced one, the guilty one, has not this right of remarriage, and such remarriage is adultery, not only on the part of the divorcee, but also the partner of the new marriage. Christ makes no provision for minor grounds of divorce, and we should be very careful in upholding the sanctity of marriage and the strictness and righteousness of His holy law.

CELIBACY AND MARRIAGE

4. The Lord then takes up the question of the rightness and wrongness of the unmarried state, and while He certainly does not place any premium on celibacy as the highest state of Christian life, yet He gives perfect freedom to

those who choose the unmarried state to do so, and He leaves this a matter of conscience for each one to settle with himself or herself. If, from our high allegiance to Christ and a desire to be more free to serve Him, we choose it "because of the kingdom of heaven" (Matthew 19:12), the Lord accepts our sacrifice and consecration, but He adds: "The one who can accept this should accept it" (19:12). We shall find no sanction anywhere in the New Testament for the extreme and fanatical teachings of a class who are waging war on the lawful marriage as a less holy state. Like all extreme teachings, this will lead to great sin in the very direction in which it is seeking for greater purity. We shall always find that the path of service, holiness and highest service will be found in simple obedience to the gentle and highest commandments of that blessed Master, who put upon us no hard conditions, but has said: "For my yoke is easy and my burden is light" (11:30).

Finally, let us remember that all human relationships are but stepping stones to our highest and divine relationship to Christ and heaven. The best of earthly marriages is but a little bit of broken glass full of the sunshine of heaven. God gives us these earthly ties as types of the heavenly that we may better understand the love of our divine Bridegroom, the tenderness of our heavenly Father and the meaning of our holy sonship.

CHAPTER 12

THE KINGDOM AND THE CHURCH

For where two or three come together in my name, there am I with them. (Matthew 18:20)

U p to this point in the Gospel of Matthew the Lord Jesus had not referred to the Church. He had frequently spoken of the kingdom of heaven, but the Church is mentioned for the first time in Matthew 16:18: "On this rock I will build my church." And here again in the 18th chapter He refers more particularly to the authority and discipline of the Church.

This naturally suggests the question: What is the difference between the kingdom and the Church? The *kingdom* is the larger term denoting the whole revelation of God's plan during the Christian age up to the coming of the Lord and including His advent and reign. The *Church* is a narrower term, denoting the body of believers called out from the world and united to Him as their Head and whom He is preparing for the high destiny of His bride.

THE IDEA OF THE CHURCH

The Greek word for church, *ekklesia,* literally means *called out.* The primary idea of the word is separation. As you will note in the New Testament, this word seems to have two distinct applications. First, it denotes a particular congregation of believers in one place, as for example, the church in Jerusalem, the church in Samaria, the church in Antioch. Secondly, it also denotes the whole body of believers, and is so used when it is said "Christ loved the church and gave himself up for her" (Ephesians 5:25), and other similar passages. It is never used to denote a Christian denomination, as the Baptist, the Methodist, the Presbyterian church. That is a purely human application of the term. While the Lord's forbearance graciously tolerates our sectarian division, they have no warrant whatever in the Holy Scriptures. It is not worth our while to quarrel with them, as the Lord's coming will soon end these sad divisions in the blessed reunion of the children of God in the "church of the firstborn" (Hebrews 12:23); but all the same, it is well for us to understand the true meaning and limitations of the words used to describe the Church of Christ.

These two passages in the 16th and 18th chapters of Matthew contain much important teaching respecting the Church of Christ:

THE FOUNDING OF THE CHURCH

1. This takes us back to the 18th verse of the 16th chapter of Matthew: "And I tell you that you are Peter, and on this rock I will build my church, and the gates of Hades will not overcome it." It is needless to say that this passage has given occasion for centuries of theological controversy. Long before the days of the Papacy, however, the Christian Fathers, like Jerome and Augustine, had suggested the interpretation which we venture to give, and which leaves no ground whatever for the primacy of Peter as the head of the Church on earth. Even the least learned reader of the English Bible can easily see that any power and authority given to Peter in this verse was equally given to the other disciples in the 18th chapter, where He says of all of them: "whatever you bind on earth will be bound in heaven, and whatever you loose on earth will be loosed in heaven" (Matthew 18:18).

But turning to the passage itself, we find a very delicate and striking distinction in the two words. *Petros* signifies a stone, *Peter* a rock; that is the bedrock from which the stone is cut. Now, the Lord Jesus Christ says: "You are *Petros*, the stone, and on this *Petra*, the bedrock from which this little stone has been cut, I will build my Church." No mason would think of building a lofty and stable edifice on a shifting stone; it is the solid rock that he seeks for a foundation. Peter is the stone, but Christ Himself is the rock; and as some of the Fathers very wisely suggested, in saying this, the Lord Jesus must have pointed to Himself in distinction from Peter.

This distinction gives a very fine meaning to the passage. Peter himself, in his own epistle, carries out the same idea with great beauty, "As you come to him, the living Stone . . . you also, like living stones, are being built into a spiritual house" (1 Peter 2:4–5). Here we have the separate stones, individual saints and the great foundation Stone, the Lord Jesus Christ Himself. Very distinctly does the Apostle Paul also refer to this when he says: "For no one can lay any foundation other than the one already laid, which is Jesus Christ" (1 Corinthians 3:11).

Christ, therefore, is the true Foundation of the Church, and only as we are united to Him do we belong to the true Church. It is not our theology, our profession, our baptism, or our confirmation that makes us members of His Church, but our vital union with Him, our Living Head.

But not only is He the Founder; He is also the Builder of the Church. "On this rock I will build my church" (Matthew 16:18a). Only the Holy Spirit can truly attach souls to this Living Head. All other work is called by the apostle "wood, hay or straw" (1 Corinthians 3:12), and will perish amid the awful tests of the last day. In the account of the Church at Pentecost, it is finely said, "And the Lord added to their number daily those who were being saved" (Acts 2:47); and in the same connection, it is added a little later in the same book of Acts: "Nevertheless, more and more men and women believed in the Lord and were added to their number" (5:14).

THE CONSTITUTION OF THE CHURCH

2. This is finely expressed in the text which we have quoted above. "For where two or three come together in my name, there am I with them" (Matthew 18:20). It is this which constitutes the Christian Church, a company of true believers gathered together, not in, but unto, the name of the Lord. It is not unto the name of some human leader or sect, but the name of the Lord; He is the true Head and front of His own Church. Even a little company of true believers thus gathered unto His name really constitute the New Testament Church, although there may be neither bishop nor presbytery nor high authority, nor long tradition, nor illustrious human names. Where there are even two or three so gathered unto His name, there is always One more.

The expression, "there am I with them" (18:20), denotes much more than the spiritual presence of the Lord Jesus in the hearts of individual believers. That is always true, but this is something quite different. It is the Lord Jesus "with them," as well as in the heart; it is the presence of the Head of the Church, the King of kings, the Lord of lords, the Glorious One, who is "head over everything for the church, which is his body" (Ephesians 1:22–23). And He is in the midst not only by His Holy Spirit, but in His providence, in His power and with all the authority of His kingly rights as the Son of God and mediatorial Lord and King. He is in the midst, as He was at the Red Sea, at the Jordan, and on the day of Pentecost. He is in the midst to clothe with His authority, to anoint with His Spirit, to defend by His power and to sanction with His name that which is done in His name and for His glory.

What a dignity this confers upon the humblest Christian assembly, and what a simplicity it gives to our equipment in the great work of evangelizing the world for Christ. We do not need to wait for ecclesiastical dignitaries or depend upon human forms and ceremonies, but in the heart of heathendom, a little flock may meet in the Master's name and know that its acts and ordinances are as sacred and effective as though they were done in the most venerable cathedral or the most imposing ecclesiastical council.

THE DISCIPLINE OF THE CHURCH

3. The Lord Jesus has provided for the government and purity of His

Church, and He has given authority to His servants to remove from this fellowship everything in opposition with its holy character. He has invested this discipline with the most sacred and binding authority, and He tells us in this passage that what we bind on earth He will bind in Heaven, and what we loose on earth He will loose in heaven. When the willful and disobedient disciple refuses to yield to loving admonition and persists in some sinful and unchristian course, the Master has given to His people the right and power to remove that member and hand him over to the divine chastening until he shall truly repent. He tells us here that such an act on the part of the Church of God will be followed by the Lord's effectual dealing with all such cases. It will not be merely a matter of outward excommunication or public censure, but God's hand will deal with the offender through temporal judgment with a view to bringing the guilty one to repentance, or, as the apostle expressed it in another place, "so that the sinful nature may be destoyed and his spirit saved on the day of the Lord" (1 Corinthians 5:5).

But He tells us that discipline must be the last resort and not the first. Therefore He says: "If your brother sins against you, go and show him his fault, just between the two of you" (Matthew 18:15). There is to be personal dealing first—tender, loving admonition and appeal; but if this fails, then He says: "take one or two others along, so that every matter may be established by the testimony of two or three witnesses" (18:16). Then, if this united appeal should fail, "tell it to the church," and "if he refuses to listen even to the church, treat him as you would a pagan or a tax collector" (18:17).

Here we learn that our Christian attitude with the erring brother is always to deal with him personally and alone. We have no right to speak even to another of our brother's faults and offenses, until we have first dealt with him ourselves in loving faithfulness. It is only when this course has failed that we are permitted to resort to more rigid discipline. The Lord Jesus has made this the law of the Christian Church. Oh, how better it would be if His people would really live up to it! What a certain preventive it would be to the slander, the evil speaking, the strife and often the falling away of brethren who might have been saved by true obedience to the loving and wise commandment of the Master. Shall we take His message to us, here and henceforth thus deal with our erring brethren and prove to the world that the resources of the Church of Jesus Christ are adequate for her preservation, purity and power?

THE SPIRIT OF LOVE AND FORGIVENESS

4. The Lord Jesus proceeds from this point to unfold to His disciples the law of love in the form of a striking parable, "the Unmerciful Servant" (18:23–35). The design of this parable is to show the estimation in which the Lord holds the spirit of charity and forgiveness and His indignation

against all uncharitableness, censoriousness and harsh judging among brethren. The two unpardonable sins of the New Testament are unbelief in Christ and unlovingness toward our brethren, and we cannot claim forgiveness of the Lord unless we are equally forgiving one to the other. Even the infidel, Gibbon, was forced to admit that one chief secret of the extraordinary success of the early Church, notwithstanding the severest persecutions, was the mutual love of the brethren, a spectacle wholly new to the world and an armor that will ever prove invincible against human criticism and Satanic hate. A church without love would be as great a contradiction as a home without affection or a Heaven without God.

THE FELLOWSHIP OF THE CHURCH

5. The fellowship of prayer is next referred to as the real source of power in the Christian Church. "Again, I tell you that if two of you on earth agree about anything you ask for, it will be done for you by my Father in heaven" (18:19). This is the real purpose of the union of Christian hearts in the Church of God. It is to bring them together in the fellowship of divine prayer. There is an added power in the element of union; there is something in the prayer of two harmonious hearts that does not seem to be promised even to the prayer of one. But they must be in unison. The word "agree" in the Greek is *symphonie*; it is a word which denotes a musical chord, and is the most perfect expression of harmony. It is more than unison; it is the unison of different notes; it is an accord of hearts that are individually distinct yet spiritually one. Only the Holy Spirit can produce such harmony. He is the true author of prayer, and He does this by laying it upon different hearts that they shall be truly one.

In the fine picture given us in the book of Zechariah of the Church of Christ in the image of the seven lamps in the temple, we have this figure of the two golden pipes conveying oil from the living olive trees to the bowl of the lamp. That was the one feature of the symbol that impressed the prophet as he gazed upon the vision. "What are these two olive branches beside the two gold pipes," he asked, "that pour out golden oil?" And the answer was: "These are the two who are anointed to serve the Lord of all the earth" (Zechariah 4:12, 14). Literally these are the "two sons of oil." This surely represents the unity of prayer on the part of God's children. It would seem as if the Lord had required such unity as essential to effective prayer. Perhaps we shall some day find that no blessing ever reaches us from the throne which does not come through someone's prayer, and thus gives occasion for the name of Jesus Christ to be honored and glorified before all heaven.

In the story of the early Church we have some remarkable instances of the power of united prayer. We are told how, after an outbreak of bitter persecution, they went unto their own company and unitedly called upon God, and it is added: "After they prayed, the place where they were meeting was shaken. And they were all filled with the Holy Spirit and spoke the word of God boldly. . . . With great power the apostles continued to testify to the resurrection of the Lord Jesus, and much grace was upon them all" (Acts 4:31, 33). This was a direct answer to a service of united prayer.

We read again in the 12th chapter of Acts a similar instance. The Apostle Peter was held in prison, caged like an animal, to be brought out on the great festival of Easter and publicly butchered before the crowd to make a more distinguished holiday, and the simple but eloquent verse is added: "but the church was earnestly praying to God for him" (12:5). We know what followed—not only the miraculous deliverance of Peter, but soon after the fearful death of Herod, his persecutor; and the chapter ends with the remarkable but brief record, "But the word of God continued to increase and spread" (12:24). This has ever been and will ever be the secret of the Church's power.

Dr. Torrey declares that the secret of the remarkable religious revival now in Great Britain is due to the fact that a few years ago some Christian friends in Chicago began to pray in unison and faith that God would bring about a religious revival throughout the world. They continued their prayer from month to month and are continuing it still. It was not long until God's working began to appear. A deputation from Australia waited on Dr. Torrey in Chicago and invited him to visit that commonwealth and conduct a series of evangelistic services. The result of those meetings was a remarkable religious awakening that spread over the whole of Australia and has been followed by similar meetings in other places. The records of answered prayer are full of similar instances, perhaps on a smaller scale, but not less encouraging to faith and prayer. This is the mightiest equipment of the Church of God, the highest ministry of the people of God.

Shall we prove its power as never before? "You who call on the LORD,/ give yourselves no rest,/ and give him no rest till he establishes Jerusalem/ and makes her the praise of the earth" (Isaiah 62:6–7).

CHAPTER 13

THE SPIRIT OF THE EARTHLY AND
HEAVENLY KINGDOMS

You know that the rulers of the Gentiles lord it over them, and their high officials exercise authority over them. Not so with you. Instead, whoever wants to become great among you must be your servant, and whoever wants to be first must be your slave—just as the Son of Man did not come to be served, but to serve, and to give his life as a ransom for many. (Matthew 20:25–28)

This is a picture of the spirit of the earthly and heavenly kingdoms. The watchword of the former is "look out for yourself," "get all you can," "make the best of life," "take care of yourself" and many phrases of similar import and familiar colloquial meaning. The spirit of the heavenly kingdom is "Love . . . is not self-seeking" (1 Corinthians 13:4–5), "deny [your]self" (Matthew 16:24), "live for others and for God" (see Philippians 2:4), "the Son of Man did not come to be served, but to serve, and to give his life as a ransom for many" (Matthew 20:28).

The various paragraphs from Matthew 19 to 28 contain a series of illustrations of this contrast:

SELFISHNESS

1. Selfishness is the essential principle of sin.

This is very finely illustrated in the incident of the one who came to Him asking, "Good Master, what good thing shall I do, that I may have eternal life?" (19:16, KJV). In answering him, the Lord Jesus paused a moment to show him that the word "good" could be applied to none but God: "If I am good I must be God, for no human being can claim that title." This must have been a rude shock to this young man's self-confidence, for he felt quite certain that he at least was good.

Then the Master proceeds to show him his own heart and convict him of his utter selfishness. He does this by meeting him first on his own plane and assuming that, according to the law of righteousness, if he is really good he will inherit eternal life as a matter of simple justice and righteousness. Therefore He answers: "If you want to enter life, obey the commandments" (19:17). "Which ones?" replies the young man. The Lord then quotes the second table of the law covering our duties to our neighbor, all summed up in one closing command, "love your neighbor as yourself" (19:19). This is familiar ground to the young man, and he confidently declares: "All these I have kept. . . . What do I still lack?" (19:20).

Then the Lord presses the keen edge of the sword of truth into his hypocrisy that had so long deceived him. It was as if He had said, "You think you have obeyed the second table of the law and loved your neighbor as yourself, for that is the real spirit of the law. Well, I am going to apply a simple test. If you love your neighbor as yourself, it will not be difficult for you to share with him your wealth; and if you love the Lord with all your heart, it will be no sacrifice to you to give up all and follow Him. Therefore, as a simple test of your love to your neighbor and your love to God, go, sell your possessions and give to the poor, and you will have treasure in heaven. Then come, follow me."

And lo, that young man's castle of self-righteousness crumbled into dust. In a moment he saw himself in his true selfishness. The very thought of parting with his wealth and becoming a humble, despised follower of the Son of God filled him with sorrow and despair. He could not make such a sacrifice. He did not love his brother or his God. He loved himself and his own wealth and comfort, and he was unwilling to give these up for any higher plane. Alas! the illusion was gone, his dream of righteousness and eternal life melted into air, and he went away sorrowful for the strangest reason in the world—because he had great wealth (19:18–22).

Most people are sorrowful because they have so little; but he found the cause of his deepest sorrow in the fact that he was unwilling and unable to part with his earthly treasures for the sake of his neighbor and his God. He had committed no act of gross immorality or open sin; he was not in any sense a bad man as the world understands it, and yet he saw himself to be utterly selfish and bound to earth and its pleasures and aims by bonds that he was utterly unable to break.

And so, when the light of God comes into the soul, we find that sin does not consist so much of gross crimes against the laws of man, or even the laws of God, as in the subtle spirit of self-love. Therefore it comes to pass that the self-righteous and moral sinners are much harder to reach than the profligate and the drunkard; and the Lord Jesus had to say to the religious Pharisees of

His own time, "I tell you the truth, the tax collectors and the prostitutes are entering the kingdom of God ahead of you" (21:31).

It is said that a celebrated rationalist preacher of France was once invited by an evangelical minister to preach in his pulpit on the text, "Love the Lord your God with all your heart," and " 'Love your neighbor as yourself.' All the Law and the Prophets hang on these two commandments" (22:37a, 39b–40). While standing in the pulpit introducing his sermon, his brother minister, who was an earnest and spiritually minded man, was praying to God for the salvation of his soul. In answer to his prayer, the strangest thing came to pass. The rationalist preacher became suddenly convicted of sin while trying to preach on this subject. The Spirit of God showed him that the one thing that even the Hebrew law demanded of all men was perfect love to man; and there and then he saw that he was destitute of this love, and, filled with alarm and despair by the view he got of his own heart, he stopped in his sermon, and with tears of earnestness besought the congregation to pray for him that he might seek and find through Jesus Christ that grace that alone could enable him to have this love of which his own unnatural heart was utterly destitute.

Dear friend, have you become convicted of the spirit of selfishness, the love of your own self, your own reputation, your own ease and pleasure, even your own religious merit and righteousness? This is the essence of human depravity, and in this begins the very first stepping of the work of grace and salvation. The Lord Jesus takes occasion, after the departure of this young man, to say, "it is hard for a rich man to enter the kingdom of heaven. Again I tell you, it is easier for a camel to go through the eye of a needle than for a rich man to enter the kingdom of God" (19:23–24). The eye of the needle to which He here referred was a certain gate in Jerusalem which was so low that a loaded camel could not pass through it. It had to unload its burden and kneel, before it could pass the gate of the needle's eye. What a striking figure of the necessity of our unloading our earthly treasures and self-righteousness before we can enter into the heavenly kingdom.

The disciples are amazed at His strong language, and ask in sorrow, "Who then can be saved?" (19:25) and the Lord replies, "With man this is impossible, but with God all things are possible" (19:26). Nothing but a miracle of grace and power can bring the proud, self-satisfied human heart to see its emptiness, to part with its idols, and to pass on its knees through the narrow gate that leads to life.

SELF-SACRIFICE

2. The measure of our eternal reward is determined by the spirit of self-sacrifice.

Peter answered him, "We have left everything to follow you! What then will there be for us?"

Jesus said to them, "I tell you the truth, at the renewal of all things, when the Son of Man sits on his glorious throne, you who have followed me will also sit on twelve thrones, judging the twelve tribes of Israel. And everyone who has left houses or brothers or sisters or father or mother or children or fields for my sake will receive a hundred times as much and will inherit eternal life. But many who are first will be last, and many who are last will be first." (19:27–30)

The words "renewal of all things" here is in the Greek *Palingenesis,* which means the new creation. It describes the coming age when the Lord Jesus will return and set up His kingdom. Then He tells His disciples the rewards of that kingdom will be determined by the sacrifices of His servants. It is not so much what we have done, as the spirit of love and sacrifice that has prompted our deeds and sufferings. But in the closing sentence which immediately follows, "But many who are first will be last, and many who are last will be first" (19:30), the Lord implies that there will be much surprise and disappointment when the testing time shall reveal the real spirit of every heart; and many that have seemed to be truly unselfish may find, to their eternal disappointment, that even their seeming sacrifices were prompted after all by some form of selfishness, even if it is sometimes religious selfishness.

There is a very solemn story told by Dr. Bonar of a dream in which he saw his own heart analyzed in the presence of God by a holy angel, who dissolved it in a crucible and took each separate element and weighed it, and when all was over the good minister looked with horror as he saw that almost all the masses of elements into which his spirit had been resolved consisted of mere earthly motives, love of applause, love of intellectual work, mere habit or tradition and a thousand other things, and there was but a trace of true divine love. He woke from his dream to humble himself before God and pray with deep earnestness: "Search me, O God, and know my heart;/ test me and know my anxious thoughts./ See if there is any offensive way in me,/ and lead me in the way everlasting" (Psalm 139:23–24).

FUTURE REWARDS

3. The highest recompenses in the heavenly kingdom will be given to those who serve not for reward, but for love.

The parable of the Laborers in the Vineyard (Matthew 20:1–16) unfolds some deep principles in connection with the subject of reward. First, let us closely understand the difference between free grace and reward. Salvation is the gift of God's free grace; but after we are saved, our services for Christ are rewarded according to the measure of our sacrifices and love. We cannot obtain the entrance into the kingdom of heaven by our own good works; this is bestowed upon the sinner freely for Christ's sake. But having entered the kingdom, we are all competitors for various prizes which are bestowed on the principle of service and love.

These rewards are various. It does not look like this at first, as we study the parable, for each of the laborers seems to receive the same amount, a penny a day. But when we look more closely into the matter, we find that the first laborers worked twelve hours for their penny and the last only one hour for the same sum, so that they really received 12 times as much pro rata as the others. The picture is a very graphic one. The Master comes to His vineyard in the morning at six o'clock and finds a lot of idle men around. He engages a number of laborers under a special contract at a penny a day, equal to about 15 cents in our money. This would be fair wages in the East today. Later, at nine o'clock, and again at noon, and again at three o'clock in the afternoon He went to the vineyard and found others standing idle and He sent them to work, but on a different contract. There was no stipulation of a penny a day, but simply the promise, "I will pay you whatever is right" (20:4). It was work for wages, but there was a degree of trust about it. But at five o'clock when the day was almost gone and only one hour was left for work, He found still others standing idle, and He sent them into the vineyard to work, but said nothing to them about wages. The reading in our old [King James] version of verse 7 is wrong. The revised version [and NIV] has given it correctly by leaving out the clause about wages. He simply sent these men to work without any promise or agreement whatever. When the evening came and all received their wages, these last laborers received the same as the men that had toiled all day long, practically 12 times as much as the first workmen.

When we come to inquire into the reason for this, we cannot forget that these last laborers worked in simple faith without any agreement at all, while the others labored under a law and contract. Truly, this represents the highest spirit of service, "all for love and nothing for reward." The first represents work done under the law; the second, perhaps, for the class of Christians that try to get through as cheaply as possible; the third for those who go purely under the principle of grace, who give their lives to God in simple faith and trust Him for everything. Their reward will be the largest of all. It is quite possible for us to be working for a reward rather than for the Master with love. And this form of selfishness, even though it is spiritual selfishness, will vitiate much of our best service. How beautiful is the picture in the 25th chapter of Matthew of the persons whom the Master praised for their ministries to Him: "For I was hungry and you gave me something to eat, I was thirsty and you gave me something to drink . . . I was in prison and you came to visit me" (25:35–36), and they were quite surprised and had forgotten all about it, and answered simply, "Lord, when did we see you hungry and feed you" (25:37). The very unconsciousness of their own merit was their highest merit, and the Lord rewarded them all the same, adding with supreme beauty: "I tell you the truth, whatever you did for one of the least of these brothers of mine, you did for me" (25:40).

FELLOWSHIP IN HIS SUFFERINGS

4. The prizes of the kingdom are given for fellowship in the sufferings of Christ.

It was in this connection that the mother of James and John came to the Master with her two boys and made a special request for them, that they might sit the one on His right hand and the other on His left in His kingdom. The answer of Jesus was very striking; He did not refuse the honor requested, but He told them that it was to be bestowed not arbitrarily, but on special grounds. The correct reading here is very expressive: "to sit on My right hand and on My left is not Mine to give, except to them for whom it is prepared of My Father." (20:23, author's translation). He does not say that there is no such reward, but He says it is prepared for certain persons and will be only given to those who meet the demands. And then He tells them what these conditions are: "Can you drink the cup I drink or be baptized with the baptism I am baptized with?" (Mark 10:38). The cup was His cup of sorrow, the baptism was His baptism of death, and He meant that only by their partnership of suffering and death could they enter into the fullness of His glory.

This is what the Apostle Paul must have meant when he said in one of his epistles that there was no glory in preaching the gospel, for that was simply duty, but there was some glory in preaching the gospel "free of charge," and in meeting gladly the sacrifices and sufferings which made him a spectacle and a gazing stock to the world and a follower of his suffering Lord in the path of danger and death (1 Corinthians 9:15–18). The words of Matthew 20:25–28, and which we have quoted above as our text, sum up the whole discussion in the strongest and most forcible language and draw a picture with vivid lines of contrast between the spirit of human ambition and Christian self-sacrifice. "Greatness in the world," he says, "consists of lording it over others; greatness in the heavenly kingdom consists in serving others and sacrificing for Him."

Two words are here employed to describe Christian service: the one is the Greek word *diakonos*, which denotes ministry, or service, for others; the second is the word *doulos*, which means a slave. It is not merely service for others, but it is humiliating service. He says, "He that would be great, let him be your *diakonos*, but he that would be supremely great, the chief among you, let him be your *doulos*, your slave." This is the ministry of the Son of Man who came "not . . . to be served, but to serve, and to give his life as a ransom for many" (Matthew 20:28), and the treasured servant will approach most nearly to the steps of his patron and Lord.

There are ministries which God appoints for us which require us not only to serve our brethren, but even to suffer indignity, humiliation and the most trying provocation at their hands. There are men and women whose lives are spent enduring the weakness, selfishness, petty annoyances, overbearing unkindnesses, exactions and misunderstandings that come from the selfish lives with whom they are called to stand in constant forbearance and loving patient service. Oh, suffering children of God, do not think your lives wasted in such trying ministries; you are following in the footsteps of the Son of Man. You are not only a minister for Him, but a slave too for His sake, and the time is coming when your exaltation yonder will be in proportion to the depths of your abasement here. These are the ministries that are forging your eternal crowns, and some day, the tear drops and the blood drops will be transformed into diamonds and rubies of surpassing glory in the recompenses of the coming age.

Even human history is glorified by just such flashes of earthly heroism. The story is told far and wide of that young girl of 14 in the fearful Chicago fire who risked her life to keep open the door of a fire escape in that burning theater until her little body was blistered almost to a cinder, and yet she bravely stood there until she had saved 50 perishing men and women.

The courageous little nation that is now facing the horrors of a terrific war with the mightiest empire on the globe, the Japanese, glory in these memorials of patriotic sacrifice. In the late war with China, when the gate of Port Arthur could not be forced open, a common soldier in the army of Japan rushed up with a dynamite bomb in his hand and dashed it against the gates. In the awful explosion that followed, he himself was torn to a thousand fragments, but that barrier was also pressed asunder and the soldiers of his country marched through to victory, and this was his sufficient reward.

At another time one of the young officers learned that the harbor of Port Arthur was closed against the fleet of Japan by a boom that crossed its mouth and which it was impossible to break through. He went to the commanding officer and explained to him that he had invented a device by which he could destroy that boom, but that he was not at liberty to explain the secret, but only asked permission to carry it out. This was given him, and with a little company of marines, he stole up at night within 100 yards of the boom and then in a little shell slipped up alone with soft paddles until near enough to fasten a bomb to the great barrier and explode it. Again, in the explosion which followed, a human being was sacrificed and little pieces of his uniform and his body were picked up as they were scattered far and wide, but the harbor was opened and the navy of Japan stole in and captured the ships of China. A few months afterward the fragments of his mutilated body were buried in state in the presence of the Mikado of Japan. It is said that the father of this brave young soldier, his face shining with joy, was called to lead the funeral procession in the presence of his emperor, and for the first time in the history of Japan, a subject walked in front of the ruler in that procession of honor.

It was a deed of sacrifice that had raised a common soldier higher than all the rank that a throne could give.

And so the time is coming when the Lord Jesus shall call His humble servants and His self-sacrificing followers and before assembled worlds shall place the crowns upon their heads and gird Himself and go forth to serve them.

God help us, like Him, for the joy set before us to endure "the cross, scorning its shame" (Hebrews 12:2), and not miss the opportunities so swiftly passing away for winning unfading crowns of glory.

CHAPTER 14

THE MANIFESTATION OF THE KING

Say to the Daughter of Zion,
"See, your king comes to you,
gentle and riding on a donkey,
on a colt, the foal of a donkey."
(Matthew 21:5)

The time had now come when the Lord Jesus was to be publicly manifested as the Son of David and the King of Israel. Hitherto He had refused the demands of the multitude, who, after His Galilean miracles, had tried "to come and make him king by force" (John 6:15). But now as the end draws near, it is proper that He should literally fulfill the announcements of ancient prophecy, and for a brief moment, at least, appear as the heir to David's throne and the answer to all the Messianic hopes of Israel.

BLIND MEN

1. The Recognition of the King

It was strange that the first to recognize Him as Israel's King should be two blind beggars. That which the rulers of Israel, with all their wisdom, failed to comprehend, was discovered by poor old Bartimaeus and his blind companion. Calling Him by His Messianic name, they cried, as the procession pressed by, "Lord, Son of David, have mercy on us!" (Matthew 20:31b). When Jesus heard that name, He instantly ordered the procession to halt, and, calling them to Him, granted their petition like a king, bidding them receive their sight and follow Him in the way.

So still it is ever true, "you have hidden these things from the wise and learned, and revealed them to little children" (11:25). The wisdom of the world and even the culture of theological science have blinded men to the vision of God, and it is the lowly and often illiterate to whom the Holy

Spirit reveals "the secrets of the kingdom of heaven" (13:11) and the blessed hope of the coming once more of our glorious King.

How did these blind men know that Jesus was the Son of David? With their inner senses they felt after Him until they found Him. It is still so that the hungry heart finds the Savior. Reaching out in our darkness and sense of need, groping for One who we feel can meet and satisfy our need, we press our way toward the light even as the blind man who, while he cannot discern the objects before him, can see vaguely at least the glare of the light and press closer to it. Even so we can press toward God, and He will meet the seeking soul and reveal Himself in the vision of light and love even as He did to them.

Seeker for Christ, follow the light you have and He will give more as you follow on, and you, too, will hear Him say, "Receive your sight; your faith has healed you" (Luke 18:42).

THE TRIUMPHAL ENTRY

2. The Manifestation of the King

Ancient prophecy had foretold the coming of the King of meekness, truth and love, and his triumphal entry into Jerusalem was a striking fulfillment. Zechariah especially had literally described the scenes portrayed in this chapter: "Rejoice greatly, O Daughter of Zion!/ Shout, Daughter of Jerusalem!/ See, your king comes to you,/ righteous and having salvation,/ gentle and riding on a donkey,/ on a colt, the foal of a donkey" (Zechariah 9:9).

For the first time in His earthly ministry, our Lord permits Himself to be borne by the beast of burden, which had always been recognized as the bearer of kings. Riding upon a little colt never ridden before, draped with the garments of His disciples as they walked beside, and accompanied by the mighty multitude surging up from the city at this, the Passover time, when the population of Jerusalem was multiplied tenfold, he slowly descended from Bethany toward the city. At every step the enthusiasm of the crowd grew higher. Cutting down branches from the palm trees, they strewed them in the way, and even their garments they flung in homage at His feet, while their voices rose to a mighty shout as they cried in the language of an old prophetic psalm, "Hosanna to the Son of David! Blessed is he who comes in the name of the Lord!" (Matthew 21:9).

But His own demeanor was in strange contrast to all these scenes of tumultuous excitement. Truly, He came as the King of meekness, lowliness and love. This became still more apparent when the city suddenly burst upon their view, and the sight of it drew from Him an outburst of sorrow and compassion, and amid all that pageant of popular acclamation He gave way to bitter tears and lamentations over the certain doom which He saw impending upon the scenes that lay spread before Him in all their glorious beauty. But the procession swept on, and in a little while He entered the city and the temple.

His triumphal entry into Jerusalem was the foreshadowing of that glorious time when He shall come again as Israel's long expected Messiah and take His place upon the throne of David, never again to leave it.

It is also typical of His entrance upon the throne of the individual heart when we receive Him as our Lord and King. The little foal on whom no man had sat before, is the exquisite type of the heart that gives Him its exclusive affection. He comes to reign, not as tyrant, but as a King of gentleness and love in all the attractive attributes so finely set forth in the ancient picture that we are considering. He does not come to repress, but to satisfy. He does not dominate us as a despot, but He meets all the needs and longings of our being, and so blends with our nature and our will that we become His willing subjects and the very partners of His kingdom and His throne. Have we thus received Him and known Him as our King?

CLEANSING THE TEMPLE

3. The King of Zion and the Lord of the Temple

Immediately upon entering the city, He passed through the gates of the temple and repeated the miracle of its cleansing which had formed the first chapter of His early Judean ministry. The difference between this miracle and the former, is that then He called it His Father's house (John 2:16); now "My house" (Matthew 21:13). He was now taking the position of being Himself the Lord of the temple and the true theocratic Head of the kingdom. A little later the phrase was changed again. As He left that temple after His solemn warnings and judgments were pronounced against the false rulers and leaders of Israel, He declared "your house"—"Mine" no longer— "your house is left to you desolate. For I tell you, you will not see me again until you say, 'Blessed is he who comes in the name of the Lord' " (23:38– 39).

The cleansing of the temple was occasioned by the abuse which was made of its courts by the class of money brokers and cheap traders who took advantage of the people's desire for silver change in order to pay the half shekel offering which was required of everyone entering the temple. Out of this there grew up a regular business and a large class of men who, at exorbitant rates of usury, supplied the silver exchange to the worshipers as they crowded into the courts without having provided themselves with the requisite coin.

Another class of tradesmen in like manner filled up another part of the court with their filthy stalls for the supply of doves and other animals for the sin offerings and burnt offerings of the daily sacrifices. These also were sold at exorbitant prices for the convenience of the worshipers, but really for the gain of the dealers.

As our Lord looked upon this unseemly spectacle in the house of God, His indignation was aroused. Taking a whip of small cords, He drove them out, overturning the tables, ordering the dove cotes immediately removed, and driving them before Him under such a spell of fear that they forgot everything but the means of escape from His holy wrath (21:12). This act was a final assumption on His part of the highest authority, not only in, but even above the temple and its worship.

The same high place He still claims in the Church of God and the individual heart. The abuses of the temple courts of old have, alas, been more than paralleled in the history of Christendom. It was the sale of indulgences, in the time of Luther, for the enrichment of the ecclesiastical parties that brought about the Reformation.

The kind of sin here described is not secular business in its own place, but the doing of things in the name of religion which are prompted by mercenary motives. The preaching of the gospel for the sake of gain; wrong financial methods in supporting the church; the desecrating of the house of God by social and secular entertainments; methods of raising money which appeal to the selfishness and frivolity of man; the use of Christianity in any way as a cloak of covetousness, as an advertisement of business, as a means of social preferment or secular gain—these are things which are so common on every side of us that the hearts of many of God's children have been filled with humiliation and sorrow, and moved to earnest prayer for the coming of the King once more to cleanse His temple and purge from His Church these shameful profanations.

The second cleansing of the temple would seem to suggest that before the Lord's coming, there is to be a profound work of sanctification among the people of God answering to the first cleansing of which we read so fully in the early chapters of the Acts of the Apostles.

Still more truly does it apply to the individual experience of the Christian. Here, too, there is a second cleansing which the Lord comes to bring when He Himself enters the consecrated heart, not only saving, but sanctifying and separating us unto Himself in a deeper sense than we can possibly know, even in the early joy of conversion. Have we received this second cleansing?

HOSANNAS OF THE CHILDREN

4. The Children's King

This was not an ordinary crowd where the children always love to be in the front, but it was a genuine outburst of heaven-inspired love and loyalty that made them cry, "Hosanna in the highest" (21:9). For the Lord Jesus Himself bore testimony of the genuineness of their praise and indeed gave it the highest place over all others as He quoted the ancient Scripture, "From the lips of children and infants/ you have ordained praise" (21:16). Others might join in the acclamations because of the contagious influence of an excited multitude, but theirs was "ordained praise." As usual, the Pharisees were ready to scorn their juvenile enthusiasm, but the Lord Jesus was also ready to vindicate them as He had once before.

Let us never forget that Jesus is the children's King. By and by, when we welcome Him to His heavenly throne, we shall find that a vast proportion of that ransomed crowd will consist of little children. Let us train our little ones to know Him and crown Him as their King. The word used here in their childish praise is the Hebrew word *hosannah*. It is not quite the same as *hallelujah*, the usual expression for worship and praise. Literally, it means "Lord save us." Our hallelujahs must begin in hosannas. Even the children, too, must learn that they are sinful children, and that they also require His cleansing blood, and only as they accept it and honor it will their hosannas become hallelujahs, and the Lord pronounce their homage "ordained praise."

MIRACLES OF HEALING

5. The Blessing of the King

Immediately after Christ's triumphal entry into Jerusalem and His cleansing of the temple, we read these significant words, "The blind and the lame came to him at the temple, and he healed them" (21:14). Purification always leads on to power. The cleansing of the temple was followed by the healing of the sick and the revelation of the great and good Physician. So, still, it will be found in our personal experience. This was not a momentary gleam of divine beneficence over a dark and suffering world, but "Jesus Christ is the same yesterday and today and forever" (Hebrews 13:8).

> And warm, sweet, tender, even yet
> A present help is He;
> And love has still its Olivet,
> And faith its Galilee.
> The healing of His seamless robe
> Is by our beds of pain,
> We touch Him 'mid life's pain and strife,
> And we are whole again.

But, of course, all this awaits its perfect fulfillment in this happier time when the King shall come to His own again, "and the ransomed of the LORD will return./ They will enter Zion with singing;/ everlasting joy will crown their heads./ Gladness and joy will overtake them,/ and sorrow and sighing will flee away" (Isaiah 35:10).

Then, when this earth is purged of all iniquity, will it be also true that the inhabitant shall no more say, " 'I am ill';/ and the sins of those who dwell there will be forgiven" (33:24).

> Come, Lord, and take away
> The sin, the wrong, the pain,
> And make this blighted world of ours
> Thine own fair world again.

THE FRUITLESS FIG TREE

6. The Curse of the King

But the King has not only blessing, but also judgment recorded in His mighty hand. The only miracle of judgment recorded in all the life of Jesus Christ immediately followed these incidents. It was the cursing of the barren fig tree, to which He came seeking fruit and from which He was encouraged to expect it by the luxuriant leaves that covered its branches; but lo! there was "nothing on it except leaves" (Matthew 21:19), and He pronounced upon it the withering words that left it leafless and dead.

This was, of course, a type of the fruitless nation that He had already referred to under the parable of the barren fig tree (Luke 13:6–9), and it forecasts the solemn judgment that awaits every professed follower of Christ who shall meet Him at last with empty hands and fruitless life. But there is a beneficent aspect, even in the curse of the King. It tells us of One that has power to consume and destroy the things which we are unable to cast out of our lives. There are fig trees of sinful habit and physical disease which our human strength cannot throw off alone. Oh, how glad we are sometimes to have a God who is "a consuming fire" (Hebrews 12:29) and from whose presence Satan, sin and sickness flee away! He tells us we may enter into His destructive power against these things and hand over to His flaming sword adversaries and obstacles too great for us to overcome. "I am so glad," said a little child once, "that I have a God that can shake the world." Our Christ is not all soft and easy benevolence. Back of His gentleness is an arm of might and a holiness as inexorable as the lightnings of the sky. Oh sinner, whatever else you dare, beware of "the wrath of the Lamb" (Revelation 6:16)!

THE FAITH OF GOD

7. The Scepter of the Kingdom

In the closing verses of our lesson, the Lord reveals the secret of His own power and tells the disciples how they may share it also. The secret of it is faith. "Jesus replied, 'I tell you the truth, if you have faith and do not doubt, not only can you do what was done to the fig tree, but also you can say to this mountain, "Go, throw yourself into the sea," and it will be done. If you believe, you will receive whatever you ask for in prayer' " (Matthew 21:21–22).

And so He passes over to us His very scepter, and tells us that we may exercise the same omnipotence of faith through which He wrought His mighty works. It was by faith that He overcame and became for us "the author and perfecter of our faith" (Hebrews 12:2). But we, too, may exercise the same faith, too. Some time in that coming kingdom we shall be like Him and exercise a power over the universe of God at which, could we fully realize it now, we would be amazed and appalled. But He is training us now in the use of this mystic scepter, and teaching us the lessons of that faith of which He once said, "With God all things are possible" (Matthew 19:26); "Everything is possible for him who believes" (Mark 9:23).

We have but touched its borderland, beloved. There are great continents of faith and power and prayer for us yet to explore. "Lord, teach us to pray" (Luke 11:1), help our unbelief (Mark 9:24) and give us "the faith of God" (Romans 3:3, KJV).

CHAPTER 15

THE KING IN CONFLICT WITH HIS ENEMIES

The Spirit of the LORD will rest on him—
the Spirit of wisdom and of understanding,
the Spirit of counsel and of power,
the Spirit of knowledge and of the fear of the LORD—
and he will delight in the fear of the LORD.

He will not judge by what he sees with his eyes,
or decide by what he hears with his ears;
but with righteousness he will judge the needy,
with justice he will give decisions for the poor of the earth.
He will strike the earth with the rod of his mouth;
with the breath of his lips he will slay the wicked.
(Isaiah 11:2–4)

T his prophetic picture of the Messiah finds a striking and marvelous illustration in the series of incidents that will form the subject of this chapter, revealing the Lord Jesus as the One "greater than Solomon" (Matthew 12:42) and as the "Wonderful Counselor," as well as the "Mighty God" (Isaiah 9:6).

Hitherto we have seen the triumphs of the Lord Jesus in His miracles of power. We are now to see a series of miracles of wisdom not less wonderful than His victories of might.

We have already noticed the account of His triumphal entry into Jerusalem and His public recognition as the Son of David, the King of Israel and the Lord of the temple. This occurred on the day corresponding to our Sunday, which was the day immediately following the Jewish Sabbath. On the following Monday He again visited Jerusalem from Bethany and spent the day in teaching and preaching in the temple. The incidents of the present chapter occurred on the next day, which would correspond to our

Tuesday. Returning to the city from Bethany early in the morning of that day, He had resumed His teaching and preaching in the presence of the multitude. Then His enemies began a battle royal against Him with the evident purpose of ensnaring Him in some hasty word and affording a basis for accusing Him before the Roman governor. Their plans were adroitly laid, and the story of their attack and defeat is one of the most thrilling dramas of all literature, sacred or profane.

THE PHARISEES

1. Questioning His Authority

The conflict begins by the Sanhedrin sending an official deputation to Him to demand His authority for the audacious things that He was daring to do and say (Matthew 21:23). The Lord tactfully answered them by propounding another question to them and promising, as soon as they answered it, that He would tell them by what authority He was acting. "John's baptism—where did it come from? Was it from heaven, or from men?" (21:25). He had a perfect right to ask this question because as the great national Council they had sent three years before to John a deputation to ask him, "Who are you? Give us an answer to take back to those who sent us. What do you say about yourself?" (John 1:22). It was only natural and right that the people should know the result of their inquiry.

Immediately the deputation found themselves on the horns of a dilemma. If they answered "from heaven," very naturally Christ would ask, "Then why didn't you believe him?" (Matthew 21:25). But if they went so far as to deny John's prophetic character, they would array the multitude against themselves, for all counted John a prophet. They were, therefore, driven to say, "We don't know," and of course the Lord replied, "Neither will I tell you by what authority I am doing these things" (21:27).

There are times when we, like the Master, are justified in avoiding or evading the foolish questions of the enemies of the truth. "Do not answer a fool according to his folly,/ or you will be like him yourself" (Proverbs 26:4). Servants of Christ should exercise the profound wisdom of their Master and claim it from Him for similar emergencies that will ever meet us in our life and work. "Let your conversation be always full of grace, seasoned with salt, so that you may know how to answer everyone" (Colossians 4:6).

The Lord followed the repulse of the Pharisees with three parables addressed immediately to the multitude, but really directed in part against them. The first was the parable of the Two Sons (Matthew 21:28–32). In this parable He contrasted the false professions of the Pharisees as represented by the second son with the conduct of the tax collectors and the prostitutes as represented by the first, who said: " 'I will not,' . . . but later he changed his mind and went" (21:29), and He applied the parable to the incident of the hour by adding, "I tell you the truth, the tax collectors and the prostitutes are entering the kingdom of God ahead of you. For John came to you to show you the way of righteousness, and you did not believe him, but the tax collectors and the prostitutes did. And even after you saw this, you did not repent and believe him" (21:31c–32).

Then He followed with a second parable still more severe and pointed, the Wicked Tenants (21:33–44). In this He represented the faithfulness of the Jewish nation to their great trust, their rejection of the messengers God had sent through successive dispensations until at last He sent to them His own Son, only to be rejected and murdered by their wicked hands. Then comes the pointed question: "What will he do to those tenants?" (21:40) and the multitude is ready with the answer: "He will bring those wretches to a wretched end . . . and he will rent the vineyard to other tenants, who will give him his share of the crop at harvest time" (21:41). The Lord takes up the words of the multitude and echoes them back: "Therefore I tell you that the kingdom of God will be taken away from you and given to a people who will produce its fruit. He who falls on this stone will be broken to pieces, but he on whom it falls will be crushed" (21:43–44).

There could be no doubt about the application of this message to the scowling rulers before Him. "When the chief priests and the Pharisees heard Jesus' parables, they knew he was talking about them. They looked for a way to arrest him, but they were afraid of the crowd because the people held that he was a prophet" (21:45–46).

And so the first battle of the conflict ended and His enemies shrank away defeated and confounded.

The Lord took advantage of the lull to continue His teachings in the presence of the multitude. He proceeded to deliver the third parable, the Marriage of the King's Son, which was addressed rather to the people than to the Pharisees, and which was intended to guard His teachings from possible abuse in the direction of free grace and unconditional salvation for the worst sinners (22:1–14). The parable begins, as in the corresponding passage in Luke, with the story of the great feast representing the gospel, and the first invited guests indifferently excusing themselves from it; upon which the master sends out his servants into the highways to gather in the outcasts to the banquet. All this teaches the same lesson of the mercy of Christ for sinners of every class, and, especially, that offer of overflowing mercy to the neglected ones, which is to mark the close of the present dispensation and immediately precede the coming of the Lord. That special message of grace to the outcast at home and abroad is the feature of the Christian work of today.

But now He adds another touch of this parable designed to correct the possible abuse of the gospel of free grace and to show that while all classes of sinners are welcome to His mercy, that mercy must not be abused as a cloak for sin, but they must accept His holiness as freely as His forgiveness. The incident of the man that came in "not wearing wedding clothes" (22:11) has a touch of emphasis added to it by the peculiar Greek word used for the negative here (22:11–12). There are two Greek words for "not" or "no," the one having reference to the outward fact, the other having reference to the inward feeling of the person respecting this fact. It is the latter that is used here, and it means not merely that he was without a wedding garment, but that he was willfully without it. These garments were provided by the host and loaned for the occasion to the guests, who passed into a dressing room near the vestibule and were robed for the feast. It is a beautiful picture of the provision Christ has made for the sanctification as well as salvation of sinners. Let us not think that because His mercy is so free we can accept it and still appear before Him in the robes of our self-righteousness. We must accept His grace in its fullness. Sanctification is not an option, but an obligation.

Dear friend, have you received the wedding garment as well as the invitation to the banquet? It was because of this willful neglect that the man was "speechless" when the master confronted him with the question, all the more terrible because it was so kindly expressed, "Friend . . . how did you get in here without wedding clothes?" (22:12). How solemn the conclusion of the scene, " 'Tie him hand and foot, and throw him outside, into the darkness, where there will be weeping and gnashing of teeth.' For many are invited, but few are chosen" (22:13–14). It will give added force and light to the concluding verse to read it: "For many are called but few are choice." God grant that we may be among the choice ones.

THE HERODIANS

2. The Tribute Money

But now the second stage of the conflict comes. The Pharisees have held a lobby and have been reinforced by a new company of auxiliaries. These are called Herodians, a political party, who, in opposition to the popular Jewish element, were adherents of the royal dynasty and Roman power and usually bitter enemies of the Pharisees. But now they united in a common hatred to the Lord and joined forces to overthrow Him. They brought to Him a subtle political question, "Is it right to pay taxes to Caesar or not?" (22:17). It placed Him in a very difficult and embarrassing position. If He had said, "No," He would at once have been open to arrest as a ringleader of sedition against the authorities and would have speedily been added to the number of those whose blood, we are told in the Gospels, about this time, Pilate "had mixed with their sacrifices" (Luke 13:1). Had He taken the other ground as a rabbi, that it was lawful to pay tribute to Caesar, He would have offended the popular sentiment of the nation, who hated the Romans and their taxes, who looked upon it as almost disloyal to Jehovah to recognize any king but God, and who had a secret hope that Jesus Christ was about to deliver them from the Roman yoke and reestablish the old theocratic kingdom.

The question was forged in the very pit of hell, it was deep as the serpent's guile, but it was not too deep for His instinctive and unerring wisdom. Fathoming instantly their purpose, He simply called for a coin, and, holding it up, He asked whose image or superscription it bore. They, of course, answered "Caesar's" (22:21). The Jewish law did not permit them to put any graven image on any coin, or indeed, on anything, and yet they accepted these coins as money and constantly received and paid them in secular business. They were already committed to this by their daily life, and habitually acknowledged the Roman authority by accepting the Roman currency. It was the simplest and most natural thing in the world to add next: "Give to Caesar what is Caesar's, and to God what is God's" (22:21).

This simple and profound answer, which has settled for 20 centuries the connection between secular and sacred duty and rendered it possible for us to be loyal citizens and yet holy saints, was so obvious and so wise that they really had nothing to say, and the evangelist adds with quiet force: "When they heard this, they were amazed. So they left him and went away" (22:22). They were struck so quietly and softly that they scarcely knew what had hit them, and yet they were no less struck and paralyzed and driven from the field feeling themselves, as everybody else felt, that they were again baffled and utterly defeated.

THE SADDUCEES

3. Questions about the Resurrection

They soon returned, however, with a third onslaught. This time they had a new auxiliary, namely, a company of Sadducees. These also were a Jewish sect of limited number but great influence. They were the educated and skeptical element, the "higher critics" of the day. They disbelieved in the supernatural and especially in the resurrection; they were materialists and would have been found today among the agnostics. They also, it is held by some, discredited a large portion of the Old Testament Scriptures. They had their question ready for the Master and it seemed also unanswerable.

It was a rather coarse story about a woman who had been married in succession to seven different brothers as they had successively died and she had married the next according to the Levitical law. At last she herself died, and now the absorbing question arises in their earnest and inquiring minds: "What are they all to do in the resurrection? What a perplexing time they will have, and which of them is to be her true husband then?"

It was a taxing question, and for a moment there must have been many in the crowd that caught the ludicrousness of the idea. Nothing but infinite wisdom could have turned aside the force of the blow. But again the Lord was equal to it. The "one greater than Solomon" (12:42) was there. With quiet dignity He turns upon them with their own words: "You are in error because you do not know the Scriptures or the power of God" (22:29). And then He proceeds to explain the true doctrine of the resurrection and to show them that it is not a resumption of the coarser material forms of our earthly life, but a higher existence in which we shall have passed beyond the laws of reproduction and shall dwell in a loftier fellowship with one another, even as the angels now, and all mere human relations shall pass into divine relationships.

Then He follows this by a striking quotation from the Old Testament Scriptures, and especially from that portion which they believe without question, the Pentateuch, where God said, "I am the God of Abraham, the God of Isaac, and the God of Jacob" (22:32). Then the Lord added, "He is not the God of the dead but of the living" (22:32). They had passed out of human sight and human touch, but not from the fellowship of God. They were with Him and He spoke of them as living men, although they had long since been moldering in their graves. The force of this argument was un-answerable and the multitude instantly caught it. "When the crowds heard this, they were astonished at his teaching. Hearing that Jesus had silenced the Sadducees, the Pharisees got together" (22:33–34). The Greek word here is "muzzled." He had muzzled the Sadducees; it was a case of lockjaw, and soon after, of paralysis too.

THE LAWYER

4. The Lawyer's Question

They next put forth one of their own number, a doctor of the law, with a subtle question respecting the interpretation of the law of Moses, "Teacher, which is the greatest commandment in the Law?" (22:36). Now, we are told that in the Rabbinical writings there were no less then 613 commandments recognized. Of these, 248 were affirmative statutes, corresponding to the number of members in the human body, and 365 were negative, cor-responding to the number of days in the year. Some of these were called "light" and others "heavy," somewhat like the distinction that the Roman Catholics make between "moral" and "venial" sins.

This Pharisee wanted to know which were the lighter and which were the heavier commandments. By a great flash of celestial light, the Lord il-luminates the subject in a single sentence and tells him that the one supreme commandment of the law is not the question of tithes or fringes, but simply love to God, and the second is but another form of it, namely, love to man. So truly there is but one great principle in the divine law, and that is love. Like the law of gravitation, which has simplified all men's former notions of the universe and swings the planets in their orbits and the constellations in their courses and holds in cohesion all the elements of matter without an effort, so love to God keeps us right with Him and one another without the bondage of a thousand petty exactions and constraints.

It was so simple, so beautiful, so conclusive that the young lawyer surrendered, and, as another Gospel tells us, acknowledged that this was "more important than all burnt offerings and sacrifices" (Mark 12:33).

THE SON OF DAVID

5. The Lord's Own Question

Christ now turns upon His baffled foes and presses upon them the question before the multitude:

> "What do you think about the Christ? Whose son is he?"
> "The son of David," they replied.
> He said to them, "How is it then that David, speaking by the Spirit, calls him 'Lord'? For he says,
> " 'The Lord said to my Lord:
> ' "Sit at my right hand
> until I put your enemies under your feet." '
> "If then David calls him 'Lord,' how can he be his son?"
> (Matthew 22:42–45)

This question, which touched the very heart of Christ's own claim as at once the Son of God and the Son of David, overwhelmed them; they could not answer it without acknowledging all His claims, and yet their silence was even a more effectual answer. So complete was their humiliation that it is added by the evangelist: "No one could say a word in reply, and from that day on no one dared to ask him any more questions" (22:46). As we have said above, it was not only a case of lockjaw, but of complete paralysis.

THE WOMAN TAKEN IN ADULTERY

There is another incident not mentioned in the Gospel of Matthew which seems to belong in this series and at this point. It is the story of the woman taken in adultery (John 7:53–8:11), and which the best authorities tell us really belongs to a later portion of John's Gospel, during this last week of the Master's life. There is no place in which it could be so fittingly introduced as here, forming perhaps a climax to this series of assaults and victories.

They dragged her into the presence of the Lord not so much to deal with her as to get some advantage over Him and force Him to some public statement which would either embarrass Him with the people or put Him in opposition to the law. The law required that such as she should be stoned, but His teaching was so mild and merciful that perhaps He would ignore the law and set her free. They wanted a decision. This is not the place to enter into an exposition of that marvelous story in detail, but we know how, without meeting their demand, He again turned the tables on them by asking that the man that was without guilt among them for the same kind of sin should cast the first stone at her; and the extraordinary fact is added that everyone, convicted by his own conscience, sneaked away in silence and left the Master and the woman alone. We may be pretty sure they did not show themselves again for a while for the confession which they had tacitly made would have ruined their reputations and perhaps driven them out of the synagogue. Then the Master, without condoning the woman's sin, forgave her and added the solemn words that she never could forget: "Go and sin no more" (8:11, KJV).

WOES UPON THE PHARISEES

6. The King Judging His Convicted Enemies

Now follows a little section on the day of judgment. The Lord Jesus turns upon His defeated foes and pronounces upon them the fearful words summed up in this entire chapter. Just as there had been eight beatitudes, so we have here eight woes.

The first charges them with being false leaders, shutting up the doors of the kingdom of heaven and neither entering themselves nor allowing the helpless sheep whom they are guiding to enter in (Matthew 23:13).

The second charges them with cloaking their own unrighteousness with mere religious forms and professions, devouring widows' houses and for a pretense making long prayers (23:14, margin).

The third accuses them of proselytizing zeal which is not zeal for God but simply human ambition seeking followers and making them worse than themselves (23:15).

The fourth refers to their duplicity and deceitfulness in the interpretation of the Scriptures on Jesuitical principles, splitting hairs and making fine distinctions, saying, "If anyone swears by the temple, it means nothing; but if anyone swears by the gold of the temple, he is bound by his oath" (23:16).

The fifth refers to their ceremonialism and tells them that their religion consists in mere questions of tithes and ceremonies while they have omitted "the more important matters of the law—justice, mercy and faithfulness" (23:23).

The sixth exposes them as mere formalists who seek to make clean the outside of the cup and the platter while the insides of their hearts "are full of greed and self-indulgence" (23:25).

The seventh draws the fearful picture of "whitewashed tombs, which look beautiful on the outside but on the inside are full of dead men's bones and everything unclean" (23:27).

And the last reminds them that while with sentimental hypocrisy they "build tombs for the prophets and decorate the graves of the righteous" (23:29) and say, "If we had lived in the days of our forefathers, we would not have taken part with them in shedding the blood of the prophets" (23:30), at the same time they are doing the very works of their fathers and murdering the messengers of God even as they. Therefore He adds,

> Therefore I am sending you prophets and wise men and teachers. Some of them you will kill and crucify; others you will flog in your synagogues and pursue from town to town. And so upon you will come all the righteous blood that has been shed on earth, from the blood of righteous Abel to the blood of Zechariah son of Berekiah, whom you murdered between the temple and the altar. (23:34–35)

Terrible indeed must have been the holy indignation and the burning force with which the holy lips of Jesus poured forth these withering words upon these self-convicted and guilty men, rising at last to the very climax of invective indignation: "You snakes! You brood of vipers! How will you escape being condemned to hell?" (23:33).

And that was Jesus. Oh, do not dream in your carelessness and sin that that gentle and forgiving One was incapable of the most awful severity and the most consuming judgment. Above all other wrath the sinner may well fear "the wrath of the Lamb" (Revelation 6:16).

But the torrent has spent its force, the heart of Jesus cannot long brook even this merited outburst of judgment and condemnation. Suddenly pausing in the midst of His fiery rebukes it would seem as if a gush of tears must have poured from His eyes and with broken voice and unearthly tenderness He cries again: "O Jerusalem, Jerusalem, you who kill the prophets and stone those sent to you, how often I have longed to gather your children together, as a hen gathers her chicks under her wings, but you were not willing" (23:37).

And that was Jesus, too. Blessed be His name, that is the Jesus that we are still permitted to approach. Oh, do not wait until He shall have put on the robes of judgment and risen up to pronounce the sinner's doom. Still He is speaking to us with the same tenderness and reminding us in the same terms how often He has sought us and how often we have rejected Him.

Is there anyone reading these lines to whom He is speaking now? Hasten beneath the shelter of His wing from the coming storm, and do not wait until He shall have nothing left for you but His compassion and His tears.

It is said that once a distinguished judge after pronouncing sentence upon a man before him and sending him forth to end his days in a penal colony, put off his judge's cap and looking the man in the face said, "Why have you forced me to do this? You were the friend of my childhood; I have loved you as I have loved few men; why have you made it necessary that I should speak these awful words that doom you to a misery worse than death?" And he could only weep, and yet his tears did not avail to avert that stroke of judgment.

And so, even Jesus, in these tender, passionate words, did not take back the sentence that He had passed. In condemning them His heart was breaking with tenderness and sorrow, but none the less did He pause and close this solemn chapter by adding, "Look, your house [Mine no longer, you can have it now] is left to you desolate. For I tell you, you will not see me again until you say, 'Blessed is he who comes in the name of the Lord' " (23:38–30).

CHAPTER 16

THE COMING OF THE KING

"Therefore keep watch, because you do not know the day or the hour." (Matthew 25:13)

Our Lord had accepted for the time the homage of the multitude and the titles and honors of the Son of David and the throne of the Messiah! If the nation had only heartily and truly received Him, we can scarcely dream of the results that might have followed. An eloquent writer has ventured to express something of such a dream, picturing the Lord Jesus completing His sacrifice, not through wicked enemies, but by His Father offering Him up even as Abraham offered Isaac on Mount Moriah, followed by His glorious resurrection and His sitting down upon David's throne and fulfilling for Israel and the world the vision of ancient prophecy without the dark and dreadful centuries of Israel's rejection and punishment.

But this was not to be. Indeed, it could not be with all the other prophecies yet to be fulfilled. And so "He came to that which was his own, but his own did not receive him" (John 1:11). Israel as a nation rejected Him, and ages had to pass before He could come to them again, as their King and fulfill to them the vision of the promised glory.

But He will surely come; and the next portion of Matthew's gospel unfolds to us, in His own prophetic words, the panorama of events that will lead up to the great appearing.

The discourses related in the 24th and 25th chapters of Matthew were delivered by our Lord on Tuesday afternoon, immediately after His great conflict with the rulers described in our last chapter, and on His way from the temple to His temporary home in Bethany. The first part of the address was no doubt uttered as they departed from the temple, probably through the Golden Gate, and walked down into the valley of Kedron. The last portion was probably concluded as He sat on the slopes of Olivet, looking down once more over the city at His feet. The interpretation of the discourse will be rendered more clear if we bear in mind the questions of the disciples to which it was intended to be an answer.

QUESTIONS OF THE DISCIPLES

They pointed out to Him the splendid stones and buildings of the temple and He told them, "Not one stone here will be left on another; every one will be thrown down" (Matthew 24:2). Immediately they ask Him three questions, "Tell us . . . when will this happen, and what will be the sign of your coming and of the end of the age?" (24:3).

The first part of His discourse would therefore naturally be a reply to their first question, "When will this happen?" namely, the destruction of Jerusalem. The later portion of His discourse would naturally refer to their other two questions, "What will be the sign of your coming and of the end of the age (world, KJV)?" It should be borne in mind that the term "world" here employed is not the usual Greek word for the material world. That would be *kosmos*; it is the word *aion*, which means "the age," the order of events, and the plan of providence. The correct translation, therefore, is "the end of the age," for the end of the age will not necessarily bring the end of the world.

We shall group the Lord's teachings concerning His coming under a number of clearly defined heads which are brought out with great distinction in His discourses.

IN RELATION TO ISRAEL

1. The Relation of His Coming to Israel and the Destruction of Jerusalem

This was the first thing that entered their minds and His, and it is also the prominent idea present to the narrator of the Gospel of Matthew, which was specially the gospel for Israel, and brings to the front, in all the Master's teachings, the special references of His addresses to the "chosen people" (Deuteronomy 7:6). From verse 4 to verse 28, with the single exception of verse 14, the entire passage in Matthew 24 seems to apply to Israel and the judgments and sufferings that were to come upon them because of their rejection of the Messiah. There would appear, however, to be two sections in the passage, the one referring to the earlier tribulations of Jerusalem under the Romans, and the other to her later trials at the end of the age. To the Master's view, it seemed like one long perspective for Israel, beginning and ending with a fearful tragedy. Between these two sections, there is thrown in a brief parenthesis in verse 14, which describes the Christian age and the gospel among the Gentiles. For Israel, however, the prospect is dark and lurid, reaching its climax in spiritual delusion and national calamity, without a precedent or parallel.

This is in exact accordance with the predictions of Daniel and Zechariah.

Referring to the first destruction of Jerusalem, Daniel had said: "The people of the ruler who will come will destroy the city and the sanctuary. The end will come like a flood: War will continue until the end, and desolations have been decreed" (Daniel 9:26). And referring to the later afflictions of Jerusalem at the end of the age Daniel had said: "There will be a time of distress such as has not happened from the beginning of nations until then" (12:1).

Zechariah also had even more explicitly described these calamities, especially in the later days of Israel.

"In the whole land," declares the LORD,
   "two-thirds will be struck down and perish;
   yet one-third will be left in it. . . ."

A day of the LORD is coming when your plunder will be divided among you.
   I will gather all the nations to Jerusalem to fight against it; the city will be captured, the houses ransacked, and the women raped. Half of the city will go into exile, but the rest of the people will not be taken from the city." (Zechariah 13:8, 14:1–2)

Our Lord's predictions are in exact accordance with these terrible forewarnings. No doubt much of this was fulfilled when the Romans captured the city under Titus and Vespasian, but much of it yet must be in store.

THE CHRISTIAN AGE

2. His Coming with Reference to the Christian Age

This is condensed into a single verse: "And this gospel of the kingdom will be preached in the whole world as a testimony to all nations, and then the end will come" (Matthew 24:14). This is all that the Master says about the Gentile parentheses which we call the Christian age and which has now been running its course for 19 centuries. A single phrase of concentrated light and truth covers all this long period. Let us not think, in our self-conceit, that we Gentiles monopolize the whole prophetic word. Writing to the Gentiles, the Apostle Paul said: "I do not want you to be ignorant of this mystery, brothers, so that you may not be conceited: Israel has experienced a hardening in part until the full number of the Gentiles has come in" (Romans 11:25).

That is to say, we Gentiles have received the gospel for a time because Israel refused it, but after our time of opportunity is over, Israel's will return. This 14th verse describes the Gentile age during which the gospel of the kingdom (and there is but one gospel) is to be "preached in the whole world as a testimony to all nations" (Matthew 24:14). When this shall have been done to the full extent, our Lord assures us "the end will come" (24:14).

The evangelization of the world and its universal accomplishment are the most distinct landmarks of the Lord's coming. Our Lord's prediction here is in exact accord with the words of the Apostle Peter and the prophets [summarized by James]: "God at first showed his concern by taking from the Gentiles a people for himself. . . . 'After this I will return/ and rebuild David's fallen tent' " (Acts 15:14, 16). This is the age in which we are living. This is the time of grace for the Gentiles. Oh, let none of us allow "the time of God's coming to you" (Luke 19:44) to pass by neglected; and let us not fail as the disciples of Christ to meet our high and holy trust to send the gospel as a witness to all nations that we may hasten the coming of our Lord.

THE TRIBULATION

3. The Great Tribulation

Coinciding with Israel's latest trials is to come that time of trouble known in prophecy as the "The Great Tribulation." Speaking of it our Lord said: "For then there will be great distress, unequaled from the beginning of the world until now—and never to be equaled again. If those days had not been cut short, no one would survive, but for the sake of the elect those days will be shortened" (Matthew 24:21–22).

This time of trouble will be brought about by a variety of conditions. One of them will be God's judgment upon this sinful world, another the outbreak of Satanic power and malignity, and still another, the power of Antichrist and his assaults upon Israel and upon all divine institutions that shall remain in the world; and yet another element will be the absence of most of God's people, for the Church will have been withdrawn at the beginning of the tribulation and its watching and holy members caught up to meet the Lord in the air. A world without the godly, a world controlled by Antichrist, a world under the personal government of Satan, and a world beneath the outpourings of God's vials of wrath—surely, that is a picture dark enough to make us watch and pray that we "may be able to escape all that is about to happen" (Luke 21:36). It is the promise of Christ to the faithful ones: "I will also keep you from the hour of trial that is going to come upon the whole world to test those who live on the earth" (Revelation 3:10).

HIS APPEARING

4. The Glorious Appearing of the Lord

"Immediately after the distess of those days 'the sun will be darkened,/ and the moon will not give its light;/ the stars will fall from the sky,/ and the heavenly bodies will be shaken.' At that time the sign of the Son of Man will appear in the sky, and all the nations of the earth will mourn. They will see the Son of Man coming on the clouds of the sky, with power and great glory" (Matthew 24:29–30).

This is the great *epiphany*, the public appearance of the Lord Jesus as distinguished from His *parousia*, which refers to His previous and secret coming for His own. Now, however, after the tribulation He is to come in the blaze of His glory openly and visibly before the eyes of all the world, and as they see Him "all the nations of the earth will mourn" (24:30). It shall be a day of terror to this godless world and destruction and judgment to the wicked nations that shall be found in opposition to His throne.

We should notice the pronoun "they" instead of "you." The Lord does not tell them that they are to see Him come; His disciples will be with Him when He comes. The world shall see Him, but we, His followers, will have no business there in that day of terror and dismay. God help us to be found ready and waiting so that we shall escape the tribulation and the day of wrath and be with Him above the storm.

> I see that last and bloody sunset,
> I see the dread Avenger's form;
> I hear the Armageddon onset,
> But I shall be above the storm.

CAUGHT UP

5. The Rapture of the Saints

This forms a separate picture (verses 40 and 41). This passage refers to the *parousia* of the Son of Man before His *epiphany*, His coming for His own. "As it was in the days of Noah, so it will be at the coming of the Son of Man" (24:37). Of this He is speaking when He says: "Two men will be in the field; one will be taken and the other left. Two women will be grinding with a hand mill; one will be taken and the other left (24:40–41).

It is a little uncertain whether the passage in verse 31 also refers to this, "And he will send his angels with a loud trumpet call, and they will gather his elect from the four winds, from one end of the heavens to the other." This may refer to the final gathering of the tribulation saints, still left on earth after the tribulation of His public appearing. There is no doubt, however, that the passage, verses 40 and 41, must refer to the rapture of His saints as one by one they shall be caught up to meet Him in the air and the unready ones left behind. Dear friend, are you ready for that *parousia* and will you be found in "that happy company"?

CHRIST BEFORE THE MILLENNIUM

6. The Parable of the Fig Tree

The Lord introduces, in the picture of His coming, the remarkable natural similitude which He calls "a parable of the fig tree" (24:32, KJV). The peculiarity of the fig tree is that the fruit appears before the leaves, and the application of this to the Lord's coming is that the Lord Jesus will appear before the Millennium. It is not first the luxuriant foliage on the tree and then the fruit as a climax, but it is first the fruit and then the foliage. Or, to drop the figure, it is not first our culture and social, scientific and religious progress, and then Christ coming to a world all ready to receive Him. On the contrary, it is first Christ Himself, and then, as the result of His coming, the revolution of modern society and the righting of all the world's ancient wrongs. The coming of Jesus Christ is not an evolution, but a revolution.

AS THE DAYS OF NOAH

7. The Condition of the World at the Time of His Coming

This is still further confirmed by the picture He gives us of the state of human society at His advent. Our postmillennial friends are fond of telling us of the gradual progress of Christian influences and the improvement of the world and that, after a little while, things will be about right and we can expect the Lord to come down to congratulate us on the good work we have been able to do without Him.

The picture Jesus gives us is entirely different: "As it was in the days of Noah, so it will be at the coming of the Son of Man" (24:37). We know that the days of Noah were marked by wickedness and crime, and it would seem as if the two crimes most rampant in Noah's time, namely violence and lust, are coming to the front again in our own day in the increasing prevalence of murder, divorce and social corruption. While it is true that the elements of righteousness and spiritual power are making progress and the good are better than they ever were before, there can be no doubt that the bad are worse, and the shadow grows as dark as the light grows bright.

SUDDEN

8. His Coming a Surprise

Matthew 24:36, 42 and 44 tell us that the Lord's coming will be a shock to this self-complacent world. It will also be a surprise to the modern prophets who have told us all about it so often and still persist in knowing the very schedule of events and the times which the Father has set by His own power.

It will not be a surprise to His waiting people. "But you, brothers, are not in darkness so that this day should surprise you like a thief" (1 Thessalonians 5:4). They may not know the day or hour, but they shall know enough to be ready. But to the world it will be a terrific and startling blow. "While people are saying, 'Peace and safety,' destruction will come on them suddenly, as labor pains on a pregnant woman, and they will not escape" (5:3). Even for us, the followers of Christ, the only safety is to be always ready.

THE JUDGMENT OF THE MINISTERS

9. The Lord's Coming in Relation to the Ministers of Christ

His first act at His coming will be to call His servants before Him in judgment. Then shall the faithful ministers receive a great reward.

> Who then is the faithful and wise servant, whom the master has put in charge of the servants in his household to give them their food at the proper time? It will be good for that servant whose master finds him doing so when he returns. I tell you the truth, he will put him in charge of all his possessions. (Matthew 24:45–47)

This is the promise which speaks of the servants who shall be found true to His message and His flock. But, oh, how awful the doom of the false minister, of the man that has ignored the truth of the Lord's coming and in his heart has secretly hoped that it might not be; and, encouraged by this false theology, has yielded to ambition and self-aggrandizement and been drawn into the spirit of controversy and worldliness. Alas for him!

> But suppose that servant is wicked and says to himself, 'My master is staying away a long time,' and he then begins to beat his fellow servants and to eat and drink with drunkards. The master of that servant will come on a day when he does not expect him and at an hour he is not aware of. He will cut him to pieces and assign him a place with the hypocrites, where there will be weeping and gnashing of teeth. (24:48–51)

PREPARATION OF THE CHURCH

10. The Lord's Coming in Relation to the Members of His Church and Their Spiritual Preparation

This is brought out in the parable of the 10 Virgins (25:1–13). These two classes both represent the followers of Christ. They were all virgins, which certainly represents purity, and they were all looking forward to the coming of the Lord, for they "went out to meet the bridegroom" (25:1). Then besides, they all had light and a certain measure of oil, and this must stand for the true light and the true life. The difference between them was essential; the one had the source of light and the other had not. The foolish virgins had a temporary supply and the wise had vessels filled with oil, a permanent provision. There can be little question about the meaning of the symbol of oil, always the type of the Holy Spirit. And so the lesson seems most plain that the wise virgins represent those Christians who have not only accepted Christ as a Savior, but have received the baptism of the Holy Spirit and been brought into a personal relation with Christ Himself as an abiding source of light and power, while the foolish virgins represent the great multitude in the Church of God who are willing to remain on a lower plane and fail to press on into the fullness of Christ. When the Master comes it is too late to rectify their mistake. They go to obtain oil and perhaps they obtain it, but the doors are shut. It would not seem that they are finally lost, but they are excluded from the marriage feast, they are left in the "darkness" (25:30) of the tribulation. They are not lost, perhaps, but oh, how much they lose!

Dear friend, do not run this fearful risk. The baptism of the Holy Spirit means much to you now for your peace, your holiness, your victory, your power, your service; but oh, it will mean everything to you then. "Did you receive the Holy Spirit when you believed?" (Acts 19:2). This is the one prerequisite for the coming of the Lord.

THE SERVANTS

11. The Judgment of the Servants

The parable of the 10 Virgins has reference to our sainthood; the parable of the Talents has reference to our service. It is found in the paragraph Matthew 25:14–30.

The endowment of these talents stands for everything in our natural, spiritual and providential conditions which God has given us for the purpose of fitting us for service and usefulness, everything in a word, which may tell in your life for the glory of God and the good of others. These talents, He says, were given "each according to his ability" (25:15). God has put each one of us in the very best position to accomplish our own work for Him. There is something you can do that no one else can do, there is someone you can reach that no one else can reach. Your talent may consist of natural ability, social influence, financial resources, position in the church or the world or special opportunities brought to you in connection with your life work. It is the sum of all the possibilities of usefulness in your life. God expects you to make the most of it for Him and others and is going to call you to account at the coming of Christ for the use you have made of your life.

The principle on which He will judge you will not be the amount of your talent, but the measure in which you have improved it. The man who had but two talents was rewarded as much as the man who had five if it was found that he had made a proportionate improvement of his little endowment. The reward that the Master is to give at His coming will be a higher form of service. The coming age and the future kingdom is not to be a luxurious sinecure, but a magnificent opportunity for higher work and holy activity.

There is one figure in this picture which stands out in awful distinctness. It is the servant who had but one talent, and because it was so little, made no use of it, but wrapped it up in a napkin and brought it back to his Lord with his trifling and insulting excuses. How solemnly it reminds us that the people that are mostly to miss the mark are the ordinary people that think they amount to very little and therefore do little or nothing. Oh, you who think you have but one talent, watch and pray, lest through false humility you lose even that and meet the Master in fearful disappointment and condemnation.

The deep secret, however, of this man's failure was his utter lack of faith and love toward Christ. He said, "I knew that you are a hard man. . . . I was afraid" (25:24–25). It was the spirit of the natural heart. Faith and love will make a very little ability go a great way; and without them, the largest gifts are vain. When the Master comes He is to judge our works. Oh, that He may find us faithful now and accepted then.

THE NATIONS

12. Christ's Coming with Reference to the Judgment of the Nations

God is judging the nations in providence now. And at the coming of the Lord Jesus He will call them before Him in final and solemn assize, and judge them according to their treatment of His people and their treatment of Israel. "These brothers of mine" (25:40), no doubt refers to Israel literally and also spiritually. According to the way in which the rulers of the earth have treated God's ancient people and also treated the gospel and the followers of Christ, will be their judgment in that day. We see a little section sometimes of that judgment now as the hand of God is breaking those powers that have oppressed the Hebrew people and opposed the gospel of Christ, but we shall some day witness the final act of this sublime tribunal when the old promise of Psalm 72:4 shall be fulfilled, and "he will crush the oppressor."

LESSONS

Such, then, is the Master's panorama of the events that lead up to His coming. Oh, how solemnly it bids us to be ready, to be faithful, to be watchful and to labor and pray that all our loved ones may be with us in that day, nay that hour, which may come at any moment, when "one will be taken and the other left" (Matthew 24:40).

Our Loved Ones

The late Dr. Gordon told of two girls, sisters, who lay down to sleep one night in the same bed. The one, a Christian, the other, a scoffer. The Christian girl had just come from a religious service in which the preacher had quoted that phrase, "one will be taken and the other left" (24:40), and had solemnly warned his hearers of the coming of the Lord. Her heart was so filled with concern for her sister that she could not sleep. She told her of the sermon and her feelings and earnestly begged her to think of her soul's salvation, but she was only met with jests and rebuffs, and soon the thoughtless girl was fast asleep. The other could only weep and pray in agony until at last she was so distressed that she rose from her bed, and stealing into a closet adjoining, she fell upon her face and poured out her heart in sobs and prayers for the salvation of her sister.

After a while the sleeper awoke, and missing her sister from her side, suddenly remembered the conversation of the earlier part of the night. Suddenly it flashed upon her, "What if the Lord had come and she was left?" Then she broke down with alarm and calling for her sister, sought her in the darkness of the room, and at last heard her sobbing in the closet. Throwing herself on her knees by her side, she besought her prayers, and together the two girls found the Savior and lay down a little later clasped in each other's arms with the joyful thought that if He should come, they would be together.

Oh, is there any motive that so tenderly appeals to us to labor and pray for our dear ones in view of the coming of the Lord?

This Passing World

And surely, out of all this there must come to the mind of every thoughtful man and woman the solemn conviction of the uncertainty of this present world and the supreme importance of being ready for that coming age which is so speedily impending. Dear friend, if these things be true, what security have you for the future?

Humboldt, the great traveler, describes in one of his books his first experience of an earthquake. He was in South America at the village of Cumana. Suddenly a shock came and everything beneath him and around him seemed dissolved. The one overmastering impression was, he says, that everything was going, and the things that he had always looked upon as substantial were no longer real. The solid ground was rocking and sinking beneath his feet; the crocodiles ran howling from the rivers into the woods in terror and dismay; the very dogs lay panting by his side unable to bark or scarcely to breathe. The houses, instead of being a refuge for their inmates, were falling in ruins upon the inhabitants, whose screams of dying agony were mingled with the roar of dissolving nature. He looked to the forests and the trees were falling; he looked to the mountains and they were flying from their bases and tossing like the billows of the sea. And then he looked up and lo, the sky and heavens alone seemed stable and unchanging, and he thought, "every earthly thing is dissolving and heaven alone remains unmoved."

The hour is coming when everything which you have counted substantial shall dissolve and disappear, and only the things that are above shall be unshaken and remain. Oh, have you found your portion there? Have you chosen "the city with foundations" (Hebrews 11:10), and "a kingdom that cannot be shaken" (12:28)?

CHAPTER 17

THE CROWN OF THORNS

And then twisted together a crown of thorns and set it on his head. They put a staff in his right hand and knelt in front of him and mocked him. "Hail, king of the Jews!" they said. (Matthew 27:29)

Our present study will lead us through the scenes of the garden, the judgment hall, the cross and the tomb. But true to the great design of the Gospel of Matthew to reveal the Lord Jesus continually as the King, we shall not see in these scenes the signs of weakness and defeat, but rather the still more signal evidence of victory and power. Even in His bitterest sorrows and His darkest hours, we shall find that Jesus Christ is still the Son of David and the Son of God. The loftiest greatness is not achieved by mere gifts of power; it needs the touch of suffering to add the supreme glory of heroism in the hour of His shame and agony and death. It has been said in language most striking and yet most true: "Socrates died like a philosopher, but Jesus died like a God." With this as our underlying thought, let us gather up the scenes of His final sufferings and the light that shines from the "crown of thorns" (27:29).

HIS DEDICATION

1. The Shadow of the Cross (26:2)

It has been said most truly of human ignorance of the future that "The veil which hides our future is woven by the hand of mercy." It would multiply tenfold all our trials if we could see them before they come, but with Jesus Christ it was entirely different. The shadow of the cross overhung all His earthly life. Day by day He saw it drawing nearer as He passed on, exclaiming: "But I have a baptism to undergo, and how distressed I am until it is completed!" (Luke 12:50). So we find Him in this passage saying to His disciples: "As you know, the Passover is two days away—and the Son of

Man will be handed over to be crucified" (Matthew 26:2). His death, therefore, was no mere accident, which came to Him through the superior power of His enemies, but a foreordained result which He had known from the beginning and toward which all His earthly life had been converging. What a dignity and a glory this adds to His voluntary sufferings. He had come to the world to die, and now death could bring Him no surprise and no defeat.

CAIAPHAS

2. The Plot of His Enemies (26:3–5)

Next we see the conspiracy of His murderers. It was led by the religious rulers of the people and was hatched in the very palace of Caiaphas, the high priest. The ancient Levitical types had provided that the sin offering should be presented by the leaders of the people for the whole nation. In exact fulfillment of this, it was thus divinely ordered that the death of Jesus Christ should be the official act of the Jewish rulers. Not only so, in the narrative given us in the Gospel of John we are even told it was revealed to Caiaphas that it was necessary that "one man die for the people than that the whole nation perish" (John 11:50), and in gathering the council together to plan for the arrest and condemnation of Christ this was the very reason that he alleged for so doing. The death of Christ thus becomes the exact fulfillment of God's ancient plan and the men that brought it about to gratify their own personal vindictiveness were unconsciously fulfilling "God's set purpose and foreknowledge" (Acts 2:23). Thus again the death of Jesus Christ is lifted above any mere accident or human aspect and placed in the divine program of redemption.

MARY

3. The Anointing of Mary (Matthew 26:6–13)

This beautiful incident in the house of Simon, the leper, who was probably the husband of Martha at Bethany, was more than a sentimental expression of Mary's love to her Teacher and Lord. It was an act of faith, a faith which had already detected the great purpose of His life and understood as none other had that He had come to die. The Lord expressed this very delicately and yet distinctly as He vindicated her from the unworthy and harsh criticism of Judas and the others and claimed her personal gift as a service accepted for Himself, and added: "She has done a beautiful thing to me. . . . When she poured this perfume on my body, she did it to prepare me for burial" (26:10, 12). Here again, we have the hand of God above the hand of man and we see the divine purpose moving calmly on and choosing every instrument and every incident to set it forth and work it out as God's great purpose of love and grace in spite of man's purpose of cruel hatred.

How impressively this incident reminds us that there are ministries our Lord asks for Himself alone which are higher far than all our works of charity and gifts for the poor and the church. Our highest service should be for Him. Are we pouring the incense of our love and worship at His feet? Still again, we are reminded that there are gifts which may be kept too late. Mary had purposed reserving this until after His death and then using it to anoint His lifeless body, but an opportunity came to give it to Him while He was still alive, and her act of timely love was lifted to the dignity of an eternal priesthood and a ministry of which even the Master said: "I tell you the truth, wherever this gospel is preached throughout the world, what she has done will also be told, in memory of her" (26:13).

JUDAS

4. The Shadow of the Betrayer (26:14–16, 27:3–8)

Over against the beauty and glory of Mary's love falls the dark shadow of Judas Iscariot. But even Judas' treachery is made to rebound to the honor of Christ. His very act was but the fulfillment of an ancient prophecy from Zechariah (11:12) specifying the very amount that was paid for his crime. Even Judas was compelled, before the tragedy was over, to come back in a fit of remorse and despair and throw his ill-gotten silver at the feet of the rulers and bear a testimony to the innocence of Christ: "I have sinned . . . for I have betrayed innocent blood" (Matthew 27:4). As he went out into the darkness that was never to end and hurled himself to destruction, even Judas became one of the long array of witnesses that gather around the cross of Jesus Christ and add to its eternal glory.

THE PASCHAL LAMB

5. The Passover Feast (26:17–25)

This ancient ordinance, the most sacred of all the national feasts of Israel, had for its central figure the slaying of a lamb and the sprinkling of its blood on the door posts of their homes, followed by the eating of the flesh of the lamb. This also must bear witness to Jesus Christ. In the providence of God, it was so ordered that His sacrificial death should come during the Paschal Feast, and thus He is set forth as Himself the Paschal Lamb, to whose shed and sprinkled blood all the types of Judaism had looked forward for more than a thousand years.

What a testimony to that cross which to the eyes of men seemed a badge of shame and failure, but which stands out as the very glory of the Old Testament as well as the New.

THE LORD'S SUPPER

6. The Memorial Feast of the Lord's Supper (26:26–30)

The Passover supper blended with a new ordinance which was henceforth to perpetuate the memory of His death among His followers and to be known in the future as "The Lord's Supper." The very object of this ordinance is to set forth, not His life, nor His works, nor His miraculous power, but His suffering and dying love. "You proclaim the Lord's death until he comes" (1 Corinthians 11:26) is the apostle's description of the deep and sacred meaning of the Lord's Supper.

Other earthly names are remembered and celebrated by the day of their birth; the day of our Savior's birth is uncertain, and our Christmas celebration is but a guess as to the time, and certainly claims no divine authority for its observance, but the commemoration of Christ's death is the most sacred duty of every Christian and lifts the Cross of Christ so high that it stands: "Towering o'er the rocks of time."

GETHSEMANE

7. The Cup that Passed (Matthew 26:36–46)

The agony in Gethsemane has usually been regarded wholly in the light of a tragedy. It is customary for preachers to quote it as the deepest and saddest evidence of the Savior's humiliation and sorrow. But there is another aspect in which it is raised to the height of a great and glorious victory.

There is a passage in Hebrews (5:7) which tells of some occasion when "During the days of Jesus' life on earth, he offered up prayers and petitions with loud cries and tears to the one who could save him from death, and he was heard because of his reverent submission." There is no occasion to which this can reasonably apply except that hour of agony in Gethsemane. If it applies to that, then it is certain that Christ's prayer in the garden that night was heard and the cup did pass from Him. We have been accustomed to tell people that the Lord Jesus prayed in vain, and that, like Him, we must submit to the will of God even when our prayers are not answered. But if this passage in Hebrews be true, His prayer was answered and the thing He dreaded did not come.

How are we to explain it? What was the thing He dreaded and escaped? It seems very plain that it was the fear that He should die then and there under the pressure and agony and through the power of Satan; that He should be crushed by the intolerable burden that He was unable to bear and should be hindered from accomplishing His sacrifice in the true order of God's time and plan. Satan resolved to crush Him and kill Him before the time, and it was against this that the Lord struggled and prayed and won the victory, for there appeared an angel strengthening Him; and He rose up from the conflict and went forth in the power of God to pass through the scenes of the judgment hall and the protracted sufferings of the cross. Then, in due time, after every Scripture had been fulfilled, He laid down His life voluntarily as He Himself had said: "No one takes it from me, but I lay it down of my own accord. I have authority to lay it down and authority to take it up again. This command I received from my Father" (John 10:18). In this view, the agony in Gethsemane is one of the most glorious victories of the Master's life, and encourages us to claim a similar triumph when Satan would kill us before our work is done. By entering into His faith and triumph, we can live on and labor on until we "finish the race and complete the task" (Acts 20:24) and have "nothing to do but to die."

LEGIONS OF ANGELS

8. His Refusal of Angelic Succor (Matthew 26:47–56)

Even His arrest would have been impossible but for His own consent. Another evangelist tells how the men that came to take Him were prostrated at first by His glance and could not have touched Him if He had not voluntarily surrendered (John 18:6). Matthew tells us how He forbade His followers to fight for Him, telling them that He had only to pray to the Father and He should presently give Him "more than twelve legions of angels" (Matthew 26:53). Twelve legions of angels would have been an army of over 60,000 angelic soldiers. Now we know that one angel was sufficient to slay in a single night an army of 175,000 Assyrians. What would 60,000 angels have meant for Christ's safeguarding? And He had only to breathe a single word and that army would have been around Him and His enemies stricken with swift destruction. But that word was never spoken, and the self-restraint of Jesus Christ in this hour of peril is one of the mightiest proofs of His deity and gives to His arrest the glory rather of a triumphal march than a shameful defeat.

ALONE

9. The Forsaking and Denial of Peter and the Disciples (26:56, 58, 69–75)

When at last His arrest had really come, and they saw Him bound and apparently helpless in the hands of His enemies, then His disciples utterly broke down. Of the others it is said: "Then all the disciples deserted him and fled" (26:56), but Peter's was a still worse treachery, for he not only fled, but under the pressure of that night of panic, he openly and repeatedly denied Him. Surely, this at least was an evidence of weakness on the Master's part that the very men who had stood nearest to Him should so easily give up their Master and testify against Him. On the contrary, it is one of the strongest and grandest testimonies to the Lord. In one of the old prophetic pictures of the Messiah, it is this very feature that is brought into prominence: "Who is this coming from Edom,/ from Bozrah, with his garments stained crimson?" and the answer comes, "I have trodden the winepress alone;/ from the nations no one was with me" (Isaiah 63:1, 3). The very solitariness of Christ's sorrow is the most majestic touch. There are times in every great and noble life when it must stand alone and even the sympathy and support of the dearest friends appear to be withdrawn. This is the very test of fortitude and heroism, and in this hour of solitary ignominy and desertion Jesus stood supreme, sublime.

HIS OWN CONFESSION

10. Confessing Judgment (Matthew 26:59–66)

He is now arraigned before the court of Caiaphas, but they are helpless to convict Him. At last they appeal to the Lord Himself, and He comes to their aid and makes a confession on which they are able to base His condemnation. He acknowledges all that they have been unable to prove against Him respecting His divine claim that He is Christ, the Son of God, and adds: "You will see the Son of Man sitting at the right hand of the Mighty One and coming on the clouds of heaven" (26:64). With great delight they listen. He has put into their hands the weapon they had sought in vain, and they cry, "He has spoken blasphemy! Why do we need any more witnesses?" (26:65). So even the condemnation of Jesus was brought about by His own act. His death was a voluntary sacrifice all the way through and the accomplishment of that great purpose for which He had come from heaven, "to give his life as a ransom for many" (20:28).

BARABBAS

11. The Substitution of Barabbas (Matthew 27:16–21)

Brought before the tribunal of Pilate, that shrewd Roman could find no cause for His condemnation. But seeing that His accusers were bent on blood, he ventured on a compromise and suggested to them that he should release, as was the custom at the feast, some one person as a concession to the multitude and an act of clemency. In order to compel them, for decency's sake, to consent to the release of Jesus, he puts as the alternative the release of Barabbas, who is called "a notorious prisoner" (27:16). This man seems to have been a very paragon of wickedness and his name was in the mouths of all as the most desperate of criminals. Pilate reckoned that they would not dare to ask for his life and so, with what he thought great adroitness, he placed the two horns of the dilemma before them and said, "Which one do you want me to release to you: Barabbas, or Jesus who is called Christ?" (27:17). To his consternation, the cry came back, "Barabbas" (27:21). Rather would they set free the vilest of men than give up their hold upon Jesus Christ. Was there ever such a testimony to His innocence and to the spirit of His murderers? But back of all this story of substitution there lies the deepest, sweetest secret of redeeming love, namely, that Jesus Christ becomes the substitute from age to age for just such men as Barabbas; that He bore that day the shame, the wrath, the cross that the vilest of men deserved in order that the sinner might go free through His vicarious suffering. That is why we, as we read these lines, are saved from condemnation and accepted by the Father as fully as if we had never sinned, because one day our blessed Substitute took our place and we were released from judgment and are now "accepted in the beloved" (Ephesians 1:6, KJV).

PILATE AND HIS WIFE

12. Pilate's Testimony to Christ (Matthew 27:18–24)

Both Pilate and his wife are compelled to give their testimony for the innocence of the Sufferer. From the very beginning Pilate knew that "it was out of envy that they had handed Jesus over to him" (27:18). But his perplexity was still greater when there came from his wife a pressing message: "Don't have anything to do with that innocent man, for I have suffered a great deal today in a dream because of him" (27:19). This was a solemn warning from the very heavens. Pilate longed to yield to all these appeals to his sense of right and justice, but at heart he was a coward. At last he yielded to pressure, vainly thinking that he could shift the responsibility to their shoulders as he washed his hands before them and added one more testimony to the Lord, "I am innocent of this man's blood. . . . It is your responsibility!" (27:24). So from the very judgment seat of His enemies, the testimony comes: Jesus Christ was righteous and died not for His own sins but for the sins of men.

HIS BLOOD BE ON US

13. The Testimony of Israel's Punishment (27:25)

"All the people answered, 'Let his blood be on us and on our children!' " (27:25). That was an awful imprecation. Had Jesus Christ been guilty, it would have fallen lightly on Israel's head. Has it fallen lightly? What is the story of these 19 centuries? The saddest and most terrible of human tragedies. Witness the sufferings of Israel's sons and daughters in every country and every clime. Recall the horrors of the siege and fall of Jerusalem under the Romans, think of the cruel persecutions of the race all through the Middle Ages, remember the latest scenes from Kishinev and Rumania, and ask what does all this mean if it is not the fulfillment of their own self-inflicted curse. Does it not declare like the voice of many waters, "Surely we are being punished because of our brother" (Genesis 42:21)? It is the very fulfillment of the curse which Israel accepted, for His blood was shed in innocency and shed for them.

THE KING OF THE JEWS

14. The Testimony of the Title on His Cross (Matthew 27:37)

Over the cross of Jesus, Pilate ordered this inscription fastened: "This is Jesus, the King of the Jews" (27:37). Another evangelist tells that they were very much displeased with this and tried to have it changed so as to read, "this man claimed to be king of the Jews" (John 19:21), but Pilate rudely answered, "What I have written, I have written" (19:22); and the record remained and stands forever as the very echo of Matthew's Gospel and God's decree that Jesus was indeed the Son of David and the King of Israel.

REFUSED THE MYRRH

15. The Unmixed Cup of Agony (Matthew 27:34)

"There they offered Jesus wine to drink, mixed with gall; but after tasting it, he refused to drink it" (27:34). This was intended as an anodyne to deaden His sufferings, a merciful provision of the executioners, but Jesus would have none of it. Not one drop of woe would He abate. He was bearing our cross and He insisted on bearing it to the full. He has done so and there is nothing left for you and me to do. "Jesus paid it all."

THEIR TAUNTS

16. His Self-Restraint in the Face of Their Taunts (27:39–44)

This verse tells how they challenged Him, if He were indeed divine, to come down from the cross and show it. How easily He could have done so, but not for one moment did He attempt His own vindication. All the humiliation and shame He bore in full and left His honor and His dignity to His Father's vindication. What but the power of His divine nature could have ever held Him in such self-restraint, knowing, as He did, how easily He might have stricken down the insulting crowd before Him and answered their buffetings with the lightness of His power? There is no strength so great as the strength of self-restraint and oh, how this shines out from the cross of Calvary.

"MY GOD, MY GOD, WHY HAVE YOU FORSAKEN ME?"

17. The Cup of Wrath (27:46)

At last there comes, from out of the darkness which had now fallen upon the scene, a strange and bitter cry. It was a quotation from the 22nd Psalm (verse 1), a prophetic psalm describing the Messiah's sufferings. It was a cry extorted by the wrath of God that was now ruling over His head. Deeper and harder than all the cruelties of men was the hiding of His Father's face, but even this was but part of the program of prophecy. That cry was but another testimony to His Messiahship as He fulfilled to the letter all that God had said should come to pass. Even that bitter cup of God's curse against sin He drank to the full, and now "there is now no condemnation for those who are in Christ Jesus" (Romans 8:1).

THE EARTHQUAKE

18. The Testimony of Nature to Christ (Matthew 27:45, 51)

"From the sixth hour until the ninth hour darkness came over all the land. . . . The earth shook and the rocks split" (27:45, 51). The very sun refused to look upon the agony of its Maker, and the earth shuddered at His dying pain. History and tradition tell us that in other lands at this very time the attention of observers was directed to the preternatural disturbance of the material world and the fact that some great tragedy must be taking place somewhere.

THE RENT VEIL

19. The Testimony of Judaism (27:51)

"At that moment the curtain of the temple was torn in two from top to bottom" (27:51). That veil, we know, was suspended between great columns about 70 feet high. It would have been impossible for any human hand to reach the top. It might have been torn from the bottom to the top by powerful hands, but when we read that is was "torn . . . from top to bottom" we know it must have been the hand of God. And so Judaism, from its most sacred shrine, bore witness that the great mystery which that sacred veil had covered, namely, the intercession of the Great High Priest, was now about to be accomplished, and the way into the holiest of all was opened by the death of Jesus.

THE CENTURION

20. The Testimony of the Centurion (27:54)

"When the centurion and those with him who were guarding Jesus saw the earthquake and all that had happened, they were terrified, and exclaimed, 'Surely he was the Son of God!'" (27:54).

This cold and unsympathizing Roman soldier, with no prejudice in favor of the suffering Victim on that cross, had taken in the whole situation—His own demeanor, His silent majesty and the portents of nature on every side. As he comprehended it all, this was his testimony: "Surely he was the Son of God." Truly of such a scene we might well say, "Death has been swallowed up in victory" (1 Corinthians 15:54).

JOSEPH

21. The Testimony of Joseph, the Counselor

One of the most remarkable testimonies to Christ was the coming of this man, a member of the Sanhedrin which had condemned Him, to ask the privilege of burying the body of Jesus in his own tomb. Thus the very council of the nation, through Joseph, bore witness to His innocence, and the old prophecy of Isaiah was fulfilled: "He was assigned a grave with the wicked,/ and with the rich in his death,/ though he had done no violence,/ nor was any deceit in his mouth" (Isaiah 53:9). His grave had been prepared among the thieves, but instead His body was laid in the tomb of this rich friend.

THE WOMEN

22. The Testimony of the Watching Women

Finally, there is no testimony to the death of Christ so deep and strong as that which comes from the hearts that love Him and that have found in His precious blood the source of their cleansing and salvation.

This was represented by that company of women who were "watching from a distance" (Matthew 27:55), and who represent that mighty crowd who, through all these ages, have stood beholding with sacred grace, until before the vision guilt and sin and sorrow fled away and faith could blend their voices in the song:

> Here I'll stand forever viewing
> Mercy's streams in streams of blood,

Plenteous drops my soul renewing
Plead and claim my peace with God.

THE POWER OF THE CROSS

The following allegory from the pen of Mark Guy Pearse, finely expresses
the power of that cross:

Once I went forth to look for Repentance. I sought her day
and night in the City of Mansoul. I asked many if they knew
where she dwelt, and they said they had never seen her. I met
one, grave and scholarly, who told me what she was like, and
bade me seek her earnestly, but he did not tell me where she was
to be found. Then, all sad at heart, I went forth without the city
walls and climbed a lonely hill, and up a steep and rugged way,
until I came in sight of the Cross, and of Him who hung thereon. And lo, as I looked upon Him, there came one and touched
me. Then instantly my heart was melted, and all the great deeps
of my soul were broken up.

"Ah, Repentance, I have been looking everywhere for you," I
said.

"Thou wilt always find me here," said Repentance; "here, in
sight of my crucified Lord. I tarry ever at His feet."

Again I went forth to look for Forgiveness. I knocked at many
a door in the City of Mansoul and asked for her. And some said
they thought she did live there sometimes; and some said she
used to once and some said she came there occasionally when the
weather was fine, to spend Sunday. Then up came one whom I
knew by name as Unbelief, with a voice like a croaking of a
raven, and he said that Forgiveness never was there and never
could be, that she was much too fine a lady to live in so low a
place as that and among such a set as they were. So I came forth
wearied and sad: and as I reached the city gate I met again the
grave scholar, and he gave me much account of her birth and
parentage and showed me her portrait, and told me of her gracious works, and he bade me seek her earnestly; but he did not
tell me where I could find her.

So I went along my way, looking, but wellnigh in despair,
when it chanced that I found myself again upon the high hill,
climbing again the steep and rugged path. And I lifted my eyes
and saw once more the Cross and Him who hanged thereon, and

lo, at the first sight of my dear Lord, Forgiveness met me and filled my poor soul with holy peace and rest like Heaven itself.

"Oh, I have had a weary search for you," I said.

"I am always here," said Forgiveness; "here at my Master's feet."

Long afterwards I wondered within myself where Holiness dwelt, but I feared to go in search of her. I knew she would never be at home in the low lands and busy streets of Mansoul. All whom I asked about her answered doubtfully. One said she had died long ago; indeed was buried in Eden before Adam came out. One said that she lived away at the end of the Valley of the Shadow of Death, her house was on the brink of the river, and that I must hope to meet with her just before I crossed it. Another argued almost angrily against this notion. "Nay," said he, "She lives farther on still; search as thou wilt, thou shalt never find her till thou art safely across the river and landed on the shores of the Celestial City."

Then I remembered how well I have fared aforetime on that Holy Hill and went forth again. So up the lonely way I went and reached the top of it and looked once more upon my blessed Savior. And lo! there was Holiness sitting at the Master's feet. I feared to say that I had been looking for her, but as I gazed upon the Crucified, and felt the greatness of His love to me, and as all my heart went out in love and adoration, Holiness rose up, and came to me all graciously, and said, "I've been waiting for thee ever since my first coming."

"Waiting where?" I asked, wondering.

"At His feet," said Holiness. "I am always there."

CHAPTER 18

THE PRINCE OF LIFE

"Come and see the place where he lay." (Matthew 28:6)

In keeping with the special design of Matthew's Gospel, it is interesting to notice the resurrection of the Lord Jesus as it shows the fulfillment of Messianic prophecy and reveals Him in His kingly character.

HIS OWN PREDICTIONS

1. First, it was in accordance with His own predictions and had been always contemplated as part of His redeeming plan. In the very beginning of His earthly ministry, when they asked Him for a sign by which to authenticate His claims, His answer was, " 'Destroy this temple, and I will raise it again in three days.' . . . But the temple he had spoken of was his body" (John 2:19, 21). Again in Matthew 16:21, which is before the transfiguration, we find Him explaining to His disciples "that he must go to Jerusalem and suffer many things at the hands of the elders, chief priests and teachers of the law, and that he must be killed and on the third day be raised to life."

In the following chapter we read again, "When they came together in Galilee, he said to them, 'The Son of Man is going to be betrayed into the hands of men. They will kill him, and on the third day he will be raised to life' " (17:22–23).

Still later, on His last journey to Jerusalem, we read: "Now as Jesus was going up to Jerusalem, he took the twelve disciples aside and said to them, 'We are going up to Jerusalem, and the Son of Man will be betrayed to the chief priests and the teachers of the law. They will condemn him to death and will turn him over to the Gentiles to be mocked and flogged and crucified. On the third day he will be raised to life!' " (20:17–19).

So widely known were these announcements that His enemies were familiar with them, and after His crucifixion they went to Pilate and said, "Sir . . . we remember that while he was still alive that deceiver said, 'After three days I will rise again' " (27:63).

These repeated announcements of His resurrection give an emphatic and conclusive significance to the value of that resurrection as an evidence of His claims. It was the one sign which He always submitted as the supreme test of His divinity and His authority as Messiah. When they demanded a sign from heaven, He had said unto them that "none will be given . . . except the sign of the prophet Jonah," and that even as Jonah had been "three days and three nights in the belly of a huge fish," so He, the Son of Man, should be "three days and three nights in the heart of the earth" (12:39–40). Therefore we find the apostles, in their preaching to the unbelieving world, always insisting upon the doctrine of the resurrection of Jesus Christ as the cornerstone of Christianity. The Apostle Paul builds up a powerful argument on it and declares: "if Christ has not been raised, our preaching is useless and so is your faith. . . . you are still in your sins" (1 Corinthians 15:14, 17).

In one of the most powerful books of a generation ago, Dr. Horace Bushnell's *Nature and the Supernatural,* there is a chapter on the resurrection of Jesus Christ which is the most conclusive piece of evidence in this class of theological literature. The writer on one occasion submitted this argument for the resurrection of Christ to a learned lawyer who had confessed himself an unbeliever in Christianity. The lawyer promised to weigh the evidence and study the case. At the end of a fortnight, he returned and frankly confessed that the argument was overwhelming and that he had no doubt, and never again could have any doubt, that Jesus Christ had really died and risen again and that the claims of Christianity were divine. At the same time, he added that he was not yet a Christian and now discovered that he did not even wish to be, and that the trouble was not in his head but in his heart.

The resurrection, therefore, of the Lord Jesus Christ was designed as His own special vindication and was announced by Himself again and again. Therefore, when it occurred exactly as He had predicted it, its effect is irresistible and overwhelming.

OLD TESTAMENT PROPHECIES

2. The resurrection of Jesus Christ was in accordance with the prophecies of the Old Testament. The ancient story of Abraham and Isaac and the offering on Mount Moriah was an obvious foreshadowing of the resurrection of Christ. Speaking of it the apostle says: "By faith Abraham, when God tested him, offered Isaac as a sacrifice. He who had received the promises was about to sacrifice his one and only son, even though God had said to him, 'It is through Isaac that your offspring will be reckoned.' Abraham reasoned that God could raise the dead, and figuratively speaking, he did receive Isaac back from death" (Hebrews 11:17–19). Isaac's release from that sacrificial altar was a figure of Christ's resurrection from the dead. Abraham

had even expected Isaac to be raised from the dead if the sacrifice had really been consummated.

The story of the prophet Jonah was a type of Christ's resurrection. Jonah's burial in the bowels of the sea monster was a distinct type of Christ's entombment in the heart of the earth, and his coming forth on the third day completed the type and foreshadowed the resurrection of the Son of Man. David in the 16th Psalm uses language which the apostle interprets as having reference exclusively to the resurrection of Jesus Christ: "my body also will rest secure,/ because you will not abandon me to the grave,/ nor will you let your Holy One see decay" (16:9–10). Speaking of this on the day of Pentecost, the Apostle Peter thus comments on it:

> Brothers, I can tell you confidently that the patriarch David died and was buried, and his tomb is here to this day. But he was a prophet and knew that God had promised him on oath that he would place one of his descendants on his throne. Seeing what was ahead, he spoke of the resurrection of the Christ, that he was not abandoned to the grave, nor did his body see decay. God has raised this Jesus to life, and we are all witnesses of the fact. (Acts 2:29–32)

To the same effect, also, the Apostle Paul quotes this passage in his address to the Jews at Antioch. "For when David had served God's purpose in his own generation, he fell asleep; he was buried with his fathers and his body decayed. But the one whom God raised from the dead did not see decay" (13:36–37).

The greatest of all prophets, Isaiah himself, does not fail to point out the resurrection of Jesus Christ. In Isaiah 53:10 we read: "Yet it was the LORD'S will to crush him and cause him to suffer,/ and though the LORD makes his life a guilt offering,/ he will see his offspring and prolong his days,/ and the will of the LORD will prosper in his hand./ After the suffering of his soul,/ he will see the light of life and be satisfied." This language evidently describes a Sufferer who survives His sufferings, prolongs His days and lives afterwards to rejoice in the fruits of His great sacrifice.

So the resurrection of the Lord Jesus Christ is true to the Messianic ideal and we may say of it as He Himself, in His conversation with the disciples on His walk to Emmaus, said: " 'Did not the Christ have to suffer these things and then enter his glory?' And beginning with Moses and all the Prophets, he explained to them what was said in all the Scriptures concerning himself. . . . Then he opened their minds so they could understand the Scriptures. He told them, 'This is what is written: The Christ will suffer and rise from the dead on the third day' " (Luke 24:26–27, 45–46).

VICTORY OVER HIS ENEMIES

3. The resurrection of Christ was a victory over the plots of His foes. They had specially feared this very thing and had laid their plans to circumvent it. They went to the governor immediately after His death and told him that they expected the disciples to come and steal His body from the tomb and then pretend that He had risen from the dead. They were given permission to place a powerful guard of Roman soldiers for three days before the tomb and also to close the sepulcher with a great stone and securely fasten it with the Roman seal, making it a treasonable crime for any one to break that seal and open the sepulcher. Everything was done that they asked for. And when, in spite of all their precautions, the resurrection was accomplished according to the divine order, their very plot only added to its significance and made it the more glorious a vindication of the Lord.

They could not say that they had been surprised; they did all that they could to prevent it and failed, and they must stand the consequences of their defeat and concede the claim of the friends of Christ.

Still more emphatically have we a right to demand from them some light on the disposal of the body. Human courts refuse to proceed with a charge of murder unless the body is produced. We may well refuse to consider the charge of the stealing of Christ's body unless our opponents can produce that body and show us what was done with it. How would it have been possible for the little company of terrified men and women who had fled from the judgment hall in dismay, who had given up their Master and their cause as lost, who were without means or influence or human resources, how would it have been possible for them in the face of the whole Roman government and the keen watching eyes of the entire Jewish nation on guard against this very thing happening. How, we ask, would it have been possible for them to have stolen away the body and succeeded afterwards in permanently concealing it from the keen scrutiny that would have hunted it down with all the detective resources of the ecclesiastical and civil authorities? The idea is simply preposterous and the question answers itself.

The story of the Roman soldiers that they had slept and been surprised by the disciples would not have stood a moment with Pilate if he had really believed it, but as a good-natured concession to the men who were sufficiently angry with him already, he took their bribe and allowed it to pass while he laughed in his sleeve and knew as well as they that they had only tried to fool him and themselves too. So the very efforts of the adversary recoiled upon his own head and left the evidence of Christ's resurrection unassailable.

ANGELIC WITNESSES

4. Christ's resurrection was witnessed by the angels of God. Not often do these mighty beings interpose in human affairs. Certainly they do not come down from heaven to play a farce such as the enemies of Christ's resurrection would imply. Their presence on this occasion intimates that some stupendous event had occurred. There were apparently three angelic parties, the one that rolled away the stone and two others that afterwards were found sitting where the body of Jesus had lain. So mighty was this glorious being that "his appearance was like lightning, and his clothes were white as snow. The guards were so afraid of him that they shook and became like dead men" (Matthew 28:3–4). But as the women drew near with their loving offerings for the body of Jesus, he answered and said unto them, "Do not be afraid, for I know that you are looking for Jesus who was crucified. He is not here; he has risen, just as he said. Come and see the place where he lay" (28:5–6).

The voice of heaven proclaims the resurrection of Jesus Christ. The mighty angels, who came down at Sinai and at the Savior's birth and who are to come once more when the Lord returns, were there to herald His victory over the grave and the ushering in of the great redemption which His death assured. Joyfully we listen to their message and echo back the glad refrain, "The Lord is risen indeed."

HUMAN WITNESSES

5. The resurrection of Jesus Christ is established by the strongest human testimony. We have in this chapter the words of the women who had gone to anoint His body in the early morning and who heard first the message of the angels and immediately afterwards the very voice of Jesus Himself as He met them on the way, saying "Greetings," and sent them on with the glad command: "Do not be afraid. Go and tell my brothers to go to Galilee; there they will see me" (28:9–10). The other evangelists add many similar testimonies respecting the various appearings of Christ after His resurrection. The whole evidence is summed up by the Apostle Paul in the strong language of First Corinthians 15:4–8:

> He was raised on the third day according to the Scriptures, . . . he appeared to Peter, and then to the Twelve. After that, he appeared to more than five hundred of the brothers at the same time, most of whom are still living, though some have fallen asleep. Then he appeared to James, then to all the apostles, and last of all he appeared to me also, as to one abnormally born.

The cases of our earthly courts are all founded upon human testimony. If we cannot believe the testimony of honest men and women, then thousands of lives have been sacrificed by public execution and thousands of sentences have been passed by men upon their fellow men which were unjust and cruel. We believe in the resurrection of Jesus Christ on precisely the same testimony on which men are convicted every day in our courts of justice, and as we have stated above, the evidence of Christ's resurrection is in every way as conclusive and unassailable.

SUPERNATURAL SIGNS

6. The resurrection of Christ was signalized by the natural world. We are told "there was a violent earthquake" (Matthew 28:2). The earth rocked at His death and it shook once more with the travail of a great birth when He came forth from its bowels, the first fruits of the new creation. This was but in keeping with the testimony of nature everywhere, for God made the little seed that germinates and bursts forth from its tomb in the dark soil of earth and the opening bud and leaf and flower, all to be types of the great doctrine of the resurrection. He made the little chrysalis which emerges from the dark womb of nature and is transformed into the gorgeous butterfly to tell of the higher transformation of grace. Truly it has been said:

> All nature dies and lives again
> The flower that paints the field,
> The trees that crown the mountains' brow
> And boughs and blossoms yield.

DEATH DESTROYED

7. Christ's resurrection was His victory over death. He had gone down into the den of the King of Terrors in single combat and come forth Conqueror, and not only had come forth alone, but brought with him a train of rescued captives. In Matthew 27:52–53, we read: "The tombs broke open and the bodies of many holy people who had died were raised to life. They came out of the tombs, and after Jesus' resurrection they went into the holy city and appeared to many people."

These were the first fruits of the resurrection and they are pledges of that great company who at His second coming will come forth from the cemeteries of earth and will be clothed upon with glorified bodies and enter with Him into the inheritance of the age to come.

Henceforth death is a conquered foe; its sting is gone and, to the child of God, it has no terrors. It may still come to him as it came to the Master, but it will be as a servant and not as a master, to open the gates of heaven and let us pass into the joy of our Lord; for "Christ Jesus . . . has destroyed death and has brought life and immortality to light through the gospel" (2 Timothy 1:10). And He Himself has told us, "if anyone keeps my word, he will never see death" (John 8:51).

SATAN OVERTHROWN

8. Christ's resurrection was His victory over Satan. Death was but one of Satan's dark disguises. When Jesus conquered death, He conquered "him who holds the power of death—that is, the devil" (Hebrews 2:14). His resurrection has guaranteed the final overthrow of the "prince of demons" (Matthew 9:34), and standing by that open grave we can put our feet upon his neck and triumph over him as a conquered foe.

SIN PUT AWAY

9. Christ's resurrection was His victory over sin. He went down into that tomb as a person might go into a dungeon under a sentence for debt and crime. Had He remained in that prison, it would have shown that the debt was still uncanceled and the sentence still in force. But when He comes forth in victory and glory, all the officers of heaven's court of justice waiting upon Him and the Father Himself recognizing Him and taking Him to sit down by His side on the Ascension Throne, then we may know that the debt is paid, the cross is canceled and the power of sin destroyed. His deliverance was your deliverance for "he was delivered over to death for our sins and was raised to life for our justification" (Romans 4:25). Therefore faith can shout its triumph: "Who is he that condemns? Christ Jesus, who died—more than that, who was raised to life—is at the right hand of God and is also interceding for us" (8:34).

But not only does His resurrection cancel the curse that was against us, it brings the power of His life to dwell within us and purifies from the dominion of sin. Our life is just an impartation of His resurrection life. He rose from the dead not for Himself but in union with His body, the Church, and that resurrection guarantees to each of us the power to rise above sin and into all the resources of His grace and the fullness of His life. Sanctification as well as salvation springs from the open tomb and the life of the risen Lord and the very secret of it is:

> In the same way, count yourselves dead to sin but alive to God in Christ Jesus. Therefore do not let sin reign in your mortal body so that you obey its evil desires. Do not offer the parts of your body to sin, as instruments of wickedness, but rather offer yourselves to God, as those who have been brought from death to life; and offer the parts of your body to him as instruments of righteousness. (6:11–13)

HEAD OVER ALL THINGS

10. The resurrection of Jesus Christ guarantees victory over every obstacle that can obstruct our way. It is the pattern of His kingly power over all forces and adversaries and guarantees to us who abide in Him and press on in the power of His resurrection that nothing can prevail against us but that all things shall be subdued under the victorious feet of overcoming faith.

There is a striking and beautiful feature about the resurrection of Christ that we may not have noticed. The rolling away of the stone which had closed His tomb was not, by any means, necessary for Christ's resurrection. He had risen and come forth before that stone was moved. The power that could pass through closed doors after His resurrection could easily pass through that mass of the intervening rock. The stone was rolled away, not for the convenience of the Lord, but for the convenience of the women that they might be able to enter in and see the proofs of His resurrection. When the women came, He was not coming from the tomb through the open gate but He was approaching the tomb from the open garden where He had already been.

This is indeed most blessed. The Lord Jesus can pass through the stones of difficulty. And if we are walking with Him, we can pass through them, too, and so rise above them that even if they still remain they cannot impede us or imprison us, but we may overleap their barriers and laugh at their resistance.

Have we spiritual difficulties, temptations and obstacles? Let us not wait for them to pass away but rise above them in the resurrection life of Christ, and instead of being hindered by them, turn them into occasions of greater victory and blessing.

God help us, like the mighty angel, to sit down upon the stones that threaten to obstruct our way and look into the face of Satan, sin, sickness and the world until, like the Roman guards, they shall be ashamed and flee away.

CHAPTER 19

THE MEDIATORIAL KING

Then Jesus came to them and said, "All authority in heaven and on earth has been given to me. Therefore go and make disciples of all nations, baptizing them in the name of the Father and of the Son and of the Holy Spirit, and teaching them to obey everything I have commanded you. And surely I am with you always, to the very end of the age." (Matthew 28:18–20)

The manifestation of the Lord Jesus here recorded was, in some respects, the most remarkable of all His appearings during the 40 days. It was the only one by special appointment, the others being merely incidental and mostly unexpected. This He had arranged for even before His crucifixion, saying to His disciples, "But after I have risen, I will go ahead of you into Galilee" (26:32); and this had been the message of the angel to the women on the morning of His resurrection: "Then go quickly and tell his disciples: 'He has risen from the dead and is going ahead of you into Galilee. There you will see him.' Now I have told you" (28:7). This also was the direct message of Christ Himself as He first met the women returning from the sepulcher: "Go and tell my brothers to go to Galilee; there they will see me" (28:10).

THE MEETING IN GALILEE

This, then, had been the special appointment for His great meeting with all His disciples; and it seems a little strange, in view of the urgency and emphasis with which the message had been given, that they were so slow in obeying it, and in meeting their appointment with Him. They tarried in the neighborhood of Jerusalem at least eight days after the resurrection, for there were certainly two Sabbaths in immediate succession in which He appeared to them there. Were they waiting for Thomas to join their number, or were they needlessly tardy in beginning their journey? Perhaps the cause of the

157

delay was in order that all the disciples might receive the message and have time to attend the solemn convocation.

The place appointed we are not told; it was a mountain in Galilee. It could scarcely be Mount Hermon, the Mount of Transfiguration, for that would be more remote and difficult of access than was necessary. It may have been the same mountain where the sermon of Matthew 5–8 was delivered, the famous Horns of Hattin, where He had first proclaimed the principles of His kingdom to the world. It is probable that the 500 brethren, of whom Paul speaks in the 15th chapter of First Corinthians as having all seen Him at once, were the persons present at this gathering. They formed the surviving few who still remained faithful after the tragedy of the crucifixion.

HIS APPEARING

At length they have come together and are waiting for His appearing. It was the first great missionary convention that the world ever held, and it is most remarkable that the only appointment that Jesus made with His disciples after the resurrection was a missionary one. What a solemn emphasis it gives to the great commission and the glorious work of evangelizing the world, to fully realize the dignity with which Christ has invested this great occasion! At length they were assembled, and the Lord appeared in their midst. His coming to them seems to have differed in the form of its manifestation from any of His previous appearings. The Greek word, translated "came to them" (Matthew 28:18), has a special shade of meaning, implying the gradual approach—"He came toward them," becoming visible at first at some distance and majestically coming nearer, until at length He stood before them, coming down, perhaps, from the lofty mountaintop which rose above their heads. His appearance was impressive enough to throw most of them upon their faces in adoring reverence; yet there were some, even here, who doubted His identity.

HIS MESSAGE

Then He addressed to them His great and important message, containing: first, the claim of His kingly power and prerogatives; secondly, His great commission to them to go forth and establish His kingdom among all nations; and thirdly, the promise of His presence through all the days until the end of the age. Let us realize, as we dwell upon these three great themes, that this was not a message to the Eleven but to all the disciples of Jesus Christ, to all the days until the end of the age. For the company He had in His mind's eye must have included all that gathered around Him and would take up His commands even unto the end of the age of which He spoke.

SECTION I—*The Royal Proclamation*

"All authority in heaven and on earth has been given to me" (28:18).

This is really the manifesto of our King, in assuming His mediatorial throne. In declaring that all power is given to Him in heaven and on earth, He does not refer to His primeval deity and His divine rights, but to that special kingdom and authority given to Him in the eternal covenant of redemption on account of His finished work. It is something that has now been given to Him; it is the throne of the Mediator which He assumes at the Father's right hand, for the purpose of accomplishing the great work of redemption, for which He has already suffered and died. It is that of which He declared, "the Father . . . has entrusted all judgment to the Son" (John 5:22). "The Father loves the Son and has placed everything in his hands" (3:35). "For he must reign until he has put all his enemies under his feet" (1 Corinthians 15:25).

The word "power" (KJV) here more exactly means "dominion, authority," and has reference to the scepter and sovereignty of a king. The Lord Jesus means that He has been appointed to administer the government, both of heaven and earth, until the consummation of redemption. It is, indeed, a glorious and transcendent claim.

AUTHORITY TO SAVE

1. He has all authority to settle the standing and destiny of every sinner, and to control all our future prospects and our relations to God. He Himself could say, "For you granted him authority over all people that he might give eternal life to all those you have given him" (John 17:2). Through His name and the acceptance of His words all sins are forgiven, and the guilty soul in a moment is translated out of the kingdom of Satan and from the curse of sin and hell into the glorious liberty of the children of God and heirship of His everlasting kingdom. He has authority, in a moment, to arrest the sentence of judgment and condemnation, and to proclaim the guilty acquitted, justified, and joint heirs with Himself of all the hopes of the gospel.

The power of salvation is in His hands. Once, when visiting the Castle of Toulon, in France, the emperor gave to a friendly king the right to set a single prisoner free, and he accepted it as a royal compliment. The Son of God has received from the Father the right to emancipate every criminal under the sun from every curse of the law of God if he will accept His mighty clemency. Well may we rejoice in the power of Jesus—His power to save. Well may the prophet cry in wonder and admiration, "Who is this coming from Edom,/ from Bozrah, with his garments stained crimson? . . . 'It is I, speaking in righteousness,/ mighty to save' " (Isaiah 63:1).

THE HOLY SPIRIT

2. He imparts and controls the power of the Holy Spirit. The mighty spirit of Pentecost is His gift. The power that convicts of sin, of righteousness and of judgment is from Him. The power that clothed the apostles with such resistless might and divine efficiency is the power of our risen Christ, for Peter said of Him, "he has received from the Father the promised Holy Spirit and has poured out what you now see and hear. . . . Therefore let all Israel be assured of this: God has made this Jesus, whom you crucified, both Lord and Christ" (Acts 2:33, 36).

"God giveth not the Spirit by measure unto Him" (John 3:34, KJV). He has power still to awaken the most insensible soul and break the most hardened heart. It was He who struck Saul of Tarsus and broke his heart by a glance and word. It was He who convicted the rude jailer in the midnight hour. It was He who opened the heart of Lydia as the sun opens the blossoms of spring. And He still has power to draw the sinner, to melt the stony heart, to conquer the stubborn will, to sanctify the sinful soul, to consecrate the whole being to Himself.

Is there anything that we need in our own spiritual life or in our work for souls? Our glorious King has all authority in heaven and on earth to accomplish it.

AS OUR INTERCESSOR

3. He has authority to give efficacy to our prayer. He is our Great High Priest as well as King. "I knew that you always hear me" (11:42). His hands receive our imperfect supplication, cleanse them from their defects and add to them His own intercessions and the incense of His perfect offering. Then He claims them as the right of His redemption, and fulfills them by the might of His omnipotence. Therefore there is nothing too hard for Him to grant to our supplications, or too difficult for us to ask of His Almightiness, when we remember that we are presenting our requests in the very name and character of Him who has "all authority in heaven and on earth" (Matthew 28:18). "Therefore, since we have a great high priest who has gone through the heavens, Jesus the Son of God . . . Let us then approach the throne of grace with confidence" (Hebrews 4:14, 16). As we go forth in our work for God and in fulfillment, especially, of the great commission of this passage, our weapon is chiefly prayer; and in the light of this mighty manifesto, what may we not dare to claim for our own efficiency and the evangelization of the world?

IN PROVIDENCE

4. He has all authority in the realm of providence. The burning wheels of

Ezekiel's vision all move at the touch of His hand; the chariots of the vision that Zechariah saw riding through the earth and putting all its conflicts at rest, go forth at His bidding. The thrones of earth rise and fall at His command. The events of history are the outworking of His plans. The book with the seven seals is held by His hand and opened by Him alone (Revelation 5:5). It is not true, of course, that He is responsible for the wickedness and willfulness of man, but His hand is over all man's ways and His providence overrules all events.

We see this constantly in His earthly ministry and in His government of the Church in the Acts of the Apostles. How easily He could send Peter to the sea for the single fish which had the golden coin in its mouth, sufficient to meet their needs! How exactly He brought the assembled multitudes to Pentecost, at the right time, to receive the Holy Spirit, and then scattered them all over the world! How wondrously He brought together Philip and the eunuch in the desert at the right moment, and then sent the converted prince to evangelize a kingdom and a continent! How easily He could lay His hand on the life of the impious Herod, and protect the trusting Peter from his violence! How marvelously He guarded the life of Paul through perils of persecuting foes, through perils of waters and perils of every enemy, until his work for Him was accomplished!

How marvelously the Old Testament illustrates His providence! He could send the child of a Hebrew slave, doomed to death, into the house of Pharaoh, to become the child of Egypt's king, and the deliverer of Israel from the man who had sought his own life in infancy. He could lead an army of three million for 40 years through the barren wilderness, and sustain them without hunger or lack. He could send a Hebrew maiden into the house of Persia's monarch and make fair Esther the deliverer of her people. He could use Cyrus, without his understanding it, to be the restorer of Israel's scattered tribes when the 70 years were literally fulfilled, and make Daniel's captivity the occasion of his life and testimony in Babylon and the subjugation of Nebuchadnezzar and Darius at the feet of Israel's God. He could give Jeremiah courage to be fearless and faithful for 40 years, amid the perils of Jerusalem's last days, and then He could protect and guard his life, alone, of all others, in the hour of her fall and amid the massacre of her inhabitants. And He who did all this is Jesus, our Lord and Christ, with power undiminished, and only waiting for faith to claim its yet mightier victories in these last days.

What God wants today in His Church, and in His work, is not so much that the world shall see the power of the Church, as the power of her Lord and the presence of Him who goes forth with His weakest servants and becomes their might and their mighty Victor. Oh, as we go forth to evangelize the nations and to represent our God amid the mighty forces of the world's last days, let it be our supreme mission to realize and show forth the might of our anointed King, and so to stand for Him that the world can see once more that He has "all authority in heaven and on earth" (Matthew 28:18).

IN NATURE

5. He has all power over natural laws and forces. While this material world is His creation, and He does not usually mar nor interrupt the uniform movement of the forces and laws that He has framed, yet He can suspend them at will and substitute higher forces if He pleases, just as the engineer can stop the engine or reverse it at his will. And so the Lord Jesus holds in His control the elements of nature, and still can quell the storm or bid it come; can counteract the poisonous malaria or render it harmless; can vitalize these exhausted physical frames with His divine life until our "weakness [is] turned to strength" (Hebrews 11:34), and can carry and sustain us through all the difficulties and apparent impossibilities that may surround our work for Him. Let us go forth, especially in the work of missions, realizing this, that nature is subordinate to redemption, and the natural subordinate to the spiritual, and the kingdom of matter is under the control of the King of saints.

OVER MEN

6. Again, He has all authority over the minds and passions of men. He can hold back the murderer from his design or render him helpless in his attempt. Dr. Paton tells us how often the savages of Tanna assembled to take his life, and some chief was led to stand up in a critical moment, and by an unlooked-for suggestion to turn them aside from their plan, and they dispersed without hurting a hair of his head. How he had gone through armed and furious crowds of naked savages, determined to murder him, and escaped their hands, turning sometimes to them and commanding them, in the name of the God of heaven, to disperse and desist, and sometimes, seeing their muskets pointed and their spears poised, and yet in a few moments fall unused to the ground, and his life miraculously spared. Our blessed Christ has still this power in every place where His servants need His protecting presence, for He has "all authority . . . on earth" (Matthew 28:18). Kings' hearts are in His hands, and He can still say to all our foes, "Do not touch my anointed ones;/ do my prophets no harm" (1 Chronicles 16:22). He can still induce men to receive us, to accept our testimony, to help us by their influence, their means and their cooperation. It was He who gave Daniel favor with his masters in Babylon, and Joseph the confidence of his king, and Mordecai his place of power in Persia, and Paul the confidence of the Roman captain and of Caesar's household. And in every age He has shown how He can put His hand on men when He needs them, and call them in a moment to the place He means them to fill.

Oh, that we might know better and trust our Almighty King! Then would we trust less in man and care less, either for his frowns or his favor. But, moving on the might of a divine dependence, we would know that God would bring to us all men that we need for His work, and help us, by many or by few, as He sees best.

OVER THE CREATION

7. Christ has all power over the lower orders of creation. "I have given you authority," He says, "to trample on snakes and scorpions and to overcome all the power of the enemy; nothing will harm you" (Luke 10:19). He that went with Daniel into the lion's den has gone many times since then with men like Arnot into the jungles of Africa, and paralyzed the fury of the savage beasts and made them slink away abashed before the keen and fearless eye of His trusting child.

OVER SATAN

8. Christ has all power over Satan and all our spiritual foes. We are so glad of this. We meet our adversary with the assurance that he is a conquered foe in the presence of our Lord. We may well fear him in our own behalf, but as we claim the abiding presence of our Christ, he is but a toothless lion, a disarmed and humiliated foe and an empty shadow and sham. Let us not dread his power nor try to evade his fury, for he will do his worst against us, but with our Master in our midst we need not be afraid. His assaults will only end in greater victories, and in all these things "we are more than conquerors through him who loved us" (Romans 8:37). Are we not afraid sometimes, and shrink from positions where we know we shall meet the adversary's wrath? Let us no longer dishonor our Lord, but know that the places of most peril are the places of the most absolute safety.

OVER ANGELS

9. Christ has all power over angelic beings. These mighty creatures who perform the executive offices of the government of God, and through the universe with their ceaseless ministries, all go forth under the orders of our anointed King. Myriads of them crowd this earth and wait upon the saints of God, but they are all subject to our Master's orders. Occasionally the curtain parts enough for us to see the shining form of one or two as they are engaged upon their ceaseless services, but when we see them not, they are doubtless ever near. The Old Testament is full of their interpositions in human affairs, and the New has many examples of it. It was an angel that opened the Redeemer's tomb, an angel that told Mary of the resurrection, an angel opened Peter's prison and smote his persecutor, an angel stood on the tossing ship by the side of Paul and promised him deliverance. And, surely,

their ministry did not end when the great apostles passed home. Unseen by mortal eyes they have still fulfilled their loving tasks through every generation. And when each of us shall close our eyes on the last human face, we shall find some shining companion by our side gazing upon us with a look of quiet recognition and tender affection, smiling at our look of wonder, and saying to us, perhaps, "I have known you for half a century, better than your mother, your wife or dearest friend. I nursed your infancy, guarded your childhood, protected your manhood, hovered over your dying bed and now am waiting to guide your spirit home."

Who of us cannot remember some moment when we had just escaped a sudden peril, or stood within a hairbreadth of death, and as our palpitating heart recovered its pulsation, a strange heavenly hush breathed over our spirit and a voice almost seemed to whisper, "For he will command his angels concerning you/ to guard you in all your ways" (Psalm 91:11)? Samuel Rutherford tells us how, when a child, he fell into a deep well. For a long time he struggled to hold on to the slippery sides and called in vain for help, and at last began to sink. Just as he was perishing, he says, a beautiful man slipped quietly down into the well, lifted him out without a word, and left him safely on the ground above and immediately disappeared. The glorious old saint did not doubt that it was, literally, an angel of the Lord.

How often they have interposed for the visible deliverance of God's servants we cannot tell. Who knows but they come in human guise sometimes, when all other help has failed. Enough to know that when we need them they are at hand in the most lonely place, and they are all under the command of the Son of God; for it is said, "Let all God's angels worship him" (Hebrews 1:6b), and in the book of Revelation we see them going forth at His bidding to fulfill His mighty purposes in these last days.

OVER EARTHLY RULERS

10. Finally, our risen Christ is yet to have all the power of earth's kingdoms under His scepter and to be the King of kings and Lord of lords. God will overturn and overturn and overturn until He comes, whose right it is. For the kingdoms of this world must become the kingdom of our Lord and of His Christ. This is Christ's covenant right and reward, and the Father's heart will never be satisfied for His Son until His will is done on earth as it is in heaven. We shall yet see our blessed King wearing the crown of all the world, and we shall see every knee bowing to Him, and every tongue confessing He is Lord.

> He shall reign, from pole to pole,
> With illimitable sway;
> He shall reign, when like a scroll

Earth and heaven shall pass away.

SECTION II—*The Great Commission*

"Therefore go and make disciples of all nations" (Matthew 28:19a).

Because of His power, and because of His right, He bids His disciples go forth to establish His kingdom among all nations.

TO THE NATIONS

1. We must be struck, first of all, with the boldness and majesty of this command. He did not send them now simply to individuals, but to nations. He looked upon the mighty communities of earth as not too great for the conquest of His kingdom, and the mission of His followers to win. He sends us forth as ambassadors to earth's great powers and as His soldiers against the mighty hosts of humanity. The work of foreign missions ought to deal very directly not only with individuals but with nations. God has a purpose in the tribes and tongues of earth. He wants them all represented in the great triumphant song which is to echo around the throne, and we ought not to be satisfied while a nation or tongue is not evangelized. Indeed, His coming is directly connected with the evangelization of all nations, not necessarily all individuals. The Church of today ought to lift up her eyes upon the fields (John 4:35) and see how far and how faithfully she has fulfilled this commission with respect to neglected nations and unevangelized races and people. It would seem to be the special call of Christ today to each of us to see, so far as in us lies, that every community that has not yet received the gospel is specially visited with the message of our King. There are still many tribes of earth who have not received the message. There are scores in Africa and several in Asia, who have yet no part in the chorus of redemption, and were the Lord to come tomorrow, their tongue would not be heard in the great millennial psalm which shall arise at His coming, when

> All people that on earth do dwell,
> Sing to the Lord with cheerful voice.

UNIVERSAL

2. The universality of the commission is sublime. It sweeps the circumference of the world. It spreads its royal scepter over an empire more magnificent than Nebuchadnezzar claimed or Caesar saw. It reaches far beyond the narrow limits of Jewish patriotism or imperial ambition. Never was an empire so grand and universal as that which, by and by, shall join in the

chorus of coronation,

> Let every kindred, every tribe
> On this terrestrial ball,
> To Him all majesty ascribe,
> And crown Him Lord of all.

Oh, as we have already said, let each missionary burn to make the victories of the gospel as universal as the commission which He has given. May each of us have the holy aspiration to add one other tongue or one other tribe that none have reached before, to the glorious song which is soon to burst forth when the ransomed hosts from every land shall, with songs, surround the throne, and it shall indeed be true,

> Ten thousand are their tongues
> But all their hearts are one.

GO

3. The commission given is an aggressive and progressive one: "Go" (Matthew 28:19a). It does not imply by any means the idea of settling down in comfortable repose and consolidating great ecclesiastical institutions; but it is a ministry of itinerance, and we very much doubt whether any church or servant of the Lord should cease to go in this sense of aggressive and progressive work. The missionary is to go until all regions are visited and all tribes evangelized; the Church is to go until all who are at liberty have become the messengers of the gospel. In the early Church we find not only Paul and Barnabas going, but Aquila and Priscilla, working people, Gaius and Aristarchus, and many of Paul's companions constantly moving with him from place to place. Evidently they were men and women from the ordinary walk of life, who counted it their commission to share in the toils and tasks of the gospel. The time has come when the heathen world needs more than stereotyped ministers to meet its awful needs, and Christ is calling a whole army of plain and practical men and women to cover its needy fields. Good Pastor Harms long before suggested a way: namely, the missionary colony. Today in Africa and India thousands of happy native Christians are the fruit of a humble missionary movement, in which a whole parish almost moved bodily to the heathen world and settled down among them to teach them how to live as well as how to know the Lord. God grant that the next few years may put such a go in the hearts of thousands of the consecrated children of God that they cannot any longer stay at home, and a great army of picked men and women, who fear no hardship and seek no rest short of the Master's coming, shall spread over all the neglected fields of the heathen world!

EVANGELIZATION

4. The first process in this great work is denoted by the term "make disciples of all nations" (28:19). This is not "teach" (28:19, KJV), which is an incorrect translation, but rather "evangelize," that is, bring to the knowledge of Christ and the fold of Christ. It is, in a word, the work of evangelization, the quick and worldwide proclamation of the gospel in every land, with a view to gathering out all who are willing to confess the truth and follow the Savior. This is the first work of missions, and until this is done the work of costly organization and education should be held in subordination. Too little has this been the object of missionary societies and too much the building up of elaborate establishments. This was the apostolic method. In his great missionary journeys Paul swept over vast fields. In a few months he had itinerated over Cyprus, Iconium and Central Asia Minor, and then was ready to go over these fields again and establish them more formally. On his later journeys he swept with similar celerity over Syria, Cilicia, Galatia, Macedonia and Achaia in a few years, preaching the gospel in many countries and gathering multitudes to Christ. This is the world's great need today. In a single generation its entire population will have passed away, and what has to be done must be done at once.

One night, in Albert Hall in London, the royal family of England and the most distinguished men and women of the nation assembled and stood upon their feet to receive and honor Henry Stanley because he had successfully penetrated Africa and rescued a brave man from isolation and peril. Oh, what honor will heaven pay to the men and women who will penetrate these dark regions for a nobler purpose and rescue their millions from the tyranny of Satan and the curse of despair! Surely all heaven will stand up some day to receive them and the Son of God Himself will make them sit down and will serve them with His own Royal hands.

ORGANIZATION

5. The work of evangelization is to be followed by the work of organization. "Baptizing them in the name of the Father and of the Son and of the Holy Spirit" (28:19b). This is the ecclesiastical part. But there is a notable absence of all ecclesiasticism. We find no name of modern sect in this organization. The only name into which they are baptized is that of God. There must of course be organization: the public confession of Christ in baptism, the uniting of the little flock in the name of Christ and the proper discipline and government of the Church. But this should be as simple as possible, and adapted in each case to the exigencies of the case, and whatever may be the denominational form, its spirit should always be as large as the one body of Christ.

TEACHING

6. The last direction respecting this great work has reference to what we might call the edification of the Church. It includes the building up of the Church of Christ in truth and holiness; "teaching them to obey everything I have commanded you" (28:20a). This, of course, includes the deeper instruction and the higher training of the flock of Christ, and this is proper and scriptural in the Church both at home and abroad, and should be carefully provided for, that the flock may be fed, not only with milk, but with meat, and prepared for the highest Christian living and the most effective work for the Master. But it is not in the traditions of men that it is to be taught, but in the commandments of Christ—in the practical observance of His will and the duties and experiences of holy living, the one simple rule of life being "everything I have commanded you" (28:20).

Such then, is the Master's great commission; the one message which He gave on this great occasion, this most important meeting with His flock after His resurrection.

SECTION III—*This Abiding Presence*

"And surely I am with you always, to the very end of the age" (28:20b).

There is something very emphatic in the note of exclamation, "surely"! It implies that they would be likely to forget it. It is intended to call perpetual attention to it. No matter how improbable it may appear, and how many other presences may seem to crowd it out, yet lo! I am with you. Look more closely and you will see Him.

There is, also, special emphasis in the present tense, "I am with you." It might have implied a presence different from that which they now enjoyed —that there was to be a break in His abiding with them, and then a subsequent appearing. But He says, "I am with you." I shall not cease for a moment to be with you. I shall be as truly with you the moment after my ascension as I am now while I am speaking these words to you.

MARK

INTRODUCTION

THE GOSPEL OF MARK

John Mark, the second evangelist, was the son of Mary, a well-known and probably wealthy lady of Jerusalem, in whose house the early church frequently used to assemble. She was the sister of Barnabas, and the entire family seem to have belonged to the better classes of society. We read of Barnabas consecrating his wealth at the feet of the apostles. If Mary retained hers, it was to spend it for the encouragement and upbuilding of the little church and to afford a place of shelter and hospitality under her generous roof.

It was to her house that Peter came when released from prison and found the apostles gathered together. Her young son, through the influence of such associations, was probably early led to embrace cordially the principles of Christianity. There is a reference in his gospel to a certain young man who followed Jesus in his night robes in the hour of His betrayal, until seized by the guard, and then tearing himself from his pursuers, he left his night robe and fled from them naked. The name is carefully suppressed, and yet the incident is related by Mark alone of all the evangelists. It looks very much like some of John's narratives of one of the disciples whose name is not given, but it was always the writer. And it has been supposed that this was the earliest incident of Mark's acquaintance with the Lord Jesus.

We soon find him an ardent disciple, perhaps more enthusiastic than steadfast, in his first fervor. And so he accompanies Paul and Barnabas on their first missionary journey. But, discouraged by the perils of the way, he shrinks from the undertaking at length and returns from the field before the campaign is completed, losing for a time, the confidence of Paul so entirely that Paul refuses to allow him to accompany them on their next journey. Barnabas, however, his genial uncle, is more indulgent and chooses to sever his union with Paul rather than to discard altogether his young relative. He was evidently justified by the result, and Paul himself was glad before the close of his life to place on record his candid and high estimate of Mark's services and to send for him with loving entreaty to accompany him on one of his most important expeditions. In Colossians 4:10 we find him side by side with the great apostle in his prison at Rome, and a little later he is with Peter at Babylon (1 Peter 5:13). Still later he seems to have been with Timothy at Ephesus when Paul sent for him to come to Rome (2 Timothy 4:11).

To this ardent young evangelist ancient tradition has universally ascribed the second gospel. And almost as universally is his authorship linked with the name and influence of Simon Peter. This was the opinion of John as quoted by Eusebius, of Iraeneus, of Clement, of Alexander, or Tertullian, and others of the Fathers. It is strongly confirmed by many internal indications in the gospel itself, where Peter is very frequently referred to, and in a manner such as we would expect from the later spirit of this apostle when his egotism had been subdued and when he was not ashamed to give the church the most humiliating pictures of his own weakness, and a most vivid view of his Master's grace and glory. There is something about the style of Mark which seems to demand the presence of an actual spectator in the vivid pictures given of the Lord Jesus and the events of His life. If Mark himself was not an eyewitness, as he could not have been, someone must have inspired his narrative.

It seems therefore probable that he obtained facts partly from Peter and really represented his version of the Master's life under the guidance of the Holy Spirit. There is indeed, much of the bold, direct and impetuous spirit of the great apostle in the whole style and structure of the second gospel. It is probable also that Mark had the same peculiarities, the same impetuousness of spirit, the same liability to reaction, and, when finally restored and reestablished, the same consecrated force which we find in Simon Peter.

It is still an unsettled question in biblical criticism whether Matthew or Mark was first written. Many have tried to prove that Mark is but a briefer synopsis of Matthew and Luke. Others again have urged that Mark's is the original composition, and these are the amplification of his more concise narrative. It is enough to show that Mark is undoubtedly an independent witness; and that even if he wrote his gospel subsequently to the others, which is extremely doubtful, he added innumerable points both in method and matter which justify his claim to be an independent writer. It is true that most of the ground covered by his gospel is also covered by the others; and yet even where this is the case, we find a remarkable fullness and vividness of detail, a graphic and dramatic character in the picture, and yet all reasonable evidence of an eyewitness. Then there are many passages in his gospel which we do not find in the others at all. The events in Mark 1:23, 8:22, 12:41 and 7:31–37 are recorded by no other evangelist. Mark 4:26–29, 11:11–14, 14:51–52 and 16:14–20 are all peculiar to this gospel. The hypothesis which all these facts lead to is that while all the matter common to the first three evangelists is derived from the early teaching of the apostles, yet this evangelist writes as an independent witness to the truth, and not as a compiler; and that the tradition that the gospel was written under the sanction of Peter, and its matter in some degree derived from him, is made probable by the evident traces of an eyewitness in many of the narratives.

It is less Jewish than Matthew and much more Gentile and Roman. The word law does not once occur. Direct quotations from the Old Testament, except by the Lord Himself, are very infrequent. Matters of special interest to the Jews are omitted; explanations are frequently given which to the Jew would seem especially needless, such as calling Jordan a river, stating that the Pharisees were accustomed to fast, describing the Mount of Olives as over against the temple, and many such things which a Jew perfectly understood. The Jewish genealogy of the Lord is entirely omitted. Where Hebrew words are used, they are explained. Latin words are very frequent. Many classical usages are found in his style, and many other features which give it a certain cosmopolitan character and have justified somehow the distinction that while Matthew wrote for the Jew, and Luke for the Greek, Mark wrote rather for the Roman, as John's afterwards was for the saint of every nation, and the spiritual of every name.

Among the other peculiarities of the gospel may be named its brevity and conciseness, its record of deeds rather than of words, the almost military march of its pictures and incidents, the intense vividness of description, the minute and graphic touches which make it live before our minds. The present tense is almost always used rather than the past; the first person rather than the third. The word "straightway" rings like a trumpet call through most all the chapters, occurring more than 40 times. He photographs for us the very look of Jesus, and almost phonographs the tone of His voice. It is he who gives us the name of Boanerges for the two disciples, the name of Peter as given to Simon by our Lord, the name of Alpheus as the father of Levi, the name of Jairus, the Ruler of the synagogue, the trade of our Lord, a carpenter, the name of Bartimeus, the blind beggar of Jericho, the sons of Simon of Cyrene who bore His cross after Jesus, the vivid picture of the demoniac of Gadara, and many more such peculiarities which the close and profound study of the gospel reveals in almost endless variety and fullness.

According to the classification of the four gospels already given, the symbol of Mark is the ox, expressing the idea of strength and service. It is, therefore, the picture of our Lord's deeds rather than His words, and represents Him as the toiling servant, pressing through His great life-work with an intense earnestness, promptness and energy. It is therefore the gospel of work, and pictures the divine Servant, and chronicles the great campaign between earth and hell. As has been well said, "It is the history of the war of Jesus against sin and evil in the world, during the time that He dwelt as a man among men." It is thus the highest example for the Christian servant as well as the most vivid picture of the Father's chosen Servant. Its motto might well be:

> Here is my servant, whom I uphold,
>   my chosen one in whom I delight;
> I will put my Spirit on him
>   and he will bring justice to the nations.
> He will not shout or cry out,
>   or raise his voice in the streets.
> A bruised reed he will not break,
>   and a smoldering wick he will not snuff out.
> In faithfulness he will bring forth justice;
>   he will not falter or be discouraged
> till he establishes justice on earth.
>   In his law the islands will put their hope.
>   (Isaiah 42:1–4)

Like a great military leader He charges at once upon the field of action without introduction or preliminary word. He is announced by His deeds rather than His words.

Before the middle of the first chapter He is through 30 years of His life, and before the end He is in the very midst of His Galilean ministry, and by the end of the ninth chapter, He is already marching to the cross and within a few months of Calvary. The closing picture of the gospel represents Him as still working on the right hand of God as busily as ever, in partnership with His faithful disciples on earth, "the Lord worked with them and confirmed his word by the signs that accompanied it" (Mark 16:20).

DIVISIONS

The whole gospel might be divided into these sections:

1. The Forerunner and the Inauguration (1:1–13).
2. His work in Galilee (1:13–9:50).
3. His work in Perea (10:1–34).
4. His closing works and sufferings in Jerusalem (10:35–15:47).
5. The resurrection, ascension, and mediatorial work at God's right hand (16).

Instead of tracing this outline in detail, which would really lead us over much of the ground already traversed, it will be more profitable for us to look first at the distinctive portions of Mark's gospel separately, and then to gather up the lessons in the one general picture which he gives of the work of Christ, with its special lessons for us as disciples and fellow-workers.

CHAPTER 1

THE PREPARATION

The beginning of the gospel about Jesus Christ, the Son of God.
(Mark 1:1)

It is a familiar truth to Bible students that the four gospels are four distinct pictures of our Lord. The Gospel of Matthew is the gospel of the King. The Gospel of Luke is the gospel of the Son of Man, the human Christ. The Gospel of John is the gospel of the Son of God, the deity of Christ. The Gospel of Mark is quite different: the gospel of the Servant of God. "Here is my servant, whom I uphold,/ my chosen one in whom I delight" (Isaiah 42:1). It is the gospel of the toiling Christ, the pattern Worker, the Man of action rather than the Teacher. Its type is the ox—patient, toiling, suffering, standing midway between the plough and the altar, ready for either or for both.

The Gospel of Mark commences without an introduction and plunges at once into the busy field of active service. It is full of action from start to finish. Its notes ring like the call of a commander leading his victorious troops, and its pages glow with the graphic and vivid touches of a living picture. It closes with a vision of the Master still at work. "Then the disciples went out and preached everywhere, and the Lord worked with them and confirmed his word by the signs that accompanied it" (Mark 16:20) is the closing verse of the gospel. Let us turn our eyes upon this pattern Worker, the Lord Jesus Christ, and learn from Him the spirit of true service for God.

PREPARATION FOR WORK

God's work is always well prepared. It is no afterthought. It is carefully planned, wisely laid out and long looked forward to. We have here the account of the preparation of this great work which Jesus came to inaugurate and finish, "the beginning of the gospel about Jesus Christ, the Son of God" (1:1). Before we look at this subject we need to find out what the Lord's work was.

WHAT IS THE LORD'S WORK?

What is the service on which Christ came? What is the ministry that Christ commits to us? What is Christian work? What was Christ's work? We have it all here—"the gospel about Jesus Christ, the Son of God." That is the work for which He came. That is the work for which He leaves us here. That is the only work that is worth doing. Striking in this picture of work is the fact that the frontispiece is the gospel of salvation. That is our business, our trust, our occupation, to give the gospel about Jesus Christ, the Son of God, to men.

The gospel means good tidings, a word of cheer from heaven and that word about Jesus Christ, the Son of God. How simple, how beautiful, how satisfactory! Good news! Good news from heaven to suffering, sinful men that God has sent Jesus Christ, the Son of God, to settle things, to remedy things, to make things right. That is the gospel.

Christian work is not trying to save the world, or reform society. You cannot reform society, and you cannot save the world, but you can tell the world that Jesus Christ has saved it. You can proclaim the gospel of Jesus Christ. Christian work is not our busybody activities, but it is holding up Jesus and giving Him to men, and nothing else is worth a thought. Our philosophies and inquiries into nature and science are all apart from real Christian service. This is the business on which Jesus came, and from start to finish the Gospel of Mark is crammed with this and nothing else, and our lives should be full of this and nothing which does not work for this.

HOW GOD PREPARED FOR THIS GREAT WORK

First of all "it is written in Isaiah the prophet" (1:2). It was laid out, and announced, and predicted in ancient prophecy. It was no afterthought. God was thinking of it when He talked to Isaiah and to Malachi and told them to say these things; "A voice of one calling:/ 'In the desert prepare/ the way for the LORD;/ make straight in the wilderness/ a highway for our God' " (Isaiah 40:3). "Built on the foundation of the apostles and prophets, with Christ Jesus himself as the chief cornerstone" (Ephesians 2:20). The whole system of truth from Adam and Abraham down was just a portraiture of the coming Redeemer and the coming gospel. "The testimony of Jesus is the spirit of prophecy" (Revelation 19:10), and how careful He was before He left them to explain, as He opened up the Scriptures, how in the Psalms and in the Prophets all these things were written concerning Him, and "this is what is written: The Christ will suffer and rise from the dead on the third day" (Luke 24:46).

And in our Christian work we must never get away from the Scriptures. The Lord Jesus worked according to the Scriptures. His business was to fulfill everything that has been written concerning Him, and He could not die until the last prophecy had been fulfilled down to the casting of the lots for His clothes. So it is our business to fulfill everything that was written concerning us. Have you found out everything that was written concerning you? This Book was written as much about you as about Jesus Christ. You must find out what it says about you. You have no business to meet Jesus in the new revelation of the coming day until you finish the old. Have you found out what it says about you as a sinner, as a child of God, as a servant of God and a witness for Jesus, and have you worked it out? "All Scripture is God-breathed and is useful for teaching, rebuking, correcting and training in righteousness, so that the man of God may be thoroughly equipped for every good work" (2 Timothy 3:16–17).

PREPARATION OF JOHN

Next is the preparation of the herald. The messenger came in advance to announce this gospel and this greater Messenger. While John was not the great Pattern, he was a very beautiful pattern. As Christian workers we will find some splendid examples in the preparatory ministry of John the Baptist.

Look at his humility. They asked him, "Who are you?" (John 1:22), and his reply was, "I am the voice" (1:23), a voice crying in the wilderness, the message that was breathed into him from heaven. He is not an original. He does not need to think out some wonderful discovery and read up the marvels of science; but he must be a good listener and echo, catching the voice from heaven and ringing it out to the world around.

And then how he constantly hides under the shadow of the greater Servant. "After me will come one more powerful than I" (Mark 1:7). There can be no service for God without humility. God cannot use you if your shadow comes in His way. The saddest picture in the Old Testament is that withered gourd at the gates of Nineveh, and that man under its shadow who was rejected after the greatest revival in the history of the world because he wanted his own glory rather than the salvation of Nineveh. Jonah is thrown aside like his withered gourd, left a spectacle of shame and failure because he thought only about his own importance. Your own natural gifts, your spiritual experience and ministry will wither and become a positive curse if you always see yourself or think about yourself. No matter how sweetly you may sing the gospel, if you are thinking of your tones, it will amount to nothing. No matter how eloquently you may tell the story of Jesus, if you are studying your elocution or seeking the praise of your admirers, it is a failure. God save us from self-consciousness and self-importance and everything but nothingness.

The ripe ears of wheat hang down because they are ripe. The greatest apostle looked around for a name, and he took "Paul the Little." He went on diminishing until he became "less than the least of all saints and not worthy to be called an apostle" (see Ephesians 3:81; 1 Corinthians 15:9), and "the chief of sinners" (see 1 Timothy 1:15). God give us this grace of humility. Then He will use us and hide us in the shadow of His hand, and the more He uses us the more He will hide us. If we do not stay hidden, He will send the devil after us to scare us into the shadow and keep out of our own sight.

JOHN'S MESSAGE

His message to men was about sin. His call to men was "repent." No honeyed words, no silly talk about developing people by drawing out what is in them. If that is all we ever get, the Lord have mercy on us. The word "education" means to lead out, to draw out, and education without God ends where you may expect. There is no greater curse in modern civilization than culture without Christ. It is the particular peril of the present century. They tell us that just as the artist sees the angel in the marble and must chisel it out, so there is a God in every human being. It is a demi-god, a devil god. You do not get God that way. You must have Him put Himself in.

John the Baptist's work started with the recognition of the great and awful fact of sin. Jesus Christ's ministry never got away from sin. He talked gently to the woman of Samaria for a time, but He did not play with her. "Go, call your husband" (John 4:16). She knew what that meant, there were five husbands, and none was her husband. Jesus was after sin. When the woman anointed His feet with her tears, He accepted the tears and love, but He did not wink at her sins. "Her many sins" (Luke 7:47) were forgiven. When He gave us the matchless picture of the prodigal, there was no home-going to the father until the cry came, "I have sinned" (15:21). That is Christian work. Start with sin and repentance and out and out dealing with souls. John handled sin without gloves. They came to him, and his cry was, "Confess your sins," and the lightning of God struck into their consciences and revealed to them their awful peril under the wrath of God. Their one thought was to flee from the wrath to come and to get right with God. That was John's work. It was honest work, foundation work, excavating deep down and not trying to put up a flimsy building without a foundation. It is the same old fallen heart you Christian workers have to deal with. It is the same old gospel He has left to you, and it is the same old preparation that it needs still—the message of sin, the message of repentance. Give it tenderly; give it always with the blood in view; give it always depending upon the Holy Spirit; but, in God's name give it.

JOHN'S BAPTISM

What did baptism mean? Up to John's day they only baptized proselytes; no Jew was ever baptized. But a Gentile entering Judaism was baptized.

When John demanded that the children of the kingdom should go down to the bottom and start at nothing, start like the heathen started and get baptized as a confession they were not even consistent Jews and had no rights or privileges, but were lost, vile sinners—that was thorough work. That was treating human nature as it has to be treated by God—as so thoroughly worthless that there is no remedy for it but death. Baptism just means death. It is God's own type of death. The burial beneath the water and the rising afterwards set forth the fact that there was no room for self-improvement. They were so steeped in sin no cathartic would cleanse them, no chemical wash them white. They must die and be raised from the dead by regeneration. That was just what John said the new religion was going to bring. "The ax is already at the root of the trees" (Matthew 3:10). Do not talk about making yourselves right. You must be baptized into death and then resurrected into supernatural life.

Dear Christian worker, that is the foundation work of all true ministry. You must recognize men as made of that kind of material and as needing that kind of radical gospel. I know it is not popular in this humanitarian age, but He that sits in the heavens is laughing at man's new religion, and in a little while He is going to overwhelm it in ruin and shame. And that which is founded upon the rock will stand when the winds rage, and the rains come, and the floods beat and the testing day will discover whether our work is built on the rock or on the sand. I would rather have half a dozen true hearts convicted of sin, and saved by the precious blood of Christ, and regenerated by the power of the Holy Spirit, than a whole mob of modern whitewashed Christians. You are not going to get the crowd this way, but you are going to get His approval when the judgment comes.

WITNESSED TO JESUS

John pointed his followers forward to Christ. He said, "Don't look at me; don't stay with me." Even his beloved disciples, John and Andrew, left him and followed Jesus; at which time he told them, "Go, He is mightier than I. I am not worthy to unloose His shoes. He is the One, go to Him, follow Him." John's ministry pointed the people to the Savior. Let yours and mine. Do not stop with even conviction of sin because that will not save men. Man's conscience may be blasted with the lightnings of heaven, and he may cry out in the agony of Judas and yet be lost. It is Jesus who saves. It is seeing Him and trusting Him that accomplishes the real work of the gospel. The other is preparatory, but this is the essence of the gospel itself. So he pointed them to Jesus. Let us so point them. Let us know the way, and let us always be crying "Behold the Lamb of God."

You will notice here especially that John points to the One that baptized with the Holy Spirit. "After me will come one more powerful than I, the thongs of whose sandals I am not worthy to stoop down and untie. I baptize you with water, but he will baptize you with the Holy Spirit" (Mark 1:7–8). "Don't take less than that," was John's message. "My washing will not keep you clean. You will be vile and foul tomorrow after I plunge you in the Jordan. You must get a supernatural power, something I cannot bring you, the Holy Spirit to fill you, to recreate you and then to keep you. This One who is coming is to bring power, to bring God into man, to be the supernatural force in the building of character and the saving of souls."

TWO KINDS OF RELIGION

We see here two kinds of religion and two kinds of Christian work. "I indeed baptize you with water unto repentance." Get people convicted, crying out for pardon, superficially saved perhaps, the baptism of John, outward reformation perhaps, but nothing more. God keep us from uncharitableness, but I am afraid nine-tenths of the members of the churches today have gone no farther than the baptism of John. I am afraid that nine-tenths of our preachers have led their converts no farther than the remission of sins. That is not the gospel. That is the scaffolding that leads to the gospel. But the gospel is the Holy Spirit filling the hearts of saved men and changing them supernaturally, sanctifying them from the power of evil and keeping them for that great day. That is what John said was to be the characteristic of this new Teacher, that He would put God into men, the power that would change them spiritually and make them stand. O Christian workers, be sure of that. The apostles did not leave their converts till they had their Pentecost.

THE PREPARATION OF JESUS

How very solemn that even our Master had to be made meet for His work. If He had to be prepared, how are you going to do it without the same divine equipment?

He was baptized by John. "Jesus came from Nazareth in Galilee and was baptized by John in the Jordan" (1:9). That was His first preparation. He had to be baptized. Why? There was no sin in Him. There is a very deep and tender lesson here. He was baptized not because He needed it, but because we needed it. He was baptized that He might be made identical with us. He was baptized into our sin and death and resurrection. They went down in the Jordan because of their sin. He went down in the Jordan because He took sin upon Himself. In that act He identified Himself with sinful men. He went down there sharing my curse and yours, and when He came out again, His resurrection was typified in that symbol; and John could point to Him and say, "Look, the Lamb of God, who takes away the sin of the world" (John 1:29). He buried it in Jordan just as He was to bury it in the grave afterwards. Before you can help people, you must be baptized into sympathy and fellowship with the men and women you are going to save. You cannot stand up on the mountain and say, "Come up," but you must go down and share their sorrow with them. You cannot save them at arm's length. You have to be baptized into their conditions.

The missionaries in Jamaica could not get near the blacks because the blacks were slaves. They tried in vain to touch them. Then the missionaries became slaves too; they gave up their freedom, went down into slavery, and then the broken-hearted men and women understood and responded and believed, and a great and mighty work for Christ was done. When our missionaries go to China, they have to go down and love these people. They do not mind the smells of the Chinese cities; love identifies them with the people. That is what the Master did, came down to where we were and took us up to where He is, and He will keep us there forever. That is the first principle of Christian work—sympathy with those you seek to save.

As the Holy Spirit comes in deeper preparation for service, you will find some strange things in your experience. People you do not love naturally, you will learn to love. There sometimes comes to us such a sense of evil. As we pray and pray, we find Christ has put into us the need of a sinful soul, some of the curse that is destroying one dear to us. We have to pray it through, take it in our arms and bear it to His blessed feet until He withers it. He will baptize you into sympathy with the need of people and the unworthiness of people until you will be patient and long-suffering with a love that never tires. That is Christian service; that is the way He did it. Are you willing that He should thus baptize you into the conditions of a sinful world?

THE BAPTISM OF THE HOLY SPIRIT

The next thing in Christ's preparation was the baptism of the Holy Spirit. As He came out of the water, there came a second baptism. The heavens were opened, and the Holy Spirit like a dove came down and abode upon Him and remained with Him from that moment. I don't know of anything so wonderful in the life of Christ. Why did He need the Holy Spirit? Jesus was born of the Holy Spirit, but He was not baptized of the Holy Spirit. The Spirit had given Him His divine humanity, but the Spirit was not yet living with Him and in Him. But now on the banks of the Jordan, the Holy Spirit came to Him as a Person. From that moment there were two persons in the life of Jesus—the Son of God and the Spirit of God—and the two were working together all through His ministry, and He did not do a thing without the Holy Spirit. "But if I drive out demons by the Spirit of God, then the kingdom of God has come upon you" (Matthew 12:28).

Beloved worker, you must have the same baptism. You may be born of the Holy Spirit, you may have the Holy Spirit with you, you may be a real

Christian, but there is infinitely more for you. There is the coming to you of the personal Holy Spirit as He came to Jesus, so that from this day there will be two people in your life, your consecrated self and the Spirit of the living God of whom you are the temple. Until that comes you are not fit for Christian work. You will be doing your work rather than His. But when He comes, it is no longer you but the Spirit of your Father. If the Son of God needed the baptism of the Holy Spirit before He began His ministry, how dare you attempt your ministry without it?

I cannot tell you how He will come to you. I do not believe we have any business to limit His coming by any sign or method. He Himself is greater than His gifts or manifestations. It is Him you want. Accept any gifts He may be pleased to give you. Do not rest in any gift or manifestation but in Him. If you need Him, you can have Him now.

"And a voice came from heaven: 'You are my Son, whom I love; with you I am well pleased' " (Mark 1:11). Beloved, you and I must have such a vision of God, you and I must have such an acceptance with the Father, you and I must have such a consciousness of living without doubts and fears. So long as you are groping through shadows and singing

> 'Tis a point I long to know,
> Do I love the Lord or no?

you will not bring anyone to Christ. Spurgeon told his doubts to his congregation one day, and they said to him afterwards, "Don't tell us them again. We have enough of our own. We want a voice of victory from the pulpit, a leader living in the light of the Lord." O beloved, keep there, and you will draw people to Christ. Keep in the place of fellowship. Keep in the place of joy. Say to people, "My God will meet all your needs" (Philippians 4:19). It is glorious to go to people with the consciousness that you have something to recommend; it is glorious to have Him so shine in your face that they will come and say, "Take me with you to your Jesus." Keep in the sunshine of victorious joy, and you will be able to bring others where you are.

PREPARATION FOR WORK BY TEMPTATION

"At once the Spirit sent him out into the desert, and he was in the desert forty days, being tempted by Satan" (Mark 1:12–13). Strange is it not that that had to come, too? That was part of the Master's preparation for work—temptation. Luther was asked what was the first qualification for the ministry, and he answered, "Temptation." What is the second qualification? "Temptation." And what is the third qualification? And once again he answered, "Temptation." The Lord had to know what sore temptations are before He could help us. The Lord had to fight the battle alone before He could stand for you.

Beloved worker for Christ, do not think it strange concerning the fiery trial which comes to you. In my early ministry a woman came up to me and said, "Don't be discouraged. If God wants to use anybody, He puts them into a furnace seven times heated." I have always found after strange, peculiar testing someone has come along I could not have helped without it, someone on the same lone path. God sent me on ahead to blaze the way. Beloved, He will test you, but remember, it is victorious temptation that helps people. If God honors you with peculiar trials, take Him to carry you through. He went into battle with the devil for the purpose that He might come back and overcome in you.

> As surely as He overcame,
> And triumphed once for you.
> So surely we who love His name,
> Shall triumph in Him too.

As workers for God we must have this same Christ in us to give us His power for service. "I worked harder than all of them—yet not I, but the grace of God that was with me" (1 Corinthians 15:10). "To this end I labor, struggling with all his energy, which so powerfully works in me" (Colossians 1:29).

> My hands were strong in fancied strength,
> But not in power divine,
> To take up many tasks at length
> That were not His but mine.
> The Master came and touched my hands,
> And might was in His own,
> But mine since then have powerless been
> Save His were laid thereon.
> For it is only thus, said He,
> That I can work My works in thee.

CHAPTER 2

THE BEGINNING OF THE MASTER'S WORK

After John was put in prison, Jesus went into Galilee, proclaiming the good news of God. "The time has come," he said. "The kingdom of God is near. Repent and believe the good news!" (Mark 1:14–15)

The second section of the Gospel of Mark, chapter 1:14–39, describes the beginning of the Master's own work. There was a place for preparation, but now the work itself begins. There is a time to tarry, but there is also a time to go, and the Gospel of Mark is the gospel of "Go." One word rings out as a sort of keynote of the whole story. It is a Greek adverb variously translated "immediately," "forthwith," "straightway," and it emphatically expresses the strenuous side of the Master's life which is so prominent in the picture of Mark. We shall see how that strenuous spirit enters into every moment of this first chapter of His ministry.

THE TIME

The Master's first word is translated "The time has come" (1:14). This is another emphatic Greek word denoting not merely a period, but a point of time. It was a crisis moment which it was important He should not miss. And the Master was there on time as all His servants should ever seek to be. How sad it is to wake up a little too late and think what we might have said or done, but the opportunity has passed never to return. There was nothing more remarkable about Christ's life than the timeliness of everything He said or did. His words were always in season and His movements in perfect accord with the divine order and plan. When action was delayed, it was because "My time has not yet come" (John 2:4). And when action was begun, He could always say, "Father, the time has come" (17:1). So here He was beginning His ministry at the very moment for which all preceding ages had prepared.

The immediate occasion was also opportune. John had just been cast into prison by his false friend, Herod, at the instigation of his own angry paramour, and also with the hearty consent of the rulers of the Jews. Herod thought he had suppressed the strong voice that was dealing too frankly with his sins, but a mightier voice was there to take up the echo and repeat the message in weightier tones. So Jehoiakim of old thought he had destroyed the disagreeable prophetic role which Baruch brought him from Jeremiah the prophet, as he cut it into ribbons and flung it into the fire. But he found soon after that the roll which he had destroyed had risen phoenix-like from the flames clothed with new terrors to avenge his presumption and his sin. So Jesus followed John; and soon after when Herod had consummated his crime by the murder of the forerunner and learned of the miracles of Jesus, his conscience terrified him with the suggestion that John had risen from the dead and had come back again to avenge his murder. It must have been a great relief to Herod when he met Jesus at the mock trial in Jerusalem to find his fears were vain. Perhaps this explains the levity with which he treated the Lord when he found that he was mistaken in his dread, and sent Him back to Pilate with mock honor, clothed in a purple robe.

THE MESSAGE

The Master's message had in it an echo of John's gospel of repentance, but it reached a higher plane and a loftier tone. "The kingdom of God is near. Repent and believe the good news" (Mark 1:15).

"The kingdom of God" was His message. The world had had its kingdoms of men, plenty of them. Nimrod, Pharaoh, Sennacherib, Nebuchadnezzar, Cyrus, Caesar had all run their despotic course and proved how little mere kings can do for the welfare of humanity. Israel, too, had had its kings, Saul, David, Solomon, Jehoshaphat, Hezekiah, Ahab, Ahaz, alternating between the best and the worst, but all that they had done for the chosen people was to leave them subject to the oppression of their heathen masters. Jesus came to announce a new kingdom, the reign of God. This is really the distinctive feature of Christianity. All other religions are based on the principle of self help. Christianity tells humanity, "You have destroyed yourself, but in Me is your help." It is a supernatural religion. It is the revelation, the incarnation, and the indwelling of the living God in human life. Its message is "In the past God spoke to our forefathers through the prophets at many times and in various ways, but in these last days he has spoken to us by his Son" (Hebrews 1:1–2a). This was the dream of Hebrew prophets, little understood, perhaps, by their own times. Isaiah had written of the coming of Immanuel, which being interpreted is God with us, and had proclaimed from the towers of vision, " 'Here is your God!'/ See the Sovereign LORD comes with power,/ and his arm rules for him" (Isaiah 40:9b–10). But now, at last, the vision was fulfilled, and that God whom even His own people were to fail to recognize was standing in their midst. He was bringing with Him a divine revelation, for His message was "Anyone who has seen me has seen the Father" (John 14:9). He was bringing in a divine redemption through the cross and the resurrection from the dead. He was leaving behind Him a divine presence, the blessed Holy Spirit, to reside and abide in the Church and in the heart of the believer. He was bestowing a divine experience in that regeneration which means to be born from above, and that sanctification which makes us partakers of the divine nature.

He was calling His people into a divine sonship as the literal children of the living God, and He was unfolding the vision and prospect of a future life higher than the angels and enthroned with God Himself in the kingdom of glory. Surely this was the kingdom of God. Nay, more, the outcome and the issue of the gospel which He proclaimed is to be realized not only for the individual and the Church but for the world itself in that glorious age which He came to usher in when the reign of God will embrace the globe itself from pole to pole and shore to shore, and the old chorus shall reverberate from earth to heaven, "The LORD reigns, let the earth be glad" (Psalm 97:1). "The kingdom of the world has become the kingdom of our Lord and of his Christ" (Revelation 11:15). "The dwelling of God is with men, and he will live with them. They will be his people, and God himself will be with them and be their God" (21:3).

The nation perhaps had caught something of this glorious vision, but to them the ideal of the kingdom was as yet one of earthly pomp and political power. And so the Master introduces this kingdom by a message wholly unlike what their national pride had looked for. "The kingdom of God is near. Repent and believe the good news" (Mark 1:15). This kingdom was to be entered not by the portals of pride and ambition, but by the lowly gateway of penitence and moral transformation. The humbling message which John had introduced is taken up by Jesus also. It was as if he had said, "You must give up your cherished ideas of being children of the kingdom and come in as Gentiles and proselytes through the gateway of repentance and a new birth from above." The gospel of Jesus Christ abates nothing of the righteousness and the heart-searching requirements of God's ancient law. There is no easy vaulting over the barrier of righteousness and condoning the guilt of sin. The message of the gospel still is "turn to God in repentance and have faith in our Lord Jesus" (Acts 20:21).

But repentance is not the whole gospel. The man who has nothing but a negative message and a call to righteousness will never move men permanently or lift them effectually into any sort of spiritual transformation. Law and judgment never can go farther than they went in the story of ancient Israel. But that story only shows us how:

Law and terrors only harden,
All the while they work alone.

Christ's message was a positive one. It was a gospel of love, of grace, of help, of salvation, of encouragement and of confidence. Its supreme message is, *Believe the gospel.* It recognized the fact that the Fall had come in when faith went out, and that only by a return to faith could there be a return to God. The difference between faith and works is just this: works bid us try to do it ourselves; faith tells us that it is all done, and we have but to believe this, rejoice in it, and enter in.

How this new message changed the whole face of religious life. As the sinful woman heard it, how it lifted her above her despair and bade her go and sin no more. As Zacchaeus heard it, how it melted his stony heart, and enlarged his little soul, and enabled him to cry out spontaneously, "Look, Lord! Here and now I give half of my possessions to the poor" (Luke 19:8). Beloved, that is the message for us Christian workers. Never let us forget it or get away from it to the petty appeals of mere moral reform or humanitarian help. We have been entrusted with the best of news, a gospel of love, and help, and victory, and all men have to do is to believe it and spring into the glorious liberty and triumphant victory which it assures. We have not to save men, but to tell them they are saved if they will but believe it and to echo the glad tidings the world around, "He is able to save completely those who come to God through him" (Hebrews 7:25).

What is it to believe the gospel? It is a very personal, practical and powerful experience. No man can believe the gospel without being instantly and infinitely changed. I remember talking to a patient in a yellow fever hospital about his personal salvation, and his easy answer was that he believed the gospel as, of course, everybody believed in Christ. "But what do you believe?" I asked. "Why, I believe that Christ lived, and died, and was a good man, and is the only Savior." "But," I asked, "do you believe that He has saved you?" "Why, no. How can I until I know that I am saved?" "Do you believe everything this Bible says about the gospel?" "Why, yes." I turned to First John 1:9 and asked him to read, "The blood of Jesus Christ his Son cleanseth us from all sin." He read it glibly, and I asked him if he believed it. "Why, yes, of course," he said. "Do you mean to say that the blood of Jesus Christ cleanseth you from all sin?" "Why, no. I believe it could cleanse me from all sin" (KJV). "Then you do not believe what it says." After a good while the light began to break on him, that believing the gospel meant actually believing that the gospel was true for him then and there, and that and nothing else saved him. How hard it is to get people to see this point. And yet the very essence of believing the gospel is appropriating it to your own soul, and saying as Hedley Bicars said that night when on the eve of a sinful dissipation this same verse first flashed like a lightning shaft into his awakened conscience, "If that be true for me, I will live from this moment as a man that has been cleansed from all sin in the blood of Christ."

SETTING OTHERS TO WORK

One of the best ministries that any of us can render to God and our fellow men is to start other lives in useful service. And so one of the very first things the Lord did was to call His first apostles. Walking by the sea of Galilee, He found two fishing parties. The first was Simon and Andrew who were casting a net into the sea. The Master called them with a strange authority of His heart-searching voice and glance, " 'Come, follow me,' Jesus said, 'and I will make you fishers of men' " (Mark 1:17). And we are told that "At once they left their nets and followed him" (1:18).

The second party was one of no greater consequence. It consisted of James and John with their father and some hired servants. They had some property and standing. But they, too, heard His urgent call, and they left their father, their property and the hired servants, and also went after Him. The word "straightway" (KJV) occurs twice in these two pictures. There was something urgent about His call and something instant about their response. The Lord is still calling for workers. He does not call idle and unsuccessful people. But He wants men and women that are already busy in the callings of earth. The man that makes a poor fisherman will very likely be a poor preacher. And Christ calls men who have something to give up. Abraham gave up his country. Moses gave up a throne. Elisha gave up 12 yoke of oxen. What have you given up for Christ? Ask these men today if they regret their sacrifice. When all earth's honors have faded, and earth's palaces are dust, "Those who lead many to righteousness, [will shine] like the stars for ever and ever" (Daniel 12:3).

What a fine suggestion is implied in the Master's figure, "I will make you fishers of men" (Mark 1:17). Our earthly callings fit us for heavenly ministries. God wants to consecrate our worldly wisdom and make us wise to win souls. They did not learn it all at once, for He said He would teach them and make them to become fishers of men. How much of heavenly tact and spiritual discernment is implied in this fine figure. Are we letting the Master teach us the art of winning souls and catching men?

PREACHING IN THE SYNAGOGUE

Next we see the Master in the synagogue at Capernaum. "They went into Capernaum; and straightway on the sabbath day he entered into the synagogue, and taught" (1:21, KJV). Here we have another "straightway." It seems intended to emphasize the fact that the first thing He did on a Sabbath morning was to go to the synagogue. We always find the Lord Jesus honoring the Sabbath and the sanctuary, and in the ministry of the apostles we note the same example.

Our modern laxity in church going receives no sanction from the Lord and His example. There was not much, humanly speaking, to attract Him to the synagogue, but He went there to meet God, and because it was the time and place for public worship. How much we need today to emphasize this lesson. We have to look to the votaries of superstition and ignorance to see the devoutest examples of religious worship today. Our Roman Catholic neighbors may well make us ashamed. There may be much ignorance and much imperfection in their religious character, but at least they are inspired with a deep and reverent regard for the house and day of God. It is a shameful reflection upon our boasted Protestant liberty and progress that in New York City there is not church accommodation for more than one-third of the citizens, and yet the churches as a rule are not more than one-third full. The supreme idea of church attendance is not to hear an attractive preacher or a pleasing address, but to meet and worship God.

But the Lord did not go to the synagogue merely to worship, but also to witness. And so we may find work to do in helping others and winning souls. But the one feature of His testimony in the synagogue at Capernaum was that "He taught them as one who had authority, not as the teachers of the law" (1:22). What an important hint for every Christian worker! Our ministry ought to have authority. If we really are speaking and acting in the name of God, it is our privilege to feel that He is behind the message and that men are answerable to Him for the way they receive it. We ought to have such a clear-cut, God-given message that we can hold men accountable to the judgment seat of Christ for the way they receive it. There is also another sense in which every Christian worker and minister should have in a very real way a prophetic message, a message not obtained from books and scribes, but warm from the mouth of God, and fresh from the Holy Spirit. Then men will recognize that it is not we who speak, but our Father who speaks in us.

POWER OVER SATAN

But we note also in the Master's ministry at this time another element of power and authority. He is immediately confronted with a demon spirit. Whenever God works, the devil will surely oppose, and the best evidence that we are sent of God is Satan's challenge. But like Him we must be ready also to claim our victory and exercise the authority which He has given us. The Lord had met the adversary alone in the wilderness, and now He was prepared to meet him on the battlefield of public service and in contending for the souls of others. So every Christian worker must be prepared, not merely for the opposition of the human heart, but for the hate of hell and the utmost resistance of the evil one. As surely as you attempt any definite work for Christ, the enemy will try to baffle you. In seeking to bring a soul to Christ, you will find yourself confronted not only by the resistance of the human will but by the wiles of Satan; and you must know how, like David of old, to rescue your lambs from the jaws of the destroyer. If you have not already won your personal victory, you will not be of much use in trying to help others. You will find in every Christian effort you make that you will be opposed not only by the indifference, willfulness and folly of men and women, but that Satan will do everything in his power to discourage and defeat you. This is the very first thing the Christian worker must learn, that we wrestle with principalities and powers and all the hosts of hell. If you allow yourself to be discouraged by difficulties, the Lord can never make much use of you. If you expect to serve God only when everything goes nicely and the people are all like angels, you had better ask the Lord to take you to heaven at once. This is part of our commission and equipment: "I have given you authority to trample on snakes and scorpions and to overcome all the power of the enemy" (Luke 10:19).

THE MINISTRY OF HEALING

The Master's pattern ministry is not complete until He has also taught us that part of our commission is to preach "freedom for the prisoners/ and recovery of sight for the blind,/ to release the oppressed [or sick, as the word really means]" (4:18). And so as He returns from the synagogue to the house of Andrew and Simon, His work is waiting for Him. Simon's wife's mother is lying sick of a fever. They seem to expect something from Him, for they tell Him of her. We read, "He went to her, took her hand and helped her up. The fever left her and she began to wait on them" (Mark 1:31). But lest it might be thought that this healing ministry was only for a favored few, we read in the next verse, "That evening after sunset the people brought to Jesus all the sick and demon-possessed. The whole town gathered at the door, and Jesus healed many who had various diseases" (1:32–34). Here we have not only the ministry of healing in a few isolated cases, but the larger gospel of physical help and health through the name of Jesus for all who can touch Him and trust Him. Matthew tells us that He did all this in pursuance of the promise of the ancient prophet, "He took up our infirmities/ and carried our diseases" (Matthew 8:17).

As Christian workers, how dare we limit our commission to mere spiritual help? If it was necessary for Christ to fulfill Isaiah's prophecy, then it is just as necessary for Him to fulfill it in every age, if Jesus Christ is indeed "the same yesterday and today and forever" (Hebrews 13:8).

THE MINISTRY OF PRAYER

"Very early in the morning, while it was still dark, Jesus got up, left the house and went off to a solitary place, where he prayed" (Mark 1:35). Here is the secret of power for the Master and all that would be master workmen. Perhaps the night before His work had so pressed upon Him that He had little leisure for communion. But no day could be passed without much waiting upon God in such a life as His; and so the morning finds Him "while it was still dark" (1:35) in a solitary place in prayer.

How often we hear people excusing themselves from much prayer for lack of time. You have all the time the Master had. Shame on your Sabbath indolence and lazy, self-indulgent slothfulness. You have no more right to rob God of two hours on Sabbath morning than you have to rob your employer on a weekday morning. Prayer and early rising have been associated in many of the most eminent Christian lives. General Gordon used to have a card fastened on his tent every morning long before sunrise forbidding any interruption for the first two hours of every day. Little wonder that such a life made its profound impression upon his age and time. No Christian can do without much solitary prayer, but every Christian worker must literally be steeped in prayer.

AGGRESSIVE WORK

Meanwhile the crowds gathered in the early morning for more of the Master's ministry, but He could not be found. Simon, however, seems to have already learned some of the Master's ways, and so they followed and found Him in His morning watch and said unto Him, "Everyone is looking for you" (1:37). They were evidently greatly excited and delighted at His popularity. To Him it meant little. He was looking over the heads of the people to the white fields and the distant cross. He knew how much there was to do and how little time was left to do it. And so we hear the quiet, touching answer, "Let us go somewhere else—to the nearby villages—so I can preach there also. That is why I have come" (1:38). The vision of the field was before Him. The regions beyond were calling Him. It was the spirit of the great apostle. It is the spirit of every true evangelist and soul winner. There is another man to be rescued. There is greater need still unreached. "So he traveled throughout Galilee, preaching in their synagogues and driving out demons" (1:39).

What a picture we have of one day of the Master's life in these last few verses—one Sabbath day's strenuous work. Beginning with the early morning, we find Him in the synagogue teaching. Going home with Him in the afternoon we find Him ministering to the sick in the house of Simon. Far into the night He is still amid the suffering, healing and helping. Long before the dawn He is wrestling in prayer alone with God, and with the sunrise He is off again to the next towns. A writer has told us of the hundreds of towns at that time in the populous province of Galilee and how no less than nine times did the Lord on foot travel these rugged pathways of toilsome service. Once only did He ride on the little colt that bore Him to Jerusalem as the Son of David. His life was one of intense, unceasing toil and service. As we gaze at that spectacle of holy earnestness, we are reminded of the description of His last march to the cross, "As the time approached for him to be taken up to heaven, Jesus resolutely set out for Jerusalem" (Luke 9:51). "And the disciples were astonished, while those who followed were afraid" (Mark 10:32). Oh, how we fail in the light of that majestic pattern! Lord, give to each of us a life in earnest, too.

> Not many lives have we, but one,
> One, only one.
> How precious should that one life ever be,
> That narrow span.
> Day after day filled up with busy toil,
> Year after year still bringing in new spoil.

CHAPTER 3

THE MASTER WORKMAN IN RELATION TO
SICKNESS AND HEALING

(Part 1)

So he went to her, took her hand and helped her up. The fever left her and she began to wait on them. (Mark 1:31)

The development of divine healing in the Gospel of Mark is full of significance for all Christian workers, and calls for fuller consideration than the brief references in our last chapter. There appears to be a distinct order in the unfolding of this truth in the incidents related in this Gospel. With divine discernment the Lord adjusted Himself to the conditions He met and step by step prepared His hearers and disciples for the full unfolding of God's plan of mercy for the bodies and souls of men. We will find it interesting to trace these steps in the several miracles of healing recorded in the first few chapters of Mark. Each suggests a different lesson and a deeper line of truth.

THE HEALING IN THE HOUSE OF SIMON

Mark 1:31

The first case of healing occurred on the memorable Sabbath to which we have referred in a former chapter. After leaving the synagogue in Capernaum He entered the house of Simon and Andrew, and they immediately reported to Him that "Simon's mother-in-law was in bed with a fever" (1:30). The fact that they promptly told Him suggests some expectation on their part of help and healing; nor were they disappointed. "So he went to her, took her hand and helped her up. The fever left her and she began to wait on them" (1:31).

In this first case of healing, there is little special or deeper teaching. His purpose appears to be to impress upon the people the general fact that He was able and willing to minister to suffering bodies as well as to sinful souls. The parallel gospels, however, add an intimation which has special significance, following as it did the casting out of the demon in the synagogue just before. They tell us that He "rebuked the fever" (Luke 4:39). This certainly suggests more than a hint of Satanic power behind that to be rebuked. There must have been some personal agent responsible for that fever. And so we get our first suggestion here of that tremendous fact which Peter, who was virtually the author of the Gospel of Mark, at least the source of Mark's direct information, refers to in his address in the house of Cornelius, "He went around doing good and healing all who were under the power of the devil" (Acts 10:38). What a dread meaning it gives to sickness to recognize it as the hideous touch of the Wicked One. How it emphasizes the prophetic words which describe the Lord's commission, "He has sent me to proclaim freedom for the prisoners/ and recovery of sight for the blind,/ to release the oppressed [sick]" (Luke 4:18). The sick are bound by chains that have been forged in the flames of the pit. Sickness may not always be directly caused by Satan, but certainly it was in this case, and this was an ordinary fever.

Again we note the simple and striking way in which her healing is described. There were no spells or incantations or mystic rites attempted. He did not even parade His miraculous power, but in the most unostentatious way He just came and took her by the hand and lifted her up. He did not override her own individuality or make her the subject of some hypnotic power outside herself. He required her cooperation. He extended His own hand, and the touch of that hand no doubt brought supernatural strength, but it was necessary for her to meet that touch and rise by her own volition. So still we cannot expect the Lord's healing unless we meet Him in responsive and active faith. We must not fail to note that it was not until she had arisen that the fever left her. The Lord does not heal us on our back, but on our feet. The paralytic must arise and take up his bed himself. The impotent man must stretch forth his hand.

Finally, it is emphatically noted that she ministered unto them. Her healing called her to higher service. The Lord does not heal people simply to gratify their selfishness or enable them to have a good time, but to enable them, like her, to minister. This is the fatal defect in much of the new Immanuelism. It is too self-centered. People are taught that they may spend the night in pleasure, and when they find themselves exhausted, nervous or ill, they may simply turn to some process of psychotherapy and take in new life and strength, only to get up the next morning and plunge again into the world of selfishness and pleasure. It is a very sacred thing to receive the Lord's healing, and it leaves upon all its subjects the solemn charge, "You were bought at a price. Therefore honor God with your body" (1 Corinthians 6:20). The corrected reading makes that passage a very impressive message to all who have learned to count their bodies the temples of the Holy Spirit.

THE HEALING OF THE MULTITUDE

Mark 1:23–34

It might have been supposed, if nothing else had followed, that the healing in the house of Simon was a special favor shown to the Lord's immediate friends, but did not give any assurance of larger promise of help for a suffering world. A great many people are willing to believe that the Lord may occasionally heal the sick today when it is His sovereign pleasure to do so and they have some special claim on His intervention. Such persons do not recognize the privilege of healing as in any sense general or common to the house of faith. And so the Lord appears to have had a special purpose in the incident which followed later in the day, "That evening after sunset the people brought to Jesus all the sick and demon-possessed. The whole town gathered at the door, and Jesus healed many who had various diseases. He also drove out many demons" (Mark 1:32–34b). Matthew adds in his fuller account of this occurrence that He did this to fulfill the prophecy of Isaiah, "He took up our infirmities/ and carried our diseases" (Matthew 8:17). Surely we cannot mistake the profound significance of this second incident and the larger scope which it gives to the gospel of healing. It is not some extra privilege of the favored few, but it is the common heritage of the children of faith. It is based not upon special personal claims, but upon Christ and upon His great atonement, His finished work for the souls and bodies of men, the fact that He bore our sickness and carried our infirmities, and we need to carry them no more. Surely if it was necessary for Christ to fulfill the prophecy of Isaiah, then it is necessary for Him to continue to fulfill it through all the generations, or Jesus Christ is not "the same yesterday and today and forever" (Hebrews 13:8).

We are not told that He healed all the sick, but He healed many of them. It was not universal, and it was not special. He does not heal all the sick yet, but He heals without distinction or respect of persons all that are able to touch Him and take His help according to the conditions of the gospel. Oh, what a gospel of love and of help this is for a suffering world! What right have we, the ministers of Christ, to deprive men of it? What a message this story is to the Christian worker! Are we, as followers of the Master and workers together with God, giving the world the full gospel He entrusted to us, and the full purchase of His precious blood? And what a foundation it gives to faith to know we are asking and believing, not because we have had some special revelation of God's will to help and heal, but because it is our redemption right and covered by His precious blood and His all-embracing Word.

THE HEALING OF THE LEPER

Mark 1:40–45

Here we note a still further advance in the order of the Lord's teaching concerning divine healing. The very condition of this sufferer was in itself an object lesson of truth. Leprosy was God's punctuation mark in the revelation of the connection between sickness and sin. It was the stamp of moral evil on the physical frame. That diseased and dissolving body literally going through a living death and dropping into the grave piecemeal was an awful picture and parable of the spiritual death which was destroying the soul within. A little later we will find the Lord emphasizing yet more the connection between sickness and sin, but here He lets the picture speak for itself. But the great lesson of this incident has reference to the question of the Lord's will respecting our healing. This poor sufferer came as a sort of "committee of the whole" representing the human race in its suffering and need to ask one supreme question for all the ages: What is God's will about our healing? What supreme interest hangs upon the answer! It comes with the very words that our own hearts would speak if they were honest, "If you are willing, you can make me clean" (Mark 1:40). Scarcely no one doubts the Lord's power to heal, but how few really believe He is willing; and yet it is much more unworthy of us, His children, to doubt His love than it would be to doubt His power. Which of us would say to an earthly parent, I know you can help me, but I do not believe you will? How this little speech reflects the heart of humanity and the unbelief even of the child of God.

But how promptly and unmistakably the answer comes. There is no hesitation; there is no qualification; there is no ambiguity, but frank and wholehearted the answer bursts from His very heart, "I will." We can almost see the Master smiling in the face of the timid, trembling sufferer at His feet, and hear Him say, "Of course I will. How could you ever doubt it?" Beloved, this is Christ's answer, not to one suffering man, but to that great multitude for whom He stood sponsor and spokesman. It is His word to you and me through all the ages, "I am willing. . . . Be clean!" (1:41). And that great "will" is seconded by His whole life of love and compassion and blessing. When did He ever refuse to help a trusting sufferer? And how often was He grieved because their unbelief prevented them from trusting Him for more! And should anyone say, "Yes, but what is the will of the heavenly Father above?" The Lord Himself has answered that question, "Anyone who has seen me has seen the Father" (John 14:9). "My food . . . is to do the will of him who sent me and to finish his work" (4:34). The will of Jesus, the work of Jesus is the will of God forevermore.

But the will of Christ does not settle the matter. There are two wills which must meet in this great transaction, and the one is as necessary as the other, and this explains the rest of His answer, "Be clean!" (Mark 1:41). Do not let us invert the order of the words. It is not the indicative mood, but the imperative. It is not a promise or a pronouncement, but a command. Christ wills it, but the leper must will it too, The two currents must meet in contact before the electric flame can burst forth from the wires. The will of God must be answered by the will of faith before the miracle can be complete. This is one of the most profound of all the teachings of the Master's life. We see it in all His later healings. It is the missing of this which explains the failure—so-called—of divine healing in so many cases. Men and women are looking for some miracle to drop from heaven upon them, as it is said the lazy poet, Thompson, used to lie under the apple trees expecting an apple to fall into his mouth. God does not give His benefits in that easy way. Faith is a spiritual force, an actual factor in the mystic process of divine working, and it is just as essential as for the electric current to have a conducting wire along which to carry its message. Faith is an act, an exercise of the human will. It is not an emotion, a feeling, a sensation, but a volition, a choice, a hand upon the helm, setting the course of the Spirit with firm, inflexible purpose.

We have to go through two experiences in our spiritual life; first, to lay down our own will in submission to the will of God, and then to take it up again from God in harmony with His will. "God wills it and I will it," was the victorious cry of an ancient conqueror. It may have been fanaticism with him, but it is faith with us if we are acting in accordance with His Holy Word. We take because God gives. We dare to believe because God has dared to bestow. Does this solemn message speak to you? Is this the weak place in your spiritual life? Listen as He speaks to you today, "I will, will you?"

There are one or two other interesting points in this story of healing that should be briefly noticed. Mark, in his graphic way, pictures the compassion of Christ. Not coldly nor from a logical necessity does the Lord help the sufferer and meet his faith; but his whole heart is in His response. He loves to heal and save. Oh suffering one, He has watched your weary way. He has carried your sick and suffering body. He has seen your pains and privations and been touched with the feeling of your infirmities, and He will be more glad than you to lift your load and change your groans and tears to songs of deliverance. You do not need anybody to persuade Him to help you. He loves you much better than any of the helpers to whom you are looking now. You do not need to make Him willing to answer your cry. He has always been willing. All you need is to get into the attitude where you can take what He is longing to give, and respond with the strength of answering faith to the overflowing of His heart of love.

Mark also tells us He touched the leper. Nobody else would have touched him; but Christ meets us on our level. There is a physical touch in divine healing that we must learn to recognize. There is a substantial reality in the meeting of God with the human soul and body which gives added emphasis to that splendid definition of faith, "Faith is being sure of what we hope for" (Hebrews 11:1). We may know that touch, and we may meet it with that other touch of which it is forever true, "All who touched him were healed" (Mark 6:56).

THE HEALING OF THE PARALYTIC

Mark 2:1–12

Up to this time the Lord had not especially emphasized the question of sin. It appeared to be His purpose to impress upon the people His ability and willingness to help and bless, but the time had come when He must go deeper and reveal that subtle poison which was the source of all human ills and infirmities. He takes occasion in this next miracle to bring out the sin question in its most vivid colors. They had brought this sufferer to Christ for healing, and expected, no doubt, that He would immediately perform a miracle upon his body. But Christ for the present paid no attention whatever to his body, but passed right on and pressed right home to the question of sin. "Son," He said, "your sins are forgiven" (2:9). And not until this question was settled and the sufferer had accepted forgiveness and sonship did the Lord take up his physical condition and complete the work of healing. What an object lesson this is for the Christian worker! In dealing with the sick we must realize the deeper causes of their physical conditions. This question is a fatal defect in psychotherapy or Immanuelism. Moral and spiritual conditions are ignored, and even faith is regarded as of importance merely as a physical force, and faith is just as good in a Hindu as in a Christian, in believing a lie as in believing on the Son of God. It is not the truth believed that explains its power, but it is the pure psychical force which faith adds to the case. Not so did the Lord deal with men. He was far more anxious to get them right than to get them healed. Let us as Christian workers follow closely in His footsteps and always recognize divine healing as a moral and spiritual ministry.

Again the Lord emphasizes in this healing the place of personal faith. Many people seem to think that the Lord healed this man because his four pallbearers brought him in the arms of faith. The Lord did nothing of the kind. He proceeded to instruct him to save him; and when he got him to the place where the man could himself believe, then the Lord challenged his own faith and said, "Get up, take your mat and walk" (2:9). A paralytic would not be likely to do that unless he had very real and adequate faith. The Lord does not heal people over the head of their unbelief. He loves them too well for that. But He first teaches them to trust Him for themselves, and then He gives them all they trust Him for. As Christian workers it is a great mistake for us to tell people we are believing for them and they are surely going to be healed. We have no right to let anybody lean over on us.

Wiser far was the word of Elisha when he refused to go to Naaman the Syrian and satisfy his superstition by a number of passes and outward manifestations, but rather sent him to go and wash in the Jordan himself seven times and he should be clean. It was thus that Paul dealt with sickness. As he preached the gospel at Lystra, he looked upon his little congregation, and we are told that another paralytic was sitting there. And Paul "looked directly at him, saw that he had faith to be healed and called out, 'Stand up on your feet!' " (Acts 14:9b–10a). The best thing we can do for people is not to get them to trust in us, but to trust in the living God.

THE MAN WITH THE WITHERED HAND

Mark 3:1–5

The next chapter leads us over this ground again and a little farther on. In the case of this man we see the same insistence on the part of Christ that he was himself to actively take hold of the Lord's help and healing. "Stretch out your hand" (Mark 3:5) was the Lord's command. How could a man with a withered hand stretch it out? He could choose to do it. The stretch could begin inside, and that is where all life and power begins. Faith is but the embryo of fact, the stardust out of which worlds are formed, the pollen lightly falling on the air which matures into the bud, the blossom and the fruit. And the Lord was there to follow the first outreaching of his faith and quicken it into victorious power and clothe it with new muscles and healthy flesh and restored functions and organism in his physical frame. We cannot stretch a paralyzed arm, but we can choose to do it, and the Lord can make our purpose real and good.

The special added truth lying back of this miracle is the relation of this healing to the Sabbath. It was a test case. They were watching to see whether He would heal on the Sabbath day, and He deliberately, and we might almost say defiantly, went on and finished His work of love in the very teeth of His scowling enemies. Why did they question His healing on the Sabbath day? The reason is a profound one and touches the whole question of physical healing. They regarded healing as a purely secular matter. It belonged to the workaday week and not to the holy Sabbath. It was remanded to the province of material and secular life. That is just where medical science places it today. It is a profession, a trade, a mere material thing. The body has ceased to be the handiwork of the Creator and become a machine at the bidding of science and skill. Here divine healing takes radical and bold issue with this present evil age. The body is not a mere material organism. The body is the temple of the Holy Spirit, a member of Christ and an embryo of the glory of the resurrection. Matter is not sinful or unholy, but is as sacred as spirit. God demands our bodies as well as our spirits. He has redeemed them. He has honored them by His own incarnation. He has destined them by His Holy Spirit's presence, and He regards their healing as a sacred matter, a part of our heritage of faith. We do not go to the Lord for healing merely because we want help, but because we are jealous of any hand but His touching the sacred vessel which He has been pleased to call His own. Therefore the Lord brought healing into the Sabbath day and brought the Sabbath day into the very heart of the Christian economy as the best of days, the day of which He said, "The Son of Man is Lord even of the Sabbath" (2:28).

CHAPTER 4

THE MASTER WORKMAN IN RELATION TO
SICKNESS AND HEALING

(Part 2)

There remain for consideration four other miracles of healing by the Lord Jesus in the Gospel of Mark, which will be found to enlarge yet more the scope of the Master's teaching with respect to the gospel of healing still committed to our hands.

THE LIVING AND LIFE-GIVING TOUCH

Mark 5:25–34

The graphic story of the woman who pressed through the crowd until she touched the hem of His garment and instantly drew from Him life for her immediate and perfect healing, has one preeminent message for us as Christian workers and subjects of the Lord's healing power and blessing, namely, the necessity on our part of that living faith which will give to us personal contact with the living Christ.

The Lord had already hinted in His striking message to the leper that a distinct responsibility rested upon the sufferer in receiving the healing which He was willing to give. There it was expressed as an act of will through which the leper was commanded to meet the Lord's will and take what was so freely given.

Here it is represented under the figure of a touch. There is no human sense more delicate and distinct in its manifold offices than the sense of touch. The grasp of a responsive hand means more than words could possibly express. The kiss of affection between still more intimate friends has always been the expression of the deepest love. The hand of the worshiper upon the head of his sacrifice identified him with his offering. The hand of the healer upon the sufferer was always the token of the Master's imparted life and blessing. Our word "contagion" simply expresses the power of contact in communicating malign influences and physical disease. In the material world and mechanical realm the meeting of two currents through the contact of the communicating wires completes the electric circuit and illuminates the darkness and turns on the power. In persons deprived of their ordinary senses, as the blind and deaf, the sense of touch becomes intensely acute. In our spiritual nature there are senses that correspond to all our physical powers, and there is a touch of faith and even of feeling which opens the channels of communication between God and our responsive being. Faith is much more than an intellectual assent to certain truths. It is also a recognizing of the divine presence and a contact with the personal life of the Lord Jesus. The apostle, speaking to the Athenians, refers to humanity even in its native blindness as seeking the Lord if they "would seek him and perhaps reach out for him and find him, though he is not far from each one of us" (Acts 17:27). And the Apostle John, speaking of fellowship with the Lord Jesus, the Living One, uses this realistic language, "which we have seen with our eyes, which we have looked at and our hands have touched—this we proclaim concerning the Word of life" (1 John 1:1). Even in the Old Testament experience of believers we find such saints as David distinctly recognizing the supernatural presence of Jehovah and using such language as this, "My soul clings to you;/ your right hand upholds me" (Psalm 63:8). There is probably in every human heart to some extent an instinctive reaching out after God. But when the Holy Spirit quickens into spiritual life and vivifies all the senses of our higher nature, then Christ becomes to us indeed, "a living, bright reality."

This woman had already that spiritual instinct that felt its way to Jesus. Something in the depths of her being told her that He had the help she needed, and that if she could but touch Him, her faith and need could draw it out and claim it for her healing. This was not a matter wholly dependent on the will of the Lord and the exercise of His voluntary help. The moment she touched Him, He was conscious instantly that virtue, or as the Greek express it, "dynamite," had gone out from Him. The Lord was so full of redundant life that He was ready to communicate it through every open channel. Like the sun in yonder heavens that does not need to put forth a special effort to reach a dark alley and a lonely chamber, but necessarily enters wherever there is an open window, so the Lord Jesus was always giving, and the moment hungry and believing hearts came within His influence they drew from His fullness all they had capacity to take. He is still the same, "on the giving hand," as a happy, stereotyped phrase so often expresses it,

> You do not need at mercy's gate,
> To knock, and weep, and watch, and wait,

> For mercy's gate is open free,
> And Christ has waited long for thee.

But there must be capacity to take. There must be a power to touch. In the science of wireless telegraphy the instruments at the receiving end must be turned up to the same pitch as those at the other end. Our faith must be in tune with God, and when it is, there is no limit to the blessing we may claim. Therefore God is always saying to us, "Open wide your mouth and I will fill it" (81:10). "Whoever wishes, let him take the free gift of the water of life" (Revelation 22:17). "He who doubts . . . that man should not think he will receive anything from the Lord" (James 1:6–7).

This is true salvation, the receiving of the Holy Spirit, and the communication of every blessing. But it is especially true in connection with divine healing. It is not enough to believe that Christ is able to heal you, nor even that He is willing to heal you, nor even that He is going to heal you. You must go farther, or rather you must come nearer. You must recognize the Healer Himself as present; and you must reach out through all the darkness and the pain and the conflict of doubt and fear until you touch Him and are conscious that somewhere in that viewless space there is a living presence, there is a loving heart, there is a mighty force that is pouring itself into every vessel of your need and continuing to pour itself as long as the contact is maintained. For it is not enough to touch Him once and then detach yourself and attempt to live an independent and self-constituted life. The secret of permanent healing and strength is to continue to live in dependence upon Him, physically as well as spiritually. It was a great physical truth that the apostle expressed when he said, "For in him we live and move and have our being" (Acts 17:28). It was the same truth the Master more profoundly expressed when He said, "Whoever eats my flesh and drinks my blood remains in me" (John 6:56). "Remain in me, and I will remain in you. . . . apart from me you can do nothing" (15:4–5).

I remember in one of my former congregations a little woman of the most ordinary type whom I had often visited, but had never been able to touch a single string of sympathy, response or life in her cold, dead nature. At one time, however, I found on calling that she was absent and she remained away for many months. On her return I called again and was surprised to find that the woman was transformed. Her face was radiant with animation and almost beautiful in its new expression of sympathy and intensity. I asked her what had happened, and she told me of the terrible trial through which she had gone in which health, life, home and everything were at stake, but nothing was left her but God. Then for the first time she learned to pray, and in her own simple, graphic way, she said, "At last I prayed and prayed and prayed until I actually touched Him." There was no mistaking the expression of her countenance as she used the words. The contact was still there and the power was still on. And then she told how the wondrous deliverance had come, and all her circumstances had changed, and all her trials had gone. But greatest of all was the change in herself, for God was now more real to her than either joy or sorrow or earthly friend or foe. Oh, beloved, that is the trouble with you. You have not touched Him.

There are many other minor lights and shades in this beautiful picture, most of which we must pass by. It has been observed by thoughtful expositors that what this woman touched was the hem of His garment. The border of the Rabbi's robe was called the phylactery. It was a fringe chiefly made up of quotations from the Word of God. It would seem as if God was intimating to us that the way to touch Him first at least is through His Word. You cannot see His face; you cannot feel the physical contact of your outstretched hands, but you can claim His promise and know that the Promisor is true and near, and it shall be your joy to know

> But warm, sweet, tender, even yet
>   A present help is He;
> And faith has yet its Olivet,
>   And love its Galilee.

> The healing of His seamless dress
>   Is by our beds of pain;
> We touch Him in life's throng and press,
>   And we are whole again.

It should be added (and it is a point of no little importance), that this woman's healing was but a prelude to a greater blessing. The Lord would not let her off with a mere outward touch, but insisted on bringing her into the inner chamber of His love and blessing. And when with trembling lips and prostrate form she fell at His feet and told her story, almost asking forgiveness for her boldness, He met her with the reassuring words and double blessing, "Daughter, your faith has healed you. Go in peace and be freed from your suffering" (Mark 5:34). A few chapters before it was, "Son," now it is "Daughter." Contact with Christ lifts us into the family of God. The touch of a king can make a royal knight, but the touch of Jesus makes us the sons and daughters of the Lord God Almighty. How often divine healing becomes, as in the case of this woman, the steppingstone to greater blessing. How many of us have found in it the introduction to a closer fellowship with God, and the key to all the chambers of faith, and prayer, and power, and heavenly blessing.

THE DEAF MUTE OF DECAPOLIS

Mark 7:23–27

This miracle is peculiar to Mark, and the record of it is in keeping with the graphic pictorial style of the writer. We will also find in this example some special additional lessons. The first is suggested by the statement that when they brought this sufferer to the Master and besought Him to put His hand upon him, He did not do so immediately, but "took him aside, away from the crowd" (7:33). Christ never performed miracles as spectacles for the gaping crowd, nor does He do it yet. The men that want to parade divine healing as a spectacular attraction belong to another world than that of the lowly Nazarene. He knew full well that the eyes of the multitude could only distract this man and hinder his faith. And still, before He can do much for us, He has to take us aside from the multitude. You must get alone with the Lord. There is so much danger of leaning on other people and looking to other people. Some of them have been healed and you are trying to get the experience that way. Some of them have not been healed, and the devil is using their failure to discourage your faith. We are too anxious to get our blessings in congregations and assemblies and meetings. The Lord's best work is done when you and He meet face to face and alone.

The next thing He did was to endeavor to reach this man's spirit through his senses. He put His fingers into his ears, where his physical infirmity was chiefly seated, and then He took a little of His own saliva and touched the tongue of the deaf mute. He was speaking to him in signs, and so He still uses a few outward signs as steppingstones to our faith. Anointing with oil in the name of the Lord is not a means in a medical sense; it is simply an outward sign to suggest through the senses more vividly the spiritual reality which it signifies. The same is true of the Lord's supper and baptism. It is a symbol, and the Lord addresses us through every vehicle which can convey to us His thought and His touch.

Then He added another sign of singular beauty and impressiveness. Looking up to heaven He sighed. This flashlight picture is worthy to stand beside the immortal words of John, "Jesus wept" (John 11:35). It speaks more than volumes could express, and no one yet perhaps has sounded the full depths of that heavenward "sigh." Was it an involuntary expression of His own intense sadness, with this spectacle of human infirmity and the great world of sufferers who seemed to stand behind him in the circle of the Master's vision; or was it an object lesson to the helpless and undeveloped soul before Him, intended to teach him how he could reach out even in his helplessness to the help that was waiting for him above?

On another occasion the Lord breathed upon them and said, "Receive the

Holy Spirit" (20:22). It would seem that the Lord was showing them how to receive the Holy Spirit by a deep inbreathing of God. So here He seemed to say to this speechless, impotent being, "You cannot pray in words; you have no voice to speak; but you have eyes, and you can look up to heaven, and you have lungs and lips, and you can breathe out your inarticulate cry, and that is prayer." And doubtless the man responded and lifted up his eyes and reached out as well as he was able to with the wordless cry of his necessity.

How finely one of our classic hymns has expressed this beautiful conception:

> Prayer is the burden of a sigh,
>   The falling of a tear,
> The upward glancing of an eye,
>   When none but God is near.

The impression of this miracle on the community was intense. The Lord modestly tried to keep it quiet, but "the more he did so, the more they kept talking about it. People were overwhelmed with amazement. 'He has done everything well,' they said. 'He even makes the deaf hear and the mute speak'" (Mark 7:36b–37). Oh, Christian workers, can you say that your work is well done? Can you accept the Master's "Well done" in all its fullness until you too have sighed like Him for human sorrow and helped, like Him, to dry its tears and heal its sickness?

THE BLIND MAN OF BETHSAIDA

Mark 8:22–26

This miracle is also peculiar to Mark, and its beautiful message is worth the whole gospel. The first lesson is a more emphatic repetition of the teaching of our last subject. "He took the blind man by the hand and led him outside the village" (8:23). There we noticed that He took the deaf mute aside from the multitude, but here we see something more deliberate and prolonged. He not only withdrew from the crowd, but from the town. It was not a momentary retirement, but it was a long continued walk; and surely it suggests that as they walked they talked. What would we not give to know the details of that conversation! The Lord saw that this man was wholly unprepared for the blessing he was seeking. There was something preliminary to his healing—spiritual preparation. The Lord was teaching us through him that the sick and suffering nature has to be put to school with God and to be led into those deeper experiences which will fit them to know and touch the Lord and afterwards abide in Him. Wise workers will always be patient, careful and thorough in the instruction of those that are seeking for help. It is so natural for human beings to want to be relieved, and then to forget the lesson of their trial when the pressure is removed, that God insists on letting them learn their lesson well. If we are wise workers, we will do likewise and always be patient, careful and thorough in the instruction of those that are seeking for help.

Then we must not fail to notice that the Lord Himself led the man out of the town. He did not hand him over to Simon Peter or some other Christian worker. He took the case in hand Himself. He went into the inquiry meeting. Still He is willing to take infinite pains and patience with us. No man can bring healing to you. No man can prepare you for divine healing but the Lord. Until you have been alone with Jesus, you cannot know Him well enough even to touch Him for the experience of healing. This is why He has compelled you to let many things go and to go aside yourself where He can reach your ear and speak to your heart. It is an old story: "I am now going to allure her;/ I will lead her into the desert/ and speak tenderly to her" (Hosea 2:14).

Once more we have another significant lesson in connection with the successive stages in the healing of this sufferer. After the Lord had touched him the first time, He asked him if he saw aught. "He looked up and said, 'I see people; they look like trees walking around' " (Mark 8:24). Now the division of this miracle into two sections has a peculiar significance. We remember that the critics of the Lord's miracles have sometimes said that a mere miracle of physical healing would not enable a blind man to see immediately, at least to see straight; for, as they correctly say, even after the perfect restoration of the organs of sight the man would still be like a child utterly inexperienced in the use of his eyes and unable to see things in their right relations and proportions. It is well known that to a child the moon appears as close as the adjoining chair. It reaches out its little hands to touch it, and only by long experience does it learn to know the difference between the near and the distant. It is said by science that the organs of vision alone reproduce the image of the object seen wrong side up as an ordinary telescope does, and then a mental operation is needed to correct this impression and give us properly adjusted sight. Now in this case the Lord divided His miracle into two sections. The first part appears to have been the physical correction of his distorted sight, the second, the correction of the mental impression. After the first touch he saw things, but they appeared to be confused and wrong side up—"men as trees walking." After the second touch the operation was complete, and he looked up and "saw everything clearly" (8:25).

Was this intended to show to a doubting world that the Lord understood their thoughts afar off and that His miracles took into consideration all conditions both mental, spiritual and physical? For us, however, the chief lesson is that the Lord's healings are not now in every case immediate and complete any more than during His earthly ministry, but they are often gradual and in successive stages. He has much to teach us, and He cannot teach it all at once. The words here employed in the beautiful original suggest that the second time this man looked up he looked with a steadier eye and unwavering vision. The first time he was looking at men, and men sometimes do look very strange to us when we are trying to trust the Lord. The second time the Lord made him look up first, and then he could see every man clearly. The blessings of the Lord are not supplied on the principle of our modern quick lunch counters. The best things come to us slowly, and as we are fully prepared to receive them. Let us be willing to wait upon the Lord and follow Him step by step as He leads us by the hand and prepares us for the unfolding of all the stages of blessing which He has "prepared for those who love him" (1 Corinthians 2:9).

CHAPTER 5

THE MASTER WORKMAN IN RELATION TO SIN

I have not come to call the righteous, but sinners. (Mark 2:17)

Our attention has been directed already to the attitude of the Lord Jesus towards sickness. In the beginning of His ministry He simply dealt with sickness from the standpoint of compassion, emphasizing no moral idea and requiring no moral conditions. His object appeared to be, first of all, to impress upon the minds and hearts of the people His power over physical suffering and His willingness to help and heal.

But we soon find Him pressing closer to the heart of things and bringing to the consciousness and consciences of men the deeper causes that lie back of physical suffering. One of these causes, Satanic power, had already been hinted at when, in healing Simon's wife's mother, He rebuked the fever and so cast out the demon spirit which caused it. In the next case of healing there was implied, if not expressed, a still closer connection between sin and sickness.

Leprosy was the especial brand of sin upon the body, and, above all other diseases, marked the intimate connection between a corrupt nature and a corrupting body. The cleansing of the leper in the Old Testament was a significant type of the cleansing of the soul from sin, and the very word used by the sufferer in this case to express his idea of healing implies his need of cleansing, "if you are willing, you can make me clean" (Mark 1:40). It is not, however, until the next miracle of healing, the paralytic (2:1–12), that the Master brings out explicitly and emphatically the doctrine of sin and its relation not only to healing but to His whole work and ministry. This object lesson of the paralytic is followed immediately by His calling as one of His disciples and apostles a man who was notoriously identified with publicans and sinners, Levi, and His allowing Himself to be associated with these classes openly and notoriously at the feast which Levi gave to the Master and his own associates. Finally, the Lord followed His remarkable action by the statement of our text which was intended to be His official and emphatic pronouncement of His attitude henceforth and forever toward lost and sinful men, "I have not come to call the righteous, but sinners" (2:17).

THE STORY OF THE PARALYTIC AND ITS LESSON ABOUT SIN

The first thing we learn from this story is that the question of sin is fundamental in all Christian ministry. Any gospel that begins and ends with mere physical healing, social reform or human philanthropy falls short of the gospel of Jesus Christ. The radical need of our fallen race is far deeper than all the apparent conditions of ignorance, misery and disease. The poison of sin is the fountain of all woes. If we would give real and lasting hope to our fellow men we must start there. There is no use trying to get people healed when the canker of evil is festering in their spiritual and moral nature. The new Immanuelism merely mocks the awful condition of our sin-cursed race. Its fatal defect is the attempt to encourage people to obtain healing from the Lord without any radical rectifying of their hearts and lives. When the heart is wrong, there can be no possible contact with the healing life of the holy Christ; and it is doubtful if mere healing would be a blessing if it only strengthened and encouraged men and women to go still deeper into sin. The Lord lets sickness come, no doubt, in many instances, to restrain people from greater wrong doing, and He is not likely to take it away until the moral cause is honestly met. This man was brought by his friends to Christ for healing, and most people seem to have concluded that the Lord healed him because of their faith. The fact is the Lord paid no attention at first to his physical need, but immediately pressed home His heart-searching probe to the moral center of his being, and insisted on beginning with the question of sin. No doubt He saw in the paralyzed and powerless condition of this body the perfect type of the diseased and helpless soul behind it, and at once prescribed the supreme remedy of forgiveness and salvation. "Son," He exclaimed, "your sins are forgiven" (2:5). The wise worker will always start where Christ did and aim to get people right before he tries to get them well.

Next we see God's remedy for sin, divine forgiveness through the Lord Jesus Christ. Here for the first time the Master claims the right and power to forgive sins. It was this that shocked the Scribes who were looking on and made them question, "Why does this fellow talk like that? He's blaspheming! Who can forgive sins but God alone?" (2:7). We need not wonder at their startled questionings. Their reasoning was correct, but their conclusion was wrong. They were justified in saying "Who can forgive sins but God alone?" (2:7) but they failed to finish the argument, "therefore this must be God." It was indeed a bold and startling announcement, and He was not slow to follow it up with the explicit statement, "The Son of Man has authority on earth to forgive sins" (2:10). The time had not yet come to unfold that wondrous plan of redemption through which this power was gained, the blood of Calvary and the great redemption. It was enough at present to announce the fact, and in this fact sin meets its remedy and love finds its message of glad tidings for a lost and ruined world. Christ has power to forgive sins. Christ has power on earth to forgive sins. We need not wait till the answer comes back from heaven to know whether we may be forgiven, but the throne of grace is ever open, and no soul can be too lost and no sin can be too great for us to say to discouraged and perishing men, "He is able to save completely" (Hebrews 7:25).

But we have not yet grasped the full meaning of this gospel until we note one point more, that the proclamation it makes to sinful men is not merely that they may be forgiven, but that the forgiveness is already actually provided, purchased, pronounced and laid at their feet waiting their immediate acceptance. Christ did not say to this man, "You may be forgiven," but "your sins are forgiven" (Mark 2:5). The very word brought actual forgiveness and all that the sinner needed was to consent, and it became an everlasting and unchangeable fact. The gospel we preach to men is not a piece of information we are reporting, as a journalist might relate the latest news. It is an official and authoritative message from the throne, carrying with it an actual change of condition the moment it is received and accepted. It is like the verdict of the jury or the sentence of the judge, not merely a matter of words, but words that mean deeds and decide conditions for weal or woe with the force of an authoritative decree. This was what the apostle meant when he declared, "I am not ashamed of the gospel, because it is the power of God for the salvation of everyone who believes" (Romans 1:16).

Brethren, do we realize as Christian workers and ministers of the gospel that we have the God-given right to go to men and carry to them not only some words of encouragement and hope about their future life if they will try to do better, but an actual and authoritative message of immediate and eternal salvation this very moment, and that all that is necessary to make it final is their endorsement, their acceptance, their confession of Christ as their Savior? Not only has the purchase been completed on Calvary, but the papers have been completed at the throne, and the title deeds are here ready for your name to be inserted, only you must write and endorse it with your own hand. In this double sense it is indeed a finished salvation and this moment I have the right to offer to every man and woman to whom this message comes instant and eternal salvation through the simple fact of your turning from sin and accepting the gift of God, eternal life through Jesus Christ our Lord.

This was what the apostle meant when he dared to utter that bold announcement, "If you confess with your mouth, 'Jesus is Lord,' and believe in your heart that God raised him from the dead, you will be saved. For it is with your heart that you believe and are justified, and it is with your mouth that you confess and are saved" (10:9–10). This is Christ's message about sin. This is our gospel to sinful men. This is the finished work not only of man's salvation, but, my brother or sister, of your salvation. All that is needed is that you shall ratify it.

We must not fail to notice the immediate effect of forgiveness in raising this poor, helpless sinner to a new place in the scale of being and the family of God. All the words of Jesus are tried words, and there is not a monosyllable that we can afford to miss. Have you noticed the way in which He addressed this poor sinner? "Son," He says, "your sins are forgiven" (Mark 2:5). What a transformation! A moment ago a sinner, a sufferer, a sick and sinking soul, now a son of God, a child of heaven, an heir of glory. Salvation brings us into a new circle and a heavenly standing, and henceforth there is nothing too hard or too high for us to ask of Him whom we have learned to call Abba, Father.

Now we see the connection, the bearing of all this on the healing of this man. Before this transformation he had no claim on Christ for healing or anything. But now he is a child of God, and his healing is a birthright blessing which he may boldly claim. He has been raised to a plane where he no longer needs four men to carry him, but he can rise up with his own faith, and carry himself and his bed, too. And so the Lord adds, as though it were a matter of course involving little effort now, "Which is easier: to say to a paralytic, 'Your sins are forgiven,' or to say, 'Get up, take your mat and walk' " (2:9). After forgiveness everything else is easy. And so He turns to the sufferer with a second command, "Get up, take your mat and go home" (2:11). Forgiveness brings faith, and faith brings both spiritual and physical strength. Instead of trying to get people helped through our hypnotic power, how much better to help them get in personal touch with the power of Jesus, and then all the resources of His power and grace are at their command.

There is a further suggestion here that the modern ministry would do well to heed. " 'That you may know that the Son of Man has authority on earth to forgive sins. . . .' He said to the paralytic, 'I tell you, get up, take your mat and go home' " (2:10–11).

How is the world to know in this age what it needed to know in the first age of Christianity, that we have in our midst a supernatural and almighty Christ whose hands are able to control our eternal destinies; how can it be made convincing and convicting to men without the continued manifestation of the healing power of that Christ who is the same yesterday, and today and forever? It is all very well to say the evidences of Christianity have been already settled, and the story can be read in the pages of Church history. But what does the blind and ignorant pagan know about the pages of

Church history? Why should we deny him the evidence which the Lord gave in the first ages of Christianity? There is no doubt that the supernatural operations of the Holy Spirit were intended for the very thing the apostle himself declares in Hebrews 2:4, "God also testified to it by signs, wonders and various miracles, and gifts of the Holy Spirit distributed according to his will." Nothing but unbelief can hinder us from claiming and proclaiming our full heritage of power and blessing.

THE CALLING OF LEVI

The Lord chooses His workers on the principle of adaptation. Sinners must be reached through saved sinners. A man who never has had much experience or contact with sin loses to that degree contact with the men that need salvation. And so the Lord called Levi that through Levi He might reach Levi's friends, that large and outcast class known in the Master's lifetime as publicans and sinners. Levi was an official of the hated Roman government, and his business was to collect tribute from the Jews. It was difficult even for an honest man to hold the respect of the community in such a position, and a bad name is very likely to lead to a bad life. Publicans or tax collectors, therefore, as a rule, had about the same reputation as Tammany officials and ward politicians, and it is probable that most of them lived up to their reputation, or lived down to it. They represented, perhaps, the most hopeless form of vice and sin, not the grosser indulgences so much as the hard spirit of graft and avarice. Nothing so closes the human soul to everything divine as the love of money. We find the Lord reaching some men of this class of whom Zacchaeus was the most prominent type in the Gospels. And the Lord wanted a representative of this class in the apostolic company, and how well His choice met expectation needs no other proof than the simple fact that this converted publican became the writer of the first Gospel, and the leading messenger of Christ to the ages to come.

We find, therefore, that the Lord has been pleased to call many of His choicest workers from the lowest depths and slums of sin. John Newton, Jerry McAuley, John Bunyan, Gipsy Smith—these are some of the honored followers of Levi, the son of Alphaeus, in the ranks of soul-winners. If it has been your sad lot to deeply fall and greatly sin, at least you may have this compensation, that it opens to you a ministry and gives to you a touch with your fellow men which no one else could have. May it be your glorious recompense to be avenged, like Samson on the Philistines, by turning the weapons that Satan used so well against you for the rescue of others and the defeat of him who once defeated you. And, oh, if this appeal might reach someone who is still in the ranks of sin, what nobler motive could appeal to you than the thought that the Lord needs you far more than some of His less erring children, and that your very shame and wrong may become elements of influence and power when turned to account through a transformed life for the service of God and the help of your fellow men. Oh, that you, like Levi, would not only turn at His call and follow the Master, but bring with you as he did a great circle of publicans and sinners!

Does it not seem very strange that Levi should so promptly respond to the Master's call, and give up his alluring gains to follow in the path of self-denial, poverty and loss in which the Master led the way? Does it not seem strange that Levi's associates and friends should be willing to meet such an One as Jesus of Nazareth, the prophet of Galilee, and spend an evening with Him around the social table? Would such people be likely to invite one of our starched modern preachers to a social function? How are we to explain it?

Well, first of all, we little understand the human heart if we imagine there is not some lingering chord, in the most lost and hopeless men and women, that is quick to respond to the voice of God and the love of heaven. The Lord had no harsh word for publicans and sinners, but the very lightnings of His displeasure blazed upon the heads of self-righteous, hard-hearted scribes and Pharisees. Many and many a time the prodigal would gladly return if there was but a voice to call and a hand held out to help him to his Father's feet. The most cheering fields of Christian work, the soil that renders quickest returns and largest harvests is not found in Fifth Avenue's fashionable churches but in Water Street and Mulberry Bend.

But there was another reason. The Christ who went to that supper in the house of Levi was not one of your conventional preachers, but a simple, unconventional, unaffected Man whose very presence and manner drew the little children to His arms and led the sin-stained woman to creep through the crowd and pour her tears of contrition on His blessed feet. Oh, to have that simplicity and approachableness which will win the world for Jesus!

Much of the Lord's work was unconventional. He did not save men through great sermons and in crowded congregations. The woman of Samaria met Him at the countryside on a tiresome journey and through asking for a cup of water. Zacchaeus was saved up a sycamore tree. The dying thief found a way to heaven from a malefactor's cross. The woman found mercy at the dinner table of Simon the Pharisee. Oh, that we might be always on duty for Christ and in touch with men and women for His work.

CHRIST'S ATTITUDE TOWARD SINNERS

The incident in the house of Levi led to a bitter controversy and the harsh criticism of the scribes and Pharisees. They said "Why does he eat with tax collectors and 'sinners'?" (Mark 2:16). As the stroke of Moses' rod brought out the waters from the rock, so the sharp blow of human hate always met some revelation of the Master's love and grace. We thank the Pharisees for giving occasion for this immortal sentence, "It is not the healthy who need a

doctor, but the sick. I have not come to call the righteous, but sinners"
(2:17). What an awful gulf this word creates between human self-righteousness, self-complacency and pride, and the Lord Jesus Christ and His gospel!
The story is told in an ancient Hebrew legend, as an addition to the parable
of the Pharisee and publican, that the Pharisee also prayed. "Lord grant that
in the day of judgment I shall be far removed from this publican." The following night an angel stood beside his bed and announced, "Thy prayer is
heard. In the day of judgment this publican shall stand by the Master's side,
and thou shalt stand afar off."

We can choose our place. If we are self-satisfied, the Lord will let us alone
to await the issue of the testing day. He can do without you if you have no
need of Him. But if you are a poor, erring, helpless, discouraged soul, to you
is the word of this salvation sent. This Christ is your Christ. This gospel is
your charter of deliverance, liberty and salvation. Perhaps no better definition was ever given of the best way to come to Christ than this: simply take
the sinner's place and claim the sinner's salvation. Oh, men and women who
are far from God, from happiness, from hope, from satisfying even your own
standards and ambitions, listen to this gentle voice, listen to this heavenly
call. This is your Friend, your Deliverer, your Christ. He has come all the
way to you. He takes His stand on your level. He "who had no sin" has been
"made . . . to be sin" for you (2 Corinthians 5:21). He asks no question
about your past. He will never upbraid you with your sin. All He asks is that
you leave it and leave it to Him to settle for you and that you let Him love
you, forgive you, cleanse you, keep you and help you to do to others as He
has done to you.

CHAPTER 6

THE MASTER WORKMAN AND THE
POWER OF SATAN

They saw the man who had been possessed by the legion of demons,
sitting there, dressed and in his right mind. (Mark 5:15)

As we have already pointed out in a previous chapter, the Christian
worker is called to deal not merely with depraved human nature but with
the powers of hell. Therefore, the Lord Jesus, our great Example, appears in
this story of service in constant and victorious conflict with Satanic power.
One of the first pictures in this graphic panorama is the temptation in the
wilderness, where the Lord Jesus met the devil alone and defeated him in
single combat, and then went forth to renew the battle on a wider field for
the deliverance of captive men and women. Immediately afterwards we read
the story of the first of these battles in the synagogue of Capernaum (Mark
1:23). There we find Him challenging the unclean spirit, who had recognized the Lord in the public assembly, and driving him out with such
authority and power that the spectators were amazed, and "they asked each
other, 'What is this? A new teaching—and with authority! He even gives orders to evil spirits and they obey him' " (1:27).

And now in the fifth chapter of Mark the conflict is renewed again, and
the incident gathers about it the most intense dramatic force and interest
and reveals to us a flood of lurid light concerning the malign powers of the
demon world, and the awful forces with which we have to contend in our
ministry in the Master's name.

THE DEMONIAC

What an awful picture we have here of the wreck of a human life and of
the power of Satan! The first dark shade in the picture is the dwelling of the
demoniac among the tombs. How it suggests to us the close connection be-

tween sin, Satan and death. How dreary, how dark, and how hopeless is the atmosphere of evil! Sin is indeed a living death, and the sinner is always dwelling in the valley and shadow of death. "For the wages of sin is death, but the gift of God is eternal life in Christ Jesus our Lord" (Romans 6:23).

Next we notice the fearful power of evil in a human subject. When possessed by the evil spirit no force could restrain this man. "No one could bind him any more, not even with a chain. For he had often been chained hand and foot, but he tore the chains apart and broke the irons on his feet. No one was strong enough to subdue him" (Mark 5:3–4). The world is beginning to learn that power is not a matter of physical organism. A live wire is mightier than 100 men. Spirit force may be either good or evil, but surely if the power of Satan could so augment the natural energy of one human frame, the power of the Holy Spirit can much more endue a weak and suffering body with health and energy for life and service. This was the source of Samson's supernatural strength. It was the moving of the Spirit of God in the frame of an ordinary man that made him mightier than multitudes of armed men.

Again we note the awful tendency of evil to self-destruction. "Night and day among the tombs and in the hills he would cry out and cut himself with stones" (5:5). This was a little section of hell let loose on earth to give us a glimpse of the world of darkness and despair. He that has ever seen that awful spectacle of wrecked humanity furnished by an insane asylum cannot fail to realize the reality and the fearfulness of the work of sin and Satan, and flee from the wrath to come. It is not only in the insane asylum that the devil shows his work. The streets and saloons and sometimes the desolate homes of our own city and country are full of parallel scenes. The drunkard is a specimen of the work of Satan and of the possession of evil spirits as real and terrible, if not quite as helpless, as the Gerasene demoniac. Oh, if men would only realize when they begin to play with the fires of drink that they have started on the downgrade that leads to a world from whence there can be no return and where there can be no hope, they would shrink back with horror from the awful peril.

We see in this man a strange contradiction. There were two men in that one human form. One was the spirit of the demon which answered back to Christ, recognizing Him as the Lord who had supreme authority even over the evil spirits and adjuring His mercy and indulgence. And the other was the spirit of the man himself, cowed and crushed and yet not wholly suppressed, but instinctively feeling that his only hope and help were to be found in Jesus and, in spite of the power within him leading him to run, throw himself at the feet of Jesus and worship Him. There are two men in every drunkard and every sinner. The one is the strong will of Satan, but the other is that mighty thing with which God has endowed every human being—his own will, the power of choosing or refusing. You may be swayed and controlled by the spirit of evil, but you are not obliged as yet to obey it implicitly and forever. You have not the power to throw it off, but you have the power to cry out against it and to ask deliverance of One who is able to overcome it and set you free. This man could not cast out the demon that raged within him, but he could flee to the feet of Jesus and throw himself upon His mercy. Oh, that your lingering power of choice would lead you likewise not to try to save yourself, not to fight against your tempter and tyrant, but to go to Christ and ask Him to set you free. Let us remember this as Christian workers. There is something in every man, no matter how lost, that may be wrought into a link that will bind him to the Savior. Let us not deceive ourselves or our fellow beings with anything less than God's supreme remedy for sin. Let us bring men to Jesus and we will find that even the most lost and helpless has something in him that will respond to that call and recognize the Master's voice.

THE DEMON POWER

What a fearful glimpse we get in this story of the myriads of those principalities and powers that have been cast down from heaven to work in the children of disobedience. In this single man there was an army of evil spirits, as much as a Roman legion, numbering several thousand persons. What vast capacity there must be in a human soul when it is able to offer a satisfying home to such powerful and numerous spirits! What a picture it gives us of the supremacy of man above nature and creation. When these demons entered into the herd of swine, although there were 2,000 of them, they were not able to stand the pressure which one human being had endured for years, and, driven mad by the awful sensation produced through the entrance of the demons, they rushed headlong into the sea and were immediately destroyed.

And what a dark and desolate conception the cry of these demons gives us of their dreadful existence. They besought the Lord that He would not send them out of the country. In a parallel gospel they are represented as beseeching Him that He would not send them into the abyss. This word represents that dark abode where the evil spirits are kept in prison. They would rather dwell in the bodies of filthy and unclean swine than be reincarcerated in their dismal dungeons. The powers of evil seem to have a plenary indulgence to visit this fallen world and find temporary respite in the souls and bodies of men. They are no doubt able so to unite themselves with our human nature that they can enjoy our conscious pleasure and share the gross and sensual lusts, appetites and passions of the men whom they control. It is not the sinner's own spirit that is made happy with a temporary thrill of sinful passion, but it is a demon within him that is drinking up his life and quaffing the cup of sensuality once more before he returns to the devouring flames and everlasting burnings. This and this alone explains the awful depths of human weakness and the fierce and fearful passions which sometimes break loose in the worst of men and fill the world with horror.

It is very obviously suggested here that the ferocity of the lower animals may be inspired to a great extent by evil spirits. The serpent, the lion, the tiger and the vulture are but embodiments for the time of fiercer natures and more awful forces. "We know that the whole creation has been groaning as in the pains of childbirth" (Romans 8:22) since the fall of man. The creatures that yielded to Adam's dominion have now been turned loose on humanity under Satan's control, and when once more Satan shall be driven out of this world and bound with chains in the bottomless pit, again it shall be true,

> The wolf will live with the lamb,
>   the leopard will lie down with the goat,
> the calf and the lion and the yearling together;
>   and a little child will lead them.
> The cow will feed with the bear,
>   their young will lie down together,
>   and the lion will eat straw like the ox.
> The infant will play near the hole of the cobra,
>   and the young child put his hand into the viper's nest.
> They will neither harm nor destroy
>   on all my holy mountain.
>   (Isaiah 11:6-9a)

THE DELIVERER

The evil spirits recognize without question the authority of the Master and they instantly obey His supreme command, "Come out of this man, you evil spirit!" (Mark 5:8). Fellow worker, have you understood the Master Workman's words to you, "I have given you authority to trample on snakes and scorpions and to overcome all the power of the enemy: nothing will harm you" (Luke 10:19)? Have you recognized this authority, and are you going forth in the Master's name not merely to instruct and counsel and plead with men to live better lives, but to bring them the message of victory and power and bid them rise up and claim their deliverance as in the days of old?

How simple and sublime is the next picture. "When they came to Jesus, they saw the man who had been possessed by the legion of demons, sitting there, dressed and in his right mind" (Mark 5:15). The wretched being that had ranged the mountains and the tombs, naked and mutilated, is now sitting down like a quiet child at the feet of Jesus, clothed with decency and modesty, looking up with a rational, intelligent and peaceful face. And so vast was the transformation that we do not wonder "they were afraid" (5:15). We do not need to go back to Gerasa to see this picture to repeat it. How often it has filled our hearts with joy and wonder! How many of those who are reading these lines have themselves furnished the materials for both pictures! How Jesus can tame the savage breast, can refine the coarse and brutal nature, and can transform the victim of passion, cruelty and lust into a life of sweetness and gentleness, love and holy usefulness! The gospel has no nobler evidences of its divinity than these triumphs of grace in the lives of the profligate, the harlot and the savage. Oh, let us accept them! Let us multiply them until the wildernesses of sin shall blossom as the rose.

THE REDEEMED ONE

> As Jesus was getting into the boat, the man who had been demon-possessed begged to go with him. Jesus did not let him, but said, "Go home to your family and tell them how much the Lord had done for you, and how he has had mercy on you." So the man went away and began to tell in the Decapolis how much Jesus had done for him. And all the people were amazed. (5:18–20)

We can all sympathize with the longing of this new convert to be with Jesus. It is the old, old story of a soul in its earliest love. Thank God, we can still be with Him even though we may not go on the boat with Him. The Lord knew that this man would be stronger to be at once thrown upon his own feet and sent back to his own people. The new convert will get a great deal more out of his testimony than anybody else. You can be with Jesus still, not as a weak and suckling infant fed with a spoon and petted by a lot of sentimental women, but as a robust man stepping out in faith and telling the story to others of what He has done for you. This man needed no very elaborate pulpit or letter of introduction. His own personality was sufficient advertisement. The Lord knew how often the children had to run at his approach, and his own family had rushed in to lock the doors against him; and when he came back the same man, but not the same, to tell of the wondrous stranger who had set him free, the Lord Jesus had a press agent a good deal better than our modern newspapers. We do not wonder that when Jesus came back through this great and populous region a little later, the people crowded around Him by tens of thousands to hear with their own ears the story of His love and power. It was the country of Decapolis, which means, "the 10 cities." It was full of people who formed a kind of link between the

Jew and the Gentile world. It was new territory, and it brought a mighty harvest. Oh, saved men and women, are you doing your best to make known to others the Savior you have found? Christian workers, are you wisely following the Master's example and getting saved men and women busy for their own sake and the world's sake in witnessing for Jesus?

THE WORLD'S HATE

The picture closes with a very sinister touch, a very dark and ugly shade. It was not long till the herdsmen of that flock of swine went back to their masters and told them of the tragedy which had destroyed so much valuable property, and also of the man that had been saved. What a lifelike picture it is! They took no interest in the story of the saved man, but they were greatly stirred at the loss of their hogs, and with a sarcastic touch Mark adds, "Then the people began to plead with Jesus to leave their region" (5:17). This was too expensive a religion for these people. Was it not rather a hard and questionable thing for the Lord to destroy so much valuable property? In answering this it is enough to remember that they had no business having swine. It was contrary to the Hebrew law to raise them and to eat them, and to ask anybody else to eat them. It was a righteous judgment on these men and probably they knew it. They were much more willing to give up the Lord than the world, and they asked Him if He would not please excuse them; and He did. He answered their prayer. He left them to their swine and those awful powers which no doubt soon found a place of refuge in the hearts of the men who had turned out the Master. We can have our choice. If you want to reject Christ, you may. If you want to crucify Him, you can now; but another day is coming soon, and what then? Which shall it be, your Savior or your swine?

CHAPTER 7

SIDE ISSUES AND ESSENTIALS

No one sews a patch of unshrunk cloth on an old garment. If he does, the new piece will pull away from the old, making the tear worse. And no one pours new wine into old wineskins. If he does, the wine will burst the skins, and both the wine and the wineskins will be ruined. No, he pours new wine into new wineskins. (Mark 2:21–22)

This striking double figure, drawn by Christ from the simple customs of everyday life in the East, suggests a world of wisdom in connection with the Master's work and ours. The Lord was introducing new principles and teachings into old and outworn forms and systems. He was dealing with men that had long grown into conventional ideas and methods of religious work and worship until they had lost the vital principle in the shell of form and ceremony, and to them religion consisted mainly in traditional observances and ceremonial acts. They were clinging to the old husk of Judaism and wholly losing the living kernel of spiritual truth and life which it had enclosed. Christ came to plant this vital seed and develop a new and nobler life which would throw off the old husk and blossom into a harvest of glory and blessing. With the keenest jealousy for all their cherished traditions and conventions they looked with suspicion and anger on what they deemed a daring and dangerous innovation and a new theology. This conflict, therefore, was bound to come; it had now reached its first acute and critical stage, bringing out on their part a storm of criticism and hostility, and on His part a series of bold, profound and far-reaching principles, covering the whole question of what is essential in Christianity and what constitutes a lot of side issues.

THE QUESTION OF FASTING

The first of these questions which they raised relates to the place of fasting in the Christian system. It would seem as if they had in mind the last inci-

dent to which our attention has been called in this Gospel, the feast that followed the calling of Levi, and the presence of the Master at that social
gathering of publicans and sinners. It had evidently struck them not only as
bad form on His part, as a Jewish rabbi, to mingle so freely with disreputable
characters, but particularly out of place that He should be present at such a
function. They were as much shocked as if one of us ministers should be
found at a theater some evening. This was the more emphatic because it
would seem that the disciples of John were at the same time observing a special fast on account of their master's having just been cast into prison by
Herod. It was as if these saintly people had said, "Did you ever hear anything like this? Here are John's poor disciples and we religious Pharisees fasting. And there is this new rabbi feasting with a lot of disreputable people."
Of course it all seemed very shocking, and they no doubt thought they were
honest in their indignant criticism.

The Master replies by taking up the question of fasting, so far as His disciples are concerned, and answering it by one of those profound and far-
reaching illustrations which seem to ignore the point at issue and yet
illuminate the whole subject in its remotest bearings. He does not condemn
fasting or even discountenance it in its true place. He even takes it for
granted that there are times when His followers should fast, and He seems to
imply that it was most natural and seemly that John's disciples should fast
when their master was gone, even as His disciples should fast when the
Bridegroom should be taken away. The reference here appears to be to the
dark and sorrowful days immediately following the crucifixion when the disciples mourned and wept for their absent Lord.

But what the Lord does discountenance is fasting for fasting's sake. Their
boast was, like the Pharisees, "I fast twice a week" (Luke 18:12). It was done
like a meritorious duty, as an enforced infliction of suffering, that was expected to give the Lord special pleasure, and add to their accumulated credit
in the books of heaven. All this God had already frequently reproved by the
ancient prophets. Any good work loses its value when it is done for effect.
And the idea that we can make God happy by being miserable is repugnant
at once to Christianity and common sense. It is the old spirit of asceticism of
which the apostle says, "Such regulations indeed have an appearance of wisdom, with their self-imposed worship, their false humility and their harsh
treatment of the body, but they lack any value in restraining sensual indulgence" (Colossians 2:23). Some people still always seem to be sailing in what
navigators call the doldrums and seem to consider it the highest achievement
of sainthood to enjoy bad health and have a miserable time.

All this the Lord Jesus repudiates as foreign to the true spirit of the gospel.
By a very striking and really scriptural figure, He lights up the whole question as He asks, "How can the guests of the bridegroom fast while he is with

them?" (Mark 2:19). This metaphor recalls the beautiful message of Hosea to God's ancient people, where Jehovah represents Himself as the Bridegroom of His people, and declares, "I will betroth you to me forever" (Hosea 2:19).

By the use of this figure, Christ really identifies Himself with the Jehovah of ancient prophecy. Indeed, John the Baptist had already identified Him in his striking proclamation, "The friend who attends the bridegroom waits and listens for him, and is full of joy when he hears the bridegroom's voice" (John 3:29). The Lord Jesus thus assumes what the ancient prophet and forerunner had predicted of Him, and takes the place of the Bridegroom of His people. If you were invited to a wedding, you would not put on mourning, especially if you yourself were the bride. And so away with the idea that the depth of piety is to be measured by the length of our countenance. "Let the people of Zion be glad in their King" (Psalm 149:2).

Christian life should be a happy honeymoon. Even here we have the place of the betrothed bride and we are looking and hastening unto the marriage of the Lamb.

There are times when the burden of the Lord will rest upon us and the Spirit will make intercession within us with groanings which cannot be uttered, but even then we should be able to say with Paul, "Now I rejoice in what was suffered for you, and I fill up in my flesh what is still lacking in regard to Christ's afflictions for the sake of his body, which is the church" (Colossians 1:24). And there are times when the brimming cup of bitter sorrow will be pressed to our burning lips, even by the Father's hand. But that is the time when most of all we need to "Rejoice in the Lord" (Philippians 4:4), and even to "also rejoice in our sufferings" (Romans 5:3).

The sanctimonious severity of Pharisaism has been crystallized too much into modern conventional religion. The grim story is told of a happy black sister who was struck with a flash of heavenly lightning in a very conservative and proper, fashionable church. Without ceremony and without the consent of the authorities, she began shouting and praising the Lord. The solemn sexton hastened to her side and ordered her to hush and keep quiet. "Oh," she said, "I've got religion. I've got religion." Raising his finger and looking sternly at her, he replied in a solemn voice, "Hush, woman, this is no place for religion. This is a church."

THE OLD AND THE NEW

The Lord follows His special message on fasting by the two striking figures of our text, which not only apply to the subject of fasting, but to the whole range of Christian life as it relates on the one side to outward form and law, and on the other, to the deeper principles of spontaneous life and love. The figures themselves are particularly fine. The new cloth sewed on the old garment literally means undressed cloth, cloth not yet fulled, as the draper would call it. Should such a piece of undressed cloth be sewn upon an old garment, the action of the heat, the dampness and the hard usage of the wearer would cause it to shrink and tear the old cloth to which it was attached and make a worse tear than before. In like manner the bottles used in the Orient were made of skin, not glass. And these skins when new were elastic and susceptible of stretching with the fermentation of the wine and expansion of its volume. The wineskin grew as the wine swelled and there was no rupture. But new wine put into old skins would have no allowance for stretching, and the result would be the rending of the wineskins and the loss of both wineskin and wine. And so the Lord teaches that it is impracticable to try to combine things that are not essentially adjustable to each other. The result will be failure and disaster. This principle is of very wide and varied application.

Primarily no doubt He had reference to the old ceremonial system of Moses which could not be carried intact into Christianity, but must yield its nonessential points to the larger life and liberty of the gospel. The story of this transition is told us in the Acts of the Apostles, and we see there how the conservative party tried to cling to the old for its own sake, and how God gradually adjusted the church to her new conditions and the simplicity and freedom of the life of the Spirit, and the love and liberty of the gospel.

The same struggle still goes on when people try to hold on to old forms, habits and methods of worship and work which are not in themselves essential. I remember terrific struggles in my early experience as a minister in the church to which I belonged, on the grave question of using an organ or simply praising God with the human voice, the question of using the Psalms of David in the old harsh version of Rousse or daring to introduce modern hymns and tunes, of the frequency and order of observing the Lord's Supper, and many other things that are simply nonessentials. There is no sacredness in antiquity. There is not always wisdom in old age. Nature adjusts herself with perpetual rejuvenation to the ever-changing seasons. Of all this the apostle well says, "These things are all destined to perish with use, because they are based on human commands and teachings" (Colossians 2:22), "the reality, however, is found in Christ" (2:17b).

Our text might be applied also to the uselessness of trying to get people to produce the fruits of the Spirit while they still are in the flesh and have unregenerate hearts. One is reminded of a Polynesian grave with a coconut tree growing above it and constantly covered with fruit tied on with strings for the supply of the wants of the departed friend in the other world. A good many Christian lives are like this tree. Their fruit is all tied on with strings, and there is a dead man at the root. How wisely and truly the Master used to reiterate, "Make a tree good and its fruit will be good, or make a tree bad and its fruit will be bad, for a tree is recognized by its fruit" (Matthew 12:33). Mere discipline, legislation and example will not make things right. God's remedy is a new garment, a new bottle, a new heart, a divine transformation, a life that springs spontaneous from within and, like the lilies, grows without trying.

This text also touches a very practical question which is always coming up among Christian workers and in our modern church life. How shall we regulate the social amusements of our Christian people? Is it possible to do this by arbitrary rules and church discipline? Or, in other words, by the works of the law? Experience has not proved it so.

The better way is that adopted by a Christian minister who announced a special sermon on "Religious Amusements." He did not mention dancing, card-playing or theater-going, but simply expounded three principles which should govern the conduct of every follower of the Lord Jesus Christ. First, will this glorify Christ? And can I take Him with me to this place and in this pleasure? "Whether you eat or drink or whatever you do, do it all for the glory of God" (1 Corinthians 10:31). "Apart from me you can do nothing" (John 15:5b). Second, is this expedient? Whether right or wrong for me, is it going to do harm to somebody else, and encourage a weak brother or sister to do at his risk what I can do with perfect safety? "All food is clean, but it is wrong for a man to eat anything that causes someone else to stumble" (Romans 14:20). "Make up your mind not to put any stumbling block or obstacle in your brother's way" (14:13). "It is better not to eat meat or drink wine or to do anything else that will cause your brother to fall" (14:21). Third, am I under the power of this thing? Is it becoming a controlling habit and necessity in my life? Is it mastering my freedom and my conscience? " 'Everything is permissible for me'—but I will not be mastered by anything" (1 Corinthians 6:12b).

After the address referred to, a good many of the young people of the church decided without any pressure that in the light of these three principles, or at least of one or the other of them, they were no longer at liberty to go to the theater, to attend the races, to play cards, to dance and to indulge in promiscuous worldly amusements. It was the operation of a principle rather than the application of a rule.

THE SABBATH QUESTION

This was destined to become one of the most burning questions of all the Master's ministry. Of course the passing of Judaism and the gradual introduction of the Christian Sabbath has greatly lessened the acuteness of this issue in our day, but it is not without its bearings still in our practical work as ministers and teachers.

At the very outset our text suggests an explicit answer to an increasing school of Sabbatarians who are trying in the present day to impose the Sabbath law of the ancient Hebrews upon the Church of Christ, and are teaching many honest but mistaken followers that we are disobedient to God when we fail to observe the seventh day of the week as the Sabbath. This surely is an attempt to put new cloth on old garments and new wine in old bottles and to project the shadow of Mt. Sinai upon the glorious sunlight of the gospel age. Let us note, in the Master's answer to these critics, a number of important points.

First, the Lord did not revoke or discountenance the Sabbath as an institution, but adopted it and incorporated it into the Christian system by declaring that the Son of Man is Lord of the Sabbath.

Second, the Lord gave the Sabbath a much wider scope, an older sacredness than a mere Jewish institution. "The Sabbath," He said, "was made for man" (Mark 2:27). He is looking back to the creation Sabbath to which also the fourth commandment looks back when it says, "Remember the Sabbath day" (Exodus 20:8). As one has finely said, "The Sabbath was a higher mountain peak than Sinai, the mountain of the law." For a time, it is true, the clouds of Sinai gathered about it and hid its ancient glory. But they have now passed and the Sabbath still stands in its primeval authority and blessedness as made for man and not for Israel or any transitory age.

Third, the Master assumes the right to regulate the Sabbath and legislate for it. If the Son of Man is Lord of the Sabbath, He is entitled to settle every question regarding it. And if He lays down certain principles respecting its observance in the spirit of liberty and love, and if He even changes the day of its observance in the spirit of liberty and love, He is only doing that which belongs to Him as Lord of the Sabbath, and His example and Word are our sufficient warrant for the New Testament Sabbath of the first day.

Certain principles and directions He does give practically reenacting the Sabbath for the Christian age with a glorious Magna Charta of liberty and love. The supreme features of His teaching respecting the Christian Sabbath are liberty and love, or liberty limited and regulated by love. The law of Christ is the law of love. We are not to do things because they have to be done, but because they are best to be done, they are necessary to be done and their doing is to help somebody. Even under the Old Testament, He shows them that there were times when the law of necessity justified David in doing things which were forbidden by the letter of the law, but necessary for the preservation of himself and his comrades. Here the law of love triumphed over the law of tradition and enactment. Then He appeals, as we find in the parallel Gospels, to the principle of humanity and asks what man would not, on the Sabbath, break the Sabbath law regarding manual labor to rescue his ox or his ass, especially if it was his own ox or ass. There is a fine suggestion here of their own selfishness which would settle all questions of conscience quickly if their own property was in danger, Sabbath or no Sabbath. And then He argues by inexorable logic, how much more valuable a man is than an ox or an ass or a sheep, and how reasonable it is even to infringe the letter of the Sabbath law to help and heal a suffering human being.

They are utterly unable to meet the calm, keen logic of His argument and only look on with ill-suppressed hate and anger, while He proceeds to demonstrate what He had just taught, by bidding the man with the withered hand stand forth in their midst on the Sabbath day. He looks into their silent faces and demands, " 'Which is lawful on the Sabbath: to do good or to do evil, to save life or to kill?' . . . He looked around at them in anger and, deeply distressed at their stubborn hearts, said to the man, 'Stretch out your hand.' He stretched it out, and his hand was completely restored" (Mark 3:4–5).

The sequel only shows how vain it is to try to teach a prejudiced and angry spirit, for "Then the Pharisees went out and began to plot with the Herodians how they might kill Jesus" (3:6). They were so distorted morally and mentally that, while they fully recognized His power to heal and all it must have meant as to His divine character, they put before all this their own theological prejudices and their own willful bigotry, and as the margin expresses it, yielded themselves up to hardness of heart. It was exactly the same thing to which their wickedness ripened later when they fully recognized His miraculous power and supernatural character after the raising of Lazarus from the dead, but in spite of light and conviction, coolly went forward and planned for His destruction. It only shows to what fearful lengths religious bigotry and theological obstinacy may go. May the Lord save us from the letter of the law and give us the spirit of love.

Returning for a moment to the Sabbath law, the happy medium of Christian practice would seem to be, not the loose and godless disregard of God's holy day, which is bringing such perilous conditions into the Church and society today, but a sacred regard for God's day which shall be controlled by the spirit of love and lead us to treat the Sabbath as we would treat the best room in our houses; not bringing into it the rubbish of the workshop, but making it a gathering place for the family circle and the service of the Lord. We should invariably connect the Sabbath and the sanctuary, and always observe it by habitual and reverent attendance at the house of God. We should avoid all our ordinary secular occupations, and such reading, letter writing, visiting and social enjoyment as are not distinctly of a more sacred character. It is not a proper day to finish up your belated correspondence, unless your letters are written with special reference to the service of God and the help of souls. It certainly is not a day to read the secular newspapers and fill your mind with all the rubbish and rottenness of this vile world. As to the use of public conveyances, it is proper to use them for the service of God to facilitate your attendance at church and your varied Christian ministries, but you have no right to use them for mere diversion and amusement. In other words, the principle of Sabbath observance is separation and dedication, the lifting of this holy day to a higher plane than other days, making it the day of God, and finding it the vestibule of heaven. Those who spend their Sabbaths thus will have cause like a good old saint to say, "If this be not heaven, it surely must be the way to heaven."

CHAPTER 8

THE FIRST APOSTLES AND THE NEW SOCIETY OF THE CHURCH OF GOD

Jesus went up on a mountainside and called to him those he wanted, and they came to him. He appointed twelve—designating them apostles—that they might be with him and that he might send them out to preach and to have authority to drive out demons. (Mark 3:13–15)

Whoever does God's will is my brother and sister and mother. (3:35)

These words introduce us to the first chapter in Church history. The Lord was founding a new society. It was already apparent, through the strife of tongues that had arisen concerning Him among the religious leaders, that His final rejection by His own people was a foregone conclusion, and that a new Israel must ultimately take the place of the old. And so, as there had been 12 tribes of Israel, there should be 12 apostles of the Lamb. We have here the account of their first calling. They were to be the princes of the kingdom of heaven, the first tier of stones in that eternal edifice built upon the foundation of the apostles and prophets, Jesus Christ Himself to be the chief Cornerstone.

The time had not yet come for the formal institution of the Church in so many explicit terms; but as the new harvest grows out of the shell of the old seed, so Christianity was emerging from the husks of Judaism, and the Lord had already anticipated it and was preparing for it. It was necessary that His first apostolic messengers should be thoroughly educated and trained under His personal supervision, and so early in His ministry He calls them to Him and invests them with their new apostleship.

This, we are told in a parallel Gospel, followed a night of prayer. He felt that a crisis had come, and that the step He was about to take was fraught

233

with the most important and lasting consequences. And so as the Pattern Worker He laid the matter before His Father, and we cannot doubt that every step which followed was the result of divine direction and according to the will of God. So let us always, like one of old, "prepare all our ways before the Lord." And the steps that are born of prayer, although they may afterwards be severely tested, will ultimately be established and confirmed to the glory of God and the blessing of the world.

As Christian leaders and workers we will find, in the example of our Lord, a pattern for ourselves. No movement that rests upon a single individual can ever be permanent or widespread. There is always a strong temptation to young Elijahs to go out without regard to the brethren or the body of Christ. The New Testament teaches us at every step that the body is just as necessary as the head and that we must learn to be workers together as well as workers with God. A narrow and bigoted party would have us believe that the Christian ministry is without scriptural warrant and that every servant of Christ has equal authority and standing as a minister of the New Testament. This is not so. While it is true that we are all priests unto God and that there is no separate priesthood under the Gospels, yet it is just as true that

> God has appointed first of all apostles, second prophets, third teachers, then workers of miracles, also those having gifts of healing, those able to help others, those with gifts of administration, and those speaking in different kinds of tongues. (1 Corinthians 12:28)

> It was he who gave some to be apostles, some to be prophets, some to be evangelists, and some to be pastors and teachers, to prepare God's people for works of service, so that the body of Christ may be built up until we all reach unity in the faith and in the knowledge of the Son of God and becoming mature, attaining to the whole measure of the fullness of Christ. (Ephesians 4:11–13)

The Lord not only recognized the apostolic office, but early in the history of Christianity, He set apart also the body of deacons and later ordained elders in all the churches and left the most unmistakable directions for the proper government and discipline of the household of faith and the full recognition of the Christian ministry both in respect to authority and support. There appears to be no rigid law in the New Testament as to precise methods of church government and exact gradations of ministry and service. It is enough to recognize the principle of government and along with the rights of the congregation, which must ever be acknowledged, the authority of those whom God has made overseers of the Church which He has purchased with His own blood.

THEIR INDIVIDUAL CHARACTERISTICS

It is an interesting study to follow the details of this picture and form our impressions of these first leaders of the Church universal. The name that stands in front in all the lists is Simon Peter. No one can ever forget the true and graphic photograph of this extraordinary man. Mark was no doubt inspired by Peter himself in writing his Gospel, and there is nothing more touching than the honest frankness with which Mark brings out the worst features in the character of his headstrong master and fellow-worker. It is Mark who tells us of Peter's boast, "Even if all fall away, I will not" (Mark 14:29). It is Mark who gives the shameful picture in all its vivid details of the successive denials, three times over, and the oaths and curses with which he emphasized the last. It is Mark also who remembers the crowing of the cock and the bitter tears of Simon as he thought thereon and wept. It is Mark who adds that dramatic word that speaks unspeakable volumes as the Master, just risen from the dead, hastens to say to the frightened women, "But go, tell his disciples and Peter, 'He is going ahead of you into Galilee. There you will see him, just as he told you'" (16:7). The Lord's chosen instruments are not always the strongest and best material humanly speaking. He chose Jacob to be the founder of Israel of old, not because he was so strong, but because he was so weak. And grace triumphed over human infirmity as in no other of the patriarchs. He chose Simon Peter likewise to be the first living stone in the temple of the New Jerusalem because he was so much like Jacob and so true an example of the transforming power of grace in a vessel that was like potter's clay. How all this comes out in Peter's first name, "Simon, son of Jonas," and the surname which the Lord gave him, Peter, the rock; or rather, the piece cut out of the living Rock, which is Christ Himself. "And Simon (to whom he gave the name Peter)" (3:16). When the Lord gives us a new name He never fails to bring us up to it. He has a new name for all His servants who will let Him surname them. "You will be called by a new name/ that the mouth of the LORD will bestow" (Isaiah 62:2b).

The two next in the list always afterwards appear together with Simon— James, the son of Zebedee, and John, the brother of James. We find these three disciples always in a class of their own. They are with Him in the house of Jairus; they are with Him on the mount, and they are with Him in the Garden.

James was not permitted to have a very long public ministry after the day of Pentecost, but he had the distinguished honor of being the first apostolic martyr, while Peter was released from prison by the angel of the Lord. We read that Herod "had James, the brother of John, put to death with the sword" (Acts 12:2). Stephen and James stand together in front of those who come out of great tribulation and have washed their robes and made them white in the blood of the Lamb. John, however, has a prominence and permanence among the disciples not less than even that of Simon Peter. We know much less of his natural peculiarities of temperament. Perhaps the surname the Master gave these brothers, Boanerges, the sons of thunder, may hint at some strong individuality in both of them along the lines of rugged and natural impulsiveness. There may have been a time in their lives when they were not unlike the noisy, swearing crowd of sailors and fishermen with whom we are all familiar. If this were so, there surely was as great a transformation in John as in Simon. He is known to the heart of the Church in a more sacred and mystic memory than belongs to any other except perhaps Mary of Bethany. The two facts that he was known as the disciple whom Jesus loved and that he was chosen to give to the Church the gospel of the Son of God and the revelation of the plan of the ages, give him a unique place in the New Jerusalem that no other can ever share. They also give assurance of qualities either natural or divine which were preeminent and unique. Just as the character of the Son of Man is too sublimely beautiful to have been invented by any human brain, so the picture of John the Divine, as he has often been called, carries with it its own attestation of heavenly origin. And yet his brother James must have had qualities even more forceful, for when on first introduction to these brothers, we do not read of James, the brother of John, but John, the brother of James. It is evident that they were the children of a family of some social standing, for when the Master called them, they left their father Zebedee in the ship with the hired servants. They had some property and more than one servant. Their mother was evidently a woman of strong character and womanly ambition, for it was she who came to Jesus toward the close of His ministry and asked for her two boys that they might sit with Him, one on His right hand and the other on His left hand in His kingdom. She wanted the whole thing. The young men themselves could not have been disinterested in this little scheme, for we read that the disciples were much displeased with James and John as well as their mother for this little piece of presumption. Indeed, Mark tells the story in such a way as make James and John themselves the principals in this ambitious request (Mark 10:35–41). But all this belongs to the first chapter of their life. The day came when they were both ready to drink the Master's cup and to be baptized with His baptism. The one is the proto-martyr in Jerusalem; the other is the prisoner on the Isle of Patmos.

The next set begins with Andrew. He is also a marked character in the apostolic circle. Scotland claims the honor of calling him her son. His name is derived from the Greek word *aner*, a man, and seems to suggest the humaneness of his nature. It was he that brought his own brother Simon to Jesus and had been the first to discover the Messiah, while still a disciple of John. It was he also who discovered the little lad in Galilee who supplied the buns and fishes that were used as the materials for the glorious miracle of the feeding of the 5,000. The boy must have naturally taken to this big-hearted man. It is a great thing in Christian work to have a human heart. Grace does not rob us of our individuality. It uses it as a point of contact with other hearts.

Philip, too, is a very distinct figure in the gospel story. He appears to have had, like Andrew, a large-hearted sympathy with men. It was to him the Greeks came, of whom we read in John 12:20–22, with the touching request, "Sir, we would see Jesus." And it was to Andrew that Philip naturally turned in arranging for an interview with these men from afar. Again it was Philip that stated, "Lord, show us the Father and that will be enough for us" (John 14:8). His heart was longing for God, but he had wholly misunderstood the Master notwithstanding his intimacy with Him, and the Lord was obliged to say with a touch of reproof, "Don't you know me, Philip, even after I have been among you such a long time?" (14:9).

Bartholomew is not a stranger to us. It was he who sat under the fig tree in Galilee and received from the Master those matchless words of commendation, "Here is a true Israelite, in whom there is nothing false" (1:47).

Matthew has also been introduced to us already by Mark himself for he is none other than Levi the publican, whose calling brought such opprobrium to Christ in the fellowship which He had with publicans and sinners.

Thomas is one of the unique figures in the story of Jesus. There is something pathetic in our first introduction to him as the Master was about to go back into Judea and risk His life among His enemies, and Thomas cried out in a burst of enthusiasm, "Let us also go, that we may die with him" (11:16). True-hearted like Simon Peter and ready impulsively to risk any peril for the Master he loved, yet that very love led him after the resurrection to doubt and question the joyful tidings that the Lord was risen. To Thomas it was too good to be true; but even he at last was not only convinced but became a most powerful argument for the conviction of others as he sank at the Master's feet and cried, "My Lord, and my God!" (20:28).

James, the son of Alphaeus, reached the pinnacle of his greatness and influence after the resurrection. A man of strong conservative nature and great uprightness of character, he was naturally chosen to be the first leader and pastor of the church in Jerusalem. He was the president of the first apostolic council and gave voice to its final decree. Paul calls him one of the pillars whom he met in his first visit to Jerusalem. Later we become personally acquainted with him in his strong epistle which retains many of the ethical qualities of the old prophetic writers, as Moses and Jeremiah, and yet imbued all through with the spirit of lofty faith and intense godliness.

The other names are less prominent and familiar, except the last one, Judas Iscariot, who is mentioned last in all the catalogues of the various evangelists. Why did the Lord choose Judas Iscariot as one of His apostles? Could He have been mistaken and deceived in this man? Certainly not. We are told more than once that the Lord knew from the beginning who should betray Him. Early in His Galilean ministry Christ had said, "Have I not chosen you, the Twelve? Yet one of you is a devil!" (6:70). How can we explain the Master's allowing such a man to be in the very bosom of primitive Christianity? Was it on the same principle that God allowed Satan to meet with the sons of God, in the story of Job, to prove that His own work can stand the inspection even of Satan? Was it that a man might come into the very heart of Christianity and know the Lord from the beginning to end with utmost intimacy, and then at last bear witness to Him and say with his dying gasp of despair, "I have betrayed innocent blood" (Matthew 27:4)? Was it that the infinite patience, long-suffering and tenderness of Jesus might be brought out against this foil, this background, this awful shadow of hypocrisy and Satanic guile? Was it that later ages might understand that even the Church of God would sometimes have in its bosom the false as well as the true and that we should not be frightened or distressed to find sometimes the intermingling of evil with the holy and the good? If the Lord could stand Judas, in His personal family circle, He can stand all who are like him to the end of the chapter. Judas was the only real Jew among all the twelve, that is, the only one who came from Judea. By some strange happening he held the bag and was the treasurer of the household. Perhaps the Lord allowed him to be there and to have this position to make His servants careful of His own oft-repeated warnings, especially to the gospel ministry, "Watch out! Be on your guard against all kinds of greed" (Luke 12:15). Perhaps the Lord meant these hints for the benefit of Judas. Happy for him if he had heeded them more, and well for every Christian worker and minister of Christ if he makes good use of the warning and cherishes a wholesome fear of filthy lucre.

THE TRAINING OF THE APOSTLES

These He ordained, we are told, "that they might be with him and that he might send them out to preach" (Mark 3:14). There has been much foolish talking about the unscripturalness of the educated ministry, and the story of the apostles is often quoted as a precedent; but never were men more thoroughly trained than the first ministers of the New Testament. For three and a half years without any vacations, which would be equal to at least five years of an ordinary college course, these men were constantly in the presence and under the instruction of the greatest of all teachers, and then from His breath they received His own imparted Spirit as well as the baptism of the Holy Spirit, which afterwards followed on the day of Pentecost.

The first of all preparations for Christian work is to be "with Him." Personal intimacy with the Lord Jesus will enable us to imbibe His Spirit, and it will be true, "For it will not be you speaking, but the Spirit of your Father speaking through you" (Matthew 10:20). There is the utmost need for the careful preparation of the Christian worker. "The things you have heard me say," says Paul, "entrust to reliable men who will also be qualified to teach others" (2 Timothy 2:2). The Lord wants no untempered mortar in the building of His temple. He carefully selected His first apostles from a great number of other followers, and we should be most discriminating in committing the mysteries of the kingdom to crude and unqualified vessels, especially in these days of false teaching and manifold error. Let us not be afraid to exercise the spirit of discernment and to insist that those who bear the vessels of the Lord shall be clean, qualified, Spirit-filled and efficient.

THEIR MINISTRY

They were to preach. That is the first business of the ministry of Christ, to proclaim the gospel of the Lord Jesus Christ. They were also to exercise the ministry of healing, and the church has been wholly wrong in remanding this to professional physicians and forgetting her sacred trust for the bodies as well as the souls of men. And they were to cast out demons. The Lord sends us forth with the distinct understanding that we are dealing not merely with the minds and hearts of men. Back of their unbelief and weakness are the powers of hell. All our words will be a mockery and all our work a disappointment unless we claim the authority which Christ has given to us to treat the devil as a conquered foe, to tread on serpents and scorpions, to drive Satan from the minds and hearts of men, not merely by logic and eloquence, but by the faith of God and the fire of the Holy Spirit.

THE SPIRIT OF THE MINISTRY

A little later in the sixth chapter of Mark we have an account of their first campaign and of the commissions and charges He gave them as they went forth. They were to go in the spirit of faith and simplicity and self-denial, and they were especially to remember that they bore the authority of the King of kings. "He who listens to you listens to me; he who rejects you rejects me; but he who rejects me rejects him who sent me" (Luke 10:16). "It will be more bearable on that day for Sodom than for that town" (10:12).

While the apostolic office ceased with the first apostles, yet the Christian ministry is permanent and its authority is as lofty and divine as that of the twelve. It is our privilege to speak to men, not in our own strength or with a claim of our personal influence, eloquence or learning, but to hide ourselves behind our Master and ever realize that we are acting and speaking with His supreme authority. This would give to the speaker a weight which no personal qualities can supply, and to the hearer a sense of responsibility which God Himself will witness to. The greatest force which we can bring to bear upon the minds and consciences of men is to make them feel that they are dealing with God and not with us, and that we are leaving our hearers face to face with Him "to whom we must give account" (Hebrews 4:13b). "I have a message from God for you" (Judges 3:20b), should be the profound conviction of every preacher of the gospel, and it will leave a corresponding impression upon the heart of the hearer. When we thus go forth, our Master is ever behind us, and it is not we who speak, but the Spirit of our Father that speaks in us.

THE NEW RELATIONSHIPS

The forming of the new society naturally created new relationships. So as a sequel to the calling of the 12 apostles and the founding of the New Testament Church, which that involved, we have a somewhat striking incident relating to the immediate family of the Lord Jesus Christ. Immediately after the calling of the apostles a great company gathered together around the Lord in the house which He had entered. So great was the crowd and so intense the interest, we are told, "he and his disciples were not even able to eat" (Mark 3:20). It was then that His friends, as they are here called, meaning no doubt His relatives and family, became greatly disturbed about it and actually tried to put Him under arrest and restraint, "for they said, 'He is out of his mind' " (3:21). This perhaps was partly caused by the bitter attacks upon Him of the officials who had come down from Jerusalem and who made an awful charge of blasphemy, saying, "He is possessed by Beelzebub! By the prince of demons he is driving out demons" (3:22).

Christ's immediate relatives, being no doubt pious Jews, would naturally have a good deal of confidence in the statement of these high religious authorities, and probably concluded that He had gone insane, and ought to be taken in charge by His friends. A little later in the chapter the incident is repeated. At the close of His reply to these bitter attacks we read, "Then Jesus' mother and brothers arrived. Standing outside, they sent someone in to call him. A crowd was sitting around him, and they told him, 'Your mother and brothers are outside looking for you.' " (3:31–32). It would appear that even Mary at last began to wonder if her boy had gone wrong, and if all these strange things simply meant some fearful fanaticism or disease. But the incident brought out, as all these things ever did, one of the noblest utterances from the lips of the Lord. He did not respond by going to them, but with calm dignity replied, "Who are my mother and my brothers?"

(3:33). And then suiting the action to the word, He looked around upon His hearers, with some striking gesture, and said, "Here are my mother and my brothers! Whoever does God's will is my brother and sister and mother" (3:34–35).

While we can in the light of 19 centuries understand the deep spiritual meaning of this announcement, it must have fallen upon their ears with startling strangeness. It seemed like an utter uprooting of old relationships and the establishing of a new family and fellowship. Henceforth the home circle has its center not even around the sweetest hearthstones of earth, but in the heart of God and the home above. Henceforth the holiest ties and the only everlasting bonds are in union with the Lord Jesus Christ. The fatherhood of God and the sonship of believers are New Testament relations. The brotherhood of man, so foolishly wanted by the lips of the socialist and sociologist, is not an earth-born tie, but wholly based on our relationship with Christ. We are children of God through regeneration; we are brethren through Jesus, our Elder Brother. The tenderest earthly ties must end with the tomb if they are not transformed and transfigured through spiritual resurrection into heavenly relationships. This does not do away with the sanctity of the home, but it gives it a higher sanction and a deeper root, and no loving father, husband, wife or friend should ever rest satisfied until the earthly love has been transformed to the heavenly and the bond become through Christ an everlasting one. The Lord Jesus had already prepared His mother in some degree for this by His own words to her at Cana on the occasion of His first miracle, "Dear woman, why do you involve me?" (John 2:4). That was to her the signal that the mere human relationship had been superseded by the higher one. So the natural must pass into the spiritual, the earthly into the heavenly. We find the apostle saying in regard even to His natural knowledge of the Savior, whom probably he had seen at some time in His earthly ministry, "Though we once regarded Christ in this way, we do so no longer. Therefore, if anyone is in Christ, he is a new creation; the old has gone, the new has come!" (2 Corinthians 5:16–17).

How close and endearing are the terms and attachments of this new relationship! "Whoever does God's will is my brother and sister and mother" (Mark 3:35). The Lord Jesus has for us a personal friendship as real as any human love and infinitely more helpful and satisfying. There is still room on His breast for you and me beside the "other disciple, the one Jesus loved" (John 20:2). The affections and friendships of earth are but feeble types of that divine and infinite fellowship which finds its center in Him. Just as He was the true Vine and all others were but figures, so is He the true Brother, Husband, Friend, who all human friendships were simply meant to reflect. Men and women follow after earthly loves in the wild and vain dream that there their hearts will find rest, but oh! how often the most intimate of human relationships has mocked a brokenhearted world. How touching is Paul's reference to marriage in his epistle to the Ephesians, where after speaking for a little of the true love which should exist between husband and wife and the sacredness of the marriage tie as a mysterious type of the heavenly union of the bridegroom and the bride, he adds, "This is a profound mystery—but I am talking about Christ and the church" (Ephesians 5:32). The true mystery is the heavenly marriage; the earthly is but a little shadow of it, a fragment of broken glass reflecting the glory of the sun, but oh! how much less than the sun. Beloved friend, have you come into this mystery? Do you know this friend that "sticks closer than a brother"? (Proverbs 18:24). Has He not said, "I will betroth you to me forever, . . . and you will acknowledge the LORD" (Hosea 2:19a, 20b)? And have you learned to say, "This is my beloved and this is my friend, the chief among ten thousand and altogether lovely" (a combining of Song of Songs 5:10, 16)?

CHAPTER 9

THE INTERTWINED MIRACLES

When she heard about Jesus, she came up behind him in the crowd and touched his cloak, because she thought, "If I just touch his clothes, I will be healed." (Mark 5:27–28)

"Your daughter is dead," they said. "Why bother the teacher any more?"
Ignoring what they said, Jesus told the synagogue ruler, "Don't be afraid; just believe." (5:35b–36)

The two miracles suggested by these two texts bear a relation to each other unlike any others in the Gospels. They are so intertwined in each other as to form one story. Before the woman touched Him, He was already on His way to answer the summons of the ruler of the synagogue, whose daughter was lying at the point of death, so that wondrous miracle of resurrection power may be said to have already begun. But right in the midst of it came the other incident of the healing of the woman with the spirit of infirmity who pressed through the crowd and touched the border of His garment. Then when that was finished and the woman sent on her way rejoicing, He continued His journey to the house of Jairus and ended the stupendous program by raising Jairus' daughter from the dead. There must be some special lesson in this interlinking of these two incidents, conveying some message to us believers and Christian workers that we ought not to miss. Let us approach this lesson through the many incidental teachings of the story.

AN EMERGENCY CALL

The first thing we note is the extreme emergency of this first case. Returning from Decapolis the Master found a great concourse of people awaiting His little boat. In front of the crowd came a distinguished man for whom the multitude made way with every token of respect. It was the ruler of the synagogue, Jairus, who immediately threw himself at the feet of Jesus in humble prostration, "and pleaded earnestly with him, 'My little daughter is dying. Please come and put your hands on her so that she will be healed and live'" (Mark 5:23). No case was ever too hard for the Lord, and so He immediately responded and went along with the distressed father with a vast throng of people surging about them on every side. Let us bring our hard cases to the Lord Jesus. Let us hear Him saying in the face of the gravest dangers, "Don't be afraid; just believe" (5:36).

THE MASTER AT LEISURE

One would have thought that, facing such an emergency, nothing would have been allowed to detain Him for a moment. It must have been a fearful trial for the agonized father when the interruption came and the Lord turned around to talk to the woman that had pressed through the concourse to touch His garment. But God is never in a hurry, and the Lord Jesus was always deliberate and had leisure. When the tidings came a little later that Lazarus was sick, we are specially told, "When he heard that Lazarus was sick, he stayed where he was two more days" (John 11:6). "He that believeth shall not make haste" (Isaiah 28:16, KJV).

Faith is always at rest. If God is in charge, nothing can get beyond Him. His eyes run to and fro throughout the whole earth and no other can anticipate or stay His hand from working. How wonderful it is for us to realize that every moment matters of emergency are pressing upon the attention of our ascended Lord! Every instant He is intensely occupied with the government of the universe and the care of His people. This very hour thousands of His people are calling upon Him from all parts of the world; some are dying; some are pleading for dying friends; some are in instant peril; some are pleading for His mercy and salvation. He is the greatest of all workers and the most occupied of all strenuous lives, and yet He is at leisure to listen to your feeblest whisper or your longest appeal, to enter into every detail of your situation and to go with you through every minute stepping of your perplexing way. Was there ever such a heart of love and such a wise and resourceful mind? Nothing takes Him by surprise. Danger and death have for Him no alarms. Oh, let us come to Him with confidence and ever live in touch with His guiding eye and upholding hand.

The family of Jairus thought no doubt that that delay had been fatal to their interests, and they sent an urgent message saying to the father, "Your daughter is dead, . . . why bother the teacher any more?" (Mark 5:35b). It was a very polite and courteous way of saying, "You have come too late. You have waited too long; it is all over." But the Lord paid no attention to this message. No doubt He saw in the father's face the same despair, but He only reassured him and bade him fear not, but only believe. Our times are in His hands as well as our lives and interests. In the parable of Luke 11, it was when the door was shut and the night was far gone that the friend in need came to the gates of prayer and found that the extremity of the case did not hinder his guest but only brought out in clearer light the grace and power of the heavenly Friend. It is never too late to call upon God or knock at the doors of almighty grace.

THE TOUCH OF POWER

Undoubtedly the overshadowing lesson of the story is the almighty power of the Lord Jesus over death. Hitherto He had appeared as the conqueror of sin, Satan and disease and the elements of nature. But now a new enemy confronts Him. It is that grim and resistless foe that well has been called the king of terrors. How little he cares for human helplessness and sorrow is evident in this pathetic picture. It was a little girl that had been gasping out her life in yonder home and now lay cold and still in death. Oh, how the picture recalls some other little girl that we have seen lying cold and silent in her coffin, and received perhaps, as some of us did, our first dreadful impression of the power of death, the mysterious power! How love had clung to her and prayer had pleaded for her; but all in vain. The ruthless destroyer had trampled her beauty and her youth into the dust, and she was dead and in a little while must be given up to the cold and silent grave. No one knew as well as He the dreadful significance of death. He had seen its ravages through all the ages since first the sentence fell at the gates of Eden. "For dust you are/ and to dust you will return" (Genesis 3:19). A little later we see Him looking into a tomb at Bethany and the awful spectacle, as it brings up before Him the vision of all who ever died and ever shall go down to the realms of death. It broke His heart, and we read that Jesus groaned in spirit and was troubled, and a little later, "Jesus wept" (John 11:35). It was to face this grim foe that He came. His mission was to "destroy him who holds the power of death—that is, the devil—and free those who all their lives were held in slavery" (Hebrews 2:14).

And now at last He was face to face with death and was about to be manifested as its master and destroyer. "Your daughter is dead" (Mark 5:35), they tell Jairus. Does He turn back or blanch before that prospect? No! He only answers, "Don't be afraid, just believe" (5:36). Calmly dismissing the multitude and taking with Him three chosen companions, Peter, James and John, He enters the home of death. There is a motley crowd of Eastern mourners, and already the dramatic scene of Oriental lamentation has begun. He meets it with strange rebuke, and then adds a mysterious word whose depths of meaning no one of us perhaps has ever yet measured, and which only filled His hearers with amusement and scorn, "Why all this commotion and wailing? The child is not dead but asleep" (5:39). Did He know something about the disembodied spirit and the thing that we call death, which we have yet to learn? Something of what He meant we know regarding those who sleep in Jesus, and we thank our blessed Lord that that sweet word has taken away half the dread of death. No wonder they laughed Him to scorn, but He as little regarded their wild professional demonstrations of grief. It was a hollow show of this cheap world which is just as silly in its fashions of sorrow as in its entertainments of pleasure and joyfulness. But putting them all out, He took the father and the mother and His three disciples and calmly entered into the chamber of death, and without any incantations or outward show, "He took her by the hand and said to her, 'Talitha Koum!'. . . 'Little girl, I say to you, get up!' " (5:41).

The simplicity and modesty of the narrative moves with a majesty that no theatrical figures of speech could add to, and we stand awed and overwhelmed with them before the advent of One who at length "has destroyed death and has brought life and immortality to light through the gospel" (2 Timothy 1:10). "Immediately the girl stood up and walked around (she was twelve years old). At this they were completely astonished. . . . and [He] told them to give her something to eat" (Mark 5:42, 43b).

This was Christ's first victory over the power of death. It was the pledge and guarantee of all that followed afterwards and that was still to come. Henceforth He holds the keys of Hades and of death. His own death was necessary for the final expulsion of the king of terrors; but that has been accomplished, and now to the believer death is but a shadow and a sleep, "a tunnel," as someone has said, "carrying us beneath the waters of the dark river to the glorious city of the New Jerusalem." In a little while even the form of death shall be swallowed up in life. This was the supreme proof of Christ's Messiahship. He had vindicated His claim to be the Son of God and the Savior of the world from all the issues of the fall.

But the one special lesson which we desire to emphasize, in connection with this part of the chapter, is the divine side of God's grace and power. Here we have a case where there was nothing that man could do. That helpless child could not put forth a single effort, nor move a muscle to approach Him. The leper could kneel at his feet, the paralytic could take up his bed and walk, the woman could press through the crowd and touch Him with her hand; but the little girl could do nothing but lie in helplessness, the passive subject of creating power. And so there is a point of view from which the whole work of salvation is divine. This is the standpoint of the Calvinist. To him man is helpless and God almighty. The sovereignty of the Lord is everything here, and we are saved through His effectual calling and almighty grace. This is all true and to the latest ages of eternity it will be our humble and joyful cry, "By the grace of God I am what I am. . . . not I, but the grace of God that was with me" (1 Corinthians 15:10).

THE TOUCH OF FAITH

But there is another side to this great philosophy of redemption. There is a human side as well as a divine. There is a touch of faith as well as a touch of God. Therefore it comes to pass that the story of the woman who reached out her hand and drew from Him, by a force within herself, His life and power is interwoven with the other story of the child whom Jesus touched without any cooperation from her will or her helpless hand. This is the other side of the great dual problem, divine sovereignty and human responsibility. Both are true and each in its place is imperative. We must trust as if all depended upon God and we must work as if all depended on us.

In a sense the Lord appeared to be at first involuntary in His response to this woman's faith. The healing virtue passed from His person without a distinct act of will on His part and in response to a touch on her part which had in it some strange power to appropriate His very life. Surely we are taught by this striking illustration that the blessings which God has to impart to us through the Lord Jesus Christ do not wait upon some sovereign act of His will, but are already granted, completed and prepared and simply awaiting the contact of a believing hand to open all the channels of communication. It is like the electric current which is already communicating with your home, and which you have only to turn on by touching the switch which connects the wires; or like the sunlight of heaven which is already pouring all around you and which you have but to open your window to let in. What a responsibility this places upon us! All things are ready and we have but to come and take of the water of life freely. This applies not only to the primary question of salvation, but to all the successive steps of Christian experience.

But we must not fail to notice that the touch of faith is a very personal one. It involves not only our hand but His personality. Faith must recognize the Lord Jesus Himself and come into immediate contact with Him before it can draw His healing virtue or His comforting love. We have already seen in the previous chapter how much more was involved in this touch than her immediate healing. Her initial act of faith had to be followed by a frank and full confession. When a soul comes into living touch with the Lord Jesus, it is introduced to a new world of infinite and endless blessing. "He who did not spare his own Son, but gave him up for us all—how will he not also, along with him, graciously give us all things?" (Romans 8:32).

LUKE

CHAPTER 1

THE SON OF MAN

Here is the man! (John 19:5)

The Gospel of Luke is the picture of the Son of Man. The very fact that it begins with a preface is significant. The other Gospels have no preface, but immediately introduce us to the very heart of the subject. Luke presents to us the human medium through which this revelation of the Master comes. It is no disparagement to inspiration to recognize the coloring of the earthly medium through which the light is communicated.

Luke tells us of his careful investigation (Luke 1:3) of all things of which he writes and leaves us to conclude that, with his trained mind, he has given the most thorough and painstaking inquiry into every fact and question that has come to him, and that while the Holy Spirit has guided and controlled, at the same time the instrument has been used with the fullest recognition of all his special qualifications for the task assumed.

The first two chapters of Luke contain a number of testimonies to our Lord, especially in connection with His birth, which have not been recorded by any other evangelist.

THE ANNOUNCEMENT OF THE BIRTH OF JOHN

The first of these is the announcement to Zechariah of the birth of John, the great forerunner. The revelation comes to him from the angel Gabriel as he is ministering in the holy place in the due course of his priesthood. The messenger informs him that his prayer is heard and that God is about to give a son to him and his godly partner after long delay, and when, in the course of human events, such a blessing had become improbable. Zechariah receives the message with astonishment and doubt, and asks for a sign to confirm his hesitating faith. The angel gives him a sign which is at once a reproof to his unbelief and a prop to his faith. He tells him that he shall be mute until the prophecy shall have been fulfilled.

There was extraordinary significance in this sign. It was not merely a miraculous testimony of the prophecy just given, but it was a striking symbol of a still greater fact.

Zechariah represented the priesthood of Israel, and his unbelief was just a type of the unbelief of the nation in the coming Messiah, and the judgment upon that priesthood for its unbelief. Israel was to be silenced as the messenger of God because she had failed to be true to her divine commission and to believe the gospel of which she had been made the trustee, and God was to put her aside and choose instead a new body of inspired messengers. And so God will silence every voice that fails to honor His well-beloved Son, and honor every voice that bears witness to Jesus Christ.

This is in keeping with Luke's special ministry to portray the Savior and His wider relation to the Gentiles rather than to Israel. With the ministry of Zechariah and John, his distinguished son, the voice of Israel was to cease and the Church of God was to come instead.

THE ANNUNCIATION

The Annunciation to Mary is in the same spirit. The angel Gabriel appears to her in the seclusion of her modest life, and bearing to her the greeting of heaven upon the high honor that was to be bestowed upon her, he announces the birth to her of a divine Son. But the name he gives Him is the name which is given to sinners of every race, Jesus. "You are to give him the name Jesus" (1:31). Then are added the majestic words which tell of His deity as the "Son of the Most High," His heirship to David's throne, and the fact that His kingdom "will never end" (1:32–33). Her modest question, "How will this be?" (1:34) was not a word of doubt, but simply of inquiry, and as the answer comes telling her how the Holy Spirit shall accomplish this stupendous and holy miracle, she believes and answers, "I am the Lord's servant . . . May it be to me as you have said" (1:38).

Here again we see the human element in our great redemption. There must be a cooperation of some believing soul before even the Son of God could become incarnate. While we guard against the exaggerations and blasphemies of the Church of Rome in giving to her equal worship and homage with God, at the same time let us not withhold from her the veneration and love which God intended that all ages should accord to that one woman whose consecration and faith rolled back the curse which the sin and folly of another woman had brought upon the human race.

The visit of Mary to her cousin Elizabeth is the next incident in this chain of testimony. It would seem that she hastened to her cousin in the hill country of Judea as soon as the angel's strange message had been fully realized. She needed the sympathy of a true sister in this tremendous crisis, and so the two women met without previous knowledge by any earthly means of their several conditions. How perfectly natural as well as supernatural is the narrative of this meeting. Taught by the Holy Spirit, Elizabeth pours out in inspired language her greeting to the mother of her Lord; tells of her own strange joy and coming motherhood, and adds the benediction, "Blessed is she who has believed that what the Lord has said to her will be accomplished!" (1:45).

THE MAGNIFICAT

The song of Mary which follows rises to a higher plane. It is Jewish throughout, breathing the very essence of the old covenant and the spirit of the ancient prophets; but it goes back beyond Moses to Abraham, and thus rises to that lofty plane from which the Apostle Paul ever grasped the gospel plan of salvation. But while a Hebrew psalm, Mary's *Magnificat* is in perfect keeping with Luke's purpose to reveal the Savior to the Gentiles. As someone has well said, it is the swan song of Judaism, the dying dirge of the old dispensation. Mary reaches the very highest point of Hebrew poetry and lofty vision, and then she stands aside lost in the light of her greater Son as the chorus of redemption begins with its worldwide and eternal refrain.

THE PROMISED FULFILLMENT

First comes the birth of John and the testimony of Zechariah. At length the promise of the forerunner is fulfilled and a child is born to aged Zechariah and Elizabeth. Her cousins and neighbors gather to hail the event with rejoicing. On the appointed day they meet to circumcise the child, calling him Zechariah, after his father. But the mother forbids and appeals to the father. He in turn declares on the writing tablet, "His name is John" (1:63). His long silence is broken, and, filled with the Holy Spirit, he begins to praise God and utters his sublime testimony not only to John, but to Jesus (1:68–79).

This is the glorious gospel of salvation. First is the keynote of the incarnation, "He has come" (1:68). Next comes the echo of the cross, "and has redeemed his people" (1:68). Then we have the fullness of the great salvation which He is about to reveal, "to rescue us from the hand of our enemies,/ and to enable us to serve him without fear/ in holiness and righteousness before him all our days" (1:74–75). This is the gospel in all its fullness.

Then follows the special introduction of John's ministry: "And you, my child, will be called a prophet of the Most High;/ for you will go on before the Lord to prepare the way for him" (1:76). Next his special ministry of repentance and remission of sins is specified: "To give his people the knowledge of salvation/ through the forgiveness of their sins,/ because of the tender mercy of our God" (1:77–78). Then the vision expands into the larger fullness of the perfect day, of which this was but the dawning, "by which the rising sun will come to us from heaven/ to shine on those living in darkness/ and in the shadow of death,/ to guide our feet into the path of peace" (1:78–79).

GOOD TIDINGS

Next, there is the message of the angels to the shepherds of Bethlehem (2:1–20). Here again the keynote is loftier and larger than in the other Gospels. Matthew opens with the question, "Where is the one who has been born king of the Jews?" (Matthew 2:2). But the message of the angels to the shepherds is, "Today in the town of David a Savior has been born to you; he is Christ the Lord" (Luke 2:11). The spirit of the message is joy and gladness. The very word the angels use is the sweet word that has passed into all Christian speech, the gospel—"I bring you good news" (2:10); that is, I bring you the gospel. The keynote of their message is gladness and great joy, and it is no longer the joy of a little exclusive company, but "I bring you good news of great joy that will be for all the people" (2:10). And then the song with which this glorious evangel is climaxed prolongs the notes in a still grander refrain: "Glory to God in the highest,/ and on earth peace to men on whom his favor rests" (2:14).

How perfectly this fits into the scene which follows. "They hurried off and found Mary and Joseph, and the baby, who was lying in the manger" (2:16). This is the inauguration of the world's redemption. Not in palace halls and amid pageants of earthly grandeur, not with princes leading the inaugural procession, but with a company of shepherds at their nightly task as the first witnesses. And the Savior Himself is introduced with a lowliness and poverty in keeping with the calling of the shepherds and the condition of the sinful world to which He has come. Thus the story of salvation is begun and the Savior of sinners enters upon the stage of human suffering as our Brother and our Kinsman-redeemer.

THE TESTIMONY OF SIMEON AND ANNA

One more testimony completes this striking chain (2:1–38). The eighth day of our Savior's life brings His circumcision, followed soon after by His presentation in the temple. How natural, yet supernatural again, is the whole scene. Without notice or invitation cards, Simeon and Anna meet at the right moment by the intuition of the Holy Spirit. The whole circumstances are very touching and intensely human. The offering which Mary and Joseph bring is the offering presented only by the very poorest of the people, a pair of turtle doves, or two young pigeons. But as the little Babe is presented and the aged priest receives Him in his arms, the whole scene is transfigured, and that sublime testimony which fittingly closes this series of witnesses to the birth of Christ flows from his lips. Taking the infant Jesus in his arms, how truly he can say, "For my eyes have seen your salvation" (2:30). What a beautiful picture of faith, not only accepting but embracing the Lord! But the salvation which He has prepared is as wide as the world "which [He has] prepared in the sight of all people." He adds, "a light for revelation to the Gentiles/ and for glory to your people Israel" (2:31–32). Here is the gospel for both Jew and Gentile. Here is the watchword of the missionary crusade and the promise of the Chosen People's final restoration. And as the scene closes, he turns to Mary and adds a message more personal to her, and yet as true for every one of us, "This child is destined to cause the falling and rising of many in Israel, and to be a sign that will be spoken against, so that the thoughts of many hearts will be revealed. And a sword will pierce your own soul too" (2:34–35).

The shadow of the cross is not only to fall upon Him, but upon her, and yes, upon all that receive Him. They must fall before they can rise. They must die before they can live. They must get down to nothingness before they can rise to holiness and heaven.

Simeon's testimony was followed by that of Anna, who, womanlike, went out to tell the joyful news to those who waited for redemption in Jerusalem.

Thus dawned the glorious light of the Sun of righteousness and the Savior of the world. Shall we catch the spirit of these opening scenes in the beautiful Gospel of Luke? Shall we hear the blessed "Do not be afraid" (2:10) which is the very keynote, and enter into the gladness of the good tidings which it brings? Shall we accept it not merely as our heritage of blessing, but our trust to pass on to all the world? And shall we fully recognize with deeper, truer love the human Christ, the Son of Man, the Kinsman-redeemer, who is bone of our bone, flesh of our flesh and heart of our heart, and go forth to walk in closer fellowship with His great human heart and constant sympathy?

> We may not climb the heavenly steeps
> To bring the Lord Christ down;
> In vain we search the lowest depths,
> For Him no depths can drown.
>
> But warm, sweet, tender, even yet
> A present help is He;
> And faith has still its Olivet
> And love its Galilee.
>
> The healing of His seamless robe
> Is by our beds of pain;
> We touch Him in life's throng and press
> And we are whole again.

CHAPTER 2

THE HOLY CHILD

*And the child grew and became strong; he was filled with wisdom,
and the grace of God was upon him. (Luke 2:40)*

*And Jesus grew in wisdom and stature, and in favor with God and
men. (2:52)*

Luke lingers over the human picture and the home life of our blessed
Lord. "The child grew" (2:40). How perfectly natural this is! How different
from the story of the first creation! Adam sprang to life full grown and fell.
The second Adam began as a helpless Babe and traversed every step of the
pilgrimage of man from the cradle to the grave, and He has lifted up and
redeemed the race.

SECTION I—*His Childhood*

There is a clear suggestion here of the threefold humanity of our Lord, and
the perfectly natural development of each part.

HIS PHYSICAL LIFE

"The child grew." This is the first thing for a child to do. The perfect
physical development and health of your child should take precedence over
all other things. Too often the body is stunted and depressed by over-am-
bitious parents in pushing the mere intellectual culture of their children.
Our Lord Jesus had a sound physical life, and all through His earthly existence we find Him giving proper care to His body, and free from asceticism
and extremes of every kind so that He even received the reproach from His
enemies, "The Son of Man came eating and drinking" (7:34). While physical culture may be carried to an extreme, and no doubt is in many modern
schools, yet a sound mind in a sound body is in perfect keeping with the

principles of the common sense religion which Christ has taught us.

HIS SPIRITUAL LIFE

Spiritual culture took the second place in the development of Jesus. It came before all educational processes for mere mental training. "The child . . . became strong" (2:40). The spirit is our higher nature, including conscience with its instinctive knowledge of right and wrong, and the faculty to know God, to pray to Him, to love Him and to obey Him. All this was carefully trained by the pious mother of our blessed Lord. Gradually He drank in from her lofty spirit those higher inspirations which formed the strength of her holy character.

FILLED WITH WISDOM

Luke next tells us that He was "filled with wisdom" (2:40). This embraces the educational processes through which His mind was trained. But there was more than the mere acquisition of knowledge. His was a practical education which turned mere knowledge into wisdom, the power to utilize knowledge and bring things to pass. Too much of our modern education lacks this. The brain is crammed, the memory stored with facts and theories which are soon forgotten and have little value as actual forces in the formation of character or the accomplishment of the work of life.

THE GRACE OF GOD

"The grace of God was upon him" (2:40). The influence behind all, and over all His early life was the recognition of God and the spirit of piety. Of course, such a mother as Mary could not bring up her child in any other way. Happy for all children if their parents would recognize the capacity of even the youngest child to spiritual influences. It is but a short step to heaven from the instincts of the youngest child, and through the medium of a loving and holy mother it is not hard to mold the earliest conceptions and thoughts of life in a heavenly pattern.

The synagogue at Nazareth no doubt was furnished like Hebrew synagogues with the regular scrolls containing the sacred volume, and also a plan of the tabernacle and temple. Once every day, and three times on the Sabbath, it was customary for pious households to gather for the worship of God. Under all these influences the childhood of Jesus developed, and His earnest spirit reached out after sacred truth in many a longing and perhaps many a question which led up to the next important incident in His young life, when the opportunity came in the temple to satisfy the deep desires and questionings which had already reached out beyond the light which even His mother was able to give.

What a beautiful example for the Christian parent and the Christian child

Luke has given us in this simple story of the "holy child Jesus" (Acts 4:27, KJV)!

THE BOYHOOD OF CHRIST

The age of 12 is a kind of turning point in the life of every boy, a narrow strait leading out from the harbor of childhood into the larger ocean of early manhood. How important to have a wise pilot to guide the little ship through the dangerous passage. It is then that the boy begins to awake to all the powers and possibilities of his being, and the world grows bigger to his eyes in response to that other world of inward consciousness, which he finds within his soul. It was at that time that the Hebrew law provided for the bringing of Jewish boys into the full recognition of their responsibilities as "sons of the law." For this purpose Jesus was taken by His parents to Jerusalem to the Passover in His 12th year. Every year they had faithfully gone up since His birth, but now He accompanies them for the first time (Luke 2:41–51). It was a long, weary journey; even today on the strongest and swiftest of beasts of burden it takes two and a half days from Nazareth to Jerusalem.

ON THE WAY TO JERUSALEM

The author of *Ben Hur* has given us an imaginary picture of that little caravan. Joseph, a man of middle age, is leading the party on foot. Mary, the modest mother, still a young woman, is seated on the donkey following close behind. And walking alongside is a lad of 12, perhaps with a face like that exquisite picture given us by Hoffman, thoughtful, pure and strangely earnest, the brow covered by the usual white handkerchief of the Bedouin, the corner turned in over the forehead, a white tunic covering His graceful frame below the knees, and His feet shod with rough sandals, while He holds in His hand a long staff higher than His own stature.

At length they reach the city, crowded at this time in the early Spring with a population six times its ordinary size, and with others they camp out on the hillsides round about and prepare for the solemn services of the Passover.

PREPARATION FOR THE PASSOVER

With what intense interest He must have watched them as they selected the lamb and kept it apart for three days, typical of the three years of the Messiah's earthly ministry, and then on the fourth day offered up its life at the appointed hour with solemn sacrificial services, sprinkling its blood upon the doorposts and then roasting its flesh for the Paschal meal. The very form in which it was prepared was significant. Two skewers were passed through the lamb crosswise, and thus it was hung above the fire and slowly roasted, presenting the perfect symbol of His own cross. At the appointed time the Passover meal began with the purging out of every speck of leaven. Then followed the cup of wine, the unleavened bread, the bitter herbs and the flesh of the lamb.

At a certain point in the feast some child in the household would ask the question, "What does this service mean?" No doubt on this occasion it would be the lad Jesus Himself, and from His lips what intense pathos that question had. In reply Joseph would tell the story of that night in ancient Egypt when the destroying angel passed by and the sprinkled blood saved Israel's firstborn from the curse of sin. And doubtless he would also tell of the coming Messiah in whom all this was to be fulfilled, and Mary's face and falling tears would bear witness to how much it meant for her and her precious child.

WITH THE DOCTORS OF THE LAW

Influences such as these naturally worked up His mind to the most intense interest in the scenes that were all around Him, and the services of that wondrous temple which for the first time He beheld. Little wonder that He soon found His way to the classroom where aged Hillel and other doctors of the law were discussing the deep questions of their national faith. As the hours flew by He took no note of time, but became intensely absorbed in hearing and asking questions, while they in turn were as much amazed at the wonderful answers which he often gave.

THE SEARCH FOR JESUS

"Why were you searching for me?" (2:49). Hours passed into days and already Joseph and Mary had turned homeward with the large caravan containing many of the kinsfolk. It was not until the evening she discovered that her precious child was missing. "A lost child!" How the words stir our hearts and set in motion the bells of the town, the wires of the telephone and the hearts of anxious mothers. But, oh, what a child was this that was lost that day! One can faintly imagine the suspense and anguish of Mary's heart as they eagerly retraced their steps and sought for Him through all the city. Three days of anxiety and despair passed before at length they found Him still absorbed in the Bible class of the temple. One can almost imagine the accents with which she cried as she embraced Him, "Son, why have you treated us like this? Your father and I have been anxiously searching for you" (2:48). But what elocution or rhetoric can give full weight to the wondrous answer that came so simply and spontaneously from His lips, "Why were you searching for me? . . . Didn't you know I had to be in my Father's house?" (2:49).

This incident gives us only one glimpse of all those early years. But, oh, how much it tells of the deep unfolding of His mind and heart, and the perfectly human yet superhuman development of the character of Jesus. How beautiful to think that this blessed Christ is the Savior and Friend of every boy and girl. Edmund of Canterbury tells how once in a dream, when a lad of 12, he met a beautiful Boy of the same age, and followed Him long, charmed with His face and conversation. As He seemed about to leave him Edmund said, "Oh, that I could be with you always." And the Boy turned and said, "Why, I am with you always. When you sit at your class in school, lo, I am there helping you. When you lie down upon your bed at home, I am there protecting you. In your work and in your prayer I am ever with you." And Edmund looked up and saw the name of Jesus upon His brow. And the Boy said, "Just whisper this name and you will always find Me by your side."

This blessed Christ is yours. Whatever your age, He was once just as old and just as young. Whatever your circumstances He was there, and if you, too, will breathe that sweet name you will hear a gentle voice reply, "Surely I am with you always, to the very end of the age" (Matthew 28:20).

And for us men and women of larger growth, the message of the holy Child is just as timely. Your Father's business, are you about it? Is your life as earnest and as consecrated as His? Is there a *must* controlling and constraining every power of your being and every moment of your existence for highest service and holiest usefulness? A simple workman whose daily toil was inscribed with "HOLINESS UNTO THE LORD," was once asked what his business was, and his answer deserves to be written over every shop and factory and office and calling, "My business is to serve the Lord, but I make shoes for a living." Are you about your Father's business?

> No time for trifling in this life of mine,
>   Not this the path the blessed Master trod;
> But strenuous toil, each hour and power employed
>   Always and all for God.

SECTION II—*His Early Manhood*

"Then he went down to Nazareth with them and was obedient to them" (Luke 2:51). This is all we know about 18 long years of the Master's life. But how much it embraces.

OBEDIENT

This is just another word for discipline. Our excessive liberty has degenerated into license, and we are growing weary of God's old-fashioned methods of training. But it is still true, as has been wisely and wittily said,

"One of life's chief missions is not foreign missions nor home missions, but submission." If we are not willing to learn our lesson at home, we will have to have it taught us in harder fashion between the millstones of life's trials. No character can be strong without learning to yield, to suffer and to obey.

TOIL

The sentence passed upon the first Adam, "By the sweat of your brow" (Genesis 3:19), must be literally fulfilled by the second Adam, and by all His followers who expect to pass with Him first through the downward progression of humiliation and suffering, and then through His exaltation and glory. A luxurious age is trying to get away from the law of labor. But to do this we must leave our Lord behind us. Idleness is the twin brother of crime, and someone has truly said of toil,

> Blest toil, if thou were cursed of God,
> What must His blessing be!

THE SHADOW OF THE CROSS

Holman Hunt has left us the vivid painting of the toiling Christ returning at sunset from His carpenter's bench and stretching His arms horizontally in a momentary paroxysm of weariness, while the sun caught His figure and threw His shadow across the opposite wall in the form of the cross. Under that shadow He always walked, and we, too, should be willing to walk with Him. Probably their lot was extremely poor. Possibly He was the breadwinner of the family as the eldest if not the only Son, and if, as has been suggested, Joseph had died during his childhood and left Him with His mother leaning upon His care. The wages of a carpenter would not exceed at the very highest 25 cents a day, and the hours were from sunrise to sunset. On this pittance He supported His loved ones and lived in a humble home which was half a cave, a stranger to all the comforts of luxuries which a modern tradesman's family can enjoy.

Someone has told us of another beautiful dream in which he seemed to be standing just outside their cottage door at Nazareth with the carpenter's shop nearby. As he watched he saw a middle-aged man working at a carpenter's bench and a Lad picking up the chips. Then a maiden came and called them into the cottage for their evening meal, and all they had was coarse bread and milk. Before they tasted, the Boy, with a face all beaming with love, looked toward the stranger at the door and said, "Why does the stranger stand outside? Let him come in and eat with us."

Blessed Christ! Blessed heart of human tenderness and divine love! Oh, that our childhood, our manhood and our latest years may be so linked with You and so filled with Your gentle Spirit that we, too, will leave behind us upon every path of life through which we pass some of the light which You have left upon the home of Nazareth and the path of life.

CHAPTER 3

THE BAPTISM OF JESUS

For this reason he had to be made like his brothers in every way, in order that he might become a merciful and faithful high priest in service to God, and that he might make atonement for the sins of the people. (Hebrews 2:17)

In no respect was the perfect humanity of Jesus Christ, and His entire identification with our fallen race, more strikingly manifested than in His submission to the ordinance of baptism at the hands of John. That ordinance was an explicit confession on the part of those receiving it of their utter sinfulness, and their need of the divine forgiveness. And the act was a striking symbol of death and resurrection on the part of the subjects of baptism. It was an actual confession that they were so utterly guilty and lost that there was no hope of self-improvement, and they must therefore yield to the judgment of God and die, so far as every personal merit was concerned, and then be brought back to an entirely new life through the sovereign mercy and grace of God.

SIGNIFICANCE OF CHRIST'S BAPTISM

The impropriety of Christ submitting to such baptism, in view of His personal innocence and utter freedom from all taint of sin, was so obvious to John the Baptist that he at first refused to allow the Lord to be baptized by him, and only consented because of Christ's insistence. Why then did our Lord insist on receiving a rite which was so explicit a confession of sin? The answer is very solemn and glorious. It was because He identified Himself with sinful men, and in symbol went down with them to the death which they deserved as He was afterwards to suffer that death in actual reality. No wonder that when He came forth from the waters of baptism the great forerunner pointed to Him on the banks of the Jordan and cried, "Look, the Lamb of God, who takes away the sin of the world!" (John 1:29). His baptism had been a rehearsal of the cross and a type of the great atonement which He was afterwards to accomplish on Calvary.

SIGNIFICANCE OF OUR BAPTISM

This is the deepest significance of the ordinance of baptism for us, His disciples today. As He went down with us to death and took away our curse and sin, so we go down with Him by baptism into death, and become partakers of His atonement and redemption. Baptism is therefore not a symbol of cleansing, but of crucifixion; not of self-improvement, but of self-effacement and resurrection life in Him, our risen Head:

> Don't you know that all of us who were baptized into Christ Jesus were baptized into his death? . . . just as Christ was raised from the dead through the glory of the Father, we too may live a new life. (Romans 6:3–4)

Luke gives a fine touch to the human picture of our Lord's baptism by a single phrase in the 21st verse of the third chapter: "When all the people were being baptized, Jesus was baptized too. And as he was praying, heaven was opened." It was when all the people were baptized that He went into the Jordan's flood unostentatiously just like anybody else. Probably to the ordinary observer there was nothing to distinguish Him from the crowds of sinful men that pressed into the waters, and but for the special sign which had been given to John, even he would not have recognized Him, for speaking of it himself he says, "I myself did not know him" (John 1:31). There was no parade of His importance. There was no halo around His brow. There was no proclamation of His divine condescension, but standing on the level of our lost humanity, going down with us into the common grave, which typified our just doom, "he had to be made like his brothers in every way, in order that he might become a merciful and faithful high priest in service to God, and that he might make atonement for the sins of the people" (Hebrews 2:17).

There is also another touch of humanness in Luke's narrative. It is found in the words "and as he was praying" (Luke 3:21). As He went down to His baptism, He was in the attitude of a dependent man, having no strength of His own, and looking up to God for grace and blessing. There is nothing more comforting than the uniform attitude of the Lord Jesus Christ to that heavenly grace upon which we are so dependent through the open gates of prayer. He, who might have commanded all the resources of the skies, took the lowly position of a suppliant at the throne of grace, and still bends with us as we also come coupling His personality with our own as we say, "Our Father in heaven,/ hallowed be your name" (Matthew 6:9).

THE BAPTISM OF THE SPIRIT

But the scene which followed gives a grander climax to this picture of the human Christ: "Heaven was opened and the Holy Spirit descended on him in bodily form like a dove. And a voice came from heaven: 'You are my Son, whom I love; with you I am well pleased' " (Luke 3:21–22). The baptism of Jesus Christ with the Holy Spirit marks an epoch in His earthly life. From this moment all His public ministry began and all His work was accomplished in dependence upon the Holy Spirit. He did not claim to work miracles through His essential deity, but acknowledged, "But if I drive out demons by the Spirit of God, then the kingdom of God has come upon you" (Matthew 12:28). He did not meet the tempter in the wilderness in His own inherent strength, but "Then Jesus was led by the Spirit into the desert to be tempted by the devil" (4:1). And He went back from the conflict "in the power of the Spirit" (Luke 4:14). He did not stand before the people as a great Teacher through His wisdom, but He stood up in the synagogue at Nazareth and declared,

> The Spirit of the Lord is on me,
>   because he has anointed me
>   to preach good news to the poor.
> He has sent me to proclaim freedom for the prisoners
>   and recovery of sight for the blind,
> to release the oppressed,
>   to proclaim the year of the Lord's favor.
>   (4:18–19)

The Apostle John, in quoting His own words, says, "I do nothing on my own but speak just what the Father has taught me" (John 8:28).

THE REAL HUMANITY OF CHRIST

Is it not true that we have been accustomed to think of the Lord Jesus as having some special and individual advantage of us through His divine nature and perhaps to say, "Christ could do that because He was the Son of God, but I cannot be expected to do such things"? Have we not failed to realize that while Christ was indeed the Son of God, and can never cease to be, yet when He came down as the Son of Man to represent our race and to work out our salvation, He suspended the prerogatives and resources of His deity, and took the place of a dependent man, drawing all His strength from God through faith and prayer even as we must do? How near this brings Him to us, and how truly He could say, "But if I drive out demons by the Spirit of God, then the kingdom of God has come upon you" (Matthew

12:28). That is to say, the same Spirit that dwelt in Him is now given to us, and through Him we may share the same enduement of power from on high.

THE HOLY SPIRIT AND JESUS

In receiving the baptism of the Holy Spirit, Jesus was our Forerunner. Let us bear in mind that up to this time He had not been without the Holy Spirit. He was born of the Spirit, for had not the angel said to Mary, "The Holy Spirit will come upon you, and the power of the Most High will overshadow you. So the holy one to be born will be called the Son of God" (Luke 1:35). In like manner we are also born of the Spirit from the moment of our conversion, and become the children of God. But that day on the banks of the Jordan something more than this came to our Lord. The Holy Spirit as a person actually moved from the heavens and came down to earth, and henceforth resided as a distinct Person in union with the Son of Man. From this time forward there were two persons united in the life and ministry of Jesus Christ, the Holy Spirit and the Lord Jesus, and all He said and did was in the power of the Spirit. This is just what happens to the consecrated believer when he receives the baptism with the Holy Spirit. He has been a child of God before. Born of the Spirit he has had the Spirit with him. But now the Holy Spirit comes to be in him, so united to him that all his life henceforth is accomplished in constant dependence upon and fellowship with that divine Presence. It is as when the bride loses her personality, in a sense, in dependence upon her husband. Down that aisle they walk alone, but from that marriage altar they return no longer alone, but united. Henceforth her name is lost in his. Her support is derived from him, or ought to be, and her will is yielded to him. Something infinitely greater than this comes to pass when our life passes out of the human into the divine, and we can truly say,

> Once it was my working,
> His it hence shall be;
> Once I tried to use Him,
> Now He uses me.

If the Lord Jesus did not presume to begin His public ministry or perform a single service as our Teacher and Example until He received the Holy Spirit, what right have we to go forth in our self-sufficiency and attempt to minister at the altar of Christian service until we be endued with power from on high?

HIS HUMAN PEDIGREE

In striking testimony to the perfect humanness of all this scene is the fact that Luke introduces the genealogy of the Lord Jesus at this very point. This genealogy, unlike that in Matthew, is traced back, not to Abraham, but to Adam. "The son of Adam, the son of God" (3:38), is the sublime climax of this long list of names which links the blessed Jesus with our fallen race. His pedigree therefore is not that of a Jew, but of a man; not the descendant of Abraham, but the son of Adam. Well may the apostle say, "Verily he took not on him the nature of angels, but he took on him the seed of Abraham" (Hebrews 2:16, KJV).

The genealogical line given us by Luke differs in all its important links from that of Matthew, and we must accept the explanation and hypothesis that it is given in the line of Mary, while Matthew's is traced in the line of Joseph. All that is necessary to make this plain is simply to interpret, as was customary among the Hebrews, the word "son" in verse 23 as "son-in-law."

How may we follow our blessed Forerunner in thus receiving the baptism of the Spirit?

THE BAPTISM OF THE SPIRIT A DEATH

1. Like Him let us yield ourselves to death. This just stands for that act of definite surrender and consecration in which every marked spiritual crisis must begin. It comes to each one of us differently, but it accomplishes the same result in each case. It searches our hearts to their inmost depths. It brings to light each hidden sin and cherished idol, and especially all the depths of our self-sufficiency and self-will, and it lays us broken, helpless and wholly yielded at the feet of sovereign grace. The deeper the death, the higher will be the life to which it leads. The more complete the surrender and the separation, the more glorious will be the blessing. Let us not be afraid to be thoroughly honest and inexorably true to the life the Spirit brings. Let us give up self as well as sin, and say as utterly as the great apostle could say, "I have been crucified with Christ and I no longer live, but Christ lives in me" (Galatians 2:20).

Usually we will find that there is some special form of self and sin to which the heart is clinging, some hidden idol in which all the roots and tendrils of the carnal heart have concentrated their strength. It is generally the last thing we are willing to see and let go. And therefore consecration often hinges upon one special decision or surrender. But it is more than a negative surrender. It is a positive accepting of and entering into all the will of God for us. It is an infinite privilege to be permitted to make such a consecration and to receive such a blessing. The consecration of Jesus Christ that day was not merely a surrender to death, but an acceptance of all His Father's will. Let us therefore come not merely to give up everything, but to receive infinitely more. When we kneel at the altar of sacrifice there is Another who kneels with us, and just as fully as we give ourselves to Him

He gives Himself to us, and His own glorious promise is, "For them I sanctify myself, that they too may be truly sanctified" (John 17:19).

NECESSITY OF FAITH

2. Therefore faith is as essential as consecration in receiving the baptism of the Holy Spirit. We must believe that God accepts us just as surely as we have surrendered ourselves to Him. We must take as well as give. We must be fully assured that the Father receives us in His beloved Son, and says of us as truly as of Him, "With you I am well pleased" (Luke 3:22). We must recognize the Holy Spirit as actually coming to us, and henceforth taking up His abode within us; and we must begin to treat Him as if He were our indwelling Guest, and our ever-abiding Comforter and Guide. We must think of God as no longer in some distant heaven, but actually within us, and the throne of grace as in our very hearts where we may pray with confidence and dwell in communion in the "Most Holy Place" (Hebrews 9:3). We must go forth expecting His presence, His power, His response to our every cry, and His all-sufficiency for our every need. Thus walking in the Spirit, we too will find that our life has been translated and transfigured from the earthly to the heavenly, from the human to the divine, from our endeavor to God's best.

Oh, what a privilege, what an honor, what a boundless possibility all this opens up to us weak and worthless children of Adam's fallen race! Truly since that morning on Jordan's strand, the heaven is open and the kingdom of God has come near to us! Let us recognize it. Let us receive it, and let us hear the voice of ancient prophecy inviting us, "Come, O house of Jacob,/ let us walk in the light of the LORD" (Isaiah 2:5).

CHAPTER 4

THE TEMPTATION OF THE SON OF MAN

We have one who has been tempted in every way, just as we are—yet was without sin. (Hebrews 4:15)

Because he himself suffered when he was tempted, he is able to help those who are being tempted. (2:18)

The baptism of the Holy Spirit is not given to us primarily as an enduement of power for service. This is one of the mistaken teachings that are abroad today. Undoubtedly power for service is one result of this blessing, but it is primarily given to us for personal character and holiness; for what we are to be, rather than what we are to do and say. This is surely demonstrated by the fact that, after receiving the baptism of the Spirit, our Lord—our Example and Forerunner—did not immediately begin His public ministry, but first went alone for a personal conflict with the adversary, and for the testing and establishing of His own personal victory and righteousness. The 40 days of Christ's temptation mean a good deal more than 40 days in the experience of His disciples and cover the whole experience of our Christian life in the conflict with sin and Satan. Indeed, the supreme factor in our service is personal character and experience. It is only the men and women who have been there themselves, who can lead others through the conflict and into the victory.

SECTION I—*The Elements of the Temptation*

THE FACT OF TEMPTATION

The fact that Jesus Christ was tempted is the most emphatic proof of His actual humanity. It was in our nature that He was tempted, for "God cannot be tempted by evil, nor does he tempt anyone" (James 1:13). It was as the second Adam, and the representative of our struggling race that the Lord

271

Jesus entered the battle that day with the great adversary and proved that no mortal again need ever despair. Temptation is still a fact in every human life. But, it is also true that "no temptation has seized you except what is common to man. And God is faithful; he will not let you be tempted beyond what you can bear. But when you are tempted, he will also provide a way out so that you can stand up under it" (1 Corinthians 10:13).

THE AGENT IN THE TEMPTATION

The agent in the temptation is called the devil. The Bible has a way of calling things by their right names which we would be wise to follow. The devil has achieved no greater triumph than to succeed in hiding his identity from this advanced age. If a brigand could only succeed in posing as one of a tourist party whom he intended to rob, he would have little difficulty in carrying out his plans. This is just what Satan has attempted and accomplished in many quarters today, and while men are laughing at the idea of a devil he is playing off his disguise and leading men captive at his will. Doubtless he came to Jesus as he still comes to us, not in some open and repulsive form, but in deep disguise and probably by such subtle suggestions as could easily be mistaken for the promptings of His own mind.

THE CIRCUMSTANCES OF THE TEMPTATION

The first great test came to man in a paradise of beauty and delight, but it ended in a tragedy. The second came in the desolate wilderness, but it led up to Paradise restored. The adversary chooses his battlefield with wise discrimination. He came to Christ when His body was enfeebled with long fasting, and His spirit perhaps clouded with the gloomy surroundings of His situation. He will always attack us at our worst. When the frame is worn with sickness, the body racked with pain, and the spirit depressed with discouragement and sorrow, then look out for the crafty and cruel adversary.

THE TIME OF THE TEMPTATION

It was after a great blessing and before a great service. Jesus had just stood at the open heaven and received the baptism of the Holy Spirit, and the message of His Father, "You are my Son, whom I love; with you I am well pleased" (Luke 3:22). And He was about to begin His great life, and His mighty assault upon Satan's kingdom. Therefore all the forces of hell were roused against Him. It was when David was crowned king in Hebron that "the Philistines . . . went up . . . to search for him" (2 Samuel 5:17). An old writer has said, "So long as Jesus was occupied with the chips of the carpenter shop, the devil paid little attention to Him; but when He came forth in the power of the Spirit to conquer him, then the gauge of battle was drawn." Let us look out for danger in the hour of spiritual elevation and glorious blessing, and let us especially be prepared for the wiles of the enemy when we are planning some high service for God and our fellow men.

THE PURPOSE OF THE TEMPTATION

Why was Jesus tempted of the devil? Why is temptation permitted to come to any man? Why does not God with one lightning stroke destroy our cruel foe and clear our way from every adversary and obstacle?

If two young men were placed in a position of responsibility and trust, and the one permitted every opportunity to be dishonest, and the other so hedged about that all graft and dishonesty were made impossible, and both came forth at the end of their period of probation with an irreproachable record, which would have the higher moral standing? Surely, the one that had been tested in the face of temptation. The moral character of the other would still be a matter of absolute uncertainty.

Therefore it was necessary that the human race should be tested in the first creation, and it is still necessary for the development and confirmation of character that we should pass through the ordeal of the tempter. "Consider it pure joy, my brothers, whenever you face trials [temptations, KJV] of many kinds, because you know that the testing of your faith develops perseverance. Perseverance must finish its work so that you may be mature and complete, not lacking anything" (James 1:2–4). All the more was this necessary in the Master's case, because His righteousness was not for Himself alone, but was to be imputed to all His followers as the ground of their acceptance, and it must be proved even in the face of the gates of hell to be without a flaw. Furthermore this conflict was a great representative battle in behalf of the race. It was the decisive conflict of human history and destiny. It was the second Adam taking up the issue where the first had failed, and winning back all that he had lost. It was as necessary for Christ to stand victorious in the wilderness as it was for Him without a murmur to lay down His life upon the cross. Both were vicarious offerings—the one the suffering of His righteousness, the other of His life. And by both He has conquered hell and opened heaven to all believers.

SECTION II—*The Method and Process of the Temptation*

In many respects it was the very counterpart of the first great conflict in Eden.

THE ATTACK ON HIS FAITH

The first attack was made upon the faith of our Lord. "If you are the Son of God" (Luke 4:3), the devil sneered; as much as to say, "You the Son of God! Well, did I ever hear anything so absurd! The Son of God left by His

Father in this desolate wilderness, exposed to wild beasts and starving for bread? Why, You are deluded. You must be insane. Come, let us dispel this dream; or, if You be the Son of God, let us have some proof of it." And so the devil dared the Lord to prove His character and claim. Remember the subject of this temptation was a real man with a mind as liable to discouragement, despondency and the depression that come from physical weakness as yours and mine. Remember also that it is your faith that the enemy assails, and discouragement is usually the gateway to doubt and unbelief. Your worst faults and falls are not so important to the great enemy of your soul as the use which he intends to make of them in crushing your spirit and destroying your confidence. Remember, therefore, the stirring message of one who himself was sorely tempted: "Resist him, standing firm in the faith, because you know that your brothers throughout the world are undergoing the same kind of sufferings" (1 Peter 5:9). Remember, also, the words of another victorious soldier of the cross, "In addition to all this, take up the shield of faith, with which you can extinguish all the flaming arrows of the evil one" (Ephesians 6:16). "So do not throw away your confidence; it will be richly rewarded" (Hebrews 10:35).

THE ATTACK UPON HIS PHYSICAL NATURE

The second assault was upon His body and His physical appetites and desires. "Tell this stone to become bread" (Luke 4:3). And so the first experiences of temptation are often through our physical nature or our temporal circumstances. How often he comes to us through sickness and the choice is between his prescription and the Lord's help. How blessed to remember at such a time the Master's answer to the enemy, "Man does not live on bread alone" (4:4). There is life in God for our bodies as well as for our spirits, and it were better even not to live than to live by the devil's help. How often the temptation comes through financial pressure. One of his fallacies is to say, "You must have a living and therefore you must do something to help yourself in this emergency." It is not always true that we must have a living. There came a time when the three Jewish men of Babylon dared to say, "the God we serve is able to save us. . . . But even if he does not, we want you to know, O king, that we will not serve your gods or worship the image of gold you have set up" (Daniel 3:17–18).

THE ATTACK UPON HIS AMBITION

The next attack was upon His ambition. In some way the glory of earthly power was brought before Him in a moment and the possibility of His attaining it, if only He would put Himself under the direction of the arch fiend. Satan was the first political boss, and ever since he has been trying to make men his dupes. Oh, how many have sold their souls for power, ambition or graft! Doubtless, in the case of our Lord, he made it all appear beautiful and beneficent and pointed out, perhaps, the splendid use He could make of such power in bringing to an end the wrongs of His people, the cruel oppressions of earth's tyrants and the manifold evils of humanity. But again Christ refused the tempting bribe simply because He would not take anything from Satan. Just as He would not have the devil's bread or the devil's medicine, He would not have the devil's crown; and the day came when from the Father He received a mightier dominion and could say without any thanks to the devil, "All authority in heaven and on earth has been given to me" (Matthew 28:18).

AN APPEAL TO SPIRITUAL PRIDE

The climax was an appeal to His spiritual pride. The devil first attacked His body, next His soul and finally His spirit. "Cast Yourself down," he cried, "from this lofty pinnacle of the temple, and God will work such a miracle for Your deliverance that the world will immediately flock to Your feet and hail You as its deliverer and its God." And then he began to quote some Scripture, but again Jesus met him word for word with the same weapon that he had used: "It says: 'Do not put the Lord your God to the test' " (Luke 4:12).

The principle of the temptation, and the principle of the victory was the same as in the other assault. He refused to take Himself out of the place of a real man. He refused to turn aside from the will of His Father and even work a miracle to save Himself. Had He done so it would have been the rejection of the cross and the renouncing of the pathway of lowly humanity and suffering through which He was to redeem the race. As a man He had gone into that place of trial, and there He should remain until deliverance came to Him not through His own rash act, but through His Father's loving hand. How perfect the picture of humanity. How truly He "has been tempted in every way, just as we are—yet was without sin" (Hebrews 4:15).

SECTION III—*The Secret of Victory*

THE WORD

The Word was His weapon. "It is written," was the sword of the Spirit which again and again He wielded with such resistless power. We cannot hope to stand in the evil day unless we know our Bibles and are taught by the Spirit how to use them. The remarkable fact about His use of the Bible was that most of His quotations were taken from the book of Deuteronomy, the very book which the devil and higher critics have always tried to depreciate and discredit. Jesus took the very weakest of all His weapons and used it to crush the serpent's head.

THE HOLY SPIRIT

Jesus "was led by the Spirit in the desert" (Luke 4:1), and He went forth in the power of the Spirit. "When the enemy shall come in like a flood, the Spirit of the LORD shall lift up a standard against him" (Isaiah 59:19, KJV). It is only as we walk in the Spirit and follow Him closely, that we can expect to overcome that crafty foe whose wisdom is too deep for us alone.

DEVOTION TO THE WILL OF GOD

The deepest secret of Christ's triumph was His devotion to the will of God. "I must be about my Father's business" (Luke 2:49, KJV), was the keynote of His life. He sought nothing for Himself. He would accept nothing for Himself. Nothing could tempt Him from the path of suffering to which He had given Himself in obedience to His Father's will, and this was the sheet anchor of His safety. This is that breastplate of righteousness wherewith we shall be armed against the great enemy. It is a great and profound truth that Jesus Christ won His victory over Satan and won our redemption, not by brilliant wisdom, or superhuman power, but by simple righteousness. It was a moral triumph. Had He for a moment failed, our redemption would have been lost, and He and we together would have perished in the ruin. Remember, the mightiest thing in your life is to be right and to do right at any cost. Against such a purpose the gates of hell cannot prevail.

SECTION IV—*The Results of the Temptation*

"Jesus returned to Galilee in the power of the Spirit" (4:14). He was stronger for the battle. And so will we be. Every victory won imparts to you the strength that you have taken from your conquered foe. And by and by there will be added the crown of recompense and the eternal reward which God is preparing not only for those that have worked for souls, but for those that have stood true in the evil day. "Blessed is the man who perseveres under trial, because when he has stood the test, he will receive the crown of life that God has promised to those who love him" (James 1:12).

CHRIST'S FELLOWSHIP WITH US IN TEMPTATION

This is the chief lesson of all this story. True to Luke's great purpose, the Son of Man appears in the conflict of the wilderness as our Brother, our Champion and our great Example. For us He won back the victory that Adam, our first father, had so shamefully lost; and with us and in us, still He overcomes as we follow His footsteps through temptation and trial. "Because he himself suffered when he was tempted, he is able to help those who are being tempted" (Hebrews 2:18). How tender and solemn His message to Peter, His tempted disciple, "Simon, Simon, Satan has asked to sift you as wheat. But I have prayed for you, Simon, that your faith may not fail. And when you have turned back, strengthen your brothers" (Luke 22:31–32). And how faithfully Peter, in his turn, sought to fulfill this trust and help the tempted ones.

CONQUERORS THROUGH HIM

The supreme lesson of all that we have been considering is that only in Christ can we hope to overcome our subtle foe. All who try this unequal conflict alone will surely fail. The sinner has ventured on the devil's territory and Satan has a right to every man who sins. There is One only who can set us free, and those who refuse His help must fall. The most fearful thing about the condition of ungodly men is that they are unable to give up sinning and are bound to fall under the power of the wicked one. "The Lord knows how to rescue godly men from trials and to hold the unrighteous for the day of judgment, while continuing their punishment" (2 Peter 2:9).

One of my saddest memories is the case of a man addicted to drink, who persistently refused to accept the Lord Jesus as his Savior, declaring that he needed nothing better than his own manhood to give him the victory. In the last interview I had with him he closed the conversation by saying, "I don't want your Jesus, I can save myself." A few months after this, the awful tidings suddenly came that he had dropped dead in a drunken spree in one of the saloons in the city, and gone to his account with all his transgressions upon his head. There is but One who can succor and save you. The Son of Man who conquered for you once, and is ready to conquer in you again.

Fainting soldier of the Lord,
Hear His sweet, inspiring word—
I have conquered all thy foes;
I have suffered all thy woes;
Struggling soldier, trust in Me,
I have overcome for thee.

CHAPTER 5

THE FIRST MESSAGE OF THE SON OF MAN

Jesus returned to Galilee in the power of the Spirit, and news about him spread through the whole countryside. He taught in their synagogues, and everyone praised him.
He went to Nazareth, where he had been brought up, and on the Sabbath day he went into the synagogue, as was his custom. And he stood up to read. (Luke 4:14–16)

The remarkable incidents attending the birth, baptism and temptation of our Lord, as recorded by Luke, would naturally prepare us to expect some unusual opening of His public ministry. And we are not disappointed. Like the frontispiece on the opening page of a volume, the incident of our text stands out in bold relief. How utterly human the picture is! Like all the other pictures which Luke gives us of the Son of Man—His coming to His own country to begin His ministry and to the city where He had been brought up; His claiming in humble dependence the direction of the Holy Spirit as He gives His message; His modest recognition of the Holy Scriptures as the authority and foundation of His address, and then the character of this message with its infinite tenderness and grace and its broad and sweeping appeal to humanity with all its needs—all this coupled with His rejection by His own people gives to the incident of our text a peculiar propriety as the opening chapter of Luke's account of the wondrous ministry that was to be so broad in its scope and so gracious in its mercy and love. We might well inscribe over the scene the touching words of another evangelist, "He came to that which was his own, but his own did not receive him" (John 1:11).

SECTION I—*The Background*

HE BEGAN AT NAZARETH

Let us note the fact that He began at Nazareth, His own city. The evangelists, Matthew and Mark, described a visit by our Lord to Nazareth much later in His ministry. We find the account in the sixth chapter of Mark and the 13th chapter of Matthew. Most of the harmonists of the Gospel identify that visit with the one recorded by Luke in our text. But it is contrary to Luke's custom to insert incidents out of their chronological order. He usually follows the law of sequence more exactly than any of the evangelists, and it would not be like him to strain a point in this record even for the sake of introducing this striking scene as a frontispiece in his Gospel. Further, when we look at the facts related in Matthew and Mark, we find them quite different from the incident in Luke. They tell us that the Lord performed several miracles of a minor character at this time and "he could not do any miracles there, except lay his hands on a few sick people and heal them" (Mark 6:5).

The accounts of these evangelists also show that the disciples were with Him. Luke's narrative makes no mention of any disciples and it seems quite certain that if they had been there, they would have interposed in some way to protect Him from the violence of the mob who tried to hurl Him from the brow of the hill on which the city was built. We are therefore justified, we believe, in regarding this as an earlier visit to Nazareth quite near the beginning of His ministry and probably just after His visit to Cana and the brief tarry in Galilee that followed, just before His journey to Jerusalem. Probably He left Capernaum for Nazareth, taking His mother with Him and leaving her there while He journeyed down to Jerusalem.

How tender the interest connected with His first message to His own people, and how full of significance for us in connection with our responsibility to be faithful witnesses to our own family circle and immediate friends. Have we been true to our testimony there? Perhaps, like Him, we will be rejected, but nonetheless we should be faithful even if it must be as true of us as of Him, "no prophet is accepted in his hometown" (Luke 4:24).

IN THE SPIRIT

Quite as remarkable is His dependence upon the Holy Spirit in this, His first message. He does not come announcing His own independent authority, but He takes the place of one dependent upon the same great Teacher to whom we all may look for our endowment of power for service. There is something very striking in the voluntary dependence of the Lord Jesus upon the power of the Holy Spirit in all His work and teaching. Surely, if He did not venture upon His ministry without the baptism of the Spirit and did not take a step except in dependence upon Him, we are guilty of the highest presumption should we attempt the slightest ministry in our human strength. How near it brings us to Him and Him to us, to find Him thus leaning upon the same Arm that sustains us in all our service.

We cannot fail to note the effects of the Spirit's baptism as manifested in our Lord. "All spoke well of him and were amazed at the gracious words that came from his lips" (4:22). The Spirit-filled worker will always have the same token, the unction of the Holy Spirit as shown in every tone and expression as a Spirit of graciousness, gentleness and power.

How may we expect to receive this power? Surely, by truly expecting it and claiming it by faith. There was no uncertain sound in the confession of His faith. "The Spirit of the Lord is on me" (4:18), He could say, and we too must claim this divine endowment as positively and confess it as steadfastly. Are we thus working in the power of the Spirit as well as walking in fellowship with Him? They that look for Him will not look in vain.

HIS DEPENDENCE UPON THE HOLY SCRIPTURES

Not only did He look to the Spirit to guide and inspire Him, but He took the Scriptures as the foundation of His messages. Already He had proved its power in the hour of temptation, and now He leans upon it as He goes forth to His work. Other teachers are accustomed, in founding a new religion, to bring out a new Bible; so we have the Bibles of Mohammedanism, Mormonism and similar delusions. Jesus Christ identified Himself with the Old Testament Scriptures, and on this occasion began His ministry by taking the prophetic scroll, from which they were accustomed to hear their morning lesson, and reading the very passage which was fulfilled that day in their ears in His own personal ministry.

We notice His familiarity with the prophetic Word. "Unrolling it, he found the place where it is written" (4:17). He knew where to find it. He was familiar with His Bible. Oh, that each of us, like Him, might be "a workman who does not need to be ashamed and who correctly handles the word of truth" (2 Timothy 2:15). The modern preacher soon exhausts his Bible and goes to the newspapers or the scientists for his sensational messages. The wise preacher will always preach the Word. Not only so, but He also knew how to apply the Word to the occasion and the audience. "Today," He said, looking directly in the faces of His hearers, "this scripture is fulfilled in your hearing" (Luke 4:21). His preaching was pointed, personal and intensely practical. So let ours be. Let us aim at men and women and let us strike hard at human consciences and hearts and let us expect immediate decisions and results.

SECTION II—*The Message*

What a wonderful message it was! How fitting to the scope and purpose of Luke's Gospel! How different from the great sermon recorded by Matthew in the opening of his Gospel! That was suited for the Jew and the Gospel of the Kingdom. It was all about "his kingdom and his righteousness" (Matthew 6:33). There is nothing of this in Luke, the Gospel to the Gentiles and the sinner. The keynote here is all grace, mercy and salvation.

THE GOSPEL OF THE JUBILEE

The first note and the supreme note in it is joyfulness. It is a message of hope to a sorrowing, despairing world. It has been well called the Gospel of the Jubilee. Its undertone and its echo are gladness, victory, deliverance from all the evils that oppress humanity. It is the "sovereign balm for every wound." It is the remedy for the ills of humanity. Back of it stands the splendid figure of the Year of Jubilee. This is just the meaning of the closing clause to "proclaim the year of the Lord's favor" (Luke 4:19).

Every 50 years there came to ancient Israel a great festival that lasted a whole year long. All labor ceased and the earth abundantly supplied, the preceding year, enough for two. Nature rested, man rested and every home and synagogue and sanctuary and spot became the scene of festival and gladness. With its early dawn, the jubilee trumpets rang out upon every mountain top and summoned the people to a year of rejoicing; and, as the year wore on, you might have seen many a family moving back to the vine-clad cottage which they had been compelled to lose years before for some mortgage debt. You might have seen sons and daughters traveling home and welcomed by rejoicing fathers and mothers as they came back from the slavery to which they had been consigned as hostages for some family debt. You might have seen bonds and mortgages, promissory notes and liens torn up or burned to ashes while every debt was canceled, every slave set free, every prison opened and every lost heritage restored. All this Jesus Christ came to fulfill in a higher and grander sense by proclaiming an everlasting jubilee for all who accept His grace. Surely, such a gospel is indeed humanity's greatest boon and the announcement of such a message a fitting and glorious inauguration of the gospel of the Son of Man.

FORGIVENESS OF SINS

Coming down to particulars, the first great blessing of this jubilee is the cancellation of our debt, the forgiveness of our sins and the discharge for us of all our obligations to a broken law and an offended God. Christ has come to set us free from the law, not only from its curse and penalty, but from its bondage as demanding our righteousness, giving us instead His better righteousness and His indwelling and enabling, so that "the righteous requirements of the law might be fully met in us, who do not live according to the sinful nature but according to the Spirit" (Romans 8:4). Have we entered into this glorious liberty? Have we taken Him for all our liabilities and responsibilities and are we proving that noble *Magna Charta* of the children of God, "So if the Son sets you free, you will be free indeed" (John 8:36)?

FREEDOM FROM SIN

He brings freedom from the bondage of sin, "freedom for the prisoners/ . . . to release the oppressed" (Luke 4:18). The sinner is helpless as well as guilty. He has gone upon the enemy's ground and has been taken captive. This does not lessen his accountability, because he is responsible for having put himself in this condition, but he is nonetheless helpless. Sinful men are spoken of in the Scriptures as those in "the trap of the devil, who has taken them captive to do his will" (2 Timothy 2:26), and those whom "[God] gave . . . over to a depraved mind" (Romans 1:28). Of course, they think they can do as they please; but they find when it comes to the test that they are "unspiritual, sold as a slave to sin" (7:14). One of the chains of sin is the force of habit. Another is an evil nature and a heart whose preference is for evil. We find an innate tendency to sin developed in the youngest children. From all this, Christ comes to set us free. "The law of the Spirit of life set me free from the law of sin and death" (8:2). The Holy Spirit puts within us a new heart, new thoughts, new desires and preferences and then He puts within us also new strength, His own power to enable us to obey these higher impulses.

> He breaks the power of canceled sin;
> He sets the prisoner free.

The bondage of sickness is also implied in this passage. "Them that are bruised" (Luke 4:18, KJV) literally means, "Them that are diseased." Sickness and death follow sin by the operation of the same great law. From sickness Christ set us free by His healing power, and from death He has delivered us by His resurrection, which is the pledge and guarantee of ours.

Oh, what a glorious announcement to a death-doomed and fallen race! What else can for a moment compare with the lofty claims and infinite and eternal possibilities of our great redemption?

OUR LOST INHERITANCE

The jubilee gave back their lost inheritances. The home that had been forfeited for debt was returned to its ancient owners and the inalienable possessions of the family were restored. Christ has come to give us back all which we, through sin, have lost—lost years, lost opportunities, lost powers, lost hopes, a lost heaven and our lost loved ones. The curse of sin is more than canceled, and in Him we boast "more blessings than our father lost."

THE GRACE OF GOD

The one underlying thought in all this glorious proclamation is grace. It is the revealing of the heart of God. It is a proclamation of infinite help to a helpless, hopeless world. "The year of the Lord's favor" (4:19) just means the day of grace, the offer of mercy, the opportunity of salvation for all who will receive and believe. It finds its parallel in that beautiful expression of the apostle in the Second Epistle to the Corinthians, "I tell you, now is the time of God's favor, now is the day of salvation" (6:2). Literally, it means, "Now is the time of loving welcome; now is the day of salvation."

The most noticeable thing about this paragraph is that the Lord stopped in the middle of a sentence and omitted the last clause of the quotation from Isaiah. That clause is "and the day of vengeance of our God" (Isaiah 61:2). He did not read this because the time for that had not yet come. The day of grace is a great parenthesis, but some time soon that parenthesis will end and the prophecy will be finished, and on a slumbering world will burst "the day of vengeance of our God." Oh, that we might catch the spirit of this glorious evangel and go forth to ring it out from all the mountaintops of earth until the glad jubilee of the world will have fully come with the coming of the King Himself in His millennial glory!

The illustrations which our Lord adds in His sermon at Nazareth are most significant. They are drawn from Hebrew history and they both anticipate the dispensation of the gospel for the Gentiles.

> I assure you that there were many widows in Israel in Elijah's time, when the sky was shut for three and a half years and there was a severe famine throughout the land. Yet Elijah was not sent to any of them, but to a widow in Zarephath in the region of Sidon. And there were many in Israel with leprosy in the time of Elisha the prophet, yet not one of them was cleansed—only Naaman the Syrian. (Luke 4:25–27)

How strange the citation of these two cases showing the overflow of God's mercy, even in their own history as a nation, to two Gentiles. The widow of Zarephath was a poor Gentile, Naaman the Syrian was a Gentile too, and yet these are the only instances of divine mercy which the Savior mentions in His argument to show how the nation has in the past rejected God, and He has reached men and women beyond the pale of Israel altogether. So once more they are to reject their Messiah and the Gentiles are to come in and inherit their privileges. It was a foreshadowing of the very reception that He was Himself to get that morning, for no sooner had these words fallen from His lips than the whole congregation fell upon Him in angry violence, and, dragging Him to the city, tried to hurl Him from the cliff on which Nazareth was built, and He was only saved by a divine miracle which suddenly took Him, we are not told how, from their midst, and enabled Him to escape their blind fury.

So Luke gives us this early intimation of the rejection of the Messiah by His own people and the coming of the Gentiles instead. How solemn and full of instruction the fact that, although clothed with the power of the Holy Spirit, the Master's first message to His own people at Nazareth seemed utterly to fail. Let us not be surprised if sometimes our messages too appear to fall upon dull or unbelieving ears. Sometimes we shall be "the fragrance of life," sometimes "the smell of death" (2 Corinthians 2:16). Let us be willing to follow the Master everywhere even when it means rejection for us too.

> I'll share the cross of Jesus,
> Its crucifixion bear;
> All hail reproach and sorrow
> If Jesus leads me there.

Beloved, have we followed the Master in the baptism of the Spirit? Have we entered into the spirit of the glorious Gospel of the Jubilee, and are we sounding out its message and sending forth the trumpets of salvation to herald on earth's mountaintops the glorious message?

> Go and tell them, go and tell them,
> Jesus died for sinful men;
> Go and tell them, go and tell them,
> He is coming back again.

CHAPTER 6

THE SON OF MAN AND THE SINNER

For the Son of Man came to seek and to save what was lost. (Luke 19:10)

This man welcomes sinners and eats with them. (15:2)

In nothing is it more true that God's thoughts and ways are as high as heaven above the earth as in His dealing with sin and sinners. Human nature goes either to the extreme of undue palliation or undue severity, either embraces or consumes the transgressor. Divine grace, while condemning sin with a holy severity unapproached by the severest human standards, at the same time meets the sinner with a tender grace and an almighty help and love of which this beautiful gospel affords a series of illustrations unequaled in any of the books of the New Testament. In this respect, Luke is indeed the gospel of the Son of Man and of Him might be written over almost every chapter, "For the Son of Man came to seek and to save what was lost" (19:10).

In the present chapter we will present five pictures of Christ's grace in relation to sinners, most of them peculiar to Luke.

SECTION I—*The Calling of Levi*

Luke 5:27–32

While this incident is not peculiar to the Gospel of Luke, yet it forms the introduction to a number of incidents that are not related by any other evangelist and it gives us the keynote of the whole. Here we see especially the unconventional character of our Lord and the simple and informal way in which He came into contact with sinful men. He sat down in the home of Levi with the company of tax collectors and sinners in the most unaffected and natural way, and by tact and sympathy He won His way to the hearts of men rather than by stately messages and formal addresses. If we would be soul winners like Him, we must learn to be "all things to all men so that by all possible means [we] might save some" (1 Corinthians 9:22).

But the special lesson of this incident is the beautiful tact which Christ used to save men as links through which He was able to reach other men. Levi represented the class from which he came, and through him the Savior was able to come in contact with a great multitude who would have naturally stood off from Him had He met them as a Jewish rabbi; but as the friend of Levi they gladly received Him, and doubtless others also "left everything and followed him" (Luke 5:28).

Have we used our past and the influence which even a sinful life may have caused over our fellow men to bring them to the Christ who has redeemed us from a life of sin?

SECTION II—*The Sinful Woman in the House of Simon*

Luke 7:36–50

In looking at this touching example of our Savior's love, it will help us to enter into the spirit of it if we recall the probable prelude to the story in Luke. This will be found in the closing verses of the 11th chapter of the Gospel of Matthew. The beautiful words of invitation with which that paragraph closes, "Come to me, all you who are weary and burdened, and I will give you rest" (11:28), would seem to have been spoken in immediate connection with this incident. Probably they form the close of an address which the Master had just been giving in some public place to the assembled crowd, and among those who heard it were both Simon and this sinful woman. On him it had made a profound impression, and with evident sincerity he had invited the Lord to come to his home and accept his hospitality. The evangelist tells us that he "invited Jesus to have dinner with him" (Luke 7:36). This word "invited" carries with it the idea of earnest and perhaps repeated importunity. He was evidently cordial and sincere in his invitation. The Master's own words in the parable that followed in the house of Simon leaves no doubt that, notwithstanding all that was wrong in his spirit, he had been forgiven. He was certainly one of the two debtors referred to in the parable and Christ says the Lord "canceled the debts of both" (7:42). We are not, therefore, to think of him as a supercilious and scornful adversary, but as an honest friend gradually emerging from the prejudices of the Pharisaism in which he had been so long schooled. The Lord appreciates his spirit, and in the scene which follows is endeavoring to help him quite as much as the sinful woman.

AN ORIENTAL SCENE

The scene in the house of Simon is a striking one. Reclining at the table in a large court, with their feet extending back from the table on the Oriental divans, the guests were assembled to eat; while around the walls of the large chamber or court a motley crowd sometimes gathered, freely passing through the open doors according to the simple etiquette of an Eastern home. There was, therefore, no reason why this poor woman of the town should not also slip in with the crowd and take her place behind the seated guests. The language of the narrative implies that all this had been carefully planned by her. She had known that Christ was to be there, and she had chosen the time to express her love and gratitude. She had heard Him utter those gracious words of invitation already quoted. Perhaps He had looked into her face and made her know that her sins were forgiven. Certainly she had taken this by faith herself, for the Lord clearly implies that her great love was the result of a sense of great forgiveness.

The language of the narrative implies that the gift she brought had been hers before. Probably it was the wages of her sin, and surely if ever a gift was "tainted" this was. But the Lord can accept the gifts of the vilest if they are accompanied by the tears that show that the heart and hands that bring them have been cleansed. She had evidently meant to be calm and proper in her thank offering, but before she knew it a storm of feeling had swept all barriers away, and she found her tears would not stay back as she had bid them, but fell in torrents of passionate love and contrition at His feet. Luke says, "she began to wet his feet with her tears" (7:38). That implies that she stopped her weeping just as quickly as she could compose herself, but already those tears covered His holy feet and made it difficult for her to anoint them as she had planned. The tears were not in the program, and so it became necessary to wipe them away. Impulsively she loosed her tresses and with her hair she wiped away the tear stains from His feet, and then she took the costly spikenard, and with many a caress of love she anointed His blessed feet until the house was filled with the odor of the oil.

THE TEMPTATION OF SIMON

It had all been so sudden that the company of guests were held spellbound, and Simon himself was the most impressed of them all. Well he knew her character, and expected his guests with becoming dignity to check or rebuke this sudden interruption. What must have been his amazement when he turned and saw the Savior Himself evidently accepting with complacency and approval this extraordinary demonstration. Immediately the confidence that had started in his own heart began to be rudely checked. Must he not be mistaken? Can this man be a true prophet and not really know the character of the woman who was touching Him; or, if He knows, can He be a good man to allow her to take such liberties? Jesus understood his thought, and quickly answered it. We do not need to speak out for the

Lord to know what is passing in our hearts. Very striking are the two expressions, "the Pharisee . . . said to himself," and "Jesus answered him" (7:39, 40). No word had come out from those cold and haughty lips, but he had spoken all the same, and Christ had heard it. It would not do to let the temptation be unmet. Simon must understand, and the woman, too. And so that matchless parable follows in which the guilt of both is pictured in such discriminating and heart-searching words. Then the grace of God to both is pictured in the matchless language of the parable, and the gentle yet unmistakable reproof is suggested to the proud heart of the Pharisee, while to the sinful woman He addresses the reassuring words that her sins, which are many, are forgiven (see 7:48), "Your faith has saved you; go in peace" (7:50).

LESSONS

For us the lesson is plain and full of the gospel of the grace of God.

1. We are all debtors.

2. There is a great difference in our debts. God does not condone gross sin, but characterizes it at its true estimation. Yes, her sins are many. There is no attempt to whitewash her life. It is all frankly conceded. She is a greater sinner than Simon, but . . .

3. Both are equally bankrupt. They have nothing to pay. Simon cannot meet his debt any more than the woman can.

4. The free grace of God frankly forgives them both.

5. Love is not the crown of forgiveness, but the proof of it. She is much forgiven, therefore she loves much. Put in the word "therefore," instead of "for," and you get the gospel truth unmixed with error.

6. It was her faith that saved her, not her love; but her faith worked by love and melted her heart with tender gratitude for her forgiveness.

7. Forgiveness brings us into peace. "Come into peace," is the literal translation of the message of her Savior; a land of rest, a new world of infinite and everlasting joy, and doubtless in the coming days she was found with loving heart and willing hands among those that ministered to the Lord. This is the gospel of the grace of God. This is the attitude of Jesus Christ toward sinful men and women.

SECTION III—*A Sinful Man*

Luke 19:1–10

Now it is not a sinful woman, but a sinful man, that meets us, and it is a new type of sin altogether. Perhaps before the world it may seem much more respectable. Here is no degrading lust, no repulsive debauchery and open vice, and yet here is perhaps the hardest and most hopeless of all the forms of human sin: the love of money. But there is a key even to the heart of Zacchaeus. That key is the love and grace of the Lord Jesus Christ. The Master did not wait until Zacchaeus had sought Him, for Christ Himself was seeking this poor lost sinner. How sublime the grace that offers itself to the sinner unsought and unconditionally! "Zacchaeus, come down immediately. I must stay at your house today" (19:5). So the Master gave Himself unreservedly, unconditionally to this hard and sinful man, and what was the result? Listen: Zacchaeus stood and cried, "Look, Lord! Here and now I give half of my possessions to the poor, and if I have cheated anybody out of anything, I will pay back four times the amount" (7:8). That was the repentance that comes from one touch of divine grace. So the sunrise melts away the fogs of night. So the summer melts away the frosts of winter. So the Gulf Stream embraces in its mighty arms the icebergs of the Pole, and lo, they fall into that warm and fertilizing stream that turns the shores of Western Europe into summer lands. And so the grace of God transforms the hardest heart.

But above all other impressions that we gather from this matchless picture, there is none more touching than what Robertson of Brighton has so happily called "Christ's estimate of sin."

Speaking of Zacchaeus, He does not seem to think of his hardness, his meanness, his selfishness, but only of his danger. In the thought of Christ, it was enough that he was lost and He had come to seek and save him. So Christ is looking at every sinner still with a deep concern that is only too glad to forgive the past, if only He may save for the present and future. Oh, that we may have that love for sinful men, for perishing men!

SECTION IV—*Christ Weeping over Jerusalem*

Luke 19:41–44

The one touching yet terrific truth that stands out above all others from this dramatic picture is that marvelous love that can still pity when it is too late to save. As Christ looked down upon that doomed city lying at His feet, He knew that the day of grace was already past, but nonetheless did He cry, "If you, even you, had only known on this day what would bring you peace—but now it is hidden from your eyes" (19:42). Blessed Heart of infinite and everlasting love, it is sweet to know that even when we will not let You save us, we cannot keep You from loving us. Surely, this should be enough to touch every sinner's heart and drive him to the feet of Jesus.

There is a day of grace, and it passes even long before the thunders of judgment roll and the lightnings of doom burst from the angry clouds. All may be calm, certain and free from alarm, and yet the soul be lost and Christ have for you only the mercy of His tears.

SECTION V—*The Dying Thief*

Luke 23:39–43

This is not peculiar to Luke in one sense, for two of the other evangelists refer to it, but only Luke gives the details. They seem to have just mentioned it, and then remembered that it was best suited for the gospel of the Son of Man and left it for Luke to tell the story in detail.

It is inexpressibly touching that Luke should make it the last scene in the Savior's life, for as he finishes his narrative we hear Jesus gently say, "Father, into your hands I commit my spirit" (23:46); and with that first ransomed sinner in His arms Jesus has entered Paradise. His last act on earth was to save a brutal murderer; His first in heaven was to present him washed and glorified before His Father's throne. Surely, this was a fitting picture for the Gospel of the Son of Man.

What is the supreme message of this scene in connection with our subject? Surely it is this: that the destiny of the sinner depends upon his attitude toward the cross of Jesus Christ. There were two sinners there that day, "one on his right, the other on his left" (23:33), and while one went with the Redeemer into Paradise, the other passed with curses upon his wicked lips from Calvary to perdition. The only reason was that one accepted Jesus as his Savior and the other refused Him. What a message of warning as well as encouragement! How awful to think that we may find the way to hell from the very side of the crucified Redeemer, as well as the way to heaven, in the last moment of life, from the depths of a life of wickedness by simple faith in the Son of Man.

On which side of that cross are you?

CHAPTER 7

THE SON OF MAN AND THE HOME

As Jesus and his disciples were on their way, he came to a village where a woman named Martha opened her home to him. She had a sister called Mary, who sat at the Lord's feet listening to what he said. But Martha was distracted by all the preparations that had to be made. She came to him and asked, "Lord, don't you care that my sister has left me to do the work by myself? Tell her to help me!"

"Martha, Martha," the Lord answered, "you are worried and upset about many things, but only one thing is needed. Mary has chosen what is better, and it will not be taken away from her."
(Luke 10:38–42)

W e have here another woman at the feet of Jesus, but how different from the former scene. This one is listening, learning, loving and leaving her sweet lesson of higher service for all the ages.

THE SON OF MAN AND THE HOME

How sacred is the home circle and the hearth stone. There we begin our life. There usually we close it. And with it the sweetest joys and the most sacred memories of life are associated. Luke and John give us a picture of the Son of Man in the home at Bethany. From the crowded city He loved to retire at night to the quiet surroundings and loving society of the household of Bethany, and we love still to think of Him as interested in our homes and the unseen Guest in every family circle. He began His public ministry at the marriage of Cana in Galilee, and every word and act of His life gave a higher sanction to the sacredness of family life.

Has Christ His true place in our homes? Do we minister to Him at the family altar, and do we sit, like Mary, at His feet and give Him the greater joy of ministering unto us?

This incident has given us two companion pictures hung up in the gal-

293

leries of time, and revealing to us two types of Christian life intensely real and strangely different.

SECTION I—*The Spirit of Martha*

1. She was a friend of Christ. With all her faults and shortcomings, she loved her Master well, and it is distinctly stated, "Jesus loved Martha and her sister and Lazarus" (John 11:5). Let us never forget, amid all our faults and the faults of our friends, that Christ loves our imperfect lives and will not leave us until He has done His very best for every one of us.

2. The motive of her service on this occasion was love. She was mistaken in her method. She was excessive in her preparations and attentions, but her heart was true. She spoiled her work, but through all its defects, the Master saw that true and tender heart and loved her nonetheless. How full of mistakes our service often is. How comforting to know that we have a Master and a Judge who loves to detach the imperfections from our gifts of devotion, and accept them through His own merits as if they were blameless.

3. Martha represents the practical Christian. Her love found expression through her hands, her eyes, her busy brain. There is a type of womanly character which a New England writer has called "faculty," which is a little in danger of detracting from the feminine qualities of many good women. They are tempted to elbow aside their quieter sisters and to fall either into masculine boldness or feminine fussiness. You practical people need the balance wheel which Mary had, of a heart that has learned to sit at the feet of Jesus as well as to run around and serve.

4. Martha was too particular about mere external things. Her housekeeping and her hospitality were overdone. This is the fault of many good women today. They are in bondage to their homes, and they are allowing style, equipage and entertainment to hinder the development of higher qualities and the fulfillment of higher ministries.

5. Martha was restless. "You are worried and upset" (Luke 10:41), might be translated, "You are fussing and fretting." Anxious care and mental agitation are always wrong. We should never be driven by our work. We should never lose our poise or peace. "Do not be anxious about anything" (Philippians 4:6). "Let the peace of Christ rule in your hearts" (Colossians 3:15).

6. Worse than all this was Martha's ill temper. This is a great fault in all, but a fatal blemish in a woman. There are two jewels she should always wear—quietness and sweetness. No matter how beautiful or brilliant you may be, ill temper will deface your beauty and neutralize your usefulness.

7. Rudeness and discourtesy also characterized Martha's conduct. She publicly exposed her irritation against her sister. She even went so far as to blame the Lord Himself for allowing her to act as she had done. We think

our irritation is all against people and things, but really it is against God. When Israel murmured against Moses, God took it all to Himself. Martha was not the first that found fault with the Lord because He did not straighten out the disagreeable people. When we come with such requests to Christ, we will usually find that He will turn the tables upon us and proceed to straighten us out. The trouble is nearer home. Love "is not rude" (1 Corinthians 13:5). A Christian woman should always be a lady. A Christian man should always be a gentleman. If you have fault to find with your brother, go to him alone and tell him. "Let your gentleness be evident to all" (Philippians 4:5).

8. Another of Martha's troubles was the many things that concerned her. Her heart was divided. Her mind was distracted. She had too many aims in life. She needed singleness of purpose. This is the trouble with us all. If we are seeking first the kingdom of God and His righteousness, we will be less worried about other things and we will leave Him to add them to us.

9. Martha's worst fault was that she failed to understand her Lord. She thought that He wanted her to do something for Him, when in reality He was just wanting to do something for her.

How Christ must be pained and disappointed with the people that are spending their lives in ecclesiastical millinery and religious ceremonies, serving tables and performing pageants of worship under the impression that this is acceptable service to Him. " 'The multitude of your sacrifices—/ what are they to me?' says the LORD" (Isaiah 1:11).

> If I were hungry I would not tell you,
>   for the world is mine, and all that is in it.
> Do I eat the flesh of bulls
>   or drink the blood of goats?
> Sacrifice thank offerings to God,
>   fulfill your vows to the Most High,
> and call upon me in the day of trouble;
>   I will deliver you, and you will honor me.
>   (Psalm 50:12–15)

SECTION II—*The Spirit of Mary*

1. In the first place, Mary had not been neglectful of her practical duties. She had done her part in the kitchen, and at a certain point, thinking that enough was done, she had left Martha and taken her place at the feet of Jesus. This is implied in the aorist tense, "my sister has left me to do the work by myself" (Luke 10:40). She had been serving and simply changed the

form of her service. Mary therefore was as practical as Martha, but she did not carry it too far. In our spiritual ministries we must be careful not to neglect our human relationships and duties. Our husbands and children should not suffer while we are sitting at the feet of Jesus. But the most spiritual people can be the most practical. "Never be lacking in zeal, but keep your spiritual fervor, serving the Lord" (Romans 12:11).

2. The secret of Mary's happier temper was that she was not living for many things, but for one thing. "One thing is needed. Mary has chosen what is better" (Luke 10:42). Hers was an undivided heart. Hers was a life that had sought the best things and let the world and its distractions go.

3. She had sought the best things. How many people take the second best! There is a fine play upon the words here in the expression, "what is better." The Romans, at their splendid feasts, were accustomed to have a choice morsel for the guest of honor. This phrase literally means "the choice bit." The Lord uses the very figure that appeals to Martha, taken from her own domestic department. She thought she knew what was the best, but Mary had the advantage of her and had chosen it and received it. With all his faults, this was the one distinguishing point between Jacob and Esau. There was very much about Jacob that was unattractive. He was selfish and contriving and full of cunning, but he knew the value of the blessing and the birthright. He appreciated the highest things, and God loved him for it and gave him what he chose. So we shall get what we choose.

4. Mary had learned to receive rather than to try to give. She understood the meaning of grace and that the Lord had come, not to get our help, but to give us His help and blessing. This is the very height of grace as taught in the Word of God. Martha still was full of the spirit of the law. She wanted to serve, to work, to do something. Mary had learned that Jesus had come to put an end to our doing and to give us in exchange His grace. Therefore today God draws a line between people at this very point. "How much more will those who receive God's abundant provision of grace and of the gift of righteousness reign in life through the one man, Jesus Christ" (Romans 5:17); while those who try to work their way will be found, like Israel of old, "going about to establish their own righteousness" (10:3, KJV) not having submitted unto the righteousness of God.

5. It all comes to this: Mary understood her Lord and Martha failed to understand Him. Mary comprehended the real heart of Jesus and the object that had brought Him from heaven, and Martha was still under the old spirit of Judaism. A little later, when once again the Master sat at that table in Bethany, Mary was the only one of all that company that comprehended the things that were pressing upon His heart and the great purpose which had brought Him to the world: to die for sinful men. It was this that cheered the heart of Jesus: that she understood Him. When she poured that

precious ointment upon His feet He declared with words of profound significance, "When she poured this perfume on my body, she did it to prepare
me for burial" (Matthew 26:12). Mary understood Him and, instead of
waiting like the other women to anoint Him after He was dead, and finding,
as they did, that He had already arisen and the opportunity was gone, Mary
came beforehand and sent Him forth to His great priesthood with an intelligent faith and devoted love that took away much of the sharpness of that
bitter cross.

Do we understand the Savior? Do we enter into His thought? Do we give
Him our sympathy, our fellowship, our deepest love? Mary represents
through all the ages the spiritual life in contrast with the practical and yet as
the true inspiration of all practical holiness. We must first come to Him and
learn to sit at His feet, hear His word and receive His grace before we can
give back to Him anything in return that will be worthy of His receiving.
God is not blaming us because we do not give more, but because we do not
take more. The keynote of redemption is grace. It is through grace alone
that we can receive the first touches of the new life, but it is equally through
grace that we must serve Him all the way. "Everything comes from you, and
we have given you only what comes from your hand" (1 Chronicles 29:14).

OUR CHOICE

There is a very practical and helpful word in this incident that will answer
for most of us the question: How can we have the best things that God has
for us? The answer is found in that little word "chosen." "Mary has chosen"
(Luke 10:42). It was not a matter of temperament with Mary, making her
contemplative rather than practical. It was a matter of will. She had chosen
deliberately, intelligently, the best that God had for her. A fine old German
saint was once asked why it was that we did not have more holiness, and his
answer was, "We have all the holiness we want. God will sanctify you, and
does sanctify every one of us just as much as we wish and choose." This is a
heart-searching truth. God gives us what we want. If you want a little of His
grace, you may get it. If you want to be halfhearted, you may. But if you
want to be wholly His and have all His fullness, His great heart is just longing to find room and vent for His love, and He "will . . . throw open the
floodgates of heaven and pour out so much blessing that you will not have
room enough for it" (Malachi 3:10).

CHAPTER 8

THE SON OF MAN AND THE FIRST DISCIPLES

Don't be afraid; from now on you will catch men. (Luke 5:10)

Nothing is more in keeping with the perfect humanity of the Lord Jesus Christ than the fact that He committed His work so fully to the hands of His disciples. His own personal ministry did not result in the conversion of as many people apparently as were added to the Church in a single day under the preaching of His servant Peter. Like David, who committed his work to the hands of Solomon and rejoiced to see it prosper in his hands, so the blessed Master loves to work through His disciples. He, the true Vine, does not bear the fruit Himself, but rather gives it to the little branches and the youngest sprouts to be loaded with the precious clusters while the Vine sustains them with His life.

While the Lord Jesus had already called His disciples at various times to follow Him, it would seem that they had not yet abandoned their ordinary vocations and devoted themselves exclusively to His service.

On His visit to Nazareth shortly before this, He was unaccompanied by His disciples, and on this occasion we find them still upon the shores of the Lake of Galilee attending to their ordinary business as fishermen. The call that comes to them at this time leads to their final separation from all other conflicting interests, and the devoting of their lives exclusively to the service of the Lord. His call to Simon and his fellow disciples reaches a wider company and teaches us many useful lessons about our service to the Lord.

GOD CALLS US THROUGH OUR SECULAR OCCUPATIONS

He found Saul seeking his father's donkeys. He found Samuel attending to his duties in the house of Eli. He found Moses shepherding the flocks of Jethro. He found David occupied with his sheep at Bethlehem. He found the shepherds of the advent morning engaged in their duties and vocations. He found Elisha ploughing his fields at Abel Meholah. And He found

299

Simon at his fishing nets in Bethsaida.

So He will meet us also at our daily tasks and enable us to turn them to higher account. We need not give up our callings to serve the Lord unless He clearly shows us that He would have us to do so, but serve Him in our secular duties with a consecrated spirit. And when He calls us to higher service, we will find the lessons we learned in the school of life to be fraught with holy power for the ministries of heaven.

HE CAME TO THEM WHEN THEY HAD FAILED IN THEIR EARTHLY CALLING

They had toiled all night and caught nothing, and then it was that He met them with the miraculous catch of fishes and said, "Don't be afraid; from now on you will catch men" (5:10). So God comes to us through our earthly trials and opens to us a vision of higher work. But for Joseph's trials, he would never have been able to save his father's house and feed the famine of the whole world. Had not poverty and widowhood come upon Naomi in the land of Moab, the beautiful story of Ruth would have been unwritten and she would have had no part in the glorious history of Israel and the Messiah. It was when the widow of Zarephath had only a single handful of meal and a single drop of oil left that the higher call came to her to feed the prophet of the Lord and to receive the most glorious manifestation of divine power in the whole history of the Old Testament. It is said that Adam Clark failed completely as a clerk in a commercial house before he found his higher ministry to teach the children of God and the churches of later centuries.

There is some lesson in your business failure. There is some blessing hidden behind the cloud if you will only watch for the coming of the Son of Man and follow as He leads.

CHRIST ASKS SERVICE FROM SIMON

"He got into one of the boats, the one belonging to Simon, and asked him to put out a little from shore" (5:3), and then turning the fishing boat into a pulpit, He began to preach to the people from the stern of the little ship.

So He came to the woman of Samaria and asked her for a drink of water, and then He gave her the living water and the glorious ministry of telling the story of Christ to her own wandering people. So again He came to Zacchaeus and asked that He might stay at his house for entertainment, but He brought with Him a whole heaven of higher blessing.

So He calls upon us for some little ministry, some gift to help a poor and suffering life, some act of self-denial for His service. And the joy it brings to us is so great that we never can rest again till we have entered upon His service and given Him all our life. He comes to us with deepest condescension.

He asked Simon for the use of his little ship that day. He is asking us to give to Him our hearts and standing, as He pleads, "Here I am! I stand at the door and knock. If anyone hears my voice and opens the door, I will come in and eat with him, and he with me" (Revelation 3:20).

Will we listen to His tender appeal and let Him lead us up to the noblest service and the most glorious and lasting blessing?

THE VALUE OF HARD PLACES

Had Daniel remained the petted courtier in the palace at Jerusalem, he never could have been God's chosen instrument to bring Nebuchadnezzar to the feet of Jehovah and glorify God before the heathen world. It was the ordeal of the lions' den that brought out the grandeur of his faith and the power of his God.

The life of Paul was one continuous succession of hardships so that he could say he was made "a spectacle . . . to angels as well as to men" (1 Corinthians 4:9) of the power of God to sustain a suffering child. Each new trial enabled him to say, "What has happened to me has really served to advance the gospel" (Philippians 1:12).

And so God has to push us out into some new place of difficulty in order to develop our faith and show us what He can do for us and through us. You will never know how God can use you until you venture upon Him and attempt more than you are equal to in your own strength and resources. The first time you attempted to give a simple testimony for Christ, you hesitated and feared the very sound of your own voice; but when you launched out and ventured upon Him, you found your voice and your work, and ever afterwards you had liberty and power in witnessing for the Master. The late Mrs. Booth was literally pushed into her public work by her husband suddenly committing to her one day a public service for which she had no experience or training whatever, and from which she shrank back with extreme sensitiveness and dread. But finding herself alone and compelled to say something, she opened her lips in dependence upon God; and to her own amazement and the delight of her hearers, she found that God had given her an unction of which she had never dreamed, and which, but for that venture, would have been unused and lost. This is why our fellow workers upon foreign fields grow so fast in their spiritual life. Their difficulties mold them. Their hard places challenge for them the richer gifts and graces of the Spirit. As they "put out into deep water" (Luke 5:4) they find the Master is with them and that great shoals of fish are to be gathered in.

Why remain in your diffidence and false humility and fail to attempt some bold service for the Master? Arise in your strength and, giving up both your strength and weakness to Him, go forth to "attempt great things for God and expect great things from God."

GOD'S PROVIDENCE

Christ manifested Himself in the miraculous catch of fishes to Simon and his brethren, and astonished and inspired them by the vision of His power.

So God meets us in some hard place in life by the angels of His providence and the interposition of His power, until we too are filled with awe and praise at some marvelous deliverance, and henceforth we never can be the same again. Such places in our life are like "the land of the Jordan,/ the heights of Hermon—from Mount Mizar" (Psalm 42:6), to which David looked back as the sunlit peaks of life's mountains; the places where God meets us, and the heavens are opened in the revelation of His love and power. This forever makes life divine and God intensely real. God is waiting to meet us along life's pathway with just such memorials which fill our hearts with confidence in His all-sufficiency and power. And if He has so met us let us not be "disobedient to the vision from heaven" (Acts 26:19), but remember that our life is a trust, and that God has simply shown us what He is able to do for us a thousand times if we will but step out upon His Word and venture upon His almighty help.

GOD'S WORD

It was the word of the Master that called Simon to higher service. "But because you say so, I will let down the nets" (Luke 5:5). It is a crisis hour in our life when first the Word of God becomes real to us. Up to that time it was just a book, but now it becomes a message. It was that Word that came to Moses, to Samuel, to Elisha, to Paul, and transformed their lives. If we will listen, we will hear it speaking with divine authority to our conscience and heart and saying, "Follow Me." When God speaks to us and sends us forth at His command, then no danger can appall us and no difficulty can discourage us. Oh, what a condescension that the Mighty One should turn aside and call us, insignificant children of the dust, to be His fellow workers and partners of His very throne. God grant that, even as you read these lines, some heart may discern that voice and answer, "Rabboni."

THE REVELATION OF SELF

This miracle brought to Simon Peter not only the revelation of Christ, but a revelation of himself. "Go away from me, Lord," he cried, "I am a sinful man!" (5:8). The vision of God always disgusts us with ourselves. There need be no discouragement in this deep consciousness of our unworthiness. It will but make larger room for God Himself and bring us into closer sympathy with weak and sinful men. May God show us Himself and ourselves.

A CALL TO A DEEPER LIFE

The call to Peter may be translated as a call to each of us to come into a deeper Christian life. Such an experience is the best qualification for Christian service. It is what we are, more than what we say or do, that God uses to impress other lives.

Have we gone down into the depths of self-surrender and have we ventured out into the ocean of His boundless grace? "Put out into deep water, and let down the nets for a catch" (5:4).

SEPARATION

The Master's message to Simon and his brethren led them to an entire separation to Him and His service. "They . . . left everything and followed him" (5:11)—their nets, their fathers, their old ties, interests and aims. Henceforth there was but one thing to live and labor for: the Master's work and will. Are we thus separated unto His service? Even if we still are led to continue in our secular callings, have we the separated spirit and the single aim?

THE PLACE OF SERVICE

The end and purpose of all God's dealings with us is service. "From now on you will catch men" (5:10). The word "men" is very emphatic in the original. There is the suggestion that many of us are fishing for very poor game. Are we catching men? Oh, the value of a single soul! Think of one such life as Ramabai, saved from the wreckage of India and the thousands of precious lives that she has brought to her King. What if God should give you one such soul in heathen lands? Oh, the glorious fruition which some day will meet us from lives of consecrated service! This is but the apprenticeship of our immortal life. There we shall enter upon unknown glories, and we shall find that they will simply be the outcome of our life below.

In a recent poem Kipling has touched with a master hand, although with a very unconventional touch, the vision of the future. His striking picture is worth repeating:

When Earth's last picture is painted,
　　And the tubes are twisted and dried,
When the oldest color has faded,
　　And the youngest critic has died—
We shall rest; and faith, we shall need it,
　　Lie down for an aeon or two,
Till the Master of all good workmen
　　Shall set us to work, anew.

And they who are good shall be happy,
  And sit in a golden chair,
And splash at a ten-league canvas
  With brushes of comet's hair.
They shall have real saints to draw from,
  Magdalene, Peter and Paul;
And work for an age at a sitting,
  And never get tired at all.

And only the Master shall praise us,
  And only the Master shall blame,
And no one shall work for money,
  And no one shall work for fame.
But each for the joy of working,
  And each, in his separate star,
Shall paint the thing as he sees it,
  For the God of things as they are.

God has provided some better thing even than this. "Even now the reaper draws his wages, even now he harvests the crop for eternal life, so that the sower and the reaper may be glad together" (John 4:36).

CHAPTER 9

THE PARABLES OF DIVINE MERCY

(Part 1)

*I have not come to call the righteous, but sinners to repentance.
(Luke 5:32)*

There are 14 parables peculiar to the Gospel of Luke, and singularly appropriate to his picture of the Son of Man. They naturally divide themselves into two series, namely, parables of divine mercy and parables of human destiny. The first seven are parables of divine mercy. The three parables of the 15th chapter of Luke form a trinity in unity. The other four also form a cluster by themselves and present a striking and complete view of the mercy of God. The first, the Good Samaritan, illustrates God's mercy to the fallen; the next, the Friend at Midnight, help in time of need; the third, the Great Supper, mercy for the suffering and outcast; and the fourth, the Pharisee and tax collector, pardon for the penitent, and rejection for the self-righteous.

SECTION I—*The Good Samaritan, or Mercy for the Fallen*

Luke 10:25–37

While in its first application this beautiful parable is of course designed to exemplify the duties of humanity and kindness to our neighbor, in answer to the man's question, "Who is my neighbor?" (10:29), and in illustration of the Lord's teaching about love; yet deeper than all this it unfolds the glorious picture of the Lord Jesus Himself as the Friend and Deliverer of ruined and helpless sinners. The unhappy traveler, attacked, robbed, almost murdered on his way down from Jerusalem to Jericho, is the type of the sinner who on his downward path has fallen into the hands of Satan, and

305

been stripped of his raiment, wounded in every part of his soul and body, and left, not only half dead, but spiritually dead in trespasses and sins.

THE PASSERSBY

The priest and the Levite who pass him by in his misery, represent the failure of all human resources, and all human schemes of benevolence and reform, to reach and relieve his distress. The first stands for Jewish sacerdotalism, and the cold and selfish priesthood of every age; and the other for humanitarianism in all its forms and failures. The lowly despised Samaritan is a good type of the rejected Nazarene. "Aren't we right in saying that you are a Samaritan and demon-possessed?" (John 8:48) was the very germ of the treatment that the Pharisees gave to Jesus; and He is willing for a time to accept the obloquy, and to glorify it by the love that puts to shame all their pretensions. And so this good Samaritan does for the unfortunate traveler what none of the others had thought of doing. Although the man has no sort of claim upon him, and has perhaps also regarded him as an enemy and an alien, yet the sight of his distress is enough to call forth all his love and strength for instant help and deliverance. First, he goes right to him, undeterred by fear of lurking enemies and a similar fate himself. Next, he has compassion on him; his whole heart swells with tenderness and pity, and all thought of selfishness is at once driven out by the one overwhelming impulse of sympathy and love. Then with his own hands, tenderly bending over him, he binds up his hideous wounds, pouring in oil and wine. And when the poor victim is able to rise, he gently seats him on his own beast, conducts him to the nearest inn, takes him to a chamber, and watches tenderly by his side all the night. On the morrow before he departs, he pays in advance for his expenses, and gives his pledge to see that all else he may need shall be honorably paid for when he comes again.

CHRIST, THE GOOD SAMARITAN

What an exquisite picture of the love and compassion of Christ. First, He pities us. Then He comes to us even before we go to Him. He heals the wounds of our sin; yes, even of our body. He pours in the oil of His Holy Spirit in comforting, quickening and healing love and power, and revives us with the wine of His own love and joy. He does not send us on our way alone, but carries us Himself, bearing us in His own arms, or walking by our side. The inn in which He shelters His rescued ones, is the blessed Church of Christ. There He Himself takes care of us, watching all through the night of our trial; and when He seems to pass on and withdraw His more manifest presence, He still leaves ample provision for all our need, and assures us that everything we can require is already paid for and may be freely drawn from the resources of grace. And best of all, He adds the precious promise that He is coming again; and that every kindness rendered to His brethren, shall receive a hundredfold recompense.

SECTION II—*The Friend at Midnight, or Help in the Time of Need*

Luke 11:1–13

This beautiful parable leads us a step in advance of the other. There the sufferer is helpless and ready to die, and does not even ask or hope for deliverance. Mercy finds him in his misery, and brings to him unsought her gracious deliverance. This parable, however, represents the divine mercy as given in response to the prayers of the needy. It is introduced by the lesson on prayer which the Lord Jesus gave to His disciples in response to their petition, "Lord, teach us to pray, just as John taught his disciples" (11:1).

First, He gives them a beautiful pattern prayer, the simplest and most universal liturgy of all Christendom. Then He illustrates the principle of prayer by this beautiful parable, in which God is represented under the figure of a friend and a father. The case of distress is one of extreme emergency. The need is not a personal, but a relative one. Help is required for a friend who has come at a late hour of the night; and his host has kindly taken him in, but has nothing to set before him. In this situation, he appeals to his friend. But it is an unseasonable, and almost an unreasonable request. The time for visitors is long past. The doors are all closed, and his children are with him in bed. The whole figure represents a case in which all probability, even of divine help, seems cut off, and every door shut. It is at such a time as this that the friend presumes upon the kindness of his benefactor. It is a case where even friendship probably would have been refused. But the parable teaches us that where the claims of human kindness would not have been strong enough, divine mercy breaks through every barrier, and meets the cry of distress with instant and ample aid. "I tell you, though he will not get up and give him the bread because he is his friend, yet because of the man's boldness (importunity, KJV) he will get up and give him as much as he needs" (11:8). Dr. Walker, in his profound book on the Holy Spirit, states that the word "importunity" here does not mean urgency on the part of the supplicant, but rather emergency in his situation—the extreme distress in which his benefactor saw he was, and on account of which his kind, compassionate heart rose above all difficulties and immediately relieved him.

First, we have God in the two figures of Father and Friend.

Second, we see His willingness to help us, not only in season, but out of season, when the door of mercy even seems to have closed, and the time to help seems to have passed.

Third, we see His consideration for the extremity of our circumstances, and the fact that the more difficult the case is, the more likely and willing He is to help.

Fourth, we see the completeness and generosity of His provision; "as much as he needs" (11:8). The three loaves for which the friend asks, may well express the threefold fullness of the gospel: salvation from past sins and future judgment; sanctification from the power of evil; and temporal deliverance both from sickness, sorrow and all the other troubles and needs of life.

OUR NEED AND GOD'S RESOURCES

Finally we find how much stronger is the claim we have upon His bounty and help, not for our selfish needs, but for those that we wish to relieve, either temporally or spiritually, who have come to us in their distress, and we have nothing to set before them. Even in our utmost helplessness and need we may venture to undertake the most difficult services for others; and then as we go to Him, we will find Him ready to meet all our need. There is something beautiful in the boldness of this man's faith, in taking in the midnight wayfarer when he knew that he had nothing to set before him. He seemed to have such confidence in his friend, that he ventured to the utmost length in the exercise of his own hospitality. Surely we may venture as far in undertaking the burdens of Christ's work and the relief of His suffering ones, in full assurance that, even in the most extreme case, He will prove faithful to us and place at our command His abundant and unfailing resources. What an encouragement to us in the work of His kingdom, that in every work before us, in charitable relief for the orphan and the helpless, when done in accordance with His wise and holy will, and in all our spiritual work where we are conscious of our own insufficiency, and must constantly venture out in the confidence that He will supply the wisdom and the power, the faith and the love, the agencies and the efficiency for all our service as we go forward!

SECTION III—*The Parable of the Great Supper, or Mercy for the Suffering and Outcast*

Luke 14:12–24

This parable represents the provisions of divine mercy, under the figure of the feast long prepared, and now at last, complete. "Everything is now ready" (14:17)—mercy to pardon, grace to purify and power to keep. The invitations are sent out, and they are issued on a scale of almost boundless generosity. Three classes are successively invited.

THE WORLDLINGS

First, the friends of the host, who here represent the ordinary hearers of the gospel; perhaps we may say the worldly and nominal adherents of Christianity. They rejected the invitation. They did it very politely, as proud and worldly sinners still do. The first class declined on account of pressing business engagements, perhaps connected with first starting in life, and beginning to acquire earthly possessions. This man has bought his piece of ground. He is just commencing to accumulate wealth, and is too busy to go to the feast. The second has bought five yoke of oxen. This represents an advanced stage of worldly success and occupation; he is now getting to be a very busy man. He is stocking his farm by the half score at a time, and rapidly growing rich. And so he, for the present, puts off the kind invitation. The third has married a wife, and is still more peremptory in his refusal. He *cannot* come; and evidently he regards the religion of Jesus as incompatible with the thorough enjoyment of the pleasures of the world. Everything in its place. The bridal party, the honeymoon, the dance and revel are inconsistent in his view with the table of the Lord; and he allows the endearments, attachments and pleasures of life to outweigh the claims of Christ, and the value of his soul.

The three forms of worldly obstruction which here stand in the way of the gospel are worldly business, worldly wealth and worldly pleasure. With some, it is the eager desire to grow rich. With some, it is the increasing preoccupation of constant drive and absorbing business. With others, it is the love of pleasure and the influence of friends. From these various causes the great proportion of the invited guests still stay away from Christ. Indeed, the parable represents every one of them as refusing. It looks as though the whole body of nominal professors was ultimately going to reject the gospel.

THE WORLD'S POOR

Next comes a different class. The Master is not going to let His bounty be lost because these proud and contemptuous worldlings did not appreciate it. He is very angry with their contemptuous excuses. He does not look lightly on the sin of rejecting the great salvation. With calm and awful dignity He declares that none of these men will taste of His bounty. He takes every one at their word, and excuses them all. And now He sends out His servants into the streets and lanes of the city; not into the fine avenues, but into the narrow alleys where the poor are found in their wretchedness. Two classes especially, are described, the poor and the sick. No doubt these are literally meant, and the provision of the gospel for the temporal needs and physical ills of humanity is surely set forth in this picture. It is, indeed, God's blessing for the world's poor. Most of its saved ones have come from their ranks. Without it, life has little for them. With it, life has not any grief to harm them, and great is their reward in heaven. It alleviates their physical condition. It is of infinite value even in improving the material condition of the poor, and leading to prosperity and success in temporal things. And for the maimed, and the halt, and the blind, it has not lost its ancient power of healing and uplifting them from their temporal distresses. What a mercy it would be for the poor if they could but fully trust the Lord Jesus as their Healer and physical Redeemer, as many of them do, and find in Him the balm for every pain and the remedy for every trial.

THE SINFUL

Thirdly, there is another class. The gospel is not satisfied when it has relieved the physical ills and social miseries of men. And so the servant comes back with the message, "There is still room" (14:22). The feast is not exhausted with all the multitudes of suffering poor that have already sat down. The tables still have room for myriads more; and nothing must remain or go to waste of all this costly provision. So the messengers are sent forth for the third time, and now they go beyond the city walls to the highways and hedges. It will at once occur to the thoughtful reader that this is the place where the lepers and outcasts herd together in homeless misery, and unpitied exclusion. These poor children of the wayside surely stand for the outcast members of society, for the lost and sinful who have passed even beyond the pale of hope, and for whom there seems to be no possibility of redemption or reformation—the degraded drunkard, the dishonored daughter of shame and every corruption, the criminal, the social pariahs of life. Yes, the gospel has ample room and almighty power for all these. But they are not expected to appreciate it or embrace it of their own accord. They are too hopeless or too corrupt to come within its pale, or even to accept it when they hear it. We must bear it to them, nay, must press it upon them, and even compel them to come in. All that the Savior meant by this strong expression the Church of God has not yet more than begun to realize. All that tact can do to win them, all that sympathy and consideration for their distress can do to awaken their confidence, and above everything, all that faith can do to bring to bear upon them the constraining power and love of God, all this is implied. A little of it is illustrated in the Christian philanthropies and blessed agencies of consecrated evangelism in our own and other days. And it is sufficiently vindicated and has proved effectual from the fact that multitudes of the most honored servants of God, and even the ministers of the gospel of Jesus Christ, have been snatched from these very ranks, rescued from the very gates of hell, emancipated from both spiritual and literal prisons and chains, miraculously saved from the wreck of drunkenness, pulled out of the seething pollutions of prostitution and saved from the gambling saloon, barroom and pickpockets' den, to leave behind them the glorious record of a Bunyan, a Newton, or a Jerry McAuley.

THE HEATHEN

But the last cluster includes a wider circle than merely the sinful and out-cast. These poor lepers, beyond the pale of the city, stand for the great heathen world in its helplessness and misery. And the sending out of the ser-vants to constrain them to come in is being fulfilled before our eyes in the great missionary movement of today. How solemn the stages represented in this parable. We have first the rejection of the gospel by the children of the kingdom. How perfectly it fits the picture of Christendom today, with the indifference of the great masses in Christian lands to the message of salva-tion. God seems to be at length excusing them and passing them by for the classes that have long been regarded as hopeless and past redemption. And so we have the second stage of the parable: the movement downward to the slums of the city. Surely that is going on around us today in a most sig-nificant manner.

Finally, there is the third movement beyond the city gates to the great lost masses of humanity beyond the pale of Christendom. This is the preaching of the "gospel of the kingdom . . . as a testimony to all nations" (Matthew 24:14), and this is to close the gospel age and bring the Master of the feast back again. How very real all this seems as we behold it happening before our eyes in these eventful days.

May God make us faithful to our trust as His messengers in working in line with His plan and so hastening His blessed coming.

SECTION IV—*The Pharisee and the Tax Collector, or Divine Mercy in Contrast with Man's Self-righteousness*

Luke 18:9–14

On the one hand we have the very highest sample of mere human good-ness, in the self-conscious Pharisee standing in the temple with head erect, and heart inflated, talking to himself and about himself and his excellencies, and calling it prayer. He is so full of self-consciousness that he forgets all about God after the first breath in which he has pronounced His name, and becomes in a sort of self-homage and the contemplation of his own virtues, a god to himself.

"God," and there he parts company with heaven, "I thank you that I am not like other men—robbers, evildoers, adulterers—or even like this tax col-lector. I fast twice a week and give a tenth of all I get" (Luke 18:11–12). On the other hand, the poor sinner stands far off, feeling himself unworthy even to approach the Pharisee, far less to lift his eyes to heaven, and simply con-fessing his unworthiness, and imploring the divine mercy for his own soul, as if there were no other sinner in the world but he. "God have mercy on

me, *the* sinner," is the real force of the language. There is a still deeper suggestion in the word he used for mercy. Literally it might be written, "God be
the propitiation for me the sinner." There seems to be the thought of an
atonement, of the divine plan of mercy through expiation, something that
God must arrange, and that he was helpless to provide, but glad to accept.
Surely this was deepest penitence and simplest faith. Nor need we wonder
that it was instantly effectual. The very moment he took the sinner's place,
and claimed the sinner's Savior, he was justified. The Lord Himself emphatically declares that "this man . . . went home justified before God"
(18:14). It is a beautiful instance of the immediate and complete forgiveness
of the soul that takes its true place at the footstool of mercy. The other went
as he came, satisfied with himself—not needing, not claiming, not having
any part in Christ's salvation.

A LEGENDARY PHARISEE AND TAX COLLECTOR

Ancient legends have left an interesting tradition that strongly resembles
this parable, and which Archbishop Trench has used with fine effect. Two
men it is said once approached the Master as he passed through the villages
of Judea. One of them, a poor sinner, besought His mercy. The other, a
robed and phylacteried Pharisee, clasped his hands in holy horror and said,
"God grant that I may stand far from this wicked man, in the last day." The
Master, it is said, quietly answered: "Both men have their petition. The sinner has asked My mercy, and has obtained it, and in that day, he shall stand
on My right hand. The Pharisee has asked that he might stand far from him
on that day. His wish is granted, for in the company of redeemed and pardoned sinners he shall never come." The Lord Himself has given us the application in the searching words, "For everyone who exalts himself will be
humbled, and he who humbles himself will be exalted" (18:14).

CHAPTER 10

THE PARABLES OF DIVINE MERCY

(Part 2)

In the same way, I tell you, there is rejoicing in the presence of the angels of God over one sinner who repents. (Luke 15:10)

The three parables of the 15th chapter of Luke are a trinity of divine love and mercy. Like the Scripture itself, they cannot be broken and never should be divided. While each has its separate lesson, they form a glorious unity of truth and grace and a picture of God which is fitted to move and attract every sinner's heart. It is like the photograph which a loving mother, seeking for her long-lost daughter, hung up on the dance halls of a great city, hoping that someday her wandering child would see it and come home. So the Son of Man has hung up this picture of divine mercy to attract and win back to God the lost sheep and the wandering prodigals of this sinful world. Let us look first at each of these parables in detail and then seek to gather up the lessons of the series.

SECTION I—*The Good Shepherd, or the Mercy of Jesus Seeking the Lost*

Luke 15:3–7

This beautiful picture centers around the person of Jesus. The sinner is represented by the foolish sheep, the weakest, most defenseless, and often the most unwise of all creatures; lost not through willful intention always, but through folly, wandering and neglect of the shepherd's voice. When lost, the sheep is the least likely of all creatures to find itself, and the least able to take care of itself. "We all, like sheep, have gone astray,/ each of us has turned to his own way" (Isaiah 53:6).

We are represented in the parable as lost in the wilderness. It is a dangerous place, even with the fold around us and the Shepherd near; but without the Shepherd it is a dreadful place to be lost in. Fierce wolves, trackless wastes, wild tempests, impassable torrents, desolate mountains, and unsheltered wilds—these are the figures which portray the misery and perils of lost souls. The value of the lost one is strangely indicated by the contrast between one and 99. Only one was lost, but that one outweighed all the flock, for the moment of peril and need. Every individual soul is missed by the Shepherd, and is worth all His toil and love and suffering. But it is the picture of the Shepherd that stands out with most glorious vividness. The moment He discovers that one is lost, He immediately leaves the 99, and goes Himself to find it. He does not send but goes. He seeks the lost one. It tells of patient love. It tells of His long-suffering pains and toils. It tells of the 33 years of His earthly love and sorrow. It tells of the long journeys through Galilee and Judea, the weary summer days, the sleepless nights, the agony, and bloody sweat, the denial, the betrayal, the crucifixion, the hideous darkness of the cross, the hidden face of God, the fierce wolves that crept upon Him in His dying anguish from the dark wilderness of His sorrow, the strange horror of the burden of sin, the love that has still followed sinful men through all the years since then. The Shepherd seeks them now so patiently, and waits so long to be gracious, and follows until He finds. And then when He finds the lost sheep there is no upbraiding, no scourging. Gently He lifts it to His bosom. In its weakness, He carries it along. He does not even feel its heavy burden. He is so glad to find it that He carries it on His shoulders, rejoicing. And when He reaches home, He calls all heaven to rejoice because the lost is found. This is the picture of that matchless love, the seeking, saving, sacrificing, keeping, overcoming and everlasting love of the Lord Jesus Christ.

SECTION II—*The Parable of the Lost Coin, or the Mercy of the Holy Spirit*

Luke 15:8–10

Here the lost soul is represented by the figure of a coin. This is one of the most familiar symbols of value; and perhaps, the most expressive to ordinary minds, to whom nothing seems so valuable as money. The soul is the precious coin. It still bears upon it the stamp of God. And although lost amid rubbish and dust, it still contains the precious gold, compared with which all other created things are poor and cheap.

The seeker and finder is a woman; fitting type of the blessed Comforter, often represented, it would seem, under the image of a mother. The lost coin is one of the 10 which she has treasured, and for which she has no doubt a plan of wise investment. Everyone is needed and this lost one cannot be dispensed with. Every soul has its place in the divine plan, and is unspeakably and eternally precious. Until saved and restored, it is out of its true place, and something is lost in the full purpose of God. Like this woman, the Holy Spirit is the great seeker of lost souls. For 1,800 years the divine Comforter has been thus engaged, seeking in dark corners and unclean recesses for the immortal treasures which man has thrown away.

The process of the search is instructive and expressive. The lighting of the candle suggests the work of spiritual illumination, the shining in of the truth upon the conscience and heart, the quickening of our spiritual apprehensions and convictions, the revealing to the soul, of sin and of God. The sweeping of the house has also its counterpart in the dealings of God with souls under conviction: the sharp and sudden trials that come, the knock of sickness, bereavement, disappointment or loss, upon the door of the closed heart, the shaking up of our circumstances, until we are compelled to look around us and realize our situation and awake to the consciousness of our danger. And all through this, the Spirit is seeking diligently, whispering to the heart, touching every chord of impression and aspiration, and drawing the soul to Jesus. How long the process sometimes lasts and how patiently the blessed Spirit waits till He finds the lost coin; and then the joy of the Holy Spirit over the newfound heart. This is the secret of the strange gladness that comes into the soul when truly converted. It is the joy of the Spirit overflowing into the consciousness of the sinner, until it becomes his joy, too.

SECTION III—*The Parable of the Prodigal Son, or the Mercy of the Father*

Luke 15:11–32

First, we see the picture of the sinner. What selfishness! "Father, give me my share of the estate" (15:12). What earthliness of desire—the portion of goods, the things that I can eat and drink, and wear, and enjoy with my senses! What self-will and false independence of control! He longs only to get away from the restraints of authority, to be his own free master, only to find at last that he has become a slave.

What heartlessness, and alienation from his father's love! He goes as far as he can from his home, and suffers no thought of compunction for the father's feelings, or consideration for a father's love.

What profligacy and riotous living! He wasted his substance; spent all. How myriads of young men today are just wasting their strength and life, expending their God-given powers in the exhaustion and self-destruction of base indulgence.

What misery at last! "After he had spent everything, there was a severe famine in that whole country, and he began to be in need" (15:14). How soon the cup of pleasure is drained. How soon even our own natures refuse to reward indulgence with delight. How soon lust ends in satiety and disgust; and that which administered pleasure becomes a stinging pain and torture. Not even the husks of the swine are afforded him. There comes a time when even the basest and coarsest gratifications lose their power to please, and the soul feels that it is starving; and even if surrounded with everything in the universe, it would seem to be perishing of hunger.

What shame and disgrace! "He went and hired himself out to a citizen of that country, who sent him to his fields to feed pigs" (15:15). He is a poor slave of Satan, and the devil uses him only for the meanest purposes. How many men that might have been useful today, and honorable, if they had only obeyed the Father's commands and trusted the Father's love, are pouring out alcoholic swill to feed the filthy swine that swarm the barroom, and yet they are unable to take any pleasure from it, but are living a life of constant torment and self-reproach, because of their wasted youth and opportunities.

And finally, how complete the wreck: "when he came to his senses" (15:17)! It looks as if even reason had been dethroned. The sinner is a madman and a fool. And when he comes to his senses he feels as one that is awakened from a dream of insane delusion and desperate folly.

HIS REPENTANCE AND RETURN

The first step was his coming to his senses. It suggests the first moment of reflection. At length, after the wild rush of years, he stops for a moment and begins to think. It is the first pause of his headlong heart since he left his father's home. Oh, if souls would only think, God could speak to them, and mercy could still reach them.

The next strand in the cord of love that at length brought him home, was the thought of his father. "How many of my father's hired men have food to spare" (15:17). It is the thought of God's love and grace that always prompts true repentance.

Next is the question of his own misery. "I am starving to death" (15:17). At length he realizes his true situation, and is willing to confess to himself his failure and misery. And everything that he has called pleasure and freedom, he sees at last to be a cruel mockery and a hideous dream.

Then comes that which must always accompany any true return, the purpose of his will: "I will set out and go back to my father" (15:18). If men would only realize that their choices and purposes are the true helms of life. Anyone can be saved who simply wills it.

Then comes the spirit of humility, penitence and readiness to confess his fault. "I will . . . say to him: Father, I have sinned" (15:18). There is nothing degrading in a sincere confession. There is nothing more manly and noble than an honorable apology for a mistake; and penitence is simply a becoming apology to our glorious and gracious Parent, and is necessary for our own true self-respect, as well as for any just or lasting pardon.

Yet with all this, there was much that was wrong in the spirit and repentance of the prodigal. There was much of pride still lingering in his heart, and he was really determined to buy his way back to his father's favor; or, at least, to earn some place as a servant at his board. It was a self-righteous idea which always clings to the fallen heart. I will do something to deserve God's mercy. "I will . . . say to him: Father, I have sinned against heaven and against you. I am no longer worthy to be called your son" (15:18–19). This is all right, but "make me like one of your hired men" (15:19) is the very self-righteousness which Christ and His apostles declared shut the Pharisees out of the kingdom of heaven. It is the sinner still comforting himself with the thought that he is going to do better, and somehow make up for his past misdeeds by trying to serve God. Happily, when he got back, his father choked all this out of him before he was able to utter it. He let him say, "I have sinned . . . and am no longer worthy to be called your son," and then he stopped short all the rest of his studied speech by his overflowing welcome, and his fatherly reconciliation (15:21–22). Therefore although our penitence may be imperfect, and our faith be weak and faltering, let us come the best we can. This is the beautiful teaching of this parable, and it comes out with still more force in the next division.

HIS RECEPTION AND RECONCILIATION

First, it was immediate. The father did not wait until he got back, and stood in the reception room and made an ample apology. Before he heard a word from his lips, when he saw him still a great way off in the distance, he ran to meet him, and, without a particle of reserve, manifested by his actions his overflowing welcome and forgiving love. So God meets on the way the first desire and endeavor of the penitent soul to return to Him, and even before we are conscious of the truth in its divine clearness, somehow, our heart has been made to feel that He is ready to receive us graciously, and love us freely.

Next, it was cordial and gracious. "His father . . . was filled with compassion for him; he ran to his son, threw his arms around him and kissed him" (15:20). It was not only a gracious acquittal, but a full hearty forgiveness. When God saves a sinner, He does not merely tolerate him, but He loves him with all His heart.

Further, it was not only gracious, but it was free. No word of any conditions was suffered. As we have seen, the ungenerous speech which the son had meditated, offering to pay his way, or earn his living as a servant, was not allowed to be uttered; but, by the father's free, unconditional mercy, he was welcomed and perfectly restored. So the sinner is received—not because of the service he is going to render, not because of the love he is going to show, not because of the value he is going to prove, but absolutely and wholly through the divine mercy, and for the sake of the atoning sacrifice of the Lord Jesus Christ, our perfect Ransom and our only plea.

Again, it was paternal. The father would not suffer him to be a servant, or anything else than a very child. He immediately commands that the symbols of sonship will be put upon him—the best robe, the ring of affection, the shoes of dignity, the feast of honor, and the assurance, "For this son of mine was dead and is alive again; he was lost and is found" (15:24). And so the soul that returns to Christ cannot go half way, and cannot stay in the kitchen and in the fields of servile bondage. There is only one place, and that is in the Father's arms, and at the Father's table. Nothing less than complete sonship is provided or permitted for the most vile and unworthy of God's ransomed ones.

Marvelous grace, unspeakable dignity! This moment reeking in sin, clothed in rags; the next, seated in honor and purity as heirs of God and joint heirs with Christ, and saying with rapturous wonder, "How great is the love the Father has lavished on us, that we should be called children of God!" (1 John 3:1). The best robe expressed perfect justification, and divine holiness. The ring is the token of covenant love. The shoes are marks of honor; slaves always walked with naked feet. The feast tells of the joy and gladness to which God receives His restored children. And the father's word proclaims how mighty the transformation, how terrible the ruin, and how literally the salvation of the soul is life from the dead.

SECTION IV—*Conclusion*

The first lesson which we are taught by this series of parables is the preciousness of the human soul. This is presented under the image of the lost sheep which was almost as dear as a child to an Oriental shepherd; of a lost coin, which with many people is the supreme standard of value; and of a lost son, which is the climax of all that the human heart holds dear. The lost soul is as dear to God as the sheep to its tender shepherd, the precious treasure to the men and women who make it the supreme object of their life, and the fondly loved child for whom a father or mother would give all the world. Still further there is a heightening scale of value and appreciation shown in the parables in the fact that in the first it is one out of 100 that is lost; in the second it is one out of 10; but in the third it is one out of two, intimating that when God lost the human race He lost one-half of the things of value in this entire universe.

The next lesson we are taught is the love of God for sinners. The whole Trinity is revealed here in the fullness of divine love. The Parable of the Prodigal Son tells of the love of the Father. The Parable of the Good Shepherd tells of the love of the Son. The Parable of the Woman tells of the love of the Holy Spirit. Father, Son and Holy Spirit are all working and waiting to save the lost sinner if he will only come.

There is a strange and touching picture here of the heavenly world and its interest in the salvation of men. What efforts men have made through the telescope to get one little glimpse of yonder worlds of space. How poor the light that even the finest telescope sheds on those celestial realms. But Christ has given us here one glimpse of heaven at the very moment when the tidings arrive that a lost son has been found. All heaven is overcome with joy; the angels rejoice, the Father rejoices, the Son rejoices, the Holy Spirit rejoices. God is not ashamed to show His joy "in the presence of the angels" (Luke 15:10), and there are other beings that rejoice still more. There is the mother whose last message was one of loving appeal that you should turn to God. There is the wife who walked by your side and whose beckoning hands are calling you to come home. There is the little child that left the gates ajar for you to follow. Oh, the tender, sacred cords that are drawing sinners home.

The next lesson is what we might call the theology of salvation. I was once asked by a Unitarian why men could not be saved by the Parable of the Prodigal Son and what need there was for all this talk about the atonement in view of the picture Christ Himself has given us of the Father's love and willingness to save. The Holy Spirit immediately suggested the answer. "The Parable of the Son is not complete in itself, but follows the Parable of the Good Shepherd. The father could not welcome his lost child back until first the Shepherd, by His sufferings, opened the way. The three parables together constitute the gospel message. The Savior must suffer and die, the Spirit must seek and find and then the sinner comes home and the Father welcomes him to His heart."

The part of the sinner in the process of salvation is made very plain here. First he must see his condition, his misery, his sin and come to himself. Next he must resolve and choose to return to God. It is not "I feel," but "I will" that turns the scale. "I will set out and go back to my father" (15:18). The salvation of every soul is a matter for his individual choice. It is simply making up your mind and then going. Then, of course, there is repentance. "I have sinned. . . . I am no longer worthy to be called your son" (15:18–19). There is nothing more honorable on the part of a gentleman than a manly apology for his fault. Repentance is just an honorable acknowledgment to God that we are wrong and a fixed purpose to change our way and turn from our sin.

Finally, we have a humbling view, at the close of the last parable, of something worse even than the sinner's sin, namely: the uncharitableness of the older brother who refused to join in the welcome to the prodigal and threw the shadow of his selfishness across that happy scene. He had his punishment in being shut out from the festival by his own spirit. Yes, the worst of all sins is the sin of lovelessness. God save us from the curse of religious selfishness and give to us the spirit of Him who came to "seek and to save what was lost" (19:10).

CHAPTER 11

THE PARABLES OF HUMAN DESTINY

(Part 1)

The four parables which we group together in this chapter present a striking view of human destiny. The first represents the destiny of the worldling in this life, up to the hour of death; the second, the fruitless professor, up to the close of life; the third, the use of present opportunities to prepare for eternal destiny; and the fourth, the contrasted destiny of the worldling and the saint in time and eternity.

SECTION I—*The Rich Fool*

Luke 12:16–21

This parable represents the character and destiny of the man of the world, up to the close of the present life. How vividly we see in this picture the restless, grasping spirit of avarice, of seeking to add to its possessions, and seemingly unsatisfied with all its gains. Even more emphatically the picture reveals the godlessness of worldliness. He omits from all his plans the very thought of God, or His sovereign will and omnipotent control of our very life and all we can call our own. "This is what I'll do. I will tear down my barns and build bigger ones, and there I will store all my grain and my goods. And I'll say to myself, 'You have plenty of good things laid up for many years' " (12:18–19). The first mention of God in the parable is when He steps in upon the scene, and the two short words, "But God" (12:20), turn to confusion and dissolve to nothingness all the vain and self-sufficient plans of human selfishness.

We see also in this miserable worldling the utter selfishness of the spirit of the world. While there is no grateful recognition of God or thought of pleasing or serving Him, neither is there any desire or purpose to use his wealth for the happiness and good of others. He regarded it as all his own, and he proposed to enjoy it by himself and for himself. "You have plenty of good things laid up for many years. Take life easy; eat, drink and be merry" (12:19). He had taught his soul no higher pleasure than that which sensuality affords, and fed its immortal needs on things of earthly nature. There is nothing said about his vices or crimes. He is simply a worldling, seeking and successfully finding for a time, his portion in the things of earth, and binding them to his bosom as his idols, his ends and his supreme enjoyments, with no sense of God and no regard for higher obligations, either to his Maker or to his fellow man.

How terrible, even here, the issue of such a life: the sudden summons of the last inevitable messenger; the awful disappointment at the loss of every earthly thing; the fearful message of a God that he has never recognized or loved; the irresistible separation of his soul from all its treasures, and its naked and terrified appearance before the eternal tribunal; and the bitter consciousness that all he has labored for and hoped to enjoy is to pass to others, who will, perhaps, not even thank him, and to be irretrievably lost forever to him and to all the higher ends for which he might have consecrated them. It is a lost life, all the more terrible because he had so much to lose.

Someone has sarcastically remarked of such a man at his death, "How much has he left?" And the answer, bitter as wormwood and hopeless as despair is, "He has left all." He had nothing but his gold, and with the loss of that, he has nothing left. Dr. Johnson once said to his friends, as he looked at the wealth and splendor of an earthly estate, "Ah, Boswell, these are the things that make death terrible."

The vision of the eternal does not pass in through the curtains that hide the future. Just a momentary glance we get that indicates the desolate spirit passing beyond, and casting one lingering look of horror on all that he has lost and left behind. But the eternal side is reserved for the later parables. Enough for the present that we fully realize the earthly wreck and the mortal side of the sad picture—the desolation and despair of the soul that has invested everything in money, and sees his house of sand collapse in a moment in ruin and despair.

The parable is chiefly intended to show the utter transitoriness of earthly things: the certainty and suddenness of their loss; the bitter disappointment which their loss will bring; the folly and shortsightedness of those who have no other treasure and hope; and the wickedness of those who, as the Lord expressed it, live to lay up treasure only for themselves, and are not rich toward God. At the same time there is a solemn intimation of the life beyond for which the soul has made no provision, where it must eternally reap the consequences of its shortsightedness and sin.

SECTION II—*The Barren Fig Tree, or the Destiny of Fruitlessness*

Luke 13:6–9

While the rich fool represents the worldling, the fruitless fig tree represents the nominal Christian, as well as the Jewish nation for whom, of course, it was primarily intended. It is not enough that we should be planted in His vineyard, and even watered by His grace and care. The only ultimate test of reality and ripeness is fruit. Long the husbandman bears with the empty branches. Patiently he waits, and seeks by careful culture to cherish the decaying life and save the fruitless tree from destruction. Lovingly the interceding Savior pleads for the faithless one, and renews the influences of His grace and Spirit—digging about its roots by trial, and seeking to fertilize them by the influences of truth, and the blessed Holy Spirit. But at last there is a limit, and even the Savior will plead no more. Love must not betray itself by displacing and injuring others for the sake of one that will not improve its opportunities. The fruitless tree cumbers the ground. It not only wastes the soil and the space of the vineyard, but disfigures it, overshadows others, and brings reproach upon the gardener. So at last, the word goes forth, "Cut it down"; and the intercessor raises no pleading voice against the fatal blow.

THE RESULTS

So Jerusalem was cut down in the days of captivity. So again, the fruitless tree that Jesus and His disciples so patiently labored to nourish into life and fruition, fell before the Roman armies. So the Master threatened the churches of Pergamos, Thyatira, Sardis and Laodicea with His judgment stroke. And so each individual soul that proves faithless to its trust, neglects its opportunities, and wastes the rich grace of a loving Savior in selfishness and negligence, shall be put aside from the place of privilege and opportunity, and summoned to the judgment of the unprofitable servant. How solemnly, sometimes, comes the stroke of death to the unfaithful Christian. And although, perhaps, the soul may not be hopelessly lost, yet it is dragged away with the awful sense of lost opportunities, neglected truths, forfeited rewards, and the disapproval at last of the Master to whom it had pledged its undivided love and service. How sad and bitter the departing cry,

> Must I go, and empty handed,
> Must I meet my Saviour so?

And how wise the solemn question,

And shall I thus the Master meet,
And at the awful judgment seat,
Bring nought but withered leaves?

SECTION III—*The Prudent Steward, or the Wise Use of Present Opportunity to Prepare for Future Destiny*

Luke 16:1–12

This is a very remarkable parable, requiring delicacy of discrimination in interpreting it so as to avoid confusion and error. The steward, in this case, had been guilty of unfaithfulness in his trust, and in consequence was about to be dismissed, and lose his present home and situation. But at the last moment, finding his impending danger, he displayed a spirit of remarkable prudence and forethought in taking advantage of his remaining days of opportunity to make provision for the future, and secure friends and a home when he should be turned out of his present situation. We are told that the Lord commended the unjust steward because he had acted wisely. This does not mean that the Lord Jesus commended him. The lord who commended him was his own master whom he had already defrauded, and now so shrewdly outwitted. He could not help acknowledging the smartness of the fellow, in making the most of his situation to provide for the future. Even men of the world can appreciate shrewdness in the man that victimizes them. The Lord Jesus does not commend his injustice, but He takes occasion from his prudence to teach us a lesson on the importance of using our little while of time and opportunity, to prepare for the destinies of the future.

We, like this steward, have been given a great and solemn trust. Like him also, we have been unfaithful to it and are about to be called to account. The time is coming when each of us will have to pass out of our present habitations, into the uncertain future; but mercy still suspends the execution of the sentence for a little while. The bailiff, death, has not yet knocked at our door; and until he does, there is an opportunity for doing something to provide for the time when we shall be houseless and homeless. We can use the present life for this great end, to prepare for the future, so that when we are driven away from this earthly tabernacle, there will be friends waiting up yonder to receive us into everlasting habitations. This is what the Savior means by saying, "use worldly wealth to gain friends for yourselves" (16:9). That is, to so use the world that when we will leave it we will have gotten out of it something that will abide forever. We will have so improved the opportunities of grace and salvation, so consecrated and turned to divine account even the money, the friendships and the secular business of life, that we will have treasure laid up in heaven, and the loss of earth will be infinitely compensated by the everlasting gain. It is the same teaching which the Lord has elsewhere given in His Sermon on the Mount: "Store up for yourselves treasures in heaven, where moth and rust do not destroy, and where thieves do not break in and steal" (Matthew 6:20). It is the idea the apostle repeats to Timothy in his letter:

> Command those who are rich in this present world not to be arrogant nor to put their hope in wealth, which is so uncertain, but to put their hope in God, who richly provides us with everything for our enjoyment. Command them to do good, to be rich in good deeds, and to be generous and willing to share. In this way they will lay up treasure for themselves as a firm foundation for the coming age, so that they may take hold of the life that is truly life. (1 Timothy 6:17–19)

Of course it does not mean that either money or the consecrated use of money will save us. But it does mean that we can use our opportunities of life and grace to accept the salvation of the Lord Jesus. And then we can so turn to account our means, our business, our entire life in loving service for Christ, that there *shall be reserved for us* through His grace an everlasting recompense and a better and enduring substance.

This parable, then, is a link between the ones that precede it, and those that follow. The two former refer to human destiny in the present life, or rather, at death. This looks on to the eternity beyond and teaches us to so use the present, even notwithstanding our failures and sins, as to prepare for it, and lay up treasure in it.

SECTION IV—*The Rich Man and Lazarus, or the Destiny of Unfaithful Souls after Death*

Luke 16:19–31

This remarkable and most solemn picture carries us forward from the present to the eternal world, and reveals the judgments and recompenses which await each individual at the close of the present life.

THE PICTURE IN LIFE

First, we have the picture of two lives in vivid contrast. The one is a man who has everything that this world can afford without God. He is not necessarily a wicked man in the common sense of that word; he is simply a worldly man without God. His portion is purely earthly; but it is as complete as such a portion can be. He is rich and lives in luxury, and every indulgence.

His taste and vanity are gratified by the most elegant and costly apparel. His sensual appetites are ministered to by every form of physical gratification. He dwells in a splendid mansion, and no doubt is surrounded by a retinue of servants and a circle of admiring friends. Perhaps he has all that affection can add to the more refined enjoyments of life, but that is all.

The other is a man that has nothing that the world values. He is a poor, diseased beggar, without the means even of obtaining his necessary food, except through the charity of this very rich man; and without a friend to minister to his sufferings except the dogs that licked his sores. It is the uttermost contrast of earthly conditions. But as the one compensation, he has God, and the hope of heaven. This is not intended to glorify poverty, or to depreciate wealth; but simply to show how little the world is worth without God, and how much God is worth without the world.

THE PICTURE IN DEATH

Next, we have the picture of death. To both of these men it comes. To the rich man it comes with all the pomp and splendor of his condition. No doubt the wisest physicians attended him and the widest sympathy cheered and encouraged his closing days. But none of them could keep the grim messenger away. And when he died he was buried. This is emphatic. No doubt he had a costly and splendid funeral. Multitudes of mourners. Sublimest music. The grandest state. And perhaps, a tomb that tried to make death seem only a splendid pageant; and the narrow house, the palace of magnificence. The beggar died too, but perhaps, was not even buried. If he was, the public wagon hustled his uncoffined bones to the pauper's field, where no headstone marked his resting place, and no tear was ever shed above his forgotten dust.

And so the first two scenes close, and Dives (rich man's traditional name) seems to have all the advantage. But now the next scene opens. It is eternity. How instantly and awfully all is changed. The narrative changes too. The beggar now comes to the front, and is first described, as he had the last place in the previous pictures. What procession of celestial forms is this we see swiftly and triumphantly passing through the fields of air and entering the heavenly portals? This is the beggar's funeral procession. But it is not death, but life he is entering. He is carried by angels into Abraham's bosom. At the very head of the table and reclining as in ancient feasts, so that his head would rest on the shoulder of the very Master of the supper, he sits down. "Never again will [he] hunger;/ never again will [he] thirst" (Revelation 7:16), or ever say again, "I am ill" (Isaiah 33:24).

It is not necessary to dwell on all the details of the heavenly picture. It looks a little like the Old Testament paradise just before the ascension of Jesus opened heaven to all believers. It was perhaps the happy home of saved ones before Jesus came. It was not the final heaven, but the blessed home of the waiting ones, under the Abrahamic covenant, who were resting with their fathers until the Lord Jesus should open the portals of heaven to all believers. But it is enough that it was home, and rest, and happiness, and all of heaven that he could then enjoy.

And now, we turn to the other side. What an awful picture! "In hell" (Luke 16:23), is the first vivid coloring on the canvas. "In torment" (16:23) is the next. "In this fire" (16:24), is the lurid light that next flashes upon the scene. "Have pity on me and send Lazarus to dip the tip of his finger in water and cool my tongue" (16:24), is the bitter cry. Abraham afar off, and Lazarus in his bosom, is the sight of heaven which adds a millionfold to the bitterness of hell. And last of all, "between us and you a great chasm has been fixed, so that those who want to go from here to you cannot, nor can anyone cross over from there to us" (16:26). There is no transition there. No second probation. No hope of reprieve or change.

> But fixed the doom of all remains
> And everlasting silence reigns.

There seems a strange consciousness still of earth. A vivid memory of all the past, and a clear sense now of the madness and folly of his earthly choice, with a strange desire to save his brothers from his terrific fate. But even that is impossible. His own anguish is enhanced by the horrible fear that his bad example has ruined others as well as himself; and that in a little while he will see their sufferings, too, which he can less easily bear than his own. Is this then the punishment of wealth? No, but it is the loss of eternal life, and the neglect of heaven for the sake of the present world. It is designed to illustrate the Master's oft repeated message, "What good is it for a man to gain the whole world, yet forfeit his soul?" (Mark 8:36). And again, "Seek first his kingdom and his righteousness, and all these things will be given to you as well" (Matthew 6:33). "It is better for you to enter life with one eye than to have two eyes and be thrown into the fire of hell" (18:9).

One lesson more should be added—namely, that our immortal destiny is settled not by our social condition, but by our faith and obedience with reference to the Word of God. The final answer of Abraham to this wretched spirit, in the depths of despair, implies that the cause of his and his brothers' ruin was that they had refused to hear Moses and the prophets, and that not even the miracle of his return from the dead would be effectual and lead to their faith and repentance. The ground of human destiny is our treatment of God and His Word. "Whoever believes and is baptized will be saved, but whoever does not believe will be condemned" (Mark 16:16).

Therefore everyone who hears these words of mine and puts them into practice is like a wise man who built his house on the rock. The rain came down, the streams rose, and the winds blew and beat against that house; yet it did not fall, because it had its foundation on the rock. But everyone who hears these words of mine and does not put them into practice is like a foolish man who built his house on sand. The rain came down, the streams rose, and the winds blew and beat against that house, and it fell with a great crash. (Matthew 7:24–27)

CHAPTER 12

THE PARABLES OF HUMAN DESTINY

(Part 2)

T he parables of the Unjust Judge and the 10 Minas present a double picture of human destiny, first in relation to the church of Christ and secondly in relation to the individual believer. The Parable of the Unjust Judge is a picture of the church in her conflict with the adversary, waiting for the coming of the Lord. The Parable of the 10 Minas represents the ministry of Christ's servants under the dispensation of the Holy Spirit and in view of the coming of Christ.

SECTION I—*The Unjust Judge*

Luke 18:1–8

THE WIDOW

There was in a city a certain widow. This widow represents the Church of Christ. While she is the bride of the Lamb, yet the Bridegroom is now absent and she is alone and exposed to the hatred and opposition of her great adversary, the devil.

THE ADVERSARY

We know who this is. From the beginning, the wicked one has sought to destroy the Church of Christ. He is represented in the book of Revelation as a dragon waiting to devour her seed.

THE RECOURSE

She appeals to God in prayer. Indeed, the specific lesson of the parable as represented in the opening verse is that "they should always pray and not give up" (18:1). She is represented as one who "[cries] out to [God] day and night" (18:7). This is our best defense against every form of opposition and trial. This is our best weapon in our warfare of work for God and men. The Church needs to learn afresh the power of collective prayer, united prayer and prayer as a real business that takes hold of God and expects Him to do real things for us.

A PICTURE OF GOD

He is here presented in contrast with the unjust judge. We are not to suppose that we need to worry Him by our importunity into granting petitions as this woman worried the indifferent magistrate into listening to her plea. The whole figure here is one of antithesis. The unjust judge is in contrast with God, and the Lord Jesus asks, "Will not God bring about justice for his chosen ones, who cry out to him day and night? Will he keep putting them off? I tell you, he will see that they get justice, and quickly" (18:7–8). In contrast with the earthly official, He will not keep them waiting but will promptly and gladly respond to their appeal.

There is a fine suggestion in the figure of the judge, full of encouragement for our prayers. God is not only a Father loving to help His children; not only a God of mercy and love willing to bless because of His goodness and grace, but we have claims upon Him on the grounds of righteousness as a Judge. We do not come to Him in prayer as mendicants to beg a pittance for which we have no claim, but we approach Him as the counselor at law approaches the judge of the court and pleads the statutes of the commonwealth and the claims of equity and asks for his client judgment not as a charity but as a right. Our great Advocate, the Lord Jesus Christ, has established our rights before the throne of prayer and has presented an equivalent for all that we can ask from heaven; so that in His name we are entitled to ask the largest things, to present our strong reasons, to bring our prevailing plea and to know that God is not only merciful but also "faithful and just and will forgive us our sins and purify us from all unrighteousness" (1 John 1:9).

THE CAUSE OF FAILURE

Why then, do we not receive more frequent and valuable answers to our prayers? The Lord Himself gives the reason. "When the Son of Man comes, will he find faith on the earth?" (Luke 18:8). It is the lack of faith. It is the spirit of unbelief. And so the great lesson of the parable comes in with "they should always pray and not give up" (18:1). The word "always" does not mean that we are to pray under all circumstances and at all times, but we are to pray through. We are not to stop until we receive our petition. We are not to be discouraged by delay or faint because of the extreme conditions of our case, but we are to "approach the throne of grace with confidence" (Hebrews 4:16) and "always keep on praying" (Ephesians 6:18).

THE FINAL LESSON

The final lesson of the parable, however, teaches the great thought of future destiny. The real deliverance of the widow is to come when her Bridegroom comes. "When the Son of Man comes" (Luke 18:8)—this is the outlook of the suffering Church and the waiting age. Then all wrongs will be righted. Then the cruel adversary will be found and cast out. Then the bride of the Lamb will shine more glorious than the sun and share through the coming ages the throne and kingdom of her Lord. Is this our blessed hope "as [we] look forward to the day of God and speed its coming" (2 Peter 3:12)?

SECTION II—*The 10 Minas*

Luke 19:11–27

This parable has reference, not to the Church, but to the individual believer in view of the coming of the Master.

HIS GOING AWAY

The first reference to our Lord and Savior is the master's going away. "A man of noble birth went to a distant country to have himself appointed king" (19:12). Christ has gone into heaven and there is gathering one by one the members of His future kingdom and preparing for that glorious age when He and His people will together reign over earth and heaven.

HIS COMMISSION

The second parallel to Christ is the master's commission to his servants. Christ left His earthly interests in the hands of His servants. While He represents us yonder, we are to represent Him here. We have charge of His affairs and stand for the interests of His kingdom on earth.

ENDUEMENT FOR SERVICE

Another reference to our Lord is enduement for service. The master gave to each of them a mina. We will notice the difference between the Parable of the 10 Minas and the Talents (Matthew 25:14–30). In the latter case, they received different investments: one five, another two and another one. In this case they all received alike. The talents seem to refer to God's special gifts to His people, the minas to the one great gift of the Holy Spirit. Our one great equipment for service is the Spirit of Pentecost. Without Him we can do no work for God effectually, either in the home, the church or the closet. He gives the Spirit to each of His servants. The differences among Christian workers are not due to favoritism or partiality on the part of God, but to the different way in which each follower of Christ improves His gift. We all have the same opportunity of claiming and using the divine power and our supernatural equipment for the work committed to our hands. We do not need many gifts but one, and that one is comprehensive of all others. The Holy Spirit is wisdom, power, holiness, faith, love, prayer—everything a Christian worker can require—all comprehended in the one living Presence that comes to abide in the heart that is yielded wholly to Him. Have we received this divine equipment and are we keeping the fire burning and fanning "into flame the gift of God, which is in [us]" (2 Timothy 1:6)?

THE USE OF THE ENDUEMENT

The fourth parallel to Christ is the use and improvement of this enduement. "Put this money to work . . . until I come back" (Luke 19:13). This word translated "put . . . to work" means to use. So we are to be active in employing the gifts of the Spirit for the work of God, and as we do so, the gift will grow and our mina will become 10 minas. This appears to be the meaning of the apostle in First Corinthians, "Now to each one the manifestation of the Spirit is given for the common good" (12:7). This profiting is a commercial phrase. We are to use our divine gifts as the businessman uses his capital and his investments. This explains the difference between different Christians. One has been more faithful and diligent in the use of his resources and they have multiplied. George Mueller used to say that after years of experience of God's faithfulness it was as easy for him to ask and receive thousands as it was to receive pounds. Oh, that it might be true of us as of the early Christians, "Your faith is growing more and more. . . . bearing fruit in every good work, growing in the knowledge of God" (2 Thessalonians 1:3; Colossians 1:10).

THE MASTER'S RETURN

Next, there is the master's return. At length Christ will come, too. This is the goal of Christian hope and longing desire. He has waited long, but He will come. He is already on the way. The signs of His appearing are on every hand. Oh, how glad the prospect and yet how solemn its significance!

THE ACCOUNTING

Like the earthly master, when Christ comes there will be an accounting. His coming means our accountability to God and His reckoning with us for our life work and our eternal reward. This is not the judgment of the Great White Throne, the day of wrath and doom. This is the Judgment Seat of Christ where His own servants are to have passed in review their earthly work, and to receive according to what they have done and be assigned their places in the coming kingdom. This was the great motive of the apostle in all his ministry. He was ever looking forward to that time when he should present his work and receive his crown.

And so the servants come before Him with their several accounts. The first two servants have a happy reckoning. They have wisely used the trust committed to them and multiplied their mina, the one tenfold, the other fivefold, and their recompense is first the commendation of their Lord, and secondly a higher trust and a nobler service. The reward is proportioned to the measure of service rendered. For every mina, there is a city in the empire of the skies. The reward is distinguished honor and noble employ. The heaven of the Bible is no luxurious sinecure, but the most glorious activity. The work we have loved to do below will be continued with nobler capacities and larger scope through the ages to come. The philanthropist, the missionary, the benefactor of his fellowmen, the consecrated genius will all have congenial work, but on a higher plane and with unbounded resources and the glorious addition that there will be no night to close the working day and no dark grave to cut short the story. The whole creation will be the empire of our high dominion and the theater of our eternal employ. How inspiring the prospect! How sublime the vision! How uplifting the motive which it gives to us in all our ministries now! We are but apprentices preparing for the manhood of the future and the sovereignty of the ages to come.

But there was one servant who had no such object or reward. He simply brought his mina carefully wrapped up in a piece of cloth and carefully preserved but utterly unimproved. He had done nothing with his trust. That was all. But the reason which he gives shows how wrong his heart had been and reveals the secret of all our failures in the sight of God. "I was afraid of you," he said, "because you are a hard man. You take out what you did not put in and reap what you did not sow" (Luke 19:21). He had wrong views of his Master. He did not know God. He did not love Him. He did not trust Him, and of course there was no incentive to serve Him. Nothing but the love of Christ can inspire true service, and if we are coming short, it is because we do not know the love of God. What a surprise it must have been to him when he saw at last the glorious recompenses of his fellow-servants. And how he wished, no doubt, that he could live his life once more. How we will wish sometime that we had better understood the generous heart of our great Master and had better used the capital which He had entrusted to our hands! The punishment of this faithless servant was the loss of the blessing he had received. The mina was taken from him and given to the one that had used his trust more wisely. Neglect and unfaithfulness rob us of what we have. If we are not growing, we are retrograding. If we are not revolving on our axles in the busy mechanism of life, we are rusting and preparing for the refuse heap and the dumping cart. There is no intimation of any other judgment upon this unfaithful servant than the rebuke of his master and the loss of his mina. There is a very clear distinction between the unfaithful servant and "those enemies of mine who did not want me to be king over them" (19:27). The "enemies" are slain. The faithless servant is deposed. There is the judgment of loss for the unfaithful Christian, but it is very different from the judgment of perdition that awaits the wicked. Both are sad enough, but the latter is irretrievable.

The two most solemn lessons which this parable teaches us are:

1. Our power for service must all come from God, and He has given to us all the equipment necessary for His work. The Holy Spirit is our enduement, and He is given to every child of God who will give Him right of way and yield himself to His direction and control. This makes our responsibility for service very great. We cannot plead our incompetency. We cannot excuse ourselves because of our inability. He is not asking us to do more, but to take more from Him.

2. We must remember both our accountability and liberty. Daniel Webster used to say that the most stupendous thought that ever came to him was man's accountability to God. It seems to us that this thought will be heightened very much when we combine with it the other thought of our personal liberty in view of our accountability to do with our lives as we will. Christ is not continually policing our life and pursuing us with detectives at every step of our way, but He is quietly letting us alone and saying to each one of us, "Put this . . . to work . . . until I come back" (19:13). And each of us is living our life ourselves in view of that great and solemn day. If we want to be selfish, we can. If we allow opportunities to pass by, we may. No lightning stroke will fall upon us. No outward pressure may be brought to bear. We are left to the motives and impulses of our own hearts, and meanwhile the phonograph of the skies is recording silently, constantly, every act and influence of our lives for the day of reckoning. Then will come the review and the recompense or retribution. Oh, how solemn it is to have such liberty and such accountability! God help us to keep it in view.

> Oh, that each in the day of His coming may say
> I have fought my way through,
> I have finished the work Thou didst give me to do.

CHAPTER 13

THE SON OF MAN AND SICKNESS

Then should not this woman, a daughter of Abraham, whom Satan has kept bound for eighteen long years, be set free on the Sabbath day from what bound her? (Luke 13:16)

The miracle recorded in this chapter is peculiar to Luke, and it sheds much light upon the subject of divine healing and the ministry of our Lord to the sick and suffering. Among the special teachings we may gather from it may be mentioned:

THE RELATION OF SATAN TO DISEASE

Our first introduction to this woman points to a deeper cause for her trouble than mere physical condition. It is said she had "been crippled by a spirit" (13:11). There is no doubt about what this means. A demon power had taken possession of her body and bound her limbs so that she "could not straighten up at all" (13:11). We must not carry this too far by concluding that all sickness comes directly from Satanic power. Sickness may come from a physical cause, and it may come from the direct stroke of God Himself in judgment. We read that "the LORD struck the child that Uriah's wife had borne to David, and he became ill" (2 Samuel 12:15). But that it is often the result of demon power, there can be no question if we are to believe the words of the Lord Himself. In this case an evil spirit had taken control of the limbs of this helpless cripple and bound her hand and foot for 18 years. This does not at all imply that she was a bad woman or under the control of the wicked one in her spirit and life. On the contrary, she is expressly described as "a daughter of Abraham" (Luke 13:16) and was evidently regarded by the Lord as a true servant of God. Satan may and does afflict God's children even as of old he inflicted on Job his loathsome boils and later tried to hinder Paul in his work in a similar way. The realization of this fact ought to be a powerful incentive to us in claiming healing and refusing to be disabled and defiled by the touch of our hated adversary.

Let us arise and repel his power, and the Lord will come to our aid as He did to hers. Submission to sickness is not always submission to God, but often to God's enemy and ours, and the exhortation is as applicable to our bodies as to our spirits: "Resist the devil, and he will flee from you" (James 4:7).

THE RELATION OF DIVINE HEALING TO THE VERY IMPULSES OF HUMANITY

The Lord appeals to the sentiment of human compassion even for a suffering brute and asks, "Doesn't each of you on the Sabbath untie his ox or donkey from the stall and lead it out to give it water? Then should not this woman . . . be set free on the Sabbath day from what bound her?" (Luke 13:15–16). Surely, God is not less pitiful than human compassion, and on the very lowest grounds of humanity we may expect Him to meet the needs of our physical life as well as of our higher nature.

SICKNESS AND THE WILL OF GOD

We know of no stronger statement of the Lord's willingness, nay more, the Lord's will to heal His trusting children than the 16th verse, "Then should not this woman, a daughter of Abraham, whom Satan has kept bound for eighteen long years, be set free on the Sabbath day from what bound her?" This word "should" expresses much more than willingness. It expresses obligation, right, something which it would be wrong not to do. It places divine healing on a very high and solid plane as not only a possible and actual intervention of God for the help of His suffering children, but as His normal provision for the believer. It is something that is included in our redemption rights, something that is part of the gospel of His grace, something that is already recognized as within His will and not requiring a special revelation to justify us in claiming it. If God expects us to do what we ought to do, surely we may expect as much from Him. There is something startling in the positiveness and force with which this is here expressed, and surely no trusting child of God should ever doubt again His perfect readiness to help and heal.

THE SACREDNESS OF DIVINE HEALING

The reason the Lord Jesus healed on the Sabbath so frequently appears to have been to lift it out of the plane of a mere material work and place it on the level of the other spiritual blessings of the gospel. The Pharisee, like our modern materialists, looked upon the healing of sickness as a piece of work very much like the mending of a broken chair. "There are six days," he said, "for work. So come and be healed on those days, not on the Sabbath"

(13:14). Therefore the Lord purposely healed on the Sabbath day that He might lift the healing of the body from a work of human professionalism to a spiritual experience and a heavenly blessing. It is the experience of most of those who have felt the Lord's touch upon their bodies that it has a spiritual value even greater than a physical benefit. The health and strength we receive from God does not seek for its exercise in worldly pleasure and sensual indulgence, but in holy service for God and our fellow men. The health and vigor the Holy Spirit imparts reach out for the highest ministries and bring to the heart a spiritual quickening and a realization of the Lord's presence and grace which we value much more than the relief from pain or infirmity. Nothing makes Christ so intensely personal as to know Him as the very life of our conscious being and our material organism. God has made our body a trinity and there is an interdependence between spirit, soul and body which we cannot ignore. The presence of disease is a hindrance not only to our spiritual usefulness but to our higher experiences, and while divine healing is not the greatest blessing of the gospel, it is a part of it and has a reflex influence on every other part of our nature.

DIVINE HEALING AND FAITH

While the Lord is willing to heal, this passage clearly teaches us that there is a distinct responsibility upon us to claim His healing by definite and aggressive faith. He did not go to her and press upon her His healing touch until she had first reached out to meet Him in response to His call. When Jesus saw her, he called her to Him and said: "Woman, you are set free from your infirmity" (13:12). He had not yet touched her or even approached her, but He announced to her the great fact of divine power and summoned her to meet it by going to Him. Remember that "she was bent over and could not straighten up at all" (13:11), but the moment that word came to her, it constituted her authority to claim deliverance and to put on His strength and step out to meet Him. This she did. Somehow she crossed the synagogue until she came to where He was. Somehow that crippled form took hold of new life and strength until she stood erect or crawled across the intervening space and acted as if His word were already true. Then it was that "he put his hands on her, and immediately she straightened up and praised God" (13:13). His actual touch followed her act of faith. She had already taken the healing, and all that was needed was for Him to complete it by the actual manifestation. So still we must go out to meet God. We have not to do this in the dark and without His hands being extended first to us. His word to her, "You are set free from your infirmity" (13:12), was authority enough for her to act upon. It was just as when He said to the paralytic, "Friend, your sins are forgiven" (5:20). But the paralytic must believe and receive that word before it could be made good to him; and so this woman must believe what the Lord had declared and act as if it were true, and when she did this He followed it with the fullness of His power and blessing. The reason we are not receiving more help from God is because we are waiting for something first to come to us in our physical senses as a manifestation of God's presence and help. This is inverting the divine order. We must first believe without sight or sign and then will come the vindication of faith and the touch of God.

THE RIGHTS OF FAITH

The question naturally arises: Has everybody the right thus to claim deliverance from sickness? Certainly not. This passage teaches that only the believer may claim the Lord's healing: "Should not this woman, a daughter of Abraham . . . be set free?" (13:16). A daughter of Abraham is a daughter of faith. "Those who believe are children of Abraham" (Galatians 3:7). It is the one who believes in the Lord for healing to whom the promise of healing applies. Surely, this truth is very obviously taught in the great commission in the 16th chapter of the Gospel of Mark. The modified translation of that passage as given by Dr. Robert Young brings this out very clearly. "Signs shall follow them that believe these things" (16:17). In the old version it is "These signs shall follow them that believe" (KJV). This, however, is not really true, for the signs of healing do not follow all believers, but they follow those who believe for the signs. It is the law of the New Testament just as binding as the laws of nature and the great law of the fitness of things that, "According to your faith will it be done to you" (Matthew 9:29).

How very solemn is the position in which all this places us. The Lord throws down to us the gauntlet, and if we dare to take it up we may have accordingly. There is a fine force in Luke 10:19, "I have given you authority to trample on snakes and scorpions and to overcome all the power of the enemy." We quite miss the meaning of this when we fail to translate it by the right word, "authority." It is not power that He gives us. We do not have the power. He has the power. But He gives us authority to act as if we had the power, and then He backs it up with His power. It is like the officer of the law stepping out before a mob and acting in the name of the government. His single word is stronger than a thousand men because he has authority, and all the power of the government is behind him.

So faith steps out in the name of heaven and expects God to stand by it, and as we thus stand we shall not be disappointed.

Are you living up to your redemption rights or are you letting them go by default?

CHAPTER 14

THE SUFFERINGS OF THE SON OF MAN

During the days of Jesus' life on earth, he offered up prayers and petitions with loud cries and tears to the one who could save him from death, and he was heard because of his reverent submission. (Hebrews 5:7)

The picture which Luke gives us of the sufferings of Christ is characteristic and touching.

HIS ANTICIPATION OF HIS SUFFERINGS AND LONGING FOR SYMPATHY

"And he said to them, 'I have eagerly desired to eat this Passover with you before I suffer' " (Luke 22:15).

The shadow of the cross was falling upon Him, and His spirit shrank from the strange horror of a great darkness. He clung closer to His beloved disciples and longed for their fellowship. This sacred feast which He was now instituting was to be through coming ages a commemoration of His sufferings and death. With deep tenderness, He took the cup and passed it on and down the line of ages. One day He is going to take it back again when the line will be completed and He will drink it anew with all the company of the ransomed in the kingdom of the Father.

HIS MESSAGE TO SIMON

"Simon, Simon, Satan has asked to sift you as wheat. But I have prayed for you, Simon, that your faith may not fail. And when you have turned back, strengthen your brothers" (22:31–32).

Here again we see a fine touch of His perfect humanity in His tender sympathy with His people in their temptations. What a fearful picture He gives of the roaring lion who goes about seeking whom he may devour, and how vividly Peter himself has reproduced the figure in his own epistle as he warns his brethren against "a roaring lion looking for someone to devour" (1 Peter 5:8). As the wild beast shakes its victim until it is shaken to death, so the devil was waiting to shake Simon and his brethren in his fierce and cruel hate. The figure of the sieve is most suggestive. The process of sifting throws out everything that is good and leaves behind nothing but the chaff. Satan's object is to shake out of us all goodness, all faith and hope and leave us a desolated ruin.

But how unselfish the Master's love. He had already anticipated Peter's danger. He had already prayed for him through his fearful test. "I have prayed for you . . . that your faith may not fail" (Luke 22:32). But Peter was not to be delivered without his own earnest cooperation. He was not to be carried like a baby or an invalid, but was to stand upon his own feet and triumph by his own faith. That prayer of Christ saved Peter from the fate of Judas. Oh, that we might have the same spirit as the Master and stand with one another in the hard places of life, saying to the tempted and tried, "I have prayed for you . . . that your faith may not fail!"

THE AGONY IN THE GARDEN

"An angel from heaven appeared to him and strengthened him. And being in anguish, he prayed more earnestly, and his sweat was like drops of blood falling to the ground" (22:43–44).

What a realistic picture of mental anguish leading to physical suffering and exhaustion and of the dependence of the suffering Savior upon heavenly relief as the angel came to strengthen Him. The mystery of that agony has been often approached by reverent minds who have sought to fathom its awful meaning. Far be it from us to presume to dictate, but let us ask our readers to consider well the parallel passage in Hebrews 5:7 which describes this season of mysterious suffering. The common idea is that our Lord was praying against the cup of anguish which He was about to drink as the Savior and Substitute of sinful men; and that His human nature, shrinking from the fearful draught, was seeking if possible some way of escape consistent with His Father's will, and finally, when that could not be, His higher will yielded in complete submission and His prayer remained unanswered.

In this view, Christ's agony in the garden is simply a pattern to us of submission to the will of God when our prayers too remain unanswered.

But when we turn to this passage in Hebrews, we find that His prayer was answered—He "was heard because of his reverent submission" (5:7). We are told also that what He asked for was to be saved from death. There can be no doubt that the passage in Hebrews refers to the agony in the garden. There is no other incident in the Savior's life that could, by any means, be adjusted to that reference. Now when we turn to the Gospel narrative, we find as Christ entered the garden that an awful shadow fell upon Him, and

He cried out, "My soul is overwhelmed with sorrow to the point of death" (Mark 14:34). We find Him also saying a little before, "But this is your hour—when darkness reigns" (Luke 22:53). Putting all this together, it would really seem as if the adversary had made a fierce attack upon our Lord in the garden with the purpose of destroying Him before the time, and so prevent His voluntary offering of His own life a little later on the cross. We know that Christ always had regard about what He called His "time." "My time has not yet come" (John 2:4), and He frequently avoided the plots of His enemies as they sought to destroy Him before His time had come.

It would seem therefore as though Satan had made one last terrific onslaught with the purpose of taking His life there and then in the Garden of Gethsemane, and that it was against this that Jesus pleaded and struggled and "was heard because of his reverent submission" (Hebrews 5:7). His life was preserved. An angel appeared strengthening Him, and He rose up and went forward with the remaining duties and sufferings of those last hours and at last laid down His own life on the cross according to His previous announcement: "No one takes it from me, but I lay it down of my own accord. I have authority to lay it down and authority to take it up again" (John 10:18). In this view, the incident is full of encouragement and inspiration. We, too, are subjected to the attacks of our cruel enemy who would often seek to crush us before our work is done. But in the strength of Him who suffered there, we also may overcome and finish our life work so that we shall have "nothing to do but to die."

HIS LOOK UPON PETER

"The Lord turned and looked straight at Peter. Then Peter remembered the word the Lord had spoken to him: 'Before the rooster crows today, you will disown me three times' " (Luke 22:61).

All the evangelists make much of our Savior's expression of countenance. There must have been something very significant in His look on that present occasion. There was everything to give that look a tender and awful meaning. The disciple, whom He had forewarned, was at that very moment rudely and brutally denying Him and even insulting His very name, and, just a moment before, the signal that the Master had given him had fallen upon his ear with the crowing of the cock in the adjacent yard. That look must have meant not only the severest reproach but the most tender compassion. It must instantly have carried back Peter's thought to what the Master had said at the supper table and reminded him of the promise, "I have prayed for you . . . that your faith may not fail" (22:32). Hastening from the court, and overwhelmed with his conflicting feelings, Peter burst into tears of reproach, penitence, and unspeakable sorrow. But that look had saved him from despair, and, instead of Judas and his awful fate, Peter comes back again a little later to receive the forgiveness of his Lord and to be more than reinstated in his old place of trust and service. How tenderly that look has been interpreted by John Newton in its application to us in our personal dealing with the Savior:

> I saw One hanging on a tree
>   In agony and blood,
> He fixed His loving eyes on me
>   As near the cross I stood.

> Sure, never till my latest breath
>   Can I forget that look;
> It seemed to charge me with His death
>   Though not a word He spoke.

> A second look He gave which said:
>   I freely all forgive,
> My life is for thy ransom paid,
>   I died that thou mayest live.

HIS MESSAGE TO THE DAUGHTERS OF JERUSALEM

> Jesus turned and said to them, "Daughters of Jerusalem, do not weep for me; weep for yourselves and for your children. For the time will come when you will say, 'Blessed are the barren women, the wombs that never bore and the breasts that never nursed!' Then

> "they will say to the mountains, 'Fall on us!'
>   and to the hills, 'Cover us!'

> "For if men do these things when the tree is green, what will happen when it is dry?" (23:28–31)

What finer picture could we have of unselfish suffering? In the hour of His extremity, the Master was lifted above His own terrible situation by the thought of the greater peril of these loving and sympathizing women who were weeping for His fate. To His loving heart, the sufferings which He was about to endure were simply a measure of the sufferings which they should have to bear for the guilt of rejecting Him, and He added the terrific figure, "If men do these things when the tree is green, what will happen when it is dry?" (23:31). Briefly paraphrased, this figure means: "If

I, innocent and dear to God, the Father's beloved Son, am going through such an awful tragedy when I stand in the place of sinful men, how much worse shall be the sufferings of sinful men themselves who reject My salvation, when they stand for themselves in the place of judgment they deserve?" The sufferings of Jesus Christ are an awful measure of the sinners' peril and doom and the most fearful expression yet which the Father's judgment has represented in the "wrath of the Lamb" (Revelation 6:16).

HIS PRAYER FOR THE FORGIVENESS OF HIS MURDERERS

"Jesus said, 'Father, forgive them, for they do not know what they are doing' " (Luke 23:34).

This is peculiar to Luke. How beautifully it is in keeping with the gracious spirit of His Gospel as a revelation of the mercy of God. He had taught His disciples to love their enemies and pray for them that "mistreat you" (6:28). Now it is His turn to live it out Himself and to show that even under the most fearful pressure it is possible to love and to forgive, but it is only possible if we have the Spirit of Christ Himself dwelling in us. Here human nature utterly fails, and only the heart of Christ within us can meet the great demand of such a love. Was the prayer of Christ fulfilled? Certainly it was, as was witnessed in the multitudes that were saved on the day of Pentecost and the conversion of Saul himself, the most bitter of all His enemies.

What a beautiful picture it gives us of Christ. He tries to find something extenuating even in the worst of men. "They do not know what they are doing" (23:34), He cries. His love will discover some excuse or palliation. Truly, there is no love like the love of Jesus. Oh, for a heart like His!

THE COMMITTAL OF HIS SPIRIT TO THE FATHER

"Jesus called out with a loud voice, 'Father, into your hands I commit my spirit.' When he had said this, he breathed his last" (23:46).

The loud voice of which this verse speaks was not used to utter this final prayer, but rather to shout the previous words, "it is finished" (John 19:30), which John has related as His dying utterance.

That was a shout of victory as He announced to the universe that His work was accomplished and His victory won. But now, doubtless, His voice sinks to a whisper, and into His Father's ear alone He breathes this dying prayer, "Father, into your hands I commit my spirit" (Luke 23:46). How beautifully it proves the voluntariness of Christ's sufferings. He gave up His own spirit. The devil tried to take it, but failed; and now victorious He yields it Himself. How clearly it also teaches the immortality of the spirit. There is something in us that cannot die. It is said of Him, "he was put to death in the body but made alive by the Spirit" (1 Peter 3:18). A moment after death, His spirit was more active than before and so will ours be. Oh, brother or sister, where?

Finally, what a pattern for the dying saint. His work all done; his warfare accomplished; every promise fulfilled and nothing left but

On Jesus' breast to lean his head
And breathe his life out sweetly there.

CHAPTER 15

THE SON OF MAN IN HIS RESURRECTION LIFE

But they urged him strongly, "Stay with us, for it is nearly evening; the day is almost over." So he went in to stay with them. (Luke 24:29)

The story of the walk to Emmaus which Luke has told us with such graphic simplicity, has left a picture of the risen Christ upon the heart of the Church of Christ unequaled by any other record of the resurrection. There is something about it that reminds one of one of those Indian summer days that come to us as a transition between the summer and winter, a sort of second summer and yet with a mystic glory about it that seems to belong to some other clime.

"The Christ of the Forty Days," as represented in this picture, while the same in Person as the old Christ of Judea and Galilee, has risen to a new plane, more spiritual, more mysterious and more supernatural. He was lifting their thoughts to that heavenly fellowship which they were henceforth to have with Him and yet losing none of the old humanness and tenderness they had known so well. Let us gather out of this story of Emmaus some of the points of light which it sheds upon the Christ of today.

THE EVER-PRESENT CHRIST

First we see the ever-present Christ. He who came to them that day still comes to us as we walk the path of life. He is an everlasting Presence, an ever-present Friend, and His gentle voice whispers down the ages, "Surely I am with you always, to the very end of the age" (Matthew 28:20). Just as simply, just as naturally as He drew near to them, so

> Still through all life's way He walketh
> Ever near our side.

THE RISEN CHRIST

Next we see the risen Chist. There is a new touch to His humanity. It has passed through the grave and come forth transformed, transfigured and glorified. Speaking of Him, the Apostle Paul says: "Though we once regarded Christ in this [worldly point of view], we do so no longer" (2 Corinthians 5:16).

As Mary clasped Him by the feet and tried to hold Him in the old relationship, He tenderly reminded her, "Do not hold on to me, for I have not yet returned to the Father" (John 20:17). She was to have a higher touch and recognize Him as in a new place of spiritual manifestation and communion.

THE CHRIST WHO WALKS WITH US

Then we see the Christ who often walks with us unrecognized. They did not know Him at first. How often He is with us unknown; and it is not until His Presence has passed and we recall how our hearts burned within us, that we wake with the joyful cry, "It was the Lord." Many a providence, many an answer to prayer, many a human touch brings Him near, and when we seem most alone He is often closest to our side.

A CHRIST WHO KNOWS OUR CIRCUMSTANCES

We see in this incident a Christ who knows our every circumstance and condition and adjusts Himself to our life. He dropped into their conversation. He noticed that they were sad. He took up the thread of life and wove it into a message of wondrous blessing. So He comes to us just where we are. We do not need to climb to strained spiritual planes to bring the Lord Christ down. There is nothing with which He cannot blend and into which He cannot bring His loving companionship.

> There's no time too busy for His leisure,
>   There's no task too hard for Him to bear,
> There's no soul too lowly for His notice,
>   There's no need too trifling for His care.
> There's no place too lonely for His presence,
>   There's no pain His bosom cannot feel,
> There's no sorrow that He cannot comfort,
>   There's no sickness that He cannot heal.

A CHRIST WHO SPEAKS

He speaks to us through His word. "And beginning with Moses and all the

Prophets, he explained to them what was said in all the Scriptures concerning himself" (Luke 24:27). And so He still comes to us through His Word. If we knew it better and studied it more, we should find the blessed Christ ever ready to meet us through its glowing pages and to speak to us through its exceeding great and precious promises. "The testimony of Jesus is the spirit of prophecy" (Revelation 19:10). Have we learned to recognize His face on every page and His voice in every promise?

A CHRIST WHO OPENS THE SCRIPTURES

He makes our heart burn within us as He opens to us the Scriptures. His Word is not mere intellectual light, but spiritual life and celestial fire. It is the eyes of our heart that need to be enlightened more than the faculties of our understanding. It is little use to read the Bible simply as a duty or a study. We want to read it with burning hearts and glowing love as the love letter of His affection and the mirror of His face.

A CHRIST WHO WANTS INTIMACY

But the Lord wants a closer intimacy than even the revelation of His word. He longs to reveal Himself to the loving heart by a personal visitation and manifestation. And so, as they came to their destination at the village of Emmaus, He allowed them to constrain Him to enter in. There is something fondly playful and intensely human in the statement that He "acted as if he were going farther" (Luke 24:28). But this was only because He wanted to be pressed. He would not stay as an unwelcome guest. He wanted their insistent love and was willing to be constrained. He will not break into our hearts or force open any door. "Here I am! I stand at the door and knock," He cries. "If anyone hears my voice and opens the door, I will come in and eat with him, and he with me" (Revelation 3:20). Therefore He sometimes holds back the answer to our prayer and the revelation of His face so that our desire may be deepened and our appeal may be pressed more lovingly upon His heart. But when He saw that He was welcome, how glad He was to respond.

How touching their appeal! "Stay with us, for it is nearly evening; the day is almost over" (Luke 24:29). How that loving appeal has echoed through the ages as the cry of lonely hearts longing for the Savior's Presence. How often since has that prayer ascended from the lonely, the sorrowing, the oppressed and the sinking soul! Never can it go up in vain to His loving heart. Just as in nature, the warm currents of the atmosphere rush to fill the vacuum, so the hungry and the empty heart will always find the Savior near. "For he satisfies the thirsty/ and fills the hungry with good things" (Psalm 107:9). There is in every Christian experience a reality corresponding to the scene at Emmaus. The Lord Jesus does come and make Himself real to the loving and longing soul. "If anyone loves me, he will obey my teaching. My Father will love him, and we will come to him and make our home with him" (John 14:23).

When He came into the house at Emmaus, He was no longer the shy and disguised Stranger, but immediately took His place and made Himself known. Sitting at the head of the table, He took the bread and gave thanks and broke it and as together they partook we read, "Their eyes were opened and they recognized him" (Luke 24:31). The old smile of recognition could not be mistaken. It was their own blessed Lord, their precious Christ, and their hearts were filled with joy, with a joy so deep that He was constrained to withdraw the vision and vanish from their sight.

THE VANISHING VISION

He vanished out of their sight. This was deeply significant. Had He lingered longer, the whole meaning of His new relation to them would have been mistaken. Henceforth it was to be by faith and not by sight. There was a moment of vision and the memory of sight, but now they must rise up and walk by simple faith and go forth by the dead reckoning of a life of trust. It is unwholesome to be always looking for spiritual feeling and emotional joy. The normal atmosphere and attitude of the Christian is trust and the fellowship of prayer. "We live by faith, not by sight" (2 Corinthians 5:7). How slow they were to learn this lesson! How, on another occasion, the doubting Thomas even demanded that he should have some outward sign of the Master's presence and how the Lord reproved him, even as He granted it: "Because you have seen me, you have believed; blessed are those who have not seen and yet have believed" (John 20:29). Let us not miss the blessing but learn to go forth leaning upon His Word, counting upon His unseen Presence and by steadfast faith testifying with the Psalmist, "I have set the LORD always before me./ Because he is at my right hand,/ I will not be shaken" (Psalm 16:8).

Someone has written a helpful leaflet on the practice of the Presence of God, and this is a spiritual exercise which we may most profitably pursue. A distinguished preacher tells how every morning as he sits down in his library, he places a chair for the Master to sit by his side, and all through the hours of study they talk together, pray together, plan together the work of the day; and when he goes forth to life's more public duties, he is conscious, not of any ecstatic vision or any supernatural revelation, but of an atmosphere illumined and fragrant with the breath of heaven and a heart all aglow from the Presence and fellowship of the Lord.

Will we thus go forth to walk with Him, until the gates of vision open at last and we will see His face and be with Him in the glory?

'Tis so sweet to walk with Jesus
Step by step and day by day,
Stepping in His very footprints,
Walking with Him all the way.

Soon with all who walk with Jesus
We shall walk with Him in white,
While He turns our grief to gladness
And our darkness into light.

Jesus, keep me closer, closer,
Step by step and day by day,
Stepping in Thy very footprints,
Walking with Thee all the way.

CHAPTER 16

THE PARTING SCENES

When he had led them out to the vicinity of Bethany, he lifted up his hands and blessed them. While he was blessing them, he left them and was taken up into heaven. (Luke 24:50–51)

After the meeting with the Lord at Emmaus, the disciples returned immediately to Jerusalem to tell their brothers the joyful news that the Lord had appeared to them. But as they entered the closed upper chamber, they were anticipated by the greeting, "The Lord has risen and has appeared to Simon" (24:34). We have no particulars of this meeting with Simon except the hint which the angel gave in his first meeting with the woman, "Tell . . . Peter" (Mark 16:7), and also the reference by the Apostle Paul in First Corinthians 15:5, "he appeared to Peter." Somewhere and some time that morning He had met the brokenhearted disciple and passed some confidential word that never has been told to other ears. Then the two disciples told their story of the walk to Emmaus and the meeting there, but even while they spoke, the Lord Himself appeared, entering through the closed doors and suddenly standing in their presence. From the mysterious shadow form, they shrank back with dread and took it for an apparition. But immediately His reassuring voice declared,

> Why are you troubled, and why do doubts rise in your minds?
> Look at my hands and my feet. It is I myself! Touch me and see;
> a ghost does not have flesh and bones, as you see I have. (Luke 24:38–39)

And then, still further to reassure them, for we are told, "they still did not believe it because of joy and amazement" (24:41), He called for food and ate before them a piece of broiled fish which probably was left from their evening meal. No longer could they doubt that it was indeed their Lord Himself strangely changed in many things and yet the very same Jesus.

THE MANIFESTATION

Nowhere in the records of the resurrection have we a picture at all approaching in realistic vividness this picture of the risen Christ. Speculation must, of course, curb all irreverent or presumptuous boldness in attempting to define and describe the resurrection life of our blessed Lord, and yet there are touches of intense humanness here which the Holy Spirit surely intended that we should realize and draw comfort and inspiration from. While on the one hand, there is much that is mysterious and supernatural and His body was possessed of powers that belong to a higher sphere of human life: passing at will through closed doors, transporting Himself in a moment to distant places and rising by the impulse of His own will without effort, in spite of the law of gravitation, until His glorified body floated away into space. While all this is true, yet on the other hand the print of the nails and the mark of the spear were still apparent. His corporeal frame was tangible to the touch of their hands and He insisted that they should examine and handle and see. There were bones and flesh in His material form. It was an actual substance as real as their own bodies. There would seem to have been an absence of blood, for He speaks only of flesh and bones. Was it that the blood was the corruptible mortal life and that He left it behind as the ransom for our lives, and that the resurrection body has some higher vital fluid than the blood which sustains our life? While He did not need the nourishment of food, yet He could eat the broiled fish. He could taste the sweetness of the honeycomb (see Luke 24:42, KJV). He could share any of the physical attributes of our humanity.

How gloriously real all this makes the Christ to us. This Man, with a body like our own, has passed out of sight, but not out of existence. He is still the same Jesus and will forever be the most glorious and perfect Representative of our humanity. This Body is the Head of our body, and from it we can draw the physical strength and life we need. It was of this He was speaking in the sixth chapter of John when He said, "Just as the living Father sent me and I live because of the Father, so the one who feeds on me will live because of me" (6:57). And when they wondered how any one could eat His flesh and drink His blood, He explained that all this was to be made plain after His resurrection; that it was in His risen body that this was to be fulfilled. "What if you see the Son of Man ascend to where he was before! The Spirit gives life; the flesh counts for nothing. The words I have spoken to you are spirit and they are life" (6:62–63).

Have you learned to draw your life from this living One and find in Him the source of strength for every physical as well as every spiritual need?

This glorified Christ is also the pattern and type of our glorified humanity.

As He is, so shall we someday be.

> As was the earthly man, so are those who are of the earth; and as is
> the man from heaven, so also are those who are of heaven. And just
> as we have borne the likeness of the earthly man, so shall we bear
> the likeness of the man from heaven. (1 Corinthians 15:48–49)

Into the fullness of this glorified life, humanity cannot enter until after the
resurrection. And yet even now "the spirits of righteous men made perfect"
(Hebrews 12:23) doubtless enter into a very real and conscious blessedness
waiting for the fullness of their glory when He shall be revealed as our coming Lord and King. "What we will be has not yet been made known. But we
know that when he appears, we shall be like him, for we shall see him as he
is" (1 John 3:2).

THE ILLUMINATION

This brings us back to more ordinary planes. His manifested Presence
may not be always visible, but there is one place where we can always find
Him and that is in His holy Word. And so He immediately began to give
them the key to the Scriptures and made it possible for them henceforth always to find Him there. "This is what I told you while I was still with you,"
He says, "Everything must be fulfilled that is written about me in the Law
of Moses, the Prophets and the Psalms" (Luke 24:44). It is remarkable that
He uses the same general division of the old Scriptures which was used
among the rabbis. The Law was the first division containing the writings of
Moses. The Prophets constituted the next division containing the historical
portions and the prophetic Scriptures. And the Psalms finished the sub-
division including not only the Psalms of David, but the other poetical
books of the Bible, Job, Proverbs, Song of Songs, etc. And so He takes up
the three divisions and gives them a lesson in Bible study, the details of
which are not recorded, but the substance of which no doubt forever
remained in their minds and hearts as the foundation principles of the entire New Testament teaching.

It is not difficult for us, in view of the deeper teachings of the apostles, to
imagine the substance of that wondrous message which they heard for the
first time that day from the Risen Christ. How their hearts must have
burned as He explained to them the sacrifice of Abel, the offering of Isaac on
Mt. Moriah, the blood of the Pascal lamb, the wondrous types of the Jewish
tabernacle, the great high priest and his robes and functions, the Day of
Atonement, the scapegoat and all the bloody sacrifices and varied offerings
of the Mosaic economy. And then would follow the prophetic psalms, the
53rd chapter of Isaiah and the varied pictures of the coming Messiah in

Jeremiah, Zechariah, Malachi and the other prophets, until at last they understood that "This is what is written: The Christ will suffer and rise from the dead on the third day" (24:46).

But a lamp was necessary as a key for the full understanding of the sacred volume, and so we read, "Then he opened their minds so they could understand the Scriptures" (24:45). Oh, what a light shines upon the sacred page when the Holy Spirit reveals to the hungry heart that wondrous Face that shines on every page of the prophetic Word, and the truth becomes clear that "the testimony of Jesus is the spirit of prophecy" (Revelation 19:10).

The story is told of some children who were trying to make the pieces of a mechanical map fit together. Vainly and patiently they adjusted the blocks, but they could not get the lines rightly to meet or the counties and countries to fit into their places. At length one of them turned over some of the blocks and noticed a picture on the other side. "Why," he said, "here is a picture of George Washington on the back of the blocks. Let's try and fit that together." This was an easier task, and it was not long until George Washington stood out from the floor, in the little mosaic picture of 100 blocks, a perfect figure. Then it occurred to them to turn over the blocks, leaving them exactly where they were, and as they did so, the map was complete. The face of the man was the key to the adjustment of the map. In a far higher sense, it is true that the Lord Jesus Christ is the key to the whole Bible. Study it scientifically, philosophically, theologically, critically and you will never be satisfied; but put the pieces together until there stands out the face and form of Jesus Christ, and lo, the problem is solved, the message is plain, the Book is as simple as A, B, C and sweet as the very heart of love.

Have you learned this solution to the mysteries of the Bible? Has it become to you the

> Love letter of your Bridegroom's heart,
> And mirror of your Savior's face.

THE COMMISSION

Now comes the Master's commission for their ministry and service, "Repentance and forgiveness of sins will be preached in his name to all nations, beginning at Jerusalem. You are witnesses of these things" (Luke 24:47–48). This is the proclamation of a universal amnesty for the whole human family, and especially for the Jewish nation which had crucified Him. He now authorizes them to go forth and proclaim through His name forgiveness to every abandoned soul throughout the whole wide world and to begin with His very murderers. The remarkable feature about this is that the message to Israel is here committed to the Gentiles. Luke is the Gospel, not for the Jew, but for the Gentile, and the fact that this commission should be found here rather than in Matthew is most significant.

Have we Gentile Christians been true to our trust for Israel, and have we given the message "first for the Jew, then for the Gentile" (Romans 1:16)? Through every generation this is our first responsibility: to offer this risen Christ to the men whose fathers crucified Him and to leave upon each individual the responsibility of accepting or rejecting Him, one by one. Have we been faithful to this trust as opportunity has come to us and the brethren of our Lord, according to the flesh, have crossed our earthly path? They will not all accept it. A strange veil is upon their hearts. We will often wonder at the indifference and hardness of heart that seems to coolly ignore the call of their Savior, but all the same He wants us to give them the message, to afford them an opportunity and to leave upon them the responsibility of accepting or rejecting Him. Sometime they will meet Him again when He comes in glory and when there will be no doubt left upon their minds that He is their rejected Messiah, and then their eternal future will hang upon the question, "How did you treat the message of salvation which My servants brought to you in the days of time?"

THE PROMISE OF THE SPIRIT

For this great trust that He is committing to them, He now promises to them a special divine equipment and enduement. "I am going to send you what my Father has promised; but stay in the city until you have been clothed with power from on high" (Luke 24:49). He calls it "the promise." It is indeed the promise inclusive of every other, because everything that the Christian's heart can need is summed up in the Holy Spirit. Do we want cleansing and purity? He is the Spirit of holiness. Do we want joy and peace? All true joy is in the Holy Spirit. Would we have our hearts fired by love? "God has poured out his love into our hearts by the Holy Spirit, whom he has given us" (Romans 5:5). Is it power for service? "You will receive power when the Holy Spirit comes on you" (Acts 1:8). Would we know how to pray until our prayers bring an answer from above? "The Spirit himself intercedes for us with groans that words cannot express" (Romans 8:26). "The Spirit helps us in our weakness" (8:26). There is nothing which is not covered by the promise of the Holy Spirit.

Have you claimed, have you received the promise of the Father? This is spoken of also as an enduement. The word "endue" means clothe. It is not a personal characteristic or a result of culture and education. It is a direct, divine enabling. When the Holy Spirit comes to us, the power He gives is not our power, but His. We wear it as a robe, recognizing Him as the Source and maintaining the attitude of personal dependence by simple faith. They were bidden to tarry until they should be endued with power from on high.

This does not imply in our case that God is not immediately ready to give us the blessing of the Spirit, but we are not always ready. The tarrying prepares our hearts to receive Him, shows to us our deeper need, enables us to put aside the things that hinder and makes room for the deeper and fuller blessing. Have we met these practical conditions? Have we claimed the promise of the Spirit? Have we been endued with power from on high? Are we in the attitude of tarrying and habitually waiting on the Lord for the fresh anointing which we need for every new service and emergency?

THE PARTING

At length the hour for parting comes. There is no announcement that He is to leave them, but perhaps there is an instinct such as that which came to Elisha before his master was taken up into heaven. But apparently it is as at other times, as He appears to them and leads them out as far as to Bethany. We are not told that it was exactly at Bethany, but it was in that vicinity, and as far from Jerusalem. He was still talking to them and His hands were raised in benediction as had often been the case before at His partings; but now, as He blesses them, He gradually rises before their very eyes, calmly majestic, with His face shining with love, His eyes perhaps moist with tears, His hands still stretched out in benediction, higher and higher and higher while their strained eyes follow Him with intense, absorbing attention until a floating cloud intervened and He had disappeared behind it, and they woke from the spell to realize that at last He had gone away into heaven. What words could express the sweet and solemn fragrance of that last parting attitude and those extended hands above their heads in loving benediction. As He blessed them He was parted from them. Their last sight of Him was an attitude of blessing. He had come with blessing. His Sermon on the Mount had opened with nothing but beatitudes. His messages were always love, and now His last act was blessing. Some day, when He comes again, He will take up the echo once more and His words will be, "Come, you who are blessed by my Father; take your inheritance, the kingdom prepared for you since the creation of the world" (Matthew 25:34).

Are you included in that blessing? It is for all that will accept Him, and the only curse which yonder heavens hold for mortals is a fearful anathema on those that do not love Him. God save you from ever coming under the lightning breath of this fearful curse, "If anyone does not love the Lord—a curse be on him. Come, O Lord!" (1 Corinthians 16:22), that is, accursed when the Lord shall come.

JOHN

INTRODUCTION

THE AUTHORSHIP OF THE GOSPEL OF JOHN

The most abundant internal evidence, and the testimony of the earliest witnesses among the apostolic fathers, including such names as Clement, Polycarp, Papias, Theophilus, Athenagoras, Apollinaris, Tatian, Justin Martyr, and many of the leading heretics of the early centuries besides, leave no reasonable ground to doubt that the fourth gospel was accepted from the earliest period as the work of John, the beloved disciple. Early tradition represents it as written at the request of his brethren and friends in Ephesus for the purpose of meeting the errors which were springing up in the Church at the close of the first century, by the personal testimony of the one who best knew the Lord's life and teachings. Through the influence of Philo and the Alexandrian school of Jewish and Hellenistic philosophy, many subtle errors were already pervading the minds even of Christians, and the seeds of the Gnostic heresy were widely sown, embodying, among other false teachings, the idea that the Logos, or Word, was a being inferior to God, and that the creator of the world was really the enemy both of God and man. There was but one voice that could give an authoritative answer to all these opinions, and he was still alive as the bishop and father of the church at Ephesus; and a tradition referred to by many of the fathers, and mentioned by Eusebius as reliable, represents his brethren as waiting upon the venerable apostle and requesting him to put in permanent form his oral testimony concerning Christ. The apostle asked them to spend three days in fasting and prayer, and at the end of that time he was so filled with the Holy Spirit that he was impelled to indite the opening words of the gospel.

Clement of Alexandria says, "St. John, the last of the evangelists, when he saw that the outward bodily facts had been set forth in the existing gospels, impelled by his friends and divinely moved by the Spirit, made a spiritual gospel."

Of the personality of the author himself, we know that he was the son of Zebedee and Salome. His mother was probably the sister of Mary, the mother of the Lord, so that he was His cousin. He was, most probably, younger than the Lord or any of the apostles. His father was a fisherman, residing, it would seem, at Bethsaida and in comfortable circumstances. We read of hired servants in the household, and of Salome as one of the women who ministered to Christ of their substance. We find John himself possessing a home, to which he took the mother of the Lord as his abiding guest.

A disciple first of John the Baptist, he was also one of the first to receive his testimony concerning Christ, and immediately followed the new Master. The name which he and his brother received was Boanerges, or sons of thunder, which may have referred to his natural temperament, or, perhaps, to his spiritual fervor; thunder signifying, in the Hebrew idiom, the voice of God. His writings certainly express intense prophetic fire. The incident of his and his mother's request that he should be one of the favorites of Christ on His kingly throne, despite all its obvious touches of earthly ambition, was really prompted by the passionate love which desired to be near Him. Even the cross could not separate the ardent disciple from the Master's side (John 19:25–27). On the mount, in the death chamber at Capernaum and in the garden he was one of the three companions of the Lord's most sacred hours of service, glory and suffering, and at the table he was nearest to the bosom of Jesus. His place was recognized by all his brethren, and when the most delicate question of their life was to be whispered in the ear of the Lord, it was "the disciple whom Jesus loved, . . . reclining next to him" (13:23), that was entrusted with the task. He was the first to believe in the resurrection of Jesus (20:8), and the first to recognize his risen Lord on the shores of Galilee (21:7).

In the early apostolic ministry, we find him associated with Peter in the first miracle at Jerusalem (Acts 3) and in the suffering, persecution and testimony that followed (Acts 4). Next we find him at Samaria associated with Peter, still in apostolic labors (8:14), and at the time of Paul's second visit to Jerusalem he is mentioned by that apostle as one of the pillars of the church (Galatians 2:9).

The next reference to him in the Scriptures is in the opening of the Apocalypse many years later, where we find him on the Isle of Patmos for "the word of God and the testimony of Jesus" (Revelation 1:9). Many well-authenticated legends and traditions fill up the traditional portrait. One represents him as pursuing a youth who had wandered from the Lord, constraining him, as he threw his arms about him, to come back to the fold of Jesus. Another, as flying from the bathroom in Ephesus because he found that Cerinthus, the heretic, was within, fearing that it would fall upon him if he entered. The third describes him as carried in his old age from Sabbath to Sabbath into the church at Ephesus and repeating week after week the simple and single message, "Little children, love one another," and when asked by the fathers why he did so, replying, "It is the Lord's command, and if this alone be done, it is enough."

And a yet more singular legend, referring to Christ's words to Peter, "If I want him to remain alive until I return, what is that to you?" (John 21:22), represents it as the widely prevalent belief that John was not really dead, but was sleeping in his tomb till Christ's second coming. It was even said that "he showed that he was alive by the movement of the dust which was stirred by the breath of the saint." Even Augustine himself, in the fourth century, refers to this tradition as one that was believed in his own day by credible persons. Without requiring us to believe this curious tradition, it is enough for us to know that John did undoubtedly tarry until after the destruction of Jerusalem, which was, in some sense the coming of the Lord to bring an immediate crisis in the Jewish dispensation. To him, also, the Master literally came, on the Isle of Patmos, to bring the vision of the coming centuries, and the panorama of His glorious coming at the end of the age. The character of John was marked by simplicity, fervor and intense spirituality. His nature was most childlike, and, therefore, most in sympathy with the divine. To trust, to love, to know were much easier for him than for natures like Peter and Thomas. Above all others, he is the apostle of love.

OUTLINE OF THE GOSPEL OF JOHN

True to this great design to unfold the person and glory of Jesus as the Messiah and Son of God, this central thought may be traced through the whole gospel.

1. The Primeval Glory of Jesus with the Father (1:1–2).

2. His Manifest Glory in Creation, the Old Testament, and His Incarnation (1:3–14).

3. His Glory as Witnessed by His Friends and Early Followers (1:15–4:54).

a. The testimony of John the Baptist to the priests and Levites who came to inquire concerning Christ (1:15–28).

b. The revelation of Jesus to the first disciples and their acceptance of Him (1:29–51).

c. The revelation of His glory in the first miracle and the faith of the disciples in consequence (2:1–11).

d. The cleansing of the temple, the other miracles in Jerusalem and the faith of the people in consequence (2:13–25).

e. The interview with Nicodemus, representing the higher classes in

Jerusalem, and their awakening interest in Him and His teachings (3:1–21).

f. The ministry in Judea, and the numerous disciples who followed Jesus and were baptized by His disciples (3:22–4:3).

g. The ministry in Samaria and the first Samaritan converts (4:4–42).

h. The successful commencement of His later ministry in Galilee and favorable reception by the Galileans, and the faith of the nobleman at Capernaum (4:43–54).

4. His Glory Manifested in Conflict with the Unbelief and Opposition of His Enemies (5:1–12:50).

The scene now changes and the whole section is a record of conflict ending at last in the victory of Christ over His adversaries, but a victory which cost Him His life.

a. The beginning of the conflict in Jerusalem through the healing of the invalid man at the pool of Bethesda (5:1–47).

Jesus is revealed as the source of life and rejected.

b. Decisive close of the conflict in Galilee after the discourse in the synagogue at Capernaum during the feast of the Passover (6:1–71).

Jesus, the Living Bread, is rejected by the Galileans (6:66).

c. Renewal of the conflict in Jerusalem at the Feast of Tabernacles (7:1–53).

Jesus, the Living Water, is rejected.

d. Continuance of the conflict in Jerusalem (8:12; 9:41).

Jesus is the Light of the World, as shown in the healing of the blind man, but is rejected by them in their blindness (9:41).

e. Next stage of the conflict: the Feast of Dedication in Jerusalem three months later (10:1–40).

Jesus, the Good Shepherd, is rejected, with a murderous attempt to take His life.

f. Final stage of the conflict: resurrection of Lazarus, demonstrating His divinity as beyond dispute, and determining them in their mad and malignant purpose to destroy Him.

Jesus is shown as the One who raises the dead (11:1–57).

g. Triumphal entry into Jerusalem—Jesus, the King of the Jews (12:1–50).

Christ's public acknowledgment of triumph is accepted by Him as the final challenge and leads to the final accomplishment of their purpose to destroy Him.

In this closing section the plot deepens with His triumph. The dark shadow of the betrayer falls upon the scene. Mary anoints His body in anticipation of His burial, and Christ Himself predicts His own approaching death under the figure of the kernel of wheat planted in the ground.

5. His Glory Manifested in His Closing Messages to His Own Disciples (13:1–17:26).

These parting words might be divided into four sections:

a. At the Passover table (chapter 13).

b. At the Lord's Supper (chapter 14).

c. On the way from the upper room through the temple (chapters 15, 16).

d. Concluding prayer, in which He speaks not to them, but of them to the Father (chapter 17).

These sublime discourses will be found more fully analyzed elsewhere.

6. His Glory Manifested in His Trial and Crucifixion (chapters 18, 19).

a. His arrest and the perfect voluntariness of His submission (18:1–12).

b. His trial before the Jewish council and His holy dignity in the face of their helplessness (18:13–27).

c. His trial before Pilate and His vindication by the governor as innocent (18:28–19:22).

d. His suffering and death with all the incidents which manifested forth His victorious patience, meekness and love, and the fulfillment of Scripture in every act, closing with His shout of triumph, "It is finished" (19:23–37).

e. Finally, His honorable burial through the intercession of Nicodemus and Joseph, according to the prophetic Scriptures, in the tomb of the wealthy councilor (19:38–42).

7. His Resurrection Glory (chapters 20, 21).

a. Witnessed by Peter and John (20:1–10).

b. Witnessed by Mary Magdalene (20:11–18).

c. Witnessed by the 11 disciples (20:19–23).

d. Witnessed by Thomas (20:24–29).

e. Witnessed by many other signs (20:30–31).

f. Manifestation of Christ's glory at the Sea of Tiberias, restoration of Peter, and prophecy concerning John (21:1–25).

g. Final testimony of John (21:24–25).

CHAPTER 1

SCOPE AND CHARACTERISTICS OF
THE GOSPEL OF JOHN

T he apostle himself expressed his special object in writing this gospel: "But these are written that you may believe that Jesus is the Christ, the Son of God, and that by believing you may have life in his name" (John 20:31).

ITS TEXT AND THEME

1. First, then, we may expect in it a revelation of Jesus in His twofold character as Christ and as the Son of God. It is not so much a record of the facts of His life, although based upon them and presenting many new facts of great importance, as it is a revelation of His divine and Messianic character, and the summing up of the testimony concering Him would be likely to produce a conviction of His divinity in the minds of men. And even more than all these testimonies, it is an unfolding of His higher nature from the Lord's own consciousness, as expressed in His wonderful discourses, and as apprehended by the love and instinct of John and reproduced in these pages as a heart picture of his Master's inmost life and being.

Next, we may expect, along with this, a revelation of "life in his name" as the blessed experience of those knowing and believing on Jesus as the Christ and the Son of God.

This word *life* is perhaps the most prominent keynote both in the Gospel and Epistles of John. Christ is the Life. Salvation is life. Not our acts, nor even ideas, are recognized in these pages as constituting our highest self; but that new and divine *life* which we receive from Jesus Christ through the Holy Spirit in our spirits, which He imparts even to our bodies from His own risen and glorified humanity, and which is to be consummated in the perfected physical and spiritual life of the resurrection. The two great themes, therefore, in John are, *Jesus Himself the Son of God*, and *life in His name*.

STYLE

2. The style is direct and personal, and the pictures he gives are evidently those of an eyewitness. He speaks of persons, places and incidents with the precision of vividness. Notice for example his reference to Cana of Galilee, Bethany beyond Jordan, Ephraim near the wilderness; the city of Samaria, called Sychar; the allusions to the temple and its feasts; the treasury, Solomon's porch and the custom of pouring out water and lighting the lamps in the temple courts at the time of the feasts; the explicit reference to details of conversations, titles, etc., as in the picture of the calling of the first disciples (John 1); the conversation with Philip about the bread (6:5), and the conversation of Philip and Andrew about the Greeks who came to see Jesus (12:21); the coming of Nicodemus by night (3:2); the vivid picture of the interview at Sychar with the woman of Samaria, the very hour of the interview is mentioned, as it is with the healing of the nobleman's son (4:6 and 4:52); the six water jars (2:6); the five loaves and two fishes (6:9), the thirty-eight years of sickness (5:5); the pool of Bethesda with its exact location by the sheep gate (5:2); the pool of Siloam with its interpretation, "Sent" (9:7); the place called Golgotha "near the city" (19:17, 20); the pavement or raised platform in the hall of judgment, named Gabbatha (19:13); all these and many other such allusions reveal the hand and presence of a personal witness and a direct observer, and all the scenes and incidents move before us like a living scene.

INCIDENTAL

3. Although the Gospel of John is the most didactic and spiritual of all the gospels, yet all the discourses in it grow out of living facts and incidents and are vividly connected with them in the mind and picture. Even the testimony of John in the first chapter rises out of the disputations of priests and Levites. The profound discourse of the third chapter, concerning the new birth, is vivified by the midnight scene and the interesting conversation with Nicodemus. The abstruse address of the fifth chapter grows out of the healing of the impotent man. The sixth chapter is enlivened by the constant allusion both to the recent miracle of the multiplied bread and also the Passover now being observed at Jerusalem. The sublimest utterances of the seventh chapter are directly called forth by the striking ceremonies of the Feast of Tabernacles going on at the time. His discourse on the light of the world (chapters 8 and 9) is illumined by the figure of the suspended lamps in the court of the temple, and illustrated by the healing of the blind man in Jerusalem as he passes out. The picture of the Good Shepherd (chapter 10) grows out of false shepherds just given in chapter 9. The profound address of his approaching death (chapter 12) is suggested by the previous resurrec-

tion of Lazarus and the incident of the coming of certain Greeks. In chapter 13 He teaches His disciples love: first, by washing their feet, and second, by interpreting and crystallizing the act in the new commandment which He gives them. The address of chapter 15 grows out of their passing the temple vine or the vineyards by the wayside; and the parting lessons of service which He gives to Simon and the other disciples are suggested and emphasized by the beautiful miracle of the draught of fishes. Thus the entire gospel is a living panorama as well as a divine oratorio.

PERSONALITY

4. Personal character is very vivid in the Gospel of John. More than any other of the gospels it is a portraiture of persons, and the pictures stand out with graphic distinctness and strongly marked individuality.

First, we have the picture of the Baptist himself, and his unselfish and lofty testimony to Christ, even at the loss of his own disciples. Then follow the vivid sketches of Andrew, John, Simon, Philip and Nathaniel. Nowhere do we get the personal view of Andrew, Philip and Nathaniel which we find in this gospel. The marriage scene in Cana brings out the personality of Jesus' mother and her relation to Christ. In the strongest light the portrait of Nicodemus is drawn, and the woman of Samaria stands before us like a photograph, and we can see not only her figure as she stands with her empty water jar, but can also read her very heart in the strong light of the Master's searching glance. The nobleman of Capernaum, the impotent man at Bethesda and the blind man (chapter 9) are unmistakable in their personality. How different Martha seems in this gospel from the picture in Luke, as we see her bravely struggle up to the faith which should claim her brother's resurrection. How lifelike the tears of Mary as they mingle with the Master's, and how real the scene as she poured out her grateful love in the anointing at Bethany, understanding alone of all His friends the meaning of His approaching death. What an awful picture chapter 13 gives us of the betrayer, as he goes out in the night with the fearful words ringing in his ears, "What you are about to do, do quickly" (13:27). How the character of Nicodemus grows, until the timid inquirer has become the bold confessor. How strongly marked the personality of Christ's enemies, Caiaphas even predicting His death, and the Pharisees using His inspired words to justify their malignant hate and murder. What a look into Peter's heart John has given us, and what an awful shadow rests upon that judgment hall as Jesus looks down into Pilate's soul and bears witness to him, while the message comes from his very wife which deepens his superstitious fear, and the Roman governor becomes the real criminal before the power of his conscience and his Lord. What can equal the garden scene where Mary Magdalene meets her risen Lord, and the love of the Master and the disciple expresses itself in two brief words of mutual recognition, "Mary" and "Rabboni" (20:16). And how full of vividness and instructiveness are the touches which from time to time reveal to us the ardent but despondent heart of Thomas, until at last the picture culminates in the resurrection scene, unfolding to us exquisitely the workings of unbelief, the triumph of faith, and the marvelous grace, as well as the unmistakable reality of the risen Christ. The last two pictures of Simon and his restoration and John himself are exquisite. We see his modest yet bold and childlike love, nestled on the bosom of Jesus, yet nameless in his own gospel, and lost in the love of Jesus, like the beautiful painting of Raphael, entitled *John on Jesus' Breast*, where we see a head buried on the bosom of Jesus but the face is unseen, while over it there bends the tender and glowing countenance of his loving Lord.

SYMBOLISM

5. Throughout the entire gospel we have a succession of impressive symbols, most of them drawn from the Old Testament. The tabernacle becomes the type of the incarnate Christ. "The Word was made flesh and tabernacled among us" (John 1:14, author's translation).

The lamb of the Passover becomes the figure of "the Lamb of God, who takes away the sin of the world" (1:29).

The descending dove represents the Holy Spirit (1:32).

The ladder of Jacob (Genesis 28:12) shines out in full Messianic meaning in the words of Jesus to Nathaniel (1:51).

The marriage scene at Cana points forward to the whole purpose of Christ's coming, and suggests the glorious figure which John plainly brings out (3:29), as the anticipation of the marriage of the Lamb.

The temple becomes the type of His body and of His Church (2:19).

The water of Sychar's well suggests the fountain of salvation (4:14).

The harvest fields of Samaria summon to spiritual work and its glorious recompense (4:35–38).

The feeding of the five thousand (6:5–13) suggests the ancient symbol of manna, and both lead on to the higher teaching of Himself as our Living Bread (6:35).

The waters of Siloam, as they are poured out upon the altar, suggest the smitten Rock of Horeb, and both are applied by the Lord to the living water, which they that believe in Him shall receive and be able to give to others, as rivers of living water (7:37–38).

The temple lamps recall the pillar of cloud and fire (Exodus 13:22) and are used to proclaim the glory of Jesus as the true Light of the world (John 8:12).

The ancient figure of the shepherd is adopted by the Lord, and applied to Himself and His flock (10:11).

The kernel of wheat becomes the parable of death and resurrection, in relation to Jesus and His disciples (12:24–26).

The washing of the disciples' feet (13:4–5) may be an allusion to the ancient laver; but, at least, it becomes a symbol of spiritual cleansing.

The golden vine carved on the temple gate or perhaps the vineyards around Jerusalem, sets forth the deep spiritual teachings of the Christ-life (chapter 15).

The familiar Old Testament figure of a travailing woman illustrates the birth pains of the new dispensation (16:21).

And the figure of the shepherd is repeated in the closing chapter and transferred from the chief Shepherd to the apostolic ministry, as the Master commits the care of His little flock to His disciples (21:15–17).

Thus the entire gospel is alive with shining emblems, unfolding the glory and the grace of Jesus in the light, both of nature and of Scripture, and all things in earth and heaven are made tributary to the revelation of Jesus.

Someone has described a drinking fountain in Germany, where, every morning or noon, the villagers throng to enjoy the flowing water as it pours through numerous statues, the figures representing all the forms of human life. The farmer drinks from the fountain adorned with figures of waving grain, from which are traced the words, "I am the bread of life" (6:35). The shepherd comes up and drinks from the outstretched hands of a shepherd holding a lamb in his bosom, and exclaims, "I am the good shepherd" (10:11). The traveler sees a guide holding a lamp in his hand, as he cries, "I am the light of the world" (8:12). The gardener drinks from a fountain where the waters seem to be crushed from the clusters of the grapes that hang above it in the stone, almost hiding the letters, "I am the true vine" (15:1). The whole realm of nature is represented, and each object proclaims in its own tongue the glory and grace of Jesus while the water which they all drink speaks loudest of all, "If anyone is thirsty, let him come to me and drink" (7:37). So this beautiful gospel speaks to man, not only in the tenderest words of human language, the most profound discourses of human thought, but it lays under tribute every figure of Hebrew history and the natural world as an alphabet to express in the glowing language of symbol and type the abundant grace of Him who is the First and the Last, both in nature, revelation and His people's hearts and lives.

CHRONOLOGICAL ORDER

6. While not a detailed narrative of Christ's life, yet the Gospel of John contains a more exact and complete reference to the leading chronological periods of Christ's life than any of the others. In perfect succession, it refers to each of the great sections of His life which we have already outlined. This will be seen by the following brief summary.

a. The inauguration of Christ's ministry is covered by the first chapter of John's gospel, containing the testimony of John the Baptist, and the calling of the first disciples, immediately after His baptism.

b. His early Galilean ministry is covered by the second chapter, giving the account of the miracle in Cana of Galilee.

c. His early Judean ministry is sketched in the early part of the second and the whole of the third, extending to the third verse of the fourth chapter.

d. His later Galilean ministry, including the journey through Samaria, falls within the fourth, fifth and sixth chapters, containing an account of a brief visit to Jerusalem made during this period.

e. His later Judean ministry includes chapters 7 to 11.

f. In the last week of His ministry chapter 12 falls, closing with the five chapters, 13 to 17, which contain His final discourses.

g. The last day of His life, with His trial and crucifixion, is described in chapters 18 and 19, and the story of His resurrection, as we have already seen in chapters 20 and 21.

SPIRITUAL ORDER

7. We find a gradual progress in the revelation of the truth in this book. The earlier chapters deal with the more fundamental doctrines and experiences of the Christian life. The sixth chapter begins with the unfolding of deeper and higher revelations of Christ, continued to the end of His discourses with the Twelve at the supper table. Then comes the mystery of His death and the glory of His resurrection. It has been compared to the approach to God's ancient temple, or tabernacle, to which, indeed, the opening verses distinctly allude in speaking of Christ. "The Word was made flesh and tabernacled among us" (1:14, author's translation). "The glory of the One and Only, who came from the Father," referred to in the same verse, might be compared to the cloud that overshadowed the ancient tabernacle. The first five chapters remind us of the court of the tabernacle with the altar and laver of cleansing. To the former, John the Baptist points at the Christ, "Look, the Lamb of God, who takes away the sin of the world!" (1:29). To the latter there is a very natural allusion in the cleansing of the temple, in the second chapter of John, and the discourse with Nicodemus in the third, concerning the denial; while the fourth and fifth chapters still more freely unfold the freeness and fullness of the great salvation of which that was the type. In the sixth chapter, we enter the next chamber, the Holy Place, where stood the table of shewbread (Exodus 25:30, KJV), the lamps of gold, and the altar of incense. The discourse about the Living Bread might well represent the first (John 6); next, the great discourse about the Light of the world (chapters 8 and 9) seems almost to allude to the golden lampstand; the door (chapter 10) and abundant pasture, suggests the meaning of the sacred chamber as the place of

priestly access and blessing; while the altar of incense, with its hallowed teachings about communion and intercession, is appropriately suggested by the parting discourses around the communion table. Then comes the sublime intercessory prayer of John 17, in which the great High Priest already stands at the heavenly altar, almost within the veil, and announces that blessed ministry of prayer of which the ancient altar was the type. Then the veil is torn asunder on the cross through His torn flesh, and the story of the resurrection admits us to the very Holy of Holies, where He has entered in and left the way open for that blessed communion with His risen glorified person, of which the closing chapters give us such beautiful examples.

REFERENCES TO OTHER SCRIPTURES

8. There are many striking allusions to other portions of the Bible. The opening words irresistibly suggest the first sentences of the book of Genesis. His words to Nathaniel allude to the vision of Jacob at Bethel, and his discourses to the Pharisees in Galilee and Jerusalem are crowded with references to the Old Testament and especially to the three ancient saints who represented the successive periods of God's dealings with His people, namely, Abraham, Moses and Isaiah (8:56, 3:14, 12:38).

Other references to the Old Testament will be found in 2:17, 6:45, 7:38, 10:34, 12:15, 13:18, 15:25, 17:12 and 19:24, 36–37.

There is a still closer resemblance between the Gospel of John and the Epistle of John. In both we find repeatedly the words life, light, love and others that we have found specially prominent in the gospel. It has been strikingly said that the epistle is an unfolding rather of the humanity, and the gospel of the divinity of Jesus. The burden of the gospel is, Jesus is the Christ; of the epistle, Christ is Jesus. The Epistle of John deals more directly with the errors of John's own time; the gospel, with the conflicts of Christ's life and surroundings. There is a progress, also, in the epistle toward the personal coming of the Lord, which we find more fully developed in the Apocalypse.

The relation of John's gospel to the other gospels is also marked and instructive. It repeats few of the facts and discourses which they contain, showing that it is supplementary. There is no real contradiction, and there are many wonderful coincidences.

The relation of John's gospel to the Apocalypse may be summed up in this single sentence: The gospel describes the coming of Jesus in its spiritual and personal aspect, chiefly as His coming to the heart; the Apocalypse unfolds His literal coming to the world, His personal second advent.

The same expressions occur repeatedly in both. We have the "Word of God," the "Lamb of God," the "beginning of the creation of God," the "Holy Spirit" and the phraseology of cleansing and salvation.

CHAPTER 2

JESUS, THE SON OF GOD

We have already seen that the Gospels of Matthew, Mark and Luke, respectively, present the picture of Christ as the King, the Servant and the Son of Man. True to the special symbols of the four gospels, the soaring eagle represents the Master in His highest aspect as the Son of God. No other was fitted so well to unveil the inmost heart and unfold the divine glory of the Master as he who had leaned on His bosom until he had felt the very throbbings of His heart. Both in his gospel and in his Epistles, we have the very loftiest revealings of the character of Jesus, and the profoundest spiritual truth. It is the heart that best beholds God, and love is the true element of vision. "Whoever does not love does not know God, because God is love" (1 John 4:8). Hence, John, the apostle of love, was especially enabled to know and reveal the Son of God.

THE ETERNAL WORD
John 1:1–2

Four great truths are here taught respecting the primeval glory of Jesus.

First, His distinct personality. The Greek word, translated "the same" in the second verse (KJV), literally means "He Himself," and is the strongest distinctive expression in that language. The same strong idea of personality is expressed in the words twice repeated, "with God." Even before His incarnation, even before there was any creature in the universe, He was a living person, distinct from and yet one with the eternal Father. These passages completely contradict the heretical view of the Trinity entertained by some, that the divine persons are just various aspects of God. In this passage, the Father and the Son are both represented as distinct individuals, as much as any being can be.

Deity

"The Word was God" (1:1). The Word possesses all the attributes that

God possesses. The ordinary form of expression is more forcible than it is possible to represent in the translation of the Greek tense, the imperfect expresses as far as human language can, "the notion of absolute existence." This is the great fundamental truth which the Gospel of John develops and unfolds. He simply states it here, and afterwards bears witness to it. Still stronger, if possible, is his statement in the closing words of his epistle (1 John 5:20): "He is the true God and eternal life."

Eternity

"In the beginning." This expression reverts back to Genesis 1:1, and there it means the moment when the created universe came into existence. At this moment John declares Jesus Christ already was, and therefore had been in the previous eternity before any created existence had come into being. It implies His preexistence. This is the truth which the Apostle Paul expresses so forcibly in Colossians 1:17, "He is before all things," and again, "the firstborn over all creation"(1:15), literally: "born before the whole creation."

The Word

His relation to the Father, as the Image and Revealer of God. This is expressed by the term "the Word." The Greek term, *logos,* was a familiar word in philosophical discussion in the days of John, both as understood in these discussions and as the word itself naturally means. It fittingly expresses the truth that Jesus Christ is the great Revealer of the Father, conveying to us God's highest and kindest thought, and exhibiting to us His nature and character. It is the same truth elsewhere expressed by John himself: "No one has ever seen God, but God the One and Only, who is at the Father's side, has made him known" (John 1:18); and also in the later epistles of the New Testament: "He is the image of the invisible God" (Colossians 1:15); "The Son is the radiance of God's glory and the exact representation of his being" (Hebrews 1:3). What a beautiful conception it gives us of the mission of Jesus. An ancient conqueror held in bondage the beautiful wife of his enemy. Again and again the unhappy prince had sent his petition for the return of her whom he loved better than his life. The conqueror sent no written reply, but one day, who should appear at the gates of the prince, but the captive wife herself, bearing this response: "The king has sent me to be myself the answer to your petitions." She was the personal word that satisfied all his desire as no language could. So in answer to all man's questionings and cries, and all the heart's deep needs, God speaks to us. God does not speak to us merely words of truth and promise, but sends the living answer, Jesus Himself, as the one great all-expressive Word, which contains in it the substance of all other words and thoughts. He is to us, not only the realization of God's purity, power and wisdom, but the expression of God's love.

THE CREATING WORD
John 1:3–4

This also leads us back to the first chapter of Genesis and the record of creation. "And God said, 'Let there be light,' and there was light" (Genesis 1:3). This was the personal Word, and by Him all things were made. This is amplified by the Apostle Paul in Colossians 1:16—"For by him all things were created: things in heaven and on earth, visible and invisible, whether thrones or powers or rulers or authorities; all things were created by him and for him." And if the literal construction of these words is "in Him were all things created," it would seem to teach that the material universe was really involved in Christ's own eternal being, and that He is its essential Head; and perhaps His own incarnation is in some sense connected with this thought. The last link in the glorious chain, which unites the universe with the throne, is the person of Jesus, combining of Himself both the Creator and the creation. Christ's relation to nature is a most practical truth. As the maker of our spirits and the framer of our bodies, He is the true Supply of all the needs that He has created, and the true Restorer of our wrecked holiness and happiness. He is the true Head of every human life, and apart from Him our being is abnormal and must be miserably lost. What an emphasis it gives to His humility to think that He who made all worlds and beings, should lie as an infant on Mary's bosom.

CHRIST'S GLORY IN THE OLD TESTAMENT
John 1:4–5, 9–10

These words refer to Christ's relation to the rational life and reason of man, and God's manifested Presence in the Old Testament revelations, which He made successfully under the patriarchal and Mosaic dispensations. He is "the true light that gives light to every man" (John 1:9), in the sense of giving reason and intelligence to the human race. And "he was in the world" (1:10), not only in the rational nature which He gave to men, but especially in the manifestations of His will which He made to the Old Testament patriarchs and prophets. And yet, with a very few exceptions, "the world did not recognize him" (1:10). The very intelligence which He gave to the human mind was prostituted to intellectual pride and idolatrous worship.

The successive revelations made to Abraham, Moses and the prophets were all connected with the person of Christ, the great Angel of the Covenant, whom we can trace through all the stages of former dispensations, and He is ever recognized in these revelations as the Son of God.

THE INCARNATE WORD
John 1:14

First we have the nature and fact of the incarnation in the literal translation of the Greek word, "He became flesh." This denotes true and actual humanity; not merely a body, but also a soul. There were not two distinct persons, however; it was the same person who was the Eternal Word, who became a visible, tangible human being, possessing both natures, but combining them in one person. It is not said He became *a man,* but He became *man;* in the widest sense "He is the Son of Man." The exact meaning of this now becomes more vivid in the light of various heresies which have arisen in the Church. Among these might be mentioned Apollinarianism, which teaches that the divine Word took on a human body, but not a human soul; Nestorianism, which teaches that He had two personalities, both a human and a divine; Eutichianism, which really makes Christ have a third nature through the incarnation; and Gnosticism, which represents His body as simply an illusion and not really belonging to the Christ, and other less noted errors. It is needless to speak concerning the process and method of the mystery of the Incarnation. It is enough for faith to know that the power of the Holy Spirit united the nature of God with the child of Mary in one divine and human personality, which includes humanity in its widest sense and links Him with every race, sex and age, as the real Brother and Head. One of the latest errors, respecting Christ, is that of so-called Christian Science, which denies the existence of matter, and therefore, the physical and material existence of Jesus Christ, regarding Him as merely a principle of rational mind. This is the heresy of which the Apostle John has said, "Every spirit that acknowledges that Jesus Christ has come in the flesh is from God, but every spirit that does not acknowledge Jesus is not from God. This is the spirit of the antichrist, which you have heard is coming and even now is already in the world" (1 John 4:2–3).

Second, the human life of Christ on earth. He "made his dwelling among us" (John 1:14). Literally, this means, "He tabernacled among us." This describes His earthly life, which was as human as His birth, and which constantly manifested not only His humanity, but also His divine glory. There is an allusion here to the Hebrew tabernacle in the wilderness as a type of Jesus in His person and life.

Third, the manifested glory of the incarnate Christ. All through His earthly life it is witnessed by the apostles: "We have seen his glory, the glory of the One and Only, who came from the Father, full of grace and truth" (1:14). His whole life was a constant testimony of His divinity. The term glory, here applied to Christ's earthly life, is also an allusion to the glory of God manifested in the tabernacle and temple (Exodus 16:10; 11:34; Ezekiel 1:28, etc.).

The Only Begotten

Another term is here introduced for the first time, which we find frequently repeated afterwards in the New Testament: "The only begotten of the Father" (John 1:14, KJV). This expression denotes the filial relation. The Son is in some ineffable sense the effulgence and offspring of the Father's life, and yet of equal and co-eternal glory. The term also specifies this relationship as peculiar to Christ, and absolutely without parallel. No other is a son of God in the sense in which He is, except, of course, His people, who through their union with Him are received into the fellowship of His very Sonship. Two other expressions are used to characterize the manifested glory of His life, namely, "grace and truth" (1:14). These express the two great ideas that run through all the writings of John so constantly, namely, "love and light." Grace is the expression of God's love, and truth denotes the light which He came to shed on the destinies of men. Thus the incarnate Word proves His own deity by the constant manifestation of His glory through His gracious words and works, and His marvelous revelation of truth and light through His own teachings and example. The word truth literally means reality, and expresses the idea that, in contrast with the mere types and shadows of the law, Christ is the actual fulfillment of the promises.

THE WITNESS OF JOHN
John 1:6, 8, 19, 30; 3:22–34

Next, we have the witness of the great forerunner introduced. His advent is described in impressive language as one sent from God, and yet, in sharp distinction from the glorious person John the Baptist came to identify, he is called "a man" (1:6). He was especially called from the priestly line to represent the official witness of Judaism to the Son of God, and to gather up the testimony of all the prophets. In his own last message, he came not to call attention to himself or his work, but for a witness of Christ, the true Light, and not merely that Israel might receive her Messiah, but with a wider scope, that "through him all men might believe" (1:7).

John's testimony involves:

a. The witness to the preexistence of Christ. "He was before me" (1:30). This necessarily implies His divinity, for, humanly speaking, John was born before Jesus. Therefore, if Christ was before Him, He must have had a prior and therefore divine existence.

b. Not only His preexistence, but His preeminence. "He is the one who comes after me, the thongs of whose sandals I am not worthy to untie. . . . [He] has surpassed me" (1:27, 30). John clearly recognizes Him as possessing the divinity and glory of the eternal God.

c. John recognizes Him as the Son of God (1:34).

d. John recognizes Him as the giver of the Holy Spirit—"he who will baptize with the Holy Spirit" (1:33). His relation to the other Person of the Trinity is as definite as to the Father. There could be no higher testimony to the glory of Jesus than to give Him His place of honor in connection with the ministry of the Holy Spirit, through whom the light of revelation had come, and was still to come from God to man.

e. John testifies of Jesus, "the Lamb of God, who takes away the sin of the world" (1:29); thus recognizing His sacrificial work and priestly character as the atoning Savior for lost men. Then, respecting his own ministry, John describes himself as simply a voice, nothing in himself, but simply as a messenger declaring the words of another prior witness of the true object of man's hope and affections. How beautiful the picture of his humility, and how glorious the vision he brings of Jesus as the eternal Son of God, the Savior of sinful men and the source of the blessed Holy Spirit, through whom we receive the light and life of His great redemption.

THE WITNESS OF THE HOLY SPIRIT
John 1:32

This was the visible descent of the Holy Spirit upon Jesus, in the form of a dove, and was designed to be an open and manifest testimony to His Messiahship and divinity, that no one could gainsay. It was also, as we learn from the other evangelists, accompanied by the voice of God proclaiming, "This is my Son, whom I love; with him I am well pleased" (Matthew 3:17). To John himself this sign had already been promised as the special token of the Messiah. The voice of God had whispered to him, "The man on whom you see the Spirit come down and remain is he who will baptize with the Holy Spirit" (John 1:33). This is ever still the highest testimony that God can give to any of His servants. The same Holy Spirit is the witness of Christianity by His unceasing manifestations of grace and power in the ministry of God's servants and the lives of His children. The form in which the Holy Spirit came to Christ, as a dove, suggests the ideas of gentleness, peace and love as the special attributes of His life and ministry.

THE WITNESS OF THE FIRST DISCIPLES
John 1:37–49

We have here the testimonies of Christ's earliest followers. Some of them had already been the disciples of John, and at his testimony they left their former master and followed Jesus. Like all true disciples, they began to testify. The first witness was Andrew, and his testimony was first given to his own brother, Simon. "We have found the Messiah" (1:41), was his glad message. Simon, in turn, comes also to the Savior, and becomes henceforth His boldest witness; and the next day Philip is called and at once follows the

Master, and immediately becomes himself a witness to his friend Nathaniel. "We have found," he says, "the one Moses wrote about in the Law, and about whom the prophets also wrote—Jesus of Nazareth, the son of Joseph" (1:45). Nathaniel's conservative spirit is disposed to question the ardor of his younger friend, but his doubts only serve to emphasize his own testimony, when a little later he meets the Master himself, and under the searching glance of His omniscient eye, recognizes immediately His divine and Messianic character and exclaims, "Rabbi, you are the Son of God; you are the King of Israel" (1:49).

CHRIST'S WITNESS TO HIMSELF
John 1:50–51

Jesus replies by appropriating to Himself the sublime symbol of Jacob's ladder, of which, perhaps, Nathaniel at the time had been reading, and representing Himself as the way of access between earth and heaven, through whom henceforth the supernatural and stupendous manifestations of God are to be made known to His people. He adopts in His reply to Nathaniel a new title, "the Son of Man" (1:51), which, while it carries with it the sense of divine majesty and His superhuman dignity, chiefly represents Him in His relations to humanity as the Brother, Redeemer and Head of the race, with which He has forever become linked in His incarnation.

This may, therefore, be called His own witness to Himself, and it fittingly closes the series of testimonies contained in this wonderful chapter, The Word, the Only Begotten of the Father, the Light, the Life of man, the Son of God, the Messiah, the King of Israel, and now, the Son of Man.

THE WITNESS OF HIS WORKS
John 2:1–11

This miracle is recorded only by John, and the closing sentence connects it with the manifestation of His divine power and glory. "This, the first of his miraculous signs, Jesus performed in Cana of Galilee. He thus revealed his glory, and his disciples put their faith in him" (2:11). It was designed, therefore, as a special manifestation of His divine glory. Its deeper spiritual teachings we will afterwards dwell more fully upon. Here it is enough to notice, it is God's first witness through the works of His beloved Son. His mother seems to have expected some remarkable exhibition of His power, and yet He is most careful to guard Himself from being misunderstood even in His relations to her. His words, "Dear woman, why do you involve me?" (2:4), have placed an infinite gulf between the glory of the Son of God and even that blessed woman whom superstition has set up in a place of equal honor. The force of the testimony is enhanced by the statement of its influence on His disciples, for in consequence of this miracle they believed on Him, so that their testimony is really added to the miracle itself. So far as this special miracle is concerned, we may notice, first, the power manifested in this instance over organic matter, where there was no element of life to act spontaneously, and it must therefore have been the direct result of omnipotence. Secondly, the symbolical ideas suggested by the transformation of a lower into a higher substance, foreshadowing the character of His work as bringing the larger and richer blessings of the gospel to take the place of the old dispensation. Thirdly, the tender sympathy with human affections and joys which it suggested, and the great fact that the ministry of Jesus was to be a ministry of love, and to raise His people to all gladness as suggested by the marriage feast.

HIS SECOND MIRACLE
John 2:13–17

This instance has already been referred to at length in the other gospels. It is well to link it with the chain of testimony to Christ's divine character, of which it formed a part. It was the unanswerable token to the officials of Judaism of Christ's authority over the temple and the institutions of Moses, which they did not attempt to resist or dispute the justice and righteousness of His stern judgment on their abuse of their sacred trust.

THE WITNESS OF HIS OWN DEATH AND RESURRECTION
John 2:18–22

The Jews having asked Him for a sign of His authority as a teacher and divine messenger, He gives them a hint in the language of a symbolism which faith might easily understand and this token, "Destroy this temple, and I will raise it again in three days" (2:19). Their traditional ideas could only interpret His words in their literal sense; but His disciples afterwards remembered that He had thus announced, in the very beginning, His death and resurrection as the supreme evidence of His being the true Messiah, the Son of God. This is still, and ever shall be, God's highest seal to His beloved Son, and the cornerstone of Christian evidence, declared to be the Son of God with power by His resurrection from the dead (Romans 1:4).

THE WITNESS OF THE COMMON PEOPLE
John 2:23–25

The miracles already referred to were followed at this time by many similar exhibitions of His power and the result was that large numbers of the people had accepted Him as the Messiah; but that conviction which comes from the evidence of signs can never be fully depended upon; so we read that Jesus did not value greatly the adherence of even this multitude. He did not commit Himself to them, because He knew what was in man;

still, their testimony to Him had its place and value. How unsuitable must have been the evidences of His authority and claims. There is undoubtedly an allusion here in the very meaning of the words employed in the superficial character to the faith of the people. It was rather the result of wonder at His astonishing power, than of a personal confidence in, and devotion to Him.

THE WITNESS OF THE RULERS
John 3:1–13

Here we find a leading Rabbi coming to Him, timidly but honestly, and expressing without reserve the confidence of the class he represented in the new Master that had come among them. "We know you are a teacher who has come from God. For no one could perform the miraculous signs you are doing if God were not with him" (John 3:2). This is a very strong testimony, and yet the Lord Himself saw in it its essential defect. It wholly lacked a deep spiritual knowledge of Christ and His teachings, and the most essential principles of the kingdom of heaven. Therefore, Christ at once ignores the confidence of Nicodemus, and presses him to unfold the true meaning of His work and mission to the wondering Pharisee. We are not told of the immediate result, but we know that a few months later this man was not ashamed to stand up in the very midst of the highest council of the nation and claim for Christ a fair hearing (7:50), and still later, to go to the very governor himself with Joseph and claim His body for honorable burial (19:39); so that the witness of Nicodemus grew at length to be one of the grandest testimonies which the Lord ever received.

JOHN'S SECOND TESTIMONY TO CHRIST
John 3:25–26

Christ had now become fully established as a teacher, and some of John's disciples, jealous of their master's honor, came to him to report and complain about the success of his rival. The spirit of the Baptist shines out again in still more beautiful and heavenly light, as he modestly takes his true place at the feet of the greater Master and bears a still higher testimony to His preeminence.

He reminds them that no man is anything in himself and can receive nothing except what is given him from heaven. His position, he again reminds them, is not one of any personal consequence or importance, but simply that of a witness to another in whose glory he is glad to be lost sight of. He is but the friend of the bridegroom and does not come to absorb the attention of the bride, or even the spectators, but simply to wait upon the bridegroom and rejoice in the greater love and honor which He receives. It is necessary, therefore, that the more successful his ministry becomes, the more prominent his Master will be, and the more will he pass out of sight. The very conditions of his ministry are such that "He must become greater; I must become less" (3:30). Like the morning star, he is the herald of the dawn, and the rising sun buries his light in a brighter effulgence. He then proceeds to give a most distinct and excellent witness to the person and glory of Jesus.

a. John declares that Jesus comes from above, and afterwards explains this to be from heaven.

b. He says that Jesus is above all, referring not only to His preeminence above all beings, but His sovereign authority over all things.

c. John declares that the things which Jesus testifies are not through the witness of another, but are the results of His own direct knowledge; what He has seen and heard, that He testifies.

d. He declares that all who receive His testimony thus bear witness that it is true. This must mean, therefore, that His testimony is God's testimony, and that He is God.

The figurative expression, "Has set his seal" (3:33, KJV), expresses very strongly the faith with which we should receive, the testimony of Christ; not only assenting to it with our mind, but committing our entire being to it by the most solemn acts and sanctions of faith.

e. Next, he declares that God has sent Christ, in a special sense not true of any other messenger—"For the one whom God has sent" (3:34). Of John it was said that he was a man sent from God; but the meaning here is stronger. This Messenger was sent by God, in a most direct sense, to represent Himself, and the words which He speaks are the very words of God.

f. He possesses the Holy Spirit without measure. This is not true or possible of any finite being, and therefore it is an attestation of Christ's divinity. "God gives [Him] the Spirit without limit" (3:34). All the fullness of the Godhead dwells in Him (Colossians 2:9); all, including both the nature of the Father and the infinite resources of the Holy Spirit.

g. John further declares that Christ is the special object of the Father's love, and that He "has placed everything in his hands" (3:35). To Him has been committed the government, the fullness of the divine attributes, and the administration of the whole plan of redemption, and even the judgment of all men in the last days. This is parallel to the expression in Hebrews 1:1–2: "In the past God spoke to our forefathers through the prophets at many times and in various ways, but in these last days he has spoken to us by his Son, whom he appointed heir of all things."

h. In consequence of this high commission and investiture of authority and power, He has therefore become the only Savior of sinful men, and their destiny depends upon their reception or rejection of Him: "Whoever believes in the Son has eternal life, but whoever rejects the Son will not see life, for God's wrath remains on him" (John 3:36).

WITNESS OF THE SAMARITANS
John 4:28–30

The testimony of these people is the more remarkable because of their traditional prejudice and jealousy with respect to everything Jewish. It is the more emphatic because it was perfectly spontaneous and called forth by no great miracle on the part of Christ or testimony to Him from others, but wholly elicited by the moral and spiritual influence of His presence and character, and His simple conversation with the Samaritan woman and her countrymen. This represents the instinctive testimony of the human heart, and even of the sinful heart to the Savior and the gospel when brought into living contact.

There is perhaps no more remarkable or beautiful evidence of the divinity of Jesus than the consciousness He impressed upon this poor woman, as He quietly talked with her, that He was the Searcher and Creator of her heart as well as its Savior. "Come, see a man who told me everything I ever did. Could this be the Christ?" (4:29). The same impression was produced upon the hearts of the rest of the Samaritans: "We no longer believe," they said, "just because of what you said; now we have heard for ourselves, and we know that this man really is the Savior of the world" (4:42). Something like this is often the result of the first contact of the gospel with heathen hearts, and the same conviction always comes to the converted soul in the moment of its first coming to the real Savior. It knows by evidence which nothing could shake and nothing could add to, that He is indeed the Christ and the divine Christ. Therefore, to every soul that knows the Savior personally, this is the supreme evidence of Christianity, its own personal experience and acquaintance with Jesus.

CHRIST'S SECOND GALILEAN MIRACLE
John 4:46–54

There are some things peculiar about this miracle. In His conversation with the nobleman, the Master implies that there is a danger even that the signs and miracles by which He has already attested His character and commission will prove a snare to those of feeble faith, and that the evidence of the people will be so based upon these, that they will not be able to believe without constant signs. Therefore, in this case, he refuses to go down to Capernaum to heal the dying boy, but requires the father to believe without any evidence, except the naked word of Jesus, that his son is really healed by that simple word. The father's faith proves equal to the great demand, and he immediately departs, to find to his unutterable joy, his child restored and his servants on their way to meet him with the glad tidings. The faith of this man was a higher testimony, therefore, to Christ than the evidence which had hitherto been based upon His visible miracles. The fact also that this healing was produced without His personal presence, and simply by His naked word, as it traversed the intervening space and commanded the forces of nature and disease to obey His almighty will, enhanced its weight.

CHRIST'S APPEAL TO THE TESTIMONY OF HIS WORKS
John 5:17–31

This testimony immediately followed one of the mightiest of His miracles, namely, the healing of the invalid man at the pool of Bethesda in Jerusalem. It had been followed by a bitter persecution on the part of the Jewish rulers, especially on account of Christ's ignoring the claims of the Sabbath by healing this man on that day. The Lord vindicates His work by the lofty claim that His works are coordinate with His Father's and of equal authority. The Father works on the Sabbath day by sustaining the material creation, and Christ claims the equal right to work in the spiritual world for the relief of His people. This was Christ's own highest testimony hitherto to Himself, and they readily understood it to mean the claim of an absolute equality with God. This Jesus fully acknowledges in the discourse which follows. He states that His works are in absolute and uninterrupted unity with the Father and are of equal power and glory, including even the resurrection of the dead, the future judgment and the quickening of the spiritually dead in the present time. In consequence of this He dares to claim what they consider blasphemy, that all men should honor the Son, even as they honor the Father (5:23). Later in the 36th verse, Christ again applies to the witness of His works. "The very work that the Father has given me to finish, and which I am doing, testifies that the Father has sent me."

CHRIST'S APPEAL TO THE WITNESS OF JOHN
John 5:32–35

They had already received John as a divine messenger, and now the Lord appeals to their consistency and the necessity of receiving John's witness concerning Himself, if they were to be consistent. At the same time He bears a very high testimony Himself to John, as "a lamp that burned and gave light" (5:35), and adds, "I know that his testimony about me is valid" (5:32). At the same time, He does not need the witness of John, but appeals directly to His Father's testimony and the evidence of His works, only referring to John as a witness, for their sakes, and because they readily received him as one of their own prophets. "Not that I accept human testimony; but I mention it that you may be saved" (5:34).

CHRIST'S APPEAL TO HIS FATHER'S WITNESS
John 5:36–38

In these words Christ appeals to the testimony which the Father had given at His baptism with His own living voice, and thus implies that the fact that they did not receive Him is the strongest evidence that they are not even the people of God, and they do not know the Father's voice or believe His word.

CHRIST'S APPEAL TO THE SCRIPTURES
John 5:39–47

Their very own Scriptures, He tells them, contain the clearest intimation of His coming and character.

> You diligently study the Scriptures because you think that by them you possess eternal life. These are the Scriptures that testify about me. . . . If you believed Moses, you would believe me, for he wrote about me. (5:39, 46)

The Mosaic system was a beautiful and instructive type and prophecy of Jesus, and we cannot understand even the institutions and teachings of Moses apart from the gospel. They had wholly misunderstood their own Scriptures, and thus rejecting Christ, even Moses would be a witness against them. Thus we triumphantly sum up the entire series of testimonies by which God has attested His divine character and Messianic claims, and over all might be appropriately recorded the verse already quoted, "But these are written that you may believe that Jesus is the Christ, the Son of God, and that by believing you may have life in his name" (20:31).

THE TESTIMONY OF THE MULTITUDE
John 6:11–15

This is the testimony of the multitude who had been fed miraculously by the multiplied bread and fishes. This is one of Christ's most impressive miracles, showing His absolute command over all the laws and forces of nature, and the scale upon which it was wrought was so magnificent that it left the profoundest impression on the multitudes who witnessed it. So much so, indeed, that in the enthusiasm of the moment they impetuously determined to compel Him to become the leader of a great popular movement and allow them to make Him their actual king. Of course, this was but a superficial, and even a selfish movement. He knew their hearts better than they themselves did, and a few days afterwards declared to them, "You are looking for me, not because you saw miraculous signs but because you ate the loaves and had your fill" (6:26). The Greek word in this last sentence denotes the grossest, the most animal satisfaction. They wanted a king that could gratify their earthly desires and give them immunity from laboring and suffering, but had no appreciation of Christ's higher character and teaching. At the same time, their testimony on this occasion was sincere and spontaneous, as far as they knew themselves, and bears witness to the power of Christ and the influence of His mighty works.

THE TESTIMONY OF NATURE
John 6:18–21

This sublime miracle is also recorded by the other evangelists, but here it is added as an emphatic testimony to the omnipotent power of Christ, that the moment He entered the ship, immediately it "reached the shore where they were heading" (6:21). Matthew and Mark tell us that the wind also ceased. The elements of nature recognized their Master's touch, and not only gave Him a pathway upon the stormy waves, but also hushed their voices in instant subservience to His will, and even space and distance were annihilated at His coming, and the little vessel dropped into her haven without a rippling wave or disturbing element. These were both signs as well as miracles, and designed to prepare the hearts of His disciples to understand that power that can work independently of all human means and agencies and can either use or ignore second causes and material things in the fulfillment of His will.

THE TESTIMONY OF PETER
John 6:66–69

The feeding of the five thousand had been followed by the remarkable discussion of the following Sabbath in the synagogue of Capernaum. In this address He had attempted to unfold the deeper meaning of the miracles and to reveal Himself as the true source and sustenance of His people's life, both for soul and body, under the figure of the Living Bread. These profound and beautiful teachings were met by captious questionings and cavilings on the part of the Pharisees, and at the close of His address the greater portion of His Galilean followers became offended and disgusted, and many of His disciples, we are told, went back and walked no more with Him. For a moment the Master seems to have almost doubted the chosen Twelve; at least, He gave them the opportunity of making their own choice. Turning to them He asks, "You do not want to leave too, do you?" (6:67). The question is immediately answered by the impetuous Peter in a noble testimony and confession of Christ, which shows that although they dimly understood as yet the full meaning of His teachings, yet they felt in their deepest hearts that these teachings were the true satisfaction and life of their own hearts, and that He was indeed the Christ, the Son of the living God. This beautiful testimony comprehends both parts of the combined witness which John's Gospel was intended to unfold, namely, that Jesus is the Christ, the Son of God, and there is life through His name. Peter recognizes Him as the Christ, the Son of the living God, and also the Author of life eternal. The words of His confession are exceedingly positive and emphatic. It is not a mere opinion, but "We believe and know" (6:69), he says. Literally, the original means, "We have believed, and have come to know." It was more than even believing. It had risen to a spiritual consciousness of and acquaintance with Himself, which had rendered doubt henceforth impossible. Thus his identification of Christ as the Messiah is equally explicit, that Christ is the Christ of prophecy and of Jewish expectation. The true reading of the next clause seems to be "the Holy One of God." This is the form found in the earliest and best manuscripts. This would indicate even more strongly the apostle's conception of His higher nature, as one who had come to earth unstained by human sin and possessing the essential nature of the infinitely holy God.

THE WITNESS OF EVERY HUMAN CONSCIENCE
John 7:14–17

Jesus here announces the true touchstone by which His teachings, and all others, may be tested. The proof is in the practice. "If anyone chooses to do God's will, he will find out whether my teaching comes from God or whether I speak on my own" (7:17). The best way to be convinced of the truth of Christianity is to test it. Any man who will take the simple and holy teachings of Jesus and honestly practice them according to the light that God gives, shall have an answering witness in his own experience which will leave no doubt of their truth. In trying this test, we must, of course, follow the Master's own directions and begin at the beginning with a life of sincere dependence and simple trust, and then follow it by implicit and loving obedience. He who does this will always find the result in his own inward peace and happiness, and the fruits of lasting blessing in his life and influence. Many of the most remarkable examples of Christian faith and usefulness in the church today have been saved from utter atheism by simply following this direction. This, after all, is the strongest evidence of Christianity.

THE TESTIMONY OF THE COMMON PEOPLE AT JERUSALEM
John 7:25–40

The events described in this chapter transpired at Jerusalem during the Feast of Tabernacles. Day after day the Savior had abundantly taught in the very midst of His enemies, until the multitudes were amazed at His fearless boldness, and the Pharisees paralyzed and afraid to arrest or hinder Him. His wonderful teachings reached the very depths of many hearts, and set all deeply questioning. Some asked, "How did this man get such learning without having studied?" (7:15). "When the Christ comes, will he do more miraculous signs than this man?" (7:31). Some said, "He is a good man"; others, "No, he deceives the people" (7:12). Even the doubters were impressed with His courage and said, "Isn't this the man they are trying to kill? Here he is speaking publicly, and they are not saying a word to him. Have the authorities really concluded that he is the Christ?" (7:25–26). Many at length dared to say, "Surely this man is the Prophet" (7:40), and the Pharisees saw that their hold upon the people was waning, and that His audacious courage and wonderful teachings were winning the hearts of the multitude, and that something must be done instantly, at least to show a consistent front on their part.

THE OFFICERS SENT TO ARREST HIM
John 7:32, 44–46

Alarmed at the influence which Christ was gaining and the effects of their own inaction, the Pharisees at length ventured to attempt Christ's arrest, and sent a body of officers with authority for that purpose. It was while they were lying in wait for Him that Christ delivered the sublime message in the last days of the feast, recorded in John 7:37–39. We can imagine something of the effect of this lofty eloquence and its striking fitness to the occasion. Doubtless there was much added which was not recorded, and filled by the situation with a thousand details of tender and impressive meaning. At least the effect upon the officers was like that of some magic spell. As they listened they forgot all about their purpose in coming, and when they awoke from the spell of His eloquence and found themselves in the presence of the Master, the only excuse they could give for their failure was the admiring testimony, "No one ever spoke the way this man does" (7:46).

CHRIST'S OWN TESTIMONY TO HIMSELF
John 8:13–30

For the second time the Lord now bears witness to Himself, and appeals to His Father's witness as confirming it. These two witnesses, He claims, are sufficient, even according to their own law, to establish His authority. Their inability to understand this testimony was no evidence of its failure, but was simply the result of their own ignorance of the Father as well as the Son. All through this chapter the Lord lays bare their absolute blindness of heart, even to the meaning of their own institutions. "If God were your Father," He says, "you would love me, for I came from God" (8:42). "He who belongs to God hears what God says. The reason you do not hear is that you do not belong to God" (8:47). Even Abraham, whom they called their father, beheld in the distance His coming day and rejoiced in the prospect of it; but they, who called themselves the children of Abraham, and the children of God, are even trying to kill the very One whom Abraham worshiped and whom God recognized as His dear Son. Their true father, therefore, is neither God nor Abraham, but the devil, who has been a liar and murderer from the beginning, and who is now prompting them in their unbelief and murderous hate toward Him.

THE TESTIMONY OF THE BLIND MAN
John 9:8–33

This miracle was intended to illustrate the special teaching of Jesus at the Feast of Tabernacles, that He was the Light of the world. As such, He gives sight to this poor sufferer, and afterwards opens his inner vision to know the truth and to behold His own divine glory. The miracle of his healing was enough to convince the blind man that Jesus was the Son of God; but to the Pharisees it only became another occasion for captiousness and questioning. With his simple common sense, the blind man was enabled to comprehend the doubts of Christ's enemies and he treated them with undisguised impatience and contempt. When they came to question him he frankly told them the wonderful story of his healing, and added with a decisive confidence, "One thing I do know. I was blind but now I see!" (9:25). As they question him still more, he sarcastically asks, "I have told you already and you did not listen. Why do you want to hear it again? Do you want to become his disciples, too?" (9:27). And then as they heap abuse on him and his Master, he gives way to his utter astonishment at these would-be teachers:

> Now that is remarkable! You don't know where he comes from, yet he opened my eyes. We know that God does not listen to sinners. He listens to the godly man who does his will. Nobody has ever heard of opening the eyes of a man born blind. If this man were not from God, he could do nothing. (9:30–33)

The second occasion of his plain speaking led to his expulsion from the synagogue with harshness and cruelty. The Lord Jesus, however, finds him, and now gives him a still deeper revelation of Himself as the Son of God. With the same simple frankness with which he believed before, he now accepts the higher truth, and falling at His feet in reverential worship, he becomes, in a deeper and higher sense, a disciple of the Lord Jesus, whom he has so nobly confessed.

CHRIST'S THIRD TESTIMONY TO HIMSELF
John 10:22–39

This is Christ's most emphatic and explicit witness. His language is intended to be unequivocal and to claim absolute equality with God. This is rendered indisputable by the interpretation which they put upon His words, and which He did not contradict. They evidently believed Him to mean equality with the Father, and denounced it as blasphemy, and so attempted to stone Him for His profanity. Had they been wrong in this idea, honesty would have compelled Him to contradict or correct them. On the contrary, He repeats more strongly His previous claims and calls upon His Father's witness, through His works, to the truth of His assumption. He says,

> Do not believe me unless I do what my Father does. But if I do it, even though you do not believe me, believe the miracles, that you may know and understand that the Father is in me, and I in the Father. (10:37–38)

THE TESTIMONY OF THE RESURRECTION OF LAZARUS
John 11:41–45

This stupendous miracle was God's most signal testimony to His Son, excepting only Christ's own resurrection. It was not only a triumph over death, but over the corruption of the grave. It was as stupendous in power as the creation of the human race, and it left no doubt of the divinity of the Christ on every unprejudiced mind. Of course, His enemies were perverted by prejudice and determined to resist the effect of such evidence, and acknowledged, "Here is this man performing many miraculous signs. If we let him go on like this, everyone will believe in him" (11:47–48).

THE TESTIMONY OF CAIAPHAS
John 11:47–52

This was a very remarkable witness by a high priest of the Jewish order, uttered in the ecclesiastical council, the Sanhedrin. We are told that it was inspired by the Holy Spirit and not his own thought or wisdom. He declared that it was expedient "that Jesus would die for the Jewish nation, and not only for that nation but also for the scattered children of God, to bring them together and make them one" (11:51–52). This extraordinary testimony, summing up, as it did, the whole spirit of prophecy and the essential facts of redemption, is one of the sublime examples of the way in which God can use even wicked men as His instruments. Henceforth it gave a spirit of religious inspiration to the wicked and malicious Pharisees, under cover of which they henceforth prosecuted with double diligence their murderous intent.

THE TESTIMONY OF MARY
John 12:3–7

This was the witness of a loving heart to its Lord, and it was not only the witness of love, but also of the most farsighted and illuminated faith. Mary saw in Him not only her Lord, but also her dying Savior, and anointed His body for burial before the cross and the tomb. She perhaps was the only one of His disciples who really understood the meaning of His life and death. It was therefore accepted by Him with peculiar delight, and the odor of the ointment has filled heaven and earth ever since.

THE WITNESS OF THE NATION TO JESUS
John 12:12–19

This popular outburst of patriotic enthusiasm, in which the whole nation was for a time united, was intended as a divine witness to His Messiahship and as a type of the time when He shall be welcomed to the throne of Israel by the race that crucified and rejected Him. The Psalms they sang, the ascriptions they uttered, were all connected with the highest hopes of Judaism and the most sacred and divine worship; and no wonder that the Pharisees were filled with consternation, and exclaimed, "See, this is getting us nowhere. Look how the whole world has gone after him!" (12:19).

THE WITNESS OF THE GENTILES
John 12:20–25

The coming of these Greeks to Jesus represented the reaching out of the heart of the Gentile nations toward God, and the deep hunger in every human heart crying out inarticulately for that which only Christ can satisfy, and the deep need of humanity is here expressed, "We would like to see Jesus" (12:21). Not always do they know their own need, but when He is truly lifted up before them, all true hearts recognize and receive Him. To Him, on the eve of His rejection, this incident was a prophecy of the time when He will draw all men unto Him. Even already we have seen this gloriously anticipated, from time to time, in the history of missions, in the strange turning of the heathen heart to the gospel and the crucified Savior when simply and truthfully presented. The savages of Greenland resisted for years all the moral teachings of the Moravian missionaries, but when they began to tell the story of Jesus and read the third chapter of John, their hearts were completely broken down, and the gospel became its own witness to their deeper consciousness. There is something in Jesus that finds a response in the hearts when the barriers of ignorance and prejudice are removed; but there is no more sublime witness to the truth of Christianity than its adaptation to the conscious needs of our lost humanity.

THE VOICE FROM HEAVEN
John 12:27–33

This was the third direct witness of the Father's voice to His Son. The first had been given at His baptism, the second on the Mount of Transfiguration. This was distinctly audible to the people, although perhaps, none of them understood it explicitly. To some it seemed like a peal of thunder, to others an angel's voice. Jesus declared that it was designed as the Father's special testimony for their sakes. It is remarkable that this glorious testimony to Jesus followed immediately His own profoundest declaration with reference to His humiliation and sufferings. He had fully recognized and expressed His great mission of suffering death as the essential condition of His ultimate glory. The kernel of wheat must die before it can bring forth fruit, and He must reach His throne by way of the cross; nor He alone, but all His followers too. For a moment He shrinks back from the awful vision and cries out in His shrinking human consciousness, "Father, save me from this hour," but instantly rises into victory, and adds, "Father, glorify your name" (12:27, 28), thus accepting the cross and all its shame and consecrating Himself to the great sacrifice. "Father, glorify your name!" Then it is that the testimony of heaven seals His consecration and witnesses to His acceptance, and the voice of God proclaims, "I have glorified it, and will glorify it again" (12:28). Jesus accepts the testimony and rises to meet it in the lofty assurance of faith and victory. "Now," He cries, "is the time for judgment on this world; now the prince of this world will be driven out. But I, when I am lifted up from the earth, will draw all men to myself" (12:31–32). A little later in this chapter (verses 47–50), Jesus refers again to His Father's witness and solemnly reminds His hearers that rejection of His message is also the rejection of His Father, and shall be the witness against them in the last day.

THE WITNESS OF ISAIAH
John 12:37–41

The Lord quotes this verse to explain the unbelief of so many of the people, showing them it was simply what Isaiah, the ancient prophet, had foretold, and referring especially to two chapters in which that most illustrious of Judah's prophets had borne witness of His sufferings and glory. The first quotation is from the 53rd chapter of Isaiah, which is the vision of the Messiah's sufferings and humiliation. The other reference, in verse 40, is to the sixth chapter of Isaiah and the sublime vision of the heavenly glory contained therein, which the evangelist tells us had special reference to Jesus Himself, and which is manifestly a vision of Jehovah in the midst of all the majesty of His heavenly throne. To ascribe such glory to a mortal would indeed be the height of profanity.

CHRIST'S OWN CONSCIOUSNESS
John 13:3

There is a profound, subtle force in this verse. The very humiliation of

Jesus and His own voluntariness in it, while, to the outward sense, it might seem to be a contradiction of His preeminence, is the most perfect proof of His real dignity. It was because He knew that the Father had given all things into His hands, and that He was come from God, and went to God, that He could so easily sacrifice and abase Himself. True dignity can afford to stoop. False pride, with no intrinsic loftiness, is always trying to lift itself up. One who knows he has an illustrious name is not always trying to proclaim it. Jesus knew that He was divine and could not be misunderstood, therefore He was willing to stoop to the lowest place and set a perfect example of sacrifice and service; and never did He seem so divine to His disciples as when He knelt at their feet in the garb of a servant to wash away their stains. When does He for a moment lose the consciousness of His dignity in all this menial service? "You call me 'Teacher' and 'Lord,'" He adds, as He sits down again, "and rightly so, for that is what I am. Now that I, your Lord and Teacher, have washed your feet, you also should wash one another's feet" (13:13). And so, like Him, the more fully we realize our divine calling, the more willingly will we take the humblest place, and the less we know of the glory of our sonship, the more will we contend for the honors of earth and preeminence among our brethren.

CHRIST'S TESTIMONY TO HIS COMING GLORIFICATION
John 13:31–32

This announcement immediately followed the withdrawal of Judas from the company of the disciples and the presence of the Lord. His retirement lifted a great load from the mind of Jesus, and His spirit rose at once to this joyful utterance. Freely accepting all the consequences of Judas' betrayal and the cross and all its shame, He declares, "Now is the Son of Man glorified" (13:31). His death was to be His glorification as the Son of Man. It was also to bring unutterable glory to God, and it was to be followed by the glorification of Christ Himself, not merely as the Son of Man, but also in His own divine being and nature. Over all the dark and overshadowed valley of the garden and the cross, He sees immediately beyond the glory of His Father and His own eternal exaltation, and "for the joy set before him endured the cross, scorning its shame, and sat down at the right hand of the throne of God" (Hebrews 12:2).

CHRIST'S DISCOURSE AT THE PASSOVER TABLE
John 14:1–11

Perhaps there is no higher testimony to the divinity of Christ than the sublime consciousness expressed in these words. For a mortal to utter such language would be offensive and unspeakably profane. No man has ever dared to use such language. The very utterance of it would carry with it its own answer in the manifest consciousness of its extravagance, but in the case of

Christ there is no such feeling as we hear Him say,

> Trust in God; trust also in me. . . . I am in the Father and the
> Father is in me. . . . If you really knew me, you would know my
> Father as well. From now on, you do know him and have seen
> him. . . . You may ask me for anything in my name, and I will do
> it. (14:1, 11, 7, 14)

All this is so calm, so free from any idea of assumption, or of having uttered anything extraordinary; such an obvious simplicity and sense of truthfulness and reality pervade it that it bears the irresistible consciousness to every unprejudiced heart of the genuineness of His claims and the loftiness of His character. Even in human character we can always detect the borrowed feathers of pretentiousness, and recognize the natural nobility that sits so easily on lofty spirits and kingly natures. So the portrait of Jesus given in His own words is its own safe witness. The sustained character which He maintains all through this marvelous address is simply superhuman and beyond the power of man's invention. Not only do we trace in every sentence this divine consciousness of His relation to His Father, but the way in which He reveals Himself as the life and strength of His people, bestowing upon them with kingly bounty His grace, His intercession, His peace, His supernatural power, His spiritual presence in their hearts and the living reality of all this, as it has been experienced and seen in the hearts and lives of millions for more than 50 generations, is to every Christian heart the deepest, most satisfying testimony to the reality and divinity of Jesus.

THE WITNESS OF THE HOLY SPIRIT
John 14:16–20, 26; 16:7–14

The Holy Spirit had already borne witness to the Lord Jesus at His baptism, but here He is introduced as His divine Successor in the consummation of His mediatorial work, and as the perpetual witness through the coming ages to His person, His truth and His glory. He is to be the interpreter of all that Christ has said, and to make real to the faith and consciousness of His people, through divine and inward illumination, that which would otherwise be but an intellectual apprehension. He was to bring the vision as well as the light. He was to bring to their remembrance all things that Christ had already said, and then to lead them into further truths which they were not now able to bear—even opening the vista of the future and showing them things to come. Above all He was to be the special witness of Christ, and testify not of them, nor even of Himself, but personally of Jesus. And even to the world, which could not yet receive Him, He was to bring persuasions as no human arguments or persuasions could come, leading them to see their sin, their Savior, and the necessity of their separation from the world and the powers of evil.

HIS INTERCESSORY PRAYER
John 17:5, 8, 23, 24

There is no place nor time where the soul is so unfolded spiritually as the hour of solitary prayer, especially in some great crisis of need or suffering. This chapter is the opening of the curtains of the inner sanctuary of Christ's heart, and the unsealing of the very Holy of Holies itself. Here, above all other places, we may expect the truest and deepest expression of His consciousness, and it is still the same as in His parting words to His disciples. Calmly and sublimely He still takes His exalted and supreme place in His Father's fellowship, speaks of the glory which He had before the world was, assumes His perfect unity with Him as the very pattern of the oneness of His disciples, and claims the sanctification, preservation and glorification of His people by kingly right, with the majestic and imperative words which none but the equal of God could utter, "Father, I want" (17:24). Surely no one can look upon this scene without the deepest conviction of His conscious Deity, and the feeling that to assume such claims and rights and constantly sustain the lofty character to the close, would have been as impossible for a mere man as it would have been profane.

HIS VOLUNTARY SUBMISSION TO HIS ENEMIES
John 18:4–8

This remarkable instance, recorded only by John, bears the strongest testimony to the divine character of Jesus and the perfect voluntariness of His death. The men who came to arrest Him had no power to hurt Him or touch Him without His free consent. A silent look into their faces was enough to paralyze their strength and prostrate them on the ground at His feet, and it was only when He willingly yielded Himself to their hands that they were able to bind Him. Throughout His entire sufferings it was every moment true that man could have no power over Him except it was given from above, and He could truly say, "I lay down my life for the sheep. . . . No one takes it from me, but I lay it down of my own accord. I have authority to lay it down and authority to take it up again" (10:15, 18).

THE TESTIMONY OF HIS BAFFLED ACCUSERS
John 18:19–25, 29–30

In all this record of His trial there was not a single specific charge laid against Him by the Jews, and even when they sent Him to Pilate, they simply assumed that the governor would take their word for it and condemn Him without trial. Their general charge that He was a criminal (18:30), and their inability to formulate a single indictment that could stand against the test of Roman law, is the highest testimony of His innocence and blameless-ness. Looking in their faces He could appeal to those who heard Him and say, "If I said something wrong . . . testify as to what is wrong" (18:23), and they had no answer but violence and vagueness. Indeed they never had any charge to bring against Him but simply that which was His supremest glory, namely, His claim that He was the Son of God, and it was really for this that He was crucified at last.

THE TESTIMONY OF PILATE
John 18:30; 19:4, 12, 19

The Roman governor, finding that they had no charge against Him, refused to take their vague and general demand for His condemnation. He asked explicitly what accusation they brought, and getting no satisfactory reply, he questioned Him personally himself. The result was a deep convic-tion of Christ's innocence, which ever afterwards filled his soul, until at last it became a terrible fear and led him into that strange conflict between his own conscience and the mean and selfish desire to please the people, which terminated at length in the Savior's crucifixion. But up to the close, Pilate's repeated testimony was borne to the Savior's innocence, and the inscription which he had placed upon His cross and refused to change was the highest testimony to this conviction. He did not say this is Jesus of Nazareth, a criminal or a pretended king, but literally and unequivocally, "JESUS OF NAZARETH, THE KING OF THE JEWS" (19:19).

THE TESTIMONY FROM THE CROSS
John 19:23, 28, 36–38

These several passages combine the witness of the prophetical Scriptures to the sufferings of Christ, showing how literally and wonderfully every particular of the ancient picture was fulfilled, thus identifying Him as the true Messiah of Hebrew promise and hope. John's purpose in recording these minute details is to establish the point which his gospel was designed to prove, namely, that Jesus is the Christ; and so we find him more frequently than any other evan-gelist, saying, "that the scripture would be fulfilled" (19:36). The very parting of His garments, the consuming thirst that parched His tongue, the premature death that exempted Him from the breaking of His limbs, and even the inter-ment of His body in the tomb of the wealthy Joseph, were all fulfillments of scriptural predictions and marks of unmistakable identity.

THE TESTIMONY OF HIS RESURRECTION
John 20:11

This, of course, is the supreme evidence of the divinity and Messiahship of

Christ. The details which were given by John have, however, a special force. First, there is the evident unexpectedness of it by these simple disciples. None of them seemed to have had the faintest dream of His literal resurrection. Peter and John were both astonished, and Mary Magdalene was so unprepared for it that she did not at first recognize the Lord until He called her very name. This gives enhanced weight to the conclusion which was forced upon them by His actual appearance again. Next we have the explicit details which the narrative gives of the persons and places and the most trifling circumstances connected with His resurrection: the open door, the linen clothes and the burial cloth that was about His head wrapped together in a place by itself. All these points have a very positive weight in the question of evidence, which every judicial mind will fully appreciate. Then we have the explicit testimony of John, that he saw and believed (20:8). It was not an afterthought, but the instant and instinctive conviction of his whole mind that the Lord was really risen from the dead. But most conclusive of all is the testimony of Mary, all the stronger because of her perplexity at first and her womanly disappointment at not finding the body, and then her delighted and enraptured surprise when she recognized the Lord Himself, and throwing herself at His feet, she poured out the fullness of her confidence and joy in the one cry, "Rabboni" (20:16). All this evidence is confirmed by the subsequent appearance of Christ to His disciples, as narrated in this and the following chapters.

THE TESTIMONY OF THOMAS
John 20:24–28

This is perhaps the strongest witness of all from the fact that it has for its background the strongest unbelief, for Thomas had fully determined that he would not be deceived. His very love of the Master had made him afraid of any false hope. He did not expect His resurrection, and he could not bear to have an impostor palmed upon his loving heart. He therefore demanded the most tangible and unmistakable demonstration and received it—even more than he asked. Indeed, after the answer came, he was not only satisfied, but ashamed that he had asked such tokens. He threw himself at the feet of his blessed Master with one inexpressible cry of unquestioning confidence and everlasting consecration, "My Lord and my God!" (20:28). The conviction of Thomas ought to be a sufficient answer to every honest doubter. It is to be observed, however, that the evidence which convinced Thomas the most forcibly was not the mere external appearance of Christ, or the physical marks of identity which he expected, but that divine omniscience which had already searched the heart of Thomas. This made him feel that he was in the presence, not only of the Nazarene, but of the all-seeing God. And so, still, the strongest evidence of Christ's divinity and reality is not outward demonstration, but the contact of the heart with His living presence, through the Holy Spirit, as He reveals to us our sin, reads our inmost soul, and makes Himself known to us in all His grace and glory.

THE TESTIMONY OF THIS LAST MIRACLE
John 21:1–9

This is in some sense the most remarkable miracle of Christ's life, for it is the only one performed by Him after His resurrection. It bears a strong resemblance, as we have elsewhere seen, to the first miracle of the catch of fishes three years before, but it is greater in every respect, especially in the spiritual lessons which it teaches us. While the former hinted at their calling to the imperfect service of their early apostleship, this foreshadowed their calling to the victorious service upon which they were now to enter in His resurrection life and power. This glorious miracle was to them an impressive testimony to His reality and identity, and John at once exclaims, as He recognizes the Master, "It is the Lord!" (21:7). Peter, too, instinctively recognizes Him, and plunges into the sea to hasten to His feet, and afterwards cries, in response to the Master's searching question, "Lord . . . you know that I love you" (21:15).

THE WITNESS OF JOHN
John 21:24

The writer of this gospel sums up all his long array of testimony by adding his own witness, and then declaring that volumes more might have been written crowded with unpublished incidents of His grace and power.

A SUMMARY OF THE ABOVE TESTIMONIES

All these testimonies to Christ might be summed up under the following heads.

1. The testimony of His Father.

This is given publicly at His baptism, and again just before His crucifixion, both times in the hearing of the people. The third time, which John has not recorded, was on the Mount of Transfiguration in the presence of the three disciples. Again and again, Jesus Himself appealed to His Father's witness as we have seen in the above references. How can we for a moment believe that God would witness thus to an impostor, or to one whose claims were in any respect blasphemous or untrue?

2. The testimony of Himself.

This He had a perfect right to give, and constantly repeats it in the simplest and most impressive manner, showing in every case and under the most solemn and difficult circumstances, that this was the deep and true consciousness of His whole being. And this claim He constantly sustained in the most dignified and solemn manner throughout His whole life, not only in His discourses among both friends and enemies, but in the last awful scenes of His trial and agony, in the immediate presence of His Father and in the very hour of death itself. His calm assumption of divinity and its perfect consistency and simplicity is the most divine thing about the portrait of the Lord Jesus, as given by John.

3. The testimony of Scripture.

This, too, He applied in the face of His enemies. He claimed to be the Messiah of Moses and the prophets, and based all His teachings upon their own Scriptures. His enemies were never once able to contradict or confound Him. All the details of His sufferings upon the cross are identified by the evangelist with Messianic prophecies, and indeed, it is as true of the gospel as it is of the Apocalypse of John, that "the testimony of Jesus is the spirit of prophecy" (Revelation 19:10).

4. The testimony of John the Baptist.

The witness of former prophets and Scriptures is summed up by the last of the Old Testament messengers, John the Baptist, in his own prophetic witness. Again and again did he declare, as the representative of the Jewish priesthood and the last voice of ancient prophecy, that Jesus was the promised Messiah, and the voice of the common people unanimously testified that "all that John said about this man was true" (John 10:41).

5. The testimony of His friends.

To this we must add the witness of Christ's disciples and friends. We have in the first chapter of John, the testimony of His earliest followers, Andrew, Simon, Philip and Nathaniel. We have it again in the witness of Nicodemus; the Samaritans; the nobleman of Cana; the blind man healed at Jerusalem; the disciples after His discourse at Capernaum; the multitudes who listened to Him in Jerusalem at the feasts; the faith and love of Mary, who anointed Him; the multitude who hailed Him as their king on His triumphal entry to Jerusalem; the testimony of Mary Magdalene, Thomas, Simon, and John, all combined in the one confession: This is He of whom Moses and the prophets did write—the Messiah, the Christ, the Son of the living God.

6. The testimony of His enemies.

The very officers who came to arrest Him acknowledged His wisdom and wonderful words. Caiaphas in the Sanhedrin confessed His power, and even prophesied His atoning death. His accusers could say nothing against Him, and Pilate publicly vindicated Him, even while he condemned Him.

7. The testimony of the Holy Spirit.

We have seen how this witness was borne at His baptism and continually rested upon Him in all His teachings, supporting Him with marvelous wisdom and enabling Him always to meet His disciples and friends with divine love and grace. But after His departure the blessed Comforter was to bear His highest and most impressive testimony to the glorious Master and His work. Ever since His ascension, through His apostles and servants, there has been a succession of testimonies to the person and glory of Jesus.

8. The testimony of His works.

He Himself appealed to this—"The miracles I do in my Father's name speak for me . . . Believe me . . . or at least believe on the evidence of the miracles themselves" (10:25; 14:11).

His first miracle in Cana was intended to show His own glory, and we are told His disciples thereafter believed on Him.

We have the record of many glorious miracles in John, every one of them bearing separate witness, as we shall see elsewhere, to some special phases of His work and glory, and proving Him to be recognized by the omnipotence of God as divine. Not only were they works of power, but of the most gracious beneficence and the most tender and thoughtful love; ministering to vast multitudes of the suffering, drying the tear of the mourner, and symbolizing the deepest and most sublime spiritual truths and blessings, they being signs as well as wonders.

CHAPTER 3

LIFE IN THE GOSPEL OF JOHN

That we might have life through His name is the great object of this little treatise. This word, "life," is the most pronounced keynote of the Gospel of John. Matthew teaches us of righteousness; Mark, of service; Luke, of mercy; but John opens the deeper fountains of the source of righteousness and the spring of service. We can trace the development of this beautiful evolution through 12 distinct stages and sections.

CHRIST THE SOURCE

1. Christ is the Source of life, and is Himself the Life. "In him was life" (John 1:4), or, as the same apostle expresses it in his epistle, "He is the true God and eternal life" (1 John 5:20). Life is not a thing, but a throb of His own heart in us.

NATURAL LIFE

2. Natural life comes through Christ. "Through him all things were made; without him nothing was made that has been made. In him was life, and that life was the light of men" (John 1:3–4). Creation is the outflowing of His life. Man's life and reason come from Him. He is the true Head of the natural creation, and He alone is worthy to be preeminent and to be the Head of the spiritual creation.

A NEW CREATION

3. He has come to bring us the life of a new creation, which takes the place of the old life which has failed through man's sin and fall. This is set forth in the miracle of Cana, the turning of the water into wine (chapter 2). The first wine at the marriage feast represents our natural life, and the failure of the wine before the feast was ended, vividly shadows forth the failure of human life and happiness through sin. The time comes in every experience when the cry goes forth, "There is no wine." The joys of youth and affection

fade, and nature has no remedy. Then it is that the new wine of His love is revealed; not made in any measure from the wine of earth, but from the pure water of the Holy Spirit poured into the empty vessels of our hearts and bodies, richer, sweeter, purer far than all the pleasures of earth, so that even the world says, when it truly tastes, "you have saved the best till now" (2:10). This miracle is a parable of Christ's entire teaching, and indeed of the gospel of His grace. Wine is the natural emblem of the deep, full pulses of life, and the blending of the two figures, the wine and the marriage feast with its love and joy, constitutes the most vivid and expressive unfolding of the fullness of life and love in our consummated redemption.

REGENERATION

4. The life of regeneration in the succeeding chapter of John next unfolds the spiritual meaning of this new wine. The first stage of our spiritual life is regeneration, and this is unfolded more clearly and completely in Christ's interview with Nicodemus than in any other portion of the Scriptures. The Jewish rabbi had come to discuss the question of doctrine, but Jesus puts His hand upon his heart and tells him that what he must have is life, and that until he possesses true heavenly life he cannot know aright, or even see the kingdom of God. This is not a matter of individual understanding, or even of moral character; it is a newborn life coming definitely and divinely from above, as real as the impartation of physical life to the newborn child. It is even more than the repentance and outward reformation which John the Baptist taught them, and symbolized in their immersion in the Jordan. That is only being born of water. The life of which He speaks must be imparted directly by the Holy Spirit and be as truly a new creation as the divine touch which made the heavens and the earth or in-breathed the physical life of man. The outward senses cannot trace, and the understanding of man cannot penetrate its mystery, even as we cannot comprehend the simplest form of physical life in the natural world. What it is we know not, although we may perceive its effects; and so of the deeper life of the Spirit, it is true that it is wrapped in mystery, like the viewless wind, known only by its power and its results. "The wind blows wherever it pleases. You hear its sound, but you cannot tell where it comes from or where it is going. So it is with everyone born of the Spirit" (3:8). Perhaps the greatest comfort implied in the beautiful teaching of this figure is that this birth begins at the lowest, weakest stage, with the simple helplessness and feebleness of a babe. Let no one therefore, despair, because he has not been born like Adam, into fullgrown manhood. If there is life enough for a cry, thank God, and praise Him for an infant's cry. Nicodemus, at this time, was scarcely even a babe, but the time came when he stood up with manly courage in the midst of the Sanhedrin to defend his Lord, and even went to Pilate and begged His body for

honorable burial. The Lord then proceeds in the discourse that follows, to show the manner in which this new life may be received. It flows from the eternal love of God in the gift of His Son that "whoever believes in him shall not perish but have eternal life" (3:16). It is obtained by simply receiving and trusting Jesus, who is Himself the life. This is the true secret of regeneration, "Yet to all who received him, to those who believed in his name, he gave the right to become children of God—children born not of natural descent, nor of human decision or a husband's will, but born of God" (1:12–13). All who thus receive the Savior are quickened into His own spiritual life and become by birth the children of God; and all who reject Him remain in condemnation with the added guilt of His rejection.

INDWELLING LIFE

5. Indwelling life comes through receiving Christ into the heart (4:13–14). In His conversation with the woman of Samaria, the Savior carries this thought farther and deeper, revealing to her, for her thirsty and unsatisfied heart, the divine source of rest and pleasure which He had come to impart, under the beautiful figure of the wellspring in the heart, which the Holy Spirit gives to those who truly receive the indwelling Christ. The life becomes now not merely a draught of water, but a perennial fountain, an artesian well with its source in the soul itself, and its supplies as lasting as eternity. This is more than regeneration; it is the fullness of Christ Himself, our life.

ETERNAL LIFE

6. Eternal life comes through our deliverance from the law and judgment of God (5:24). Here life is regarded in its judicial aspect as secured to the believer through the eternal decree of the righteous Judge, absolving forever from condemnation and preserving from future failure. It is not mere probation; but it is a decree of life from the very Judge upon the throne, based upon the redeeming work and unchanging word of Jesus Christ, and delivering from death and even judgment all who receive it. Believing in His name we pass into a new world out of death into life, and shall not come into judgment. He who is our Savior is to be the future Judge, and accepting Him and saved by Him, we can stand without fear now, and shall meet His coming without condemnation. It is everlasting life for those who receive it. The judgment is already past, and the resurrection is already past in its spiritual and most immediate sense, for the dead have heard the voice of the Son of God and have come forth in a spiritual resurrection to die no more. Therefore they need not fear the future call which shall be the same voice which has already spoken through their souls to everlasting life. This life is inseparably linked with Jesus Himself, and all who reject Him must in-

evitably lose it, and therefore in closing this paragraph, His one complaint against His enemies is, "yet you refuse to come to me to have life" (5:40).

THE LIVING BREAD

7. We receive spiritual and physical life day by day through vital union with Jesus (6:32–35, 47–51, 53–58, 62–63).

We have now come to the deeper waters of Ezekiel's river. They are waters to the loins. They touch the very springs of our entire being. Many of His disciples could not receive teachings so spiritual and profound. This discourse was the turning point in His Galilean ministry. From that time many went back and walked no more with Him.

Such teachings are still the turning point in the lives of many Christians. They require a closer union and a more abiding fellowship with the Master than most people care for. He reveals Himself in this beautiful discourse as the very substance of His people's life. His flesh and blood give complete life for both body and spirit, and are the true supply of our spiritual and physical need. After the resurrection, His living person, through the Holy Spirit, is to be the imparted life of all who dwell in Him. In the closing verse of the paragraph, He distinctly points forward to His ascension, and the revelation which the Holy Spirit is to bring, and the time when all this is to be fully realized. It is scarcely necessary to say that the Lord intended no such idea as that implied in the gross and literal doctrine of Roman transubstantiation. Even if they could eat the literal flesh of Jesus it would be of no avail. But we can partake of the essence of His life and strength, imparted to our flesh by the Holy Spirit, as the subtle and yet supernatural force and vitality of our being. It is this that gives quickening and power to the spiritual life, and this is the true secret of divine healing; it is the life of Jesus made manifest in our mortal flesh. Thus He Himself lived upon His Father's life, and thus we are to live upon His. "Just as the living Father sent me and I live because of the Father, so the one who feeds on me will live because of me" (6:57). Therefore, He could say in the temptation, when Satan tried to persuade Him to seek for physical strength from forbidden sources, speaking for us as well as Himself, "Man does not live on bread alone, but on every word that comes from the mouth of God" (Matthew 4:4).

This, then, is the true ideal of Christian life, complete and continual dependence on the person of Jesus through the Holy Spirit for our entire life and strength; not only through outward and inward means of grace and strength, but personally and directly by the impartation of Himself. This requires the most intimate and uninterrupted communion with Him; therefore, He says, "Whoever eats my flesh and drinks my blood remains in me, and I in him" (John 6:56). It is a union as close as that of the branches and the vine, the head and the body, the throbbing heart and its physical members, the mother and the babe that lives upon her very life.

OVERFLOWING LIFE

8. We receive a life overflowing in service for others (7:37–39). Here we find the deep fountain of life running over the spring and finding vent in rivers of living water that go out to bless and save the world around us. It is beautiful to notice that as the blessing grows unselfish it grows larger. The water in the heart is only a well (in the fourth chapter), but when reaching out to the needs of others, it is not only a river, but a delta of many rivers, overflowing in majestic blessing. This overflowing love is connected with the person and work of the Holy Spirit who was to be poured out upon the disciples after Jesus was glorified. This is the true secret of power for service, the heart filled and satisfied with Jesus, and so baptized with the Holy Spirit that it is impelled by the fullness of its joy and love to impart to others what it has so abundantly received; and yet each new ministry only makes room for a new filling and a deeper receiving of the life which grows by giving.

LIFE MORE ABUNDANTLY

9. We receive life more abundantly (10:10). There are still deeper and richer experiences in the blessed Christ life, as the soul now passes into the experience of this precious chapter. Here we find ourselves in the fold of Christ and in the intimacy of His discipline and love, as He leads us in and out through richer pastures, as He goes before us and makes us know His voice, and receives us into an intimacy with Himself as close as His intimacy with the Father, and as He makes us know the meaning of His blessed covenant, "I give them eternal life, and they shall never perish; no one can snatch them out of my hand" (10:28).

RESURRECTION LIFE

10. We receive resurrection life (11:25; 12:24–25). We now rise to the very highest teaching about our life in Christ. We come to the central principle of Christianity, death and resurrection. Not in the old natural sphere is this life perfected. Like the kernel of wheat it must fall into the ground and die, or it abides alone. Like Lazarus it must pass to the tomb and come forth again. Like the Lord Himself it must pass through the gates of death and come forth in union with His resurrection life. This was the symbolic meaning of His baptism; this was the profound significance of the cross, and this is the very heart of all true spiritual experience. The life of nature, the strength of self-will, the affections of earth, the self-confidence of impulse, the ideas and opinions of the flesh, must all be laid down in the grave; and we must come forth as those who are dead and their life is hid with Christ in God, and drawn henceforth, each moment, from Him alone. This was why

Lazarus had to die, to foreshadow the greater resurrection. This was why the cup could not pass from Him, that it might bring the better resurrection. And this is why it is still true of all who follow Him, "The man who loves his life will lose it, while the man who hates his life in this world will keep it for eternal life" (12:25). The two Greek words used here for life are different; the first signifying our self-life and the second our higher and everlasting life in Him.

ABIDING LIFE

11. We receive life through abiding union and fellowship with Him (15:1–16). We are now ready for the fullness of that personal communion which He had foreshadowed in the sixth chapter of John, but between that and their actual experience lay the floods of death. These have now passed, and the way is open for the fullness of His indwelling. There is a double union, "Remain (abide, KJV) in me, and I will remain in you" (15:4). The first secures our standing and justification, the second our quickening and deeper life. The word "abide" expresses the habitual and moment by moment character of our walk with Him. Everything depends on the uninterruptedness of this life. It is simply a moment at a time, and Christ sufficient for that moment. The fruits of this blessed union and abiding are: first, our sanctification—"You are already clean" (15:3); second, our fruitfulness—"he will bear much fruit" (15:5); third, answered prayer—"ask whatever you wish, and it will be given you" (15:7); fourth, the Father glorified—"This is to my Father's glory" (15:8); fifth, a consistent example before the world—"showing yourselves to be my disciples" (15:8); sixth, the fellowship of His love—"As the Father has loved me, so have I loved you. Now remain in my love. If you obey my commands, you will remain in my love, just as I have obeyed my Father's commands and remain in his love" (15:9–10); seventh, the fullness of His joy—"I have told you this so that my joy may be in you and that your joy may be complete" (15:11); and eighth, His own personal friendship and intimacy—"I no longer call you servants, . . . Instead, I have called you friends" (15:15).

GLORIFIED LIFE

12. The perfection of our life comes in the glorious and final union of the whole body of believers in the Father and in the Son, in the unity of the Church below, and through the ages of glory beyond (17:21–26). These words express our Savior's loftiest ideal for the life of His people, that it should be one of perfect union with Him and the Father, even as he is one with the Father; not only thus in each individual, but the perfect union of the whole body of the believers together, with each other and with Him. This should be realized even in the present life; for it is the Master's will and

prayer for all His disciples, and it will be the glory of the New Jerusalem and the perfection of the Bride. Even yet it will be fulfilled before the world, we believe, in such a manner that they will believe that the Father has sent Him. But its full realization is anticipated in the closing prayer, "to be with me where I am, and to see my glory" (17:24). Let us so live, and labor and pray that we may hasten the accomplishment of His dearest desire and hope for the Church for which He died.

CHAPTER 4

LIGHT IN THE GOSPEL OF JOHN

This is another word which is very prominent and significant in the Gospel of John, and one of the keynotes of its deeper teaching. We may trace it through almost the entire gospel.

THE WORD

1. Christ is the Word, or primeval Light, manifesting and revealing God (John 1:1).

The very expression, "Word," suggests the idea of light. It is primarily the revealing of the thought of God. Christ is essentially light, inasmuch as He is God's expression to the universe of what He is Himself. The Epistle to the Hebrews calls Him "the radiance of God's glory and the exact representation of his being" (1:3).

THE CREATOR

2. Christ is the Creator of nature and reason (1:4).

Physical light is the work of His hand. God said, " 'Let there be light,' and there was light" (Genesis 1:3). This was the first act of the creating Word. So, also, the light of reason in man has all come from Him. "That life was the light of men" (John 1:4). The power of human thought, the understanding which men have used to deny God and dishonor Him, is a ray of divine intelligence.

OLD TESTAMENT LIGHT

3. Christ is the Light that shines in the Old Testament.

"He was in the world" (1:10); "the light shines in the darkness" (1:5). All the light of ancient revelation was but the radiance of the Son of Righteousness. It was He who spoke to Abraham and Moses, and He was the Angel of the covenant in all the preparatory dispensations.

INCARNATE LIGHT

4. Christ has become the Light of the world through His incarnation (1:14–18). In this glorious person we behold the Father's face and His beneficent character and purposes of grace toward sinful men. He is truly a "light for revelation to the Gentiles/ and for glory to your people Israel" (Luke 2:32).

INNER LIGHT

5. Christ is the Light of those who receive Him, dispelling their doubts and bringing to their hearts the light of faith and joy (John 1:38–49).

How beautifully we see this illustrated in the first disciples that followed Jesus. How promptly He answers their questions. How tenderly He receives them, instructs them and leads them to cry in glad assurance, "We have found the Messiah. . . . Rabbi . . . you are the King of Israel" (1:41, 49). This is the light which brings its own evidence. It is enough to say to the questioning world, "Come and see" (1:46).

This Christ is the Light foreshadowed by the ancient types and prophecies. They could say of Him, "We have found the one Moses wrote about in the Law, and about whom the prophets also wrote—Jesus of Nazareth, the son of Joseph" (1:45); and He Himself could personally apply the glorious vision of Jacob's ladder and claim its fulfillment in His intercession which has opened heaven and restored men to fellowship with God.

THE REVEALER

6. Christ is the only Revealer of true heavenly light.

> I tell you the truth, we speak of what we know, and we testify to what we have seen, but still you people do not accept our testimony. I have spoken to you of earthly things and you do not believe; how then will you believe if I speak of heavenly things? No one has ever gone into heaven except the one who came from heaven—the Son of Man. (3:11–13)

He, alone, had been in heaven and could bring to men the secrets of the unseen and unfold the will and love of His Father. Even as He spoke He could say of Himself, "the one who came from heaven—the Son of Man" (3:13). And what wondrous light He did reveal upon the character and love of God, lighting up the midnight interview with Nicodemus with a glory which has shone on millions of hearts and will continue to all eternity. That one sentence, "For God so loved the world that he gave his one and only Son, that whoever believes in him shall not perish but have eternal life" (3:16), is worth a million times more than all the literature of the ages.

CONVICTION OF SIN

7. Christ is the Light that reveals sin.

This is the verdict: Light has come into the world, but men loved darkness instead of light because their deeds were evil. Everyone who does evil hates the light, and will not come into the light for fear that his deeds will be exposed. But whoever lives by the truth comes into the light, so that it may be seen plainly that what he has done has been done through God. (3:19–21)

The only reason, therefore, that people reject Him is because the light of His teaching condemns all sin and hidden evil that will not come to the light. It exposes their sin, only that it may lead them to the fount of cleansing which takes it all away.

SEARCHES THE HEART

8. Christ is the Light that searches and reveals the human heart.

"Come, see a man who told me everything I ever did. Could this be the Christ?" (4:29).

Thus He searched this woman's heart and made her feel His omniscience and divinity; and this drew her to Him for salvation. So still, His word is the mirror of human nature and makes every convicted heart conscious of the searching eye of the holy God. "Everything is uncovered and laid bare before the eyes of him to whom we must give account" (Hebrews 4:12), and yet amid all the searching light we need not shrink from His eye, for He searches only to save.

INTERPRETER OF THE SCRIPTURES

9. Christ is the Light which explains the Scriptures.

"You diligently study the Scriptures because you think that by them you possess eternal life. These are the Scriptures that testify about me" (John 5:39).

The key to the Bible is Jesus. Its pages are obscure and dim until we learn to search in every part for His face of love and suffering, and when we see Jesus we have the key to all mystery and all knowledge.

THE ONLY LIGHT

10. Christ is the only true Light.

Well might they ask, "Lord, to whom shall we go? You have the words of eternal life" (6:68). There is no other name by which we must be saved. "No one comes to the Father except through me" (14:6).

SATISFYING

11. Again, Christ brings the light of conviction and of consciousness to every obedient heart.

"If anyone chooses to do God's will, he will find out whether my teaching comes from God or whether I speak on my own" (7:17).

This is the divine criterion of truth, and the remedy for doubt. True-hearted obedience will always bring satisfying light and certain conviction that the teachings of Jesus are true and divine. They must, however, be proved and practiced to be absolutely known.

THE TESTIMONY OF HIS ENEMIES

12. Christ is the Light that transcends all human teachers; even in the judgment of His enemies.

This was the testimony of the rude men who came without a thought of seriousness, to fulfill their official functions as officers of the law; but they were captivated by the Savior's wisdom and eloquence, and said, "No one ever spoke the way this man does" (7:46).

THE LAMPS IN THE TEMPLE

13. Christ is the Light of the world symbolized by the lamps of the temple, and shedding on the path of human life the direction and instruction required for all our practical needs. He is the Light of life, not only that which leads to life beyond the grave, but also of our present life in all its perplexities and perils.

LIGHT AND LIBERTY

14. Christ is the Light that liberates us from the fetters of ignorance and sin.

"Then you will know the truth, and the truth will set you free" (8:32).

Slavery is often the result of mental degradation. Education and moral elevation often rescue the oppressed from human bondage, and spiritual light sets the soul free from the heavier bonds of sin and Satan. When we know our rights in Christ, and that Satan is a conquered foe, we spring into liberty and claim our true place as sons of God and freeborn citizens of the kingdom of heaven.

SIGHT

15. Christ is the Light that brings us vision as well as truth, sight as well as light (9:1–7).

This was beautifully illustrated by the healing of the blind man at Jerusalem. It was intended and used to emphasize the spiritual illumination He came to bring to benighted hearts, but which in their blind self-conceit the Pharisees refused to receive, and so remained in deeper darkness (9:39–41).

GUIDANCE

16. Christ is the Light of personal guidance, step by step, in our daily life (10:3–5, 14–15).

This is the light of His personal guidance; not merely a way-mark, but a hand to lead the trusting disciple, and a voice that he cannot mistake if he is willing to be led. This is the light of which the psalmist sang, "I will counsel you and watch over you" (Psalm 32:8).

LIGHT BEYOND THE GRAVE

17. Christ is the only Light which shines beyond the grave.

"Jesus said to her, 'I am the resurrection and the life. He who believes in me will live, even though he dies; and whoever lives and believes in me will never die. Do you believe this?' " (John 11:25–26).

Through this blessed promise the Lord has brought life and immortality to light through His own open grave. He has left the windows of glory forever open to the vision of faith and to the souls of His departing saints.

TRANSIENT LIGHT

18. Christ is a transient Light which will soon pass away (12:36).

Touchingly is added this beautiful expression, "Jesus left and hid himself from them" (12:36). And so from those who reject Him the light has at length gone. The spirit of grace ceases to plead, and the soul does not have even light to know the meaning of its darkness and sorrow. Therefore, while we have the light, "put your trust in the light," and walk in the light, and be "sons of light" (12:36).

THE LIGHT OF JUDGMENT

19. Christ's word is the searching light which will judge us in the last day (12:46–48).

The gospel of Jesus Christ and the words which He has spoken are to be the standard of future judgment, and the manner in which we receive and obey them will determine our eternal destiny. The word which He has spoken to us, the same word will judge us in the last day (12:48). The very lamps of the throne are let down to shine upon our earthly path, and in the hour of the last assize they shall reveal our life and character. In some sense, therefore, every man may pass through His judgment here, and may receive the conscious witness of the very authority which is at last to decide his fate.

THE HOLY SPIRIT

20. Christ has left us the light of the Holy Spirit to continue and complete the teachings of His own personal life and work.

It is deeply interesting to trace the revelation of the Holy Spirit in the Gospel of John.

We see Him as He rests upon Jesus, the inspiration of all His teachings, and the agent in all His supernatural works (1:33).

We see Him as the author of conversion in the individual soul. "No one can enter the kingdom of God unless he is born of water and the Spirit" (3:5).

We see Him as the indwelling fullness and overflowing life of the believer (7:38–39). This, however, was an experience that was not to be fully realized until after Christ's resurrection, for we are told that the Spirit was not yet given because Jesus was not glorified.

We see Him revealed by Jesus as the Comforter who was to succeed Him, and complete His redeeming work in the hearts of His people and in the history of the Church.

a. The name by which He is revealed is beautifully expressive. It means "one called to us," or one on whom we may call in every emergency for instant and perfect help.

b. He was to be the substitute for Jesus, and at this stage of our experience to be even more to us than Jesus could be, for it was expedient for Christ to go away, in order that the Spirit might come again. The physical presence of Christ could not be as internal and omnipresent as the Holy Spirit, who brings His actual life and presence into the depths of our being and to all the myriads of His people irrespective of place or time.

c. He was to come in the name of Jesus, that is, the same Spirit that had dwelt in Jesus and who still was to bring His personal presence, and to be the medium of His indwelling life and personal revelation to the soul; so that when we have the Holy Spirit, we also have the presence of Christ.

d. He was to bring to their remembrance all things that Christ had said of Him, and thus preserve and perpetuate the Master's teachings.

e. He was to reveal to them new truths which Jesus had not yet imparted, because they were not yet able to receive them, but the Spirit would lead them into all truth (16:12–13).

f. He was to be more than a teacher—also a personal Guide, not only teaching, but leading, disciplining and educating with a mother's tenderness the life and character of the disciples of Christ.

g. He was to unveil the future and complete the prophetic vision of the coming ages and the glorious appearing of the Lord Jesus in the end of the dispensation (16:13).

h. Above all else, He was to reveal Christ and testify to the person and character of Jesus Himself. "He will testify about me. . . . He will bring glory to me by taking from what is mine and making it known to you" (15:26; 16:14).

i. He was to convict the world of sin, of righteousness and of judgment, using disciples as instruments and witnesses of the truth, but being Himself the effectual power by which the barriers of unbelief and sin were to be broken down, and sinners convicted, comforted and led to Christ. Such was the glorious light that Jesus left behind Him as He passed within the veil; a light which still shines in this dark world "until the day dawns and the morning star rises in your hearts" (2 Peter 1:19).

Once more we trace the revelation of the Spirit in this gospel (John 20:22), as imparted by the risen Lord through the touch of His own living breath. He breathed on them and said, "Receive the Holy Spirit" (20:22), so that this blessed Spirit comes to us, not merely in His absolute deity, but with the warm breath of Christ's living love, softened and humanized, if we may so speak, by passing through the medium of the Savior's own heart and flesh. It is only as we get near enough to Jesus to feel the touch of His lips and the very kiss of His love, that we can receive the fullness of the Spirit's power. The impartation here described was for service, and accompanied by the great commission, "As the Father has sent me, I am sending you" (20:21). Though it was not fully realized until the day of Pentecost, it was in anticipation of that day that the words were spoken. But since Pentecost the Holy Spirit is already come, and each of us must receive His touch of fire and His enduing presence, from the very lips and breath of our ascended Lord.

CHAPTER 5

LOVE IN THE GOSPEL OF JOHN

This is another of the emphatic words in this beautiful gospel. It runs like a golden thread through almost every incident and utterance; like a majestic rainbow, it spans the heavens with its seven splendid tints of grace and beauty.

GOD'S LOVE TO THE SON

1. God's love to the Son shines out again and again in John 1:18. It is implied in the beautiful phrase, "God the One and Only (only begotten, KJV), who is at the Father's side." He is not only the Son, but the Only Begotten, and His place is ever in the bosom of the Father's love.

Again in John 3:35, it is declared, "The Father loves the Son and has placed everything in his hands." (See also 5:20–23).

In John 6:57, He speaks of His intimate relation to, and dependence upon the Father, drawing His love every moment from Him, speaking His Word, fulfilling His law, and supremely desiring to please Him.

Again He speaks of His peculiar dearness to His Father's heart, "The one who sent me is with me; he has not left me alone, for I always do what pleases him" (8:29).

In John 12:28 the Father bears public witness to His acceptance, by a voice from heaven. Again and again, throughout the entire gospel, He speaks of His absolute oneness and unceasing communion with the Father.

In John 16:27 He tells them that the very reason that the Father loves them is because they have loved the Son, and believed upon His name. And in His sublime prayer (17:5–23, 24–26), He speaks of the glory which He had with the Father before the world was, and the love of which He has been the object from before the foundation of the world, and which love He asks for even them also. The veil is lifted from the most sacred and ineffable mystery in the universe, the heart of God, and the fellowship of the Father and of the Son. There is a unity and a love, of which all the highest forms of creature love are but a drop to the ocean and a spark to the sun. "God only knows the love of God."

There is yet one touch added to this picture in the account of the resurrection (20:17), where Jesus, just emerging from the tomb, lingers a moment to comfort the weeping Mary Magdalene, and then hastens to lay His completed offering at His Father's feet and receive His approval and welcome, before He can receive the touch of even His dearest friends. "Do not hold on to me," He says to her, "for I have not yet returned to the Father. Go instead to my brothers and tell them, 'I am returning to my Father and your Father, to my God and your God.' "

GOD'S LOVE TO THE WORLD

2. "For God so loved the world that he gave his one and only Son, that whoever believes in him shall not perish but have eternal life" (3:16).

Following the thought just expressed, this announces a mystery still more incomprehensible. It would seem as if the Father's love to His Son was for a moment outweighed by His love for the world. Inexpressibly dear as His beloved and only begotten Son was to Him, yet dearer was the salvation of His ruined children on this fallen earth, and for them He spared not the treasure of His heart and the glory of heaven. Well may the apostle add, "He who did not spare his own Son, but gave him up for us all—how will he not also, along with him, graciously give us all things?" (Romans 8:32).

This is not the only place in the beautiful Gospel of John where the Father's love to sinners is declared. Again and again Jesus announces that His coming is the Father's own act and purpose of love, and that redemption originated, not in His cross and incarnation, but in the ancient and everlasting mercy of our Father to ruined men. Very beautifully is this expressed in John 6:38–40:

> For I have come down from heaven not to do my will but to do the will of him who sent me. And this is the will of him who sent me, that I shall lose none of all that he has given me, but raise them up at the last day. For my Father's will is that everyone who looks to the Son and believes in him shall have eternal life, and I will raise him up at the last day.

Back of all His words and works of love, Jesus ever recognized the Father's coworking grace. Of His miracles of beneficence He says, "My Father is always at his work to this very day, and I, too, am working" (5:17). Of His people's security He declares, "No one can snatch them out of my hand. . . . no one can snatch them out of my Father's hand" (10:28–29). Of our future reward He says, "My Father will honor the one who serves me" (12:26). Of the coming of the Comforter He declares, not only that He will send Him, but that the Father will send Him in His name. His own indwelling presence in our hearts is followed by the Father's love and indwelling. "If anyone loves me, he will obey my teaching. My Father will love him, and we will come to him and make our home with him" (14:23). Not only does He love His disciples, but He assures them that His Father loves them likewise, even with the same love that He bears the Son. And thus the revelation of the Savior's love coordinately reveals the love of the Father, too, and His deep, divine, tender and everlasting interest in the salvation of sinful men through the redeeming work of His dear Son. Indeed, Jesus, as a loyal Son, ever sought to glorify His Father's grace, and to teach His disciples to know and trust that Father's perfect love.

CHRIST'S LOVE TO THE SINFUL AND LOST

3. Next we see Christ's love to the sinful and lost. It is difficult to select any single passage out of the many pictures of His grace and love to sinful men. One of the most beautiful of these is the fourth chapter of John, and the story of His interview with the woman of Samaria. The Bible contains no lovelier illustration of the wisdom and love which sinful souls have shared. For this poor sinner's sake "he had to go through Samaria" (4:4). For love of her thirsty heart, He forgets His weariness at Jacob's well. With unspeakable tenderness and delicacy, He lays His hand first upon her aching heart and then upon the dark secret of her sin. When He has awakened her interest, her longing and her guilty conscience, then with divine simplicity, He reveals Himself to her as her Savior as well as the Searcher of her heart. And when the disciples come and ask Him to think a little about Himself, and eat the food they brought Him, He explains Himself by telling them that the work of love in which He has just engaged is the meat and drink of His life.

Another touching and equally beautiful incident in this gospel is of less certain authority as a part of the chapter where it occurs. It is the story of the woman taken in adultery (8:2–11). Still there is no reasonable doubt of its being part of the sacred volume, and even of this gospel. Yet it cannot properly be assigned to the place it occupies in the old version, and must have occurred at a later period, probably in the last week of the Savior's life, in connection with the final conflict with the Scribes and Pharisees in the temple; but these questions are of less importance than the spiritual teachings of this beautiful incident. Here was a case of flagrant sin for which no excuse was offered, and all the hostile use His enemies would make of any necessities of the situation, especially the leniency on His part toward her, seemed to demand that He should act with righteous severity, at least according to the strict letter of the law. By a stroke of infinite wisdom He silences her accusers in a moment and sends them from the room, more confounded than she, under the conviction of their own consciences; and then by an act of sovereign grace, He forgives her sin without condoning or excusing it in the least degree, and dismisses her with the tender, solemn charge, "Then neither do I condemn you. . . . Go now and leave your life of sin" (8:11).

One beautiful act of His delicate grace shines preeminent in all this incident. It was the refusal to look in the face of this poor woman while her accusers were present. Stooping down, He busied Himself writing on the ground and seemed to pay no attention to their bitter charges. This is the beautiful attitude which He still occupies in regard to His people's sins and the devil's charges against them. He listens as though He heard them not. "Who will bring any charge against those whom God has chosen?" (Romans 8:33). But although He forgives, He forgives with a purity as beautiful as His grace is blessed, and speaks to her heart the solemn charge, which the truly forgiven never can forget, "Go now and leave your life of sin."

CHRIST'S LOVE TO THE NEEDY AND SUFFERING

4. John shows us Christ's love to the needy and suffering. No quality of the Savior's character was more constantly manifested than that which Mark has expressed so often by the word "compassion." We find many instances of it in the Gospel of John. We see it for the hungry multitudes in the wilderness (John 6:5). We see it in His coming to the toiling disciples in the tempest (6:19). We see it in His compassion for the poor cripple at Bethesda (5:6). We see it in His loving appeal to the multitudes at the Feast of Tabernacles: "If anyone is thirsty, let him come to me and drink" (7:37). We see it in His compassion for the blind man (9:1–6), and in His gracious visit to this poor man when they had cast him out of the synagogue (9:35), and we see it most beautifully of all in the story of Bethany, and His love and tears at Lazarus' grave (11:33–38), revealing a heart that was as human as it was divine, and that still is liable to "sympathize with our weaknesses" (Hebrews 4:15).

CHRIST'S LOVE TO HIS OWN

5. The true place to know Christ's love is on His own bosom. The love of Jesus is known by His loved ones. Very tenderly and fully does John unfold his Master's love to His disciples.

a. We see it in the parable of the Shepherd and His flock (John 10:3–29). He calls His own by name. He knows them intimately. He has a special voice for them alone. He leads them out gently by the hand. He always goes before them. He brings them into rich and abundant pastures. He stands in the place of danger. When the hired hand flees, He defends them from the wolf. He gives His life for them. He holds them in His hand, so that they can never perish, nor any pluck them out of His or His Father's hand. He is indeed the Good Shepherd, fulfilling all the tender and gracious meaning which this figure had foreshadowed in all the utterances of the Psalms and prophets.

b. We see it next in the picture of the home at Bethany, where we have an excellent picture of Christ's love to His personal friends, with all the fine discriminations which personal friendships always unfold. We know something from the other Scriptures of the faults of Martha, but notwithstanding, she is first named in this picture of Christ's personal friendship. "Jesus loved Martha and her sister and Lazarus" (11:5). But this heavenly friendship has its strange tests; and therefore, in the darkest hour of their life, the best friend they had seemed to fail them, and Jesus lingered in the rear until Lazarus was cold in death and even corrupting in the grave. But His resources were, and still are, sufficient for every extremity. He came to them at last, not only to weep the tears of tender sympathy, which is often the best that human love can do; but, also, with His omnipotent love, to undo the work of death and give back to their arms the lost treasure of their affections. We have elsewhere pointed out the strange beauty of Christ's conversations with Martha and Mary, respectively. To the one He talks freely; with the other He only weeps. So, still, His love is exquisitely given to all His children's needs and temperaments, and His affection is as wise as it is strong and tender.

c. The picture of the washing of the disciples' feet is our next example of His love. (13:1–15).

This is the love that stoops to cleanse us from our defilements, and to minister at our very feet. So, still, His blessed hands are daily cleansing and keeping our erring feet and stooping to depths of humiliation for us, which we could not dream of doing for others. Not only with His hands, but with the very blood of His heart, He ever keeps us cleansed from all sin. Well may we say with John in another place, "To him who loves us and has freed us from our sins by his blood . . . be glory and power for ever and ever!" (Revelation 1:5-6).

d. We see His love in the last discourses and His parting words (John 14–16).

Volumes could not fully unfold the depths of love expressed in these divine words. How lovingly He comforts them. "Do not let your hearts be troubled" (14:1), He cries, when we might rather have expected them to say to Him, "Lord, let us comfort You." Then He promises them His personal comfort and deepest love if they will but obey Him: "Whoever has my commands and obeys them, he is the one who loves me. . . . and I too will love him and show myself to him" (14:21). This is the central thought in these, His parting words, that He is still to be linked with them by an unspeakable union and communion, and that He will so abide in them and they in Him that His love shall flow into theirs, His peace shall be their peace, His joy their joy, His love their love, and His works even shall be performed in them, and all the power of His ascension glory be at their command for their necessities and their work.

e. We see His love in His intercession for them (17:23, 26).

It is not merely that this one prayer for them exhausts His interest and love, for this is but a sample of the work on which He was just entering and which 1,800 years have not finished. Thus He still represents their interests at the Father's side, and whatever they ask in His name, He claims for them in His higher, priestly, and all-prevailing intercession.

f. We see His love in His great request for them, that they shall be objects of the very same love which His Father has for Him. Which of us would give away, or even share with another, the love of our dearest friend? This is the one thing that the human heart claims as its exclusive possession. There are some whose love we want supremely for ourselves, but Jesus gives to His disciples and asks the Father to give to them the very same love that He has for His beloved Son. We are received into His own actual Sonship, and take the place in the Father's heart which He Himself possesses. It is indeed unspeakable, and prostrates our hearts in adoring wonder at His blessed feet.

g. We see His love in His tender concern for their safety (18:8).

"If you are looking for me, then let these men go." Here, even in the moment of His arrest, His thoughts are all for them. Offering His own body to His cruel enemies, He claims their exemption, just as He was about to offer His own body on the cross to all the horrors of the judgment, which we deserved, and from which we have now exemption through His sacrifice and substitution.

h. We see His love to His mother as He hung on the cross (19:26).

This is a little gleam of human tenderness which shines the brighter because of the suffering through which He was at this moment passing. How it reveals His utter unselfishness, thoughtfulness, and tender consideration for every human right and claim. What love it reveals on His part to His mother, how it honors the instinct of filial devotion in every human heart. What love it shows to the beloved disciple in the confidence reposed in his care and the trust committed to his keeping.

i. We see His love to Mary Magdalene (20:16).

One word expresses it all, and that one word her name. So, still, He speaks to the hearts that greatly love Him. There were some special reasons for His tender love to Mary; we love those best for whom we have done most, and she had been saved by His mercy. She, too, loved Him as perhaps few others ever loved Him; and while Peter, and even John, had left the sepulcher without beholding Him, she could not and would not go until she had seen

Him. Such persistent love He ever prizes and rewards by the manifestation of Himself. If we would know all the fullness of His love, we must constrain it by a love that will not be consoled without Him.

j. We see His love of Thomas (20:27).

This is the pattern of His tenderness toward His questioning and doubting disciples. Still, often He makes us ashamed by the way in which He satisfies our doubts; let us rather, however, trust Him with the love that will not need to be reproved, even while its request is granted.

k. We see His love of Peter (21:15).

This represents His love to the backslider, and His readiness to restore even the erring one who still loves Him; and restore not only to His forgiveness, but even to the highest service—service, perhaps, all the more useful because of the lessons of humility it has learned through its own inconsistency.

l. We see His love to John.

One single expression tells the whole of this secret; an expression often repeated in this gospel, "the disciple whom Jesus loved" (21:20). It is very beautiful to find John claiming this place for himself. Perhaps this was one reason why Jesus loved him, that, like a child, he claimed the tenderest love and was not afraid to insist upon it and take it as unreservedly as the babe presses close to its mother's breast and assumes its right to all the love which it can claim. It is not necessary to say that such a babe is always the best loved. Jesus forbids none the closest place to His heart, but loves us better the more closely we nestle to His bosom. John's place was one where we might well covet to lie, so near the Master's heart that he could know its very secrets and ask Him what others dare not, and receive from Him the tenderest commission of service, and write as no other could the record, and unfold the mysteries of His divine character and His future kingdom and coming.

May the Lord enable each of us to aspire to this high place and name, "the disciple whom Jesus loved . . . reclining next to him" (13:23).

OUR LOVE TO CHRIST

6. We see ample lessons and illustrations that point to our love to Christ.

a. The absence of love is the fatal source of all sin.

"You are the ones who justify yourselves in the eyes of men, but God knows your hearts. . . . I know that you do not have the love of God in your hearts" (Luke 16:15; John 5:42).

b. We learn from the love of Mary (12:3).

Mary's gift was not only an expression of faith, but a sacrifice of love, teaching that Christ expects our personal affection and gifts for Himself, and that all that we do for the Church and the poor can never be a substitute for His own personal claims.

c. Love is the condition of His indwelling (14:23).

It is to the loving heart that He loves to come and dwell, where He finds a welcome and a home. The root of piety is not intellect, but heart. Saintly souls are not cherubim, but seraphim, burning, rather than shining.

d. Love to Jesus makes us dear to His Father.

"The Father himself loves you because you have loved me and have believed that I came from God" (16:27).

e. The best proof of love is obedience.

> If you love me, you will obey what I command. . . . If anyone loves me, he will obey my teaching. . . . He who does not love me will not obey my teaching. . . . If you obey my commands, you will remain in my love . . . You are my friends if you do what I command. (14:15, 23, 24; 15:10, 14)

f. Love to Jesus is the best medium of spiritual revelation. The hearts that loved Him best were the quickest to recognize Him (20:16; 21:7).

Mary Magdalene saw the Lord first, because her love would not let her go away. With weeping eyes and willing hands she waited at the grave, ready to bear in her own arms His dear body, out of the way of those who she supposed had removed it from the sepulcher. To such a heart, Christ is ever near; and the tear of love, like a heavenly lens, is quick to reveal His presence. John, too, through the mist of the Galilean morning, instantly knows his beloved Lord. It is the instinct of love, and he has finely expressed it by the beautiful words in his epistle, "Whoever does not love does not know God, because God is love. . . . Whoever lives in love lives in God, and God in him" (1 John 4:8, 16).

g. Love is the true impulse of service (John 21:15–17).

Christ is still asking, "Do you love me?" of every worker, before He commits to their hands His lambs, His sheep or His feeble suffering ones. No one is qualified to minister in His name without love. She is the queen of all the graces and the greatest of all the gifts. Burning glasses can be made of ice, and will set on fire the object on which they are concentrated, but hearts can only be kindled by hearts that are themselves on fire.

> It needs the overflow of heart
> To give the lips full speech.

OUR LOVE TO ONE ANOTHER

7. Our love to one another is the new commandment of the ethics of Jesus and the Gospel of John.

It was promulgated, not at Sinai, nor even in the Sermon on the Mount, but at the supper table. The Mosaic law of love was, "love your neighbor as yourself" (Leviticus 19:18), but the New Testament commandment transcends it, as far as the heaven is above the earth. "Love each other as I have loved you" (John 15:12). This is impossible for human nature. Such love must be itself divine; and it is, indeed, nothing less than the very indwelling of the heart of Christ in our breast. Therefore, love in the New Testament is always recognized as a divine gift. Its very name, Charity, has the same root as the word "grace." It is a grace, and the gift of the Spirit of God.

One of the most devoted ministers of the Evangelical Church of France was a rationalist in the beginning of his ministry. A neighboring pastor, who was evangelical, a most godly man, had long prayed for his conversion, and one day invited him to preach in his pulpit on the subject of love, the text being "Love the Lord your God with all your heart and . . . your neighbor as yourself" (Matthew 22:37, 39). As he began to preach, the Holy Spirit brought to his heart, with irresistible conviction, the sense of his own inability to love according to the divine standard. Standing in the pulpit, with the tears running down his face, he confessed to his congregation that the love of which he had been preaching to them was something he did not possess, and could not, himself, produce. Then there flashed upon his soul, by the same blessed convicting Spirit, the thought of Christ as the one who had come to do for us what the law could not do, and not only to atone for our failure to meet the divine standard, but also to work in us the love which nature could not originate. And he began to preach, for the first time in his life, the gospel of Jesus Christ. This, and this alone, must ever be the spirit of love. It is the love "God has poured out . . . into our hearts by the Holy Spirit, whom he has given us. You see, at just the right time, when we were still powerless [even to love], Christ died for the ungodly" (Romans 5:5–6).

CHAPTER 6

FAITH IN THE GOSPEL OF JOHN

This is one of the keynotes of the gospel as stated by the author himself. "But these are written that you may believe that Jesus is the Christ, the Son of God, and that by believing you may have life in his name" (John 20:31).

THE TOUCHSTONE

1. We see it in the very beginning of the gospel, as the touchstone that separates between His friends and foes and divides all men into two great irreconcilable classes. Of the one it is said, "his own did not receive him" (1:11), of the other, "Yet to all who received him, to those who believed in his name, he gave the right to become children of God" (1:12). Faith lifts us into the very family of God and becomes the gate of heaven, and unbelief excludes even the chosen people from any share in their inheritance.

THE FIRST DISCIPLES

2. We see the faith of the first disciples resting on the message of John the Baptist, and afterwards on the personal testimony of individual disciples. Andrew and John believe on the word of their master, the Baptist; Simon believes on the testimony of Andrew, and Philip and Nathaniel believe on the direct words of Jesus Himself.

THE FIRST MIRACLE

3. We see next the still bolder faith of His disciples in His divine character in consequence of His first miracle and the manifestation of His glory. "This, the first of his miraculous signs, Jesus performed in Cana of Galilee. He thus revealed his glory, and his disciples put their faith in him" (2:11).

THE EFFECT OF HIS MIRACLES

4. We see the faith of the common people of Jerusalem in consequence of His supernatural works at the feast (2:23).

427

Jesus however, perceived the shallowness of a faith that merely rested upon the evidence of miracles. Therefore He did not place any permanent dependence upon these people, for He knew what was in man. We see the same kind of faith in Nicodemus himself when he first came to Jesus and was faithfully taught the necessity of a deeper life than that of mere intellectual conviction.

SAVING FAITH

5. The Lord Jesus unfolds the deeper meaning of faith in His conversation with Nicodemus as the condition of everlasting life, through which we receive Christ and spiritual life through Him. Here faith is presented with the most solemn emphasis as the sole and imperative condition of salvation, and unbelief as the cause of condemnation and eternal ruin (3:15, 18).

THE RESULT OF KNOWLEDGE

6. We see the faith of the Samaritans, founded upon their own personal acquaintance with the Lord and His heart-searching revelation of their souls, and His own grace and love (4:29, 41–42).

The woman of Samaria believed because she felt in her inmost soul that He had searched her heart and was no other than her Lord and Maker, and therefore abundantly able to become her Savior. Her neighbors gave their own independent testimony. They, too, had believed Him, not through her word merely, but through their own personal acquaintance with Him. True faith must ever rest upon our own knowledge of the Savior and be able to say, "now we have heard for ourselves, and we know that this man really is the Savior of the world" (4:42).

FAITH IN HIS WORD

7. We see the faith of the nobleman of Capernaum, resting on the naked word of Christ (4:48–50). Jesus had felt that much of the faith hitherto manifested had been based only on His miraculous power. He therefore determined to lead this soul to the higher place of naked faith in His own simple word. Therefore He refuses any sign and complains that the people are abusing His very miracles by resting on them rather than on His word. Then, testing this man's faith by a bold promise, He bids him go forth without any other token of His child's healing than His own simple word. The man rises to meet his test and dares to believe the simple promise of the Savior, and he goes his way to find it literally fulfilled, teaching us through all time, the simplicity of faith and the instantaneous results which it will ever bring.

CLAIMING ETERNAL LIFE

8. Faith delivers from condemnation and claims eternal life (5:24). This

mighty word has power to cancel the very curse of the law, to turn back the fiery sword of judgment, and to open the portals of immortal life to the soul that dares to claim it.

HINDRANCES TO FAITH

9. These, He shows them, are mainly a spirit of worldliness and a subserviency to the opinions of men (5:44). This is fatal ever to true faith in God, and indeed any unholy condition must always be fatal to true faith. In a previous verse He intimates that their own willfulness was the cause of their rejecting Him. "You refuse to come to me to have life" (5:40).

LIVING BY FAITH

10. Faith receives Jesus as the Bread of Life for our souls and bodies (6:35).

Not only does faith secure our future salvation, but it enters into the fullness of Jesus for our present needs. This the Galileans could not and would not receive; and this, today, is equally incomprehensible and offensive to the majority of professing Christians. A life of faith upon the Son of God, and the habit of trustful dependence upon Him for the nourishment of our spirits and the health of our bodies is regarded as the foolishness of mysticism and sentimentalism; but to those who thus know Him, it is the very balm of life, the bane of care and sorrow and the secret of the Most High.

FAITH TESTIFYING

11. Faith testifies to Christ (6:68–69). As we have already seen, this testimony was called forth by the withdrawal of the great majority of Christ's Galilean followers. Peter and his brethren did not yet fully understand all that the Master's profound teachings had meant, but they believed and received as far as they could, and their own experience in its true form, expresses more than one beautiful truth, "We believe and know that you are the Holy One of God" (6:69). These are the two stages of faith: first we believe, and then we know by actual consciousness and heart-satisfying experience the truth of these precious promises.

RECEIVING THE HOLY SPIRIT

12. Faith brings us into the fullness of the Spirit (7:38). We have already referred to this promise of the overflowing fullness of the Holy Spirit. Here it is connected with believing. Thus only can we ever receive the Holy Spirit. We must expect to accept Him, trust Him, and treat Him as having fully come. Moses was commanded to speak to the rock and it would flow forth, but not to strike it in any doubt or uncertainty; so, still, the whisper of trust ever brings the fullness of blessing.

THE LIFE OF FAITH

13. It is a life of believing and continuing (7:30–32).

Here we find the Lord encouraging the disciples who had taken the first steps of faith, to continue in His word and pass on into all the fullness of spiritual freedom and conscious experience of the truth. So faith must ever be rooted and grounded and built up in Him, for "we have come to share in Christ if we hold firmly till the end the confidence we had at first" (Hebrews 3:14).

THE BLIND MAN

14. We have in the story of the blind man (John 9:5–38) a beautiful example of the beginning of faith. This man had followed all the light he had, and had fully confessed it as he received it. Healed by the Lord, he had briefly and constantly borne witness to Him in the face of persecution, until at last he had been excommunicated from the synagogue for Christ's sake. Then the Lord met him and led him into fuller light, as He ever does the soul that uses all the light it has. And as the new light came, he accepted it without reserve, believing and worshiping his Lord. He became a monument of that simplicity which has often put to shame the pride and unbelief of the world's boasted wisdom.

THE FAITH OF MARTHA

15. We have here a very remarkable example of faith. Martha's heart had sunk when she saw her brother die and the Master fail to come, and for a moment she reproached Him with the neglect; but then there rises in her heart a sudden gleam of hopeful expectation that even yet it is not too late for His almighty power to remedy the disaster. "I know," she says, "that even now God will give you whatever you ask" (11:22). This was undoubtedly a literal intimation that even Lazarus could be raised from the dead. The Lord encourages it and reveals Himself as the One who possesses in Himself all the powers of resurrection life, and more than hints His consent to her amazing request, "Your brother will rise again" (11:23). For a little while Martha does what we all do at such times, she drops down her faith a little and slips it forward into the future. "I know he will rise again in the resurrection at the last day" (11:24). Jesus meets her retort by holding her to the present moment and to His own sufficiency. "I am the resurrection and the life" (11:25), He replies. Poor Martha does not quite meet the issue with definite present assurance, but she rolls her burden over upon Him and rests in Himself as the Almighty Son of God and the promised Messiah. "Yes, Lord . . . I believe that you are the Christ, the Son of God, who was to come into the world" (11:27). He must have read in her words a deeper faith than

she expressed, and He evidently felt it essential that she should stand fast in this faith. This is one of the conditions of the miracle that He is about to perform, for He adds a little later, when she expressed concern and doubt about removing the stone because Lazarus was so long buried, "Did I not tell you that if you believed, you would see the glory of God?" (11:40). Therefore the resurrection of Lazarus was, in some measure, connected with the faith of Martha. But there was a mightier faith than Martha's. He is still the faith as well as the power in all His works of omnipotence through His trusting children. How calm and lofty is the confidence of that marvelous prayer, "Father, I thank you that you have heard me. I knew that you always hear me . . ." (11:41–42). So, still, He waits to work and believe in us.

THE FAITH OF MARY

16. Next we see the faith of Mary (12:3–7). This, at first, looks like an act of love, but deeper than love was the root of faith from which it sprang. This is revealed in the seventh verse by the testimony of Jesus concerning her. It was because she knew that He was about to die as her suffering Savior, that Mary had kept this costly ointment, and now she comes with hands of loving faith to set Him apart for the altar of sacrifice, with an intelligent appreciation of His character and work which perhaps no other of His disciples in any such measure shared. So, still, the faith which best understands the cross of Calvary will most effectually work by love, and lay the richest and costliest offerings at His feet.

TIMID BELIEVERS

17. We also see a faith that fears to confess Jesus (12:42–43). In contrast with Mary we see here another kind of faith which has plenty of counterparts in the Church today; a faith which has no doubt of Christ's divinity and Messiahship, but dares to go only as far as is consistent with worldly interest and reputation, for it loves the praise of men more than the praise of God. Jesus challenges all such cowardly hearts to the bar of God, and appeals to the hour when they shall stand in the judgment and find that to have confessed Jesus amid reproach and shame was to have stood for God and won His acknowledgment when all other faces shall be covered and one smile from Him will be worth a thousand worlds.

BELIEVE ALSO IN ME

18. We see faith in Jesus Himself as a divine person, equal with the Father, and as the very expression and image of the Father (14:1, 10–11). The Lord Jesus seeks here to link their faith in Him with all that had been sacred in their conceptions of God, and to assume to Himself as the object of their confidence, all the majesty and fullness of all previous revelations of the

Father. "Trust in God; trust also in me" (14:1). What a softened light this sheds upon the name of God and the glory of His majesty, and what a majesty it sheds upon the name of Jesus. They had learned to trust His love, they must now add to this the conception of His transcendent, infinite power and Godhead. So our faith in Him must recognize His divine glory.

FAITH AND POWER

19. Faith in Christ is the secret power for our Christian work (14:12). Not only must they believe in His union with the Father, but they must likewise believe as fully in their union with Him. The works they are to do are not to be their works, but His works in them. And as He is now entering upon a high stage of His mediatorial work, they must expect to be the channels and instruments of even greater power than they have yet witnessed, even in His ministry. But the vital link of this power must ever be a living faith, a faith that receives Him constantly to work His own works in them, and dares to expect Him to do even greater works than in the days of His flesh. Do we thus believe in Him, does He thus work in us, are our works His work, and does He work the greater works in our lives?

FAITH AND PRAYER

20. Faith is the condition of effectual prayer (15:7–16, 23–27). Faith is expressed in these passages by abiding in Him and asking in His name, that is, His very character, as if He Himself were asking. This is true faith, to identify ourselves with Jesus and pray with His rights and claims. Such prayer will ever be in accordance with His will and must prevail.

FAITH IN THE RISEN SAVIOR

21. The first to believe in the resurrection was John (20:8–16). The beauty of his faith was that it was immediate, implicit and without waiting for visible evidence other than what God had already given. He saw and believed. He saw not yet the Lord, but he saw enough to rest his faith upon and to recall to his mind the previous words of his Master which he, with the others, had forgotten. No doubt, his faith now rested on the recollection of the simple promise which Jesus had made before His death, and which he refers to in the next verse. Mary's faith was different—it was the result of a personal manifestation of Christ, inspired by His own living voice; and thus, in both these cases, faith rested on the Savior's words.

THOMAS

22. We see the unbelief of Thomas and the lesson it teaches us of the highest faith (20:29). The other disciples all believed on the testimony of those who had seen the Lord. Thomas refused to be satisfied with less than a

complete series of tests. He was a regular materialist, and wanted signs and evidences to rest his faith upon. The Lord condescended to give him what he demanded; but when it came, there came also the higher witness of Christ's own presence, and His searching revelation of Thomas' unbelieving heart, so that he did not now need the visible sign, but threw himself at the Master's feet, exclaiming in the language of irresistible conviction and unconditional submission, "My Lord and my God!" (20:28). Jesus takes occasion from this to teach the great truth which He had hinted at in the beginning of the gospel, in connection with the healing of the nobleman's son, that the true resting place of faith is not material signs, but the word of Jesus Himself. He pronounced the lasting benediction which it is possible for every one of us to obtain. "Blessed are those who have not seen and yet have believed" (20:29).

FAITH IN THE WORD

23. We see faith resting on the written Word. It is the record which the Holy Spirit has *written*—"these are written that you may believe" (20:31). This is the great truth which John unfolds so simply in his epistle:

> We accept man's testimony, but God's testimony is greater because it is the testimony of God . . . Anyone who does not believe God has made him out to be a liar . . . And this is the testimony: God has given us eternal life, and this life is in his Son. . . . I write these things to you who believe in the name of the Son of God so that you may know that you have eternal life. (1 John 5:9–11, 13)

By believing the record, therefore, which God has given of His Son, we know that we have eternal life. And then we receive the second witness in ourselves, His Holy Spirit, and the peace and joy He brings into the believing soul.

DEVELOPMENT OF FAITH

It is interesting to trace the development of faith and unbelief in the Gospel of John, on the part of His friends on the one side, and His adversaries on the other. In the first four chapters we trace the gradual development of faith. First we have the inquiries the priests and Levites made of John the Baptist (John 1:19), showing considerable interest.

Next we see the open adherence of some of John's disciples, as they leave him to follow Jesus (1:37).

Next we find Philip and Nathaniel, two typical Galileans, joining the little band of new disciples (1:43–49).

In the second chapter the manifestation of Jesus becomes more marked and the faith of His disciples more pronounced. "This, the first of his miraculous signs, Jesus performed in Cana of Galilee. He thus revealed his glory, and his disciples put their faith in him" (2:11). From Galilee the scene is changed to Jerusalem, and there we see the steady development of faith in Him.

First, we see it among many of the common people (2:23).

Next, we see it in the spirit of earnest inquiry in Nicodemus (chapter 3).

And then we see it in the wide extension of His Judean ministry in the country, where many became His disciples. And His ministry grows larger and wider even than John's (4:1–2).

The development still goes on, removing from Judea to Samaria, where we see the remarkable faith of the Samaritans, and finally culminates in the strong faith of the royal official of Capernaum (4:45–54).

DEVELOPMENT OF UNBELIEF

We now come to the second series in this development, namely, the manifestation of unbelief on the part of His enemies in connection with the healing of the invalid man (chapter 5); and its issue is summed up in the Lord's words, "you refuse to come to me to have life" (5:40). In the sixth chapter, the conflict changes to Galilee and speedily terminates in the close of that chapter by His rejection, on the part of the Galileans, on account of His deeper spiritual teachings and His refusal to enter into their ambitious project—to establish an earthly kingdom (6:66). The Galilean contest is now over, and the scene again changes to Jerusalem in the seventh and eighth chapters.

We have His disputations with them at the Feast of Tabernacles, ending in their attempt to stone Him (8:59).

The next conflict is at the Feast of Dedication three months later, and it is closed with a similar attempt (10:39) and his retirement to Perea.

HIS GLORY MANIFESTED AND BELIEVED

The series closes with His supreme manifestation of His power and glory in the resurrection of Lazarus, and the final and determined plot of the entire Sanhedrin to destroy Him, which led soon after to His crucifixion.

Each of these stages of unbelief and hostility on the part of His enemies is characterized by corresponding faith on the part of His friends. Over against their rejection in chapter 5 is the faith of the invalid man at Bethesda's pool. In contrast with the rejection of the Galileans is the confession of Peter and the disciples (6:68–69). The unbelief of the rulers at the Feast of Tabernacles is met and confounded by the faith of the poor blind beggar (chapter 9), and the mad and reckless opposition aroused by the resurrection of Lazarus stands out in bolder relief from the faith and love of Mary and Martha (12:9–11) and the enthusiasm of the common people (chapter 12) as they publicly hail Him as the Son of David and the King of Jerusalem.

The final stage in this process of development of faith, we see in the closing chapter of John on the part of His disciples. Their perplexities and questionings come out most truthfully in the discourses at the table (13:36; 14:6, 8, 22; 16:18).

They enter into clearer light as He closes His address. "Now we can see that you know all things and that you do not even need to have anyone ask you questions. This makes us believe that you came from God" (16:30). Then comes the dark shadow of Peter's fall (18:27), followed and counterbalanced by the devotion of John and the brave women who still lingered around the cross (19:25–26), also the courage of Nicodemus and Joseph (19:38–40).

With the morning of the resurrection comes the faith of John himself (20:8), the joyful recognition of Mary (20:16), the confession of Thomas (20:28) and the restoration of Peter (21:15, 19)—all summed up by the final testimony of John himself, as the foundation of our unfaltering faith through the coming generations.

CHAPTER 7

TEN INCIDENTS IN THE GOSPEL OF JOHN

Wₑ find in this wonderful gospel some remarkable incidents, illustrating the grace, glory and character of Jesus.

VARIETIES OF CONVERSION
John 1:29–51
1. Interview with the first disciples or the varieties of conversion.

Through the Gospel
We have here an illustration of the varieties of conversion. The first of these disciples was led to Christ by the preaching of John the Baptist. It would be well if all preaching were as definite and evangelical. There would be more Andrews if there were more John the Baptists. The great preacher knew that he was sending away his own disciples, but he did not shrink from pointing them to the greater Master. He was not ashamed to repeat the same sermon the next day. This is a text in which no minister need ever be ashamed to repeat himself. The story of the cross is a gospel that never grows old.

Through Personal Effort
Andrew, like every true convert, becomes an evangelist, and for the rest of his life the notices that we have of him represent him in this aspect of helping others. In the present case, he first finds his own brother and brings him to Jesus; so the second conversion here is through personal influence on the part of our own immediate relatives. What a lesson it teaches us of our obligation to the souls of those who are nearest to us. Forever Andrew will be a partner of the fruits of Simon's life, for he brought him to Jesus. The way he brought him was by his own personal testimony; the reason he was able to give so clear a testimony was because he himself had come so near to Jesus. He had not only gone to Him, but he had gone with Him. The whole

previous day he and John had spent at home with the new Master, which was a wonderful type of that deeper fellowship which the converted soul may enter and must enter if it would be able to bring others to Christ.

A Day with Jesus

What a sweet picture of the soul's introduction to the Savior. These two disciples had followed Jesus at the invitation of John, but no one ever follows Christ unnoticed. Turning around and recognizing them, He asks them a very simple but searching question: "What do you want?" (John 1:38). If they had been seeking anything but Himself, the interview would have ended here; happily for them, however, that they could answer, "Rabbi . . . where are you staying?" (1:38). They did not have to wait for the welcome to His presence and His home; they went with Him and abode that whole day, and many a wondrous unfolding of heavenly truth entered their hearts as they waited the happy hours at His blessed feet. So, still, He waits to receive His humblest disciples to abide. Peter is welcomed with no less frankness and simplicity; the Lord knows him from the beginning and intimates in His first words His honest opinion of Simon, the son of John, the impulsive and unsteady man; but He also reveals the stronger qualities which are to come to him through the grace of God and make him the very rock cut out from the Rock of Ages, which is to be one of the foundation stones of the Christian Church.

The Call of Jesus

The next conversion in this group is through the direct call of Christ Himself. It is Philip of Bethsaida. He, too, responds immediately, and becomes in turn, like Andrew, a messenger to others and afterwards, along with Andrew, he is the instrument of bringing to Jesus the strangers in the temple who came to seek the Savior.

The Call of a Friend

The last of this group of disciples was brought to Christ by the personal influence, not of a relative, but of a friend. Philip found Nathaniel and brought him to Jesus. Nathaniel, however, was not willing to take so great a matter on the word of Philip; yet, like a wise man, was willing to come and see. As he met Jesus, a single sentence from Him made the old Israelite feel that he was in the presence of the searcher of his heart; and falling at His feet, gave Him homage in the loftiest faith as the "Son of God . . . the King of Israel" (1:49). Nathaniel was a true Israelite, a man of upright and blameless character, and yet even the highest morality needs something more, even the revelation of Jesus Christ and the spirit of childlike faith in the divine Savior.

In these five disciples we have a beautiful picture representing, in miniature, the story of Christianity and the various ways in which, since then, Christ has been leading myriads of souls to Himself.

NICODEMUS
John 3:1–21
2. Nicodemus, or the first inquirer.
We have already seen in this incident the spiritual teaching of the Lord Jesus with regard to the new life and the necessity of regeneration. We also may learn from it many precious lessons respecting Christ Himself and His method of dealing with souls. This man, like many other inquirers, came to talk and argue, but Jesus declined all speculations and questionings about even the truth, and threw him at once back upon himself and his need of a radical change of heart. Indeed, He tells him that without a new spiritual nature his ideas and opinions are of no value, for he cannot even see the kingdom of God until he is born again. Nicodemus' first word was, "We know," and most people, like him, are hindered by what they know. He represented the highest type of an ancient moralist and formalist, still destitute however, of true spiritual life. His first step therefore, is to humble him and show him his deep spiritual need; His next step is to lead him sweetly to see in the gospel God's full provision for this need. We should never preach regeneration apart from Christ and simple faith in Him. The true place to obtain a new heart is not by looking into our old one or trying to improve it, but by bowing at the feet of Jesus and believing in Him as our sin-atoning Savior.

SOUL WINNING
John 4:1–38
3. The woman of Samaria, or the wisdom that wins souls.
We have already referred to this incident in connection with the love of Christ for sinners. For a moment let us still glance at it as a lesson in soul-winning. The first thing that strikes us about it is the incidental character of His work in saving this woman. It was one of those opportunities which come to us constantly by the way, and which He was always ready to meet and improve. Much of our best work should be unstudied and spontaneous.

The real secret of His usefulness in this and in every case, was His intense love for souls. He could truly say to His disciples, "My food . . . is to do the will of him who sent me and to finish his work" (4:34). Work like this was His very life and joy. And so, if we are to win souls, it must be our delight, and we must be watching for them. The literal translation of the word, "welcomes" (Luke 15:2), is, "this man lies in wait for sinners."

We also see in this case the finest tact in His interesting the woman before He attempts to impress her. He awakens her interest and confidence by meeting her in an easy and friendly manner and asked a little favor of her. He stooped to her level, and even surprised her by His entire freedom from all the prejudices which she expected from a Jewish rabbi. If we would save people we must come near them. The earliest Moravian missionaries to the West Indies became slaves that they might win the confidence of the degraded natives.

Then He awakens her curiosity and spiritual hunger by hinting at the needs of her own sad heart, and the blessings He is able to give in return, if she but knew. There is always a sore place in every human heart that a loving hand can touch and find in it a point of contact with the gospel. To speak of the living water is often enough to awaken the thirst.

Her Conscience

But there is a deeper need, and that is her sin. It would not do to tell her of it, for this might offend her; she must see it herself, and so a simple question, "Go, call your husband" (John 4:16), becomes the occasion of awakening her conscience and bringing from her lips the frank confession that lays her poor guilty heart at the feet of the Savior. But now she tries for a moment to turn aside and evade her conscience and the leadings of God's Spirit by a spirit of controversy about the difference between Jewish and Samaritan worship.

Revelation of Jesus

The Master refuses to enter into the controversy further than to use it to awaken her own sense of God's spirituality and her need of a personal acquaintance with Him in her secret heart. She feels the lack of this, and her soul instinctively cries out for someone to lead her to God, and she exclaims, " 'I know that Messiah' (called Christ) 'is coming. When he comes, he will explain everything to us' " (4:25). She has been led thus step by step up to the very portals of faith, and all that is necessary now is to draw aside the veil and reveal Himself to her heart. No human language can express all that is meant in that little sentence that follows, "I who speak to you am he" (4:26). We must go back to the moment when He revealed Himself to us to understand it. It is proper that a curtain should here fall upon the scene, and she be left, with the secret of her new and eternal joy. She is saved, she has found her Lord, but she cannot keep the secret, and she, too, in turn, becomes a messenger of love, to bring her countrymen to the same wondrous Teacher that has searched and saved her own soul.

THE SINFUL WOMAN
John 8:2–11

4. The sinful woman, or the mercy that pardons without palliating sin.
We refer elsewhere to the critical question connected with this passage;

here it is enough to see in it the heartless severity of weak man toward sin in others, in contrast with the tenderness and long-suffering of Christ to the erring. These Pharisees were, by their own confession, as impure as this poor woman, and yet they could drag her forward into shameful exposure, and without a touch of mercy demand her instant death and all the eternal ruin it must bring. Jesus, on the other hand, with an infinite hatred of sin, being free from a spot or stain of defilement, could see deeper than her sin. He could feel the tenderest compassion and mercy toward the poor sinner, while giving no indulgence or countenance to the sin.

What a lesson we also learn about the necessity of our own blamelessness if we would sit in judgment upon others. When we are without sin then we can cast the stone of censoriousness at our fellows, and "be ready to punish every act of disobedience, once your obedience is complete" (2 Corinthians 10:6). What a beautiful example we learn of being blind to the faults of others when in the presence of the accuser. While they were talking against this poor woman, Jesus wrote upon the ground as though He heard them not. Happy for us all if we had thus learned not to listen to the backbiting tongue. How vividly the power of conscience appears in the presence of innocence. One look from His honest face into their hearts and they felt all their secret sin exposed and hurried from His presence to hide themselves from their own consciences and His searching gaze.

His Delicacy

Jesus dealt with this poor woman, too, but He deals with her alone; not in the presence of others can we tell the soul of its faults, nor when it feels we have listened to evil reports, or unfriendly tongues. How beautifully He preserved the confidence of this poor heart by His manly and lofty sensitiveness to her feelings, refusing even to look in her face or to see her blush of shame while her enemies were near; but only when they are alone He looks into that weeping countenance and speaks the word of mercy and yet of faithfulness. Christ's first word to her is forgiveness, free and full, not founded upon her innocence or promises of amendment, but springing only from His own undeserved grace; but His next word is a word of infinite holiness, "Go now and leave your life of sin" (John 8:11). "But with you there is forgiveness;/ therefore you are feared" (Psalm 130:4).

There is no such remedy for sin as love. "We have tried everything to reform him," said the Duke of Wellington about a deserter they had punished till it seemed vain. "We have tried everything to reform him, and it is useless; there is nothing left but to execute him." "Please your highness," said a poor soldier, "there is one thing you have never tried." "What is that?" asked the duke. "Please your highness, you have never tried forgiving him." And so it was tried, and not in vain, for the hardened deserter became the noblest and truest heart of all the soldiers of the Peninsula.

MARY OF BETHANY
John 12:1–11

5. The anointing at Bethany, or the preeminence of love.

This beautiful incident is the highest expression of love to Jesus that we meet with during His earthly life.

We have already seen that it was from one who best of all understood the meaning of His death, and that it was an act of faith quite as much as a gift of love. It was this that inspired Mary's love, that she understood so well that He at whose feet she sat with delight was about to die for her. And so our love must still draw its inspiration from the cross. But the chief lesson of this scene is that Jesus appreciates and requires our personal and highest love directly for Himself. Judas, like many people still, thought that the ointment was wasted because it had not been given to the poor. Christ replies that there is something even more than giving to the poor, namely, the offering that is placed directly at His feet and offered only to Himself. Each of us has a vessel we can break and a fragrance we can pour at those sacred feet, namely, our own heart with all its treasures of love. It is possible to do much work and even give all our goods to feed the poor, and yet be strangers to true love to Jesus. Nothing can be a substitute for love to Jesus. The very perfume of Christianity has ever been the incense of fervent pity and personal love to Christ. The world may call it waste, but Jesus treasures it in vials full of odors sweet before the throne.

HUMILITY
John 13:1–10

6. Washing the disciples' feet, or the humility that springs from true greatness.

The first lesson taught by this picture is that of Christ's humility. Like Him, we cannot truly stoop until we have learned our high calling and know that we are indeed the sons of God. Then we shall not fear the most menial service or think that the lowliest place can degrade our true dignity, but shall prove that we are the chief by becoming the servant of all. The next lesson is love, that, instead of exposing the stains of one another, seeks to wash them away. But the deepest spiritual teaching of these words is the unfolding of Christ's own constant cleansing as our ever-living Advocate and High Priest. Still He is girded with the towel, and still He stoops to cleanse the stains of defilement from our feet day by day.

Cleansing

This is not the act of justification by which He forgives the sinner, but it is the constant keeping of His own disciples. Two expressive words are used in the passage for cleansing; the first, *luo,* signifying a complete washing of the whole person; the second, *nipto,* meaning a partial washing, as the feet. The first of these, He says, does not need to be repeated; once for all they have been justified, but day by day they need to be thoroughly and constantly cleansed from the travel stains of the way. The tense used for the first is the perfect tense, "A person who has had a bath [in his justification] needs only to wash his feet; his whole body is clean" (13:10). In the first chapter of his beautiful epistle, John has taught the same truth in the words:

> But if we walk in the light, as he is in the light, we have fellowship with one another, and the blood of Jesus, his Son, purifies us from all sin. . . . If we confess our sins, he is faithful and just and will forgive us our sins and purify us from all unrighteousness. (1 John 1:7, 9)

HIS MOTHER
John 19:25–27

7. The message concerning His mother, or the humanity and divinity of Christ.

Of course, the first thought suggested by this exquisite picture is the love of Jesus to His mother and the enduring example which exalts filial piety and affection to so high a place. But following this, comes the other lesson of His transcendent superiority to her and to all His earthly relationships, and the unmistakable protest which He leaves by this incident against any undue exaltation of even His holy mother unto a place of peculiar veneration and worship. Therefore He calls her "woman" instead of mother, and transfers her, not to some place of deification, but to the humble protection of John and the relationship of a mother to him. Therefore, if Mary has been lifted into a place of divinity, what place shall we give to John, her son? The third lesson of this scene is the duty we owe to friends of Christ and the spiritual relationships into which we come to them through our union with Him, so that they are to us truly as Mary was to John, as mother, and brothers, and sisters. Here we see the dream of the household of faith and the family of God in its mutual as well as its divine relations, and the bonds of affection and care which are far too weak in the Church of God.

MARY MAGDALENE
John 20:1–18

8. Mary at the sepulcher, or the new revelation of the risen Lord.

This woman was singularly honored by the love of her risen Lord, as the first witness of His resurrection. She had been saved from more than perhaps any of His disciples. His strong arm of love had rescued her from the seven-fold possession of demoniac power. There is no reason to suppose that her womanhood had been degraded by the sin which has been associated with her name, but something more terrific, and on her part involuntary and irresistible, had bound perhaps all the powers of her body and soul. Set free by His almighty love, her heart was now bound to Him by cords of everlasting love. No sadder or truer heart lingered at the cross through the dark hours of His dying agony, and no more fearless or devoted feet hastened on the Easter morning to anoint His body in Joseph's sepulcher. Finding the stone rolled away and the door open, she hastens to tell His brethren, Peter and John. When they have come and gone, she lingers still in the garden believing that the body has been removed by the gardener's hands, perhaps because of its being inconvenient to keep it longer. It is then that Jesus appears to her, disguised at first in a form that she mistakes for the gardener; but the disguise only brings out more beautifully her tender love. Her willing hands are ready to bear away the precious body, but His living voice dispels the illusion, and her hands clasp with rapture the feet of her Lord.

His New Resurrection Life

Dear as was her love to Jesus, and tenderly as He welcomed and responded to it, yet He saw that there was too much of the old human apprehension in her faith, and that she must be gently taught now to rise to the higher realization of His resurrection and His ascension life, and therefore He adds, "Do not hold on to me" (20:17). It was as if He had said, "Think of Me henceforth as ascended to My Father and your Father, and go and tell My brethren." This was the same thought expressed by the apostle, namely, that though he had known the Lord Jesus after the flesh, yet now henceforth He knew Him thus no more. Thus the cords that bound Mary's heart to Him were transformed from earth to heaven, and her spirit taught to recognize Him as a spiritual presence, while His body was to be enthroned at the right hand of God. Perhaps she also had to be taught to lose her own self-consciousness and joy by thinking of her brethren and the higher ministry of service, and that henceforth her hands were not so much to clasp her Lord, for her own exclusive possession, as to give Him forth for the salvation and consolation of others. Among the many sweet lessons of this beautiful incident we may learn:

a. Love is the element of highest vision. Mary's affection for her Lord led to her being the first to see Him.

b. Jesus is often with us unrecognized, even as Mary supposed Him to be the gardener.

c. Christ's love to us is personal. He called her by her own name, and then there was no mistake about His identity. They who know Him personally know Him unmistakably.

d. We must know Jesus spiritually, not by the touch of flesh, but by the contact of faith as the living and ascended One at God's right hand, and yet the Ever-present in our hearts and lives.

e. We must be unselfish in our love to Christ and remember that every revelation and blessing He bestows upon us is a trust for others and must not be held as a selfish joy.

THOMAS

John 20:24–28

9. Thomas, or Christ's patience with our doubts.

a. Many of our doubts arise from neglected duty. Had Thomas been in his place on the first Sabbath evening, he would have been saved a week of agony. And were we always where Christ comes to meet us or bids us go, we should escape many conflicts. Much of our spiritual darkness comes from disobedience.

b. Much of Thomas' unbelief arose from self-will. He had ample evidence in the testimony of his brethren, but he had made up his mind that he must have his own way and his own kind of proof, and nothing else would satisfy him. So many persons have a preconceived plan of blessing or salvation, and their own will is the hindrance to the blessing they seek.

c. Much of Thomas' doubt arose from his deep love to Christ and his fear lest it might not be true. Many truehearted Christians are chronic doubters, and their very love to the cross of Christ and the interests committed to them keep them in constant unrest as they bear their own burdens and anxieties. Christ has much sympathy for the doubts and fears He sees in the true-hearted, and while He chides and reproves them, yet He gently bears with these troubled ones and constantly proves to them how useless are their fears.

d. Christ sometimes meets our unreasonable and willful demands, but when He does, as in the case of Thomas, He makes us ashamed of our will-fulness and shows us how little we needed the thing we so insisted upon. When Thomas was allowed to thrust his hand into his Savior's side he did not want to do it, and, no doubt, was thoroughly ashamed that he had ever asked it. The patience of Jesus in stooping to our unreasonableness may well break our hearts with love.

e. Thomas sets a good example to other doubters in putting himself in the way of getting light by assembling the next time with the disciples. And so, if the doubter would only come into the light, or even come to meet it, he would soon find, like Thomas, his Lord ready to shed the light of life on all his darkness.

f. Thomas was convinced, not by material evidence, but by the spiritual character of his Lord, by the heart-searching omniscience which read his own secret thoughts, and by the tender grace and love which dealt so generously with his unbelief. And so we shall find the best answer to all our questionings in the manifestation of Jesus Himself to our hearts, as the Searcher of all their secrets and the Supply of all their needs.

g. Let us not miss the blessing here pronounced on the higher kind of faith which we all may have and for which all the discipline of life is the best school, the faith of him who has not seen and yet has believed.

PETER
John 21:15–22
10. Peter's restoration, or Christ's love and grace for the backslider.

Already Peter had met the Lord alone and, doubtless, had poured out his penitential confession at His feet, and received, we may be sure, the Master's forgiveness. But weeks have elapsed since their return to Galilee, the Master has not come as He appointed, and Peter's faith has begun to fail. This is doubtless the reason why he returned to his fishing nets, and led with him, as his strong nature usually did, so many of his brethren. But their labor was all in vain, as it ever is when God is calling us from a forbidden path to Him.

On the incidents of the miracle that followed we do not dwell here, with all its significant teachings regarding their future service. Perhaps their thoughts had already reverted to that first miracle of the catch of fishes where they had been called to become fishers of men, and Peter may have been already wondering about the significance of this second call as they sat together at their morning meal on the shore. Then the words of Jesus fell upon his ear, "Simon son of John" (21:15). It was a good while since he had been called by that name, and it may have reminded him of his human weakness; but there could be no question now of his Lord's meaning as He follows the name with the humiliating question, "Do you truly love me?" (21:15), especially as the word He uses is the strongest word for love *(agapao)* and seems to imply a doubt of the disciple's devotion. There is also a little hint in the words, "more than these," reminding him of his claims of superior devotion the night on which Peter betrayed Jesus. And in the threefold question as it is at length repeated, there is an unmistakable allusion to the threefold denial on that dreadful night. But Peter appeals to his Lord's omniscience, and using a less intense word *(phileo)* than Christ had used for love, he answers, "Yes, Lord . . . you know that I love you" (21:15). The Lord accepts the answer and then gives him the first apostolic charge, "Feed My lambs" (21:15). A second time Christ asks the question in the very same words, still using the stronger term for love, and the second time Peter answers with the weaker profession, and the Lord adds the second apostolic charge, "Take care of my sheep" (21:16). The third time Jesus asks the question, using now at length the same word for love which Peter had employed. Peter, grieved that he had again been doubted, appeals most solemnly to Christ's all-searching wisdom and repeats his former asseveration, "Lord, you know all things; you know that I love you" (21:17). Then Jesus gives the third apostolic command and the tenderest of all, "Feed my sheep" (21:17), giving him that special ministry of consolation to the weak and tired which we find so exquisitely fulfilled in Peter's epistle of consolation.

One lesson more is to be learned; it is the lesson of self-crucifixion, the surrender and subjugation of Peter's strong self-will and the suppression of his strong hand and curious inquiring mind with respect to others, even to John, his truest friend. "Someone else will dress you and lead you where you do not want to go" (21:18), is the message which sends him forth henceforth with bowed spirit and head to follow his Lord to the very cross itself. The other message with respect to John, "What is that to you? You must follow me" (21:22), silences all his questionings, takes his eyes off all but Jesus, and lays at last all that is left of Simon, son of John, in the bottomless sepulcher of his risen Lord.

CHAPTER 8

TEN MIRACLES IN THE GOSPEL OF JOHN

We find 10 remarkable miracles in John, which are "signs" as well as wonders.

THE FIRST MIRACLE
John 2:1–11
1. The marriage at Cana.

This miracle was especially, as indeed all Christ's miracles were, a sign as well as a wonder, setting forth many underlying spiritual truths. This sign was especially significant of the whole teaching of John's gospel, expressed in a single sentence; its chief lesson is the failure of the life of nature, and the deeper and fuller life which Jesus brings us in the new creation. The feast and wine of Cana represent earth's highest felicity, and the failure of Cana's wine expresses the blight which has fallen on all our human life and happiness. The new wine which Jesus brings is the figure of that divine life which He has come to impart to our lost humanity. All He needs is that the earthly vessel of our being shall be empty and then filled with the living water of His Holy Spirit, and that we shall begin to pour it out in love and service. We find that it has become new wine, making all life a marriage feast and a foretaste of the marriage supper of the Lamb. He that would enter into this blessed life must not forget the charge of Mary to the servants at Cana, "Do whatever he tells you" (2:5). As we follow His word in faith and obedience, we shall find, as they did, that all our wants are supplied at His bidding, and our life's deepest extremities transformed into occasions of overflowing blessing.

There is also in the marriage scene an obvious hint of that divine relationship with Himself, into which Jesus has come to bring us, as the Bridegroom of His Church, and the satisfaction of the deepest affections of the consecrated heart, so that back of this picture there shines, in living characters, not only the glorious word Life, but the still loftier name of Love. There is also a delightful suggestion of the sympathy of Jesus with all human life in its innocent joys and the pure affections and pleasures of that sweet sanctuary which His own example has ever hallowed, the home.

THE TEMPLE CLEANSED
John 2:13–22
2. The cleansing of the temple.
Among the deeper teachings of this impressive miracle may be mentioned:

a. The authority of Jesus over the institutions of Judaism and the sanctuary of His Father's worship. This act was a bold assumption of His Messiahship.

b. The typical meaning of the temple as the symbol of His own body, and especially His mystical body, the Church, gives a deeper spiritual importance to His act of authority and judgment. He refers in the passage to this typical significance and speaks of His own body as the true temple which was to be destroyed and raised up again. The conception of the Christian Church as the body and also as the temple of Christ is common to the New Testament epistles. In this aspect the miracle emphasizes the necessity of the purity of the Church and her separation from the world, and especially all worldly methods for her support. It would not be hard to find in a majority of the churches of today many a counterpart of the oxen, the sheep, the doves, and the money changers of the ancient temple. We see it in the spirit of worldly conformity in the lives of many Christians; in the unhallowed entertainments which so often defile the sanctuary of God, covered by the flimsy excuse of the need of helping out the finances of the church; in the hired worldlings that so often lead the service of praise with the flavor of the opera or the associations of the beer garden concert; and alas, in the mercenary spirit that too often controls the very ministry itself and reproaches the name of the Master. The scourge of small cords which the Master used might explain many of the petty trials, afflictions, disappointments and failures of many a church which does not understand the chastening of its God and the lessons of its barrenness and failure.

c. The miracle, however, has a more personal application to the individual heart. If the Lord would come into this individual temple, it, too, must be cleansed. But He Himself is the only true Deliverer, and sometimes the first stage of His work is one of deep pain and sharp chastisement. As the first miracle teaches us the lesson of the new life, the second emphasizes the necessity of purity as the result of love and the very element of all Christ's blessings and teachings.

FAITH WITHOUT SIGHT
John 4:46–54
3. The royal official's son.
The emphatic lesson of this miracle is, as we have already shown, the neces-

sity of faith as the condition of Christ's work and blessing, especially the faith that rises above the visible and rests on His simple word. This also becomes a sign of the special teaching of John, and is an object lesson in the beginning of the gospel, of the principle which He declares in words at the end; "Blessed are those who have not seen and yet have believed" (20:29). Over more than 20 miles of intervening space we see the instant working of Christ's mighty word and this man's immediate faith. With explicit detail it is added that the fever abated the very hour the man believed.

We see here, also, two stages of faith: faith, in the first instance, before he saw the result (4:50); and faith afterwards in its fuller developments when he and his household witnessed the consummation of the miracle: "So he and all his household believed" (4:53). The first was a belief in Christ's word of healing, the second was a complete committal of his heart to Christ Himself in His character and teachings, and a deep and settled confidence arising from his deeper knowledge of Christ. This is what the apostle expresses when he says, "I know whom I have believed" (2 Timothy 1:12).

THE GREAT PHYSICIAN
John 5:1–14
4. The invalid man at Bethesda.
The emphatic teaching of this miracle is the restoring ministry of Jesus in contrast with all man's superstitions and human attempts to help himself. The pool of Bethesda, with all its supposed virtues, is a fair specimen of man's various methods of help and healing both for soul and body. The very corruptions of the passage are an amusing hint of the foolish superstitions that human religions and remedies have heaped up through the centuries, and the wretched failure of all for nearly half a century to help this poor sufferer is a fair commentary on the value of man's best attempts to save himself. It is scarcely necessary to explain that the words of verse four about the angel troubling the waters are an interpolation and do not belong to the text.

The sufferer, too, is an excellent illustration both of the physical and spiritual condition of most sinners. His greatest need is strength, his chief symptom, impotence both of muscle and of will. In healing him the Lord pays no regard to the pool of Bethesda or his feeble complaints about getting somebody to help him when the waters are troubled, but simply asks him if he has will enough, or will exercise sufficient desire to choose to be whole.

Faith an Act of Will
The Lord here teaches us that both in spiritual and physical healing the secret of faith is a decisive act of will, and the moment we are ready to commit ourselves to God, definitely and irrevocably, He is willing to carry us through. Therefore, Christ requires of this man an instantaneous and

decisive act of faith, "Get up! Pick up your mat and walk" (5:8). And the moment he obeys, the power already communicated to his will passes into his entire being, and the victim of nearly 40 years is well.

This miracle led to an important discussion about the limitations of the Sabbath which we shall elsewhere refer to. We have already seen that the fact of Christ's so often healing on the Sabbath was directly designed to rebuke the prevailing idea that sickness was a purely secular thing, and the physician's art a matter of worldly business. Jesus ever taught that the body was as sacred as the soul, and divine healing as much a part of His sacred ministry as salvation.

Another hint is given in this miracle of the spiritual cause of his diseases. This was not always the case, but in the present instance it is certain that the long and weary sufferings of this man's life were the direct results of his own personal sin, and that the continuance of his healing would depend upon a life of purity and obedience, while the neglect of this would bring him still more aggravated judgments.

THE MULTITUDE FED
John 6:1–14
5. The feeding of the five thousand.
We notice in this miracle a beautiful progress in the spiritual truths unfolded by these signs.

The last miracle revealed Jesus as the Restorer of life, this as the Sustainer and Support of both our spiritual and physical life—the Living Bread by whom our entire being must be supplied with vital strength from day to day. The bread distributed to these multitudes did not cease with the setting sun on those Galilean hills, but still through all the ages since His ascension, it has been repeated, not always to the multitudes, but to every single heart that will come to Him and feed upon Him.

Some of the details which John gives us of this miracle are richly instructive. Two of the disciples are introduced in the preliminary conversation, and their perplexity and unbelief stands out in striking contrast with His own calm faith and power. Philip, like many of us, sees only the vastness of the multitude; Andrew, only the smallness of the resources, the five loaves and two small fishes. But Jesus calmly commands them to go forward and make all the arrangements for the feast. When the few loaves and fishes have been brought to Him, He gave thanks, and distributes them through the disciples. As they hand them to the people, one by one, the bread is multiplied until all are satisfied, and the fragments that remain are enough to fill to overflowing the baskets of all the disciples.

We have here, therefore, not only a sign of the Living Bread which we ourselves can feed upon, but of our responsibility to give it to the world, and of the sufficiency of the feeble resources we may possess for our work. If we only bring them to Him and go forth with His blessing in the simple steps of faith and obedience, then not only will we have enough for the world's need, however wide the world of our work may be, but when the work is done, our own baskets shall be overflowing, and our own souls shall have been blessed, replenished, and strengthened a hundredfold.

THE TEMPEST STILLED
John 6:16–21
6. The stilling of the tempest.

This is a revelation of Christ as He meets the next need of our human life. In our trials and dangers Christ is the Deliverer and Comforter.

First, He lets trial come to them, nay, often sends them forth before Him alone in the midst of the storm and the darkness of the night. So He sent His little Church out into the future without His visible presence, and knowing the tempests of persecution and opposition that were to assail her through the long night of the Dark Ages. So also He sends forth each of us upon the path of life, through waves and clouds and storms; but we need not fear if He has sent us.

Second, He sees us from the mountaintop, and, indeed, is praying for us there amid all the tempests' rage; nor will He allow the trial to become too great, but will come in the right moment.

Third, His coming to us as a spiritual presence, both in the Church's history and in the individual heart, is often misunderstood and unperceived. We are even afraid of the form of our Lord, as unbelief distorts it, and even changes it, until it is a structure of terror. But we may always know Him by His voice, "It is I; don't be afraid" (6:20). The true remedy for all our trials is just this personal Christ. He does not say it is morning, or it is calm weather, but, "It is I." Not in circumstances, nor in ourselves, but in His blessed presence, is our security and consolation.

Fourth, there is something better still: He is coming in person, perhaps on the tempest and billows of the wildest storm that the Church has ever known; but when He comes, it will be true again, "immediately the boat reached the shore where they were heading" (6:21). Her trials will be past, and long deferred hopes will be realized, and she will be where tempests cease and surges swell no more.

THE BLIND MAN HEALED
John 9:1–38
7. The blind man at Jerusalem.

This is also a progressive unfolding of Jesus, now as the Light of the world; and not only the Light, but the Giver of sight as well as external light; and the Quickener of all our powers of spiritual vision, if we are but willing to acknowledge our blindness and receive Him as our Teacher. Many definite lessons are taught us by this remarkable case of healing.

a. We learn that disease is not always caused by sin, but is sometimes permitted in order that the power of God to heal may be more signally displayed. This man's blindness was not the result of special sin, either on his own part or his parents', but that the works of God might be made manifest in him, that is, of course, in his healing. What a blessing it would be if we would ever feel that our troubles have been permitted, not that we should sink under them, but that God might have an adequate occasion to show what He can do in our deliverance.

b. He definitely implies that his blindness was not the work of God, but of another hand. The works of God were to be manifested in his healing. Not only was this Christ's work, but the Father's work which He had come to do; and so He seems to imply that when He shall have gone, night will again begin to fall upon the world, and the works of the Father in healing and restoring wrecked humanity will in some measure, cease, not through lack of the Father's will, but rather of a willing instrument (9:4–5).

c. The method of this man's healing was through a double sign: first, the anointing of his eyes with clay, and second, the washing away of the clay in the pool of Siloam. Did Christ mean by this double sign to intimate the cause and the cure of our spiritual blindness; clay implying the touch of earth which has dimmed our vision, and then the pool, significant of the sent One, representing the washing from on high by which earth's clay is put away and our eyes are opened to the heavenly vision?

Not a Remedy

To say that this application was the use of a remedy for his blindness and was a recognition of human remedies seems too absurd to need answer. If the clay was the remedy, it seems strange that he was not healed until it was washed away. If the pool was the remedy, why should it not be as efficacious in other cases? This was a case where no remedy could avail, for he was a man born blind, and remedy means something adapted to produce a result. Now nothing could be adapted in this case to produce the result, because it was impossible; therefore these two acts were but symbols of the divine touch and of the deeper spiritual lessons unfolded, as today, the anointing of oil in the name of the Lord is not a means of cure, but it is a visible sign of the divine touch upon the suffering one.

d. The testimony of this man is full of manly courage and keen discernment. He faces the whole synagogue and stands fearlessly for his Deliverer, amazed that anybody could doubt that One to whom God could give such power was a true Teacher and divine Messenger. Like many still who are not afraid to witness for all that God has done for them, his persecution ended in his being expelled from the synagogue. But like every similar trial, it brought him a greater blessing, for then the Master met him and led him into a deeper revelation of His own character and love; and prostrate at Jesus' feet his spiritual vision was now open and he recognized and worshiped the Son of God as his own Savior and Lord. It teaches us that as we are true to Christ and to the light and blessing He gives us, He will lead us on and more freely meet us in every trial and suffering with the higher revelation of Himself.

HIS SUPREME MIRACLE
John 11:1–45
8. The resurrection of Lazarus.

This completes the progress of development in this series of Christ's miracles, unfolding the last and highest stage of His work of grace and power, not only as the Restorer, Comforter, Sustainer and Healer of His people, but as the Conqueror of death and the Author of resurrection life. No other miracle of resurrection can be compared to this. Here corruption had already begun its work, and only Omnipotence could ever call back the spirit now four days in the world of the unseen. There was no possible cavil against this miracle. The Pharisees were silenced before its majesty and felt that their only resource was violence and murder.

It is not necessary to repeat here what has been said elsewhere upon this passage further than to call attention to the faith which He sought to awaken in Martha's mind, and which, there can scarcely be a doubt, He saw in Mary's simpler heart, but, above all, to the sublime faith of the Lord Himself. No mightier prayer has ever been uttered than this, "Father, I thank you that you have heard me" (11:41). It is the pattern of victorious faith in the hour of all our trials, in the face of every dark disaster and consuming sorrow. It will open the gates of brass and break in pieces the doors of iron, and bring to us every deliverance consistent with the will of God and the possibilities of faith.

It was also the foreshadowing of the future resurrection. His words to Martha seem to include two classes who shall take part in the stupendous change which shall occur at His coming. First, there will be those who, like Lazarus, have long been sleeping in their graves, of whom it shall be true, "He who believes in me will live, even though he dies" (11:25). But secondly, there will be those who will be still alive at His appearing, and of them the next sentence shall be also true, "whoever lives and believes in me will never die" (11:26). Thus also does this miracle become a sign of spiritual truth, foreshadowing the resurrection and containing the pledge and guarantee of every victory and blessing we need to claim from Him who is still for each one of us, as we will receive Him and trust Him, the Resurrection and the Life.

HIS VOLUNTARY SURRENDER
John 18:4–12
9. The prostration of the officers who came to arrest Him.

There is no doubt that this manifestation of Christ's power was miraculous and was designed to impress these men with His ability to resist their force if He so desired, and with the perfect voluntariness of His surrender and submission to their hands. Perhaps, also, it was designed to give weight to His demand that His own disciples should be exempted from arrest. "If you are looking for me, then let these men go" (18:8), is the condition of which He yields Himself to their power.

This incident gives a sublime meaning to all the events that immediately followed, culminating with His death. It makes His crucifixion an act of perfect self-sacrifice, and invests the cross with all the grandeur of infinite love. Indeed, this is the view which predominates in John's picture of the last sufferings and death of Christ. The darker shadows are all omitted from the picture, and the cross is represented, not as His defeat and humiliation, but as the hour when the Son of Man was glorified. Therefore, the garden scene of conflict and agony is omitted and we behold Him rather as the Master of the situation, dictating His own terms to the very officers who stand before Him. So again, in the presence of the Sanhedrin He stands in holy majesty, not challenging a single word of testimony against Him. So, in Pilate's judgment hall He is the real judge, and Pilate himself the witness for His innocence. So, even on the cross the pall of darkness is omitted and the parting word is a shout of victory.

THE LAST MIRACLE
John 21:1–10
10. The second catch of fishes.

This is the last sign recorded in this gospel, and its significance is connected with the great theme of service for Christ to which the apostles were now to be called in a higher and mightier sense than during His earthly ministry.

a. There is an undoubted allusion to the former catch of fishes three years before and its significance of their first call to apostolic service. This would naturally be associated with a similar call, although of course, in a higher sense.

b. There is a suggestion in the background of the miracle, of their having in some measure gone back from their high calling and begun at last to falter in their faith and courage. And so the lesson is in some sense a message to the Master's discouraged and unfaithful disciples, those who, doubting their

Master's faithfulness, have gone back to some old place of worldly compromise or earthly occupation, from which He had previously separated them. In such a place it is a great mercy if, like the seven disciples, we too have a wretched time and find all our efforts unavailing and lost.

c. The appearance of Jesus on the shore in the gray dawn was unrecognized; and the disciple who is out of his Lord's will, will be very likely to miss even the vision of his Lord through the blinding influence of unbelief and worldly occupation.

d. The command of Christ to cast the net on the other side and the immediate results in the miraculous catch of fishes, reveal the Master. John is the first to recognize Him, because his spirit was the least clouded by unbelief, and Peter is the first to plunge for the shore. The other disciples followed in a little fishing boat, dragging the loaded net and landing it, with Peter's help, with its enormous store of great fishes, every one of which is safely landed and the net unbroken. All this is so different from the former miracle, where the net broke and the ship began to sink, and Peter in guilty awe, begged the Master to depart from him, because he felt unworthy of His presence, that it must itself have suggested to their minds the higher lessons it has taught the Church of service for Christ and the Church.

e. The chief of these lessons is the higher service upon which they were now to enter into fellowship with their risen Lord, and of which Peter, who had just dragged the net to land, was to be the first illustrious example through his harvest of souls on the day of Pentecost. They were to learn the vanity and selfishness of all their wisdom and strength in the Master's work, and the necessity of His presence and guidance as they cast the gospel net into the sea of sinful men. Only as He stood upon the shore were they able to cast it upon the right side, and only as they spoke and acted in fellowship with Him would they be able to bring to land the souls they sought to save. But henceforth that presence and power was to be their resource.

Henceforth, the imperfect work which had ended in their desertion and denial of the Lord was to be repeated no more. Abiding in Him they should bring forth much fruit and their fruit should remain. Their fishes should be brought to land, and in the great day should be all counted upon the heavenly shore, like the great fishes on the Galilean morning, the glorious and eternal memorials of their work.

Not only so, but their morning meal upon the beach, upon the very fishes which they had caught, was intended to teach them that their work should be their future reward, and that in a very blessed sense they should feed upon its fruits, both now and in the eternal morning. In a little while, for every true worker, the vision will be fulfilled, the last long night of sorrow will be over, and the golden shore will be just ahead, with His blessed face and His beckoning hand, calling us to His presence. One last plunge like

Peter's into the dark waters, and we shall be there; the last wave shall be passed, the last shadow gone; and as He seats us at His table and says to us, "Come and have breakfast" (21:12), we shall know it is the Lord; and we shall recognize among the richest joys and recompenses of the eternal banquet the tears we have dried on earth, the sins we have covered with His blood, the steps we have recalled from the paths of sin, the souls we have warned from death, the lives we have given to His love, and the blessed ones we shall find awaiting us in His presence and hailing us as the instruments of their eternal happiness.

CHAPTER 9

CHRIST'S DISCOURSES IN JOHN 3–4

T he Gospel of John contains several discourses of the Lord Jesus. Some of them were addressed to individuals, some of them were public addresses in the temple, and the last two were parting discourses to His immediate disciples at the table and on the way to the garden. Let us first notice two of His personal discourses, the first with Nicodemus, the second with the woman of Samaria.

THE NEW BIRTH AND THE NEW LIFE
John 3
1. The necessity of the new birth and the new life.

It is more than knowledge, and it is essential to all true spiritual knowledge. Nicodemus can say "We know" (3:2), but Jesus replies, "No one can see the kingdom of God unless he is born again" (3:3). The very first glimpse of spiritual truth is impossible without the new birth. Nicodemus was, undoubtedly, a man of superior morality, but morality without spiritual life can no more lift the soul into the kingdom of God than nature and pruning can change a bramble into a man, or even into an apple tree.

A poor man once brought the two hands of a clock to a watchmaker to be repaired, complaining that they would not keep time. The watchmaker laughed at his ignorance and told him to go home and bring the clock, or, at least, the works of the clock. The man explained that the clock was all right, the trouble was all in the hands, that they would not keep proper time. He went away complaining that the tradesman wanted to draw him into an unnecessary bill for the repairing of the clock and trying to find some other workman that would repair his irregular clock hands.

A good many people are like the poor man, trying to repair the hands of their poor broken-down human nature, not knowing or thinking that the fatal ruin is in the deeper springs of the heart, and that what they need is not reformation, but regeneration.

2. The nature of regeneration.

It is described as a new birth; elsewhere it is called a new creation. It is the addition of a new element in human nature, namely, spiritual life—spoken of in the latter Scriptures as nothing less than a new man. It is not the creation of new intellectual faculties or physical powers, but a new spiritual principle. Here it is contrasted with John's baptism, "born of water" (3:5). This is more, being born from above and of the Spirit. Again, it is contrasted with being born of the flesh. This term flesh includes not only the physical, but also the psychical nature.

It is not always possible to perceive the processes, any more than it is to follow the viewless wind, but we may know the reality and power of both by their effects.

Regeneration is not complete sanctification; it is the birth, not of an Adam, full grown, but of a feeble infant; but it will mature into all the fullness of the stature of a man in Christ, and it is real and complete in all its parts, in its infancy, as in its manhood, just as the babe is as perfectly human as its grandfather, though not as old or as fully developed.

3. The Author of the new birth is the Holy Spirit.

He is the source of all life, and His highest work is to bring souls into the life of God. The regeneration of the soul is as divine a result as the creation of a world, and involves the putting forth of a mightier effort of omnipotence (John 3:5, 8).

4. The new birth is brought about through the gospel of the Lord Jesus Christ.

Therefore, the Lord Jesus adds the beautiful words from the 13th to the 18th verses respecting His coming and the necessity of faith in Him.

The new life is received by believing in the Son of God, even as the wounded Israelites received life and healing by looking at the uplifted serpent of brass in the midst of the camp. The ancient symbol vividly expresses both sides of the process of salvation. The uplifted serpent prefigured the crucified Savior, held up as the object of our faith, and the steadfast gaze upon it finely expresses the look of faith toward Jesus, by which the soul receives His imparted life.

And in the closing sentences the Lord refers to the instrumentality of the truth in the great work of regeneration. The new creation, like the old, begins with the coming in of Light (3:19). And they who receive the Light are soon led into the life of God, but they who hate and reject the Light receive a double condemnation, simply on the ground of its rejection. "This is the verdict: Light has come into the world, but men loved darkness instead of light because their deeds were evil" (3:19).

SPIRITUAL LIFE, WORSHIP AND SERVICE
John 4:10–38

1. Spiritual life.

The Lord sets forth the blessedness of the life which He has come to bring into our hearts by the figure of the water of Sychar. Like all of her race, this poor woman had been seeking for life from the broken cisterns of earthly pleasure, but Jesus reveals to her the deeper fountains of life which she may have from Him, and henceforth carry in her very heart, as a well of water in her, springing up into everlasting life.

2. Spiritual worship.

He next leads her thoughts from her sectarian prejudices and her external ritualism to the higher principles of true religion which He had come to unfold. He points to the fact that God was not confined to places or temples made with hands, but that His true temple is the spirit of man, and the worship which He requires is the spiritual devotion of the heart, the conformity of the life to His word and truth, and the knowledge and love of Him in His divine Fatherhood.

"True worshipers will worship the Father in spirit and truth, for they are the kind of worshipers the Father seeks. God is spirit, and his worshipers must worship in spirit and in truth" (4:23–24).

3. Spiritual service.

Although verses 32 to 38 were addressed to His own disciples after the woman left, they contain the true sequel to the former discourse. From the figure of the natural harvest now ripening upon the fields, He passes to the thought of the great spiritual harvest to which He was calling His disciples, and of which He had just given them an illustration in the salvation of this woman, and the still larger fruitage which was coming, even as He spoke, in the thronging Samaritans whom she brought to Him. He tells them that such service is the very food and nourishment of His own soul, and will bring to them, not only the partnership of His joy, but a glorious recompense besides, in the hour of His coming. There are wages now which the true worker receives from day to day, but there is a still more blessed partnership in the harvest itself, for "the reaper draws his wages, even now he harvests the crop for eternal life" (4:36). And then He refers to the indirect results of our work through the work of others, and especially of those that we have led to Christ, as illustrated in the beautiful example of this woman who has not only been saved herself, but has now gone forth and multiplied the fruit in the salvation of hundreds of others. So, He teaches them that their work shall thus involve the fellowship of others, and together they shall share the eternal recompense, "The sower and the reaper may be glad together" (4:36).

One more lesson He adds in connection with this spiritual harvest, namely: the necessity of immediate and prompt action. We are always in danger of dreaming of the future, but in spiritual service opportunity is a passing angel and must be held by the hand of instant decision. "Do you not say, 'Four months more and then the harvest'? I tell you, open your eyes and look at the fields! They are ripe for harvest" (4:35). And as in the natural, so also in the spiritual husbandry, the fields will not wait our convenience or caprice, but the ripened grain will perish if it is not garnered. Every day brings its irrevocable opportunities, and if lost they, at least, will never return.

CHAPTER 10

CHRIST'S DISCOURSES IN JOHN 5–6

Continuing the discourses of our Lord in the Gospel of John we come to:

CHRIST AND THE FATHER
John 5:17–23

1. **His first public claim to deity.**

In this passage Christ makes His first public claim in the presence of the Jews of equality with His Father, and gives this as the reason for His healing the invalid man on the Sabbath. In doing this He was simply coworking with God, who, from the beginning of the creation, has exercised His active omnipotence every moment in sustaining the universe and giving life and strength to all beings. Christ was doing only the same thing in restoring strength to this man on the Sabbath day. The Jews perfectly understood His meaning, and now, with a double ground of hostility against Him because He has insulted the Sabbath law and His alleged blasphemy in claiming equality with God, they began seriously to plot His destruction. Christ follows up His statement by declaring His absolute dependence upon the Father for all His works, and at the same time His equal partnership in all the Father's works, and then announcing that He is yet to manifest still mightier works in the Father's name, which will fill them with astonishment. Two of these He specifies, namely, the raising of the dead, and the prerogative of judgment upon every human soul. The purpose of all this He declares to be the Father's glory, that "all may honor the Son just as they honor the Father" (5:23).

2. **The Son's message and gift of love and salvation to men in His Father's name.**

Invested with this high authority and power, He comes to men and now offers them through faith in His word, the gift of everlasting life. First, it is a present quickening through His living voice and almighty power: "a time is coming and has now come when the dead will hear the voice of the Son of God and those who hear will live" (5:25). This, of course, refers to the spiritual life which Jesus now imparts to the soul dead in trespasses and sin. Second, it is a life that delivers from condemnation and judgment by the law, and which takes us out of the place of guilt altogether and gives us eternal acquittal and justification through the decree of the very One who is Himself the Judge (5:24–27). Third, it unfolds the future resurrection of the body (5:29). This, then, is Christ's great message and gift to men in His Father's name: life spiritually, life judicially, and life immortal in the resurrection.

3. The credentials of this divine message.

What evidence does He bring to prove His high authority and the truth of His wonderful message? He does not ask them to receive Him on His own mere word, but He brings four great credentials (5:31–39):

> a. The witness of John, which they have already accepted in other respects.
> b. The witness of His Father, which has been explicitly given in His behalf.
> c. The witness of His own works as proof of His divinity.
> d. The very Scriptures on which they founded all their institutions and hopes bear unequivocal testimony to Him who is the fulfillment of all prophecy and the end of all the teachings of even Moses, in whom they trust (5:46–47)—credentials they cannot and do not attempt to dispute.

4. Their rejection of Him and the message of love He brings.

In the face of all this evidence they willfully refused to receive Him. "You refuse to come to me to have life" (5:40). Or it might be made even more emphatic, "You will not to come." It is a perverse obstinacy in spite of truth and evidence. The reason for their unbelief He also tells them. First, it is because they have not the love of God in them; their heart is not single unto Him, and where this is the case there can never be the true light of faith. Secondly, they are under the influence of human opinions and selfish aims. "How can you believe if you acccept praise from one another, yet make no effort to obtain the praise that comes from the only God?" (5:44). What a solemn intimation of the danger of a divided heart in perverting the soul and blinding it even to the light of life. And yet, He warns them as He closes that, although so unwilling to believe Him with all the light and evidence He brings, they will become the willing dupes of a thousand impostors, and perhaps, at last, of the very Anti-christ who will deceive them as the counterfeit of the true Messiah.

CHRIST, THE LIVING BREAD

This address, as we have already seen, was given in Galilee at the close of His ministry there, and immediately after the feeding of the 5,000 and perhaps on the Sabbath of the Passover which was then being celebrated in Jerusalem. Its one great theme, the revelation of Jesus Christ in His person, as the satisfaction of all the soul's needs, stands in contrast with their earthly expectations of a Messiah, who was to give them mere human bread and relieve them from their temporal burdens and disasters. They were eager to make Christ their king if He would always feed them with such bread as His great miracle had furnished, but when He came to lead them to a closer fellowship with Himself and to require a deeper and more spiritual apprehension of Him, they turned away and rejected Him altogether.

This discourse consists of seven sections, marked by the interruptions of His audience, and rising in succession to the final climax when the crisis is reached and their decision is made.

1. The True Bread in contrast with the food that spoils.

"Do not work," He says, "for food that spoils, but for food that endures to eternal life, which the Son of Man will give you. On him God the Father has placed his seal of approval" (6:27). This latter expression seems to refer to the ancient habit of putting a stamp or trademark on bread to indicate that it was the genuine production of a responsible tradesman. Christ bears the stamp of heaven as the True Bread of the world. They are seeking rather that which satisfies their earthly appetites, and He desires to elevate their thoughts and desires to the true source of spiritual life.

2. The true way to receive this Bread.

"Do not work," He says to them, "for food that spoils" (6:27). "What," they ask, "must we do to do the works God requires?" And He answers, "The work of God is this: to believe in the one he has sent" (6:28–29). The one thing He requires of you is not that you labor for His free salvation, but that you receive it with simple trust, by believing on Him whom He has sent.

3. The heavenly character of this Bread in contrast, even with the manna of the desert.

They now appeal (6:30–33) to their own history and the great miracle of Moses in giving them manna in the desert for 40 years, and they ask for some corresponding sign of His claims to the faith which He has demanded of them. In this request we see already the beginning of their perverse unbelief. Had He not already given them in the miracle in Galilee a sign as great as the miracle of Moses? So He does not meet them on their own plane by contrasting the greatness of His power with that of Moses, but seeks to raise their thoughts to a more spiritual plane by telling them that even the bread which Moses gave them, with all its manifestation of power, was not from heaven, after all, but mere earthly food, and that even if He should give them such bread continually, it would not be the real satisfaction they needed; and therefore He brings them bread from heaven itself, even the life which man has lost, and which only the divine love can restore.

4. Simpler and fuller explanation of this spiritual Bread.

For a moment they seem to grasp His meaning, and they respond, "Sir . . . from now on give us this bread" (6:34).

He tells them that this bread is nothing less than His own personal life imparted to them. It is all wrapped up in Himself. It is not "I give the bread," but "I am the Bread of Life," and to possess it there must be a personal relation to the fellowship with Him.

This is the source of the only true rest and satisfaction. "He who comes to me will never go hungry, and he who believes in me will never be thirsty" (6:35).

This is available and welcome to all who will truly receive it. There is no barrier in the way of any willing heart, either on the part of His Father or Himself. For Himself, He is so willing to receive any seeking soul that He puts on record the most absolute and unconditional of all His promises, "whoever comes to me I will never drive away" (6:37). This is an invitation which admits anybody and everybody who is desirous not only of the saving mercy, but also of the sanctifying, satisfying and all-sufficient grace of Jesus to the last moment of life. Nor is His Father less willing to welcome sinful men. His very purpose in sending the Son, and His very will for men is that they should thus be saved and satisfied. And even if Christ were less willing than He is, He would yet be bound by His Father's will, to save men (6:38–39).

This life and satisfaction shall be eternal, reaching down beyond the grave and including the resurrection of the body in the last day (6:40).

5. Opposition and reiterations.

Next we see the opposition of the Jews to His teachings concerning His own person as their life, and reiterations by Christ of this especial truth, with an additional reference now not only to His life, but also to His death (6:41–51).

The opposition of the Jews was on account of His high pretensions in contrast with what they knew of His obscure human origin. "Is this not Jesus, the son of Joseph, whose father and mother we know? How can he now say, 'I came down from heaven'?" (6:42). Jesus answers them that no one can understand His divine character without divine teaching. "No one can come to me unless the Father who sent me draws him" (6:44). And this, He adds, lest they should excuse themselves by saying that the Father had not drawn them: "Everyone who listens to the Father and learns from him comes to me" (6:45). That is to say, the Father is teaching and willing to teach all who will learn; but they are not willing to be thus definitely taught and drawn. Then He adds two new thoughts to His former teaching, respecting the life He brings to men. First, the life it brings is not like the nourishment imparted by the manna, mere mortal life, but it is everlasting life. "He who believes has everlasting life. . . . Your forefathers ate the manna in the desert, yet they died" (6:47, 49). The other thought is that this life must come through His death: "This bread is my flesh, which I will give for the life of the world" (6:51).

6. This life must be received through vital union with the Person of Christ and living communion with Him.

More and more His hearers become perplexed with this idea of eating His flesh. He now adds to it the other expression, drinking His blood. These together express most perfectly the idea of an actual participation in His death and risen life. Like many since, they understood it literally, and naturally asked, how can this man give us His flesh to eat? Jesus, however, now explains that what He means is such a union with Him as He has with the Father, by virtue of which His life is constantly sustained not by natural means alone, but by the constant impartation of the divine life. "Just as the living Father sent me and I live because of the Father, so the one who feeds on me will live because of me" (6:57). And then He adds, to show how close the union thus involved is, "Whoever eats my flesh and drinks my blood remains in me, and I in him" (6:56). This was the constant support of His own physical and spiritual life, so that when tempted by the devil in the wilderness to make the stones into bread, He answered, "Man does not live on bread alone, but on every word that comes from the mouth of God" (Matthew 4:4). This was not only for Himself, but it is implied in the expression "man," not the Son of Man only.

7. This can be fully understood and realized through the Holy Spirit's teaching and after His death, resurrection and ascension.

Not in His present life among them as they see Him with their eyes and touch Him with their hands can He become to them fully the Living Bread. But after He has ascended to His Father's right hand and sent forth the Holy Spirit to be the teacher and revealer of His truth and grace, and to lead His disciples to know and receive Him in His fullness, then shall these words be understood and appreciated. "What," He says, "if you see the Son of Man ascend to where he was before! The Spirit gives life; the flesh counts for nothing. The words I have spoken to you are spirit and they are life" (John 6:62–63). Therefore Mary Magdalene, as she clasped His feet with her loving arms, must be taught that there was a higher touch and a more spiritual communion to which she must rise: "Do not hold on to me, for I have not yet returned to the Father. Go instead to my brothers and tell them, 'I am returning to my Father and your Father, to my God and your God' " (20:17).

This was too spiritual for their carnal hearts, and so we read, "many of his disciples turned back and no longer followed him" (6:66). And this is the reason today that the multitudes of professing Christians know little of these great spiritual mysteries. They bring them too close to Christ, and require too pure an element of living for their earthly tastes and aspirations.

SUMMING UP THE TEACHINGS OF THIS CHAPTER

a. The earthly bread is the type of the higher needs and supplies of our being, which Jesus comes to bring.

b. Jesus Christ, in His own person, is the Supply of all our needs and is able and willing to impart His own very life as the strength and support of our entire being, spirit, soul and body. God has put into this one ideal Man all that man needs and needs to be, and He offers Himself to each one of us as the very Substance of our life.

c. This divine provision began with His death for us as our ransom. His flesh was given for the life of the world in the sense of substitution, first. This therefore, is the primary meaning of drinking His blood, namely, partaking of the benefits of His death and atonement.

d. But there is a far deeper meaning. Not only His death, but His risen life becomes for us the source of life—not only did He give His life for us, but He also gives it to us. His blood represents His life, and His flesh represents, especially, His physical life. And both together express the fact that Jesus Christ, in His entire humanity, offers Himself to His people as their imparted life and strength; His holiness, love, joy, power and even His physical vitality will be the support and supply of our every spiritual and physical need.

e. In order to receive Him thus, there must be a very intimate union with Him expressed by the language "Whoever . . . remains in me, and I in him" (6:57). There must also be a habitual receiving of Him, expressed by the figure of eating and drinking, and also by the less figurative expressions, "he who comes to me," "he who believes in me" (6:35), etc.

f. Not in His earthly, but in His ascension life was this to be realized, and therefore, since Christ's resurrection, He has been real to His people as He could not be before (6:62).

g. We must be led into this knowledge of Christ and this best fellowship with Him by divine teaching. No man can thus come without the Father's drawing and the Spirit's revealing (6:44, 63, 65).

h. But the Father is always drawing and the Spirit always teaching, and the Son always ready to receive all that come. Nowhere in all His teachings, do we find such an assurance of the willingness of Christ to receive the soul that comes to Him as in the very midst of these present teachings. This is not the exclusive privilege of a favored class, but without limitation it is said of all who are willing to come, "Whoever comes to me I will never drive away" (6:37). This is true not only of the soul that comes to Christ for salvation, but just as true of every advancing stage of our Christian life; and, especially, of this deeper experience into which the Lord is ever waiting and willing to lead His hungry and thirsty children.

i. The climax of all this experience will be reached in the future resurrection. Therefore Christ adds repeatedly in this passage, "I will raise him up at the last day" (6:40). Then shall we know all that is involved in perfect union and fellowship with the person of our Lord, as we share both in our body, our spirit and our future glory, all the fullness of His life and all the riches of His glory.

CHAPTER 11

CHRIST'S DISCOURSES IN JOHN 7–9

T here were two discourses Jesus delivered at the Feast of Tabernacles.

THE LIVING WATER
John 7:16–38
The first, on the Living Water, consists of a number of broken paragraphs spoken successively during the feast, and culminating in the striking address delivered on the last day of the feast, recorded in verses 32–38. It might be divided into five sections:

1. **The condition of true spiritual knowledge.**
This seems to be intended as an answer to their question respecting His wonderful wisdom in view of His obscure origin. He then tells them the true principle on which the divine knowledge depends, namely, a right spirit and an obedient heart. "If anyone chooses to do God's will, he will find out whether my teaching comes from God" (7:17). He seems to imply that this is the reason why He Himself has been so divinely taught, because His own aim and spirit are true to the Father's glory (7:18). But still more must this be true of all who hear Him, if they would understand His doctrine, which is not to be apprehended by the mere intellect, but its true organ is the heart and the will. The word for "chooses" here is the strongest in the Greek language; literally, it means, "If any man *wills to do His will,* He shall know the doctrine." The things of God, especially the deeper truths of Christianity, must become living experiences. God loves us too well to give us more light than we will really follow, for it would but add the greater condemnation.

2. **Healing on the Sabbath.**
Jesus next proceeds to vindicate His own conduct in healing the invalid man on the Sabbath by citing the case of circumcision, which they frequently administered on the Sabbath and yet were held blameless, while He is ac-

471

cused of breach of the law by healing a sufferer on this day.

3. His origin.

He next bears witness again to His divine descent and His heavenly origin. Still, His enemies listen with exasperation, but so great is His hold upon the people that none of them dare to touch Him. At length, however, the Pharisees are compelled to make some show of boldness, and they send a band of officers to arrest Him (7:32).

4. "I am with you for only a short time."

Jesus intimates in these words that He will soon be withdrawn from their midst, and that many will seek Him in vain and, indeed, never find Him. Perhaps He refers to the mournful days which were coming so soon to them when, beset by their enemies and by the resistless legions of Rome, they should look in vain for their Messiah. Perhaps some of them even should remember how they had neglected and mocked His blessed teachings, but they should see Him no more—"Where I am, you cannot come" (7:34).

5. "Come to me and drink."

This was His great discourse on the last day of the feast.

It is the final Sabbath of the Feast of the Tabernacles, and processions of priests are carrying the vessels of water from the pool of Siloam and pouring it out on the sacred altar. Dense crowds fill all the courts, and the interest of the whole festival is at its height. Suddenly, in the midst of the celebration, Jesus lifts up His voice and cries aloud in words which, no doubt, run through all the corridors and courts, in the ears of thousands, "If anyone is thirsty, let him come to me and drink. Whoever believes in me, as the Scripture has said, streams of living water will flow from within him" (7:37–38). The allusion to the chief ceremony of the feast was so vivid, and the language so striking, while no doubt His manner added unutterable weight to the entire scene, that the profoundest impression was made upon multitudes of the hearers, and even the officers who had come to take Him were overwhelmed with awe and went away, not daring to touch Him. The address itself leads us into spiritual truths as deep and precious as the preceding chapter. In that Jesus had not only alluded to the feeding of the 5,000, but also to two of the most ancient and venerable types of Judaism, namely, the Passover which was being observed in Jerusalem, and the manna with which the people had been fed in the wilderness. In the present passage He alludes not only to the ceremony just being observed in the temple, but also to another of the most sacred of the Mosaic types, namely, the smitten rock of Horeb and the flowing water which had supplied the thirst of God's ancient people in the wilderness. Thus He dares to attribute to Himself two of the most significant of the types of their history by claiming to be at once the Bread and the Water of life. But true to the spirit of the New Testament, He carries the figure farther than Judaism could. Here it is not merely received in selfish enjoyment and blessing, but it is given forth in still larger streams of beneficence to others. The same figure had been alluded to in His conversation with the woman of Samaria, but here it is much bolder and grander. There, the grace of Jesus was presented as the fountain in her own heart, but here it is the overflowing floods of many rivers pouring out their fullness in blessing to the world.

The evangelist himself has given us the interpretation, referring as it does to the Holy Spirit as He was to be poured out upon the disciples at Pentecost and to become henceforth the impulse of Christian life and the separation and power of consecrated service. He adds that the Holy Spirit was not yet given, or, literally, was not yet, because Jesus was not yet glorified. It was necessary that the work of the Son should be finished on earth and He glorified at the Father's right hand before His divine Successor could come to administer the next stage of the kingdom of God. We may, therefore, believe that under the ancient dispensation and even during the life of Christ the Holy Spirit was not imparted to the people of God in His personal fullness as He has been since Christ's ascension. There is a solemn personal lesson for every one of us in the expression here used; not only was it true dispensationally, but it must ever be true individually: "The Holy Spirit will not be given until Jesus is fully glorified." He comes still when Christ is fully exalted and all is laid at His feet, and He comes not to exalt us or to witness to us, but to glorify still Jesus only in our lives and services.

JESUS THE LIGHT OF THE WORLD
John 8:12–9:41

Another beautiful custom connected with the Feast of Tabernacles is referred to in this discourse, namely, the hanging up of brilliant lamps in the Court of the Women. Pointing, perhaps, to these, Jesus exclaims, "I am the light of the world. Whoever follows me will never walk in darkness, but will have the light of life" (8:12). There may also have been an allusion to another Old Testament type, namely, the pillar of fire which led ancient Israel in the wilderness, thus connecting Christ with the whole system of Mosaic types, the manna in the wilderness, the rock in Horeb, and the guiding presence of the cloud and Shekinah.

1. The light of life.

Christ is the Light of life; not merely a teacher of truth in the abstract, but a practical and personal Guide. The light He gives is the light of life, that is, light that men can live by, shining on the path of duty, perplexity and trial, illuminating and cheering every step of Christian life. The essential condition is humble obedience. And the reason they could not understand it was because they were not willing to submit themselves to His will and direction.

2. The divine light.

It is divine light authorized by the witness of heaven and shed forth by One who has Himself come down from heaven and knows all worlds, and all the possibilities of existence, and all the secrets of time and eternity (8:14–19).

3. The indispensable light.

It is indispensable light, and without it they must perish in their sins (8:21–24).

4. The true light.

It is light which they themselves shall yet recognize as true, but too late to be of any avail for them. After they have rejected Him and wrecked themselves, they shall see their fatal error. Perhaps He intimates that some of them shall even then believe on Him (8:28).

5. The light that leads to liberty.

It is light that leads to liberty and holiness (8:41–47).

They are the slaves of a master whom they are not willing to acknowledge, and the subjects of a bondage more bitter than that of Egypt. "Everyone who sins is a slave to sin" (8:34). They are bound by its fetters, and notwithstanding all their claims of descent from Abraham, they are not only the captives, but the very children of Satan. But He is the great Liberator as well as the Light of the world. If they will believe the truth which He brings and enter into the Sonship which He offers to share with them, they shall become free from the power of guilt and sin, and rise to all the dignity of His own Sonship, and all the privileges of the freeborn children of God. Hence, the apostle says to those who receive Him, "Because you are sons, God sent the Spirit of his Son into our hearts, the Spirit who calls out, 'Abba, Father.' So you are no longer a slave, but a son" (Galatians 4:6–7). True spiritual freedom springs from the belief of the truth and personal union with the Son of God. To believe God's promises saves us from the consciousness of guilt and brings us into the power of full salvation. But this full salvation involves the indwelling presence and life of Christ Himself in our heart, as the divine and overcoming power that breaks the bonds of evil. "Through Christ Jesus the law of the Spirit of life set me free from the law of sin and death" (Romans 8:2). A mere abstract faith, therefore, is not enough; there must be a living fellowship with Christ. Therefore, He says to the new converts who have accepted His word, "If you hold to my teaching, you are really my disciples. Then you will know the truth, and the truth will set you free" (John 8:31–32). "So if the Son sets you free, you will be free indeed" (8:36). Is there any soul under the bondage of guilt? The remedy is Christ's blessed word of redemption and forgiveness. "I tell you the truth, whoever hears my word and believes him who sent me has eternal life and will not be condemned; he has crossed over from death to life" (5:24). Is there any soul under the power of sin? The same word waits to emancipate the soul, if it will but believe it, and step forth upon it. "You are already clean because of the word I have spoken to you" (15:3). Is there any soul bound by physical evil and suffering? Only let it believe His gracious word, that He has come to bear our sicknesses and carry our infirmities, and it has the strong and immovable resting place for a faith that can claim all needed strength and deliverance. Is there any soul oppressed by Satan's temptations? All it needs is to know the truth that it is free, and that he is a conquered foe, and to stand upon the glorious promise, "having disarmed the powers and authorities" (Colossians 2:15), "you will tread upon the lion and the cobra" (Psalm 91:13), and lo! it steps out into victory and claims its full redemption rights.

During the Civil War, some of the slaves were held by their former masters for many months after the Emancipation Proclamation had been issued, and the poor captives were helpless and hopeless in their ignorance of their new freedom; but when the message reached them they knew the truth, and the truth made them free. And they arose at once to claim their lawful rights under the President's decree. So the gospel is the divine proclamation of emancipation, and all men may claim it for themselves and enter into the fullness of their liberty. But not only have they the decree of liberty, but also the living power of the Son Himself, as the Captain of their salvation, to lead them into their freedom and conquer for them all the power that would resist their emancipation. Therefore, He adds, "So if the Son sets you free, you will be free indeed" (John 8:32).

6. The light in the valley.

It is light in the valley of the shadow of death (8:51–55).

Not only does this glorious light lead us forth from our captivity, as the pillar of cloud and fire led Israel out of Egypt, but it also goes down before us as the ark went through the Jordan into the valley and shadow of death. "If anyone keeps my word, he will never see death" (8:51). This does not mean that the act and effect of mortality will never touch his life. It means that his spiritual consciousness shall be lifted above it, and that, though the body may sink, and the eyes of our dearest friends may see what seems to be death, yet the triumphant spirit shall be carried above it and be so enwrapped with the presence of Christ and the consciousness of His enfolding life and indwelling joy that there shall be no real consciousness of death. The victorious spirit shall pass through without a shadow into the intenser, purer and more delightful joys of the heavenly world without a moment's interruption of its conscious life and perfect felicity. Has this not often been witnessed as the last experience of God's departing saints? Standing on the very brink of two worlds, they have whispered back to all around them. "There is no river here; it is light and joy." There was indeed no death.

7. The light of past ages.

It is the light of past ages, and ancient saints and prophets (8:56).

"Your father Abraham rejoiced at the thought of seeing my day; he saw it and was glad" (8:56). This was the light that shone in the lamps of fire that passed through Abraham's vision on the night of sacrifice. This was the light which rose on the altar of Mt. Moriah when Isaac was given back to his arms from the funeral pile. This was the light that shone above the midnight stars in the promise of the everlasting covenant and the future Seed—the Light of Ages.

8. The light of spiritual vision.

It is the light of spiritual vision (chapter 9). The connection of this chapter is uncertain. The sense seems to link with the eighth chapter which we have just been considering, but many judicious interpreters consider it really a part of chapter 10 and spoken at the Feast of Dedication a few months later. The passage (10:22), they think, points back to the whole preceding section, and not merely to the verses that immediately follow. If this were so there would be a double allusion in the figure of light still employed, not only to the healing of the blind man and the previous discourse about light, but also to the name often given to this feast as the Feast of Lights. One part of this imposing ceremony consisted of the suspension of burning lamps from day to day in the temple, in celebration of its deliverance from the abominations of Antiochus. On the other hand it seems more natural to connect the miracle of the closing words of John 9 with the discourse of John 8 respecting light. Without determining, therefore, the question of historical connection, we shall be guided by the spiritual significance of the two chapters and treat them as one discourse.

The lesson in the ninth chapter seems the true sequel and close to the previous address. It leads us up to the very highest aspect of light, as bringing not only external illumination, but what is more important, the power to receive it, and the internal vision which brings sight as well as light. What is the use of a thousand suns or a million lamps to a poor blind beggar? Therefore this is the true climax of His previous teaching. The Lord heals this poor blind man somewhere near the temple gates and then makes him an object lesson of deeper spiritual teaching, adding as He performs the miracle:

> "Neither this man nor his parents sinned," said Jesus, "but this happened so that the work of God might be displayed in his life. As long as it is day, we must do the work of him who sent me. Night is coming, when no one can work. While I am in the world, I am the light of the world." (9:3–5)

The subject of this miracle received something better than even his sight, for we find him springing into the freedom and boldness of a very beautiful faith, standing up in manly vindication of Christ before all the scorn and sarcasm of the Jewish rulers, and suffering even excommunication at last rather than compromise his testimony. Jesus comes to him in the hour of His expulsion and reveals Himself in His higher character as the Son of God; and the true heart that has followed the light that was previously given still follows Him and comes into all the blessedness of the life of faith. Jesus closes the chapter with a solemn reference to the readiness of the blind man to receive the light, in contrast with the willful self-conceit and blindness of the Pharisees, who, claiming that they had the light, remained in darkness, while this simple-hearted beggar, by taking the place of blindness and help-lessness, had entered into all the fullness of the light of God. The first condition, therefore, of spiritual vision is to see our blindness and the insufficiency of natural light and wisdom to bring us into the knowledge of God. This is the deeper teaching of the apostles. This was the lesson which Jewish pride and Jewish wisdom constantly stumbled at in later years, and which is hiding from modern culture the truth as it is in Jesus. "The man without the Spirit does not accept the things that come from the Spirit of God, for they are foolishness to him, and he cannot understand them, be-cause they are spiritually discerned" (1 Corinthians 2:14). A brilliant intel-lect is as helpless to know Jesus and the gospel without the special illumination of the Holy Spirit as the musical faculty is helpless to study mathematics, or the mathematical faculty to write the *Iliad* of Homer or the odes of Horace. We must have the mind of Christ even to understand the thoughts and words which Christ has spoken.

CHAPTER 12

CHRIST'S DISCOURSES IN JOHN 10–12

The next two discourses were delivered during the Feast of Dedication and the Feast of Passover.

THE GATE AND THE SHEPHERD
John 10

This discourse was delivered at Jerusalem during the Feast of Dedication. As we have already noticed, there is some uncertainty about the 22nd verse as to whether it looks backward or forward, to the discourse which precedes or that which follows; or does it include both? For our present purpose, however, as both sections of the discourse refer to the one theme, thus making it ethically but one address, we shall treat it as one discourse. There is an evident allusion implied in the figure to the conduct of the Jewish rulers and their blindness, selfishness, harshness and cruelty as false guardians of the flock of God which had been intrusted to their keeping—more especially to their harsh treatment of the blind man whom they had just expelled from the synagogue for being true to his conscience and the Savior. They had proved themselves to be false shepherds. In contrast with them the Lord now assumes the beautiful title and character which the Old Testament types and prophecies had made so familiar in connection with the hope of the Messiah, and contrasts the Good Shepherd with the selfish hirelings and the thieves and robbers who had usurped the place of shepherds in the flock of God and who so shamefully abused their trust and imposed upon the helpless flock. There are three divisions in the discourse around which the various thoughts may be clustered:

1. The Gate (verse 7).
2. The Shepherd (verse 2).
3. The Sheep (verses 14–15).

Let us keep clearly before our minds the two distinct figures running through this discourse, and then all the symbolism will become plain. These are the sheepfold and the flock.

With reference to the sheepfold, Christ is the gate; with reference to the flock, He is the Shepherd. There is a mistranslation in the 16th verse of our revised version which tends to confuse the figure and also to mislead in the deeper spiritual teaching. The true meaning is, "Other sheep I have which are not of this fold. Them also must I bring . . . and there shall be," not one fold, but "one flock." There may be many folds, that is, many branches of the visible Church among agencies for the nurture of Christians, but there is only one flock.

1. The Gate

This figure had been used in the symbolism of the tabernacle to denote the curtains by which the priests had access to the Holy Place, which was a type of our fellowship with the Lord and our place of privilege and blessing. The simple and fundamental idea is that Christ is the only way of access, both into the Church and the kingdom. The Church is not the gate of Christ, but Christ is the gate of the Church, and also of salvation in its every stage, and its full and final consummation. He is the gate of pardon, of holiness, of access and communion with God, of prayer, of power, of service, and of heaven. He is an open gate for all who will enter in, and yet He is a closed gate, shutting His people in so that they shall never perish, nor shall any pluck them out of His hand. And He is a personal gate; not our states or acts, not any ceremony, form or external condition, but union with Himself admits us to all the privileges and immunities of the flock. The one condition of salvation is union with Jesus Christ. This is the simplicity and glory of Christianity. It has but one gate, and the test of all false teachers and false ways is simply this, that they climb up some other way. The touchstone of Christianity is the name of Jesus, and its glory His person and His cross.

2. The Shepherd

This figure had been invested with peculiar beauty and sacredness in the Psalms of David and the prophetic visions of Ezekiel, and possessed a certain divine character which no mere human teacher would ever have dared to assume. Christ's application to Himself of the figure is a virtual claim of divinity. Twice, already, among His parables had He used this beautiful symbol of His own seeking love. He now applies it, not so much to the seeking of the lost, as to the care and nurture of the flock.

Five things are attributed to the Good Shepherd:

a. He loves and suffers for His flock. The Good Shepherd gives His life for His flock. The hireling makes no sacrifice, but seeks only his own interest and safety. The Good Shepherd suffers, and even sacrifices His life for His own (10:11, 15, 17).

The good shepherd lays down his life for the sheep. The hired hand is not the shepherd who owns the sheep. So when he sees the wolf coming, he abandons the sheep and runs away. Then the wolf attacks the flock and scatters it. The man runs away because he is a hired hand and cares nothing for the sheep. . . . I lay down my life—only to take it up again. No one takes it from me, but I lay it down of my own accord. I have authority to lay it down and authority to take it up again. (10:11–13, 17–18)

Thus did He anticipate and prepare His disciples for His approaching death; and thus, voluntarily, did He look forward to it Himself, as a willing sacrifice of love.

b. He knows His flock personally and calls them by name (10:2–14).

"He calls his own sheep by name. . . . I am the good shepherd; I know my sheep and my sheep know me" (10:3, 14). The Oriental shepherd is personally acquainted with each member of his flock. How beautifully Nathan describes this intimacy in Second Samuel 12:3. "The poor man had nothing except one little ewe lamb he had bought. He raised it, and it grew up with him and his children. It shared his food and drank from his cup, and even slept in his arms. It was like a daughter to him." Thus Jesus owns His sheep; for each of us He has a personal love and a personal voice, and, as the mother gives her whole heart to each of her children, although she may have many, so He loves us individually and perfectly. Thus, to His weeping disciple in the garden did He come on the resurrection morning, calling her by her own name. Thus did He adapt himself to the different temperaments of Martha and Mary, and thus each of us has learned to know Him. The voice is different from the written word; He speaks to us all in the latter, but to each of us He has besides a living voice which we may know and follow. It is the revealing of His person and love to the heart.

c. He leads His flock.

He calls his own sheep by name and leads them out. When he has brought out all his own, he goes on ahead of them, and his sheep follow him because they know his voice. But they will never follow a stranger; in fact, they will run away from him because they do not recognize a stranger's voice. (John 10:3–5)

He does not merely lead them by His command, but He precedes them in person. There is not a step of the difficult pathway which they must go but He has already gone before them all the way. There is not a hard place still where He pushes them out in advance, but they may always hear His voice in front saying, "Arise, let us go hence." The personal companionship of

Christ, and His direct and conscious guidance in every step of our pathway, is the most certain and delightful fact of Christian experience.

d. He feeds them, supplying all their needs and leading them into the fullness of His grace. "Whoever enters through me will be saved. He will come in and go out, and find pasture" (10:9). "I have come that they may have life, and have it to the full" (10:10). "He makes me lie down in green pastures,/ he leads me beside quiet waters" (Psalm 23:2). His word and its precious promises, His Holy Spirit, His tender consolation, His public ordinances, and all their blessed fellowship, instruction and inspiration, these are the pastures of His love and bounty, in which we find not only life, but the life more abundantly.

e. He keeps them, guards them, defends them, and will never let them fall from His hands or be lost from His flock:

> I give them eternal life, and they shall never perish; no one can snatch them out of my hand. My Father, who has given them to me, is greater than all; no one can snatch them out of my Father's hand. (John 10:28–29)

Locked in the double clasp of the Father and of the Son, the trusting soul is safe forever if it only heeds this simple condition, "My sheep listen to my voice; I know them, and they follow me" (10:27). There is a cast-iron way of stating the doctrine of the saint's security which would seem to sanction rash and unholy confidence. God's Word is never spoken in a one-sided manner, so as to encourage confidence in any course of disobedience and sin; but for those who have fled for refuge to the hope set before us and are humbly abiding in Him, there is indeed strong consolation and a hope which is an anchor of the soul, both sure and steadfast, and which enters into that within the veil.

3. The Sheep

a. The sheep hear His voice (10:3–27).

"My sheep listen to my voice" (10:27). "You do not believe because you are not my sheep" (10:26). This is the mark of true sheep, they listen to the shepherd's voice and are willing to be led and taught. This listening spirit, both through the Old Testament and the New, is the very secret of the Lord and the mark of His spiritual followers.

b. They follow the Shepherd (10:4–27).

The sheep follow Him for they know His voice. "My sheep listen to my voice . . . and they follow me" (10:27). This expression includes the whole life of humble and holy obedience to the commandments and leadings of the Lord. It implies His personal presence and leadership. We do not have to walk alone, but He goes before. It makes the way easy to have only to follow. This was the first word to the disciples in the first chapter of John, and this was the last word to Peter in the 21st: "Follow me."

c. They know Him (10:4, 14–15).

The sheep follow Him for they know His voice, and a stranger will they not follow, for they know not the voice of strangers. "I know my sheep and my sheep know me—just as the Father knows me and I know the Father" (10:14–15); that is, we know the Shepherd as He knows the Father. Our personal intimacy with Jesus is the same as His with His Father in heaven.

The translation of the 15th verse obscures this thought a little, and it ought to read, "I am known of mine as the Father knows Me and as I know the Father." These thoughts lead us into depths and heights which, as yet, His disciples could not understand. We do not wonder therefore to read in the sixth verse, "Jesus used this figure of speech, but they did not understand what he was telling them." But the time came when the same Apostle John could use that word *know* with even a deeper fullness than this chapter anywhere expresses, and say of the flock:

> You have known him who is from the beginning. . . . But you have an anointing from the Holy One, and all of you know the truth. . . . We know that we belong to the truth, and how we set our hearts at rest in his presence. . . . We know that he lives in us: We know it by the Spirit he gave us. . . . And so we know and rely on the love God has for us. . . . We know that we have passed from death to life. . . . We know that we have what we asked of him. . . . We know that we are children of God, and that the whole world is under the control of the evil one. We know also that the Son of God has come and has given us under-standing, so that we may know him who is true. And we are in him who is true—even in his Son Jesus Christ. He is the true God and eternal life. (1 John 2:13, 20; 3:19, 24; 4:16; 3:14; 5:15, 19–20)

This discourse has reference not only to the individual believer, but also to the entire flock, and contains a beautiful reference to the time when its scattered fragments shall be all united, Jew and Gentile, out of every nation and class and age of time, "and there shall be one flock and one shepherd" (John 10:16), "For the Lamb at the center of the throne will be their shepherd;/ he will lead them to springs of living water./ And God will wipe away every tear from their eyes" (Revelation 7:17).

This beautiful discourse, instead of touching the hearts of His enemies, only stung them to fiercer exasperations, and was followed by a malignant attack upon Him and an attempt to stone Him in the temple, from which He escaped through the same supernatural power by which He had already evaded their fury more than once, and departed from Jerusalem to Perea for the last stage of His Jewish ministry.

THE GLORY OF THE CROSS
John 12:20–36

The occasion of this discourse was the arrival of certain Greeks who had come to attend the feast of the Passover, to ask for an introduction to Jesus through Philip. They may have had some slight acquaintance with him, or he may have had, perhaps, some Gentile blood in him. Philip consults with Andrew, and then together they go to the Master and tell Him of the request. It seems to make a profound impression upon His heart, and doubtless He sees in it the type and beginning of the conversion of the Gentiles through the gospel, which the Christian age is soon to usher in. The innumerable multitudes who are to follow in their train passed before Him in vision. Perhaps the prospect of these ransomed millions, saved through His suffering and death, lifts His spirit into exulting joy, even under the immediate shadow of the cross itself, and He exclaims, "The hour has come for the Son of Man to be glorified" (12:23). He then proceeds, in profound and beautiful language, to unfold the great principle of death and resurrection, of which His life was to be the greatest expression. First, He traces it even in the laws of nature, and then applies it both to His disciples and to Himself.

1. The Kernel of Wheat

The principle of death and resurrection in the natural world: "Unless a kernel of wheat falls to the ground and dies, it remains only a single seed. But if it dies, it produces many seeds" (12:24). This is the law of natural life. We see it in the decay of winter and revival of spring; we see it in the chrysalis and in the butterfly; we see it in the bulb of autumn and the lily of spring; we see it in the buried seed and the harvest resurrection.

> Life, evermore, is fed by death,
> And joy, by agony,
> And that a rose may breathe its breath
> Something must die.

2. Death and Resurrection

He makes the application of this principle to all discipleship. "The man who loves his life will lose it, while the man who hates his life in this world will keep it for eternal life" (12:25). Every follower of the Master must be willing to rise to life and kingliness by way of the cross, by the death of self and the portals of suffering. The word "life" here is expressed by two Greek terms having quite a different sense. The first means our lower life; the second, our higher and divine life. He that loves the former shall lose the latter, but he that yields it for the higher shall gain the life eternal. The first might be translated "soul"; it is the Greek *psyche*. He that loveth his own soul shall lose it, he that hateth it shall keep it unto life eternal.

Not only must Christian life be animated by the spirit of self-sacrifice, but it must really begin in the renunciation and death of self in its very germ, in the surrender of our natural self to Jesus, and the reception of the new resurrection life in fellowship with Him; of which we can say, "I have been crucified with Christ and I no longer live, but Christ lives in me" (Galatians 2:20). Not only must it have its source in this great principle, but it must, all the way, enter into fellowship with Christ's sufferings. "Whoever serves me must follow me; and where I am, my servant also will be" (John 12:26). But the cross is not forever; there is a glorious and everlasting reversion. "My Father will honor the one who serves me" (12:26); if we die, we shall also live with Him; and the sufferings of this present time are not worthy to be compared with the glory which shall be revealed in us.

3. Christ's Cross

He makes the application of this principle to Himself. He, too, must bear the cross in all its terrible reality; and for a moment, as the realization of it touches His sensitive spirit, He shrinks from the awful vision and cries, "Now my heart is troubled, and what shall I say? 'Father, save me from this hour'?" (12:27). It was the instinctive recoil of His humanity from the cup of trembling; it was the foretaste of Gethsemane, as that was the foretaste of Calvary. But it was only a moment's recoil, nor was it really accepted by His consecrated will; instantly He answers His own cry, "No, it was for this very reason I came to this hour. Father, glorify your name!" (12:27–28). And His holy will is still immaculately held on the altar of sacrifice in a very real sense. It is with Him in the hour of sacrifice and death. There are moments when we live over in the soul all the history of coming hours of anguish, and this was such a moment. But immediately the shadow is illumined by the glory beyond.

a. First, we have the Father's witness to His sacrifice by an audible voice from heaven in response to His prayer, proclaiming, "I have glorified it, and will glorify it again" (12:28). This is the highest glory of the cross, that it honors the Father and glorifies His name. It is the sublimest exhibition of His justice, holiness, wisdom and love, and the one offering which satisfies His heart with the perfect obedience of His beloved Son and the all-sufficient ransom for a lost and guilty world.

In these Greeks He saw the prototypes of the world's coming myriads, as they have been coming, and shall still come to Him for salvation; until, at length, an innumerable company that no man can number, out of all nations, and kindreds, and people, and tongues, shall gather around the throne, and before the Lamb, clothed with white robes, and palms in their hands, shouting, "Salvation belongs to our God,/ who sits on the throne,/ and to the Lamb" (Revelation 7:10).

b. The cross is also the judgment of this world. "Now," He cries, "is the time for judgment on this world" (12:31); not only was it the hour when the world was revealed in the deepest and darkest element of its wickedness and hatred toward God, but it was literally the hour when, in the person of the Substitute, the judgment of heaven was really passed upon sinful men. And for all who accept the atonement of Jesus the day of judgment is really passed, so far as their former sins are concerned, and the Lord Jesus Himself declares, "Whoever hears my word and believes him who sent me has eternal life and will not be condemned; he has crossed over from death to life" (5:24).

c. It is also the way of assured victory over Satan. This is another of the glories of the cross, that through death it has destroyed him that had the power of death, that is the devil. The very act by which he sought to destroy the Redeemer and the hopes of men has ruined the foundations of his kingdom and sealed his everlasting fate. Never did Satan do a rasher deed than when he incited Judas and Pilate to crucify the Son of God. By His death Jesus has spoiled principalities and powers and made a show of them openly, triumphing over them in His cross. The strong figure of the apostle implies that Satan has been hung up as a scarecrow on the cross of Calvary, with his head pierced with the nails of crucifixion. We all may know henceforth that he is a slain and conquered foe.

4. The Crowning Glory

The crowning glory of the cross is its attractive power to draw all men unto Jesus for salvation.

This was the meaning of His joyful cry, "But I, when I am lifted up from the earth, will draw all men to myself" (12:32). The lifting up referred, primarily, to His crucifixion, but also might include His resurrection and His exhibition in the preaching of the gospel, for it is only as we lift up a crucified and risen Savior that we shall ever be honored to draw men unto Him.

Soon after this beautiful discourse Jesus withdrew Himself from the people, hiding Himself, as it is expressed, from them, and adding the solemnly tender warning,

You are going to have the light just a little while longer. Walk while you have the light, before darkness overtakes you. The man who walks in the dark does not know where he is going. Put your trust in the light while you have it, so that you may become sons of light. (12:35–36)

And to those who believed on Him in secret and were afraid to confess because of others, He gave this parting admonition,

> When a man believes in me, he does not believe in me only, but in the one who sent me. . . . There is a judge for the one who rejects me and does not accept my words; that very word which I spoke will condemn him at the last day. For I did not speak of my own accord, but the Father who sent me commanded me what to say and how to say it. I know that his command leads to eternal life. So whatever I say is just what the Father has told me to say. (12:44, 48–50)

This solemn thought was enough to lift them above all the thoughts and fears of men. They were dealing with the Son of God, with the Word of God, with the issues of judgment. They were receiving not only the wisdom of a man and the kind and Christian words of a divine messenger, but the commandment of the Father, and a decisive message on the acceptance of which their eternal destiny should be settled before the throne. The offer of salvation comes to us not merely as a well-meaning opportunity, but as an authoritative command. God commands us to receive life everlasting. The law of faith is the test now of judgment and destiny. And in the day of His coming there shall be two classes, described in the earlier verses of this gospel by the solemn words, "Whoever believes in him is not condemned, but whoever does not believe stands condemned already because he has not believed in the name of God's one and only Son" (3:18).

CHAPTER 13

THE PARTING WORDS OF JESUS TO HIS OWN DISCIPLES AT THE TABLE

John 13:12–14:31

This entire discourse was given while they sat at the table in the upper room. It is naturally divided into six sections by the six questions or statements to Him; each contains His answer.

CHRIST'S QUESTION

1. His own question to the disciples: "Do you understand what I have done for you?" (John 13:12).

The answer to this contains His beautiful teachings concerning humility and brotherly love, as expressed in the example He had just set them by washing their feet.

> Now that I, your Lord and Teacher, have washed your feet, you also should wash one another's feet. I have set you an example that you should do as I have done for you. I tell you the truth, no servant is greater than his master, nor is a messenger greater than the one who sent him. Now that you know these things, you will be blessed if you do them. (13:14–17)

JOHN'S QUESTION

2. The question of John: "Lord, who is it?" (13:25).

This question refers to the betrayer, and Jesus answers it by giving the sign to Judas, and so addressing him that the betrayer is forced to withdraw from the presence of the Master and the disciples. This is what Jesus desired before speaking His words of tender and confidential farewell. He could not bear the pressure of this hideous consciousness of treachery and evil, and yet He did it so tenderly that the act was Judas' own. His departure is followed by a solemn and emphatic declaration, suggested by what He knows of the dark purpose of the traitor: "Now is the Son of Man glorified and God is glorified in him" (13:31). He does not say now is the Son of Man crucified, but above all the shame and anguish of the cross He sees the spanning rainbow of the glory it will bring to His Father and the subsequent recompense which it is also to bring to Him, for He adds, "If God is glorified in him, God will glorify the Son" (13:32). Then there falls upon His loving heart the shadow of the separation which it is to involve for His beloved disciples: "I will be with you only a little longer. . . . Where I am going, you cannot come" (13:33). But this separation is to bind them closer to each other, and bring them that blessing which will be next to His own presence and love: the bond of brotherly love. And so, in this way, the new commandment of Christianity is instituted and promulgated. "A new command I give you: Love one another," not, as the old law expressed as you love yourselves, but "as I have loved you" (13:34). This is indeed the divine principle of Christianity, and was, by the admission of its enemies, among the divinest causes of its successful progress in the early centuries. It is not a natural affection, based on congenial affinities and qualities, but born of the Holy Spirit, imparted from the heart of Jesus, and measured only by His own measureless love.

PETER'S QUESTION

3. The question of Peter: "Lord, where are you going? . . . why can't I follow you now?" (13:36–37).

The first answer Jesus gave was an assurance to the impulsive disciple that he shall yet follow Him where He goes, which must have been a comfort in view of all the words and experiences that followed. The next reply is a solemn intimation of his own great sin, which must have fallen like a shock of unutterable, and perhaps of long continued silence on the little group. "I tell you the truth, before the rooster crows, you will disown me three times!" (13:38).

The effect of these three tremendous announcements, that one should betray Him, another, even His boldest follower, deny Him, and He Himself soon pass out of sight where they cannot even follow Him, we can easily believe was a shock of intense distress and almost complete prostration to the little band of disciples. Dark shadows must have gathered on their faces, and perhaps their eyes were filled with tears of anxious grief. It was then that the Master spoke again and uttered those sweetest words of consolation perhaps ever expressed by Him, in which He most fully answers Peter's question, "Where are you going?"

> Do not let your hearts be troubled. Trust in God; trust also in me. In my Father's house are many rooms; if it were not so, I

would have told you. I am going there to prepare a place for you. And if I go and prepare a place for you, I will come back and take you to be with me that you also may be where I am. You know the way to the place where I am going. (14:1–4)

a. He comforts their hearts by sympathy, with the words, "Do not let your hearts be troubled" (14:1); and the tone in which they were doubtless uttered was meant to cheer them by the very tenderness of His love and sympathy for them, even before He spoke a single word of faith or hope, and still that loving sympathy is throbbing in His heart toward every one of His troubled children. He would shield us from our heart troubles and pillow our heads upon His gentle bosom. If the heart can but rise above its troubles they will not overwhelm us, even as the billows of the ocean cannot submerge the struggling ship, so long as the hatchways are closed and the water does not enter the hold. Christ, and Christ alone, can keep the heart victorious and still in the wildest conflict.

b. He comforts them by encouraging their faith, "Trust in God," He says, "trust also in me" (14:1). It is not "you believe in God," but a command. Over against every difficult place let us write the words, "but God." Let us remember that we have a divine Protector and Shield, but let us also add to the transcendent thought of God, this sweet thought of Jesus, "Trust also in me." Let us clothe His sweetness with the divine omnipotence, and let us color the divine omnipotence with the soft light of His love. This is the Lamb in the midst of the throne, the gentleness in the midst of the Almightiness. "Trust also in me." Faith is the true source of abiding comfort. Sympathy alone is not enough, we must also trust, and the first resting place of our trust is His person. "Trust in God." Then He adds the following words to lift their faith to the throne where He is about to ascend and the work on which He is immediately to enter in their behalf, "I am going there to prepare a place for you" (14:2). Faith not only rests upon the person of Christ, but also loves to dwell upon the place where He has gone, the right hand of God, and the work which He is doing, representing us and preparing our future home. And once more He reveals the way by which they are still to have communion with Him even in His absence and in a little while to rise to meet Him. "You know the way to the place where I am going" (14:4). It is not enough to know that He is there, and there for us, but we also need to know how we may communicate with Him and ultimately follow Him. This, too, He says, we know. And a little later He tells them it is He Himself. Faith thus rests upon Jesus, the way of access to God, and if we will only thus believe, our hearts will never be troubled.

c. He comforts them not only by faith, but also by hope. He intimates first that He Himself is coming again for them in a little while. This is the church's chief hope, oft obscure and even forgotten, but her one supreme consolation, the coming of her Lord. "I will come back and take you to be with me" (14:3). This is not death, but the brighter, better hope of His own personal return.

d. He gives them a glimpse of the glory that awaits them at His coming, and speaks of the rooms, and the Father's house, and the place prepared.

All this is suggested by the figure of the Father's house, the metropolis of this magnificent universe, the rooms with which His infinite power and glory will adorn that celestial city, and the preparation which His loving hands are about to give to their future home. We may be assured there will be nothing wanting which thoughtful love could plan, and all this may well suggest a vision of glory and happiness which should dry their tears and fill their hearts with hope and consolation. There is still another thought suggested by the word "many" which hints at the happy reunion which His coming will bring with the many that are linked with their affections and hopes. It shall not be a solitary grandeur, but a restoration of broken ties and a healing of broken hearts in everlasting love. And there is a still finer hint in one sentence which suggests an inexpressible meaning of comfort, "If it were not so, I would have told you" (14:2). But how much this covers; hopes that we scarcely dare to utter, but still feel that He has not forgotten, and a whole world of unrevealed and unutterable satisfactions which our bursting hearts cannot regulate.

THOMAS' QUESTION

4. The question of Thomas: "Lord, we don't know where you are going, so how can we know the way?" (14:5).

Thomas is a natural doubter, partly because of his ardent love. His heart takes so intense a hold on things that he cannot bear to be deceived. He, therefore, cannot rest in any indefiniteness, but must know without doubt or vagueness, not only the certainty of these bright hopes, but the very way by which they are to be fulfilled. This Jesus answers by giving a more emphatic announcement of His own personality as the one answer both to this and all their questionings. "I am the way," He says, "and the truth and the life" (14:6). It is not in a physical or material manifestation that you are to be led into these hopes and maintain this communication with Me, but through your spiritual union and fellowship with Me, for I am not only the Way, but I am also the Truth and the Life. And as you know Me and abide in communion with Me, you are also to know the Father and have access to His presence, and also to know of the truth of My teachings, and the deepest experiences of spiritual life. For I am also the Life as well as the Truth and the Way. The first of these beautiful expressions may well describe our justification, the second, our deeper teaching, and the third, our deeper life in Christ.

We are saved by simply coming to Him and becoming united to Him.

There is no way but He, and there is no need of any way to Him, for He Himself is the way. And so, as regards our higher teaching, it is not truth in the abstract that we need to know, but the truth as it is in Jesus. He is the substance of all the teachings of the Old Testament and the deeper revelations of the New. They all terminate with Him; the object of each is to reveal Him and have us know Him as our personal light, and the substance of all knowledge and wisdom. And so of our life, whether it be of soul or body; it is not an impartation from Him, but it is His own very life shed abroad in us, sustaining us by constant dependence upon Himself, so that, as He says a little later, "Because I live, you also will live" (14:19).

PHILIP'S STATEMENT

5. The question of Philip: "Lord, show us the Father and that will be enough for us" (14:8).

This whole passage is, in some sense, the answer to this question.

a. He tells them that He is the manifestation of the Father, and that all His works on earth have been through the energy of the Father working in Him. And He expresses surprise that Philip should not yet have known Him in His divine character and relationship.

b. He tells them that He is about to go to the Father. However, He will still reveal His power and grace, no less than when on earth, but even more mightily through His disciples, that just now as He represents the Father on earth, so they, then, shall represent Him; "He will do even greater things than these, because I am going to the Father" (14:12).

c. He tells them that the answers to their prayers are about to be revealed after His ascension. They will be the evidence to them of His union with the Father. "And I will do whatever you ask in my name, so that the Son may bring glory to the Father" (14:13).

d. The Holy Spirit, who is about to descend upon them, will be another proof of His union with the Father, and will come from the Father at His intercession, and will dwell in them both as the Revealer of the Father and of the Son, and as the Representative of the Godhead henceforth on earth.

e. The Comforter, the Holy Spirit, shall not be so distinct from Him that He shall be another presence, for He shall be the spirit which has hitherto dwelt in Christ, and He shall come as the Spirit of Christ, and thus bring the personal presence of Christ in abiding union and conscious fellowship, and shall reveal to the soul the person of Jesus and His relation to the Father with glorious vividness and blessedness; for, He says, "I will not leave you as orphans; I will come to you" (14:18). That is, through the coming of the Comforter. And then He adds,

On that day you will realize that I am in my Father, and you are
in me, and I am in you. Whoever has my commands and obeys
them, he is the one who loves me. He who loves me will be loved
by my Father, and I too will love him and show myself to him.
(14:20–21)

Thus the question of Philip is fully answered. Not only does Jesus say that
the Father is in His own incarnate person, but after His ascension, He is to
send the Holy Spirit to reveal Himself to them in closer intimacy and to
bring the presence of the Father Himself into their hearts, so that they shall
know that He is in the Father and they in Him and He in them, and thus
the whole mystery of the Trinity will be revealed in the living experience of
the consecrated heart. This, indeed, is the only way in which any soul can
ever fully grasp and find comfort and support in the doctrine of the Trinity.

As a speculation, it is as cold as it is lofty; but as an experience, brought to
the heart by the Holy Spirit through the indwelling presence of Jesus, it is a
threefold cord of infinite joy and everlasting love.

JUDE'S QUESTION

**6. The question of Jude: "But, Lord, why do you intend to show your-
self to us and not to the world?" (14:22).**

First, He tells them the very secret of this manifestation is obedience and
love. The world cannot, therefore, know Him, because it neither loves nor
obeys Him. But he that will obey Him shall know this, not as an occasional
flash of light and glory, but as an abiding joy, making the heart a literal
heaven where the Father, Son and Holy Spirit erect their throne and make
their continual abode. "If anyone loves me, he will obey my teaching. My
Father will love him, and we will come to him and make our home with
him" (14:23).

CONCLUSION

**7. Summing up of all these teachings and closing benediction as He rises
from the table.**

First, He tells them that these parting words have been spoken to them in
view of His separation from them; but that these and all other things which
they shall need to know, and many of which they may indeed forget, will be
brought to their remembrance and more fully revealed by the manifestation
of the Holy Spirit who is about to come in His very name, as His Substitute
and Successor, to represent Him and to finish His work. "The Holy Spirit,
whom the Father will send in my name, will teach you all things and will
remind you of everything I have said to you" (14:26). Therefore, although
there may be much at present that they cannot fully comprehend, and much

they may fear they shall forget, yet He shall be their faithful and patient Teacher, and all that now seems strange shall be made perfectly plain. Next, He gives them His parting benediction and bequest, His own divine peace: "Peace I leave with you; my peace I give you. I do not give to you as the world gives. Do not let your hearts be troubled and do not be afraid" (14:27). They had seen this wonderful peace in Him and felt its majestic power, now He breathes it into their very hearts and leaves it to all of His disciples as His last will and testament, the peace of God which passes all understanding to keep their hearts and minds through Jesus Christ.

Then He tries to rouse them to the still higher thought of love to Him and awaken in their breasts the unselfish consideration of His needs and feelings in this trying hour. "If you loved me," He says, "you would be glad that I am going to the Father" (14:28). There is no higher consolation to the troubled heart than to be lifted out of itself and think of the greater sufferings of others. If they had only realized their Master's condition and immediate prospects, their own troubles would have seemed like a dream, and they would have thrown their arms about Him and cried, "Master, let us comfort You, let not Your heart be troubled." Then, with a brief reference to the conflict which is just coming, and the victory which He is already sharing, and the solemn consideration of His Father's will and glory, which is His chief support, He slowly rises from the table and summons them to follow with the words which might well look forward to every future place of difficulty and duty. "Come now; let us leave" (14:31).

The whole of this beautiful chapter might be summed up under two divisions: First, His going, and second, His coming again. His going is to prepare a place for them, to open a way for them, to intercede for them with the Father, to work through them from the throne His greater works, and to send to them the Comforter to represent Him and continue His work. His coming again looks forward ultimately to His glorious second advent (14:3), but also includes His personal indwelling in their hearts (14:18, 20, 21, 23), and His giving to them as His ever-present legacy of blessing, His own perfect peace (14:27).

CHAPTER 14

CHRIST'S PARTING WORDS TO HIS DISCIPLES ON THE WAY FROM THE TABLE TO THE GARDEN

John 15–16

T his long discourse consists of three parts:
1. The Parable of the Vine and the Branches, and its application (15:1–25).
2. A fuller promise of the coming of the Comforter (15:26–16:15).
3. A concluding conversation between the disciples and the Lord about various questions (16:16–33).

THE VINE AND THE BRANCHES
John 15:1–25

The occasion of this discourse may have been their passing through the court of the temple and observing the magnificent carving of the vine in stone, which was one of the most remarkable decorations of the building, or it may have been suggested by the overhanging vines by the roadside as they passed down to the valley of the Kidron or the burning of the withered branches and prunings of the vineyards in the open places as they went out of the city. It was not a new figure, but drawn by Him from the beautiful imagery of the Psalms and the prophets (Psalm 80:8; Isaiah 5:1; Jeremiah 2:21; Ezekiel 15:2).

The most valuable, perhaps, of the products of the plant creation, God has chosen it as the most significant figure of Christ and His relation to His people. The devil has tried to prostitute it, perhaps for this very reason, to the most unholy and wicked purposes.

1. **Union with Christ as represented by this figure.**

a. Let us observe that the vine consists not only of the stem, but of the branches; so Christ identifies Himself with all His members, and counts them part of Himself. We are of the very same substance as our living Head, and partake of His own personal life.

b. The fruit is borne, not by the stem, but by the branches, and, especially, by the little branches. So the Lord Jesus did not, in His own personal ministry, bring many souls to God, but left the most glorious fruit of the gospel to be gathered by His disciples, and still honors His feeblest members by permitting us to bring forth much fruit.

c. The great essential of Christian life is to be united to Jesus. "Apart from me you can do nothing" (John 15:5).

Two things constitute this union. The first is expressed by the words, "In me" (15:4); this denotes our faith in Christ for salvation and our union with Him in justification. The second, "I . . . in you" (15:4), expresses a closer union, even His personal coming into the heart, in the hour of our full surrender, to abide in us by the Holy Spirit as our Lord and life.

This is the secret of sanctification, communion, power and fruitfulness.

d. We must abide in this union and communion. It is not enough that it be formed, it must be maintained, moment by moment, in watchful, obedient dependence and fellowship.

e. In connection with our abiding in Christ, it is necessary that there should be much faithful divine discipline, and therefore we read of the pruning of the vine and the Father's thoughtful, patient care as the heavenly Gardener.

f. On our part there must be obedience if we would abide in Christ. "If you obey my commands, you will remain in my love" (15:10). And again, "You are my friends if you do what I command" (15:14). And again: "My command is this: Love each other as I have loved you" (15:12).

2. The fruits of union with Christ.

a. They are fruits, not works of the flesh and the will; they spring spontaneously and delightfully from the life within, just as the vine bears fruit without effort and the fruit seems to grow from very gladness.

b. The first of these fruits is holiness. "You are already clean because of the word I have spoken to you" (15:3). All true holiness must spring from the indwelling life of Christ.

c. The next fruit is holy usefulness. This is expressed by the figure of much fruit, for fruit is reproduction, some 30, some 60, and some a hundredfold. "This is to my Father's glory, that you bear much fruit" (15:8).

d. The next fruit is answered prayer. "If you remain in me and my words remain in you, ask whatever you wish, and it will be given you" (15:7).

e. The next fruit is fullness of joy. "I have told you this so that my joy may be in you and that your joy may be complete" (15:11). If His life is in us, His joy will fill us, and His joy is fullness of joy.

f. The next fruit is the fellowship of His sufferings. If we are one with Him the world will hate us, as it hated Him (15:18–21); but we will not shrink from His cross or seek to be greater than our Lord or more exempt from persecution and suffering, for trial will be sweet as it comes with the recollection, we are suffering with Jesus. We shall be also glorified together.

THE COUNSELOR
John 15:26–16:15

In the previous discourse, He had referred to the coming of the Holy Spirit as their teacher and guide, but here He unfolds His special ministry with more explicitness.

1. The necessity and importance of His coming.

His presence is so essential to the next stage of their experience and work, that it is even expedient that their beloved Master go away in order that He may come. Anything that could require the withdrawal of such a friend must be valuable indeed. And yet, the Holy Spirit's presence with the Church is better than the continued physical presence of the Lord Jesus would have been. For in the first place, it is an internal and not an external presence. Further, He is omnipresent, not limited, as the visible person of Christ, to one place, but equally accessible to all God's people wherever they may be, and at all times. Moreover, the mission of the Spirit is to act as the Executive of the divine plan of redemption, and the time has now come when this stage of the work must follow the personal ministry and accomplished sacrifice of Jesus Himself.

2. His mission with respect to the Father.

He was to proceed from the Father in response to the prayer of Jesus. "I will ask the Father, and he will give you another Counselor" (14:16). "When the Counselor comes, whom I will send to you from the Father, the Spirit of truth who goes out from the Father, he will testify about me" (15:26).

3. His mission with respect to the Son.

He was to come in the name of Christ (14:26). He was to be the very Spirit that had dwelt in Christ; and, as has been beautifully expressed, He comes to us not in His essential deity, but colored by the humanity of Jesus, in whom He has resided. And He comes to unite us with the person of Jesus. "On that day you will realize that I am in my Father, and you are in me, and I am in you" (14:20). He comes to testify of Jesus, to make His presence real and vivid to our consciousness, and to illuminate our spirit with the revelation of Jesus Christ in all His fullness. "He will testify about me. . . . He will bring glory to me by taking from what is mine and making it known to you" (15:26; 16:14). The Holy Spirit is to Christ what the atmosphere of our globe is to the sun; we do not see the atmosphere, but the light of the sun; yet the light would be invisible but for the atmospheric medium through which it is diffused. The viewless air brings to us the vision of the sun, and so the Holy Spirit, hiding His own personality behind the person of Jesus, brings Him into our consciousness and life, to glorify Him. The telescope may be beautiful and costly in its construction, but it would be a mistake for a visitor to the great observatory of yonder Sierra Nevada mountains to concentrate his whole attention on the superb telescope, which the munificence of a wealthy patron of science has erected. Much wiser and grander would it be to use the telescope to gaze upon yonder celestial spheres, and see, not the medium of vision, but the heavenly worlds themselves. Let us honor the Holy Spirit just because He does not seek to honor Himself; but we shall ever please Him best and have His most gracious approbation when we unite our gaze with Him upon the face of Jesus.

4. His mission with respect to the disciples.

Already in the preceding discourse, has He been revealed as their indwelling Teacher and Monitor. Here He is represented still more fully in this respect, as the patient and gentle Guide, who will supplement the present instructions of the Master by such fuller unfoldings of the truth as they may be able to bear from time to time, and, especially, the truths respecting the future and the second coming of the Lord—the whole prophetic horizon, which was to be opened to their view a little later. "He will guide you into all truth. . . . he will tell you what is yet to come" (16:13). He was also to be to them the Spirit of testimony. "He will testify about me. And you also must testify, for you have been with me from the beginning" (15:26–27).

5. His mission with respect to sin, righteousness and judgment.

> When he comes, he will convict the world of guilt in regard to sin and righteousness and judgment: in regard to sin, because men do not believe in me; in regard to righteousness, because I am going to the Father, where you can see me no longer; and in regard to judgment, because the prince of this world now stands condemned. (16:8–11)

His first work upon the hearts of sinners is to convict them of sin, the deepest need of the unconverted heart; and the special sin for which He arraigns the human conscience, is that which is to be the ground of final condemnation, the rejection of Jesus Christ.

Next, His work is to reveal to the soul the righteousness of Christ as the ground of its justification and the source of its sanctification, and enable it to accept the righteousness of God as witnessed by the resurrection of Jesus

Christ in both of these aspects.

The exact meaning of the third specification of His work has been variously interpreted. Some apply it symbolically and literally, to the future judgment. It seems a little difficult, however, to connect, intelligibly, with this, the next sentence, with regard to the Prince of this world being judged. It would seem relevant and clear to apply this to the revelation of Christ's second coming—the next great theme of the gospel—and its glorious result, in the judging and casting out of Satan and the power of his kingdom. It would seem to unfold, also, the idea of the world and the devil as now already judged by the Lord, and therefore, to be treated by the disciple of Christ as a conquered foe. This is the closing echo of this very discourse: "But take heart! I have overcome the world" (16:33). The world and the devil, its master, are already judged, and the judgment will be made manifest in all its fullness at His second coming. We are, therefore, to be separated from it as a forbidden world of evil, and to testify against it. We are not to fear it in its opposition and persecution, or its malignant and mighty prince, the devil, but to treat him as a conquered foe. All this the Spirit reveals to the soul, after convicting it of sin and righteousness; leading it out of the world, giving it victory over temptation, and inspiring the blessed hope of Christ's second coming and the new world of righteousness and glory.

CLOSING CONVERSATION BETWEEN CHRIST AND HIS DISCIPLES

John 16:16–33

The remaining utterances of this discourse are somewhat broken by the questionings of His disciples. The first subject referred to is His expected separation from them, and His speedy reappearance to them. His own remark, "In a little while you will see me no more, and then after a little while you will see me" (16:16), had perplexed them. He tenderly anticipates their question, and more fully explains His meaning in verses 20–22.

He plainly intimates in these words, His approaching death and the sorrow it will bring them, as well as the malignant triumph of the hostile world. But it will be followed immediately by His reappearance to them—a joy, which, thenceforth, shall never pass away.

This dark hour, that is approaching like the anguish of a travailing woman, is but the birth throe of a new creation which is about to come, even the birth of the Church of Christ, which is to emerge from the cross and the resurrection, and go forth into a cloudless and everlasting day.

The reference is, undoubtedly, to His appearance to them after His resurrection, and to the exalted fellowship and privileges into which they are then to be raised. He proceeds next to unfold these privileges:

In that day you will no longer ask me anything. I tell you the truth, my Father will give you whatever you ask in my name. Until now you have not asked for anything in my name. Ask and you will receive, and your joy will be complete. . . .

In that day you will ask in my name. I am not saying that I will ask the Father on your behalf. No, the Father himself loves you because you have loved me and have believed that I came from God. (16:23–24, 26–27)

The first word translated, "ask," in verse 23, does not mean to pray, but to inquire about matters with respect to which they are in perplexity. He means that in the coming day, the light will be so plain and clear, that they will not need to inquire, as they do now, "What does he mean? . . . We don't understand what he is saying" (16:17–18), but they shall plainly understand His will and teachings and His Father's love. And, as to prayer, they shall have a higher place of access and confidence, for they shall ask in His name, even as He asks, which they have not yet been able to do, because His redemption work was not complete and His heavenly priesthood, in their behalf, had not begun. Henceforth He shall be at the Father's side in their interests, and their petitions shall be received at the heavenly throne even as His own. He will not need to plead for them as for strangers, or aliens, for the Father Himself loves them, even as He loves His Son. His intercession is not so much to propitiate an angry Father and constrain from His reluctant hands the answer to His people's prayers, as that He is to be the Channel through whom the answer will come, and the Mediator who receives our petitions as they ascend to heaven, in their imperfection and ignorance, purifying them with His holy intercession and then presenting them with the added incense of His own merits as His own very prayers.

There is one more word, and then this tender discourse closes. There is a touch of deep sorrow in its tone, but it soon rises to the notes of triumph. "You believe at last!" He answers their honest but superficial confession, "But a time is coming, and has come, when you will be scattered, each to his own home. You will leave me all alone" (16:31–32). Thus was the dark shadow of Gethsemane anticipated; but He quickly rises and adds, "Yet I am not alone, for my Father is with me" (16:32). And then, looking forward to their Gethsemane, too, He tenderly says, "In this world you will have trouble" (16:33); they, too, shall have their crosses and their conflicts, but their one source of rest and victory is Himself, and His triumph for them. "I have told you these things, so that in me you may have peace. In this world you will have trouble. But take heart! I have overcome the world" (16:33). That victory is the pledge of ours; as we cry out for strength, His answer ever is, "I have overcome for you." And so,

As surely as He overcame,
And triumphed once for you,
So, surely, ye that trust His name,
Shall triumph in Him, too.

CHAPTER 15

THE PARTING PRAYER

John 17

Perhaps on the brink of the Kidron, or possibly even within the temple courts, before they finally withdrew, these last words of love were spoken. Wherever His human feet may have stood last, His Spirit was on the threshold of heaven as He uttered these sentences, standing as the divine High Priest on the very borders of the inner sanctuary, hard by the veil that was just about to be torn in two, by His dying agony.

CHRIST'S PRAYER AS IT RESPECTS HIMSELF
John 17:1–5

1. The Crisis Hour
"Father, the time has come" (17:1). It was the hour of the world's destiny, the Father's glory, and His own consummated work; not only was His work done, but it was all done on time. Each moment had been filled with the Father's perfect will, and now there was nothing to do but to die.

Oh! that we might all follow Him, not only in the faithfulness, but in the timeliness of His finished life.

2. The Finished Work
"For you granted him authority over all people that he might give eternal life to all those you have given him. . . . I have brought you glory on earth by completing the work you gave me to do" (17:2, 4). He recalls His mighty commission to give eternal life to His people through the knowledge of the Father and the Son, and acknowledges publicly the complete resources which the Father has supplied for this mighty task. You have given Him authority over all people that He might thus administer the great work of salvation. What an unfolding of the purpose and glory of redemption, Christ its mighty

administrator, the whole human family its beneficiaries. His own people His especial objects, and eternal life its glorious aim. And this eternal life is not a definite future existence, but is a relation of intimacy and love with God. It is God Himself through Jesus Christ revealed in the soul. This mighty task, He declares, He has fully accomplished. He has revealed the Father, He has made known His Word and stood among men as His Representative and Expression. He has so done this as to glorify His Father on the earth. Not only has He fulfilled His work, but He has fulfilled it for the glory of God. What a pattern to all His followers—a finished task, and God supremely glorified. Oh! that it may be ours to echo it.

3. The Last Request

"Glorify me in your presence with the glory I had with you before the world began. . . . Glorify your Son, that your Son may glorify you" (17:5, 1). He asks that He may be glorified and raised up from the depths of shame and sorrow to which He is about to stoop. He asks back again, as His right, the glory which, for a little while He had voluntarily laid aside—the glory He had with the Father before the world was. He asks still more the joy of His Father's heavenly fellowship. "With you" (17:5)—it is the cry of the lonely heart to be again upon the Father's bosom. How poorly can we understand that loneliness and that love of His great heart. He had said a little before, "If you loved me, you would be glad that I am going to the Father" (14:28). But, even then, He did not ask for Himself; still, His true heart turns instinctively to His Father's glory, and He hallows even this holy prayer by the added request, "that your Son may glorify you" (17:1).

CHRIST'S PRAYER WITH RESPECT TO HIS IMMEDIATE DISCIPLES

John 17:6–19

1. He commends them to His Father and He tells Him:

a. That they have been given Him by the Father Himself (17:6).

b. That they have kept His word.

c. That they have received the messages of the Son, knowing surely that He came from God and believing in Him with all their hearts. And in Him they have also recognized the Father, and "know that everything you have given me comes from you" (17:7).

2. He pleads for them on the ground that they are already His Father's and also His own, and that His glory is linked with their blessing. "They are yours. . . . all you have is mine. And glory has come to me through them" (17:9–10).

3. He refers to His own care and keeping of them hitherto, and commits them from His hands, as He is now about to leave them to His Father's

keeping, telling Him that they are all safe, except the one who has wrecked himself, as the Scriptures had already predicted, the wicked son of perdition.

> I will remain in the world no longer, but they are still in the world, and I am coming to you. Holy Father, protect them by the power of your name—the name you gave me—so that they may be one as we are one. While I was with them, I protected them and kept them safe by that name you gave me. None has been lost except the one doomed to destruction so that Scripture would be fulfilled. (17:11–12)

4. He refers to their lonely, bereaved and perilous situation, left in the world without Him, and hated by the world for His sake. "The world has hated them, for they are not of the world any more than I am of the world" (17:14).

5. He speaks of His desire for them that they may have His joy fulfilled in themselves.

6. He prays for their preservation in the world and from the evil one (17:15). He would not have them withdrawn from the world by death, for the world needs them, and they need to finish their work; but He does ask that while remaining in the world they may be preserved from evil or from the evil one and all his malignant power both upon their souls and bodies.

7. He asks for their sanctification, including their separation from the world (17:16) and their purification and dedication to God, through the truth.

8. He claims for them the same service as He Himself has done, and sets them apart in His Father's presence, to represent Him and finish His work, with the same authority which the Father hath given to Him. "As you sent me into the world, I have sent them into the world" (17:18).

9. He solemnly consecrates Himself to them for their sanctification, service and complete salvation, and lays Himself with them in His death as a living sacrifice upon the altar of His Father's will; so that their sanctification does not depend upon their own personal strength and resources, but is pledged by His own love to them, and His own life in them. We think of our consecration as we lay ourselves upon the altar. Let us rather think of that other Sacrifice who lies down beside us, and becomes by His own consecration with us, the strength and the security of our sanctity and service. "For them I sanctify myself, that they too may be truly sanctified" (17:19).

CHRIST'S PRAYER AS IT RESPECTS BELIEVERS THROUGHOUT THE WHOLE CHRISTIAN AGE

John 17:20–24

From the little band that are kneeling close to Him, His vision expands until He sees the whole circle of His redeemed, each one of us personally; then He adds this all-comprehensive prayer, "My prayer is not for them alone. I pray also for those who will believe in me through their message" (17:20).

The simple condition which includes us in His prayer, is that we "will believe in [Him] through their message." If we can meet this, the Master's prayer has been offered for us, and will surely be fulfilled if we will let it. And this prayer not only looks forward to the words which follow, but back also to the words which he has just expressed for the 11 disciples.

Three things He asks for them in the coming ages, and one bequest He bestows upon them.

First, their unity with each other: "that all of them may be one" (17:21).

Second, their union with Him: "Just as you are in me and I am in you. May they also be in us" (17:21).

And, third, the perfecting of each one of them in their personal life, and of the whole body in the one complete Church the Bride of the Lamb: "May they be brought to complete unity" (17:23). This is also the apostle's prayer, as he echoes the Master's thought: "until we all reach unity in the faith and in the knowledge of the Son of God and become mature, attaining to the whole measure of the fullness of Christ" (Ephesians 4:13).

This complete unity, He tells the Father, is to be the great evidence through which the world will believe that the Father has sent Him, and will know that He has loved them even as Himself. Christian unity must have its deeper root in divine union, and Christian perfection can come only through such union between the soul and God. There is no self-perfection, but as God has revealed and ministered to each one of us, and together, so united us in Him, we shall be "made perfect in one" (John 17:23, KJV). Perfection here includes, not only the completeness and maturity of individual character, but also of the Church, as a collective body, at the coming of the Lord.

There is still a deeper, sweeter thought lying in the bosom of His precious words and not yet expressed in this analysis. The issue of this divine union with the Father and the Son shall be that the soul thus linked with God shall enter into the same love which the Father has toward the Son. If Jesus be truly formed in us, the Father will love us in Jesus and as Jesus Himself. These are the two sublime heights in this prayer, so far as we are concerned—the love of Jesus and the love of the Father revealed in us through our union with God.

From this great thought naturally follows the remaining prayer (17:22), which contains His last bequests to His beloved followers. At the table He had bequeathed to them His peace, and now He adds to it His glory, too. All the riches, all the splendor of the infinite and everlasting wealth of His throne and His glory, He shares with them; empties Himself of all but love, and finds His sole inheritance in them and in His Father. "I have given them the glory that you gave me, that they may be one as we are one" (17:22). And as though to complete even the very form of a will, and claim for them, by every right of His Sonship, this glorious consummation, He adds, "Father, I want those you have given me to be with me where I am, and to see my glory, the glory you have given me because you loved me before the creation of the world" (17:24).

CHRIST'S PRAYER AS IT RESPECTS HIS FATHER
John 17:25–26

The closing thoughts and words have reference to the highest of all thoughts and themes.

1. The Father and the world.

Apart from Christ, the world has no God. Man's conceptions of the Father are all distorted and false. Jesus alone has revealed Him. "No one has ever seen God, but God the One and Only, who is at the Father's side, has made him known" (1:18). The altars of false religion are dedicated "to an unknown God" (Acts 17:23). "Now this is eternal life: that they may know you, the only true God, and Jesus Christ, whom you have sent" (John 17:3). Nothing is more pathetic than the groping of lofty minds in every age to find out God. Yes, it is true as Christ said, "The world does not know [the Father]" (17:25).

2. The Father and the Son.

"They know that you have sent me. I have made you known to them" (17:25–26). Jesus is the revelation of God to the world and to the believer, and only as we receive Him can we know God and enter into union with Him through Jesus Christ. When we receive His Son, we at once pass into direct and personal acquaintance with the Father. This was the very purpose of His coming, to "bring us to God" (1 Peter 3:18, KJV), and one with Him, we become one with the Father also.

3. The Father and the believer.

Receiving Christ and through Him united to God, there comes to us the stupendous blessing expressed in these words: "that the love you have for me may be in them and that I myself may be in them" (John 17:26). We become the objects of the very same love which the Father has for His Son. We are recognized as part of Him even as the bride is taken into her husband's family and loved even as her husband. This is, indeed, the mystery of mysteries: that we are permitted to share the intimate and exclusive affection of the eternal Father toward His only begotten Son. He loves us now, not for ourselves, nor in proportion to our personal claims upon His affection, but precisely as He loves Jesus Christ, with infinite complacency and unlimited measure.

The secret of all this is expressed in the last three words in this sublime prayer, "I in them" (17:26, KJV). This is the mystery hid from ages, and at last made known to the saints, "Christ in you, the hope of glory" (Colossians 1:27), "I in them." This explains why God can love us even as He loves His Son, for to the Father we are accepted and counted as sharing His peculiar sonship—"we are like him" (1 John 4:17).

Even the Master's prayer cannot go higher or deeper than this. The curtain falls upon these parting words, and henceforth their echoes keep forever sounding through the ages as the very voices of the ministry of His intercession within the veil and the acknowledgment forever of our high place of unity and fellowship with Him as we, in His name, may come, and come boldly, to the throne of grace.

> So near, so very near to God,
> More near I cannot be;
> For in the Person of His Son
> I am as near as He.
> So dear, so very dear to God,
> More dear I cannot be;
> The love wherewith He loves His Son,
> That love He bears to me.

ACTS

CHAPTER 1

THE DISPENSATION OF THE SPIRIT

He said to them: "It is not for you to know the times or dates the Father has set by his own authority. But you will receive power when the Holy Spirit comes on you; and you will be my witnesses in Jerusalem, and in all Judea and Samaria, and to the ends of the earth." (Acts 1:7–8)

The "Acts of the Apostles" has been variously called "The Acts of the Holy Spirit" and "The Acts of the Ascended Lord." Both names are appropriate, much more appropriate, indeed, than the more ordinary title of "Acts of the Apostles." This book records not only the first chapters of Church history, but the first acts of the Holy Spirit on earth and the ascended Lord in heaven.

THE PERSPECTIVE

It is important at the very outset that we should get the right projection of the dispensation of the Spirit—the perspective, as it were, of faith and hope as it looks out from Christ's ascension to the close of the dispensation and the eternal purpose of God in redemption. In order to do this, there are three points that we must definitely and vividly fix in our thought and conception: first, the departing Lord; secondly, the returning Lord; thirdly, the descending Holy Spirit. These three points stand closely related to each other and can only be rightly understood when viewed in their mutual bearing.

SECTION I—*The Departing Lord*

The opening verses of Acts give us the picture of His ascension.

FORETOLD HIS GOING

1. This had been definitely foretold by Him. "I came from the Father and

entered the world"; again, "I am leaving the world and going back to the Father" (John 16:28), "It is for your good that I am going away. . . . If you loved me, you would be glad that I am going to the Father" (16:7; 14:28). In these and many similar intimations, the Lord had prepared them for His departure, and made them understand that His work on earth was now finished and that His ascension was only part of His great redeeming plan.

PREPARATIONS

2. His preparations for the ascension were deliberate and complete. He did not go with unseemly haste, but lingered for 40 days, meeting with them often and finishing all that remained of His prophetic ministry on earth before He assumed His priestly and kingly functions in the heavens. "He showed himself to these men and gave many convincing proofs that he was alive" (Acts 1:3). He left no doubt whatever of His identity, and He gave them full instructions concerning the kingdom of God. John tells us that if all the things He said had been recorded, the whole world could not contain the books that should be written. We may be sure then that the practice and example of the apostles, as recorded in the book of Acts, were covered by explicit directions from the Master's lips in messages that have not come to us except as we can infer them from the manner in which the apostles themselves obeyed them.

THE SCENE

3. The incidents of His departure were most impressive and glorious. Talking with them in His ordinary way, He had led them out as far as Bethany. Then, as if to close the little service, He raised His hands in benediction; but instead of disappearing as was His custom during the 40 days, with a calm, majestic power that neutralized without an effort the law of gravitation, He slowly began to rise before them, while His hands were still outstretched in blessing, His face beaming with love, and His lips, perhaps, still parted with farewell messages, until the vision of His majestic form grew more distant and dim in the receding space, and at length a floating cloud passed between and received Him out of their sight. Perhaps it was a cloud of angels awaiting Him as his escort. And as they steadfastly gazed, His blessed form appeared no more, but passed up into the heavens, while the next object that claimed their attention was a sudden message from two angelic beings who had dropped from that heavenly company to bring them yet one message more from their loving and departed Lord.

STILL THE SAME

4. His ascension did not change His person or character, for He distinctly sends them word that He is to remain "this same Jesus" (1:11) until they shall

see Him again on His more glorious return. So in heaven where He dwells, He is still the old Christ of Galilee and Bethany, as human, as loving, as near to the race with whom He has become forever identified.

> Though now ascended upon high,
> He bends on earth a brother's eye;
> Partaker of the human name,
> He knows the frailty of our frame.

> In every pang that rends the heart
> The Man of Sorrows has a part;
> He sympathizes with our grief,
> And to the sufferer sends relief.

STILL WORKING

5. His ascension did not terminate His work, for Luke tells his friend, Theophilus, that his former treatise related only to those things which Jesus "began to do and to teach" (Acts 1:1). His present treatise, therefore, by inference, is to relate to the things which Jesus will continue to do and teach. Jesus' ascension simply introduces another stage of His ministry. Now He officiates as our great High Priest and our sovereign Lord and King. Girded for constant service, He ever appears in the presence of God for us, and governs the universe with unceasing power and wisdom, as Head over all things for His body, the Church. Not for a moment is He idle or occupied with His own happiness. His ascension was as unselfish as His crucifixion, and He is finishing His glorious work and preparing the kingdom which He is soon to reveal to His waiting Bride.

WHERE IS HEAVEN?

Where did He go when He rose that day into the blue dome of heaven? While, undoubtedly, heaven is a character and state, it is just as surely also a place. There the real body of our living Lord resides, and there with Him are the actual spirits of the just made perfect, real subsistences and not ghostly shadows; persons who dwell somewhere and have a home as real as the earth they left. But which of yonder glorious worlds was the goal of that glorious journey? Was it the mighty "Arcturus and his sons," that mightiest sun in yonder ether; or was it one of those marvelous systems which astronomy has revealed, where two suns revolve in their heavens, and while one has sunk beneath the horizon the other rises to its meridian and there is no night there? Or was it to one of those celestial empires where a group of colored suns sheds a radiance so glorious as to turn every object on which their light might fall into a flashing gem of untold beauty? Or was it one of those brilliant star clusters where the eye of the telescope can discern a thousand suns in a single system? Whither did He go from Bethany that day and where is the home of the ascended Lord? Is it possible to find an answer to our eager question from these pages of revelation?

ABOVE ALL HEAVENS

There is one passage which tells us that "he ascended higher than all the heavens, in order to fill the whole universe" (Ephesians 4:10). Surely, that means that there is a sense in which all those glorious suns and stars are at His feet and around His throne, and yet that somehow He fills all the empires where their light and power extend with His presence and His actual consciousness. May this not be true? We know that the telephone and the telescope have practically annihilated distance, the one bringing the voices of the remotest regions to our side, the other bringing the distant heavenly bodies right into our immediate view. Now, suppose that in yonder heavenly world the inhabitants should have in their own brains, their ears, their eyes, their refined and perfect physical senses, all the powers of the telescope and the telephone, and this would not be hard; then, from that heavenly throne you could look out and see the most distant stars as if they were just at hand, and hear the farthest voices of the universe as distinctly as you hear the friend that is talking by your side. And thus all things would be gathered into unity together, and all the luminaries of the heavens become the lamps that light up the palace of the King, and all the voices of every planet and star one sublime harmony, one celestial chorus, ever rising in symphonies divine, and saying, as John heard every creature that was in heaven and in earth and under the earth saying, "To him who sits on the throne and to the Lamb/ be praise and honor and glory and power, for ever and ever!" (Revelation 5:13). If that is heaven, oh, how glorious it must be! Doubtless, that is the power Christ possesses now, and that makes it as easy for Him to bend His ear to our faintest cry as if He were still at Bethany. And that is the power which we one day shall share with Him when we behold His glory and shall be like Him, when we see Him as He is. Then we shall thank Him for His ascension just as much as for His lowly incarnation and His dying love.

SECTION II—*The Returning Lord*

HIS COMING

1. But now upon our vision is projected another picture just as necessary to complete the conception of God's perfect plan. It is the picture of the returning Lord. He had just disappeared from their view, and they were in danger of thinking that He had gone forever; therefore it is necessary to

arouse them by another vision. And so, as they intently watch the distant and receding cloud, lo, two shining angels stand beside them, who speak to them as visitors from another world: "Men of Galilee, . . . why do you stand here looking into the sky? This same Jesus, who has been taken from you into heaven, will come back in the same way you have seen him go into heaven" (Acts 1:11).

Just as when you have been sailing out of the harbor of New York on a distant ocean voyage, you have just said farewell to that beloved group on the dock and have seen their forms and faces and waving handkerchiefs fade in the dim distance, while your eyes grew more dim with tears, and suddenly you have been recalled to yourself by the steward telling you to get ready to send ashore whatever mail you had to give the pilot at Sandy Hook, and you realized that you had time to send one more parting message to your friends, and that brief but loving word was swiftly penned and sealed and sent, and in it you compressed your last and best message of love, until you should come again yourself. So the Lord was sailing out of the harbor of the terrestrial atmosphere into the great ocean of space, and He tarried a moment on the way to send these two angelic messengers with one more word of love. But that word, how important! For it was to mark the goal of all their future hopes and expectations, and to reveal something even more glorious than all He had taught them hitherto, namely: that His going away was but the prelude to His coming back again, and that the one key to all the problems of life, the one remedy for all the wrongs of time, the one solution of all the question of truth, the one outlook of faith and the one supreme goal of hope, was to be this blessed prospect and promise of His own literal and visible return.

But first He tells them that He is coming back actually and literally. It is not to be fulfilled in their death or their closer union with Him, by the coming of the Holy Spirit or the spreading of His kingdom on earth, but He Himself is coming, and all the rest is but a preparation for the King.

2. He tells them that they shall see Him come. "This same Jesus . . . will come back in the same way you have seen him go into heaven" (1:11). It will be visible, personal, and beyond all possible mistake or confusion.

3. It will be the same Jesus that will come, arrayed, no doubt, in the majesty of the Father, the glory of the angels and the forces of the universe. He will still have the same form, the same face, the same loving heart, and we will know Him as our brother and our Christ. Our hearts will instantly and instinctively recognize Him and reach out to Him in the presence of His majesty, even as we do when He comes to dwell in the heart, its welcome Guest.

4. He will come as He went away. And how did He go away? He went away blessing them, with His hands extended in benediction. So will He

come again with those arms stretched out in greeting to welcome us to His breast. Oh, not in terror, not in judgment, not as the dread Avenger is Jesus coming! Banish from your hearts these unscriptural and unbelieving specters. It is the Bridegroom that is coming. Let us love His appearing. Let us be preparing to welcome Him with joy and not with grief.

This, then, is the goal of prophecy and the outlook of faith. Now place these two points clearly in your spiritual view like the two centers of a great ellipse, and you will be prepared for the next point.

SECTION III—*The Descending Holy Spirit*

HIS RELATION TO CHRIST'S COMING

The Holy Spirit comes, not to be the final factor in the Christian dispensation, but as a temporary administration: first, to finish Christ's earthly work, and secondly, to prepare the way for His second coming. But we are not prepared to understand the coming of the Spirit until we first see these two clear points—the departing and returning Lord—and between them, like a parenthesis, the dispensation of the Holy Spirit to follow the one and herald the other. The business therefore, of the Holy Spirit, and the Church through which He operates, is to bring Christ back again, and so to complete the ministry which He began on earth that He can come to bring its final stage in the setting up of His millennial kingdom on the very place where He was rejected and crucified.

Having understood this, the place of the Spirit's dispensation, let us look at the promise of the Spirit as given us by the departing Lord.

A PERSON

1. He was to be a Person as real as Christ Himself. It is not something that we receive from God in this deeper life, but Somebody who comes to make Himself known to us, to make Himself real to us, and to be in us the source of all strength and happiness.

POWER

2. He was to come as the Spirit of power. Man is the weakest of beings, weaker than his own sinful nature, weaker than the elements around him, weaker even than the brutes over whom he was sent to exercise dominion. But the Holy Spirit comes to give him power, to make his life effectual, and when the Holy Spirit comes into our life He does something. He accomplishes something. He is more than a sentiment, a feeling, a fancy. He is an infinite force that makes our life powerful, and enables us to accomplish all for which we are called as the disciples of Christ. It is power over sin, power over self, power over the world, power over sickness, power over

Satan, power to be, to do, to suffer and to overcome.

IN US

3. The Holy Spirit does not work apart from us. The Master died and trod the wine press alone, single-handed, and went to the dragon's den and destroyed him. But the Holy Spirit is not like Christ. We are His temple. He resides in us and works through us, and unless we yield ourselves to be His instruments, He is unable to carry out His supreme purposes, and the great exalted Head is like a man with a paralyzed body that refuses to perform the functions for which that brain has power sufficient, but the paralyzed members are unequal to the effort. Therefore, the Spirit claims us as the subjects of His working.

WITNESSES

4. The Spirit's power is to be shown chiefly in our witnessing for Christ. That is the form of our service. We are not to witness of truth merely, not to become wise and wonderful orators or teachers, but we are to be witnesses of Him. I do not know how to express this better than to say that our business is to make Jesus real to men, so to live and so to speak that they shall see in us and through us a power and a Presence that will make them long for the same loving and almighty help in their lives. Thus to minister Christ to men is the highest service to which we can be called, and the most helpful thing we can do for weak and erring men.

AGGRESSIVE WORK

5. The sphere of their ministry was to be an ever-expanding one: "in Jerusalem, and in all Judea and Samaria, and to the ends of the earth" (1:8). Of course, we cannot now stop to follow this widening circle as the apostolic Church followed it through their great missionary campaign until the whole inhabited world had received the message of Christ. This remarkable verse is just a table of contents of the whole book of Acts, and the chapters that follow are the best commentary upon it, as successively we see the gospel planted first in Jerusalem, then throughout all Judea, next in Samaria, and finally in the remotest heathen nations.

Doubtless, also, we have here a hint for the individual Christian, of the Spirit-filled life and service that will always begin at home, our Jerusalem; and then reach out to our relatives ("all Judea"); and next find its way to our very enemies, those farther removed from us and having, perhaps, no natural claim upon us—Samaria; and then finally will lead us out in sympathy and service to be in some sense missionaries to the very heathen lands and send the gospel to the uttermost part of the earth.

TARRY

6. They were to tarry for this baptism of power. Without it they must not attempt their work, nor must we. If the Lord Himself would not begin His earthly ministry until He had received the baptism of the Holy Spirit, how much less dare we presume to go forth in our own strength and represent Him!

Why should they need to tarry? First, perhaps because the fullness of the time must first come, and the Pentecostal hour which, according to the Hebrew calendar, was to be interpreted and fulfilled in the coming of the Spirit, should have arrived. But secondly, and doubtless much more probably, because they themselves were not ready, and the waiting days were necessary for their spiritual preparation, to bring them to the end of themselves, to show them their need, to give them time to search their hearts, to deepen the hunger and the longing which were necessary for them to appreciate the blessing, and to make full room and right of way in their hearts for His indwelling and outworking.

And so let us wait for the promise of the Father. Let us receive in all His fullness the blessed Holy Spirit; and if any reader has not yet proved this promise true, be encouraged, dear friend, to follow even the dim light that is now shining in your heart, even the faintest longing that is springing in your soul. No words that we could speak would make you understand this experience until it comes to you. If there is within you a sense of something that you need and do not have—a cry for God in some way to give you purity, victory, power and rest—that is the blessing already begun. If you follow on to know the Lord, then surely will you know Him. He would never give you that longing desire and disappoint it when you came to tarry at His feet. Wait for the promise of the Father, "Seek the LORD while he may be found;/ call on him while he is near" (Isaiah 55:6), and "you will receive power when the Holy Spirit comes on you; and you will be my witnesses in Jerusalem, and in all Judea and Samaria, and to the ends of the earth" (Acts 1:8).

CHAPTER 2

PENTECOSTAL POWER

These men are not drunk, as you suppose. It's only nine in the morning! No, this is what was spoken by the prophet Joel:

> *"In the last days, God says,*
> *I will pour out my Spirit on all people.*
> *Your sons and daughters will prophesy,*
> *your young men will see visions,*
> *your old men will dream dreams." (Acts 2:15–17)*

We have glanced at the great points that were to mark the beginning and close of the Christian age, the departing and the returning Lord, and touched upon the great event that stands between these two—the coming of the Holy Spirit to administer the dispensation until the Lord Jesus shall come again. The Holy Spirit was to fulfill the work that Christ left undone and to prepare the way for the greater work which Christ Himself is coming back some day to complete. The great theme of the Acts of the Apostles is the Holy Spirit's coming and the power which He was to bring.

THE IMPORTANCE OF HIS COMING

1. Let us look first at the event itself, its magnitude, its stupendous importance and far-reaching power. What was it? It was something like the difference between the reign of David and the reign of Solomon. David came to lay the foundation for the work which Solomon followed to fulfill. When David had made his preparations he passed out of view and Solomon came to complete the work and rear that splendid temple. And so Jesus Christ in His earthly ministry had prepared the way for the building of His Church, the spiritual temple. Now He withdraws for a season from the scene, and the Holy Spirit comes to erect the edifice of the Church of God out of living stones. When this is done Jesus will come again to enter His temple and

reign over it, even as David is coming back again in the millennial age to sit once more upon his throne.

The event which this book of Acts records is nothing less than the actual descent of the Deity to this globe, the coming of the third Person of the Godhead, on a visitation of 2,000 years to one of the smallest orbs of space. It is a stupendous event. Jesus came to visit it as the Son of God for 33 years. Here we have a Divine Person just as great as Jesus—the Holy Spirit— leaving heaven, for He is no longer a resident there, and making His home on earth for 2,000 years. As a missionary might go to some leper hospital, to some outcast race, to some scene of barbarism and degradation, and, with his refinement and culture and higher tastes, settle down among these people and spend his lifetime—so this gentle, glorious Being, the Spirit of God, the Mind that made every mind in the universe, that garnished the heavens, made the beautiful stars, the glories of earth and all things that are lovely— the Holy Spirit—the Intelligence, the Executive of the Godhead, actually left heaven and moved down to this little planet and has been living upon it, making it His headquarters ever since that Pentecostal day.

WHAT WAS THE DIFFERENCE OF PENTECOST?

What was the difference between the Holy Spirit's coming and His Old Testament manifestations? In the Old Testament He only came to certain persons, prominent leaders, to men called to be prophets or priests or kings and perform some distinguished service. He came to such and gave them special qualifications for their work. He did not come to the great mass of people. There is no single example of a slave or a person of lower stage in the Old Testament being filled with the Holy Spirit. Now we are told He will come to all flesh, even the handmaidens and slaves without distinction of sex, rank or education. In the Old Testament the Holy Spirit came upon them. On this day of Pentecost He came in them. He was with them, but now He enters and becomes part of the inner life of the one in whom He dwells. It is a presence not with us, but in us.

Then again the Holy Spirit comes to us now for witnessing and service. The Jewish dispensation knew nothing of this. Their business was to keep the light among themselves and be exclusive and separate from the Gentiles. It is all different now. The Holy Spirit comes to spread the light, to make every man a reflector, a messenger and witness of Jesus Christ, and to expand and distribute this glorious gospel until it shall reach the uttermost parts of the earth.

Then again the Holy Spirit often came upon a bad man like Saul, yet did not change Saul's heart. He did not make Balaam a holy man. He gave power to these men for a purpose and an occasion. The Holy Spirit now comes to good men and to make men good. He comes for moral cleansing and quickening. He will not dwell in a heart that is willfully unholy.

Once again, the Holy Spirit differs in this age from the past because He comes now as the Spirit of Jesus. In the Old Testament He came as the Deity, the Spirit of the Father, distant and mighty. Now He comes as the Spirit of the Son, as the gentle heart of Jesus, the One that wept in His tears, loved in His tenderness, suffered in His pains, sympathized in His compassion. Now the Holy Spirit is the very embodiment and expression of the love and sweetness of the Christ of Galilee.

THE TIME OF HIS COMING

2. The day of Pentecost was the time He chose for His descent. It was a special day. He did not vaguely drift into time, but there was a line of demarcation, a point of contact, an instant when He entered this planet and settled in this world as His abiding home. There are reasons why He should not have come before. There were reasons why He should come then. The day of Pentecost was a Jewish feast of little interest to the Gentiles, but intensely interesting to Israel. Their ecclesiastical year was divided into 12 months, seven calendar months and five left blank because God did not give them a full plan of all the ages. The rest is to be filled up when He comes again. The ecclesiastical year began with the Passover, which stands for Calvary, where all our eras begin. Then came Pentecost in the next month. That is the second chapter of Church history. The Holy Spirit comes after Calvary also in the individual experience. Later came the Feast of Trumpets implying testimony for Christ, the Day of Atonement and the Feast of Tabernacles in the seventh month representing the coming of the Lord. The Feast of Pentecost was specially the one which celebrated the beginning of their harvest. The Feast of Tabernacles represented the full harvest.

Then Pentecost was also the anniversary of the law. It was on that very day that Moses gathered Israel around Mount Sinai, God came out in majesty and gave His law with His thunders and lightnings and they stood trembling and entered into the covenant of works with Him. Now the Holy Spirit comes on that anniversary because the Holy Spirit is the new law of the Christian. The old law was written on stone. The new law is written on the tablets of the heart. The old law was outside, while the new law is put within you as an instinct and intuition of your being, something that is part of your very nature.

"I will make a new covenant/ with the house of Israel. . . . This is the covenant . . . I will put my law in their minds/ and write it on their hearts./ I will be their God,/ and they will be my people" (Jeremiah 31:31, 33). Therefore the Holy Spirit came on the anniversary of the law that He might be to us, instead of the words of Sinai, the mere sense of duty which will never make anybody good.

Pentecost was the feast of the first harvest—so the Holy Spirit comes to bring the first harvest of the earth. That is the key to the whole missionary question. God is not saving the world, but He is saving the first sheaves out of the world. We are sent, not to convert everybody, but to gather out of the nations a people for His name.

We must not wonder if nine out of every 10 refuse the gospel. We must not be disappointed if results seem limited. It is a selective age, only every man makes the selection for himself. God gives everybody the call, and "all who were appointed for eternal life believed" (Acts 13:48). God sends us to gather samples of the nations, and do not think that God is disappointed or the Holy Spirit is baffled if the great mass of our countrymen are going on the broad road to ruin. They have been going and will keep on going all through the dispensation of the Holy Spirit. Pentecost is the gospel of first fruits.

There is another beautiful thing about this. In Leviticus 23, God is describing the way they are to keep the Passover, and also the Feast of Pentecost. He tells them that in the Passover they are to eat unleavened bread because it represents the spotless Lamb of God, leaven standing for human imperfection. After the Passover they had a wave offering of a sheaf, marking the first sheaf of harvest. Then they counted 50 days to Pentecost, and when that came it was celebrated by two loaves waved and also given to God for His food. But those loaves were baked with leaven, the only instance where leaven was allowed in the Levitical ceremony. Why? Surely it teaches that the Holy Spirit would not stay away from us even if we were still poor, imperfect disciples; that the Holy Spirit would come to Peter with his imperfection, and to Thomas with his doubting heart. In other words, you don't need to wait until you are faultless and sinless to receive the Holy Spirit. There is a kind of teaching about sanctification, telling people they must get sanctified and all right themselves, and then the Holy Spirit will come. If you can get ready for the Holy Spirit without Him, you can get along without Him afterwards. You have to have Him to make you ready and to make you right. You must have Him come down to where you are, "outside the camp" (Hebrews 13:11–13), and take you in. It is He that sanctifies, and sanctification is not a man all cleaned up himself and saying "Blessed Holy Spirit, I am all right and I will be glad to have your company." It is your coming as a poor leper and handing yourself over to Him. The Holy Spirit will take a poor sinner just as graciously as the Savior. And He will never leave you until He has you white and spotless, "without stain or wrinkle or any other blemish" (Ephesians 5:27). That is the meaning of the old Levitical Feast of Pentecost where the loaves had the leaven in them; but God took them and undertook to take the leaven out of them. Don't wait until you have yourself adjusted; come as you are. Take Him to be the First and the

Last, for "he is able also to save them," from the uttermost, "to the uttermost that come unto God by him" (Hebrews 7:25, KJV).

THEIR PREPARATION FOR HIS COMING

3. There was preparation for this great event. "When the day of Pentecost came, they were all together in one place" (Acts 2:1). Rotherham translates it thus: "While the day of Pentecost was being filled up they were all in one place with one object." They were not there at the moment only. They came all the week and were ready because they had been there. It wasn't keeping appointments with God and just sparing one hour out of seven days for His service. It was a time of daily waiting. They were there 10 days and were ready, and that was why He came. They were "all in one place with one object." They took pains to get everything fixed up. They had a sort of housecleaning. Some think Peter was all right in proposing to elect an apostle in place of Judas. It seems, however, as if God ignored Peter's apostle. You never hear of him again. He paid no attention to this new apostle, but He chose Paul a little later when he was ready. John speaks of only 12 apostles of the Lamb in Revelation. Peter tried to get everything adjusted. God help us to do the same.

SUPERNATURAL SIGNS OF HIS COMING

4. There were some signs and accompaniments of His coming. We are told there was some kind of a sound, "a sound like the blowing of a violent wind" (Acts 2:2). There was no wind, but the sound of a wind. A little later we are told, "when this was noised abroad" (2:6, KJV), literally, "when the people heard the sound they came running together." There was some strange supernatural voice, some supernatural demonstrations which they and all Jerusalem heard.

It was like wind. Wind is one of the tokens and symbols of the Spirit. Wind, with its tremendous force, so destructive and often so helpful, stands for the Holy Spirit, the mightiest of powers.

Again the symbol of fire is implied in the tongues which sat upon them.

They seem to have appeared like intoxicated men. They were lifted by a divine stimulus to a higher plane. So the apostle says, "Do not get drunk on wine, . . . Instead, be filled with the Spirit" (Ephesians 5:18).

Further the tongues suggest that it was their voices He was to change and use.

EFFECTS OF HIS COMING

5. There were the effects of His coming. It was in general supernatural power. He came to give them a force stronger than sin, disease, Satan or the spirit of popular opinion and the willfulness of the human will, power to

make things move; to lift this world and place it in its true orbit around the throne of God. Let us look at these signs of power.

a. The Gift of Tongues

This was the first of the Pentecostal signs, and the first to disappear.

b. Power of Testimony

It was not merely the voice, but the message that they spoke had strange power in it. They told about Jesus, His resurrection and coming, and many were stirred, convicted and saved. If you have received the Holy Spirit you are able to speak for God, perhaps not magnificent words, but loving, living words.

c. Power of Conviction

Again it was the power of supernatural conviction, a power that rested on the audience quite apart from the power in the message or the speaker. This is the greatest mark of the Holy Spirit's presence. Oh, for the power that brings people face to face with God, and holds them by a spell that we may not see, but God sees. Ask God for the power of conviction, so that every time the voice of the gospel is uttered there shall be stricken hearts, even as we are told of them that many were cut to the heart and said, "Brothers, what shall we do" (Acts 2:37)?

Will you look for that kind of power; and when you hear no shouts or tears, take the mighty God to move upon the people as a great electric current that will thrill them to their consciences and bring to their knees? It is power from on high. Not power from the man, but power that comes from God every time.

d. Power of Supernatural Boldness

The men were awed when they saw the boldness of these timid, uneducated fishermen, and they marveled and said "these men had been with Jesus" (4:13). They had courage and authority to speak, knowing God is behind.

e. Power of Healing

We find right away the power of the Spirit began to touch men's bodies, and the next morning the lame man at the gate Beautiful sprang to his feet leaping and praising God because the Holy Spirit had come. Then each new stage was marked by some manifestation of healing. When they went to Samaria the people were healed and the attention of the multitude was attracted. Peter went to Joppa and Lydda and the people there were healed. Then Paul started out on his missionary journey and the people were healed all along the way. Each new stage seemed to be marked with a new manifestation of the healing power of God.

f. Power of Holiness

Best of all was the power of holiness, for the Holy Spirit does not come to make men great, but He comes to make you real and true first, and then let your life reflect its reality and power on others. Therefore we are told "much grace was upon them all" (4:33). Their lives were beautiful. There was power over selfishness and sin and there was the power of love.

> Every day they continued to meet together in the temple courts. They broke bread in their homes and ate together with glad and sincere hearts, praising God and enjoying the favor of all the people. (2:46–47)

No one could say a word against them. "No one claimed that any of his possessions was his own" (4:32). God taught the Jew all through the Old Testament that property was a sign of God's blessing, prosperity in temporal things was the sign of God's approval, and there was no instinct so strong in the Jews as that of possession. But now they reckoned themselves as trustees, holding it for God. That was power, and it is real still when it works that way. If your consecration and blessing have not opened your purse strings and made it a joy to give to God you have not much of the Holy Spirit.

Communism was established at Pentecost. It was simply the overflow of hearts in a beautiful spectacle of unselfishness. Later all the social boundaries were recognized and Peter clearly intimated that every man had a right to do with his money as he wished. Communism is not, therefore, Christianity. Back of it is the bigger thing—love that gives up your rights when anybody else is wronged by your rights. Love is the law of the New Testament, and while love does not lead to communism, it will lead to sacrifice and live out John Wesley's famous sermon on practical love, which was:

1. Get all you can.
2. Save all you can.
3. Give all you can.

g. Power of Guidance

Again, it was the power of guidance, the power that led men in the right way. You can trace this through the Acts of the Apostles. See Him leading Philip to the desert to meet the eunuch. So He will lead you to the mission field. See Him leading Paul on that marvelous journey to Rome when everything conspired to stop him. A man with his hand in the hand of God, a woman grasping infinite power and wisdom as her protection, is safe. The Holy Spirit is strong enough to lead you safely and will not leave you until He has done all that He has spoken of.

h. Power of Providence

There is nothing that impresses one more in this book of Acts than the power of providence; that is, the power of the Holy Spirit in men's hearts to change circumstances. If God is on the throne inside your heart, as you go forth the winds and waves obey Him and the passions of men subside, the perils of earth and hell fall back and you live a charmed life because the Holy Spirit is upon the throne. You will find this all in the Acts of the Apostles. We see Peter in prison and the curtain falls on the darkest drama. Tomorrow is Passover and the appetite of the brutal mob is whetted for a feast, for Herod has told them they shall have Peter's blood. But God had not been consulted. Oh, how mighty that little "but" in the beginning of the chapter. "Peter was kept in prison, but the church was earnestly praying to God for him" (12:5). At midnight the prison door swung open and a shining guide is by the side of Peter, and he goes forth into liberty. Before yonder sun goes down Herod is seized with an awful pain and dies convulsed in terrible agony.

Many a time since has God worked the same. There was a day when the sultan of Turkey said that on that very day Christianity should be banished from his dominion, and every Christian found without having recanted must be put to death. But on that very day, less than a century ago, there was a strange panic yonder in Constantinople, for the Sultan was dying, and ere the sun went down on that fated day the Sultan was dead. The heart that is filled with the Holy Spirit can walk safely amid arrows and whirlwinds and death, for "in all things God works for the good of those who love him, who have been called according to his purpose" (Romans 8:28).

i. Power to Suffer

Finally there is power to suffer, power to be sweet amid wrong and persecution, to stand like Stephen when they gnashed upon him with their teeth, and made them gnash the more when they saw his face like an angel and they dared not look upon him, power like him to say, "Lord, do not hold this sin against them" (Acts 7:60). That was the mightiest power of the Holy Spirit, a power to be gently victorious even in suffering, and to stand with the Master in the garden and judgment hall.

j. Power of Salvation

But we must close the picture. Perhaps the most glorious power of all was the power of salvation, for Peter, quoting that prophecy of Joel, says, "And everyone who calls/ on the name of the Lord will be saved" (2:21). When the Holy Spirit comes it is so easy to be saved. If you are not saved, come while the door is open and the Lord is nigh. You have only to call. The work is done. Salvation is ready. The Spirit is here.

We have spoken about the earlier experiences of the Holy Spirit. There is not time to dwell on the fact that there were several later outpourings of the Spirit even in Pentecostal times. So He is not exhausted when He first comes. But, dear child of God, He has many times of refreshing for you. Have you got your baptism for today? Have you got the filling of the Spirit? He will come to the leavened loaf, but, oh, He comes to take the leaven out and sanctify you wholly and fill you so full that there will be no room for self, the world or sin. God help you to take it in His way.

Once again, the baptism of the Holy Spirit was not meant for higher Christians only. Peter says, "Repent and be baptized, every one of you, in the name of Jesus Christ for the forgiveness of your sins. And you will receive the gift of the Holy Spirit" (2:38). It is for the youngest Christian, and indeed, no soul should leave the altar of salvation until it has been sealed with the Spirit and taught to say:

> Let the water and the blood,
> From Thy riven side which flowed,
> Be of sin the double cure,
> Cleanse me from its guilt and power.

CHAPTER 3

GOD'S PLAN FOR THE AGE

You will be my witnesses in Jerusalem, and in all Judea and Samaria, and to the ends of the earth. (Acts 1:8)

W e have already seen that this remarkable verse is an epitome of the whole book of Acts. Were we to express in three words the design and contents of this story of primitive Christianity, those words would be the perspective, the power and the plan of the Christian age.

THE PERSPECTIVE

First, we have the perspective given in the first 11 verses of the Acts of the Apostles. Perspective is the relation of objects to each other in the line of vision. The book of Acts gives us the outlook of Christian faith and hope. In its true perspective four great promontories stand out. First the cross, expressed by the word "suffering" in the opening verses of Acts—"his suffering" (1:3). Next is His resurrection and ascension described so vividly in the same passage. Now His cross would not have had the same meaning if it had been looked at alone. It could have signified only death, disaster and utter despair. But when looked at with the resurrection in perspective just beyond, it becomes a stepping stone to glory and victory. Next comes the ascension, but this would have only meant separation from His loving disciples had it not been for the third object that meets our view, namely, the descent of the Holy Spirit, the Comforter, who came to take His place and fill the void of His absence. But even the dispensation of the Holy Spirit is not final. This has been the great mistake of the Church, to look upon it as the end of the Christian age. There looms beyond a still more sublime vision, namely the return of the Lord Jesus, the message of the angels to the bereaved disciples: "This same Jesus . . . will come back in the same way you have seen him go into heaven" (1:11). Thus, as we look at all together, they have upon each other the most vital bearing, and the whole truth is

531

necessary in order rightly to understand each part of the whole.

THE POWER

Next, the word power expresses that deep underlying truth that runs through the entire book of Acts, impressing us with the fact of a supernatural Person in the bosom of the Church, the power of the Holy Spirit as the heart of Christianity, while Jesus on the throne is its Head. The whole story of primitive Christianity is supernatural. There is no rational explanation for the sudden and widespread movement that brought into the bosom of the Church the men that crucified the Lord and the bitter enemy that pursued Stephen to his death and afterward ravaged the Church of God in the name of religious zeal. The triumphs of the gospel were miracles of grace and power, and the same power must still be recognized or we shall cease to have a living Christianity.

THE PLAN

But we have already followed these thoughts and facts in some measure, at least, through their unfolding in this history; and so we come to the third of these great outline words: the plan according to which this mighty and divine Person was to evolve the Church and prepare for the coming of the Lord. This is also most clearly given in our text and as clearly unfolded through the entire book. The movement was to begin at Jerusalem, and so we find the earlier chapters of Acts describing the origin, growth and constitution of the Church in Jerusalem. Next it was to reach the scattered Jews throughout all Judea. And so we find the story expanding in the evangelistic work of Peter and Paul among their countrymen scattered abroad. Then Samaria was to be reached, and so the eighth chapter of Acts introduces us to the gospel in Samaria, and late references continue the story. But the final and supreme triumph of Christianity in the Christian age was to be in the remoter realms of heathenism. And so the last half of the book of Acts, from the 13th chapter, is chiefly occupied with the origin and growth of foreign missions and the spread of the gospel to the "ends of the earth" (1:8). Such was the plan of campaign given by the Master and faithfully followed by His first field officers; and such is still the divine order for the Church of God in the aggressive work of Christianity—or, at least, such it ought to be—and only as we follow this plan will we have the Master's approval and blessing. Let us follow in detail these successive stages of aggressive Christianity.

SECTION I—*Jerusalem*

THE CHURCH IN JERUSALEM

This picture occupies the opening pages of Acts. Some striking features of this primitive Church are well worthy of our imitation.

1. It was born upon its knees. It came into being at Pentecost in the spirit and atmosphere of prayer.

2. It was baptized as soon as it was born. Its youngest members were taught to receive the Holy Spirit the moment they had accepted Jesus. "Repent and be baptized, every one of you, in the name of Jesus Christ for the forgiveness of your sins. And you will receive the gift of the Holy Spirit" (2:38). So still we should lead the convert to the altar of consecration, and never leave him until he has been sealed and sanctified by the same Spirit and saved from backsliding and defeat.

3. It was a household of love. Joy, praise, mutual affection, self-sacrifice, consideration for others, the care of the poor and the stranger, and the spirit of gladness and love made it a center of attraction and a blessed home circle which drew to it the sad and hungry world, as it still will draw men if it has the same Pentecostal spirit.

4. It was not without a very heart-searching discipline. The incident of Ananias and Sapphira left an awful lesson of the holiness of God and the sin and folly of trifling with His grace; and great fear, as well as great joy, fell upon the infant Church.

5. It had its baptism of fire in the martyrdom of Stephen and James, the imprisonment of Peter, and the cruel hatred of Herod and the Jews. And so still, if we have anything worth attacking, the devil will attack it, and if we have anything worth hating, the world will hate it as much as in the days of old.

6. It was scattered abroad by trial, that it might sow the seed in wider fields. When its members were in danger of clinging too closely to their congenial home circle, the Lord had to send them forth by persecution and kindle the fire on other altars.

7. But at length it became established and settled, and "It was strengthened; and encouraged by the Holy Spirit, it grew in numbers, living in the fear of the Lord" (9:31b).

Our Jerusalem

They were first commanded to begin at Jerusalem; and so, when we receive the Holy Spirit, our first witness should be at home in the family circle, to husband or wife, children or parents, brothers and sisters. In the church where God has placed us we should make the name of Jesus felt as "the aroma of Christ among those who are being saved and those who are perishing" (2 Corinthians 2:15). We are not justified in running away from our kindred, or even from our Christian associates because they do not agree with us and are not congenial to us. We are to stay until we have finished the testimony and learned the lesson God has for us. Have we been true to those at home, or have we found it harder to live and witness for Christ in these closer circles of love and intimacy than from some public pulpit or to some company of strangers?

SECTION II—*Judea*

THE CHURCH AMONG THE SCATTERED JEWS

God has distributed the children of Abraham by many vicissitudes and providences in all parts of the world. They formed a little nucleus in almost every important center of commercial life, and became a starting point for the apostolic missions in almost every land. Peter was chiefly their apostle, and we find him going down to Lydda and Joppa, while it is significantly added that he "traveled about the country" (Acts 9:32). Later he seems to be writing from Babylon, where we know there were some 70,000 Jews residing. We know also that there were many Jews in Rome, for we read in Acts of a decree banishing the Jews from Rome, in consequence of which Aquila and Priscilla and others were driven forth to Corinth. Paul also ministered much to his own countrymen and had an insatiable longing, amounting even to self-sacrifice, for their salvation (see Romans 9:3). James writes to them as "the 12 tribes scattered among the nations" (James 1:1), and there seems to have been an understanding that these scattered Jews were not merely remnants of the two tribes of Judah and Benjamin, but that they represented all the 12 tribes of the dispersion. If this be so, the recent theory which has been widely propagated in favor of the identity of the 10 tribes with the Anglo-Saxons, is, of course, without foundation, and the 10 tribes form part of the mass of Hebrews scattered among all nations still. To the Jews, therefore, everywhere the gospel was to be presented first, and this is still its message and its scope. The Gentile portion of the Christian Church has largely forgotten its sacred trust to Christ's kindred according to the flesh. This duty is not entirely fulfilled when we seek out the Jews separately and try to form our class missions for them as a race distinctively, as though they were scarcely fit to be included in our Christian congregations. Surely, this is a mistake. Why should we not preach to them in our common congregations just as directly as to the Gentiles? Why should we know either Jew or Gentile in the one Church of Jesus Christ? Why should we not seek and expect to attract them as hearers of the gospel in all our places of worship, and receive them to equal membership and love in all our Christian fellowships? Surely, this is the intention of the apostolic commission, "first for the Jew, then for the Gentile" (Romans 1:16); and we have reason to thank God that many Christian Hebrews are to be found in the ordinary membership and even the ministry of the churches of Christ.

Our Judea

But for us as individual Christians, what does this second stage of the great commission mean? Assuredly, that having begun at home, we are next to go with our testimony to our friends, to the whole circle of those we love and with whom we have personal influence and who belong to our sphere of fellowship and affection. Have we done so? Have you been true to your friends in witnessing for Christ? Have you, like Andrew and Philip, brought your brother and your friend to Jesus? Is your personal correspondence, your social conversation, your whole influence flavored and fragrant with the love of Christ and interwoven with tactful and wise appeals for the best and highest things; or has your selfishness, timidity and shame led you to betray your Master and neglect the very highest claims of holy friendship?

SECTION III—*Samaria*

THE GOSPEL IN SAMARIA

The Samaritans were a mongrel race descended from the old Jewish remnant left in Northern Palestine after the Assyrians took most of the people captive, and the heathen colonies with whom they intermarried after these immigrants were planted in the land by the Assyrian conquerors. Contrary to the laws and traditions of Israel, these poor Jews allowed themselves to be drawn into family relationships with the strangers, and thus there grew up a new hybrid race partly Jewish and partly heathen, with a mixture of Mosaic teaching and ritual along with much that was loose and uninspired. These people were called Samaritans, and as traitors to their race they were hated much worse than the heathen. The Jews, therefore, had no dealings with them; but the Lord during His own earthly ministry several times visited Samaria and opened the doors of salvation to these people. Now therefore, when giving the commission He was particular to include them, and at a very early date the Holy Spirit directed the first evangelists to go to them with the gospel. The pioneer of this work was Philip, the deacon. His work was marvelously successful, and in a short time a great revival ensued, multitudes flocking to Christ, so that the apostles and elders at Jerusalem were compelled to send a special deputation to visit these new churches and share with them the fuller blessings of the Holy Spirit. A little later we read of many churches in Samaria, as well as Judea, which were in a prosperous condition.

Our Samaria

Now what for us is the personal application of this third stage of apostolic witnessing? Where is our Samaria? Can we fail to recognize it in that great outlying world around us in the homeland, consisting of the multitudes that lie beyond the pale of Christian influences, whether it be by poverty or race distinctions or the awful effects and ravages of sin? They have grown up in every Christian land, a great multitude of outcast ones who never go to the house of God, whose synagogue is that of Satan, who worship the world, the flesh and the devil, who are held captive by Satan at his will, and for whom respectable Christianity remanded long ago to a place of hopeless despair. For the drunkard, the harlot, the thief, the convict, the foreign population who infest our alleys and slums, the multitudes that somehow struggle for life in the dark underworld of poverty and sin, it is only a little while since the very thought of salvation and rescue was seriously entertained among the activities of the Church of God. Thank God that it is coming to pass, and Christian love is now going out into the streets and lanes of the city to find the poor and the maimed, the halt and the blind. But oh, how much has yet to be done, and how little some of us have even attempted! Have you, beloved, been faithful there? This wonderful movement of rescue mission work in the homeland is one of the features of Christian life today and one of the signs of the end. The Holy Spirit is moving out and moving down from the old planes, and perhaps, leaving the gospel-hardened children of the kingdom and finding the chief trophies of grace today among these neglected and hopeless children of wretchedness and sin. When this task is fully done, and along with it the great outcast heathen world has been equally invited, then the Lord Himself will come.

SECTION IV—*The World*

THE GOSPEL FOR THE HEATHEN

"You will be my witnesses . . . to the ends of the earth" (Acts 1:8). This is the final stage and the supreme work of the witnessing Church. We shall find it the deep underlying thought of the whole book of Acts. It is quite wonderful and touching to see how the Lord patiently and gradually endeavored to bring His Church to understand this high calling and to be true to this trust. Naturally the Jew regarded the outlying Gentile world beyond the pale of God's purpose of grace. He believed he could not please God better than by keeping as far from them as possible, holding himself in a place of rigid separation, and leaving them to their wickedness and doom. It was very difficult, therefore, to thoroughly infuse into the minds of the apostles themselves God's larger thought of love and salvation for the heathen. It is interesting to trace the unfolding of this purpose and plan through the book of Acts.

1. Pentecost

We notice in the gathering of the multitudes at Pentecost from all nations a providential movement in connection with the spread of the gospel. These people were brought from the remotest regions of the globe to attend the great annual Jewish festivals, and then God gave to them the marvelous lesson of Pentecost and sent them forth to tell the story in their own language and to their own people of this wonderful gospel. That in itself was a stupendous missionary movement and laid the foundation, no doubt, of many a church in far scattered lands.

2. Philip

Next we find Philip suddenly called from Samaria, in the midst of his work, to meet a heathen prince down in the desert of Gaza as he was returning disappointed and hungry-hearted to his distant home. Peter might have argued with Philip that there was work enough to do at home, for never were hands so full as his with that great revival in Samaria. But Philip left it all for the greater work of foreign missions, even as Judson and the early missionaries left the attractive fields of their own home churches, refusing the most flattering calls that they might go far hence unto the heathen. And Philip found his obedience was not misplaced. God never misfits. When the man is ready the field is ready, and lo, the gospel has been carried to Ethiopia, and the first convert of foreign missions has been sent forth as the pioneer of a nation and of a continent. Surely, it paid. And so no matter how busy or how needed you may seem to be at home, if God is calling you to the work of missions, do not hesitate, do not spare the best you have to give, do not fear to leave your work in other hands; enough that the "Lord has need of you."

3. Peter

Next, we have Peter's call to Caesarea and the house of Cornelius. First Peter himself had to be prepared, and there on the housetop God did most thoroughly prepare him, breaking up his old Jewish prejudices by that never-to-be-forgotten lesson of his strange, supernatural meal, and then calling him, when he had become enlarged enough to understand the call, to go to the capital of the country and the innermost circle of Roman influence and power and begin a new Pentecost in the very heart of the Roman Court. From that wonderful scene Peter went to Jerusalem with a testimony that they could not resist. "Who was I," he might well say, "to think that I could oppose God?" (11:17). And the apostles began to understand and to rejoice that the door of faith was at last open unto the Gentiles.

It was some such process as this that God had to go through in the beginning of this century in breaking our ecclesiastical fathers from their old theological shells and having them understand that it was our business to care for the heathen and send them the gospel. But, alas, even yet how little the ministry of the Church of God realizes the claims of foreign missions!

We have no hesitation in saying that the lack of liberality, sacrifice and consecration in the churches of Christ lies much more at the door of the ministers than of the people themselves, and that when a pastor is thoroughly awakened to the claims of the perishing heathen and really baptized with the missionary spirit, there will never be any real difficulty in getting the people to give largely and to give freely. This is, perhaps, the most needed revival of missions in the Church of today.

4. Antioch

The next step in the development of the missionary idea was the church in Antioch. God had to have a new center from which to send out the great missionary movement. Jerusalem was too conservative and too exclusive, and so in Antioch a new center was started and a new mother church was formed—consisting of spirits like Barnabas, the noble merchant prince; Saul, the educated teacher; Manaen, the courtly gentleman; Simeon, the consecrated black man; Luke, the large-hearted cosmopolitan, and such men as these with a large mass of common people that had been brought into the church not even by apostolic preaching, but by the simple testimony of men and women like themselves. From this new center the gospel could go forth with peculiar power.

And so in our day God has been raising up His Antiochs again. The deep spiritual movements of our time all form a sort of Antioch from which are going forth the most vital missionary agencies of our time. It was this church that sent forth the early missionaries. Let us, therefore, not forget that it is God's plan to send forth the missionary from a warm home center. The idea of independent missions apart from that supporting center is not scriptural. There must be two ends to the work, the home and the foreign, both equally responsive and helping.

5. Barnabas and Saul, the First Missionaries

Time will only permit us to lightly touch this stirring theme. God has His men ready. Saul had been called from the ranks of the enemy, and Barnabas had also been prepared from another class. There were three men in the first missionary party. One was an educated teacher, and such men are needed still. The second was a consecrated businessman, and there are no better missionaries than such laymen. And there was a young man, a little fresh, a little immature, a little soft, a little weak, a little like some of our missionaries still—poor Mark. And he had his failure, as some of our boys and girls have at first, and for it Paul even would have none of him; but he came out all right at last. Let us learn the lesson of patience, for God even uses imperfect material and patiently waits until it is trained. And so they went forth, and in due time came back to tell the story of their wonderful beginning and to gather in that great missionary convention at Jerusalem, where the plan was more fully settled and their subsequent missionary work wrought out with still more intelligent and holy zeal. Let us learn the lessons of their victories and defeats, and let us catch the thought of the Master they followed so fully, so that He can use us to finish what they so gloriously began.

CHAPTER 4

WITNESSING FOR CHRIST

You will be my witnesses in Jerusalem, and in all Judea and Samaria, and to the ends of the earth. (Acts 1:8)

"I have appeared to you to appoint you as a servant and as a witness of what you have seen of me and what I will show you." . . . I have had God's help to this very day, and so I stand here and testify to small and great alike. (26:16, 22)

Testimony is the foundation of all jurisprudence in earthly courts and all faith in the economy of grace. The lives of men are determined every day by the word of a credible witness. And so God has rested the foundations of Christianity upon human testimony and required of us the faith that believes on the word of the true witness. God Himself meets us as a Witness.

> Anyone who believes in the Son of God has this testimony in his heart. Anyone who does not believe God has made him out to be a liar, because he has not believed the testimony God has given about his Son. (1 John 5:10)

Faith is not believing because we have seen a mathematical demonstration, but it is believing someone's word. Therefore God has sent forth the most credible witnesses to bear testimony to men of the death and resurrection of Jesus Christ and the offer of salvation which He has made through His name. He has been most careful in the appointment of such witnesses. This was the primary meaning of the apostolic office to be witnesses of His resurrection (Acts 1:22). And for this purpose they were to be endued with supernatural power, that their testimony might be that of the Holy Spirit as well as of faithful men.

Our ministry, therefore, is that of witness-bearing. "You will be my witnesses in Jerusalem, and in all Judea and Samaria, and to the ends of the earth" (1:8).

PERSONAL KNOWLEDGE

1. The witness must have personal knowledge of the matters concerning which he testifies. Hearsay evidence cannot be admitted. We must know Christ personally before we can testify to Him.

A personal experience is essential to effectiveness in all work for Christ. Men instinctively become sensible of the lack of it. It gives a fine tone and color to all we say, and its absence is quickly detected even by the unsaved. During the earlier years of the writer's ministry, before he knew the Holy Spirit personally, no one ever came to him to talk about the deeper life, but within 24 hours after he knew the Lord as an indwelling personal reality, hungry hearts began to come and ask the way to Jesus. You cannot deceive human souls with painted fire and spiritual illusions. We cannot make burning glasses for the heavenly altars out of lumps of ice as they do in Arctic regions to kindle fires.

> We must ourselves be true,
>   If we the truth would preach;
> Our hearts must overflow, if we
>   Another's heart would reach.

A PERSONAL CHRIST

2. We are witnesses of a personal Christ. We are not sent to unfold a scheme of doctrine, a logical creed, a system of truth merely, but primarily, to tell about a Person, to make Jesus Christ real to men and make them long to know Him for themselves. We are not to testify of our personal experience so much as of Him; but we are to testify from our personal experience and have it give warmth, reality and force to the message of Jesus, as the heathen child so plaintively expressed it when she cried to the missionary, "Take me with you to your Jesus." We must have them feel that He is our Jesus, but it is Jesus and not ourselves that we are to preach. Your glowing experiences may only perplex or discourage them and make them feel how unlike their experience is, or still worse, try to copy you. But let Christ be your theme, and you, like the transparent glass, reveal the light without projecting your own shadow.

DEFINITE TESTIMONY

3. Their witness of Jesus was at the same time very definite. It was not a vague metaphysical dream, such as Christian Science would give us, of some

manifestation of Deity, some idea of love which God was projecting upon the human mind, but it was a real personal, individual Christ of whom they could tell with authority who He was, whence He came, how He suffered, died, and rose again, where He is now and how He is coming once again.

Their testimony embraced four points especially.

First, they witnessed His divinity. He was "Jesus . . . the Son of God" (9:20). "The God of our fathers raised Jesus from the dead—whom you had killed by hanging him on a tree" (5:30). "God has made this Jesus, whom you crucified, both Lord and Christ" (2:36). That was the way they testified to Him.

Second, they saw His death and atonement. They witnessed to His sufferings and His precious blood as the ground of justification and forgiveness for sinful men.

Third, they witnessed of His resurrection. "God has raised this Jesus to life, and we are all witnesses of the fact" (2:32). They announced Him as a risen and glorified Being, seated on a throne of supreme power, and showing by the might of His very name that He was still alive and was the Son of God.

Fourth, their witness included His second coming. They preached Him to men as "judge of the living and the dead" (10:42). They proclaimed a day when God "will judge the world with justice by the man he has appointed. He has given proof of this to all men by raising him from the dead" (17:31). "He must remain in heaven until the time comes for God to restore everything, as he promised long ago through his holy prophets" (3:21). These were some of the terms in which they witnessed to His coming again. And so our witness of the Christ must always include His deity, His atonement, His resurrection and His coming again.

SCRIPTURAL TESTIMONY

4. They testified according to the Scriptures, and they based their arguments on the Scriptures. In Peter's sermon in the second chapter of Acts we find him quoting with singular appropriateness from the prophet Joel and the patriarch David, arguments which they could not gainsay because they were from their own Scriptures. Again, in Acts 3:22 and 24, Moses and Samuel are called as witnesses to corroborate the apostolic testimony. So again we find Stephen basing his entire argument on the Old Testament history, and they were powerless to resist the inexorable logic of his appeal. Philip in his interview with the eunuch, Acts 8:35, immediately turns to the Scriptures and from the book of Isaiah preaches unto him Jesus. Again in his great sermon at Antioch, Acts 13, Paul appeals to their own history as the foundation of his argument and quotes from David and the prophets (verses 33 and 41) to clinch his arguments and rivet his messages. So our testimony

for Christ must be through His own Word, for the Bible is just one successive testimony of Jesus and every page a glowing portrait of His face.

IN THE HOLY SPIRIT

5. Our witnessing must be in the power of the Spirit. "We are witnesses of these things," said Peter, "and so is the Holy Spirit, whom God has given to those who obey him" (5:32). It is the joint testimony of the Spirit and the messenger. Without Him our witness is cold and fruitless. "No one can say, 'Jesus is Lord,' except by the Holy Spirit" (1 Corinthians 12:3). And if we have the Holy Spirit the message cannot be kept back.

OFFICIAL WITNESSES

6. There were official witnesses and unofficial. There were the appointed messengers and officers of the church, and there were the hearts and voices that overran the limits of conventional ministry and just witnessed because they could not help it, going beyond their own province, but gloriously irregular through the power of the Spirit.

First there was the apostolic body, consisting only of those who had seen the Lord in the flesh and were qualified thus to be witnesses of His resurrection. Therefore there can be no apostolic succession, for John saw on the foundations of the New Jerusalem the names, not of all the apostles of later times, but the 12 apostles of the Lamb.

Then there were the prophets, whose ministry Paul defines thus: "Everyone who prophesies speaks to men for their strengthening, encouragement and comfort" (1 Corinthians 14:3). The prophet, therefore, is a God-touched messenger who brings to men some living message of instruction or appeal or consolation fresh from the heart of God. He is not necessarily the foreteller of future events. Certainly he is not inspired to give a new Bible or authoritative revelations of the will of God in addition to the Holy Scriptures, but he is just a voice to speak from time to time in living power what God has already spoken through His written Word.

Then the evangelist came next, the soul winner, the messenger of salvation to men, with a wider parish than a single church, an office which still God uses and honors, and should be recognized as the special ministry of those whom the Holy Spirit thus calls.

Next was the office of pastor and teacher. He was the shepherd of the particular congregation, and associated with him was the elder, an office that included two classes apparently, the teaching and the ruling elder, for the apostle speaks of elders that labor both in word and doctrine as worthy of double honor.

The deacon was the servant of the church as the word literally means. His duty was to minister to the poor, the stranger, the neglected, to stand with open heart and hand at the threshold of the church, bidding its children welcome to the Father's house and helping to make it indeed a household of faith and a home of love.

The deaconess, too, had her place, for Phoebe, "a servant of the church in Cenchrea" (Romans 16:1), was literally a deaconess as the words mean.

Then there were the irregulars of the Lord's army, the people that went beyond their formal line of ministry, and like Joseph, allowed their fruit to "climb over a wall" (Genesis 49:22). Such was Stephen, the deacon, who became the most illustrious evangelist and the first martyr of the infant Church, confounding even Saul in the synagogues of the Cilicians with his matchless arguments and heavenly wisdom, and bringing him by his dying prayers to follow in the same pathway. Such was Philip, also a deacon, who through his zeal and faith promoted to be the great evangelist of Samaria and afterwards pioneer missionary of Africa, calling the prince of Ethiopia to Christ and sending him back to his own land, perhaps, to lay the foundations of the great churches which we afterwards find in those regions.

And then woman's ministry, too, found its place; good Priscilla getting ahead even of her husband Aquila in the ranks of service, and Dorcas with her spirit-baptized fingers and heart strings so necessary to the apostolic Church that she had to be brought back even from the dead, while James the apostle was permitted to pass away in martyrdom. Such were the apostolic witnesses in whose footsteps we are permitted to follow in the closing days of the same dispensation. There was a glorious irregularity as well as a divine order, for order was never intended to cramp, but only to direct the forces of the spiritual world. Therefore we find in Acts 8:4, that when persecution came all the Christians were scattered abroad except the apostles, and "those who had been scattered preached the word wherever they went." This word "preached" is an unusual word, meaning literally, talking informally, or as some have translated it, "gossiping the gospel." It was the witness-bearing of plain men and women who just talked about Jesus wherever they went, and so talked that, as we read a little later in Acts 11:19–21, they brought a great multitude to Christ and laid the foundations of the mother church at Antioch, which became henceforth the head and heart of the missionary activities of the apostolic Church.

EXAMPLES

7. Here are some examples of their witness-bearing:

Peter on the Day of Pentecost

a. We have Peter's testimony on the day of Pentecost, which Prof. Stiffler characterizes as the most compact and convincing piece of sacred oratory in the New Testament. And yet it was an address that could be delivered in less than 10 minutes, and had none of the shallow tricks of modern oratory about it, but was the simple eloquence of truth and earnestness on fire with the Holy Spirit.

Peter before the Council

b. Next were Peter's messages before the Council, splendid examples of a holy courage that cared not for his own safety, but sought only to make the occasion an opportunity to witness for his Savior and Master. And so convincing was the testimony that the rulers were compelled to let him alone and keep their hands off the word of God.

Stephen's Testimony

c. Again we have the testimony of Stephen, so bold and fearless of his own safety, so wise and convincing in its arguments, and so heavenly in its spirit, that the only argument left them in their baffled rage was a shower of stones, making him, as the word witness literally means, a martyr too, the proto-martyr of the Church of God.

Philip's Witness

d. Then we have the witness of Philip in Samaria, and later to the eunuch in the desert, and in both instances it was the same simple testimony: "Philip went down to a city in Samaria and proclaimed the Christ there" (8:5). "Then Philip began with that very passage of Scripture and told him the good news about Jesus" (8:35)—the same old gospel whether in Samaria or Africa:

> Jesus only, Jesus ever,
> Jesus all our theme shall be.

Peter's Testimony

e. Next we have the witness of Peter in the house of Cornelius, a beautiful model of gospel preaching. It took a good deal to get him ready for it. God had to take him on the housetop and put him through some pretty hard classes, not only in theology, but also in biology, before he was ready to go to a Gentile congregation and preach Jesus unto them. But he was ready at last, and preach he did, so that the Holy Spirit came like a second Pentecost, and the door of faith was opened unto the Gentiles. What a sermon that was in Acts 10:34–43, only 200 words all told, less than five minutes long and yet the whole gospel compressed into it without the slightest stiffness: all about John's baptism, Jesus Christ's life on earth, His death on the cross, His resurrection and its infallible proofs, His coming again as the Judge of the quick and the dead, and His offer of salvation to all that believe witnessed by all the prophets. Nothing lacking. Everything complete and glowing with the very love of Christ.

Paul the Witness

f. Next we have Paul's witness-bearing. It began immediately after his conversion. "At once he began to preach in the synagogues that Jesus is the Son of God" (9:20). Time will not permit us to follow all the recorded testimonies of his life and work: at Antioch, Acts 13, a scriptural testimony to the Jews; at Derbe and Lystra, Acts 14, an entirely different but equally appropriate testimony to a heathen audience; at Athens, Acts 17, a still more wonderful and wisely adapted appeal to the extraordinary audience gathered at the Acropolis at Athens representing all the art, learning and idolatry of Greece, but all woven into the exquisite web of his testimony of Jesus, the coming Judge of all, and the risen Son of God—a message followed even in cold Athens by the conversion of a poor prostitute and a noble councilor. Then we might trace also with equal interest his witness to the jailer of Philippi: "Believe in the Lord Jesus, and you will be saved" (16:31); his strenuous testimony at Corinth (18:5); and the long retrospect he gives us in Acts 20 of his three years' ministry and his faithful witness-bearing at Ephesus until he could say, "I am innocent of the blood of all men" (20:26). Again we have his testimony from the stairs of the castle in Jerusalem (chapter 22), addressed to his own countrymen; his heart-searching message to Felix and Drusilla (chapters 24, 25), until the old Roman debauchee trembled on his very throne and for a moment felt himself in the presence of the judgment day; and his longest testimony with the story of his conversion as told by himself in the presence of Agrippa in the 26th chapter of Acts—all these messages are brimming with the glory and the name of Jesus Christ, and his one object is not to clear himself, but to introduce his Master. Later on we see him on the deck of the tossing vessel in the Adriatic storm, taking command of the ship when all hearts failed with terror, and testifying of Jesus Christ, "whose I am and whom I serve" (27:23), until he himself becomes the central figure in the drama, and for his sake all on board are saved. At Rome it is the same story. Daily in his own hired house they come to him, and the book of Acts leaves him there preaching the kingdom of God and teaching those things which concerned the Lord Jesus Christ with all confidence, no man forbidding him, for two long years. His later epistles give us innumerable glimpses of subsequent testimonies.

In the closing scenes unveiled in his last letter to Timothy, we see him brought before the cruel Nero on trial for his life. We hear him say with no bitterness of spirit, only sorrow for them,

At my first defense, no one came to my support, but everyone deserted me. May it not be held against them. But the Lord stood at my side and gave me strength, so that through me the message might be fully proclaimed and all the Gentiles might hear it. And I was delivered from the lion's mouth. (2 Timothy 4:16–17)

We can almost hear the growls of the fierce Nubian lions that were appointed for his death. We can see the great crowd of Gentiles gathered round the court of Nero waiting for the verdict, and whether their thumbs shall be turned upward for his acquittal or downward for his doom. But what do we see on the part of Paul? No thought of danger, no fear of death, no notice of the angry lion, but only one purpose, that "the message might be fully proclaimed" (4:17). It is the chance of his life. For the first and last time he has the ear of Nero, and the old sinner shall hear the gospel now if he never did before. And Paul just preaches it with all his might until not only he, but all the Gentiles, hear once at least the story of Jesus Christ. That was his business. What about the lion? That was God's business. And in the most incidental manner he just adds, "I was delivered from the lion's mouth. The Lord will rescue me from every evil attack and will bring me safely to his heavenly kingdom. To him be glory for ever and ever. Amen" (4:17–18). It was his business to take care of Christ's glory, and it was Christ's business to take care of him.

LESSONS

In conclusion:

1. Have something to tell and something to give, and it will get out like the testimony of which Peter had to say, "We cannot help speaking about what we have seen and heard" (Acts 4:20).

2. Always hold up Jesus Christ and try to make Him real to the world. That is the only thing that will attract, that will save, that will satisfy, that will help lost men and bring God's blessing.

3. Begin at home. That is your Jerusalem. Then go to every widening circle of influence and opportunity until you reach the uttermost part of the earth.

4. Recognize every situation that comes to you as an opportunity for testimony. Look at every person you meet as a subject for God's blessing through you in some way, and thus all your life will be a ministry for Him.

5. Live your testimony, be a Bible. If you cannot be an apostle you can be a "letter . . . known and read by everybody" (2 Corinthians 3:2).

6. Ask God to put into your life supernatural things that will themselves be His witness to your testimony and commend it to an unbelieving world.

Every Christian ought to have answered prayers in his body, in his business, in his trials and temporal circumstances, that will speak for God and make them know that there is a real and a living Christ, and that our Christianity is not a theory but is supernatural and divine.

7. Remember that though you may never be a missionary in Africa or China, you can still be a witness to the uttermost part of the earth. You can shine afar through other lives even where your feet may never go. At a country crossing and beside a village pump, Brainerd Taylor met a young man and spoke to him a few simple, burning words that sent him to seek and find the Lord, and at length become a missionary to the heathen. He never knew the name of his benefactor until long years had passed and Brainerd Taylor had been a good while in heaven. Then one day there fell into his hands a little book containing the story of that saintly life and the portrait of the man on the frontispiece. Then for the first time he knew to whom it was he owed his salvation and his life's work, and falling upon his knees he thanked God for the saintly man who had never been able himself to go to Africa, but whose witness was being repeated through another life in that dark land. God give us grace to receive our Pentecost and fulfill our testimony.

CHAPTER 5

TO THE REGIONS BEYOND

Some time later Paul said to Barnabas, "Let us go back and visit the brothers in all the towns where we preached the word of the Lord and see how they are doing." (Acts 15:36)

Paul and his companions traveled throughout the region of Phrygia and Galatia, having been kept by the Holy Spirit from preaching the word in the province of Asia. When they came to the border of Mysia, they tried to enter Bithynia, but the Spirit of Jesus would not allow them to. So they passed by Mysia and went down to Troas. During the night Paul had a vision of a man of Macedonia standing and begging him, "Come over to Macedonia and help us." (16:6–9)

In a previous chapter we have reviewed the plan of the Holy Spirit and the apostolic Church for the wider witnessing of the gospel from Jerusalem to the uttermost part of the earth, and we have seen how God's supreme thought for the evangelization of the world was slowly impressed upon the early Church until the great work of foreign missions had been fairly started with the first missionary journey of Barnabas and Paul. All this was, indeed, a marked advance on Jewish conservatism, and forcibly recalls the slow awakening of the modern Church during the past century to a sense of its obligations to the heathen world.

But it was merely a beginning. They were as yet but feeling their way to this new department of work and finding out its limitations and spiritual laws. At the end of their journey it was necessary that the Church should come together and have a more perfect understanding of God's great plan for the evangelization of a world, so that they might go forth and work intelligently in cooperation with their divine Leader.

THE COUNCIL AT JERUSALEM

For this purpose the first Council at Jerusalem was held, to which we referred in the close of the last chapter. The effect of this was to clearly determine in the minds of both Jewish and Gentile Christians the divine method for the present age, namely, the gathering out from the Gentiles a people for His name; second, the personal coming of the Lord Jesus immediately afterwards; third, the millennial age and the salvation of all the world. With all this settled and communicated in the form of a fraternal letter to the brethren in all the churches, they were now ready to enter fully upon the great business of the world's evangelization, and the present section beginning with the second great missionary journey marks the next epoch in this mighty movement.

REVISITING THEIR STATIONS

It began with the revisitation of the stations already planted, and then followed the evangelization of the Celtic tribes of the highlands of Asia, known as the Galatians. But at this point God called a halt in all their home work in the continent of Asia, and marked a new epoch by sending them forth to the yet unoccupied continent of Europe, in connection with which the rest of their campaign was entirely occupied.

Let us make a passing note of time at this point, that we may the more intelligently follow this great historical movement. It was now about 17 years since Pentecost. The events of the last section, from the sending out of the first missionaries to the Council at Jerusalem, had occupied about three or four years; and the present section, embracing their work in Galatia and Greece to the close of their second missionary journey, covered about three years more, from A.D. 51 to 54. While the narrative sweeps rapidly over these stirring events, let us not forget that what we are told is but a fragment of the whole story of apostolic missions, and that these are but sample pages from God's book of remembrance intended to give a connected thread of the development of missions, especially in connection with the life and work of the great apostle of missions, Paul.

SECOND MISSIONARY JOURNEY

Let us mark some of the stages of this second missionary campaign (Acts 16 to 18):

1. Voluntary

We note the absence of the special call of God to go forth as in their first missionary journey. It was voluntary, and came directly from the prompting of Paul himself. "Let us go back," he said to Barnabas, "and visit the brothers" (15:36). And so we learn that when God has once called us to His work we are to be about our Father's business and not wait for some special revelation for each new ministry, but "each man, as responsible to God, should remain in the situation God called him to" (1 Corinthians 7:24).

2. Timothy

We note in the next place the solicitude of Paul about his fellow workers. He wanted the best material only for this great work, and he would have nothing to do with Mark, who had proved a failure in their former journey and gone back from Perga when the difficulties began to thicken. We can scarcely doubt that Paul was right in wanting the best missionaries, and we are quite safe in following his example. We cannot doubt that Barnabas was right, too, in standing by Mark as his nephew and helping to restore him to the Lord and the work, and so successful was he that the outcome justified him, and the day came when Paul was manly enough to acknowledge Mark's merits and even to send for him in the hour of his need and add, "he is helpful to me in my ministry" (2 Timothy 4:11). Doubtless Paul's firmness was as much used as Barnabas' kindness in restoring the young and yet undisciplined lad.

But the best lesson of all is the beautiful picture we have here of the way in which love can settle the differences of consecrated Christians. There are two ways of separating from our fellow workers: one, which leaves an unhealed scar, and weakens both of our lives for all the future; the other, like the separation of Abraham and Lot, or Barnabas and Paul, which sheds honor on the character of both and starts two centers instead of one of holy influence and service. If you cannot work together in perfect harmony as Christians, separate in perfect frankness and Christian love.

3. Silas

We soon find God supplying Paul with new companions as he sets out on his missionary journey, leaving Barnabas to divide the field and go back to Cyprus, his native island, while Paul takes his own home province of Cilicia and moves on to Asia Minor. Paul chooses Silas as his fellow worker, and a little later God gives him Timothy who had been converted three years before during the apostle's former visit to Derbe and Lystra. Timothy was the son of a godly mother, Eunice, a Jewess, and indeed had enjoyed the blessed teaching of a godly grandmother, Lois. There is, perhaps, a hereditary piety; at least there is an early influence in the first teaching and training of childhood that nothing can be a substitute for. God have mercy on the children of worldly, shallow, heartless mothers, and have mercy on mothers who bring into being neglected lives to a fate worse than orphanage. We little dream how soon the infant mind begins to receive religious impressions. I know a little child, little more than three years old, who can tell the whole story of the Acts of the Apostles, and often goes aside with her Christian nurse at her own request, with the tears streaming down her little face, to pray for the conversion of the manservant in the house to whom she is much attached, but who, she has lately found, is going to dancing school, and she greatly fears he will lose his soul. In Timothy's case the soil was all prepared, and he needed only the seed of the gospel and the quickening of the Spirit to bring into birth the most beautiful Christian life of the apostolic story, except, perhaps, the Apostle Paul himself. From the first he became like a very child to his spiritual father.

> I have no one else like him, who takes a genuine interest in your welfare. For everyone looks out for his own interests, not those of Jesus Christ. But you know that Timothy has proved himself, because as a son with his father he has served with me in the work of the gospel. (Philippians 2:20–22)

Timothy was the son of a Gentile father and a Jewish mother, and in order to smooth down the prejudices of the Jews, Paul on this occasion consented to his being circumcised, and so Timothy became a sort of bridge between the two classes who were united among Paul's hearers.

4. Former Fields Revisited

The revisiting of the churches already planted was first carefully attended to. There seem to have been many of these, and it is added, "So the churches were strengthened in the faith and grew daily in numbers" (Acts 16:5). The nurturing of that little flock was quite as important a missionary work as the planting of the gospel in new fields. In our zeal for evangelization we must never lose sight of edification, the building up of the body of Christ. The Lord Jesus has covered both in the great commission, "Go and make disciples of all nations, baptizing them in the name of the Father and of the Son and of the Holy Spirit" (Matthew 28:19). That is the work of planting the gospel. But we must never forget the other work which follows: "teaching them to obey everything I have commanded you" (28:20).

5. Galatia

One new church, at least, was planted during this journey. Luke passes over it in the narrative with a single word, but the epistle to the Galatians tells the story of its planting. It was among the highlanders of Asia, the Celtic ancestors of the French, the Irish and the Gaelic people of the north of Scotland. Like their descendants still, they were a fiery, passionate race, full of enthusiasm for a new doctrine and as ready to follow some brilliant, false teacher into error. Therefore Paul tells us, "You welcomed me as if I were an angel of God" (Galatians 4:14), but a little later we find them going away after Judaizing teachers into ritualism. To them we owe one of the richest of the Pauline epistles. But with this new station their work in Asia came to a close.

6. A Halt

The time had now come for a new departure even in foreign missions. The old world which for 4,000 years had been the cradle of the race, and the seat of all its religious movements, must now give place to the new continent of Europe and its children, which were to fill a larger place in the history of the future than even Asia had in the past. And so a strange incident occurs. They find their evangelistic work apparently arrested, "having been kept by the Holy Spirit from preaching the word in the province of Asia" (Acts 16:6), whither they were pressing forward to the ancient city of Ephesus. "When they came to the border of Mysia, they tried to enter Bithynia, but the Spirit of Jesus would not allow them to" (16:7). It must have seemed strange at first and hard to understand. They had been so accustomed to the presence and blessing of the Spirit in all their meetings that they may have been tempted to think there was something wrong in them. And so, perhaps, for several weeks they persevered and tried to push forward into these new fields. But everywhere it was the same. God would not go with them. They were evidently out of His order and will. And so, like wise men, they stopped and waited.

Have you never found at some point in your Christian work that God seemed to call a halt, and that the blessing that you had enjoyed appeared to desert you and the work to grow heavy and fruitless? And yet you could find nothing in your own heart to condemn. After a while, perhaps, it dawned upon you that God did not want you there, but had some other calling which He was trying to show you. Is this perhaps the reason why so much of our Christian work at home is dead, and worse than dead—corrupt? And why our theological seminaries and pulpits are teaching higher criticism, and our church members are dancing down in the great whirl of worldliness and sin to apostasy and ruin? God is not blessing His Church, because she is not where He wants her. She is wasting her energy, her money, her ministry, in religious selfishness, ecclesiastical extravagance and ritualistic forms in the name of religion, while her people are spending their God-given prosperity in every form of indulgence and selfishness. If she would only call a halt like Paul and Timothy and wait before the Lord as they did, the light would soon come, and she would find that her blessings are cursed because she is spending them on herself and neglecting the perishing world.

7. Europe

While they wait at Troas the situation immediately becomes plain. God does not want them any longer in Asia because He needs them more in Europe. And so there appears to Paul a vision by night, a man of Macedonia beckoning and crying, "Come over to Macedonia and help us" (16:9). And when the morning dawns the little company confer together and immediately conclude God is calling them to Macedonia. Taking passage at the earliest moment they sail for Philippi, the chief city of a miniature Roman state. Finding work, no doubt, as skilled laborers, they spend the week quietly, and on the Sabbath day they search in vain for the usual synagogue of Jewish worshipers. But they learn that there is a little company of pious Jews accustomed to meet outside the town by the riverside, and thither they find their way.

And so the gospel in the great continent of Europe begins with a woman's prayer meeting, and indeed with the opening of a woman's heart, for "The Lord opened her heart to respond to Paul's message" (16:14). Why not? Hers has ever been the glory of undoing the shame of the fall. The conversion of Lydia opened the doors of her home, and the little church was immediately transferred to that loving household. It is not strange that henceforth the spirit of the Philippian church and Paul's relation to it were marked by a tenderness not found in any other case.

8. Opposition at Philippi

Soon, however, the dark shadow of the adversary falls upon the scene. Satan understands the situation and tries to meet it in its worst form. A priestess of Apollo, inflated with demoniac possession, and yet constrained somehow to bear testimony to the divine character of the missionaries, pursues them from day to day with her insane ravings, and at the same time with her witness to them and to their message, until they are constrained to meet the issue. Then Paul, in the name of Jesus Christ, demands the demon to depart and sets her free from Satan's power. But this, of course, immediately stops her profession and brings upon the disciples the anger of her employers, who used her clairvoyant gift for purposes of gain. A riot ensues, and by a skillful appeal to the prejudices of the multitude on the ground that they are subverting Roman customs, they are condemned. They are cruelly beaten, bound with stocks and chains and cast into the inner prison. It seems, indeed, as if Satan has triumphed.

9. The Victory

It is never defeat so long as we do not lose our song of praise, and that was something the Philippian dungeon could not take away from these early missionaries. They prayed in their dismal dungeon until they could pray no more, for prayer had changed to praise, and they sang their gladness and their triumph until the strange sounds echoed through the dreary corridors and woke up the wondering prisoners. But soon the answer came from the heavenly listeners. There was a great earthquake, but such an earthquake was never known before. Instead of destroying the prison and crushing the inmates to death, it acted with the strangest intelligence, only slipping back the prison bolts and shaking off the fetters from the apostles and the prisoners. That was indeed a grand encore to their song of praise. No wonder the jailer was terrified. No wonder next morning the officials were alarmed. There was something more than a political complication in the situation. The hand of God was here. The victory of faith had been followed by the victory of Almighty power, and best of all, of saving grace, for the brutal jailer who had so needlessly aggravated the torture of his prisoners, casting them into the inner prison and making their feet fast in stocks, was now pleading for mercy, and a little later rejoicing in his new-found Savior and entertaining his prisoners with his converted household in his own home. Next morning witnessed a still more marked triumph. The very authorities, learning that they had beaten a freeborn Roman and thus insulted the majesty of the empire, sent the pleading message to Paul and his companions to please get out of prison as quietly as possible and say nothing about it. But Paul was a man as well as a missionary, and he stood upon his dignity for Christ's sake and for the sake of the little flock he represented, as the true Christian ever should. Nothing less than an honorable discharge would he accept, and so God vindicated him before the whole community and the highest authorities of the city. But now his victory being complete, it is fitting that he should show a triumph of another kind in the spirit of meekness, which is even higher than the spirit of manhood. His work in Philippi is done, and he determines quietly to retire without pressing his advantage or humiliating his enemies, and so he quietly takes his leave of the beloved little flock, and passing on along the old Roman road 100 miles westward, he pauses next at Thessalonica.

10. Thessalonica

We cannot linger over the triumphs of the gospel in Thessalonica and Berea, marked as they were by the usual introduction through the Jewish synagogue, the first fruits that always followed in Jewish and Gentile converts, and then the bitter persecution of the angry Jews from which the apostle withdrew when his pioneer work was done and hastened on to new fields.

11. Athens

We must linger over that dramatic scene on the Acropolis of Athens, where Christianity came face to face with the cultured heathenism of Greece and the world. If there be an atmosphere more difficult than any other to penetrate with the message of the gospel, it is that of intellectual and fashionable frivolity. Luke aptly describes Athenian society by a phrase that might not unfittingly be applied to many of our modern social circles. "All the Athenians and the foreigners who lived there spent their time doing nothing but talking about and listening to the latest ideas" (17:21).

Against this frivolous spirit the gospel strikes as a cannon ball upon a wall of sandbags. If it was solid rock it might be battered down, but the soft sand just falls over it and fills the vacuum, like the waves after the keel of the passing ship, leaving no impression behind. No wonder that such congregations break the hearts of earnest ministers and wear out even the long-suffering of God. Such an audience now confronted the great apostle. Little cared he for the sights of Athens. "He was greatly distressed to see that the city was full of idols" (17:16). At length the opportunity came, and the message was equal to the occasion. It deserves to be written in letters of gold.

First it began with inimitable tact; complimenting his religious audience, he politely reminded them that he perceived that they were "very religious" (17:22). Then he told them the happy incident of the altar that he had just discovered to an unknown god whom they were endeavoring to worship, and about whom they must wish to know. He had come to tell them all about Him. And then began that marvelous setting of Christianity over against Greek philosophy and mythology. Standing in the midst of an audience that had no faith in God, he began by pronouncing that one name, "God," with an emphasis that must have rung in thundering accents from all the splendid array of sculpture and architecture around. Addressing a people that were materialists and denied the doctrine of creation, he next added, "God who made the world and everything in it" (17:24). Looking in the face of a crowd of Pantheists, who identified matter with God, he declared, "God . . . is the Lord of heaven and earth and does not live in temples built by hands" (17:24). Addressing an audience of exclusive Greeks who looked upon the rest of the world as barbarians, he dared to tell them, "From one man he made every nation of men" (17:26). Surveying a whole forest of sculptured statues of innumerable gods and goddesses, he reminded them that "we should not think that the divine being is like gold or silver or stone—an image made by man's design and skill" (17:29). Then growing more deeply solemn, he told them that "in the past God overlooked such ignorance, but now he commands all people everywhere to repent" (17:30), and soon would meet them in the great judgment day, face to face with that Man of whom He witnessed, "He has given proof of this to all men by raising him from the dead" (17:31).

The whole address could be repeated in five or six minutes, and yet it outweighs whole volumes of philosophy, theology and diluted homiletics. It was cut short by ironical sneers and a mocking and polite request to defer the remainder of his address to some other occasion. But out of this five minute address came the conversion of one of the distinguished council of the Areopagus, and Damaris, who seems to have been a woman of the town, with others not named. Even in cold, heartless Athens, God's Word could not return to Him void.

12. Corinth

Our space will only permit us to touch for a moment the closing scene of this great missionary journey. Forty-five miles south, and almost visible from the heights of Mars Hill, was the rich commercial city of Corinth. It was the maritime capital of the western world and the metropolis of its vice and sin. Here for a year and a half Paul continued to labor, until he had closed his successful ministry in Greece and the gospel was firmly established in the continent of Europe. The story of Corinth was a record of faith, trial and marvelous victory.

CONCLUSION

The whole section emphasizes again and again that great missionary plan which God had so clearly projected upon their vision at the commencement. The keynote of every incident was "to the ends of the earth" (1:8). The watchword of every step was "farther on." The heart of God was reaching out with intense solicitude to the unevangelized, and it is needless to say that still that heart is as intensely concerned for the "regions beyond" (2 Corinthians 10:16). Along with this we constantly hear the echo of that other message, "from the Gentiles a people for himself" (Acts 15:14). It is not an evangelistic movement to convert the world, but to gather out of the world an elect people for His coming. We find this again at Antioch, where "all who were appointed for eternal life believed" (13:48); and we find it in the last scene at Corinth, where the Master's message to His apostle is, "I have many people in this city" (18:10). Corinth is not to be converted, Greece is not to be a Christian nation, but God has people there whom He must find.

And finally, the supreme lesson that accompanies us all the way is that the work is God's and the power must be God's alone. It was not Paul that converted Lydia, but the Lord opened Lydia's heart. Your camera may be all right, your lens may be perfect, your focus may be exact, your film may be chemically prepared and everything ready for the picture, but without yonder sun there will be no impression on that film. It is the sun that makes the photograph, not the artist. And so the work of the Acts of the Apostles, the work of the Church of God to the end of time, the work of every minister and every missionary, the conversion and sanctification of every soul is God's and God's alone, to whom be glory forever and ever. Amen.

CHAPTER 6

A CHAPTER FROM ONE OF PAUL'S MISSIONARY JOURNEYS

One night the Lord spoke to Paul in a vision: "Do not be afraid; keep on speaking, do not be silent." (Acts 18:9)

Finally, brothers, pray for us that the message of the Lord may spread rapidly and be honored, just as it was with you. And pray that we may be delivered from wicked and evil men, for not everyone has faith. But the Lord is faithful, and he will strengthen and protect you from the evil one. (2 Thessalonians 3:1–3)

We have been sweeping with rapid flight over Paul's great missionary journeys. Today we shall tarry for a while with him at one of his stations, and see the closing of his second great missionary journey in the city of Corinth. It is full of incidents fraught with instruction and inspiration to every Christian heart and missionary worker.

HIS COMING TO CORINTH

We saw him last at Athens, in a city cold and utterly heartless. He must have been glad to leave its cheerless atmosphere. He had probably seen from Athens, 45 miles to the south, a sharp cliff rising off the horizon, and perhaps he may have discerned the town nestling at its feet. Certainly he would have seen the beautiful harbors on either side and the countless ships docked there.

Down this well-traveled highway he took his way to Corinth probably on foot, for we find him on other occasions walking many long miles. He went alone, for he had sent Timothy and Silas from Athens to Thessalonica to cheer the brethren there, for they needed them more. Paul was a bighearted friend and loved congenial company. His solitude, therefore, was due to his unselfishness.

On his approaching Corinth the first thing he would have seen was the citadel known as the Acrocorinthus. It was a splendid crag rising 2,000 feet, a sheer cliff against the sky, and stood above the city of Corinth. The city was built at its foot, and at the top was a little city and powerful fortress. As he drew nearer he reached the narrow isthmus which joins the peninsula to the mainland of Greece.

On each side was a splendid harbor—one the emporium of all the commerce of the East, the other reaching out to the western Mediterranean. These two harbors were crowded with the commerce of the world, and Corinth was the commercial metropolis of the earth. It was filled with Jews, Greeks and Italians. It was a place of immense wealth and vast trade; also, alas, of great wickedness, where all colors and classes of men constantly came together. So wicked was it that the word "Corinthian" has come down to our own day to describe the worst class of women.

This was the city to which Paul was now coming, but with all its wickedness, it was a great relief to get out of cold, heartless Athens. It is easier to preach the gospel in Wall Street or the Bowery than in the chilling atmosphere of Fifth Avenue fashion.

Paul was wise in choosing the great centers of life for his headquarters in mission work. The cities of the world control its life. And so God would have us as we go to preach the gospel, to work from the center to the circumference.

AQUILA AND PRISCILLA

What were his business and domestic arrangements when he came to his mission field? He did not have a big society behind him to send him large drafts each month, and it is not likely he had very many coins in his wallet. But he had a skilled and strong right hand. He knew how to weave hair cloth and put a tent together. When he reached Corinth he began to "look for a job," as we would say. He soon found it in the factory or shop of two good people, Aquila and Priscilla, Jews, his own countrymen, who had been expelled from Rome through a decree of Claudius Caesar.

The incident is given in profane history. Claudius Caesar had become so disgusted with the quarrels of the Jews about One named Christos or Christ, that he turned all the Jews out. Aquila and Priscilla went to the provinces to find a resting place. It is quite evident that at this time Aquila and Priscilla were not Christians. If so, we would have been told that Paul went to them because they were believers. Instead we are simply told they were of the same craft. They met in the workshop and then they invited him to their home, and he went with them. This was the beginning of that splendid stream of holy helpfulness that filled so large a place in ancient Christianity and in the story of Paul himself.

There are two things well worthy of our notice right here: First, the honest, manly independence of the missionary. He did not carry his hat in his hand asking people to give him help, but worked for his needs and the needs of them that were with him. And he could do this and trust God, too. It is all right to trust God as well as your own right hand. The people that work can best trust. The businessman has just as good a chance to live the faith life as the man that has no business. Manhood is always at a premium in personal influence and Christian work. So Paul was always independent. Speaking from this very place a little later to the Thessalonians to whom he wrote, he speaks of his honest industry and tells them how "we worked night and day in order not to be a burden to anyone while we preached the gospel of God to you" (1 Thessalonians 2:9).

Then again what a beautiful picture he gives of their fellowship in their daily calling. It was the beginning of a lifelong fellowship in higher things. What are you doing for the man that works alongside of you? And what about that woman that comes to help you in your household with her manual toil? Think about this, dear men and women, for most of us are called of God to the most honorable of all callings, that of honest independent labor, and in these days of restless speculation we cannot too much emphasize the honor and importance of honest labor and simple independence as honest working men and examples to our fellow men. May the day never come when labor will be discounted! Paul's father, though he must have been rich, and certainly gave Paul a good education, taught him a trade, and every true father and mother should teach their children some trade or occupation by which they may be independent.

Still another question comes up—what about the people that live with you, and the people with whom you live? Aquila and Priscilla took Paul home; they were true home missionaries. That is where the greatest of all preachers begins, the mother, and where our influence tells more intimately, more continuously and more eternally than anywhere else. Beloved, is your family circle, where they live with you, a place where your life is speaking for God, even as the story of Paul and Aquila and Priscilla? Their friendship is one of the most blessed pictures in the whole story of Acts. Here we have the beginning of it. They were thrown together in the same family circle, and Paul's influence over them led them to Christ, and their influence with Apollos and others made them his helpers in the gospel.

A SABBATH AT CORINTH—HIS PUBLIC MINISTRY

Now the Sabbath has come. There is a synagogue there. On the Sabbath day they are gathered in it, and Paul, of course, finds his way there. He keeps the Sabbath. No man ought to be so busy that he loses God's day of rest— the day that God wants not so much for Himself as for the good of man.

You will never lose anything by taking care of God's holy day.

Next we find him in the synagogue, in his place in the congregation. He began at doors that God had opened and he did not turn his back upon the Jews and the synagogue until they turned him out. That is the place for us to begin, and if they turn us out God will open other doors. We are told very simply that he went to the synagogue and reasoned with them on the Sabbath, and persuaded the Jews and the Greeks. Those two words "reasoned" and "persuaded" give us the whole gist of Paul's splendid ministry. He gave them facts, foundations, the truth; he appealed to their understanding, he took the Scripture and opened it up to them. But it was no cold logic nor all logic. When he was through reasoning, he began to persuade them. Oh, how the tears would get into his voice and the fire would burn in his tones! The first appealed to the intellect, and the second appealed to the conscience, the heart and the will.

So he began his ministry, and for a time there seemed to be little result. But now something happens.

REINFORCEMENTS—SILAS AND TIMOTHY

We come to the next act in the drama, and we find a new inspiration coming to our missionary. "When Silas and Timothy came from Macedonia, Paul devoted himself exclusively to preaching, testifying to the Jews that Jesus was the Christ" (Acts 18:5). Something happened; two dear hearts had arrived. It was the touch of the hand of a friend, and thank God for the touch of the hand of a friend! How it cheers the heart of the lone worker on the field when he sees the new missionary coming! It is like fresh waters to a thirsty soul to have news from a far country. Let us think of our lone workers and help to cheer them by sending reinforcements. Now Paul could preach. He got up the next day and they wondered what was the matter with him as his face glowed and his voice rose into notes of passion, and he pleaded and warned and wept until they thought something must have happened. Do you help people that way? Does your coming to them make any difference in their work? Have you a bright face and a warm handclasp? We sometimes receive more help from faces than from words. God has ordained this blessed ministry of comradeship. Are you standing true to it?

OPPOSITION—THE JEWS

Next the devil comes upon the scene. The new inspiration with which Paul had been baptized was met by a countermove of the adversary. "The Jews opposed Paul and became abusive" (18:6). Speaking of them in his letter at this time from Corinth, he refers to them as those,

who killed the Lord Jesus and the prophets and also drove us out. They displease God and are hostile to all men in their effort to keep us from speaking to the Gentiles so that they may be saved. In this way they always heap up their sins to the limit. The wrath of God has come upon them at last. (1 Thessalonians 2:15–16)

The situation now became impossible, and in the most solemn manner, as directly commanded by the Lord on such occasions, he shook his raiment and said unto them, "Your blood be on your own heads! I am clear of my responsibility. From now on I will go to the Gentiles" (Acts 18:6). The crisis had come. The Jews in Europe had rejected their Messiah as they had already done everywhere in Asia.

HIS LETTER TO THE THESSALONIANS

He had written one epistle to the beloved disciples in Thessalonica, and soon after he adds his second; and now begins that marvelous ministry of the written epistle, and later the printed page which has created through the progress of Christian literature the largest pulpit and constituency in the world. There is no doubt that today the printed page reaches a far wider circle than even the spoken message, and that the Bible Society is doing more, perhaps, to evangelize the world than even the multiplied voices of many thousands of missionaries.

One of the special features of this letter to Thessalonica was a request for prayer with which he closed his second epistle, "Finally, brothers, pray for us that the message of the Lord may spread rapidly and be honored, just as it was with you. And pray that we may be delivered from wicked and evil men" (2 Thessalonians 3:1–2). The rest of this chapter is a remarkable illustration of the way God answered this prayer.

ANSWERED PRAYER

1. First it was answered by the opening of a wider door at Corinth in the house of Justus, hard by the synagogue, where the two congregations doubtlessly met every Sabbath, and the Jews could see how God was blessing the apostle's work.

2. Next followed the conversion of Crispus, the chief ruler of the synagogue, and the most influential of the Jewish party. This was followed by many conversions, including well-known families, like the household of Stephanas, and Gaius, afterwards so familiar a name in the writings of both Paul and John. There was also a large number of the humbler classes, for, writing later to the Corinthians, the apostle reminds them, "Brothers, think of what you were when you were called. Not many of you were wise by human standards; not many were influential; not many were of noble birth"

(1 Corinthians 1:26). There was another class whom Paul welcomed most gladly of all, that immoral and depraved multitude, the drunkard, the thief, the prostitute, of whom he says, "And that is what some of you were. But you were washed, you were sanctified, you were justified in the name of the Lord Jesus Christ and by the Spirit of our God" (6:11). So there came into the Corinthian church a blessed revival and a glorious company of ransomed sinners.

3. The next answer was a voice from heaven. Paul no doubt had been deeply discouraged by the opposition of the Jews, and affected still more by the painful stand which he had taken in withdrawing from the synagogue. Was he justified in this? The Lord saw that he needed the reassuring word, and how sweetly it now came and moored his tossing ship to the throne with an anchorage that would hold amid all the testings of the coming years. "Do not be afraid," the Master says, "keep on speaking, do not be silent. For I am with you, and no one is going to attack and harm you, because I have many people in this city" (Acts 18:9–10).

4. Next came the open assault of his enemies and their ignominious defeat. At this time a new governor had come to Corinth in charge of the great province Achaia, of which it was the capital. It was Gallio, the brother of the famous philosopher, Seneca, who speaks of him in one of his writings as a man of high character and uprightness, and at the same time of easy indifference such as we see in his later treatment of the Jews at Corinth. Supposing that he would be ready to please their party by a little bit of favoritism, and at the same time, taking advantage of his supposed ignorance of the local situation, they summoned Paul from his tribunal under grave charges of promoting a new religion contrary to their law. Paul was about to answer for himself, when Gallio turned on the prosecutors and sharply rebuking their miserable quibbling about questions, about words and names and their own law, he nonsuited them. And as they still seem to have lingered and pressed the case upon him, he finally and evidently with some impatience "had them ejected from the court" (18:16). The mob waiting outside as usual to join the winning and fall on the losing side, immediately turned on Sosthenes, the chief prosecutor, and beat him before the judgment seat, while Gallio, true to the character that his brother had given him, "showed no concern whatever" (18:17).

LEAVES CORINTH

Finally the trial ended, Paul quietly settled down to a long season of successful work, planting numerous churches throughout Achaia and finding, it would seem, his sweetest revenge even in the conversion of Sosthenes himself, the leader of the mob that brought him before the tribunal of Gallio. We cannot, of course, demonstrate the fact that the Sosthenes who attacked

Paul was the same Sosthenes whom Paul a little later, writing back from Philippi by the hand of Stephanas, associated with himself in his epistle to the Corinthians as "our brother Sosthenes" (1 Corinthians 1:1), but it does look as though he was drawing a very strong contrast between Sosthenes the bitter enemy and Sosthenes the now loving brother. May it not be that we shall some day find that as he lay there bleeding under the blows of the mob, Gallio caring not, and the crowd crying, "served him right," that Paul went up to him and kneeling by his side prayed him back to life, took him home under his loving care and won him to Christ? Surely that would be the most supreme triumph of faith and love.

Finally, we have not space to follow him as he closes his successful work in Corinth, sails across to Ephesus for a brief stay accompanied by Aquila and Priscilla, and then presses on to Caesarea, Jerusalem and Antioch.

CLOSE OF SECOND MISSIONARY JOURNEY

As we thus close with him his second missionary journey, we cannot fail to note, first, the presence of the Master all through these missionary scenes, and the fact that He who "began to do and to teach" (Acts 1:1) is still continuing to work and lead his missionary army. Secondly, that the power promised at Pentecost is still the equipment and enduement of the militant Church—power to win souls, power to pray until both earth and heaven answer, power to hold back the hate of men and control the very officials in the judgment hall, and power to build up and establish the Church of God in the face of the opposition of earth and hell.

Thirdly, we cannot fail to notice the ever-aggressive spirit of the gospel witness. Pressing forward from center to circumference, we still find it reaching out to the uttermost part of the earth. Rejected by the Jew it is given to the Greek, and now from its home in the continent of Asia we have seen it spreading over all the cities of Greece, and from the great commercial world-center of commerce, sending forth its influence through all the earth.

And last of all we have not only seen the splendid example of the great apostle to the Gentiles and felt our own lives dwarfed into littleness beside the grandeur of his life and work, but we have also seen that there is room for the humblest of his brethren by his side. If you cannot be a Paul in the pulpit, you can be an Aquila in the workshop and a Priscilla in the home. Or you can be a Timothy, bringing a word of cheer and the handclasp of comradeship to the tired worker. Or you can be a Thessalonian saint praying over yonder until it reaches both earth and heaven as it was so marvelously answered at Corinth. God help us so to help as in those days of old.

CHAPTER 7

PAUL AT EPHESUS

Did you receive the Holy Spirit when you believed? (Acts 19:2)

The word of the Lord spread widely and grew in power. (19:20)

T hese words reveal to us at once the secret and the story of one of the most glorious chapters in the life of Paul, the missionary. It is known as his third missionary journey. We left him closing his second journey at Jerusalem and Antioch, having called on his way home for a brief visit to Ephesus to prepare the way for his contemplated campaign and leave behind him Aquila and Priscilla to direct these preparations. His proposed visit to Ephesus had been divinely interrupted three or four years before in order that he might plant the gospel in Europe first. But now God's time has come, and the next three years find him in this splendid Oriental metropolis and engaged in the most remarkable and successful of all his missions.

EPHESUS

The city of Ephesus, the scene of his labors, was to Asia what Corinth was to Europe. They faced each other across the sea somewhat as Liverpool and New York, only while Corinth was marked by all the energy of the western world, Ephesus was a luxurious and splendid eastern city, and given up to the magic arts and idolatrous superstitions of the Orient. Its supreme glory was the temple of Diana, one of the seven wonders of the world. But the Diana of Ephesus was a wholly different character from the Diana of the Greeks. This famous temple covered a rectangle 425 feet by 225 feet. It was enclosed by a colonnade of 127 pillars, 60 feet in height and finely carved in the richest Ionic style. Unlike our sanctuaries, ancient temples were not roofed, so that most of the enclosed space was open to the sky, the shrine of the goddess being covered and more completely enclosed. A great number of eunuchs and priestesses ministered in its courts, and its worship and festivals were maintained by a number of distinguished and wealthy citizens called Asiarchs, or "chiefs of Asia," who met the expenses of these magnificent festive occasions from their personal means and counted it a distinguished honor to be permitted to do so.

To this great city Paul now came, not as he had wandered into Philippi, Athens and Corinth, a lonely stranger, but to find the hospitable home of Aquila and Priscilla awaiting him and his future work at least in some measure prepared.

But we are to look at this time at four pictures that stand out in bold relief from the story of his Ephesian ministry and speak to us lessons of peculiar appropriateness and practical power.

SECTION I—*Aquila and Priscilla: The Picture of a Home Missionary*

The story of a great life is sometimes discouraging because so few can reach the high station of a great apostle and missionary, but the Bible was written for humble disciples and everyday Christians, and the story of Paul is filled with innumerable side lights and companion pictures illustrating the infinite varieties and possibilities of Christian service. Among these no characters were more interesting than Aquila and Priscilla, whom we met in our last chapter at Corinth, and whom we meet again here and frequently afterward as Paul's friends and fellow workers. They could not be apostles, but they were indeed living "letter[s] . . . known and read by everybody" (2 Corinthians 3:2). Soon after coming to Ephesus they met with a distinguished and eloquent teacher and preacher from Alexandria named Apollos. Finely educated, mighty in the Scriptures and full of zeal and fervor, he had yet got no further than John's baptism and was eloquently preaching of a Messiah to come. With fine tact and wisdom they introduced themselves to him and took him to their home and lovingly led him into the deeper knowledge of the truth. Soon afterwards he went over to Corinth and successfully continued the work which Paul had there begun, becoming in many respects as popular and successful as the great apostle himself.

The word used to describe the reception given by these good people to Apollos is a strong one, expressing cordiality and hospitality. They did not "go for him" as some modern Christians do for ministers with whom they may not agree, but they took him to them and by love and winning example quite as much as by wise teaching led him into the deeper life. There are today many ministers as defective and as sincere as Apollos, men that have never yet been brought into favorable conditions for seeing and receiving the fullness of spiritual truth. Their ministry would be multiplied in value a hundredfold if they would but receive the Holy Spirit. They cannot be argued into it. Controversy only antagonizes. They must be won. Oh, for the wise Aquilas and Priscillas that can love them into the better way! When the story of the most useful and successful life comes to be told in all its fullness, doubtless it will be found that some holy mother, some faithful teacher, some judicious friends, some silent personal influence was the factor behind their deeper experience and wider usefulness. The chief value of the Sunday school class is not even the Bible knowledge conveyed. Perhaps there is even too much of the normal mechanical element about our Christian work today, but it is the strong and constant personal influence of a holy woman or a godly man upon the young minds and hearts under their care, and who perhaps have no other Christian friend on earth. Some of us remember our early teachers and the veneration and emulation with which we regarded and copied them. Oh, mothers, teachers, Christian friends, do not wait and wonder till some great occasion comes, but meet the simple opportunities of life and pass on the ministry of Aquila and Priscilla to the end of the history of the Church.

SECTION II—*The Holy Spirit: The Picture of a Whole Gospel*

The incident of Apollos naturally introduces the next scene at Ephesus and teaches the same spiritual lesson. On arriving there Paul found a number of disciples, perhaps from the congregation of Apollos, who, like that teacher, had got no farther than John's baptism. In answer to the inquiry "Did you receive the Holy Spirit when you believed?" (Acts 19:2) they astonished him by telling him, "No, we have not even heard that there is a Holy Spirit" (19:2). The apostle then instructed them in the gospel of Christ and immediately on their baptism they received the gift of Pentecost, and from this new Spirit-filled company the work in Ephesus began. That is the right and only place to begin any deep spiritual movement.

The condition of these Ephesian disciples is, we fear, representative of a great majority of professing Christians today. They have accepted the ministry of repentance. They have experienced to some extent conversion. They have begun to "quit their meanness" and change their course of life. But they do not know Christ as a personal and abiding presence. They have not received the Holy Spirit. They make no claim to sanctification, and, indeed, rather criticize and repudiate it as something for people that are inclined that way. And they hold themselves in some measure free to live a worldly and imperfect life because of the lower plane on which they are content to remain. Unfortunately many of their teachers are little farther on themselves. It is to these that God is sending home the question of our text, "Did you receive the Holy Spirit when you believed?" (19:2).

And this question is supreme. It was supreme in the life of the Master, for

He did not begin His public ministry until on the banks of the Jordan He had made the full consecration of His life and received the descending Paraclete. It was supreme in the lives of the apostles. They were not permitted to go forth and begin their ministry, notwithstanding their long acquaintance with Christ and their undoubted conversion, until they had tarried at Jerusalem for the power from on high. It was supreme in the early Church and in her message to her first converts. "Repent and be baptized . . . in the name of Jesus Christ for the forgiveness of your sins" was their first message, but immediately it was followed by the rest, "And you will receive the gift of the Holy Spirit. The promise is for you and your children and for all who are far off—for all whom the Lord our God will call" (2:38–39). It is the heritage of the whole Church of Christ and none can be excused from it.

Beloved, have you asked to be excused? Have you received the Holy Spirit since you believed? Have you had as a definite experience the baptism of the Spirit? Is Christ to you a living constant reality? It is this that gives holiness. It is this that brings rest. It is this which fills the heart with victorious joy. It is this which heals and keeps the body. It is this which brings love, patience and sweetness of spirit. This alone can give you victory. Without this you are powerless to pray, to witness, to work for Christ. This is your panoply and equipment for warfare and work, and this is awaiting every willing and earnest heart. If you really want Him more than anything else you will not be long in finding Him. He will meet you on the way. He will lead you all the way. He will bring you to Himself and abide with you forever.

SECTION III—*Revival: The Picture of a Mighty Spiritual Movement*

With this deep spiritual beginning the work moved on, and soon we are in the midst of an extraordinary revival.

PREACHING IN THE SYNAGOGUE

1. It commences in the synagogue, and for three months the apostle preaches to his Jewish brethren and others concerning the kingdom of God. The best evidence of the power of the work is the anger with which many of the Jews turned against him and openly denounced him before the multitude, and then the usual crisis comes and he withdraws.

IN THE SCHOOL OF TYRANNUS

2. The next phase of the work is in the school or academy of a prominent teacher named Tyrannus, where for two years the apostle is hospitably received and continues his teaching until this strong language was employed concerning the spread of the movement, "All the Jews and Greeks who lived

in the province of Asia heard the word of the Lord" (19:10). There must have been a constant concourse from the city and province and a ceaseless ministry of teaching and preaching, excepting only the hours of toil which Paul always spent in laboring with his hands and thus ministering to his necessities and those that were with him.

SUPERNATURAL SIGNS

3. His ministry in Ephesus was now marked by a peculiar dispensation of divine healing. The spirit of power so rested upon Paul that something occurred which was unusual even for him. The very handkerchiefs which he touched were laid upon the sick and they recovered. This and a similar statement about Peter should not be twisted into an authorization of the fantastic claims of some modern teachers and workers. This is the peculiar method of spiritualism, and we should be most guarded in anything that approximates to it. But in the case of Paul at Ephesus there had been special claims made for heathen magic, and especially the images of Diana and the mystic inscriptions upon them were supposed to possess a healing charm. Therefore God met this thing once for all on its own ground, even as Moses met the magicians of Egypt in order to show the genuine and the false. We will find that in the story of early Christianity special manifestations of divine healing accompanied special advances into new territory. While the ordinary operation of the Lord's healing is uniform and constant in the Church, the miraculous features seem to be intended as special signs to call attention to the truth and the gospel under circumstances where the divine seal is called for, for a time.

SATAN DEFEATED

4. In connection with this a signal victory over the devil is brought to pass. Seven young pretenders, the sons of a priest, possessed of a reckless ambition to imitate Paul, attempted to cast the evil spirit out of a possessed victim. But to their amazement the evil spirit turned upon them and, repudiating their pretended powers, cried out, "Jesus I know, and I know about Paul, but who are you?" (19:15). And then the possessed man leaped upon them and beat them within an inch of their lives, until they were glad to fly from the place naked, wounded and half dead. An incident so dramatic and even ludicrous as this was sure to take the popular fancy and spread like wildfire over the city. No better vindication of Paul could have happened. The people were profoundly impressed, and even those that had been hesitating or compromising were brought to deep conviction.

CONFESSION

5. This was immediately followed by a remarkable and public confession on the part of a number of professed believers who up to that time had ac-

cepted the new faith, but had still held on to some of their old idolatrous traditions and practices. Filled with awe when they saw the power of God upon the wicked men that had tried to imitate the apostles, they became convicted of their hypocrisy and were led to make a complete renunciation and bring their books to a public bonfire, so that from day to day, as the Greek term implies, the spectacle was presented of one after another bringing these mystical volumes and throwing them into the fire with humble and probably tearful confession of their wrongdoing. Ancient books were 10 times as costly as our literature, and the destruction of a library involved a large part of one's fortune. The total value of these books is given by Luke as an intimation of the stupendous importance and extent of this breaking down of idolatry. If we count these coins in Greek figures the amount was nearly 10,000 dollars. If the pieces of silver were Hebrew shekels it would be 35,000 dollars. Either sum is large enough to show the fruits of a revival that can bear comparison with any similar movement in the history of the Church.

TRADE RIOT

6. We next find the power of this movement expressed in a business way. It literally broke down one of the industrial trades of Ephesus and caused a trade riot on the part of the silversmiths who had made their living by manufacturing silver shrines or little models of the goddess Diana for sale. These men came together under excited leaders—and a great concourse assembled in the theater where political assemblies were held, until the peace and safety of the town were threatened—denouncing Paul for having destroyed their business and challenged the very existence of the worship of Diana. A gospel that goes down to the heart of Wall Street and turns business upside down must have some power in it. Would to God that the gospel of today might strike our crooked financial schemes, our reckless speculations, our dishonest methods, and bring to confusion the mammon worship of New York as surely as the Diana worship of Ephesus.

THE CHIEFS OF ASIA

7. But even this was not so significant as the spirit of sympathy with the apostle which it brought out from the leading citizens of Ephesus. When Paul with his usual nobility and self-sacrifice was about to rush into the theater to save his friends from suffering on his account, the very rulers of the temple already spoken of by us as the Asiarchs, or "chiefs of Asia," were the men who acted as his friends and begged him not to expose himself to danger. The gospel had reached even these men that were the official protectors and supporters of the worship of Diana. A little later we find even the town clerk himself tactfully taking the part of Paul, dismissing the mob with the official

assurance that these men had broken no law, and anyhow whatever complaint was held against them should be presented in the lawful assembly and not made the occasion for a disgraceful mob which threatened to bring down the Roman army in one of its usual demonstrations upon them.

These are some of the signs on the surface of events which showed the tremendous power of the religious current that for the time had carried all before it in the old capital of the East.

SECTION IV—*Worldwide Evangelism: The Picture of a Mightier Ambition*

But not all this could satisfy the heart of Paul or turn him aside from his grander ambition to carry the gospel to the uttermost part of the earth. It was at this very time that there rose before his mind the supreme conception of one more advance movement upon the heathen world destined to capture Rome itself, the capital of universal paganism. Here again we see the same aggressive mission of the Church breaking through every obstacle and hindrance. Just as the Church had to be driven out by persecution from her first home in Jerusalem until "those who had been scattered preached the word wherever they went" (8:4); just as Philip was hurried on from the great revival in Samaria to meet in a desert the heathenism of Africa in the person of the Ethiopian eunuch; just as Peter was pressed beyond his Jewish conservatism and compelled to go to Caesarea, the Roman capital, and begin the great work of Gentile missions; just as the center of apostolic Christianity was removed in due time from Jerusalem to Antioch and the first missionaries sent out from that church, and just as a few years before this present story Paul himself had been pushed out of Asia, forbidden to come to Ephesus and compelled to go across to Macedonia to a more remote heathen world; so now the ever-irrepressible forward movement reaches on even to Rome itself, and neither his affection for his Philippian friends, his interest in the splendid work at Corinth, nor his magnificent success in Ephesus can interrupt the supreme necessity that is laid upon him to go into the very heart of heathenism, Rome itself.

"I must visit Rome" (19:21), is strong language for mortal man, but there is a must in every divine calling. There is a resistless impulse. There is a conscious heavenly calling. There is the faith of a mighty destiny beckoning us on and assuring us of victory. The missionary calling is always a supreme one: "I am compelled to preach. Woe to me if I do not preach the gospel!" (1 Corinthians 9:16). Oh, that God would put this *must* upon some heart that reads these lines!

The reason his strong language was not presumptuous was because he purposed it in the Spirit. It is right sometimes to have such purposes and plans.

The Holy Spirit does not always lead us a moment at a time, but gives us far-reaching visions for faith, hope and holy service. Such purposes, when in the Spirit, will stand the tests that came to Paul—the mob at Jerusalem, the prison at Caesarea, the storm on the Adriatic, the viper at Malta, and even the warnings and entreaties of the too-fond friends that begged him to desist from that purpose for the sake of his own life and usefulness—none of these things moved him, but on to the end he followed that purpose and saw it all fulfilled.

The mighty mechanical forces which are driving our factories, our locomotives and our swift ocean racers are not of recent origin. Were I to ask you where this power comes from, of course you would say, "coal." But where did the coal come from? Perhaps you would answer, "from the mine." But where did the mine come from? Ah, that is an ancient story. Ages ago yonder sun flashed down upon one of the tropical forests of ancient geological periods a consuming flame, burned it up and turned it into coal and packed it away by no human hand in those great depositories in the rock-ribbed mountains where today men find their coal. And so, God comes in some early period of a Christian life and there falls from heaven the fire of the Holy Spirit upon some chosen heart and life, and a mighty call, a heavenly purpose, a divine ambition and a supernatural enabling are granted to that life hidden away perhaps for years under the discipline of God's providence. But when God's hour strikes, the power is there, the instrument is ready, the missionary comes to the front, and that silent purpose is wrought out in living characters of mighty and everlasting blessing. Oh, that that purpose might rise today in some of your hearts! Oh, that that fire might fall, and the brief and coming years which precede the consummation might see it as divinely fulfilled as in the story of Paul and Rome!

CHAPTER 8

ON TO JERUSALEM AND ROME

After all this had happened, Paul decided to go to Jerusalem, passing through Macedonia and Achaia. "After I have been there," he said, "I must visit Rome also." (Acts 19:21)

Then Paul answered, "Why are you weeping and breaking my heart? I am ready not only to be bound, but also to die in Jerusalem for the name of the Lord Jesus." (21:13)

The following night the Lord stood near Paul and said, "Take courage! As you have testified about me in Jerusalem, so you must also testify in Rome." (23:11)

Our survey of the life of the great apostolic missionary leads us at this time through the fair Isles of Greece where many an excursion party is sailing at this time of the year on voyages of pleasure and study. Had we voyaged through these isles in the time of Paul we should have beheld many a magnificent city where today the traveler finds but broken columns and buried ruins on shores of desolation. The temple of Diana and Colossus of Rhodes, the splendid amphitheaters of Assos and Mitylene, and the walls and palaces of Troas, are all since gone, but Paul remains a loftier, nobler figure today than 1,800 years ago. The only thing that is immortal is that which has been touched by the name of Jesus and the glory of consecration to His cross. Our survey at this time will take us through a swiftly passing panorama of vivid scenes, on each of which we can only pause to glance for a few moments.

HIS PLAN

1. Months before, this journey had been mapped out in conference with the Holy Spirit, and Paul had "decided" (19:21) to pass on even from the

577

thrilling scenes of his ministry in Greece and Ephesus to the two supreme goals that yet awaited him, Jerusalem and Rome. Deeper than any other feeling upon his heart, except the love of Jesus, was his devotion to his own countrymen and his desire to present to them the testimony of Jesus. Writing about this time his great Epistle to the Romans, we find him exclaiming,

> Brothers, my heart's desire and prayer to God for the Israelites is that they may be saved. . . . For I could wish that I myself were cursed and cut off from Christ for the sake of my brothers, those of my own race. (Romans 10:1; 9:3)

And now the time had come, so intensely interesting to him, so solemn and momentous to them, when he would give them the last message of mercy and the last opportunity of receiving at length the Savior they had so long rejected. Then it was Rome, the world's great capital, the citadel of Satan, the center of organized heathenism. No grander ambition had ever fired a human soul than the sublime purpose with which Paul now pressed on to the supreme achievements of his life.

PREPARATIONS FOR HIS GREAT CAMPAIGN

2. The first preparation was the revisiting of the churches in Greece. It might be long ere he should see them again. Indeed, the presentiment was upon his heart that he should see their faces no more. And so he makes a prolonged pastoral visitation of Corinth and the churches of Macedonia, sending all his companions but Luke forward to Troas while he lingers a little longer among his cherished friends at Philippi. In view of his going to Rome, he takes occasion while at Corinth to write his great epistle to the Roman church, in which he tells them of the deep desire that he has long cherished to visit them and his earnest prayers that "now at last by God's will the way may be opened for me to come to you" (1:10), adding,

> I long to see you so that I may impart to you some spiritual gift to make you strong—that is, that you and I may be mutually encouraged by each other's faith . . . I am so eager to preach the gospel also to you who are at Rome. (1:11–12, 15)

THE DEPARTURE FROM TROAS

3. Seven centuries before, a little colony had left this same city of Troy, as told by Virgil in the famous story of the Aeneid, to found the great city of Rome. Now another colony was leaving the same Troy to win this very Rome for the kingdom of Christ. It was a curious and appropriate coin-

cidence. But how much greater in its consequence the present departure than even the story of Virgil.

A MEMORABLE SABBATH

4. It is significant that the party waited at Troas seven days in order that they might meet the brethren at their stated service on the Lord's day. They had probably arrived just after the Sabbath, and so they tarried nearly a week for this purpose. What a significance it gives to the Christian Sabbath, that eager as the apostle was to reach Jerusalem in time for Pentecost, yet he tarried a whole week in order to have the privilege of joining in the Sabbath services of the brethren at Troas. It is evident that the congregation consisted of humble working people who could not afford the time from their daily toil, and therefore met at night. The day began at six o'clock in the evening at the close of the Jewish Sabbath. Paul's address would doubtless commence soon after this hour, and we are told that it continued long, even into midnight. The evening was hot, for it was the beginning of summer. The hall was lighted with many lamps; the air was heavy and the service was long. Quite naturally, one of the congregation fell asleep, and suddenly fell from the window upon the pavement below and was picked up dead. It is a little singular that Luke was not sent for, but Paul. Very quietly and unostentatiously the story is told of that marvelous miracle, how the apostle fell upon the lifeless corpse, embracing him and claiming his life from God, and then in the most unostentatious way quieting the tumult of the people and telling them that "he's alive!" (Acts 20:10). And then the service quietly proceeds as though nothing had happened, and the narrator does not turn aside to paint in sensational or glowing colors the wonderful miracle that stands beside the mightiest achievement of ancient prophets. It is evident that the Lord's Supper was administered at the same time. The service proceeded during the whole of that memorable night, and the awful shadow that had for a moment fallen was turned into unspeakable joy and praise, and an impression left behind that many a generation would doubtless retain in the early Church.

A MEMORABLE JOURNEY

5. Next morning the rest of the party embarked on their little ship at Troas, but Paul chose to remain a few hours longer and walk to the next station, about 20 miles south, there joining the ship again. His first reason probably was that he might be a little longer with the disciples, might comfort some sorrowing hearts, might lead some inquirer to Christ, might finish some work already well begun which would have had to be neglected if he had hurried on with the ship. We can imagine the little company clinging to him, following him out of the town, walking by his side, one by one taking their leave

with many tears, until, perhaps, one or two lingered still. Then the apostle was left alone to pursue his solitary walk that Monday morning along the old Roman road that looked upon the Isles of the Aegean. What a light it sheds on the apostle's missionary methods! How often was this his only way of transportation! No palace car to bear him on his missionary journeys; no chariot or beast of burden to convey him and his effects, but, like his Master, on foot, walking around the world with the message of love. What a picture of self-denial, simplicity and devout faithfulness for all other missionaries!

A MEMORABLE PARTING

6. Joining his friends and ship at Assos, they sailed past Ephesus, as Paul's haste to reach Jerusalem would not allow him to venture again amid the scenes of his longest ministry. But he sends for the elders of the church at Ephesus to meet him a few miles distant at the next port, Miletus, and there occurs that memorable leave-taking, which has fixed the standard for every subsequent minister and flock so high as to put to shame most of his followers. First he reviews the past and reminds them of his labors, not only publicly, but from house to house, of his faithful preaching of the whole counsel of God, of his many tears and temptations, and of his humble labors among them, supporting himself by his own hands and ministering to the needs of others. Next he forewarns them of their dangers from false teachers and deceivers from among themselves and solemnly commends them to God and the Word of His grace, which is able to build them up and give them an inheritance among all that are sanctified. And finally he forecasts his own future, telling of the bonds and afflictions that await him, but the immovable purpose and fearless courage with which he presses on to meet his future, intent on one thing only: "if only I may finish the race and complete the task the Lord Jesus has given me—the task of testifying to the gospel of God's grace" (20:24). The meeting closes with a touch of pathos, as he tells them that they shall see his face no more, and they kneel down together on the shore in parting prayer, falling upon his neck and kissing him with many a fond and reverent expression of their devoted love. In the second century there were doubtless men and women living who could tell how, when they were little boys and girls, they looked upon this touching scene, and had the hand of the venerable apostle laid upon their heads in blessing and farewell. Such a spectacle would be an inspiration and an anchorage for the faith and loyalty of the primitive Church, stronger than all the power of persecution.

A HARD TEST

7. We pass many an interesting scene on their rapid voyage; the Island of Cos, the seat of the great medical colleges of that age; Rhodes, with its im-

mense commerce and famous Colossus; and Patara, a great emporium of trade, but now a neglected ruin. There they embarked in a Phoenician vessel, and sighting Cyprus after a two or three days' sail, they landed at the old city of Tyre, where their voyage ended, and whence they set out on foot to Caesarea and Jerusalem. Here again there is a stay of seven days, doubtless for the same reason as at Troas, and here there comes to Paul his first great trial of faith. The disciples at Tyre, we are told, "through the Spirit . . . urged Paul not to go on to Jerusalem" (21:4). This was not a mere personal appeal, but a prophetic message, and it must have been a severe trial of his faith; but we find him calmly moving on, unshaken even by these impressive messages. A severer trial comes to him at Caesarea, for there not only the brethren, but the prophet Agabus, recognized by all as one owned of God, actually bound himself with Paul's belt and told the apostle that so would he be bound at Jerusalem and delivered to the Gentiles. Then followed a universal appeal from all of Paul's companions not to go to Jerusalem, but it only called forth a more decided resolve that nothing should hinder the sacred purpose to which God had called him. "Why," he answered, "are you weeping and breaking my heart? I am ready not only to be bound, but also to die in Jerusalem for the name of the Lord Jesus" (21:13). They seem to have at once accepted his conclusion as the higher will of God, and answering, "The Lord's will be done" (21:14), they henceforth stood with him for good or ill. Thus we see the apostle's leading by the Spirit apparently contradicted by another leading of the Spirit, and yet in the end we find his first leading was sustained, the second appearing to be only a test that brought out the more fully his fidelity to God in the commission already given him directly from the Holy Spirit.

AT JERUSALEM

8. Passing rapidly over the incidents of his journey to Jerusalem where he lodged with an old disciple of Cyprus, named Mnason, along with the other brethren, we find him paying his respects soon after to James, the head of the church at Jerusalem, and being cordially received by him and by the elders while he rehearsed to them the story of his ministry, and they accepted the testimony and glorified God. Doubtless, he also presented to them the valuable offerings that he had brought with him from the Asian and European Christians for the poor saints in Jerusalem. It was a joyful occasion, and demonstrated that the Church of Jesus Christ, whether Jew or Gentile, was at last really one.

AN INEFFECTUAL COMPROMISE

9. But now we find the apostle entering into a step which, while cheerfully acceded to by him, really seems to have been one of those compromises

which seldom or never does any good. Yielding to the advice of James and the brethren, he consented to take a step at Jerusalem which might have the effect of propitiating the evident prejudice of the Jews and convincing them that the stories about his disloyalty to the institutions of Moses were false. This expedient was that he should assume the expense of certain men who had a vow, and with them purify himself in the temple and perform the customary ceremonial rites in the sight of the people, so that they might all see that he was still a good and faithful Jew.

We cannot too highly commend the sweetness of Paul's spirit in consenting to this, although we need not be surprised to find that, like all such compromises, it failed. In the midst of the ceremonial rites incident to this vow, Paul was seen in the temple by some of the Jews of Asia who knew him abroad as a missionary to the Gentiles, and who now accused him of bringing Gentiles into the temple and openly defiling it. A riot ensued, during which Paul was violently attacked and almost torn to pieces by the mob, and only escaped through the Roman garrison of the Castle of Antonia, which stood at the corner of the temple court, who with the captain of the guard suddenly came upon the scene and rescued Paul from their murderous hands, supposing him to be some revolutionary fanatic.

A LAST APPEAL

10. At this point Paul saw an opportunity for his long-desired message to his countrymen, and begged the captain to be permitted to address the mob. This was granted, and standing on the barracks' steps under guard of the soldiers, Paul beckoned with his hand, and in Hebrew language, which at once awakened their respectful attention, Paul began to address them. First he told them that he was a Jew like themselves, zealous for the law, brought up at the feet of Gamaliel, and bitterly persecuted the sect of the Christians. Then he told them of his sudden conversion in the midst of his persecuting hate, and how it was through a Jew at Damascus, the godly Ananias, "a devout observer of the law and highly respected by all the Jews living there" (22:12), he was led into the light in the early stages of his conversion and baptized in the name of Jesus. Then he told them how it became the longing desire of his heart to testify to his countrymen, and how the Lord Himself had sent him out of Jerusalem and given him the commission in this very temple years before: "Go; I will send you far away to the Gentiles" (22:21). So far they had listened respectfully, but that last word was too much. They suddenly broke into an awful uproar, crying out that he was unfit to live, tearing off their garments, throwing dust into the air, and going through all the demonstrations of religious frenzy. His message to Israel had been given and rejected. That hour meant much more to Jerusalem than it did for him. Their turning away from that loving appeal was the last act but one in the

tragedy that culminated in the awful story of the fall of Jerusalem and the burning of their temple. Again and again had mercy lingered and God prolonged Israel's day of grace, but at every step it became more and more apparent that the heart of the people was hopelessly hardened and they had been given over to the spirit of unbelief and the final rejection of their Messiah. The solemn inexorable wheels of destiny were rolling on, and in a few years more they would bring the Roman eagles, and that devoted city should sink in a cloud of blood and flame.

How solemn it is that as Jerusalem turns herself against the apostle and the Lord, Rome stands forward as his defender. It was Paul's citizenship that saved him now, and it was the Roman guard that stood between him and his own people. Henceforth Rome is to take the place of Jerusalem and the Gentiles would inherit the privileges of the Jew. How wonderfully God had prepared the way for the spread of His gospel by creating the very power of Roman law and citizenship, under which Paul now took refuge when about to be scourged by the chief captain as a preliminary investigation of this strange riot. Paul at once demanded his rights as a Roman citizen, and immediately we find how the shield of that citizenship was henceforth thrown open to him forbidding any indignity to his person, and finally giving him the right of direct appeal to Caesar himself, by means of which at length the way was open for his very journey to Rome.

A DIVINE REASSURANCE

11. The sudden and exciting events of these days must have left Paul's spirit in deep confusion and oppression. Especially the incidents of the following day must have been peculiarly trying to him. Brought before the Council or Sanhedrin of the Jews by the Roman authorities in order to find out what the real trouble was, Paul saw an opportunity of tactfully throwing a bone of contention between the two parties that composed the Council, the Sadducees and the Pharisees. He knew that they took direct issue on the doctrine of the resurrection, and seizing upon this as a pretext, he at once announced with singular shrewdness that it was for the hope of the resurrection that he was called in question that day. This was, indeed, strictly true in one sense, and yet in another it was an evasion, for while he held and taught the resurrection, there was no other common ground between him and the Pharisees. However, it availed for the present to start a wrangle between the two parties in the Council, which took sides immediately, until the quarrel became so bitter that the chief captain had to remove Paul and close the Council in confusion.

That night as Paul lay in his dungeon, in the prison, many conflicting thoughts must have passed through his mind, and doubtless there came to him the temptation to question some of his leadings. Had not the prophets told him that he should not go to Jerusalem? Had he not forced his own will and wishes against the will of God, and had he, indeed, been quite straightforward in all this matter? Was his attitude in yielding to the compromise with James and the brethren independent? Was his plea in the Council perfectly candid or slightly evasive? And, perhaps, the brave heart began to question and to sink, as we have all done in such a trying hour. It was just then that his blessed Master came to the rescue, as He ever comes when we are overwhelmed and in perplexity, appearing to him as He had done a few times in the direct crisis hours of his life. He said, "Take courage! As you have testified about me in Jerusalem, so you must also testify in Rome" (23:11). How those words were linked in his memory with the days that followed, and through every dark night and troubled day, like a beacon light, would guide him on to his final goal, until at last he could say on the threshold of martyrdom at Rome, "I have finished the race, I have kept the faith" (2 Timothy 4:7).

Beloved, the Friend of Paul is still our Friend. The voice that spoke to him in the dark hour of trial is still ready to speak to us. He did not justify all that Paul had done; He simply passed over it with divine magnanimity. To Him of great importance was that Paul's heart was true. There might be errors of judgment, and there are ever such errors with us all, but the supreme question is, "Do you truly love me?" (John 21:15). Before that every other issue was passed over, and the Lord accepted His servant and stood back of him for good and ill until his life work should be finished. And so, as we close this rapid survey, above all other messages it speaks this to us: to have some great purpose for Him, and from Him to get our marching orders directly from the Commander, and then to press forward unhindered, whether by good or ill, undismayed by calamity, undiscouraged by even the counsels of the dearest friends, satisfied to know that He is leading, and that we have but one supreme purpose—to follow Him, to please Him, to trust Him, and have Him say at last, "Well done!" (Luke 19:17). If that is your purpose then you cannot fail. If you can go forth saying with this glorious pattern, "I consider my life worth nothing to me, if only I may finish the race and complete the task the Lord Jesus has given me" (Acts 20:24), then you may be sure that, like the great apostle, you shall ever hear Him saying what Jehovah said to Jacob: "I am with you. . . . I will not leave you until I have done what I have promised you" (Genesis 28:15).

CHAPTER 9

PAUL, THE PRISONER

*As a prisoner for the Lord, then, I urge you to live a life worthy of
the calling you have received. (Ephesians 4:1)*

W e have been looking at Paul, the missionary, in his devoted zeal and
worldwide evangelism, and we have felt how all other lives and labors
dwarfed in comparison with the splendid example of his character and
achievements. Now we are to see him in a character much more difficult to
sustain, and one where human character is much more likely to break down.
Many a man who can stand the test of the most intense labor and even the
severest suffering, wholly fails when laid aside from active service and compelled to sit in inactivity or languish in prison. The bird that can soar above
the clouds and stand the longest and strongest flights, pines away when
compelled to languish in a cage and beat its helpless wings against its prison
bars. For the next two years of his life Paul enters upon this new experience
as a captive and a prisoner; but the grace of God in his marvelous life is
equal to the strain. Looking over the walls of his prison and the heads of his
enemies, he sees only the hand of God in his trial, and he signs himself, not
the prisoner of Caesar, not the prisoner of Festus, nor the victim of the Sanhedrin, but "prisoner of Christ Jesus" (Ephesians 3:1). He recognizes the
divine will and goodness even in this painful solitude of his cell, in the visits
of his friends, and in the very trial of his case before his judges as a new pulpit of service and a new place of testimony; and perhaps some of the most
precious messages and fruitful ministries of his whole life came forth from
the dark shadows of his captivity in Caesarea.

In this he was not alone. There was another prisoner of the Lord whose
lips they silenced and whose life they shut up in Bedford jail; but John
Bunyan could write from his gloomy cell, "I was at home to prison, and I sat
down and wrote because joy did make me write." and so from that cell came
forth the wondrous dream that has lighted up the whole pathway of the

Pilgrim's Progress for many a child of God through all the years that have come and gone. Another sweet spirit, Madame Guyon, of France, spent many a day within prison walls, and like a caged bird which sings the sweeter for its confinement, her heavenly song has echoed beyond her dungeon walls and lighted up the desolation of drooping hearts with heavenly consolation. True, indeed, it is that

> Stone walls cannot a prison make,
>> Nor iron bars a cage;
> His presence ev'n a cell can make
>> A holy heritage.

Let us take three looks at Paul's prison.

SECTION I—*A Providential Protection*

ROMAN CITIZENSHIP

When Jerusalem turned against Paul, Rome opened her doors for his refuge. Back of the story of his life, we see the mighty hand of God and the executive sovereignty of the ascended Christ overruling both the history of nations and the smallest incidents of human life for the interests of His cause and His children. The same power that raised up Babylon to punish Jerusalem for its former sins, and then raised up Persia to protect the exiles of Babylon a little later, in turn gave the sovereignty of the world to the Greek race, in order that that perfect language might be spread among the nations as a vehicle in which the gospel was to be given to the world. When the mission of Greece was completed, Rome was raised up to take its place and consolidate the government of the nations under one powerful organization, which afforded the largest facilities for universal travel and the spread of the gospel rapidly through the known world. Rome was the providential preparation of God for laying the foundation of Christianity. Roman citizenship was a panoply in every part of the world, protecting its possessor from assault and injury and giving him the right of way in every land. This was Paul's safeguard, and behind it he took refuge when his own countrymen sought his life. The fortress of Caesarea, therefore, became for the time being the shelter and home of the persecuted apostle, and the bulwark of Roman law and the right of his appeal to Caesar guarded him from any injustice either on the part of his Jewish enemies or the unprincipled Roman governors who were only too willing to please them by cowardly compromises.

JEWISH HATE FOILED

But again we see the particular providence of God in discovering and revealing the wicked plot of the Jews to assassinate the apostle when they found themselves baffled in their legal prosecutions. We do not know who this nephew was that God raised up at the right moment to intercept their plotting and report the matter to Paul and the governor, but God knew all about him and had him there ready for the occasion, as He ever has His instruments ready. So, many a time has He interposed by some trifling providence to save the lives of His servants. So, once He caused a spider to weave its gossamer web over the entrance to a cave where a venerable Covenanter had taken refuge a few minutes before. The cruel soldiers, who would have pursued and searched the cave, when they saw the newly made spider's web, concluded that no one could have entered, and passed on. So, once in answer to prayer He caused a Scotch mist to gather like a curtain over a valley where the Dragoons of Claverhouse were about to pounce upon a little company of Christians worshiping in their mountain conventicle, and lo! the pavilion of God was spread over them, rendering them invisible to their pursuers and enabling them in safety to escape. So once He sent a hen to lay her eggs in the loft where one of His servants was in hiding, and supplied him his daily food until he was able to escape to a place of security. So still His hand is guarding us in all dangers, and His covenant fulfilled to those who are true to Him. "I am with you and will watch over you wherever you go. . . . I will not leave you until I have done what I have promised you" (Genesis 28:15).

SECTION II—*A Place of Persecution*

For while he was protected from their power, he was not free from their persecution, and so in a few days his enemies pursued him from Jerusalem to Caesarea, where the governor had removed him to prevent the assassins from carrying out their secret plot. They lose little time about it. Five days after the scene in the Sanhedrin, in which he had declared that he was called in question for the hope of the resurrection, we find them at the Roman capital ready to press their charges against him with their attorney, Mr. Tertullus, all primed for the attack, and an eager mob of Jews, including even the high priest and the elders, on hand to echo his charges. The speech of Tertullus is a good sample of plausible and dishonest pleading. He begins by the usual flattering exordium, to which no doubt, the keen Roman was well accustomed and knew how to estimate its value. He told him how happy they were under his benevolent government, while Felix knew in his heart that a very slight pronunciation would transform "lawyer" into "liar." He was well aware how odious both he and his government were to the Jewish authorities and people, and how gladly they would hurl them from power if they dared. Then Tertullus goes on with his case, and begins it, as weak cases generally begin, with a little cheap abuse, calling Paul a pestilent fellow; then he grows more serious and charges sedition, but ere long reaches the real point of the offense, which is that he is the leader of the sect of the Nazarenes. Then he launches out into a lot of lying, telling how they would have tried him according to their own law, had not the Roman governor violently taken him from their hands. Felix knew how false this was, and that instead of trying him, they were trying to kill him, and that the Roman captain had simply rescued him from murder at the hands of the mob and afterwards defeated their plot to assassinate him by a band of cowardly cutthroats that had entered into a conspiracy with the very high priest himself that they should neither eat nor drink until they had slain Paul.

PAUL'S DEFENSE

Paul's turn now comes, and his defense is in dignified contrast with the enemies'. There is not one word of weak adulation or praise for the governor, but a manly, courteous acknowledgment of his confidence in answering before him, simply because through his long residence as a governor he was enabled to have thorough knowledge of the whole matter. Then comes his plea, in which he denies the charges and defies the accusers to prove them. He shows that there has not been time for any seditious plot, for it is only 12 days since he arrived in Jerusalem and six of these have been spent under the guard of Roman soldiers.

During the immediately preceding days he challenges any of his enemies to prove that at any time he was found disputing or causing dissension or tumult of any kind either in the temple or in the city. He acknowledges having been found in the temple, purified in the usual way, but without any disorder or unbecoming act on his part, the only tumult having been caused by certain Jews of Asia who were noticeably absent, and who ought to have been here now if they had any accusation to bring against him. He declared that he has simply been worshiping God according to the law and the prophets which they also accept, and that the one issue raised when he stood before their Council was the resurrection of the dead, which the Pharisees themselves believed.

At the end of his defense Felix postponed his decision, but evidently showed his leaning toward Paul by ordering the centurion to give him liberty to see his friends at any time, and keep him in prison with the most moderate measure of restraint possible. A little later Felix intimated that he would look more fully into the matter, and the narrator hints that his secret motive was that he hoped to utilize this opportunity in some way to gain some personal advantage out of it for himself. So far as the prosecution was concerned, it had failed, and the next move of his enemies was, under some pretext of law, to have him sent back to Jerusalem for trial before the Council, in order that on the way he might be attacked and assassinated. This Paul defeated by refusing to go back to Jerusalem for retrial, and appealing directly to Caesar, which was the only way apparent by which he could have been saved from a violent death.

SECTION III—*A Pulpit and Place of Holy Ministry*

We now come to the deeper purpose of Paul's imprisonment. When the Lord Jesus forewarned His disciples that they should be brought before kings and governors, He had added, "This will result in your being witnesses to them" (Luke 21:13). That is, He meant that their public trials should be an occasion for witnessing for Christ. And so we find the apostle and his brethren always looking beyond the mere temporary occasion of their trial, to the greater object of bearing testimony for Jesus. The time had now come when the apostle was to have the privilege of speaking for his Master before the rulers of the world. He was to begin with the Roman governors and the Jewish king, and later was to stand before Caesar himself, as a messenger of Jesus Christ. The first of these opportunities comes in a few days. Felix sends for Paul to make a statement concerning the faith in Christ in the presence of Drusilla, his Jewish wife, whose relations to her husband, by the way, were not altogether lawful and right. Paul rises to the occasion.

PAUL AND FELIX

A little while ago we saw Paul standing before Felix. We are now to see Felix before Paul. The tables are turned and the Roman governor is the trembling prisoner at the bar—the bar of conscience, the bar of truth, the bar of God's judgment seat. A little hint is given to us of how Paul addressed himself on this occasion. "Paul discoursed on righteousness, self-control and the judgment to come" (Acts 24:25). He did not plead for himself, he did not denounce his enemies, he did not dogmatize about his opinions, he did not try to show his eloquence or learning; he went straight to the point. This was a case of conscience, a case of sin, a case where a soul was standing at the crossroads of life and the gates of decision. And so with inexorable logic, with deep solemnity, and, no doubt, with much tenderness, he reasoned about the very things which affected Felix and Drusilla most solemnly and immediately. He told them, no doubt, about the holiness of God, the necessity of righteousness, the awful penalty of sin, the wickedness of sensuality, immorality and intemperance, and the certainty and awfulness of the judgment to come. We have some examples in his epistles of such reasonings. We remember how he told the Romans that "all have sinned and fall short of the glory of God" (Romans 3:23), and that "every mouth may be silenced and the whole world held accountable to God" (3:19), and how "the wrath of

God is being revealed from heaven against all the godlessness and wickedness of men" (1:18). We remember how he told the Galatians that "God cannot be mocked. A man reaps what he sows" (Galatians 6:7). Doubtless, in similar terms he pressed the charges home upon the guilty consciences of his hearers. Perhaps, the guilty woman flushed indignant under his keen home-thrusts, then hardened herself against his appeals, while her less skillful partner in sin was unable to conceal his deep and growing feeling, until his very frame gave evidence of the awful strain upon his soul, his knees smote together, his whole frame trembled with deep agitation, and arousing himself from an embarrassment which was becoming intolerable, curtly cut short the address and dismissed the preacher by the memorable words, "That's enough for now! You may leave. When I find it convenient, I will send for you" (Acts 24:25).

A CRISIS

No wonder that this passage has become historical and this scene typical of many a decisive moment in other human lives. The sequel in the case of Felix is very sad. Luke tells us that he sent for Paul more than once afterwards, and for two whole years kept him in prison until his own term of office closed, when he left him bound as a heritage for his successor. But Luke does not tell us that he ever trembled again or came near that decisive place where once for a moment he had stood at the gates of life. On the contrary, Luke tells us how an ignoble, mercenary spirit took possession of his hardened heart, and he held his prisoner for the base hope of getting some bribe from him or his friends for his release. Failing in this, at last, with shameful cruelty, Felix left Paul bound as a criminal after he himself had given him liberty, and thus witnessed to his innocence. That heart, for a moment touched and softened, grew only harder and more wicked when it turned from the light, until we have before us the spectacle of a soul going steadily down into ever deeper degradation and sin, until, as it passes from our view, it is given over past feeling to its sin and doom. May it be that in that first moment of feeling Felix came within reach of eternal life; that that was his day of visitation, his brief day of grace, and when he missed it by procrastination, not only did it never come again, but it left him a hardened heart and more hopeless future than if it had never come at all? Would that soul remember some day in eternal darkness, how once the angel of mercy had visited him, once the gates of light were open to him, once Jesus Christ had stood with pleading, loving and open arms to forgive even him, and by one act of procrastination he had forever closed the door and sealed his own wretched fate?

There are some tragedies that come suddenly, as when Herculaneum and Pompeii fell under the flames of Vesuvius, or some soul is stricken down in the blossom of its crime going quick to hell, as Dathan and Abiram of old

(Numbers 16). But there are other tragedies more slow and yet more terrible. There is no lightning stroke of judgment; but little by little, moment by moment, the heart grows harder, the conscience more insensible, the life more depraved, the soul more incapable of feeling or repentance, like a man slowly sinking in the quicksand and dying before our eyes by inches and moments of horror. So Felix went back from the hour of opportunity, and so still men and women are missing their chance and losing their souls.

I remember a pathetic story once told me by a brother minister with tears and bitter sorrow. "Last night," he said, "one of my college friends came late to my study. We were boys together in Baltimore and close friends. One night we both knelt at the same altar, where I gave my heart to God and he refused to give his. We parted that night. Ever since my pathway has been up to God, his has been downward. Farther and farther we drifted apart, until I seldom met him, and always when I did, noticed that he was on the downward road. Last night he nearly broke my heart. He was a bloated drunkard. 'John,' he said, 'it is probably the last time I shall ever ask you. It is nearly over. One of these nights, perhaps tonight, I will drop in my tracks, and they will hustle my old bones to the Potters' Field. Don't talk to me about Christ and heaven. I know all about it. It is all gone. I looked once in His face and turned away. It is not for me now. I haven't heart enough to want it; I have not soul enough to seek it. I am dying, spiritually, as well as physically, and I am almost dead now. All I want is one drink more, one dime more, one dime more, one more chance to forget my misery. I will not trouble you again. Just a dime, and good-bye forever.' " A few months later my friend told me that the poor waif had gone. A few weeks after that night he had been picked up on the street—an accident, a fall, perhaps a collision with a passing car had given him the finishing stroke and his own prophecy was fulfilled. Ah, that is sadder than the sudden stroke of judgment.

Beloved, if you would only realize that when you say "No" to Christ today, or even put Him off until tomorrow, it means for you a slowly hardening heart, a gradually lessening interest, the power to sin without compunction, to lie down and sleep without prayer or fear, and so on down until the last act of the tragedy and it is forever too late, and the awful lines once written by Dr. Alexander, of Princeton, are true:

> There is a time, we know not when,
>   A place, we know not where,
> That marks the destiny of men,
>   For glory or despair.
>
> To pass that limit is to die,
>   To die as if by stealth;

It may not dim the sparkling eye,
  Or pale the bloom of health.

He thinks, he feels that all is well,
  And every fear is calmed;
He wakes, he sleeps, he walks in hell,
  Not only doomed, but damned.

How long may we go on in sin?
  How soon will God depart?
While it is called today, repent,
  And harden not your heart.

PAUL AND AGRIPPA

One more opportunity came to Paul at Caesarea, and one more lesson has come down to us from his message. It is a lesson that deserves to stand beside his message to Felix. It was before Agrippa this time, with Festus the new governor. Agrippa was one of the kings of Herod's line, and his dominion lay east of the Jordan. As a distinguished visitor at Caesarea, he was invited with the court to hear the famous prisoner. The occasion was most distinguished, the audience illustrious, and the message of Paul was worthy of the circumstance. It was the longest testimony published from his lips. It began with the story of his early life, his loyalty to Judaism and the marvelous revelation of Jesus Christ on the way to Damascus that had made him a Christian. Then it was followed by the modest confession of his high calling to be a witness of Jesus, and his solemn declaration that he had been faithful to the heavenly vision and had continued to this day witnessing both to the Jews and to the Gentiles the message of his great commission, the substance of which was as Moses and the prophets foretold, "that the Christ would suffer and, as the first to rise from the dead, would proclaim light to his own people and to the Gentiles" (Acts 26:23).

We can imagine the impassioned tones and the glowing fervor with which he must have poured out this eloquent appeal. So intense was the excitement that Festus, the cool Roman, could not stand it any longer, but called out, "You are out of your mind, Paul! . . . Your great learning is driving you insane" (26:24). To Festus, like many cultured people today, any religious excitement is a sign of lunacy. Even the old-fashioned Methodist "Amen" has become unfashionable in modern congregations. But Paul appeals from Festus to Agrippa, to whom all these great religious facts are not new. Seizing his opportunity Paul turns his testimony into a personal message, and asks his hearer, "King Agrippa, do you believe the prophets? I know you do"

(26:27). It is this which elicits from the king his cool, and perhaps ironical, reply, "Do you think that in such a short time you can persuade me to be a Christian?" (26:28).

Our version of this text probably does too much credit to Agrippa. It was probably meant as a somewhat scornful reminder that Paul considered him an easy subject. "Easily wouldst thou persuade me," or "by a very little wouldst thou persuade me to be a Christian," is the literal meaning of the original. Agrippa probably meant that he was not to be so easily persuaded to accept the new faith about which Paul was so enthusiastic; but as the passage has come to us and has spoken its message to millions of souls, it has a meaning well fitted to go along with the other lesson from the story of Felix. While that lesson warns us against the danger of procrastination, this one warns us equally against halfheartedness in our decision for Christ. A reservation is as fatal as a delay. "Now and fully all for Jesus, and all for Jesus now." That is the gospel message, that is the warning lesson of the story of Paul at Caesarea.

Surely we need go no further than to Paul's own life to see the grandeur and the value of uttermost decision. Look at the compromising halfhearted men before him, and think of where and what they are today. Look at him bound, shackled and imprisoned at their bar once, but today higher than the stars, brighter than the sun. Oh, how gladly would all the Caesars exchange places with Paul now. And what was the reason for the difference? The one was out and out, all and always for Christ; the other self-seeking, halfhearted, compromising and of the earth, earthly, and "the world and its desires pass away, but the man who does the will of God lives forever" (1 John 2:17). Is there any soul reading this message and committing the mistake of Felix and Agrippa? Not far from the kingdom of God, just one step between, and yet that one step is sufficient to separate you forever from Christ and happiness and heaven. May the Holy Spirit help you to give up the last reserve and come to Him today and forevermore.

CHAPTER 10

A VOYAGE AND ITS LESSONS

I planned many times to come to you (but have been prevented from doing so until now) in order that I might have a harvest among you, just as I have had among the other Gentiles. . . . That is why I am so eager to preach the gospel also to you who are at Rome. (Romans 1:13, 15)

W e are to look this time at a missionary journey, perhaps the greatest ever made, whose expenses were paid by the Roman Empire, a journey in which a prisoner became himself the captain and the crew his converts, and a journey which became a sort of type of the whole missionary work and future history of the Church, and a pattern of the principles upon which God in the coming ages was to work out the evangelization of the world. We have already called attention to the fact that the book of Acts has no formal conclusion, but like a broken column, it closes in the very midst of the story and leaves the later ages of Christianity to add the finishing chapters. The lessons of Paul's voyage, recorded so minutely in the 27th chapter of Acts, divide themselves into two groups.

SECTION I—*Lessons for the Future History of the Church*

THE CHURCH'S VOYAGE

It has been pointed out by a discriminating writer, Professor Stiffler, that the stormy sea through which Paul had to pass to Rome is the type of this tempestuous world wherein the Church has to work out her mission and destiny like a ship sailing over storm-swept seas. It recalls the picture in the Gospels where the Master ascended the Mount to pray and left the disciples to battle with the storm on the Galilean lake, coming to them at length in the fourth watch of the morning walking upon the sea. So the little ship of the Church is struggling through the tempests of time, while the Master is praying beyond at God's right hand and coming soon in His blessed advent. Perhaps the same lesson was suggested by the later scene on the same Galilean Sea, when the Master stood on the shore and called to His struggling and disappointed disciples as they cast their fishing nets into the sea. In the present instance we see the Church represented by Paul's ship passing through the stormy deep to reach the goal. That goal is Rome, which represents the heathen world. That voyage stands for the Church's great mission to evangelize the world. Opposition of the most formidable kind from the hosts of earth and hell assails her at every point, but with God in command and faith at the helm she passes triumphantly to her goal, and adversaries and difficulties are only met to contribute to the final result. But even when Rome is reached and the message given, we find that it is the old story, "Some were convinced . . . but others would not believe" (Acts 28:24). The evangelization of the world is a very different thing from the conversion of the world. As in the case of Paul, so it is still true and will be to the end of the story, "Some were convinced . . . but others would not believe." We are sent to give the gospel as a witness and gather out a people for His name; but the conversion of the world as a universal fact will never come until He comes Himself to establish His kingdom of victorious power and universal righteousness and peace.

SECTION II—*Lessons for Our Individual Life*

TRIAL

1. Trial turned to opportunity.

The whole story of the apostle's life was one of uninterrupted trial, opposition and persecution. God might have made it different; but the way of difficulty was for the education of His servants and the introduction of His kingdom. The Master Himself had foretold that His disciples should be brought before kings and councils in the course of their ministry, but He had added, "This will result in your being witnesses to them" (Luke 21:13). And so they recognized every situation as just an opportunity to preach the gospel. Instead of looking at their side of the trial and planning for their defense and deliverance, their first thought was how this affected the cause of the Master and the work of their testimony.

What a difference it would make in our lives if we accustomed ourselves thus to look at our trials. Have you thought of it, that perhaps the difficulty with which you are now contending, the uncongenial people and uncomfortable surroundings that so distress and apparently hinder you, are just a providential pulpit and congregation which God has given you for the purpose of reaching people that you could reach in no other way, and teaching or learning lessons which could only thus be exemplified? Stop looking at your end of it, and begin to think what it means for your Master and your fellow men, and so your hardest trials will become your most precious opportunities. Paul's arrest at Jerusalem seemed unfortunate, but it gave him his long-desired opportunity of giving his testimony to his fellow countrymen on the Castle steps in the Temple Square. His detention at Caesarea for two years seemed like a fearful loss of time in his busy life, and yet it enabled him to preach the gospel to governors and kings who never could have listened to him otherwise. The plot of the Jews to assassinate him, which was most cruel and cowardly, and the injustice of the Romans in working into the hands of his enemies by threatening to send him back to Jerusalem for trial and thus putting him in the power of his assassins, forced him to make a direct appeal unto Caesar for his protection. This appeal made necessary his journey to Rome and provided the long sought opportunity for carrying the gospel to the great metropolis of the world. Even the shipwreck and the "northeaster" (27:14) had their place, for they brought Paul to the front with his victorious faith and his splendid example, winning for him the hearts of soldiers and sailors, and enabling him to show the power and faithfulness of God to that heathen multitude under the most impressive circumstances. So God is ever giving to us new opportunities even in dark disguises. Let us not fail to recognize them and use the opportunities His providence sends us.

DISOBEDIENCE

2. Disobedience leading to danger.

It was not long until the first vivid lesson was painfully taught the class in which Paul was now to be the leader. Disregarding his prudent message advising them to remain and winter in the harbor of Lasea, the centurion and pilot and owner of the ship decided to venture forward to the Port of Phoenix. Deceived by the south wind, which blew softly, they determined to make the venture in spite of Paul's warning, so they cast loose from Lasea, and sailed along the coast of Crete toward their intended harbor. But soon the soft south wind was exchanged for the wild "northeaster," a cyclone sweeping across from the African desert at certain seasons, rendering navigation most perilous. They soon found themselves helpless in the fury of the storm and were driven before it for many days upon a sea of foam and under a starless sky. Soon they had to undergird the ship to keep her from falling to pieces, and throw overboard the heavy freight and even the tackling of the vessel. The end was soon in sight, and the story records it in a few unmistakable words: "we finally gave up all hope of being saved" (27:20). Then it was that Paul stepped forward and reminded them frankly of their presumption and folly in neglecting his warning. "Men, you should have taken my advice," he tells them, "not to sail from Crete; then you would have spared yourselves this damage and loss" (27:21).

Disobedience always leads to danger. The way of wrong is the way of peril; the way of transgressors is hard. God has said so, and you can never make it otherwise. Right is always safe and wrong is always perilous. You can no more make a crooked line straight than you can make a wrong act wise or happy in its final issue. Oh, that the young minds and hearts of this seductive age would learn and remember that it pays to be true, honest, upright and good, and that "the wages of sin is death" (Romans 6:23), and the fruit of iniquity is bitterness and sorrow. Must God teach you this by breaking your own heart and wrecking your life? Will you not learn it from the lessons of the past and the uniform story of His own faithful Word?

DIVINE HELP

3. Mercy in emergency.

The world is willing to echo the lesson of warning. Its philosophy is full of the maxims of prudence and practical retribution, but the world utterly fails to provide a way of escape when the mischief has been done. There is the difference between Christianity and ethical systems. They can tell us when we are wrong, they can upbraid us for having disobeyed the law of righteousness, but they cannot remedy the wrong or save us out of the consequence of our own sin and folly. The poor Chinese man was right when he told his people how Confucius and Buddha had come to him in the pit into which he had fallen, and gave him the best advice, explaining just why he had fallen in through his own fault and telling him what to do if he ever got out, but passing on in cold neglect and leaving him to his fate; while Jesus of Nazareth, without a word of blame, leaped down into the mire, lifted him out of the quicksand, cleaned and clothed him, and then took him by the hand and led him all the way. That is the beauty and glory of the gospel of the grace of God. How finely we see it in the story of Paul's shipwreck! "You should have taken my advice," he says, "then you would have spared yourselves this damage and loss. But now I urge you to keep up your courage, because not one of you will be lost; only the ship will be destroyed" (Acts 27:21–22). Then Paul tells them of his God and His promise and his own confidence in that promise, and from that hour takes command, as the messenger of hope and cheer and the instrument of the great deliverance.

It is only when you are at the end of all earthly help and hope that you find God and learn real faith. There is no situation so desperate but God can help it if we only will let Him. Even Judas might have been saved if he had listened to the gentle appeal in that crisis hour: "Friend, why have you come?" (Matthew 26:50, margin). The difference between Judas and Peter was that Judas would not believe in the mercy of Christ, and Peter would.

Oh, how many today are taking their lives in remorseful suicide just because they do not know the infinite tenderness, love and grace of this heavenly Friend! Let us tell them of Jesus, the Friend of the helpless, the Hope of forlorn, lost men and women. Is there anybody reading this message, given up by your friends, given up by yourself, with no light or hope or prospect? Oh, beloved, listen to One who says, "Thou hast destroyed thyself; but in me is thine help" (Hosea 13:9, KJV). God is ready to forgive and forget all the past and make all the present and the future right if you will but trust Him and let Him have you. All He wants is a man who has come to the end of himself and is willing to begin again with God. There is mercy for the worst emergency, for the worst man or woman. There is mercy this moment for you.

THE SALT OF THE EARTH

4. The secret of Paul's safety.

Why was it that Paul could offer such a hope and lead such a rescue? Why was it that other ships went down in that storm, and his company were all safely landed? Why is it that some carry charmed lives and are immortal in the face of danger, death and even despair? Paul tells the secret. Here it is: God, "whose I am and whom I serve" (Acts 27:23). Do you belong to God? Then you are His property and He must take care of His property. Are you serving Him? Then His work is more important than anything else in the world, and nothing can be allowed to hinder it. Consecration is the secret of faith, and a life that is all the Lord's is panoplied by omnipotence and protected by every angel in heaven and every force on earth. But there is another element of safety. "Last night an angel of . . . God . . . stood beside me and said, 'Do not be afraid, Paul. You must stand trial before Caesar' " (27:23–24).

That was one of God's "musts." Men sometimes have their "musts," but, oh, they are shattered like the ships they sail on by the buffeting waves. But God's "musts" always get through. If God has a purpose for you it must be fulfilled. If God has a plan for your life and you have accepted it and committed it to Him for execution, neither earth nor heaven nor hell can prevail against it. If God has sent you to India, China, Africa or even Tibet you must get there. Oh, to have such a "must" in our life! What invincible power, what momentous impulsive force it would give to us! What confidence it will afford our faith as we quietly lean back upon the everlasting arms and see God triumph!

I know a woman who was dying of consumption and given up by all physicians, when it was distinctly recalled to her mind that in her early girlhood she had consecrated herself as a missionary to India and God had entered into a covenant with her to send her to that land. This recollection took possession of her and became interwoven in her prayer and faith, until she felt she must not die until she had fulfilled her heavenly calling. Need we say that the cable held, the faith founded on God's "must" was stronger than the power of disease or the word of physicians. She came forth from the last stage of consumption restored to perfect health, went out to India, preached the gospel there for nearly 20 years, and is today a woman in the full vigor of life, so hardy and robust that one would never imagine that she had ever known the awful disease. Have you got any of God's "musts" in your life? Ask Him to give you something to do, to put a mission in your life and a "must" in your future, and then go forth invincible to be one of the eternal forces in the world.

BELIEVING GOD

5. The power of faith, hope and cheerfulness.

"So keep up your courage, men, for I have faith in God that it will happen just as he told me" (27:25). That single verse is worth all the philosophy and poetry of the world's literature. What else could inspire such a scene as that tossing deck presented, with the man who had gone on board as a prisoner, standing in the midst of 276 desperate men and making them eat and drink in the teeth of the storm, and put their hearts and hands together to save the sinking ship simply at his command! Beloved, if you want to be a power in the world and have an influence over your fellow men, give up your groaning, whining, fretting and complaining. Arise and shine! "Shake off your dust;/ . . . Free yourself from the chains on your neck" (Isaiah 52:2). Throw off your gloom, depression, despondency and foreboding, and clothe yourself with the sunshine of hope and cheer, and go forth among your fellow men radiant as the spring, bright as the morning, and helpful as the light. Let your face be an epistle of joy and hope, let your bearing and your step tell of victory and gladness, and let your life be an evangel of hope and inspiration in a world where there are enough tears and clouds, and where God has sent us to be the lights of the world and the comforters of the sorrowing.

A SOUND MIND

6. Faith and common sense.

We have some fine examples in this story of the perfect harmony between the most sublime trust and the most severe practical wisdom. "Not one of you will be lost," was Paul's announcement. "I have faith in God that it will happen just as he told me" (Acts 27:22, 25). More explicit and unquestioning faith we could not find. But a little later we hear him saying, as the sailor crew were trying to escape and leave the ship and the soldiers to their fate, "Unless these men stay with the ship, you cannot be saved" (27:31). Here are the two horns of the dilemma, the two sides of the great question of

God's purpose and man's responsibility, but a common sense faith can easily recognize them. The God that ordains the end also ordains the means to that end. Faith and obedience are but the two oars of the boat, the two hands that grasp the hand of omnipotence; and if we truly believe God for the promise, we shall as certainly obey Him with respect to the command. The faith, therefore, that lies down in indolent inertness and fails to watch and work in the line of God's plan and as the instrument for answering its own prayers, if such be God's way, is not intelligent, scriptural faith, but ignorant and foolish presumption. The man that pleases God always obeys God and watches and hearkens to know His will and to be used by Him in carrying out the promise on which that faith was supremely realized. God gives us wisdom to understand at once the confidence of faith, and, while we trust Him with all our heart, to obey Him with responsive feet and willing hands.

HARD PLACES

7. The value of hard places.

One has often been tempted to wonder why God allowed His distinguished servant to have so hard a struggle with the elements. Why did not some mighty angel come with a lifeboat from the skies to transport the great apostle through the surf and storm and let the world see how mighty was his God? Why did God allow him to drift for days in the tempest, and at last narrowly to escape like a waif flung ashore on a floating plank or fragment of the broken wreck? Oh, that is God's way of hiding His power and teaching us the lesson of true power ourselves. Only by the discipline of difficulty do we ever learn to put on His strength.

One day an amateur naturalist saw a butterfly struggling out of its cocoon or shell, and he thought he would help the little worm to liberty. So he gently cut a larger opening in the mouth of the shell, and the struggling worm found it easier to get out and duly emerged into the light and liberty of his new birth. But, alas, that worm never could fly. The others came out later with hard struggling through their narrow cells, and soon were beating the summer air with their buoyant wings. But this lazy grub lay around on the leaf in indolent apathy and sordid helplessness, and in a little while died of uselessness, while the others went forth into their heaven of summer glory, among the blossoms and the branches. Ah, dear friends, that is what would happen to us if God made it too easy for us. We would grovel on the ground and would be ruined by ease and self-indulgence. Let us thank Him for the wholesome discipline and the inexorable love that will not let us miss our life's lesson and our eternal recompense.

CHAPTER 11

PAUL AT ROME

And so we came to Rome. The brothers there had heard that we were coming, and they traveled as far as the Forum of Appius and the Three Taverns to meet us. At the sight of these men Paul thanked God and was encouraged. (Acts 28:14–15)

We left Paul swimming ashore on the coast of Malta on a piece of broken wreck, having saved the whole company and crew of the ship by his faith and courage, and doubtless having endeared himself to the hearts of all the 276 souls whom God had given to him. We now find him in the midst of a barbarous crowd of natives who received the refugees with rude hospitality and kindness. It was wet and cold, for it was now the depth of winter, probably the month of December, and the people kindled a fire on the shore and proceeded to minister to the comfort of their unexpected guests. Paul, just like himself, without waiting to be waited upon, went to work to help himself and his companions and began to gather sticks for the fire. Suddenly a viper sprang from the flames and seized upon his hand, and immediately the superstitious natives concluded that he must be some notorious criminal whom vengeance was pursuing; but when Paul quietly flung off the viper into the flames again, and instead of his hand swelling and some terrible fit seizing him, he appeared to suffer no harm, their suspicions were changed to superstitious awe, and they were ready to worship him as a god. At the same time an opportunity was afforded by the sickness in the home of Publius, the chief man of the island, for Paul to go to him and minister in the name of the Lord. The prayer of faith, and his healing in answer to prayer, produced a deeper impression upon the hearts of the people, so that from other parts of the island the sick were brought to him, and doubtless the good missionary took advantage of the opportunity to preach to them the gospel and turn to good account the three months they were compelled to linger on the island. On their departure they were loaded with gifts and honors, and no doubt, a blessed missionary work had been accomplished and a seeming calamity turned into a blessed opportunity.

REACHING ROME

With the opening of navigation early in March, a corn ship of Alexandria, which had wintered in the island and was on its way to Naples, took them on board and they resumed their journey. Calling at Syracuse, the principal city of Sicily, they tarried three days. Then, passing Rhegium, they entered the harbor of Naples and moored at the destination of the trade ship at the wharves of Puteoli. Here they found a little company of disciples with whom they tarried the usual seven days, waiting, no doubt, over the Lord's day. Their march was next resumed overland along the famous Appian Way toward Rome. This famous road had been trodden by mighty armies and famous travelers often before, but no such distinction ever came to it as when it was trodden by the feet of Paul on his way to Rome and martyrdom. About 30 miles from Rome there was a little station called the Forum of Appius, where an important crossroad struck the Appian Way, and here the first party of Christians in Rome had come out to meet and greet their venerable visitor. Ten miles nearer the city was another town known as the Three Taverns, also a junction with an important road and a place of public resort, and here the second party of his hosts and visitors were waiting. Less vigorous, perhaps, than the others, they had not been able to take the longer walk; but now all reunited, and as a joyous procession, walked back by his side under the escort of his Roman guard and entered Rome.

The city was at its best. Two million people crowded within its walls and overflowed its suburbs, covering every hillside with the villas of the wealthy, while the crossings of the great avenues and the many hills that covered the site of seven-hilled Rome were crowned with arches, monuments, palaces, public baths and imposing edifices. Paul's destination was the Praetorium, or barracks, near the imperial quarters in the Palatine Hill. Here he was delivered over by Julius, who had charge of his escort, to the captain of the guard, a distinguished Roman named Burrus, whose name has come down to us from contemporary Roman history as a worthy and upright man. For the present, Paul's trial was postponed until his accusers could come from Palestine with their witnesses. Meanwhile, he was treated with marked courtesy. While, of course, he was a public prisoner and never could be separated from the Roman soldier who was chained to his arm, yet he was allowed to live in his own private lodging and receive such friends as he chose to come to him, with perfect freedom. Just as soon as he had become settled in his lodgings and had had a brief rest from the fatigue of his journey, after three days he sent for the Chief of the Jews and made an appointment for a meeting with his countrymen, that he might lay before them his message.

On the appointed day they came in great numbers, for Rome had then its Jewish quarter, even as it has today its famous Ghetto, and they formed a distinct and important element in its population. It was a memorable day in the history of Israel. From morning until night Paul reasoned with them and laid before them the proofs of Christ's Messiahship from the Old Testament Scriptures, and when the day was over it was found that while some believed, many still refused to receive the message and the chief body of his people seemed to have not only left his apartment, but separated themselves from his fellowship; for the language employed denotes a formal and final separation, and Paul's solemn message to them as they left him leaves no doubt that he so understood it. Affectionately, but very solemnly, he applies to them the warning words of the Prophet Isaiah, and formally turns from them to the Gentiles, declaring that to them the message now is sent and they will receive it.

WORK AT ROME

The two years that followed were filled with constant work on the part of the apostle. Many came to him and many we know became followers of Jesus, and the church in Rome grew in numbers and influence. The soldiers who successively guarded him became in turn the subjects of his prayers and his messages and his effectual influence, so that in writing to the Philippians, he could say that the things that had happened to him had turned out for the furtherance of the gospel, and that through all the barracks his bonds in Christ had been made manifest and his testimony honored of God. Writing from Rome he could send greetings to the distant churches from those that were of Caesar's household, and quote name after name that was remembered among the disciples of the Lord. The sequel of Paul's story is gathered from various sources, partly from his own later epistles, partly from ancient traditions and Church history. It seems to be beyond doubt that, shortly after the two years mentioned by Luke in Acts, his hearing before Nero occurred and he was acquitted and released. Then he returned to the West to preach the gospel in Spain, revisited his old churches in Greece and Asia Minor, and was again arrested, sent to Rome for trial, condemned, and finally beheaded about six years after this, probably in the year 68, just a little before the capture and fall of Jerusalem.

LESSONS

But it is time to turn from the narrative of facts to spiritual facts and spiritual lessons to be gathered from these incidents and scenes.

1. Satan not only defeated, but turned into an ally.

The savage attack of that viper upon the hand of Paul was but a stroke from the old serpent, the devil, who employed him; but it reacted against its intended purpose, and when Paul was not only uninjured but victorious over its malignant power, it gave him double influence for God. So every blow of the devil may be turned to our own advantage, and God be glorified by the strange spectacle of even Satan being forced to be our ally and really help on the cause he hates. Let us not fear our conquering foes. Let us never forget this verse: "without being frightened in any way by those who oppose you. This is a sign to them that they will be destroyed, but that you will be saved—and that by God" (Philippians 1:28).

2. Adjusting ourselves to our circumstances.

How perfectly Paul fitted into the providential framework of his life. Put him on a storm-tossed vessel, or on a floating spar, or on a savage shore at Malta, or chain him to a Roman soldier in the Praetorium—he was equally at home in all. He did not quarrel with circumstances, but he adjusted himself to them and turned them to account. Look at him gathering sticks for that fire, with simple-hearted, unaffected freedom, helping to make himself and others comfortable, instead of complaining about the wet and cold. This is the true missionary spirit and this is the true secret of happiness and healthiness in every station in life.

3. The immortality of goodness.

The scenes through which Paul passed on his voyage to Rome have derived much celebrity from many distinguished names. But the name of Paul has given them a higher distinction than all the story of the Caesars. The very bay where his ship ran ashore is known today as St. Paul's bay. The place where he landed at Naples has been sought throughout all the centuries by loving and admiring followers, ever since the day when old Ignatius tried to trace his every footstep along the Appian Way to Rome. And as the ages go by, every other memory will pass into oblivion; but the name, the words, the works of Paul will possess an interest and claim a love and veneration before which all other associations must pale.

4. The rejection of Israel.

No sadder, darker shadow falls upon this story than that last meeting of Paul with his countrymen at Rome. Could we but see its mournful issues as it must have impressed the heavenly beings, it could only seem unutterably sorrowful. It was the last opportunity of Israel. During his earthly ministry how often had the Master called them; then at Pentecost they had received the message once more, and again and again Paul himself had pleaded with them. His love was so deep that he could even almost wish himself accursed from Christ for his brethren according to the flesh. At Antioch he had pleaded with them once more, and then with deep sorrow had turned from them to the Gentiles. On the barracks steps at Jerusalem he had once more appealed to them and given them his own testimony and his Master's message, but they had rejected it and sought his very life, even as they had martyred Stephen because he had witnessed to them of the same hated name. One more opportunity, however, is afforded. As Israel has heard at Jerusalem, at Antioch, and in all the synagogues of the world the message of her Messiah, she must hear it once more at Rome, but it is the old story. Again it is met by unbelief; and now the voice of mercy ends, the day of grace is over, the sentence is pronounced, the salvation of God is sent unto the Gentiles and they will hear it, and Jerusalem is left to her fate. Already the Roman eagles are preparing to descend upon their prey; and ere many years have passed, the terrible presentiments will begin, the fluttering wings will be heard within that Holy Place, while voices murmur, "Let us depart," and Israel will be led forth "as prisoners to all the nations. Jerusalem will be trampled on by the Gentiles until the times of the Gentiles are fulfilled" (Luke 21:24). Paul's loving eyes and ears shall be spared the spectacle. He shall be with his Lord before the final tempest breaks, and almost as soon as his martyr spirit shall have reached the arms of Jesus, the fatal cordon will be fastened around Jerusalem and the day of her visitation will have begun.

Oh, that the children of the kingdom, who like Israel of old, are trifling with this great salvation and missing their birthright, even as Israel missed hers—oh, that they would remember the warning: "If God did not spare the natural branches, he will not spare you either" (Romans 11:21). Israel had her day of opportunity and grace. Christendom is having hers. Soon that, too, will close, and Israel's day may return once more. Let us learn the lesson of her rejection, and "Today, if you hear his voice,/ do not harden your hearts" (Hebrews 3:7–8).

5. The open door of the Gentiles.

"Therefore I want you to know that God's salvation has been sent to the Gentiles, and they will listen!" (Acts 28:28). As the door of grace for Israel closed, it opened for the Gentiles, and now it was fully opened. The gospel henceforth was to make rapid progress at Rome and throughout the Roman world, and the epistles of Paul written from Rome showed how rapid and substantial that progress was. In his own hired house he daily received inquirers, "Boldly and without hindrance he preached the kingdom of God and taught about the Lord Jesus Christ" (28:31). He wrote the epistles to the Ephesians, the Colossians, the Philippians and Philemon during these two years. Many in Caesar's household, and many in the Roman Praetorium became followers of Jesus Christ, and from Rome, the center of the world, the light went forth among all nations. Paul himself a little later passed again over the familiar scenes of his former labors and went far beyond the old boundaries, even to distant Spain. And ever since, that door has been opened more and more widely, until today the gospel of the kingdom has been preached for a witness unto almost all nations, and the glorious work the apostle began is nearing its consummation. More widely than ever God has opened the last closed doors during the present generation, and now there is scarcely a region of the globe where the messenger of Christ may not enter, and where, indeed, the pioneers of the gospel have not already begun their final proclamation before the end shall come.

6. A pattern missionary.

The profoundest of all impressions that come to us as we follow to its close the story of Paul, is the character of the man himself. We have seen it in many lights. The last picture is one of exceeding brightness, helpfulness and suggestiveness. "Paul thanked God and was encouraged" (28:15). What a light it sheds on that glorious, radiant life! There at the gates of Rome, there on the threshold of the cruel Nero, there where he was to suffer and die, there is no shrinking; there is only gratitude and fortitude, thankfulness for the past, fearlessness for the future. "Paul thanked God and was encouraged"! There he stands waving the banner of victory for every succeeding soldier of the cross, and begging us to follow in the path of trial and triumph with the same hopefulness and the same heroic courage.

Why did he thus thank God and take courage? First, because it was his spiritual temperament to be cheerful, hopeful and brave. Perhaps it was not his natural temperament; but Christian character does not come by birth, but by second birth. It is not our disposition, but Christ's disposition that should determine our spirit and character. And wherever the Holy Spirit dwells and Christ is enthroned, there must be the spirit of joy, of peace and of confidence. Next, it was the presence of his friends that cheered and inspired him. We know who some of these were. He had sent greeting to them in the 16th chapter of Romans. There were Aquilla and Priscilla, his oldest and perhaps his dearest friends; there was Mary, who bestowed much labor on him; Tryphena and Tryphosa, who labored in the Lord, and the beloved Persis that labored much in the Lord. There, too, were Timothy and Mark, and other friends who had labored with him in Asia and in Greece. What a joy it must have been to meet them! How their coming seemed to him a signal and a token of blessing and victory! With what tears and smiles and handclasps they must have met and then journeyed on together side by side those thirty miles to Rome! Thank God for Christian friendship. Thank God for true laborers in Jesus Christ.

Thank God for the love that seeks not her own, and that brings with it a fresh touch of the love of the Master. Beloved, how shall you have that hallowed blessing which was so dear to Paul? Let us whisper the secret. It is a very important one, but a very simple one. It is this: Love your friends, not for your sake but for their own; not for what you can get out of them, but for what you can be to them in unselfish blessing. Is not this the trouble with many of you? Is not this the reason why you are so often complaining of slight and neglect? That very complaint shows that what you are thinking of most is your side of the friendship and how it affects you. Rather learn to think of it as it affects them and makes you a blessing rather than a subject of blessing, and be well assured that if God makes you a blessing to another life it must inevitably come back to you in return. Ask God to give you an unselfish interest in the joy of ministering to others and forgetting self in helping them. This is the love of God, and this is the love that God loves and blesses. Be well assured that this is the real cause of all your disappointments in Christian love and fellowship. Paul had not one selfish thought. He loved his friends as few men did. He could say to them that they were in his heart to live and die with them, and that from the very beginning of the gospel they all had been partakers of his grace. Night and day he prayed for them and carried their every burden. Was ever soul more enriched by the treasures of love and prayer? Look at them falling on his neck yonder on the shores of Miletus and by the ship as it sailed from Tyre. Look at them walking out 30 miles from Rome to meet him on his way. Was not that enough to repay a man for the toils and sacrifices of a lifetime? God give us the same spirit of helpful love!

Again, Paul thanked God and took courage because of the wonderful providences that had led him hitherto. How could he help thinking of all the way he had come, and the hand that had led him to this hour, and that, notwithstanding the appeals of friends, the threats of enemies and the hate of hell, kept him true to his purpose and carried him safe to his goal. But the deeper secret of Paul's courageous spirit was his confidence in God and his close union with the spirit of his Master. Writing from Rome about this time to the Philippians, and giving us a glimpse of his very heart, he gives utterance to the same spirit of trustfulness and victory. He says:

> I have learned to be content whatever the circumstances. I know what it is to be in need, and I know what it is to have plenty. I have learned the secret of being content in any and every situation, whether well fed or hungry, whether living in plenty or in want. I can do everything through him who gives me strength. (Philippians 4:11–13)

That was the secret of it all—the Christ who was his strength, the Spirit of the Master, the indwelling presence of the Lord, the deep lessons that he had learned in the school and under the discipline of the Holy Spirit. Not always could he say this, but now at last he says, "I have been instructed, I have learned my lesson and it is settled."

Again Paul was cheerful and hopeful because he was about to begin his cherished lifework. He had longed for this open door. Now it had come and he was about to enter upon the supreme work of his life. How he had loved that work; how he had lived for it; how he devoted himself to it and buried every private interest and every personal aim in the one purpose, to witness to Jesus and glorify His name. This is the true missionary spirit, and with this we are ready for the hardest service or the homeliest trial.

The story is told of a missionary candidate who applied for appointment for service on the field. His case was referred to a wise old clergyman who was to examine him and report upon his case. The good minister invited him to call at his study on a certain morning, naming the hour at 3 o'clock in the morning. Of course, it was a most unusual hour, but true to his appointment the young man was there on time. The servant, duly instructed, met him at the door and showed him into the waiting room. There he sat until 8 o'clock in the morning, when the host received him without a word of explanation. He asked him a few very ordinary questions. Among other things he inquired if he had a good English education, had studied grammar, could spell correctly, and finally wound up the humiliating examination by asking him if he could spell the word "fox." This was duly done, and then he asked him if he had studied arithmetic, and this examination closed by a sum in addition, consisting of the two figures, 2 and 2 are 4. The young man meekly answered every question and was duly dismissed and told that was all. He went away wondering whether he had been taken for a fool, but in due time he received word that his examiner had reported very favorably upon him and that he had been accepted. The report of the old gentleman was something like this: "I have examined Mr. So-and-So, and I consider him well fitted for missionary work. In the first place I examined him in punctuality, and I found that when I invited him to call at 3 o'clock in the morning he was there on the minute. Next I examined him on humility, and I found him to be proficient there, for when I asked him questions that any infant might have answered, he answered them meekly without asking any questions. I examined him in patience, gentleness, meekness and love, and I found him equal to the test. He waited for five hours for my coming to receive him, but he made no complaint. He must have been perplexed at the way I examined him, but he showed no trace of irritation. His whole spirit seemed to be under the control of Christ, and I have much pleasure in recommending him as a graduate in the school of his Master, and a worthy witness for His name."

Whether the incident is true or not, the lesson is, beyond all question; and happy would it be for many a missionary, more proficient, perhaps, in the culture and theology, if they could meet the same tests of all those spiritual qualities which constitute the testimony of our lives, and the absence of which will surely defeat all our words and works. While we thank God for the glorious achievements of the great apostle, while we look with wonder and amazement at his labors and sufferings, greater than all is his life and character, and best of all his testimonies is this: that he could say, "Follow my example, as I follow the example of Christ" (1 Corinthians 11:1).